Pro jQuery 2.0

Second Edition

■ ■ ■

Adam Freeman

Apress®

Pro jQuery 2.0

ISBN-13 (pbk): 978-1-4302-6388-3

ISBN-13 (electronic): 978-1-4302-6389-0

President and Publisher: Paul Manning
Lead Editor: Ewan Buckingham
Technical Reviewer: Fabio Claudio Ferracchiati
Editorial Board: Steve Anglin, Mark Beckner, Ewan Buckingham, Gary Cornell, Louise Corrigan, Morgan Ertel, Jonathan Gennick, Jonathan Hassell, Robert Hutchinson, Michelle Lowman, James Markham, Matthew Moodie, Jeff Olson, Jeffrey Pepper, Douglas Pundick, Ben Renow-Clarke, Dominic Shakeshaft, Gwenan Spearing, Matt Wade, Tom Welsh
Coordinating Editor: Katie Sullivan
Copy Editor: Lori Jacobs and Karen Jameson
Compositor: SPi Global
Indexer: SPi Global
Artist: SPi Global
Cover Designer: Anna Ishchenko

Distributed to the book trade worldwide by Springer Science+Business Media New York, 233 Spring Street, 6th Floor, New York, NY 10013. Phone 1-800-SPRINGER, fax (201) 348-4505, e-mail orders-ny@springer-sbm.com, or visit www.springeronline.com. Apress Media, LLC is a California LLC and the sole member (owner) is Springer Science + Business Media Finance Inc (SSBM Finance Inc). SSBM Finance Inc is a Delaware corporation.

For information on translations, please e-mail rights@apress.com, or visit www.apress.com.

Apress and friends of ED books may be purchased in bulk for academic, corporate, or promotional use. eBook versions and licenses are also available for most titles. For more information, reference our Special Bulk Sales–eBook Licensing web page at www.apress.com/bulk-sales.

Any source code or other supplementary materials referenced by the author in this text is available to readers at www.apress.com. For detailed information about how to locate your book's source code, go to www.apress.com/source-code/.

Dedicated to my lovely wife, Jacqui Griffyth.

—Adam Freeman

Contents at a Glance

Contents

About the Author

Adam Freeman is an experienced IT professional who has held senior positions in a range of companies, most recently serving as chief technology officer and chief operating officer of a global bank. Now retired, he spends his time writing and running.

About the Technical Reviewer

Fabio Claudio Ferracchiati is a senior consultant and a senior analyst/developer using Microsoft technologies. He works for Brain Force (www.brainforce.com) in its Italian branch (www.brainforce.it). Fabio is a Microsoft Certified Solution Developer for .NET, a Microsoft Certified Application Developer for .NET, a Microsoft Certified Professional, and a prolific author and technical reviewer. Over the past ten years, he has written articles for Italian and international magazines and has coauthored more than ten books on a variety of computer topics.

Acknowledgments

I would like to thank everyone at Apress for working so hard to bring this book to print. In particular, I would like to thank Ewan Buckingham for commissioning and editing this title and Katie Sullivan for keeping track of everything. I would also like to thank the technical reviewer, Fabio, whose efforts made this book far better than it otherwise would have been.

—Adam Freeman

■ ■ ■

Putting jQuery in Context

At its heart, jQuery does something that sounds dull: it lets you modify the contents of web pages by manipulating the model that the browser creates when it processes the HTML, a process known as *DOM (Document Object Model) manipulation*, which I describe in detail later. If you have picked up this book, then you have probably already done some DOM manipulation, using either another JavaScript library or the built-in web browser API (application programming interface), and now you want to do it in a better way.

jQuery goes beyond *better*. It makes DOM manipulation a pleasure and, on occasion, an actual joy. There is something elegant and graceful about the way that jQuery works that transforms a task that can be pure drudgery into something that is simple and easy. Once you start using jQuery, there is no going back. Here are the top reasons that I use jQuery in my projects.

- *jQuery is expressive.* I can do more work with much code.

- *jQuery methods apply to multiple elements.* The DOM API approach of select-iterate-modify is gone, meaning fewer for loops to iterate through elements and fewer mistakes.

- *jQuery deals with implementation differences between browsers.* I don't have to worry about whether Internet Explorer (IE) supports a feature in an odd way, for example; I just tell jQuery what I want, and it works around the implementation differences for me.

- *jQuery is open source.* When I don't understand how something works or I don't quite get the result I expect, I can read through the JavaScript code and, if needed, make changes.

The genius of jQuery is that it takes something that is a major grind in web development and makes it simple, quicker, and easier. I can't ask for more than that. Not everything is perfect, of course, and there are one or two rough edges, which I'll explain as I get into the details. But even with the occasional flaw, I love working with jQuery, and I hope you will find it equally compelling and enjoyable to use.

Understanding jQuery UI and jQuery Mobile

In addition to the core jQuery library, I also cover *jQuery UI* and *jQuery Mobile*, which are user interface (UI) libraries built on top of jQuery. jQuery UI is a general-purpose UI toolkit intended to be used on any device, and jQuery Mobile is designed for use with touch-enabled devices such as smartphones and tablets.

Understanding jQuery Plug-ins

jQuery plug-ins extend the functionality of the basic library. Some plug-ins are so good and so widely used that I have covered them in this book. There are a lot of plug-ins available (although the quality can vary), so if you don't like the plug-ins I describe in this book, you can be confident that an alternative approach is available.

What Do I Need to Know?

Before reading this book, you should be familiar with the basics of web development, have an understanding of how HTML and CSS (cascading style sheets) work, and, ideally, have a working knowledge of JavaScript. If you are a little hazy on some of these details, I provide refreshers for HTML, CSS, and JavaScript in Chapters 2, 3, and 4. You won't find a comprehensive reference for HTML elements and CSS properties, though. There just isn't the space in a book about jQuery to cover HTML in its entirety. If you want a complete reference for HTML and CSS, then I suggest another of my books: *The Definitive Guide to HTML5*, also published by Apress.

What Is the Structure of This Book?

This book is split into six parts, each of which covers a set of related topics.

Part 1: Getting Ready

Part 1 of this book provides the information you need to get ready for the rest of the book. It includes this chapter and primers/refreshers for HTML, CSS, and JavaScript. Later in this chapter, I'll describe the software that you will need in order to follow along.

Part 2: Working with jQuery

Part 2 of this book introduces you to the jQuery library, starting with a basic example and building up to include each of the core features: element selection, DOM manipulation, events, and effects.

Part 3: Working with Data and Ajax

Part 3 of this book shows how jQuery makes it possible to work with inline or remote data. I show you how you can generate HTML content from data, how you can validate data entered into web forms, and how you can use jQuery to perform asynchronous operations, including Ajax.

Part 4: Using jQuery UI

jQuery UI is one of the two user interface libraries that I describe in this book. Built on, and integrated with, the core jQuery library, jQuery UI allows you to create rich and responsive interfaces for your web applications.

Part 5: Using jQuery Mobile

jQuery Mobile is the other user interface library that I cover in this book. jQuery Mobile is built on top of jQuery and incorporates some basic feature from jQuery UI but has been optimized for creating smartphone and tablet interfaces. Fewer UI widgets are available in jQuery Mobile, but those that are supported are optimized for touch interaction and for presentation on smaller displays.

Part 6: Advanced Features

The final part of this book describes some jQuery and jQuery UI features not commonly used but which can be helpful in complex projects. These are advanced features that require a better understanding of HTML, CSS, and jQuery itself. When reading Chapter 36, a basic knowledge of asynchronous programming is very helpful.

What's New in This Edition?

Since the first edition of this book, jQuery, jQuery UI, and jQuery Mobile have all undergone substantial changes.

What's New for Core jQuery?

The API for the core jQuery library is remarkably stable. Some years ago, the jQuery team starting listing changes that they intended to make, and these were implemented with the release of jQuery version 1.9. Some of these changes are quite substantial and I have indicated the changes in each chapter throughout Part 2 of this book.

The good news is that these changes are very rare and the API is likely to remain stable for several years. That's not to say that new features won't be added, but the code that you develop today will continue to work without modification for some time to come.

The bad news is that the jQuery team did something unusual when they released jQuery 1.9—they also released jQuery 2.0, and thus they split development into two *lines* of parallel releases: jQuery 1.x and jQuery 2.x. Both release lines have the same API but jQuery 2.x doesn't support versions 6, 7, and 8 of IE.

The older versions of IE are notorious in their non-standard approach to HTML, CSS, and JavaScript, and removing all of the checks for odd behavior and the associated workarounds makes jQuery 2.x smaller and faster.

■ **Tip**   At the time of this writing, the current versions of jQuery are 2.0.2 and 1.10.1. It is important to understand that jQuery 2.0.2 doesn't supersede version 1.10.1. They are both the latest release and the only difference is that jQuery 1.10.1 preserves support for older versions of Internet Explorer.

You should use jQuery 2.x if you are sure that none of your users will have Internet Explorer 6, 7, or 8. If that is not the case—or if you are not sure—then you should use jQuery 1.x. These versions of IE are still widely used, especially in large corporations, and you should think carefully about the effect of using the 2.x line.

There are no legacy users in the idealized world of programming books, and I'll be using the jQuery 2.0.2 library throughout most this book—but you can substitute any version of the jQuery 1.x line (from version 1.9 onward) and get the same result and preserve support for the old versions of IE.

■ **Tip**   I use jQuery 1.x in Part 4, when I describe jQuery Mobile. jQuery Mobile tends to lag behind the main jQuery release and, as I write this, only supports jQuery 1.x.

What's New for jQuery UI?

jQuery UI has also been updated. The API for using the existing user interface widgets has been updated to be more consistent and to work more closely with the HTML elements that underpin them and some new widgets have been added. Throughout Part 3 of this book, you will find that I show the important changes at the start of each chapter, just as I did for the changes to jQuery itself in Part 2.

What's New for jQuery Mobile?

jQuery Mobile has matured a lot since the previous edition of this book. The API has been normalized, new widgets have been added, and the overall developer experience is much more consistent with jQuery and jQuery UI. To reflect this maturity, I have completely rewritten Part 4 to bring it in line with the rest of the book. There are more examples, reference tables, and demonstrations of specific features.

What Else Is New?

From Chapter 12 onward, I use templates to generate HTML elements from data. This is an important technique and I use it liberally. The library that I used in the previous edition has reached the end of its life and I have chosen a replacement. The new library doesn't come with direct integration into jQuery and so in Chapter 12, I provide a custom plug-in that makes using the template library I selected easy to use with jQuery. All of the examples that follow Chapter 12 have been revised to use the new library.

I changed the toolset that I use for testing mobile applications, preferring to use a cloud-based testing service rather than maintaining my own emulators. I explain why I have done this in Chapter 27.

Are There Lots of Examples?

There are *loads* of examples. One of the nice aspects of jQuery is that almost any task can be performed in several different ways, allowing you to develop a personal jQuery style. To show the different approaches you can take, I have included a lot of different examples—so many, in fact, that I include the complete HTML document you are working with only once in some chapters in order to fit everything in. The first example in every chapter is a complete HTML document, as shown in Listing 1-1, for example.

Listing 1-1. A Complete Example Document

```
<!DOCTYPE html>
<html>
<head>
    <title>Example</title>
    <link rel="stylesheet" type="text/css" href="styles.css"/>
    <script src="jquery-2.0.2.js" type="text/javascript"></script>
    <script type="text/javascript">
        $(document).ready(function () {
            $("img:odd").mouseenter(function (e) {
                $(this).css("opacity", 0.5);
            }).mouseout(function (e) {
                $(this).css("opacity", 1.0);
            });
        });
    </script>
</head>
<body>
    <h1>Jacqui's Flower Shop</h1>
    <form method="post">
        <div id="oblock">
            <div class="dtable">
                <div id="row1" class="drow">
                    <div class="dcell">
                        <img src="aster.png"/><label for="aster">Aster:</label>
                        <input name="aster" value="0" required>
                    </div>
                    <div class="dcell">
                        <img src="daffodil.png"/><label for="daffodil">Daffodil:</label>
                        <input name="daffodil" value="0" required >
                    </div>
                    <div class="dcell">
```

```
                    <img src="rose.png"/><label for="rose">Rose:</label>
                    <input name="rose" value="0" required>
                </div>
            </div>
            <div id="row2" class="drow">
                <div class="dcell">
                    <img src="peony.png"/><label for="peony">Peony:</label>
                    <input name="peony" value="0" required>
                </div>
                <div class="dcell">
                    <img src="primula.png"/><label for="primula">Primula:</label>
                    <input name="primula" value="0" required>
                </div>
                <div class="dcell">
                    <img src="snowdrop.png"/><label for="snowdrop">Snowdrop:</label>
                    <input name="snowdrop" value="0" required>
                </div>
            </div>
        </div>
    </div>
    <div id="buttonDiv"><button type="submit">Place Order</button></div>
    </form>
</body>
</html>
```

This listing is taken from Chapter 5. Don't worry about what it does; just be aware that the first example in each chapter is a complete HTML document, similar to the one shown in Listing 1-1. Almost all of the examples are based around the same basic HTML document, which displays a simple flower shop. It isn't the most exciting example, but it is self-contained and includes all of the things we are interested in when working with jQuery.

For the second and subsequent examples, I only show you the elements that change. This is generally just the `script` element, which is where your jQuery code lives. You can spot a partial listing because it starts and ends with ellipsis (. . .), as shown in Listing 1-2.

Listing 1-2. A Partial Listing

```
...
<script type="text/javascript">
    jQuery(document).ready(function () {
        jQuery("img:odd").mouseenter(function(e) {
            jQuery(this).css("opacity", 0.5);
        }).mouseout(function(e) {
            jQuery(this).css("opacity", 1.0);
        });
    });
</script>
...
```

Listing 1-2 is a subsequent listing from Chapter 5. You can see that just the `script` element appears, and I have highlighted a number of statements. This is how I draw your attention to the part of the example that shows the jQuery feature I am using. In a partial listing like this, only the element I show has changed from the complete document shown at the start of the chapter.

I have kept the examples in this book very focused on individual features. This is to give you the best coverage of how jQuery operates. But in doing this, you can lose sight of how different features fit together, so at the end of each part of the book, there is a short chapter in which I refactor the example document to incorporate all of the topics in the previous chapters and present a joined-up view of what's possible.

Where Can I Get the Example Code?

You can download all the examples for all the chapters in this book in the Source Code/Download area of the Apress web site (`www.apress.com`). The download is available without charge and includes all of the supporting resources that are required to re-create the examples without having to type them in (including images, JavaScript libraries, and CSS style sheets). You don't have to download the code, but it is the easiest way of experimenting with the examples and cutting and pasting techniques into your own projects.

■ **Tip** Even though I list just the changes in a lot of the code listings in the chapters, each example in the source code download is a complete HTML document that you can load directly into your browser.

What Software Do I Need for This Book?

To follow the examples in this book, you will need various pieces of software, as described in the following sections.

Getting jQuery

The very first thing you need is the jQuery library, which is available from `http://jquery.com`. There is a download button right on the front page of the web site and an option to choose either the production or development release, as shown in Figure 1-1.

Figure 1-1. *Downloading the jQuery library*

You will need to download jQuery 2.x for Parts 1–4 and 6 of this book and jQuery 1.x for Part 5. You'll be using the development versions for this book. I explain the difference between these versions and show you how to set up the jQuery library in Chapter 5.

■ **Tip** I tell you how to obtain and install the jQuery UI and jQuery Mobile libraries in Chapters 17 and 27, respectively.

Getting an HTML Editor

One of the most important tools for web development is an editor with which you can create HTML documents. HTML is just text, so you can use a very basic editor, but there are some dedicated packages available that make the development smoother and simpler, and many of them are available without charge.

When I wrote the first edition of this book, I used Komodo Edit from Active State. It is free; it is simple; it has good support for HTML, JavaScript, and jQuery; and there are versions for Windows, Mac, and Linux. See http://activestate.com for details.

Recently, however, I have switched to Microsoft's Visual Studio. Many of my books are about Microsoft's web stack and I write my code on Windows. The recent versions of Visual Studio have outstanding support for HTML editing and can be used without any dependency of the Microsoft web stack. I used Visual Studio 2012 Express for this book, which is available for free—see http://www.microsoft.com/visualstudio. (There are paid-for versions as well—this is Microsoft, after all—but you don't need the extra features for jQuery development.)

As an alternative, JsFiddle is a popular online editor that provides support for working with jQuery. I don't get on with it (it is structured in a way that conflicts with my development habits), but it does seem pretty flexible and powerful. It is free to use and is available at http://jsfiddle.net.

■ **Note** I recommend a few products in this book, but only because they are the ones that I use and like. I don't have any relationship with Active State, Microsoft, or any other company aside from Apress, which publishes all of my books. I pay full price for every web service and development tool that I use; I don't get any special support or secret access to the development teams and the only money that I receive comes from royalties (and I am very grateful for your purchase—thank you).

Getting a Web Browser

You need a web browser to view your HTML documents and test your jQuery and JavaScript code. I like Google Chrome: I find it quick, I like the simple UI, and the developer tools are pretty good. Whenever you see a screenshot in this book (which is often), it will be Google Chrome that you see.

That said, you don't have to use the same browser I do, but I do recommend you pick one with good developer tools. Mozilla Firefox has some excellent JavaScript tools available through the Firebug extension, which you can get at http://getfirebug.com.

If you don't like Chrome or Firefox, then your next best bet is Internet Explorer. A lot of web programmers have moral objections to IE, but version 10 is pretty good and I often use it as a quick sanity check when Chrome behaves in an unexpected manner.

Getting a Web Server

If you want to re-create the examples in this book, you will need a web server so that the browser has somewhere from which to load the example HTML document and related resources (such as images and JavaScript files). A lot of web servers are available, and most of them are open source and free of charge. It doesn't matter which web server you use. I have used Microsoft's Internet Information Services (IIS) in this book, but that's just because I have a Windows Server machine already set up and ready to go.

Getting Node.js

Starting in Part 3, you'll be using Node.js in addition to a regular web server. Node.js is very popular at the moment, but I have used it for the simple reason that it is based on JavaScript, so you don't have to deal with a separate web application framework. You won't be digging into any detail at all about Node.js, and I'll be treating it as a black box (although I do show you the server scripts so you can see what's happening on the server if you are interested).

You can download Node.js from http://nodejs.org. There is a precompiled binary for Windows and source code that you can build for other platforms. In this book, I am using version 0.10.13, which is likely to be superseded by the time you read this, but the server scripts should still work without any problems.

Setting Up and Testing Node.js

The simplest way to test Node.js is with a simple script. Save the contents of Listing 1-3 to a file called NodeTest.js. I have done this in the same directory as my Node.js binary.

Listing 1-3. A Node.js Test Script

```
var http = require('http');
var url = require('url');

http.createServer(function (req, res) {
    console.log("Request: " + req.method + " to " + req.url);

    res.writeHead(200, "OK");
    res.write("<h1>Hello</h1>Node.js is working");
    res.end();

}).listen(80);
console.log("Ready on port 80");
```

This is a simple test script that returns a fragment of HTML when it receives an HTTP GET request.

■ **Tip**   Don't worry if that last sentence didn't make complete sense. You don't need to know how HTTP and web servers work to use jQuery, and I provide a crash course in HTML in Chapter 2.

To test Node.js, run the binary specifying the file you just created as an argument. For my Windows installation, I typed the following at the console prompt:

```
node NodeTest.js
```

To make sure everything is working, navigate to port 80 on the machine that is running Node.js. You should see something very similar to Figure 1-2, indicating that everything is as expected.

Figure 1-2. *Testing Node.js*

I run Node.js on a machine different from the regular web server, which means that using port 80 doesn't cause me any problems. If you have only one machine available, run the web server on port 80 and change the Node.js script to use another port. I have highlighted the part of the test script in Listing 1-3 that specifies which port is used.

Image Attribution

Throughout this book, I use a set of images in the examples. Thanks to the following people for kind permission to use their photographs: Horia Varlan, David Short, *Geishaboy500*, Tanaka Juuyoh, Mervi Eskelinen, *Fancy Speed Queen*, Alan "*craigie3000*" Craigie, notsogood, and *melalouise*.

Summary

In this chapter, I outlined the content and structure of this book and set out the software that is required for jQuery web development, all of which can be obtained free of charge. The next three chapters refresh your basic skills in HTML, CSS, and JavaScript. If you are familiar with these topics, then skip to Chapter 5 where I introduce jQuery.

CHAPTER 2

■ ■ ■

HTML Primer

We are going to spend a lot of time in this book working on HTML documents. In this chapter, I set out the information you'll need to understand what we are doing later in the book. This isn't an HTML tutorial but rather a summary of the key characteristics of HTML that I rely on in later chapters.

The latest version of HTML, which is known as *HTML5*, is a topic in its own right. HTML5 has more than 100 elements, and each of them has its own purpose and functionality. That said, you need only a basic knowledge of HTML to understand how jQuery works, but if you want to learn about the details of HTML, then I suggest another of my books: *The Definitive Guide to HTML5*, also published by Apress.

Introducing a Basic HTML Document

The best place to start is to look at an HTML document. From such a document, you can see the basic structure and hierarchy that all HTML documents follow. Listing 2-1 shows a simple HTML document. I use this document throughout this chapter to introduce the core concepts of HTML.

Listing 2-1. A Simple HTML Document

```
<!DOCTYPE html>
<html>
<head>
    <title>Example</title>
    <script src="jquery-2.0.2.js" type="text/javascript"></script>
    <style>
        h1 {
            width: 700px; border: thick double black; margin-left: auto;
            margin-right: auto; text-align: center; font-size: x-large; padding: .5em;
            color: darkgreen; background-image: url("border.png");
            background-size: contain; margin-top: 0;
        }
        .dtable {display: table;}
        .drow {display: table-row;}
        .dcell {display: table-cell; padding: 10px;}
        .dcell > * {vertical-align: middle}
        input {width: 2em; text-align: right; border: thin solid black; padding: 2px;}
        label {width: 5em;  padding-left: .5em;display: inline-block;}
        #buttonDiv {text-align: center;}
        #oblock {display: block; margin-left: auto; margin-right: auto; width: 700px;}
    </style>
</head>
```

```
<body>
    <h1>Jacqui's Flower Shop</h1>
    <form method="post">
        <div id="oblock">
            <div class="dtable">
                <div class="drow">
                    <div class="dcell">
                        <img src="aster.png"/><label for="aster">Aster:</label>
                        <input name="aster" value="0" required>
                    </div>
                    <div class="dcell">
                        <img src="daffodil.png"/><label for="daffodil">Daffodil:</label>
                        <input name="daffodil" value="0" required >
                    </div>
                    <div class="dcell">
                        <img src="rose.png"/><label for="rose">Rose:</label>
                        <input name="rose" value="0" required>
                    </div>
                </div>
                <div class="drow">
                    <div class="dcell">
                        <img src="peony.png"/><label for="peony">Peony:</label>
                        <input name="peony" value="0" required>
                    </div>
                    <div class="dcell">
                        <img src="primula.png"/><label for="primula">Primula:</label>
                        <input name="primula" value="0" required>
                    </div>
                    <div class="dcell">
                        <img src="snowdrop.png"/><label for="snowdrop">Snowdrop:</label>
                        <input name="snowdrop" value="0" required>
                    </div>
                </div>
            </div>
        </div>
        <div id="buttonDiv"><button type="submit">Place Order</button></div>
    </form>
</body>
</html>
```

This is a short and basic HTML document, but it contains some of the most important characteristics associated with HTML. You can see how this document appears in a browser in Figure 2-1.

Figure 2-1. *Displaying the example HTML document in the browser*

Understanding the Anatomy of an HTML Element

At the heart of HTML is the *element*, which tells the browser what kind of content each part of an HTML document represents. Following is an element from the example:

```
...
<h1>Jacqui's Flower Shop</h1>
...
```

This element has three parts: the start tag, the end tag, and the content, as illustrated by Figure 2-2.

Figure 2-2. *The anatomy of a simple HTML element*

The *name* of this element (also referred to as the *tag name* or just the *tag*) is h1, and it tells the browser that the content between the tags should be treated as a top-level header. You create the start tag by placing the tag name in angle brackets, the < and > characters. You create the end tag in a similar way, except that you also add a / character after the left-angle bracket (<).

13

Understanding Attributes

You can provide additional information to the browser by adding *attributes* to your elements. Listing 2-2 shows an element with an attribute from the example document.

Listing 2-2. Defining an Attribute

```
...
<label for="aster">Aster:</label>
...
```

This is a `label` element, and it defines an attribute called `for`. I have emphasized the attribute to make it easier to see. Attributes are always defined as part of the start tag. This attribute has a *name* and a *value*. The name is `for`, and the value is `aster`. Not all attributes require a value; just defining them sends a signal to the browser that you want a certain kind of behavior associated with the element. Listing 2-3 shows an example of an element with such an attribute.

Listing 2-3. Defining an Attribute That Requires No Value

```
...
<input name="snowdrop" value="0" required>
...
```

This element has three attributes. The first two, `name` and `value`, are assigned a value. (This can get a little confusing. The names of these attributes are `name` and `value`. The value of the `name` attribute is `snowdrop`, and the value of the `value` attribute is `0`.) The third attribute is just the word `required`. This is an example of an attribute that doesn't need a value, although you can define one by setting the attribute value to its name (`required="required"`) or by using the empty string (`required=""`).

The id and class Attributes

Two attributes are particularly important in this book: the `id` and `class` attributes. One of the most common tasks you need to perform with jQuery is to locate one or more elements in the document so that you can perform some kind of operation on them. The `id` and `class` attributes are useful for locating one or more elements in the HTML document.

Using the id Attribute

You use the `id` attribute to define a unique identifier for an element in a document. No two elements are allowed to have the same value for the `id` attribute. Listing 2-4 shows a simple HTML document that uses the `id` attribute.

Listing 2-4. Using the id Attribute

```
<!DOCTYPE html>
<html>
<head>
    <title>Example</title>
</head>
<body>
    <h1 id="mainheader">Welcome to Jacqui's Flower Shop</h1>
    <h2 id="openinghours">We are open 10am-6pm, 7 days a week</h2>
    <h3 id="holidays">(closed on national holidays)</h3>
</body>
</html>
```

I have defined the id attribute on three of the elements in the document. The h1 element has an id value of mainheader, the h2 element has an id value of openinghours, and the h3 element has an id value of holidays. Using the id value lets you find a specific element in the document.

Using the class Attribute

The class attribute arbitrarily associates elements together. Many elements can be assigned to the same class, and elements can belong to more than one class, as shown in Listing 2-5.

Listing 2-5. Using the class Attribute

```
<!DOCTYPE html>
<html>
<head>
    <title>Example</title>
</head>
<body>
    <h1 id="mainheader" class="header">Welcome to Jacqui's Flower Shop</h1>
    <h2 class="header info">We are open 10am-6pm, 7 days a week</h2>
    <h3 class="info">(closed on national holidays)</h3>
</body>
</html>
```

In Listing 2-5, the h1 element belongs to the header class, the h2 element belongs to the header and info classes, and the h3 element belongs just to the info class. As you can see, you can add an element to multiple classes just by separating the class names with spaces.

Understanding Element Content

Elements can contain text, but they can also contain other elements. Following is an example of an element that contains other elements:

```
...
<div class="dcell">
    <img src="rose.png"/>
    <label for="rose">Rose:</label>
    <input name="rose" value="0" required>
</div>
...
```

The div element contains three others: an img, a label, and an input element. You can define multiple levels of *nested* elements, not just the one level shown here. Nesting elements like this is a key concept in HTML because it imparts the significance of the outer element to those contained within (this is a theme I return to later). You can mix text content and other elements, as follows:

```
...
<div class="dcell">
    Here is some text content
    <img src="rose.png"/>
    Here is some more text!
    <input name="rose" value="0" required>
</div>
...
```

15

Understanding Void Elements

The HTML specification includes elements that may not contain content. These are called *void* or *self-closing* elements and they are written without a separate end tag. Following is an example of a void element:

```
...
<img src="rose.png"/>
...
```

A void element is defined in a single tag, and you add a / character before the last angle bracket (the > character). Strictly speaking, there should be a space between the last character of the last attribute and the / character, as follows:

```
...
<img src="rose.png" />
...
```

However, browsers are tolerant when interpreting HTML and you can omit the space character. Void elements are often used when the element refers to an external resource. In this case, the img element is used to link to an external image file called rose.png.

Understanding the Document Structure

There are some key elements that define the basic structure of any HTML document: the DOCTYPE, html, head, and body elements. Listing 2-6 shows the relationship between these elements with the rest of the content removed.

Listing 2-6. The Basic Structure of an HTML Document

```
<!DOCTYPE html>
<html>
<head>
    ...head content...
</head>
<body>
    ...body content...
</body>
</html>
```

Each of these elements has a specific role to play in an HTML document. The DOCTYPE element tells the browser that this is an HTML document and, more specifically, that this is an *HTML5* document. Earlier versions of HTML required additional information. For example, following is the DOCTYPE element for an HTML4 document:

```
...
<!DOCTYPE HTML PUBLIC "-//W3C//DTD HTML 4.01//EN"
    "http://www.w3.org/TR/html4/strict.dtd">
...
```

The html element denotes the region of the document that contains the HTML content. This element always contains the other two key structural elements: head and body. As I said at the start of this chapter, I am not going to cover the individual HTML elements. There are too many of them, and describing HTML5 completely took me more than 1,000 pages in my HTML5 book. That said, I will provide brief descriptions of the elements I use so that you have a good idea of what a document does. Table 2-1 summarizes the elements used in the example document from Listing 2-1, some of which I describe in a little more detail later in this chapter.

Table 2-1. *HTML Elements Used in the Example Document*

Element	Description
DOCTYPE	Indicates the type of content in the document
body	Denotes the region of the document that contains content elements (described in the section "Understanding the Content Elements")
button	Denotes a button; often used to submit a form to the server
div	A generic element; often used to add structure to a document for presentation purposes
form	Denotes an HTML form, which allows you to gather data from the user and send them to a server for processing
h1	Denotes a header
head	Denotes the region of the document that contains metadata (described in the section "Understanding the Metadata Elements")
html	Denotes the region of the document that contains HTML (which is usually the entire document)
img	Denotes an image
input	Denotes an input field used to gather a single data item from the user, usually as part of an HTML form
script	Denotes a script, typically JavaScript, that will be executed as part of the document
style	Denotes a region of CSS settings; see Chapter 3
title	Denotes the title of the document; used by the browser to set the title of the window or tab used to display the document's content

Understanding the Metadata Elements

The head element contains the metadata for the document—in other words, one or more elements that describe or operate on the content of the document but that are not directly displayed by the browser. The example document contains three metadata elements in the head section: title, script, and style. The title element is the most basic and the contents of this element are used by browser to set the title of the window or tab, and all HTML documents are required to have a title element. The other two elements are more important for this book, as I explain in the sections that follow.

Understanding the script Element

The script element lets you include JavaScript in your code. This is an element that you will see often once I start covering jQuery in depth. The example document contains one script element, which is shown in Listing 2-7.

Listing 2-7. The script Element from the Example Document

```
...
<script src="jquery-2.0.2.js" type="text/javascript"></script>
...
```

When you define the src attribute for the script element, you are telling the browser that you want to load the JavaScript contained in another file. In this case, this is the main jQuery library, which the browser will find in the file jquery-2.0.2.js. A single HTML document can contain more than one script element, and you can include the JavaScript code between the start and end tags if you prefer, as shown in Listing 2-8.

Listing 2-8. Using the script Element to Define Inline JavaScript Code

```
<!DOCTYPE html>
<html>
<head>
    <title>Example</title>
    <script src="jquery-2.0.2.js" type="text/javascript"></script>
    <script type="text/javascript">
        $(document).ready(function() {
            $('#mainheader').css("color", "red");
        });
    </script>
</head>
<body>
    <h1 id="mainheader" class="header">Welcome to Jacqui's Flower Shop</h1>
    <h2 class="header info">We are open 10am-6pm, 7 days a week</h2>
    <h3 class="info">(closed on national holidays)</h3>
</body>
</html>
```

This example has two script elements. The first imports the jQuery library to the document, and the second is a simple script that uses some basic jQuery functionality. Don't worry about what the second script does for the moment. I'll get into jQuery properly starting in Chapter 5. The script element can appear in the head or body element in an HTML document. In this book, I tend to put scripts only in the head element, but this is just a matter of personal preference.

■ **Tip** The order of script elements is important. You have to import the jQuery library before you can make use of its features.

Understanding the style Element

The style element is one of the ways you can introduce Cascading Style Sheets (CSS) properties into your documents. In short, you can use CSS to manage the way your document is presented when displayed to the user in the browser. Listing 2-9 shows the style element and its contents from the example document.

Listing 2-9. Using the style Element

```
...
<style>
    h1 {
        width: 700px; border: thick double black; margin-left: auto;
        margin-right: auto; text-align: center; font-size: x-large; padding: .5em;
        color: darkgreen; background-image: url("border.png");
        background-size: contain; margin-top: 0;
    }
    .dtable {display: table;}
    .drow {display: table-row;}
    .dcell {display: table-cell; padding: 10px;}
    .dcell > * {vertical-align: middle}
    input {width: 2em; text-align: right; border: thin solid black; padding: 2px;}
```

```
label {width: 5em;  padding-left: .5em;display: inline-block;}
#buttonDiv {text-align: center;}
#oblock {display: block; margin-left: auto; margin-right: auto; width: 700px;}
</style>
...
```

The browser maintains a set of properties, the values of which are used to control the appearance of each element. The `style` element allows you to select elements and change the value of one or more of those properties. I get into this in more detail in Chapter 3.

The `style` element, like the `script` element, can appear in the `head` and `body` elements, but in this book you will find that I place them only in the head section, as in the example document. This is another matter of personal preference; I like to separate my styles from my content.

Understanding the Content Elements

The body element contains the *content* in an HTML document. These are the elements that the browser will display to the user and that the metadata elements, such as `script` and `style`, operate on.

Understanding the Semantic/Presentation Divide

One of the major changes in HTML5 is a philosophical one: the separation between the semantic significance of an element and the effect an element has on the presentation of content. This is a sensible idea. You use HTML elements to give structure and meaning to your content and then control the presentation of that content by applying CSS styles to the elements. Not every consumer of HTML documents needs to display them (because some consumers of HTML are automated programs rather than browsers, for example), and keeping the presentation separate makes HTML easier to process and draw meaning from automatically.

This concept is at the heart of HTML. You apply elements to denote what kind of content you are dealing with. People are good at inferring significance by context. For example, you immediately understood that the header for this section on the page is subordinate to the previous header because it is printed in a smaller typeface (and because this is a pattern that you have seen in most nonfiction books you have read).

Computers can't infer context anywhere near as well and for this reason, each HTML element has a specific meaning. For example, the `article` element denotes a self-contained piece of content that is suitable for syndication and the `h1` element denotes a heading for a content section. Listing 2-10 shows an example document that uses elements to confer structure and significance.

Listing 2-10. Using HTML Elements to Add Structure and Meaning to Content

```
<!DOCTYPE html>
<html>
<head>
    <title>Example</title>
</head>
<body>
    <article>
        <header>
            <hgroup>
                <h1>New Delivery Service</h1>
                <h2>Color and Beauty to Your Door</h2>
            </hgroup>
        </header>
```

```
        <section>
            We are pleased to announce that we are starting a home delivery service for
            your flower needs. We will deliver within a 20 mile radius of the store
            for free and $1/mile thereafter. All flowers are satisfaction-guaranteed and
            we offer free phone-based consultation.
        </section>
        <section>
            Our new service starts on <b>Wednesday</b> and there is a $10 discount
            for the first 50 customers.
        </section>
        <footer>
            <nav>
                More Information:
                <a href="http://jacquisflowershop.com">Learn More About Fruit</a>
            </nav>
        </footer>
    </article>
</body>
</html>
```

There are no hard-and-fast rules about when to apply a section or article element, but I recommend you apply them consistently in your content. Elements like section and article don't provide any information to the browser about how the content they contain should be displayed. This is the heart of the semantic/presentation divide. The browser has a *style convention* for most HTML elements that determines how they will be displayed if the presentation is not changed using CSS, but the idea is that you will make liberal use of CSS to create the presentation you require for your document. This is something you can do with the style element and that jQuery makes easy to do in a script element.

Some of the elements that existed in HTML4 were created when there was no notion of separating presentation from meaning, and that puts us in an odd situation. An example of this oddity is the b element. Until HTML5, the b element instructed the browser to show the content contained by the start and end tags as bold text. In HTML5, elements are not intended to be solely presentational and so the definition for the b element was revised, as follows:

> *The b element represents a span of text offset from its surrounding content without conveying any extra emphasis or importance, and for which the conventional typographic presentation is bold text; for example, keywords in a document abstract, or product names in a review.*

> —HTML: The Markup Language, w3c.org

This is a long-winded way of way of saying that the b element tells the browser to make text bold. There is no semantic significance to the b element; it is all about presentation. And this weasel-worded definition tells us something important about HTML5: we are in a period of transition. We would *like* there to be a complete separation between elements and their presentation, but the reality is that we also want to maintain compatibility with the countless documents that have been written using earlier versions of HTML, and so we have to compromise.

Understanding Forms and Inputs

One of the most interesting elements in the body of the example document is the form element. This is a mechanism you can use to gather data from the user so that you can send it to the server. As you'll see in Part 3, jQuery has some excellent support for working with forms, both directly in the core library and in some commonly used plug-ins. Listing 2-11 shows the body element from the example document and its contents, which includes the form element.

Listing 2-11. The Content Elements of the Example Document

```
...
<body>
    <h1>Jacqui's Flower Shop</h1>
    <form method="post">
        <div id="oblock">
            <div class="dtable">
                <div class="drow">
                    <div class="dcell">
                        <img src="aster.png"/><label for="aster">Aster:</label>
                        <input name="aster" value="0" required>
                    </div>
                    <div class="dcell">
                        <img src="daffodil.png"/><label for="daffodil">Daffodil:</label>
                        <input name="daffodil" value="0" required >
                    </div>
                    <div class="dcell">
                        <img src="rose.png"/><label for="rose">Rose:</label>
                        <input name="rose" value="0" required>
                    </div>
                </div>
                <div class="drow">
                    <div class="dcell">
                        <img src="peony.png"/><label for="peony">Peony:</label>
                        <input name="peony" value="0" required>
                    </div>
                    <div class="dcell">
                        <img src="primula.png"/><label for="primula">Primula:</label>
                        <input name="primula" value="0" required>
                    </div>
                    <div class="dcell">
                        <img src="snowdrop.png"/><label for="snowdrop">Snowdrop:</label>
                        <input name="snowdrop" value="0" required>
                    </div>
                </div>
            </div>
        </div>
        <div id="buttonDiv"><button type="submit">Place Order</button></div>
    </form>
</body>
...
```

When there is a form element, the input element can usually be found nearby. This is the element you use to get a particular piece of information from the user. Listing 2-12 shows an example input element from the document.

Listing 2-12. Using the input Element

```
...
<input name="snowdrop" value="0" required>
...
```

This input element gathers a value from the user for a data item called snowdrop, which has an initial value of zero. The required attribute tells the browser that the user should not be able to send the form to the server unless he has supplied a value for this data item. This is a new feature in HTML5 called *form validation*, but frankly you can achieve much better validation using jQuery, as I demonstrate in Part 3.

Closely related to forms is the button element, which is often used to submit the form to the server (and can also be used to reset the form to its initial state). Listing 2-13 shows the button element I defined in the example document.

Listing 2-13. Using the button Element

```
...
<button type="submit">Place Order</button>
...
```

Setting the type attribute to submit tells the browser I want the form submitted when the button is pressed. The contents of the button element are displayed within the button control in the browser, as you can see in Figure 2-3.

Figure 2-3. *Using the content of the button element*

Understanding Structural Elements

You will notice that there are a lot of div elements in the body of the example document. This is an element that has no specific semantic significance and is often used just to control the layout of content. In the case of the example document, I use the div element to create a *table* layout, such that the elements that the div elements contain are presented to the user in a grid. The layout is applied to the div elements by some of CSS contained in the style element. I'll be using CSS throughout this book and I give a quick primer in Chapter 3.

Understanding Elements with External Resources

Some elements allow you to bring external resources into your document. A great example of this is the img element, which you can use to add images to documents. In the example document in Listing 2-1, I used the img element to display pictures of the different flowers on sale, as shown in Listing 2-14.

Listing 2-14. Using the img Element to Refer to an External Image

```
...
<img src="snowdrop.png"/>
...
```

The src attribute is used to specify the image. I have used the image snowdrop.png. This is an example of a *relative URL* (uniform resource locator), which means the browser will use the URL of the document that contains the element to work out the URL of the image I want.

The alternative to a relative URL is an *absolute URL* (also known as a *fully qualified URL*). This is a URL that has all of the basic components defined, as shown in Figure 2-4. (I have included the port in Figure 2-4, but if this is omitted, then the browser will use the default port associated with the scheme. For the http scheme, this is port 80.)

Figure 2-4. *The basic structure of a URL*

It can be tiresome to have to type out fully qualified URLs for every resource you want, which is why relative URLs are so useful. When I specified a value of snowdrop.png for the src attribute of the img element, I was telling the browser that it could find the image at the same location that it obtained the document that contains the img element. Table 2-2 shows the different kinds of relative URL you can use and the absolute URLs that are created from them. These all assume that the document has been loaded from http://www.jacquisflowershop.com/jquery/example.html.

Table 2-2. *Relative URL Formats*

Relative URL	Equivalent To
snowdrop.png	http://www.jacquisflowershop.com/jquery/snowdrop.png
/snowdrop.png	http://www.jacquisflowershop.com/snowdrop.png
/	http://www.jacquisflowershop.com/jquery/
//www.mydomain.com/index.html	http://www.mydomain.com/index.html

The last example in the table is rarely used because it doesn't save much typing, but it can be useful to ensure that resources are requested using the same scheme as was used to retrieve the HTML document. This avoids a problem where some content is requested over an encrypted connection (using the https scheme) and other content is requested over an unencrypted connection (using the http scheme). Some browsers, especially Internet Explorer and Google Chrome, don't like mixing secure and insecure content and will warn the user when it occurs.

■ **Caution**   You can use the two periods (..) to navigate relative to the directory on the web server that contains the main HTML document. I recommend avoiding this technique, not least because many web servers will reject requests that contain these characters as a security precaution.

Understanding the Element Hierarchy

The elements in an HTML document form a natural hierarchy. The html element contains the body element, which contains content elements, each of which can contain other elements, *ad infinitum*.

Understanding this hierarchy is important when you want to navigate the document, either to apply styles using CSS (which I describe in Chapter 3) or to use jQuery to find elements in the document (which I explain in Part 2).

The most important part of the hierarchy is the relationships that exist between elements. To help me describe these relationships, I have represented the hierarchy for some of the elements from the flower shop example document in Figure 2-5.

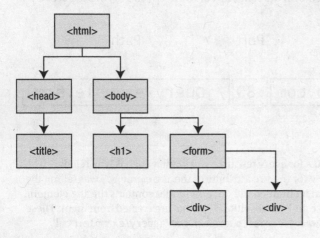

Figure 2-5. *Part of the document hierarchy*

Figure 2-5 shows just part of the hierarchy of elements from the document so you can see that the relationships correspond directly to the way that one element can contain another. There are various kinds of relationships, as described in the following sections.

Understanding Parent-Child Relationships

A parent-child relationship exists when one element contains another, for example. The form element is a *child* of the body element in the figure. Conversely, the body element is the *parent* of the form element. An element can have more than one child but only one parent. In Figure 2-5, the body element has two children (the form and h1 elements) and is the parent to both of them.

The parent-child relationship exists only between an element and elements that are directly contained within it. So, for example, the div elements are children of the form element, but they are not children of the body element.

There are some variations on the child relationship. The *first child* is the child element that is defined first in the document. For example, the h1 element is the first child of the body element. The *last child* is the last child element defined in the document. The form element is the last child of the body element. You can also refer to the nth-child, where you start with the first child element and start counting children until you get to n (you start counting at 1).

Understanding Ancestor-Descendant Relationships

An element's descendants are its children, its children's children, and so on. In fact, any element contained directly or indirectly is a descendant. For example, the descendants of the body element are the h1, form, and both div elements, and all of the elements shown in Figure 2-5 are descendants of the html element.

The opposite relationship is *ancestors*, which are an element's parent, the parent's parent, and so on. For the form element, for example, the descendants are the body and html elements. Both div elements have the same set of ancestors: the form, body, and html elements.

Understanding Sibling Relationships

Siblings are elements that share a common parent. In Figure 2-5, the h1 and form elements are siblings because they share the body element as their parent. When working with siblings, we tend to refer to the *next siblings* and the *previous siblings*. These are the siblings defined before and after the current element. Not all elements have both previous and next siblings; the first and last child elements will have only one or the other.

Understanding the Document Object Model

When the browser loads and processes an HTML document, it creates the *Document Object Model* (DOM). The DOM is a model where JavaScript objects are used to represent each element in the document, and the DOM is the mechanism by which you can programmatically engage with the content of an HTML document.

■ **Note**   In principle, the DOM can be used with any programming language that the browser cares to implement. In practice, JavaScript dominates the mainstream browsers, so I am not going to differentiate between the DOM as an abstract idea and the DOM as a collection of related JavaScript objects.

One of the reasons you should care about the relationship between elements that I described in the previous section is that they are preserved in the DOM. As a consequence, you can use JavaScript to traverse the network of objects to learn about the nature and structure of the document that has been represented.

■ **Tip**   Using the DOM means using JavaScript. If you require a refresher in the basics of the JavaScript language, then see Chapter 4.

In this part of the chapter, I demonstrate some of the basic features of the DOM. For the rest of the book, I focus on using jQuery to access the DOM, but in this section I show you some of the built-in support, in part, to emphasize how much more elegant the jQuery approach can be.

Using the DOM

The JavaScript object that defines the basic functionality that is available in the DOM for all types of elements is called HTMLElement. The HTMLElement object defines properties and methods that are common to all HTML element types, including the properties shown in Table 2-3.

Table 2-3. *Basic HTMLElement Properties*

Property	Description	Returns
className	Gets or sets the list of classes that the element belongs to	string
id	Gets or sets the value of the id attribute	string
lang	Gets or sets the value of the lang attribute	string
tagName	Returns the tag name (indicating the element type)	string

Many more properties are available. The exact set depends on the version of HTML you are working with. But these four are sufficient for me to demonstrate the basic workings of the DOM.

The DOM uses objects that are derived from HTMLElement to represent the unique characteristics of each element type. For example, the HTMLImageElement object is used to represent img elements in the DOM, and this object defines the src property, which corresponds to the src attribute of the img element. I am not going to go into any detail about the element-specific objects, but as a rule, you can rely on properties being available that correspond to an element's attributes.

You access the DOM through the global document variable, which returns a Document object. The Document object represents the HTML document that is being displayed by the browser and defines some methods that allow you to locate objects in the DOM, as described by Table 2-4.

Table 2-4. *Document Methods to Find Elements*

Property	Description	Returns
getElementById(<id>)	Returns the element with the specified id value	HTMLElement
getElementsByClassName(<class>)	Returns the elements with the specified class value	HTMLElement[]
getElementsByTagName(<tag>)	Returns the elements of the specified type	HTMLElement[]
querySelector(<selector>)	Returns the first element that matches the specified CSS selector	HTMLElement
querySelectorAll(<selector>)	Returns all of the elements that match the specified CSS selector	HTMLElement[]

Once again, I am just picking the methods that are useful for this book. The last two methods described in the table use *CSS selectors*, which I describe in Chapter 3. Listing 2-15 shows how you can use the Document object to search for elements of a specific type in the document.

Listing 2-15. Searching for Elements in the DOM

```
<!DOCTYPE html>
<html>
<head>
    <title>Example</title>
    <script src="jquery-2.0.2.js" type="text/javascript"></script>
    <style>
        h1 {
            width: 700px; border: thick double black; margin-left: auto;
            margin-right: auto; text-align: center; font-size: x-large; padding: .5em;
            color: darkgreen; background-image: url("border.png");
            background-size: contain; margin-top: 0;
        }
        .dtable {display: table;}
        .drow {display: table-row;}
        .dcell {display: table-cell; padding: 10px;}
        .dcell > * {vertical-align: middle}
        input {width: 2em; text-align: right; border: thin solid black; padding: 2px;}
        label {width: 5em;  padding-left: .5em;display: inline-block;}
        #buttonDiv {text-align: center;}
        #oblock {display: block; margin-left: auto; margin-right: auto; width: 700px;}
    </style>
</head>
<body>
    <h1>Jacqui's Flower Shop</h1>
    <form method="post">
        <div id="oblock">
            <div class="dtable">
                <div class="drow">
                    <div class="dcell">
                        <img src="aster.png"/><label for="aster">Aster:</label>
                        <input name="aster" value="0" required>
                    </div>
                    <div class="dcell">
                        <img src="daffodil.png"/><label for="daffodil">Daffodil:</label>
                        <input name="daffodil" value="0" required >
                    </div>
                    <div class="dcell">
                        <img src="rose.png"/><label for="rose">Rose:</label>
                        <input name="rose" value="0" required>
                    </div>
                </div>
                <div class="drow">
                    <div class="dcell">
                        <img src="peony.png"/><label for="peony">Peony:</label>
                        <input name="peony" value="0" required>
                    </div>
                    <div class="dcell">
                        <img src="primula.png"/><label for="primula">Primula:</label>
                        <input name="primula" value="0" required>
                    </div>
```

```
                    <div class="dcell">
                        <img src="snowdrop.png"/><label for="snowdrop">Snowdrop:</label>
                        <input name="snowdrop" value="0" required>
                    </div>
                </div>
            </div>
        </div>
        <div id="buttonDiv"><button type="submit">Place Order</button></div>
    </form>
    <script>
        var elements = document.getElementsByTagName("img");
        for (var i = 0; i < elements.length; i++) {
            console.log("Element: " + elements[i].tagName + " " + elements[i].src);
        }
    </script>
</body>
</html>
```

In Listing 2-15, I have added a script element at the end of the body element. When browsers find a script element in a document, they execute the JavaScript statements right away, before the rest of the document has been loaded and processed. This presents a problem when you are working with the DOM because it means your searches for elements via the Document object are performed before the objects you are interested in have been created in the model. To avoid this, I have placed the script element at the end of the document. jQuery provides a nice way of dealing with this issue, as I explain in Part 2.

In the script, I use the getElementsByTagName method to find all of the img elements in the document. This method returns an array of objects that I enumerate to print out the value of the tagName and src properties for each object to the console. The output written to the console is as follows:

```
Element: IMG http://www.jacquisflowershop.com/jquery/aster.png
Element: IMG http://www.jacquisflowershop.com/jquery/daffodil.png
Element: IMG http://www.jacquisflowershop.com/jquery/rose.png
Element: IMG http://www.jacquisflowershop.com/jquery/peony.png
Element: IMG http://www.jacquisflowershop.com/jquery/primula.png
Element: IMG http://www.jacquisflowershop.com/jquery/snowdrop.png
```

Modifying the DOM

The objects in the DOM are *live*, meaning that changing the value of a DOM object property affects the document that the browser is displaying. Listing 2-16 shows a script that has this effect. (I am just showing the script element here to reduce duplication. The rest of the document is the same as for Listing 2-15.)

Listing 2-16. Modifying a DOM Object Property

```
...
<script>
    var elements = document.getElementsByTagName("img");
    for (var i = 0; i < elements.length; i++) {
        elements[i].src = "snowdrop.png";
    }
</script>
...
```

In this script, I set the value of the src attribute to be snowdrop.png for all of the img elements. You can see the effect in Figure 2-6.

Figure 2-6. *Using the DOM to modify the HTML document*

Modifying Styles

You can use the DOM to change the values for CSS properties. (Chapter 3 provides a primer in CSS if you need it.) The DOM API support for CSS is comprehensive, but the simplest technique is to use the style property that is defined by the HTMLElement object. The object returned by the style property defines properties that correspond to CSS properties (I realize that there are a lot of *properties* in this sentence, for which I apologize).

The naming scheme of properties as defined by CSS and by the object that style returns is slightly different. For example, the background-color CSS property becomes the style.backgroundColor object property. Listing 2-17 demonstrates the use of the DOM to manage styles.

Listing 2-17. Using the DOM to Modify Element Styles

```
...
<script>
    var elements = document.getElementsByTagName("img");
    for (var i = 0; i < elements.length; i++) {
        if (i > 0) {
            elements[i].style.opacity = 0.5;
        }
    }
</script>
...
```

In this script, I change the value of the opacity property for all but the first of the img elements in the document. I left one element unaltered so you can see the difference in Figure 2-7.

Figure 2-7. *Using JavaScript to change CSS property values*

Handling Events

Events are signals sent by the browser to indicate a change in status of one or more elements in the DOM. There is a range of events to represent different kinds of state change. For example, the `click` event is triggered when the user clicks an element in the document and the `submit` element is triggered when the user submits a form. Many events are related. For example, the `mouseover` event is triggered when the user moves the mouse over an element, and the `mouseout` event is triggered when the user moves the mouse out again. You can respond to an event by associating a JavaScript *handler function* with an event for a DOM element. The statements in the handler function will be executed each time the event is triggered. Listing 2-18 gives an example.

Listing 2-18. Handling an Event

```
...
<script>
    var elements = document.getElementsByTagName("img");
    for (var i = 0; i < elements.length; i++) {
        elements[i].onmouseover = handleMouseOver;
        elements[i].onmouseout = handleMouseOut;
    }

    function handleMouseOver(e) {
        e.target.style.opacity = 0.5;
    }

    function handleMouseOut(e) {
        e.target.style.opacity = 1;
    }
</script>
...
```

This script defines two handler functions, which I assign as the values for the onmouseover and onmouseout properties on the img DOM objects. The effect of this script is that the images become partially transparent when the mouse is over them and return to normal when the mouse exits. I don't intend to get too deeply into the DOM API event handling mechanism, because the jQuery support for events is the topic of Part 2. I do, however, want to look at the object that is passed to the event handler functions: the Event object. Table 2-5 shows the most important members of the Event object.

Table 2-5. *Functions and Properties of the Event Object*

Name	Description	Returns
type	The name of the event (i.e., mouseover)	string
target	The element at which the event is targeted	HTMLElement
currentTarget	The element whose event listeners are currently being invoked	HTMLElement
eventPhase	The phase in the event life cycle	number
bubbles	Returns true if the event will bubble through the document; returns false otherwise	boolean
cancelable	Returns true if the event has a default action that can be canceled; returns false otherwise	boolean
stopPropagation()	Halts the flow of the event through the element tree after the event listeners for the current element have been triggered	void
stopImmediatePropagation()	Immediately halts the flow of the event through the element tree; untriggered event listeners for the current element will be ignored	void
preventDefault()	Prevents the browser from performing the default action associated with the event	void
defaultPrevented	Returns true if preventDefault() has been called	boolean

In the previous example, I used the target property to get hold of the element for which the event was triggered. Some of the other members relate to *event flow* and to *default actions*, which I briefly explain in the next section. I am just laying the groundwork in this chapter.

Understanding Event Flow

An event has three phases to its life cycle: *capture, target,* and *bubbling.* When an event is triggered, the browser identifies the element that the event relates to, which is referred to as the *target* for the event. The browser identifies all of the elements between the body element and the target and checks each of them to see whether they have any event handlers that have asked to be notified of events of their descendants. The browser triggers any such handler before triggering the handlers on the target itself. (I'll show you how to ask for notification of descendant events in Part 2.)

Once the capture phase is complete, you move to the *target phase,* which is the simplest of the three. When the capture phase has finished, the browser triggers any listeners for the event type that have been added to the target element.

Once the target phase has been completed, the browser starts working its way up the chain of ancestor elements back toward the body element. At each element, the browser checks to see whether there are listeners for the event type that are not capture-enabled (which I'll explain how to do in Part 2). Not all events support bubbling. You can check to see whether an event will bubble using the `bubbles` property. A value of `true` indicates that the event will bubble, and `false` means that it won't.

Understanding Default Actions

Some events define a default action that will be performed when an event is triggered. As an example, the default action for the `click` event on the a element is that the browser will load the content at the URL specified in the `href` attribute. When an event has a default action, the value of its `cancelable` property will be `true`. You can stop the default action from being performed by calling the `preventDefault` method. Note that calling the `preventDefault` function doesn't stop the event flowing through the capture, target, and bubble phases. These phases will still be performed, but the browser won't perform the default action at the end of the bubble phase. You can test to see whether the `preventDefault` function has been called on an event by an earlier event handler by reading the `defaultPrevented` property. If it returns `true`, then the `preventDefault` function has been called.

Summary

In this chapter, I took you on a tour of HTML, albeit without describing any of the 100+ elements in detail. I showed you how to create and structure a basic HTML document, how elements can contain a mix of text content and other elements, and how this leads to a hierarchy of elements with specific types of relationship. I also showed you basic use of the DOM API and how it handles element selection and events—as you'll see throughout this book, one of the main reasons to use jQuery is because it hides away the details of the DOM API and makes working with HTML elements and the JavaScript objects that represent them simple and easy. In Chapter 3, I provide a quick primer to Cascading Style Sheets, which are used to control the presentation of HTML elements.

CHAPTER 3

■ ■ ■

CSS Primer

Cascading Style Sheets (CSS) are the means by which you control the appearance (more properly known as *presentation*) of HTML elements. CSS has a special significance for jQuery for two reasons. The first is that you can use *CSS selectors* (which I describe in this chapter) to tell jQuery how to find elements in an HTML document. The second reason is that one of the most common tasks that jQuery is used for is to change the CSS styles that are applied to elements.

There are more than 130 *CSS properties*, each of which controls an aspect of an element's presentation. As with the HTML elements, there are too many CSS properties for me to be able to describe them in this book. Instead, I have focused on how CSS works and how you apply styles to elements. If you want detailed coverage of CSS, then I suggest another of my books: *The Definitive Guide to HTML5*, which is also published by Apress.

Getting Started with CSS

When the browser displays an element on the screen, it uses a set of properties, known as *CSS properties*, to work out how the element should be presented. Listing 3-1 shows a simple HTML document.

Listing 3-1. A Simple HTML Document

```
<!DOCTYPE html>
<html>
<head>
    <title>Example</title>
</head>
<body>
    <h1>New Delivery Service</h1>
    <h2>Color and Beauty to Your Door</h2>
    <h2>(with special introductory offer)</h2>
    <p>We are pleased to announce that we are starting a home delivery service for
    your flower needs. We will deliver within a 20 mile radius of the store
    for free and $1/mile thereafter.</p>
</body>
</html>
```

You can see how a browser displays the document in Figure 3-1.

33

Figure 3-1. *Displaying a simple document in the browser*

There are a *lot* of CSS properties—too many to cover in detail in this book—but you can learn a lot about how CSS works by looking at just the small number of properties in Table 3-1.

Table 3-1. *Some CSS Properties*

Property	Description
color	Sets the foreground color of the element (which typically sets the color of text)
background-color	Sets the background color of the element
font-size	Sets the size of the font used for text contained in the element
border	Sets the border for the element

I haven't defined values for these CSS properties but the browser has still managed to display the content and, as Figure 3-1 shows, each of the content elements has been presented in a different way. The browser still has to display the elements even if you haven't provided values for the CSS properties, and so each element has a *style convention*—a default value that it uses for CSS properties when no other value has been set in the HTML document. The HTML specification defines style conventions for elements, but browsers are free to vary them, which is why so you will see variations in the style convention between, say, Google Chrome and Internet Explorer. Table 3-2 shows the default values that are used by Google Chrome for the properties I listed in Table 3-1.

Table 3-2. *Some CSS Properties and Their Style Convention Values*

Property	h1	h2	p
color	black	black	black
background-color	transparent	transparent	transparent
font-size	32px	24px	16px
border	none	none	none

You can see from the table that all three types of element have the same values for the color, background-color, and border properties and that it is only the font-size property that changes. Later in the chapter, I describe the units used for these property values—but for the moment, though, we are going to focus on setting values for properties without worrying about the units in which those values are expressed.

Setting an Inline Value

The most direct way to set values for CSS properties is to apply the style attribute to the element whose presentation we want to change. Listing 3-2 shows how this is done.

Listing 3-2. Using the style Attribute to Set a CSS Property on an Element

```
<!DOCTYPE html>
<html>
<head>
    <title>Example</title>
</head>
<body>
    <h1>New Delivery Service</h1>
    <h2 style="background-color: grey; color: white">Color and Beauty to Your Door</h2>
    <h2>(with special introductory offer)</h2>
    <p>We are pleased to announce that we are starting a home delivery service for
    your flower needs. We will deliver within a 20 mile radius of the store
    for free and $1/mile thereafter.</p>
</body>
</html>
```

In Listing 3-2, I have used *style declarations* to specify values for two of the CSS properties. You can see the anatomy of the attribute value in Figure 3-2.

Figure 3-2. *The anatomy of a style attribute value*

Each style declaration specifies the name of a property you want to change and the value that you want to use, separated by a colon (:). You can put multiple declarations together using a semicolon character (;). In Figure 3-2, I set the value of the background-color to grey and the value of the color property to white. These values are specified in the style attribute of the h2 element and will affect only that element (other elements in the document remain unaffected, even if they are also h2 elements). You can see the effect that these new property values have in the presentation of the first h2 element in Figure 3-3.

Figure 3-3. *The effect of changing CSS values in the style attribute of the h2 element*

Defining an Embedded Style

Using the style attribute is easy but it applies to only a single element. You could use the style attribute for every element that you wanted to change, but it becomes difficult to manage and error-prone quickly, especially if you need to make revisions later. A more powerful technique is to use the style *element* (rather than the style *attribute*) to define an *embedded style* and direct the browser to apply it with a *selector*. Listing 3-3 shows an embedded style.

Listing 3-3. Defining an Embedded Style

```
<!DOCTYPE html>
<html>
<head>
    <title>Example</title>
    <style>
        h2 { background-color: grey; color: white;}
    </style>
</head>
<body>
    <h1>New Delivery Service</h1>
    <h2>Color and Beauty to Your Door</h2>
    <h2>(with special introductory offer)</h2>
    <p>We are pleased to announce that we are starting a home delivery service for
    your flower needs. We will deliver within a 20 mile radius of the store
    for free and $1/mile thereafter.</p>
</body>
</html>
```

We still use declarations in an embedded style, but they are enclosed in braces (the { and } characters) and are preceded by a *selector*. You can see the anatomy of an embedded style in Figure 3-4.

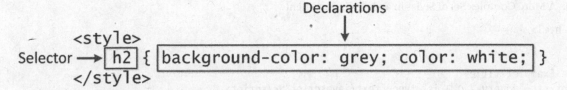

Figure 3-4. *The anatomy of an embedded style*

■ **Tip**   I have placed the style element within the head element, but I could have equally put it inside the body element. I prefer using the head element for styles because I like the idea of separating the content from the CSS that controls its appearance.

CSS selectors are important in jQuery because they are the basis by which you select elements in order to perform operations on them. The selector I used in the example is h2, which means that the style declarations contained in the braces should be applied to every h2 element in the document. You can see the effect this has on the h2 elements in Figure 3-5.

Figure 3-5. *The effect of an embedded style*

You can use a style element to contain more than one embedded style. Listing 3-4 shows the flower shop document that you first saw in Chapter 2, which has a more complex set of styles.

Listing 3-4. A More Complex Set of Styles in an HTML Document

```
<!DOCTYPE html>
<html>
<head>
    <title>Example</title>
    <script src="jquery-2.0.2.js" type="text/javascript"></script>
    <style>
        h1 {
            width: 700px; border: thick double black; margin-left: auto;
            margin-right: auto; text-align: center; font-size: x-large; padding: .5em;
            color: darkgreen; background-image: url("border.png");
            background-size: contain; margin-top: 0;
        }
        .dtable {display: table;}
        .drow {display: table-row;}
        .dcell {display: table-cell; padding: 10px;}
        .dcell > * {vertical-align: middle}
        input {width: 2em; text-align: right; border: thin solid black; padding: 2px;}
        label {width: 5em;  padding-left: .5em;display: inline-block;}
        #buttonDiv {text-align: center;}
        #oblock {display: block; margin-left: auto; margin-right: auto; width: 700px;}
    </style>
</head>
<body>
    <h1>Jacqui's Flower Shop</h1>
    <form method="post">
        <div id="oblock">
            <div class="dtable">
                <div class="drow">
                    <div class="dcell">
                        <img src="aster.png"/><label for="aster">Aster:</label>
                        <input name="aster" value="0" required>
                    </div>
                    <div class="dcell">
                        <img src="daffodil.png"/><label for="daffodil">Daffodil:</label>
                        <input name="daffodil" value="0" required>
                    </div>
                    <div class="dcell">
                        <img src="rose.png"/><label for="rose">Rose:</label>
                        <input name="rose" value="0" required>
                    </div>
                </div>
                <div class="drow">
                    <div class="dcell">
                        <img src="peony.png"/><label for="peony">Peony:</label>
                        <input name="peony" value="0" required>
                    </div>
                    <div class="dcell">
                        <img src="primula.png"/><label for="primula">Primula:</label>
                        <input name="primula" value="0" required>
                    </div>
```

```
                    <div class="dcell">
                        <img src="snowdrop.png"/><label for="snowdrop">Snowdrop:</label>
                        <input name="snowdrop" value="0" required>
                    </div>
                </div>
            </div>
        </div>
        <div id="buttonDiv"><button type="submit">Place Order</button></div>
    </form>
</body>
</html>
```

The style element in Listing 3-4 contains several embedded styles, and some of them, especially the one with the h1 selector, define values for many properties.

Defining an External Style Sheet

Rather than define the same set of styles in each of your HTML documents, you can create a separate *style sheet*. This is an independent file, with the conventional .css file extension, into which you put your styles. Listing 3-5 shows the contents of the file styles.css, into which I have placed the styles from the flower shop document.

Listing 3-5. The styles.css File

```
h1 {
    min-width: 700px; border: thick double black; margin-left: auto;
    margin-right: auto; text-align: center; font-size: x-large; padding: .5em;
    color: darkgreen; background-image: url("border.png");
    background-size: contain; margin-top: 0;
}
.dtable {display: table;}
.drow {display: table-row;}
.dcell {display: table-cell; padding: 10px;}
.dcell > * {vertical-align: middle}
input {width: 2em; text-align: right; border: thin solid black; padding: 2px;}
label {width: 5em;  padding-left: .5em;display: inline-block;}
#buttonDiv {text-align: center;}
#oblock {display: block; margin-left: auto; margin-right: auto; min-width: 700px;}
```

You don't need to use a style element in a style sheet. You just define the selectors and declarations directly. You then use the link element to bring the styles into your document, as shown in Listing 3-6.

Listing 3-6. Importing an External Style Sheet

```
<!DOCTYPE html>
<html>
<head>
    <title>Example</title>
    <script src="jquery-2.0.2.js" type="text/javascript"></script>
    <link rel="stylesheet" type="text/css" href="styles.css" />
</head>
```

```
<body>
    <h1>Jacqui's Flower Shop</h1>
    <form method="post">
        <div id="oblock">
            <div class="dtable">
                <div class="drow">
                    <div class="dcell">
                        <img src="aster.png"/><label for="aster">Aster:</label>
                        <input name="aster" value="0" required>
                    </div>
                    <div class="dcell">
                        <img src="daffodil.png"/><label for="daffodil">Daffodil:</label>
                        <input name="daffodil" value="0" required>
                    </div>
                    <div class="dcell">
                        <img src="rose.png"/><label for="rose">Rose:</label>
                        <input name="rose" value="0" required>
                    </div>
                </div>
                <div class="drow">
                    <div class="dcell">
                        <img src="peony.png"/><label for="peony">Peony:</label>
                        <input name="peony" value="0" required>
                    </div>
                    <div class="dcell">
                        <img src="primula.png"/><label for="primula">Primula:</label>
                        <input name="primula" value="0" required>
                    </div>
                    <div class="dcell">
                        <img src="snowdrop.png"/><label for="snowdrop">Snowdrop:</label>
                        <input name="snowdrop" value="0" required>
                    </div>
                </div>
            </div>
        </div>
        <div id="buttonDiv"><button type="submit">Place Order</button></div>
    </form>
</body>
</html>
```

You can link to as many style sheets as you need, referencing one per link element. The order in which you import style sheets is important if you define two styles with the same selector. The one that is loaded last will be the one that is applied.

Understanding CSS Selectors

Notice that there are different kinds of selectors in the flower shop style sheet: some are element names (such as h1 and input), others start with a period (such as .dtable and .row), and yet others start with a pound (#butonDiv and #oblock). If you are particularly observant, you will notice that one of the selectors has multiple components: .dcell > *. Each CSS selector selects elements in the document, and the different kinds of selector tell the browser to look for elements in different ways. In this section, I describe the different kinds of selectors that are defined by CSS, starting with the *core selectors*, which Table 3-3 summarizes.

Table 3-3. *The Core Selectors*

Selector	Description
*	Selects all elements
<type>	Selects elements of the specified type
.<class>	Selects elements of the specific class (irrespective of element type)
<type>.<class>	Selects elements of the specified type that are members of the specified class
#<id>	Selects elements with the specified value for the id attribute

These selectors are the most widely used (they cover most of the styles I defined in the example document, for instance).

Selecting by Attribute

Although the basic selectors work on the id and class attributes (which I described in Chapter 2), there are also selectors available that let you work with any attribute. Table 3-4 describes them.

Table 3-4. *The Attribute Selectors*

Selector	Description
[attr]	Selects elements that define the attribute attr, irrespective of the value assigned to the attribute
[attr="val"]	Selects elements that define attr and whose value for this attribute is val
[attr^="val"]	Selects elements that define attr and whose value for this attribute starts with the string val
[attr$="val"]	Selects elements that define attr and whose value for this attribute ends with the string val
[attr*="val"]	Selects elements that define attr and whose value for this attribute contains the string val
[attr~="val"]	Selects elements that define attr and whose value for this attribute contains multiple values, one of which is val
[attr|="val"]	Selects elements that define attr and whose value is a hyphen-separated list of values, the first of which is val

Listing 3-7 shows a simple document with an embedded style whose selector is based on attributes.

Listing 3-7. *Using the Attribute Selectors*

```
<!DOCTYPE html>
<html>
<head>
    <title>Example</title>
    <style>
        [lang] { background-color: grey; color: white;}
        [lang="es"] {font-size: 14px;}
    </style>
</head>
```

```
<body>
    <h1 lang="en">New Delivery Service</h1>
    <h2 lang="en">Color and Beauty to Your Door</h2>
    <h2 lang="es">(Color y belleza a tu puerta)</h2>
    <p>We are pleased to announce that we are starting a home delivery service for
    your flower needs. We will deliver within a 20 mile radius of the store
    for free and $1/mile thereafter.</p>
</body>
</html>
```

The first selector matches any element that has the lang attribute, and the second selector matches any element whose lang attribute value is es. You can see the effect of these styles in Figure 3-6.

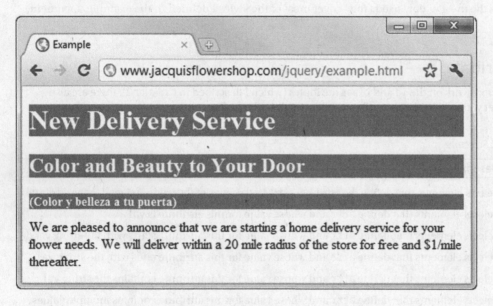

Figure 3-6. *Applying styles using attribute selectors*

■ **Note**   There is something important to note in this figure. Look at how the h2 element has been affected by *both* of the embedded styles. The first style is applied to all elements with a lang attribute. The second style is applied to all elements that have a lang attribute whose value is es. The second h2 element in the document meets both of those criteria, and so the values for the background-color, color, and font-size properties are all changed. I'll explain more about how this works in the section "Understanding Style Cascading."

Selecting by Relationship

In Chapter 2, I explained that elements (and the object that represents them in the DOM) have a hierarchy that gives rise to different kinds of relationship. There are CSS selectors that allow you to select elements based on those relationships, as described in Table 3-5.

Table 3-5. *The Relationship Selectors*

Selector	Description
`<selector> <selector>`	Selects elements that match the second selector and that are descendants of the elements matched by the first selector
`<selector> > <selector>`	Selects elements that match the second selector and that are children of the elements matched by the first selector
`<selector> + <selector>`	Selects elements that match the second selector and are the next sibling to an element that matches the first selector
`<selector> ~ <selector>`	Selects elements that match the second selector and that are siblings to (and that appear after) an element that matches the first selector

I used one of these selectors in the flower shop example document, as follows:

```
.dcell > * {vertical-align: middle}
```

This selector matches all of the elements that are children of elements that belong to the dcell class, and the declaration sets the vertical-align property to the value middle. Listing 3-8 shows some of the other relationship selectors being used.

Listing 3-8. Using the Relationship Selectors

```
<!DOCTYPE html>
<html>
<head>
    <title>Example</title>
    <style>
        h1 ~ [lang] { background-color: grey; color: white;}
        h1 + [lang] {font-size: 12px;}
    </style>
</head>
<body>
    <h1 lang="en">New Delivery Service</h1>
    <h2 lang="en">Color and Beauty to Your Door</h2>
    <h2 lang="es">(Color y belleza a tu puerta)</h2>
    <p>We are pleased to announce that we are starting a home delivery service for
    your flower needs. We will deliver within a 20 mile radius of the store
    for free and $1/mile thereafter.</p>
</body>
</html>
```

I have used both of the sibling selectors in Listing 3-8. The first selector, the one that uses the tilde (~) character, matches any element that has a lang attribute and that is defined after and is a sibling to an h1 element. In the example document, this means that both the h2 elements are selected (since they have the attribute and are siblings to and are defined after the h1 element). The second selector, the one that uses the plus character, is similar but matches only the immediate sibling of an h1 element. This means that only the first of the h2 element is selected. You can see the effect in Figure 3-7.

Figure 3-7. *Using the sibling relationship selectors*

Selecting Using the Pseudo-element and Pseudo-class Selectors

CSS supports a set of *pseudo-element and pseudo-class selectors*. These provide convenient functionality that doesn't correspond directly to elements or class membership in the document. Table 3-6 describes these selectors.

Table 3-6. *The Pseudo-selectors*

Selector	Description
:active	Selects elements that are presently activated by the user; this usually means those elements that are under the pointer when the mouse button is pressed
:checked	Selects elements that are in a checked state
:default	Selects default elements
:disabled	Selects elements that are in their disabled state
:empty	Selects elements that contain no child elements
:enabled	Selects elements that are in their enabled state
:first-child	Selects elements that are the first children of their parent
:first-letter	Selects the first letter of a block of text
:first-line	Selects the first line of a block of text
:focus	Selects the element that has the focus
:hover	Selects elements that occupy the position on-screen under the mouse pointer
:in-range :out-of-range	Selects constrained input elements that are within or outside the specified range
:lang(<language>)	Selects elements based on the value of the lang attribute

(continued)

Table 3-6. (*continued*)

Selector	Description
:last-child	Selects elements that are the last children of their parent
:link	Selects link elements
:nth-child(n)	Selects elements that are the nth child of their parent
:nth-last-child(n)	Selects elements that are the nth from last child of their parent
:nth-last-of-type(n)	Selects elements that are the nth from last child of their type defined by their parent
:nth-of-type(n)	Selects elements that are the nth child of their type defined by their parent
:only-child	Selects elements that are the sole element defined by their parent
:only-of-type	Selects elements that are the sole element of their type defined by their parent
:required :optional	Selects input elements based on the presence of the required attribute
:root	Selects the root element in the document
:target	Selects the element referred to by the URL fragment identifier
:valid :invalid	Selects input elements that are valid or invalid based on input validation in forms
:visited	Selects link elements that the user has visited

Listing 3-9 shows the use of some pseudo-selectors.

Listing 3-9. Using Pseudo-selectors

```
<!DOCTYPE html>
<html>
<head>
    <title>Example</title>
    <style>
        :nth-of-type(2) { background-color: grey; color: white;}
        p:first-letter {font-size: 40px;}
    </style>
</head>
<body>
    <h1 lang="en">New Delivery Service</h1>
    <h2 lang="en">Color and Beauty to Your Door</h2>
    <h2 lang="es">(Color y belleza a tu puerta)</h2>
    <p>We are pleased to announce that we are starting a home delivery service for
    your flower needs. We will deliver within a 20 mile radius of the store
    for free and $1/mile thereafter.</p>
</body>
</html>
```

You can use the pseudo-selectors on their own or as a modifier to another selector. I have shown both approaches in Listing 3-9. The first selector matches any element that is the second element of its type defined by its parent. The second selector matches the first letter of any p elements. You can see the application of these styles in Figure 3-8.

Figure 3-8. *Using pseudo-selectors to apply styles*

Unions and the Negation Selectors

You can get additional flexibility by arranging selectors together. Specifically, you can create unions by combining selections and inverting a selection through negation. Both of these approaches are described in Table 3-7.

Table 3-7. *Flexibly Arranging Selectors*

Selector	Description
<selector>, <selector>	Selects the union of elements matched by the first selector and the elements matched by the second selector
:not(<selector>)	Selects the elements that are not matched by the specified selector

Listing 3-10 shows how you can create unions and negations.

Listing 3-10. Using Selector Unions and Negation

```
<!DOCTYPE html>
<html>
<head>
    <title>Example</title>
    <style>
        h1, h2 { background-color: grey; color: white;}
        :not(html):not(body):not(:first-child) {border: medium double black;}
    </style>
</head>
```

```
<body>
    <h1 lang="en">New Delivery Service</h1>
    <h2 lang="en">Color and Beauty to Your Door</h2>
    <p>We are pleased to announce that we are starting a home delivery service for
    your flower needs. We will deliver within a 20 mile radius of the store
    for free and $1/mile thereafter.</p>
</body>
</html>
```

The first selector in Listing 3-10 is the union of the h1 and h2 selectors. As you might imagine, this matches all h1 and h2 elements in the document. The second selector is a little more esoteric. I wanted to demonstrate how you could use pseudo-selectors as modifiers to other pseudo-selectors, including negation.

```
...
:not(html):not(body):not(:first-child) {border: medium double black;}
...
```

This selector matches any element that is not an html element, that is not a body element, and that is not the first child of its parent. You can see how the styles in this example are applied in Figure 3-9.

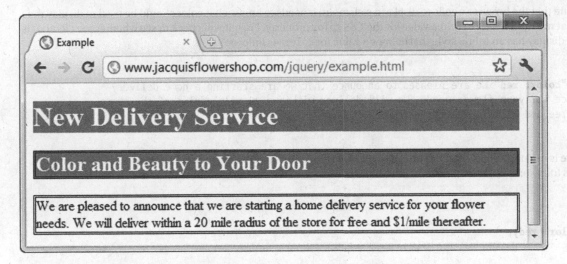

Figure 3-9. Creating selector unions and negations

Understanding Style Cascading

The key to understanding style sheets is to understand how they *cascade* and *inherit*. There can be multiple sources for CSS properties in an HTML document and cascading and inheritance are the means by which the browser determines which values should be used to display an element. You have seen three different ways you can define styles (inline, embedded, and from an external style sheet), but there are two other sources of styles: *browser styles* and *user styles*.

The *browser styles* (more properly known as the *user agent styles*) are the style conventions that a browser applies to an element if no other style has been specified. You saw an example of style conventions being used at the start of this chapter.

In addition, most browsers allow users to define their own style sheets. The styles that these style sheets contain are called *user styles*. This isn't a widely used feature, but those users who do define their own style sheets often attach great importance to being able to do so, not least because it provides a way of making pages more accessible.

Each browser has its own mechanism for user styles. Google Chrome on Windows, for example, creates a file in the user's profile directory called `User StyleSheets\Custom.css`. Any styles added to this file are applied to *any* site that the user visits, subject to the cascading rules that I describe in the following section.

Understanding How Styles Cascade

Now that you have seen all of the sources of styles that a browser has to consider, you can look at the order in which the browser will look for a property value when it comes to display an element.

1. Inline styles (styles that are defined using the `style` attribute on an element)

2. Embedded styles (styles that are defined in a `style` element)

3. External styles (styles that are imported using the `link` element)

4. User styles (styles that have been defined by the user)

5. Browser styles (the style conventions applied by the browser)

Imagine that the browser needs to display a p element. It needs to know what color should be used to display the text and that means it needs to find a value for the CSS `color` property. First, it will check to see whether the element it is trying to display has an inline style that defines a value for `color`, as follows:

```
...
<p style="color: red">We are pleased to announce that we are starting a home delivery
    service for your flower needs. We will deliver within a 20 mile radius of the store
    for free and $1/mile thereafter.</p>
...
```

If there is no inline style, then the browser will look for a `style` element that contains a style that applies to the element, as follows:

```
...
<style>
    p {color: red};
</style>
...
```

If there is no such `style` element, the browser looks at the style sheets that have been loaded via the `link` element, and so on until the browser finds a value for the `color` property, and that means using the value defined in the default browser styles if no other value is available.

■ **Tip** The first three sources of properties (inline styles, embedded styles, and style sheets) are collectively referred to as the *author styles*. The styles defined in the user style sheet are known as the *user styles*, and the styles defined by the browser are known as the *browser styles*.

Tweaking the Order with Important Styles

You can override the normal cascade order by marking your property values as *important*, as shown in Listing 3-11.

Listing 3-11. Marking Style Properties as Important

```
<!DOCTYPE html>
<html>
<head>
    <title>Example</title>
<style>
    p {color: black !important; }
</style>
</head>
<body>
    <h1 lang="en">New Delivery Service</h1>
    <h2 lang="en">Color and Beauty to Your Door</h2>
    <p style="color: red">We are pleased to announce that we are starting a home delivery
    service for your flower needs. We will deliver within a 20 mile radius of the store
    for free and $1/mile thereafter.</p>
</body>
</html>
```

You mark individual values as important by appending !important to the declaration. The browser gives preference to important styles, irrespective of where they are defined. You can see the effect of property importance in Figure 3-10, where the embedded value for the color property overrides the inline value (this may be a little hard to make out on the printed page, but all of the text is black).

Figure 3-10. *Important property values overriding inline property values*

49

■ **Tip**   The only thing that will take precedence over an important value that you define is an important value defined in the user style sheet. For regular values, the author styles are used before the user styles, but this is reversed when dealing with important values.

Tie-Breaking with Specificity and Order Assessments

We enter a tie-break situation if there are two styles that can applied to an element defined at the same cascade level and they both contain values for the CSS property that the browser is looking for. To decide which value to use, the browser assesses the *specificity* of each style and selects the one that is most specific. The browser determines the specificity of a style by counting three different characteristics.

- The number of id values in the style's selector

- The number of other attributes and pseudo-classes in the selector

- The number of element names and pseudo-elements in the selector

The browser combines the values from each assessment and applies the property value from the style that is most specific. You can see a simple example of specificity in Listing 3-12.

Listing 3-12.   Specificity in Styles

```
<!DOCTYPE html>
<html>
<head>
    <title>Example</title>
    <style>
        p {background-color: grey; color: white;}
        p.details {color:red;}
    </style>
</head>
<body>
    <h1 lang="en">New Delivery Service</h1>
    <h2 lang="en">Color and Beauty to Your Door</h2>
    <p class="details">We are pleased to announce that we are starting a home delivery
    service for your flower needs. We will deliver within a 20 mile radius of the store
    for free and $1/mile thereafter.</p>
</body>
</html>
```

When assessing specificity, you create a number in the form a-b-c, where each letter is the total from one of the three characteristics that are counted. This is not a three-digit number. A style is more specific if its a value is the greatest. Only if the a values are equal does the browser compare b values. The style with the greater b value is more specific in this case. Only if both a and b values are the same does the browser consider the c value. This means that a specificity score of 1-0-0 is more specific than 0-5-5.

In this case, the selector p.details includes a class attribute, which means that the specificity of the style is 0-1-1 (0 id values + 1 other attributes + 1 element names). The other selector has a specificity of 0-0-1 (it contains no id values or other attributes and one element name).

When rendering a p element, the browser will look for a value for the color property. If the p element is a member of the details class, then the style with the p.details selector will be the most specific, and the value of red will be used. For all other p elements, the value white will be used. You can see how the browser selects and applies values for this example in Figure 3-11.

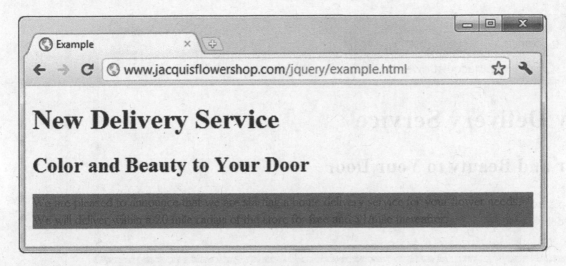

Figure 3-11. *Applying values from styles based on specificity*

When there are values defined in styles with the same specificity, then the browser selects the value it uses based on the order in which the values are defined. The one that is defined last is the one that will be used. Listing 3-13 shows a document that contains two equally specific styles.

Listing 3-13. *Styles That Are Equally Specific*

```
<!DOCTYPE html>
<html>
<head>
    <title>Example</title>
    <style>
        p.details {color:red;}
        p.information {color: blue;}
    </style>
</head>
<body>
    <h1 lang="en">New Delivery Service</h1>
    <h2 lang="en">Color and Beauty to Your Door</h2>
    <p class="details information">We are pleased to announce that we are starting a home
    Delivery service for your flower needs. We will deliver within a 20 mile radius of
    the store for free and $1/mile thereafter.</p>
</body>
</html>
```

Both styles defined in the style element have the same specificity score, and both apply to the p element. When the browser displays the p element in the page, it will select the blue property for the color property since that is the value defined in the latter style. You can see this in Figure 3-12.

Figure 3-12. Selecting property values based on the order in which styles are defined

---

■ **Tip** These specificity rules are applied only to styles that are defined at the same cascade level. This means that a property defined in a style attribute will always take precedence over a style defined in a style element, for example.

Understanding CSS Units

Earlier in the chapter, I showed you the values that the browser uses by default for some CSS properties. These are the style conventions for some of the elements in the examples, and I have duplicated this information in Table 3-8.

Table 3-8. Some CSS Properties and Their Values

Property	h1	h2	p
color	black	black	black
background-color	transparent	transparent	transparent
font-size	32px	24px	16px
border	none	none	none

CSS defines a broad range of different unit types, and in the sections that follow I'll show you some of the more commonly used ones, including those that I use in this book.

Working with CSS Colors

Colors are used by a lot of the CSS properties, including the color and background-color properties I have been using in this chapter. The simplest way to specify a color is to use a predefined color name or to use a decimal or hexadecimal value for each of the red, green, and blue components. Decimal values are separated by a comma, and hex values are usually prefixed with #, such as #ffffff, which represents white. You can see some of the predefined names for colors and their decimal and hex equivalents in Table 3-9.

Table 3-9. *Selected CSS Colors*

Color Name	Hex	Decimal	Color Name	Hex	Decimal
black	#000000	0,0,0	green	#008000	0,128,0
silver	#C0C0C0	192,192,192	lime	#00FF00	0,255,0
grey	#808080	128,128,128	olive	#808000	128,128,0
white	#FFFFFF	255,255,255	yellow	#FFFF00	255,255,0
maroon	#800000	128,0,0	navy	#000080	0,0,128
red	#FF0000	255,0,0	blue	#0000FF	0,0,255
purple	#800080	128,0,128	teal	#008080	0,128,128
fuschia	#FF00FF	255,0,255	aqua	#00FFFF	0,255,255

These are known as the *basic* color names. CSS also defines the *extended colors*. There are too many to detail here, but you can find a complete list at www.w3.org/TR/css3-color. In addition to the basic colors, a lot of slight variations are available. As an example, Table 3-10 shows the extended set of grey shades that can be used.

Table 3-10. *Selected CSS Colors*

Color Name	Hex	Decimal
darkgrey	#a9a9a9	169,169,169
darkslategrey	#2f4f4f	47,79,79
dimgrey	#696969	105,105,105
grey	#808080	128,128,128
lightgrey	#d3d3d3	211,211,211
lightslategrey	#778899	119,136,153
slategrey	#708090	112,128,144

Specifying More Complex Colors

Color names and simple hex values aren't the only way you can specify colors. A number of functions allow you to select a color. Table 3-11 describes each of the functions available.

Table 3-11. *CSS Color Functions*

Function	Description	Example
rgb(r, g, b)	Specifies a color using the RGB (red, green, blue) model.	color: rgb(112, 128, 144)
rgba(r, g, b, a)	Specifies a color using the RGB model, with the addition of an alpha value to specify opacity. (A value of 0 is fully transparent; a value of 1 is fully opaque.)	color: rgba(112, 128, 144, 0.4)
hsl(h, s, l)	Specifies a color using the hue, saturation, and lightness (HSL) model.	color: hsl(120, 100%, 22%)
hsla(h, s, l, a)	Like HSL, but with the addition of an alpha value to specify opacity.	color: hsla(120, 100%, 22%, 0.4)

You can use the rgba function to specify a color with transparency, but if you want a completely transparent element, then you can use the special color value transparent.

Understanding CSS Lengths

Many CSS properties require you to specify a *length*, such as the font-size property, which is used to specify the size of font used to render an element's content. When you specify a length, you concatenate the number of units and the unit identifier together, without any spaces or other characters between them. For example, a value of 20pt for the font-size property means 20 of the units represented by the pt identifier (which are *points*, explained in a moment). CSS defines two kinds of length unit: those that are absolute and those that are relative to another property. I explain both in the sections that follow.

Working with Absolute Lengths

Absolute units are real-world measurements. CSS supports five types of absolute unit, which Table 3-12 describes.

Table 3-12. *CSS Absolute Units of Measurement*

Unit Identifier	Description
in	Inches
cm	Centimeters
mm	Millimeters
pt	Points (1 point is 1/72 of an inch)
pc	Picas (1 pica is 12 points)

You can mix and match units in a style and mix absolute and relative units. Absolute units can be useful if you have some prior knowledge of how the content will be rendered, such as when designing for print. I don't use the absolute units that much in my CSS projects—I find the relative units more flexible and easier to maintain and I rarely create content that has to correspond to real-world measurements.

■ **Tip**   You might be wondering where pixels are in the table of absolute units. In fact, CSS tries to make pixels a relative unit of measurement, although, sadly, the specification makes a botched attempt at doing so. You can learn more in the section "Working with Pixels."

Working with Relative Lengths

Relative lengths are more complex to specify and implement than absolute units and require tight and concise language to define their meaning unambiguously. A relative unit is measured in terms of some other unit. Unfortunately, the language in the CSS specifications isn't precise enough (a problem that has plagued CSS for years). This means CSS defines a wide range of interesting and useful relative measurements, but you can't use some of them because they don't have widespread or consistent browser support. Table 3-13 shows the relative units that CSS defines and that can be relied on in mainstream browsers.

Table 3-13. *CSS Relative Units of Measurement*

Unit Identifier	Description
em	Relative to the font size of the element
ex	Relative to x-height of the element's font
rem	Relative to the font size of the root element
px	A number of CSS pixels (assumed to be on a 96 dpi display)
%	A percentage of the value of another property

When you use a relative unit, you are effectively specifying a multiple of another measurement. Listing 3-14 gives an example that sets a property relative to the font-size.

Listing 3-14. Using a Relative Unit

```
<!DOCTYPE html>
<html>
<head>
    <title>Example</title>
    <style>
        p.details {
            font-size: 15pt;
            height: 3em;
            border: thin solid black;
        }
    </style>
</head>
<body>
    <h1 lang="en">New Delivery Service</h1>
    <h2 lang="en">Color and Beauty to Your Door</h2>
    <p class="details information">We are pleased to announce that we are starting a home
    delivery service for your flower needs. We will deliver within a 20 mile radius of
    the store for free and $1/mile thereafter.</p>
</body>
</html>
```

In this example, I have specified the value of the height property (which sets the height of an element) to be 3em, which means that p elements should be rendered so that the height of the element on the screen is three times the font-size. You can see how the browser displays these elements in Figure 3-13. I added a border (using the border property) so you can see the size of the element more readily.

***Figure 3-13.** The effect of using relative measurements*

Working with Pixels

Pixels in CSS are not what you might expect. The usual meaning of the term *pixel* refers to the smallest addressable unit on a display: one picture element. CSS tries to do something different and defines a pixel as follows:

> *The reference pixel is the visual angle of one pixel on a device with a pixel density of 96 dpi and a distance from the reader of an arm's length.*

This is the kind of vague definition that plagues CSS. I don't want to rant, but specifications that are dependent on the length of a user's arm are problematic. Fortunately, the mainstream browsers ignore the difference between pixels as defined by CSS and pixels in the display and treat 1 pixel to be 1/96th of an inch. (This is the standard Windows pixel density; browsers on platforms with displays that have a different pixel density usually implement a translation so that 1 pixel is still roughly 1/96th of an inch.)

■ **Tip**　Although it isn't much use, you can read the full definition of a CSS pixel at www.w3.org/TR/CSS21/syndata.html#length-units.

The net effect of this is that although CSS pixels are intended to be a relative unit of measure, they are treated as an absolute unit by browsers. Listing 3-15 demonstrates specifying pixels in a CSS style.

Listing 3-15. Using Pixel Units in a Style

```html
<!DOCTYPE html>
<html>
<head>
    <title>Example</title>
    <style>
        p.details {
            font-size: 20px;
            width: 400px;
            border: thin solid black;
        }
    </style>
</head>
<body>
    <h1 lang="en">New Delivery Service</h1>
    <h2 lang="en">Color and Beauty to Your Door</h2>
    <p class="details information">We are pleased to announce that we are starting a home
    delivery service for your flower needs. We will deliver within a 20 mile radius of
    the store for free and $1/mile thereafter.</p>
</body>
</html>
```

In Listing 3-15, I have expressed both the `font-size` and `width` properties in pixels (the `width` property is the complement to the `height` property and sets the width of an element). You can see how the browser applies this style in Figure 3-14.

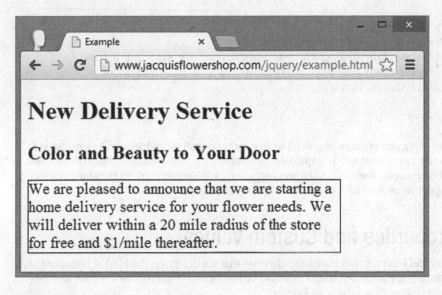

Figure 3-14. *Specifying units in pixels*

■ **Tip**   Although I often use pixels as units in CSS, it tends to be a matter of habit. I find em units more flexible. This is because I have to alter the size of the font only when I need to make a change, and the rest of the style works seamlessly. It is important to remember that while CSS pixels were intended to be relative units, they are absolute units in practice and can be inflexible as a consequence.

Working with Percentages

You can express a unit of measurement as a percentage of another property value. You do this using the % (percent) unit, as demonstrated in Listing 3-16.

Listing 3-16. Expressing Units as a Percentage of Another Property Value

```
<!DOCTYPE html>
<html>
<head>
    <title>Example</title>
    <style>
        p.details {
            font-size: 200%;
            width: 50%;
            border: thin solid black;
        }
    </style>
</head>
<body>
    <h1 lang="en">New Delivery Service</h1>
    <h2 lang="en">Color and Beauty to Your Door</h2>
    <p class="details information">We are pleased to announce that we are starting a home
    delivery service for your flower needs. We will deliver within a 20 mile radius of
    the store for free and $1/mile thereafter.</p>
</body>
</html>
```

There are two complications in using percentages as units. The first is that not all properties can be expressed in this way, and the second is that each property that *can* be expressed as a percentage individually defines which *other* property the percentage refers to. For example, the font-size property uses the inherited font-size value from the parent element, and the width property uses the width of the containing element.

Using Shorthand Properties and Custom Values

Not all properties are set using units and colors. Some have special values that are unique to the kind of behavior they control. A good example of this is the border property, which I used in some of the listings to draw a border around elements. You set the border property using three values, as follows:

```
...
border: thin solid black;
...
```

The first value is the thickness of the border, the second value is the style of the border, and the final value is the color of the border. Table 3-14 shows the values you can use to specify the thickness of the border.

Table 3-14. *Values for the Border Width*

Value	Description
<length>	A length expressed in CSS measurement units such as em, px, or cm
<perc>%	Percent of the *width* of the area around which the border will be drawn
thin medium thick	Preset widths, the meanings of which are defined by each browser, but which are progressively thicker

Table 3-15 shows the values you can use for the style of the border.

Table 3-15. *Values for the Border Style*

Value	Description
none	No border will be drawn
dashed	The border will be a series of rectangular dashes
dotted	The border will be a series of circular dots
double	The border will be two parallel lines with a gap between them
groove	The border will appear to have been sunken into the page
inset	The border will be such that the content looks sunken into the page
outset	The border will be such that the content looks raised from the page
ridge	The border will appear raised from the page
solid	The border will be a single, unbroken line

By combining values from these tables with a color, you can achieve a wide range of border effects. You can see the range of styles displayed in the browser in Figure 3-15.

Figure 3-15. *The border styles*

The border property is also a good example of a *shorthand property*. These properties allow you to set the value of several related properties in a single declaration. This means a border such as the one shown earlier is equivalent to the following 12 declarations:

```
border-top-color: black;
border-top-style: solid;
border-top-width: thin;
border-bottom-color: black;
border-bottom-style: solid;
border-bottom-width: thin;
border-left-color: black;
border-left-style: solid;
border-left-width: thin;
border-right-color: black;
border-right-style: solid;
border-right-width: thin;
```

CSS allows you to dig into the details and set individual properties for fine control or to use the shorthand properties when all of the related values are the same.

Summary

In this chapter, I gave you a brief overview of CSS, showing you how to set properties using the style attribute, how to use the style element (including the wide range of selectors that are available), and how the browsers use cascading and specificity to work out which property values should be applied to elements when they are displayed. I finished with a tour of the CSS units, custom values, and shorthand properties. You can express values for properties in a number of different ways, which adds flexibility (and a little confusion) to CSS styles.

In Chapter 4, I introduce the basics of JavaScript, which is the means by which jQuery functionality is defined and applied to HTML content.

CHAPTER 4

■ ■ ■

JavaScript Primer

jQuery is a JavaScript library that you add to your HTML documents and that is executed by a browser. You employ the features of the jQuery library by adding your own code to the document as well – and this requires a basic understanding of how to write JavaScript. In this chapter, I provide a primer for the JavaScript language, focusing on the features that are most pertinent when working with jQuery.

JavaScript has a mixed reputation as a programming language. It is true that JavaScript has had a difficult life and was rushed through standardization before it had a chance to mature properly, leaving some oddities in the way that JavaScript works. But most complaints about JavaScript are from developers who find that JavaScript doesn't work in exactly the same way as their preferred back-end language, such as C#, Java, or Python.

Once past the hurdle of accepting that JavaScript is a language in its own right, you will find a language that is flexible, dynamic, and pleasant to work with. There are still oddities, of course, but the overall experience is positive and with just a little effort you will find JavaScript an expressive and rewarding language.

■ **Tip** If you are new to programming, a good starting point is a series of articles posted on the popular site Lifehacker.com. No programming knowledge is assumed, and all of the examples are in JavaScript. The guide is available here: http://lifehacker.com/5744113/learn-to-code-the-full-beginners-guide.

Getting Ready to Use JavaScript

JavaScript code is added to an HTML document as a *script* – a block of JavaScript statements that the browser will execute – and there are different ways you can add scripts. You can define an *inline script*, where the content of the script is part of the HTML document. You can also define an *external script*, where the JavaScript is contained in a separate file and referenced via a URL (which is how you access the jQuery library, as you'll see in Part 2). Both of these approaches rely on the script element. In this chapter, I will be using inline scripts. You can see a simple example in Listing 4-1.

Listing 4-1. A Simple Inline Script

```
<!DOCTYPE HTML>
<html>
<head>
    <title>Example</title>
    <script type="text/javascript">
        console.log("Hello");
    </script>
</head>
```

```
<body>
    This is a simple example
</body>
</html>
```

This script writes a message to the *console*. The console is a basic (but useful) tool that the browser provides that lets you display debugging information as your script is executed. Each browser has a different way of showing the console. For Google Chrome, you select JavaScript console from the Tools menu. You can see how the console is displayed in Chrome in Figure 4-1; the other browsers have similar features.

Figure 4-1. *The Google Chrome JavaScript console*

You can see that the output from calling the console.log method is displayed in the console window, along with the details of where the message originated (in this case on line 6 of the example.html file). In this chapter, I won't show screenshots; I'll show just the results from some of the examples. So, for example, for Listing 4-1, the output is as follows:

```
Hello
```

I have formatted some of the results later in the chapter to make them easier to read. In the sections that follow, I'll show you the core features of the JavaScript language. If you have had any experience programming in any other modern language, you will find the JavaScript syntax and style familiar – albeit, as I said at the start of the chapter, with some oddities.

Using Statements

The basic JavaScript building block is the *statement*. Each statement represents a single command, and statements are usually terminated by a semicolon (;). The semicolon is optional, but using them makes your code easier to read and allows for multiple statements on a single line. Listing 4-2 shows a pair of statements in a script that is defined using a script element.

Listing 4-2. Using JavaScript Statements

```
<!DOCTYPE HTML>
<html>
    <head>
        <title>Example</title>
        <script type="text/javascript">
            console.log("This is a statement");
            console.log("This is also a statement");
        </script>
    </head>
    <body>
        This is a simple example
    </body>
</html>
```

The browser executes each statement in turn. In this example, I simply write out a pair of messages to the console. The results are as follows:

```
This is a statement
This is also a statement
```

Defining and Using Functions

When the browser reaches a `script` element, it immediately executes the JavaScript statements, one after the other. You can also package multiple statements into a *function*, which won't be executed until the browser encounters a statement that *invokes* the function, as shown in Listing 4-3.

Listing 4-3. Defining a JavaScript Function

```
<!DOCTYPE HTML>
<html>
<head>
    <title>Example</title>
    <script type="text/javascript">
        function myFunc() {
            console.log("This is a statement");
        };

        myFunc();
    </script>
</head>
<body>
    This is a simple example
</body>
</html>
```

The statements contained by a function are encompassed by braces ({ and }) and are referred to as the *code block*. This listing defines a function called myFunc, which contains a single statement in the code block. JavaScript is a case-sensitive language, which means that the keyword function must be lowercase. The statement in the function won't be executed until the browser reaches another statement that calls the myFunc function, like this:

```
myFunc();
```

Executing the statement in the function produces the following output:

```
This is a statement
```

Other than demonstrating how functions are defined, this example isn't especially useful because the function is invoked immediately after it has been defined. You will see some examples with more useful functions in Part 2.

Defining Functions with Parameters

In common with most programming languages, JavaScript allows you to define parameters for functions, as shown in Listing 4-4.

Listing 4-4. Defining Functions with Parameters

```html
<!DOCTYPE HTML>
<html>
<head>
    <title>Example</title>
    <script type="text/javascript">
        function myFunc(name, weather) {
            console.log("Hello " + name + ".");
            console.log("It is " + weather + " today");
        };

        myFunc("Adam", "sunny");
    </script>
</head>
<body>
    This is a simple example
</body>
</html>
```

I added two parameters to the myFunc function, called name and weather. JavaScript is a dynamically typed language, which means you don't have to declare the data type of the parameters when you define the function. I'll come back to dynamic typing later in the chapter when I cover JavaScript variables. To invoke a function with parameters, you provide values as argument when you invoke the function, like this:

```
...
myFunc("Adam", "sunny");
...
```

The results from this listing are as follows:

```
Hello Adam.
It is sunny today
```

The number of arguments when you invoke a function doesn't need to match the number of parameters in the function. If you call the function with fewer arguments than it has parameters, then the value of any parameters you have not supplied values for is undefined. If you call the function with more arguments than there are parameters, then the additional arguments are ignored.

The consequence of this is that you can't create two functions with the same name and different parameters and expect JavaScript to differentiate between them based on the arguments you provide when invoking the function. This is called *polymorphism*, and although it is supported in languages such as Java and C#, it isn't available in JavaScript. Instead, if you define two functions with the same name, then the second definition replaces the first.

Defining Functions That Return Results

You can return results from functions using the `return` keyword. Listing 4-5 shows a function that returns a result.

Listing 4-5. Returning a Result from a Function

```
<!DOCTYPE HTML>
<html>
<head>
    <title>Example</title>
    <script type="text/javascript">
        function myFunc(name) {
            return ("Hello " + name + ".");
        };

        console.log(myFunc("Adam"));
    </script>
</head>
<body>
    This is a simple example
</body>
</html>
```

This function defines one parameter and uses it to produce a result. I invoke the function and pass the result as the argument to the `console.log` function, like this:

```
...
console.log(myFunc("Adam"));
...
```

Notice that you don't have to declare that the function will return a result or denote the data type of the result. The result from this listing is as follows:

```
Hello Adam.
```

Using Variables and Types

You define variables using the var keyword and can optionally assign a value to the variable in a single statement. Variables that are defined within a function are *local variables* and are available for use only within that function. Variables that are defined directly in the script element are *global variables* and can be accessed anywhere, including other scripts in the same HTML document. Listing 4-6 demonstrates the use of local and global variables.

Listing 4-6. Using Local and Global Variables

```
<!DOCTYPE HTML>
<html>
    <head>
        <title>Example</title>
        <script type="text/javascript">
            var myGlobalVar = "apples";

            function myFunc(name) {
                var myLocalVar = "sunny";
                return ("Hello " + name + ". Today is " + myLocalVar + ".");
            };
            console.log(myFunc("Adam"));
        </script>
        <script type="text/javascript">
            console.log("I like " + myGlobalVar);
        </script>
    </head>
    <body>
        This is a simple example
    </body>
</html>
```

Again, JavaScript is a dynamically typed language. This doesn't mean JavaScript doesn't have types: it just means you don't have to explicitly declare the type of a variable and that you can assign different types to the same variable without any difficulty. JavaScript will determine the type based on the value you assign to a variable and will freely convert between types based on the context in which they are used. The result from Listing 4-6 is as follows:

```
Hello Adam. Today is sunny.
I like apples
```

Using the Primitive Types

JavaScript defines a set of primitive types: string, number, and boolean. This may seem like a short list, but JavaScript manages to fit a lot of flexibility into these three types.

Working with Strings

You define string values using either the double quote or single quote characters, as shown in Listing 4-7.

Listing 4-7. Defining String Variables

```
<!DOCTYPE HTML>
<html>
<head>
    <title>Example</title>
    <script type="text/javascript">
        var firstString = "This is a string";
        var secondString = 'And so is this';
    </script>
</head>
<body>
    This is a simple example
</body>
</html>
```

The quote characters that you use must match. You can't start a string with a single quote and finish with a double quote, for example. There is no console output for this listing.

Working with Booleans

The boolean type has two values: `true` and `false`. Listing 4-8 shows both values being used, but this type is most useful when used in conditional statements, such as an `if` statement. There is no console output from this listing.

Listing 4-8. Defining Boolean Values

```
<!DOCTYPE HTML>
<html>
<head>
    <title>Example</title>
    <script type="text/javascript">
        var firstBool = true;
        var secondBool = false;
    </script>
</head>
<body>
    This is a simple example
</body>
</html>
```

Working with Numbers

The number type is used to represent both *integer* and *floating-point* numbers (also known as *real numbers*). Listing 4-9 provides a demonstration.

Listing 4-9. Defining number Values

```
<!DOCTYPE HTML>
<html>
<head>
    <title>Example</title>
    <script type="text/javascript">
        var daysInWeek = 7;
        var pi = 3.14;
        var hexValue = 0xFFFF;
    </script>
</head>
<body>
    This is a simple example
</body>
</html>
```

You don't have to specify which kind of number you are using. You just express the value you require, and JavaScript will act accordingly. In the listing, I have defined an integer value, defined a floating-point value, and prefixed a value with 0x to denote a hexadecimal value. (There is no console output from the listing.)

Creating Objects

JavaScript supports the notion of objects, and there are different ways in which you can create them. Listing 4-10 gives a simple example.

Listing 4-10. Creating an Object

```
<!DOCTYPE HTML>
<html>
<head>
    <title>Example</title>
    <script type="text/javascript">
        var myData = new Object();
        myData.name = "Adam";
        myData.weather = "sunny";

        console.log("Hello " + myData.name + ". ");
        console.log("Today is " + myData.weather + ".");
    </script>
</head>
<body>
    This is a simple example
</body>
</html>
```

I create an object by calling new Object(), and I assign the result (the newly created object) to a variable called myData. Once the object is created, I can define properties on the object just by assigning values, like this:

```
...
myData.name = "Adam";
...
```

Prior to this statement, my object doesn't have a property called name. After the statement has executed, the property does exist, and it has been assigned the value Adam. You can read the value of a property by combining the variable name and the property name with a period, like this:

```
...
console.log("Hello " + myData.name + ". ");
...
```

The result from the listing is as follows:

```
Hello Adam.
Today is sunny.
```

Using Object Literals

You can define an object and its properties in a single step using the *object literal* format. Listing 4-11 shows how this is done.

Listing 4-11. Using the Object Literal Format

```
<!DOCTYPE HTML>
<html>
<head>
    <title>Example</title>
    <script type="text/javascript">
        var myData = {
            name: "Adam",
            weather: "sunny"
        };

        console.log("Hello " + myData.name + ". ");
        console.log("Today is " + myData.weather + ".");
    </script>
</head>
<body>
    This is a simple example
</body>
</html>
```

Each property that you want to define is separated from its value using a colon (:), and properties are separated using a comma (,). The effect is the same as in the previous example, and the result from the listing is as follows:

```
Hello Adam.
Today is sunny.
```

69

Using Functions as Methods

One of the features that I like most about JavaScript is the way that you can add functions to your objects. A function defined on an object is called a *method*. I don't know why, but I find this elegant and endlessly pleasing. Listing 4-12 shows how you can add methods in this manner.

Listing 4-12. Adding Methods to an Object

```
<!DOCTYPE HTML>
<html>
<head>
    <title>Example</title>
    <script type="text/javascript">
        var myData = {
            name: "Adam",
            weather: "sunny",
            printMessages: function() {
                console.log("Hello " + this.name + ". ");
                console.log("Today is " + this.weather + ".");
            }
        };
        myData.printMessages();
    </script>
</head>
<body>
    This is a simple example
</body>
</html>
```

In this example, I have used a function to create a method called printMessages. Notice that to refer to the properties defined by the object, I have to use the this keyword. When a function is used as a method, the function is implicitly passed the object on which the method has been called as an argument through the special variable this. The output from the listing is as follows:

```
Hello Adam.
Today is sunny.
```

Working with Objects

Once you have created objects, you can do a number of things with them. In the following sections, I'll describe the activities that will be useful later in this book.

Read and Modify the Property Values

The most obvious thing to do with an object is to read or modify the values assigned to the properties that the object defines. There are two different syntax styles you can use, both of which are shown in Listing 4-13.

Listing 4-13. Reading and Modifying Object Properties

```html
<!DOCTYPE HTML>
<html>
<head>
    <title>Example</title>
    <script type="text/javascript">
        var myData = {
            name: "Adam",
            weather: "sunny",
        };

        myData.name = "Joe";
        myData["weather"] = "raining";

        console.log("Hello " + myData.name + ".");
        console.log("It is " + myData["weather"]);
    </script>
</head>
<body>
    This is a simple example
</body>
</html>
```

The first style is the one that most programmers with be familiar with and that I used in earlier examples. You concatenate the object name and the property name together with a period, like this:

```
...
myData.name = "Joe";
...
```

You can assign a new value to the property by using the equals sign (=) or read the current value by omitting it. The second style is an array-style index, like this:

```
...
myData["weather"] = "raining";
...
```

In this style, you specify the name of the property you want between square braces ([and]). This can be a convenient way to access a property because you can pass the name of the property you are interested as a variable, like this:

```
...
var myData = {
    name: "Adam",
    weather: "sunny",
};

var propName = "weather";
myData[propName] = "raining";
...
```

71

This is the basis for how you enumerate the properties of an object, which I describe next. Here is the console output from the listing:

```
Hello Joe.
It is raining
```

Enumerating an Object's Properties

You enumerate the properties that an object has using the for...in statement. Listing 4-14 shows how you can use this statement.

Listing 4-14. Enumerating an Object's Properties

```
<!DOCTYPE HTML>
<html>
<head>
    <title>Example</title>
    <script type="text/javascript">
        var myData = {
            name: "Adam",
            weather: "sunny",
            printMessages: function() {
                console.log("Hello " + this.name + ". ");
                console.log("Today is " + this.weather + ".");
            }
        };

        for (var prop in myData) {
            console.log("Name: " + prop + " Value: " + myData[prop]);
        }

    </script>
</head>
<body>
    This is a simple example
</body>
</html>
```

The for...in loop performs the statement in the code block for each property in the myData object. The prop variable is assigned the name of the property being processed in each iteration. I use the array-index style to retrieve the value of the property from the object. The output from this listing is as follows (I have formatted the results to make them easier to read):

```
Name: name Value: Adam
Name: weather Value: sunny
Name: printMessages Value: function () {
    console.log("Hello " + this.name + ". ");
    console.log("Today is " + this.weather + ".");
}
```

From the result, you can see that the function I defined as a method is also enumerated. This is as a result of the flexible way that JavaScript handles functions.

Adding and Deleting Properties and Methods

You are still able to define new properties for an object, even when you have used the object literal style. Listing 4-15 gives a demonstration. (The listings in this section do not produce any console output.)

Listing 4-15. Adding a New Property to an Object

```
<!DOCTYPE HTML>
<html>
<head>
    <title>Example</title>
    <script type="text/javascript">
        var myData = {
            name: "Adam",
            weather: "sunny",
        };

        myData.dayOfWeek = "Monday";
    </script>
</head>
<body>
    This is a simple example
</body>
</html>
```

In this listing, I have added a new property to the object called dayOfWeek. I have used the dot notation (concatenating the object and property names with a period), but I could as readily used the index-style notation. As you might expect by now, you can also add new methods to an object by setting the value of a property to be a function, as shown in Listing 4-16.

Listing 4-16. Adding a New Method to an Object

```
<!DOCTYPE HTML>
<html>
<head>
    <title>Example</title>
    <script type="text/javascript">
        var myData = {
            name: "Adam",
            weather: "sunny",
        };

        myData.SayHello = function() {
          console.write("Hello");
        };
    </script>
</head>
<body>
    This is a simple example
</body>
</html>
```

73

You can delete a property or method from an object using the delete keyword, as shown in Listing 4-17.

Listing 4-17. Deleting a Property from an Object

```
<!DOCTYPE HTML>
<html>
<head>
    <title>Example</title>
    <script type="text/javascript">
        var myData = {
            name: "Adam",
            weather: "sunny",
        };

        delete myData.name;
        delete myData["weather"];
        delete myData.SayHello;
    </script>
</head>
<body>
    This is a simple example
</body>
</html>
```

Determine Whether an Object Has a Property

You can check to see whether an object has a property using the in expression, as shown in Listing 4-18.

Listing 4-18. Checking to See Whether an Object Has a Property

```
<!DOCTYPE HTML>
<html>
<head>
    <title>Example</title>
    <script type="text/javascript">
        var myData = {
            name: "Adam",
            weather: "sunny",
        };

        var hasName = "name" in myData;
        var hasDate = "date" in myData;

        console.log("HasName: " + hasName);
        console.log("HasDate: " + hasDate);
    </script>
</head>
<body>
    This is a simple example
</body>
</html>
```

In this example, I test for a property that exists and one that doesn't. The value of the hasName variable will be true, and the value of the hasDate property will be false, as follows:

```
HasName: true
HasDate: false
```

Using JavaScript Operators

JavaScript defines a largely standard set of operators. I've summarized the most useful in Table 4-1.

Table 4-1. *Useful JavaScript Operators*

Operator	Description
++, --	Pre- or post-increment and decrement
+, -, *, /, %	Addition, subtraction, multiplication, division, remainder
<, <=, >, >=	Less than, less than or equal to, more than, more than or equal to
==, !=	Equality and inequality tests
===, !==	Identity and nonidentity tests
&&, ||	Logical AND and OR
=	Assignment
+	String concatenation
?:	Three operand conditional statement

Using Conditional Statements

Many of the JavaScript operators are used in conjunction with conditional statements. In this book, I tend to use the if/else and switch statements. Listing 4-19 shows the use of both (which will be familiar if you have worked with pretty much any programming language).

Listing 4-19. Using the if/else and switch Conditional Statements

```
<!DOCTYPE HTML>
<html>
<head>
    <title>Example</title>
    <script type="text/javascript">

        var name = "Adam";

        if (name == "Adam") {
            console.log("Name is Adam");
        } else if (name == "Jacqui") {
            console.log("Name is Jacqui");
```

```
        } else {
            console.log("Name is neither Adam or Jacqui");
        }

        switch (name) {
            case "Adam":
                console.log("Name is Adam");
                break;
            case "Jacqui":
                console.log("Name is Jacqui");
                break;
            default:
                console.log("Name is neither Adam or Jacqui");
                break;
        }
    </script>
</head>
<body>
    This is a simple example
</body>
</html>
```

The results from the listing are as follows:

```
Name is Adam
Name is Adam
```

The Equality Operator vs. the Identity Operator

The equality and identity operators are of particular note. The equality operator will attempt to coerce operands to the same type in order to assess equality. This is a handy feature, as long as you are aware it is happening. Listing 4-20 shows the equality operator in action.

Listing 4-20. Using the Equality Operator

```
<!DOCTYPE HTML>
<html>
<head>
    <title>Example</title>
    <script type="text/javascript">

        var firstVal = 5;
        var secondVal = "5";

        if (firstVal == secondVal) {
            console.log("They are the same");
        } else {
            console.log("They are NOT the same");
        }
    </script>
</head>
```

```
<body>
    This is a simple example
</body>
</html>
```

The output from this script is as follows:

```
They are the same
```

JavaScript is converting the two operands into the same type and comparing them. In essence, the equality operator tests that values are the same irrespective of their type. If you want to test to ensure that the values *and* the types are the same, then you need to use the identity operator (===, three equals signs, rather than the two of the equality operator), as shown in Listing 4- 21.

Listing 4-21. Using the Identity Operator

```
<!DOCTYPE HTML>
<html>
<head>
    <title>Example</title>
    <script type="text/javascript">

        var firstVal = 5;
        var secondVal = "5";

        if (firstVal === secondVal) {
            console.log("They are the same");
        } else {
            console.log("They are NOT the same");
        }
    </script>
</head>
<body>
    This is a simple example
</body>
</html>
```

In this example, the identity operator will consider the two variables to be different. This operator doesn't coerce types. The result from this script is as follows:

```
They are NOT the same
```

JavaScript primitives are compared by value, but JavaScript objects are compared by reference. Listing 4-22 shows how JavaScript handles equality and identity tests for objects.

77

Listing 4-22. Performing Equality and Identity Tests on Objects

```html
<!DOCTYPE HTML>
<html>
<head>
    <title>Example</title>
    <script type="text/javascript">

        var myData1 = {
            name: "Adam",
            weather: "sunny",
        };

        var myData2 = {
            name: "Adam",
            weather: "sunny",
        };

        var myData3 = myData2;

        var test1 = myData1 == myData2;
        var test2 = myData2 == myData3;
        var test3 = myData1 === myData2;
        var test4 = myData2 === myData3;

        console.log("Test 1: " + test1 + " Test 2: " + test2);
        console.log("Test 3: " + test3 + " Test 4: " + test4);
    </script>
</head>
<body>
    This is a simple example
</body>
</html>
```

The results from this script are as follows:

```
Test 1: false Test 2: true
Test 3: false Test 4: true
```

Listing 4-23 shows the same tests performed on primitives.

Listing 4-23. Performing Equality and Identity Tests on Objects

```html
<!DOCTYPE HTML>
<html>
<head>
    <title>Example</title>
    <script type="text/javascript">
```

```
        var myData1 = 5;
        var myData2 = "5";
        var myData3 = myData2;

        var test1 = myData1 == myData2;
        var test2 = myData2 == myData3;
        var test3 = myData1 === myData2;
        var test4 = myData2 === myData3;

        console.log("Test 1: " + test1 + " Test 2: " + test2);
        console.log("Test 3: " + test3 + " Test 4: " + test4);
    </script>
</head>
<body>
    This is a simple example
</body>
</html>
```

The results from this script are as follows:

```
Test 1: true Test 2: true
Test 3: false Test 4: true
```

Explicitly Converting Types

The string concatenation operator (+) has a higher precedence than the addition operator (also +), which means that JavaScript will concatenate variables in preference to adding. This can cause confusion because JavaScript will also convert types freely to produce a result – and not always the result that is expected, as shown in Listing 4-24.

Listing 4-24. String Concatenation Operator Precedence

```
<!DOCTYPE HTML>
<html>
<head>
    <title>Example</title>
    <script type="text/javascript">

        var myData1 = 5 + 5;
        var myData2 = 5 + "5";

        console.log("Result 1: " + myData1);
        console.log("Result 2: " + myData2);

    </script>
</head>
<body>
    This is a simple example
</body>
</html>
```

The result from this script is as follows:

```
Result 1: 10
Result 2: 55
```

The second result is the kind that causes confusion. What might be intended to be an addition operation is interpreted as string concatenation through a combination of operator precedence and over-eager type conversion. To avoid this, you can explicitly convert the types of values to ensure you perform the right kind of operation, as described in the following sections.

Converting Numbers to Strings

If you are working with multiple number variables and want to concatenate them as strings, then you can convert the numbers to strings with the toString method, as shown in Listing 4-25.

Listing 4-25. Using the Number.toString Method

```
<!DOCTYPE HTML>
<html>
<head>
    <title>Example</title>
    <script type="text/javascript">
        var myData1 = (5).toString() + String(5);
        console.log("Result: " + myData1);
    </script>
</head>
<body>
    This is a simple example
</body>
</html>
```

Notice that I have placed the numeric value in parentheses, and then I called the toString method. This is because you have to allow JavaScript to convert the literal value into a number before you can call the methods that the number type defines. I have also shown an alternative approach to achieve the same effect, which is to call the String function and pass in the numeric value as an argument. Both of these techniques have the same effect, which is to convert a number to a string, meaning that the + operator is used for string concatenation and not addition. The output from this script is as follows:

```
Result: 55
```

There are some other methods that allow you to exert more control over how a number is represented as a string. I have briefly described these in Table 4-2. All of the methods shown in the table are defined by the number type.

Table 4-2. *Useful Number.toString Methods*

Method	Description	Returns
toString()	Represents a number in base 10	string
toString(2) toString(8) toString(16)	Represent a number in binary, octal, or hexadecimal notation	string
toFixed(n)	Represents a real number with the n digits after the decimal point	string
toExponential(n)	Represents a number using exponential notation with one digit before the decimal point and n digits after	string
toPrecision(n)	Represents a number with n significant digits, using exponential notation if required	string

Converting Strings to Numbers

The complementary technique is to convert strings to numbers so that you can perform addition rather than concatenation. You can do this with the Number function, as shown in Listing 4-26.

Listing 4-26. Converting Strings to Numbers

```
<!DOCTYPE HTML>
<html>
<head>
    <title>Example</title>
    <script type="text/javascript">
        var firstVal = "5";
        var secondVal = "5";

    var result = Number(firstVal) + Number(secondVal);

        console.log("Result: " + result);
    </script>
</head>
<body>
    This is a simple example
</body>
</html>
```

The output from this script is as follows:

Result: 10

The Number method is quite strict in the way that is parses string values, but there are two other functions you can use that are more flexible and will ignore trailing non-number characters. These functions are parseInt and parseFloat. I have described all three methods in Table 4-3.

Table 4-3. *Useful String to Number Methods*

Method	Description
Number(str)	Parses the specified string to create an integer or real value
parseInt(str)	Parses the specified string to create an integer value
parseFloat(str)	Parses the specified string to create an integer or real value

Working with Arrays

JavaScript arrays work much like arrays in most other programming languages. Listing 4-27 shows how you can create and populate an array.

Listing 4-27. Creating and Populating an Array

```
<!DOCTYPE HTML>
<html>
<head>
    <title>Example</title>
    <script type="text/javascript">

        var myArray = new Array();
        myArray[0] = 100;
        myArray[1] = "Adam";
        myArray[2] = true;

    </script>
</head>
<body>
    This is a simple example
</body>
</html>
```

I have created a new array by calling new Array(). This creates an empty array, which I assign to the variable myArray. In the subsequent statements, I assign values to various index positions in the array. (There is no console output from this listing.) ().

There are a couple of things to note in this example. First, I didn't need to declare the number of items in the array when I created it. JavaScript arrays will resize themselves to hold any number of items. The second point is that I didn't have to declare the data types that the array will hold. Any JavaScript array can hold any mix of data types. In the example, I have assigned three items to the array: a number, a string, and a boolean.

Using an Array Literal

The array literal style lets you create and populate an array in a single statement, as shown in Listing 4-28.

Listing 4-28. Using the Array Literal Style

```
<!DOCTYPE HTML>
<html>
<head>
    <title>Example</title>
    <script type="text/javascript">

      var myArray = [100, "Adam", true];

    </script>
</head>
<body>
    This is a simple example
</body>
</html>
```

In this example, I specified that the myArray variable should be assigned a new array by specifying the items I wanted in the array between square brackets ([and]). (There is no console output from this listing.)

Reading and Modifying the Contents of an Array

You read the value at a given index using square braces ([and]), placing the index you require between the braces, as shown in Listing 4-29.

Listing 4-29. Reading the Data from an Array Index

```
<!DOCTYPE HTML>
<html>
<head>
    <title>Example</title>
    <script type="text/javascript">
        var myArray = [100, "Adam", true];
        console.log("Index 0: " + myArray[0]);
    </script>
</head>
<body>
    This is a simple example
</body>
</html>
```

You can modify the data held in any position in a JavaScript array simply by assigning a new value to the index. Just as with regular variables, you can switch the data type at an index without any problems. The output from the listing is as follows:

```
Index 0: 100
```

Listing 4-30 demonstrates modifying the contents of an array.

Listing 4-30. Modifying the Contents of an Array

```
<!DOCTYPE HTML>
<html>
<head>
    <title>Example</title>
    <script type="text/javascript">
        var myArray = [100, "Adam", true];
        myArray[0] = "Tuesday";
        console.log("Index 0: " + myArray[0]);
    </script>
</head>
<body>
    This is a simple example
</body>
</html>
```

In this example, I have assigned a `string` to position 0 in the array, a position that was previously held by a number and produces this output:

```
Index 0: Tuesday
```

Enumerating the Contents of an Array

You enumerate the content of an array using a `for` loop. Listing 4-31 shows how to apply the loop to display the contents of a simple array.

Listing 4-31. Enumerating the Contents of an Array

```
<!DOCTYPE HTML>
<html>
<head>
    <title>Example</title>
    <script type="text/javascript">
        var myArray = [100, "Adam", true];
        for (var i = 0; i < myArray.length; i++) {
            console.log("Index " + i + ": " + myArray[i]);
        }
    </script>
</head>
<body>
    This is a simple example
</body>
</html>
```

The JavaScript loop works just the same way as loops in many other languages. You determine how many elements there are in the array by using the length property. The output from the listing is as follows:

```
Index 0: 100
Index 1: Adam
Index 2: true
```

Using the Built-in Array Methods

The JavaScript Array object defines a number of methods that you can use to work with arrays. Table 4-4 describes the most useful of these methods.

Table 4-4. *Useful Array Methods*

Method	Description	Returns
concat(otherArray)	Concatenates the contents of the array with the array specified by the argument. Multiple arrays can be specified.	Array
join(separator)	Joins all of the elements in the array to form a string. The argument specifies the character used to delimit the items.	string
pop()	Treats an array like a stack and removes and returns the last item in the array.	object
push(item)	Treats an array like a stack and appends the specified item to the array.	void
reverse()	Reverses the order of the items in the array.	Array
shift()	Like pop, but operates on the first element in the array.	object
slice(start,end)	Returns a section of the array.	Array
sort()	Sorts the items in the array.	Array
splice(index, count)	Removes count items from the array, starting at the specified index.	Array
unshift(item)	Like push, but inserts the new element at the start of the array.	void

Handling Errors

JavaScript uses the try...catch statement to deal with errors. For the most part, I won't be worrying about errors in this book because my focus is on explaining the features of jQuery and not general programing technique. Listing 4-32 shows how to use this kind of statement.

Listing 4-32. Handling an Exception

```
<!DOCTYPE HTML>
<html>
<head>
    <title>Example</title>
    <script type="text/javascript">
```

```
        try {
            var myArray;
            for (var i = 0; i < myArray.length; i++) {
                console.log("Index " + i + ": " + myArray[i]);
            }
        } catch (e) {
            console.log("Error: " + e);
        }
    </script>
</head>
<body>
    This is a simple example
</body>
</html>
```

The problem in this script is a common one. I am trying to use a variable that has not been initialized properly. I have wrapped the code that I suspect will cause an error in the try clauseof the statement. If no problems arise, then the statements execute normally, and the catch clause is ignored.

However, since there is an error in this code, then execution of the statements in the try clause stops immediately, and control passes to the catch clause, producing the following output on the console:

```
Error: TypeError: Cannot read property 'length' of undefined
```

The error that you have encountered is described by an Error object, which is passed to the catch clause. Table 4-5 shows the properties defined by the Error object.

Table 4-5. *The Error Object*

Property	Description	Returns
message	A description of the error condition.	string
name	The name of the error. This is Error, by default.	string
number	The error number, if any, for this kind of error.	number

The catch clauseis your opportunity to recover from or clear up after the error. If there are statements that need to be executed whether or not there has been an error, you can place them in the optional finally clause, as shown in Listing 4-33.

Listing 4-33. Using a finally Clause

```
<!DOCTYPE HTML>
<html>
<head>
    <title>Example</title>
    <script type="text/javascript">
        try {
            var myArray;
            for (var i = 0; i < myArray.length; i++) {
                console.log("Index " + i + ": " + myArray[i]);
            }
```

```
        } catch (e) {
            console.log("Error: " + e);
        } finally {
            console.log("Statements here are always executed");
        }
    </script>
</head>
<body>
    This is a simple example
</body>
</html>
```

The listing produces the following console output:

```
Error: TypeError: Cannot read property 'length' of undefined
Statements here are always executed
```

Comparing undefined and null Values

JavaScript defines a couple of special values that you need to be careful with when you compare them: undefined and null. The undefined value is returned when you read a variable that hasn't had a value assigned to it or try to read an object property that doesn't exist. Listing 4-34 shows how undefined is used in JavaScript.

Listing 4-34. The undefined Special Value

```
<!DOCTYPE HTML>
<html>
<head>
    <title>Example</title>
    <script type="text/javascript">
        var myData = {
            name: "Adam",
            weather: "sunny",
        };
        console.log("Prop: " + myData.doesntexist);
    </script>
</head>
<body>
    This is a simple example
</body>
</html>
```

The output from this listing is as follows:

```
Prop: undefined
```

JavaScript is unusual in that it *also* defines null, another special value. The null value is slightly different from undefined. The undefined value is returned when no value is defined, and null is used when you want to indicate that you have assigned a value but that value is not a valid object, string, number, or boolean; that is, you have defined a value of *no value*. To help clarify this, Listing 4-35 shows the transition from undefined to null.

Listing 4-35. Using undefined and null

```
<!DOCTYPE HTML>
<html>
<head>
    <title>Example</title>
    <script type="text/javascript">

        var myData = {
            name: "Adam",
        };

        console.log("Var: " + myData.weather);
        console.log("Prop: " + ("weather" in myData));

        myData.weather = "sunny";
        console.log("Var: " + myData.weather);
        console.log("Prop: " + ("weather" in myData));

        myData.weather = null;
        console.log("Var: " + myData.weather);
        console.log("Prop: " + ("weather" in myData));

    </script>
</head>
<body>
    This is a simple example
</body>
</html>
```

I create an object and then try to read the value of the weather property, which is not defined:

```
...
console.log("Var: " + myData.weather);
console.log("Prop: " + ("weather" in myData));
...
```

There is no weather property, so the value returned by calling myData.weather is undefined, and using the in keyword to determine whether the object contains the property returns false. The output from these two statements is as follows:

```
Var: undefined
Prop: false
```

Next, I assign a value to the weather property, which has the effect of adding the property to the object:

```
...
myData.weather = "sunny";
console.log("Var: " + myData.weather);
console.log("Prop: " + ("weather" in myData));
...
```

I read the value of the property and check to see whether the property exists in the object again. As you might expect, the object *does* define the property and its value is sunny:

```
Var: sunny
Prop: true
```

Now I set the value of the property to null, like this:

```
...
myData.weather = null;
...
```

This has a specific effect. The property is still defined by the object, but I have indicated it doesn't contain a value. When I perform my checks again, I get the following results:

```
Var: null
Prop: true
```

This distinction is important when it comes to comparing undefined and null values because null is an object and undefined is a type in its own right.

Checking for null or undefined

If you want to check to see whether a property is null or undefined (and you don't care which), then you can simply use an if statement and the negation operator (!), as shown in Listing 4-36.

Listing 4-36. Checking to See Whether a Property Is null or undefined

```
<!DOCTYPE HTML>
<html>
<head>
    <title>Example</title>
    <script type="text/javascript">

        var myData = {
            name: "Adam",
            city: null
        };
```

```
        if (!myData.name) {
            console.log("name IS null or undefined");
        } else {
            console.log("name is NOT null or undefined");
        }

        if (!myData.city) {
            console.log("city IS null or undefined");
        } else {
            console.log("city is NOT null or undefined");
        }

    </script>
</head>
<body>
    This is a simple example
</body>
</html>
```

This technique relies on the type coercion that JavaScript performs such that the values you are checking are treated as boolean values. If a variable or property is null or undefined, then the coerced boolean value is false. The listing produces this output:

```
name is NOT null or undefined
city IS null or undefined
```

Differentiating Between null and undefined

You have a choice if you want to compare two values. If you want to treat an undefined value as being the same as a null value, then you can use the equality operator (==) and rely on JavaScript to convert the types. An undefined variable will be regarded as being equal to a null variable, for example. If you want to differentiate between null and undefined, then you need to use the identity operator (===). Listing 4-37 shows both comparisons.

Listing 4-37. Equality and Identity Comparisons for null and undefined Values

```
<!DOCTYPE HTML>
<html>
<head>
    <title>Example</title>
    <script type="text/javascript">

        var firstVal = null;
        var secondVal;

        var equality = firstVal == secondVal;
        var identity = firstVal === secondVal;
```

```
        console.log("Equality: " + equality);
        console.log("Identity: " + identity);

    </script>
</head>
<body>
    This is a simple example
</body>
</html>
```

The output from this script is as follows:

```
Equality: true
Identity: false
```

Summary

In this chapter, I showed you the core JavaScript features that you will use throughout this book. Understanding basic JavaScript is essential to using jQuery, as you'll see in the chapters ahead. In Part 2 of this book, I introduce jQuery properly and show you how to use it.

CHAPTER 5

■ ■ ■

jQuery Basics

In this chapter, I will introduce you to your first jQuery script. The script is simple, but it demonstrates many of the most important characteristics of jQuery, including how you select elements in the document, how such selections are presented to you, and the nature of the relationship between jQuery and the built-in DOM API that is part of the HTML specification. Table 5-1 provides the summary for this chapter.

Table 5-1. *Chapter Summary*

Problem	Solution	Listing
Add jQuery to an HTML document.	Use the link element to import the jQuery element, linking either to your web server or to a CDN. Add a script element to define your jQuery script.	1
Dynamically select the jQuery 1.x or 2.x lines.	Use conditional comments.	2
Select elements in the document.	Pass a CSS selector to the $ or jQuery function.	3, 4, 10
Rename the $ function.	Use the noConflict method.	5, 6
Defer execution of your jQuery script until the document has been loaded.	Register a handler for the ready event on the global document variable or pass a function to the $ function.	7, 8
Take control of when the ready event is triggered.	Use the holdReady event.	9
Restrict element selection to part of the document.	Pass a context to the $ function.	11, 12
Determine the context used to create a jQuery object.	Read the context property.	13
Create a jQuery object from HTMLElement objects.	Pass the HTMLElement objects as the argument to the $ function.	14
Enumerate the contents of a jQuery object.	Treat the jQuery object as an array or use the each method.	15, 16
Find a specific element in a jQuery element.	Use the index or get methods.	17–19
Apply an operation to multiple elements in the document.	Use a jQuery method on a jQuery object.	20
Apply multiple operations to a jQuery object.	Chain methods calls together.	21–23
Handle an event.	Use one of the jQuery event handler methods.	24

JQUERY CHANGES SINCE THE LAST EDITION

In the first edition of this book, I described the use of the `selector` property to get a selector string from jQuery that could be used to repeat queries in the future. As of jQuery 1.9, the `selector` property has been deprecated and should not be used.

The selector engine that jQuery 1.9/2.0 uses (known as *Sizzle*) implements support for some new CSS3 selectors even in browsers that don't support them. The selectors are: `:nth-last-child`, `:nth-of-type`, `:nth-last-of-type`, `:first-of-type`, `:last-of-type`, `:only-of-type`, `:target`, `:root`, and `:lang`.

Setting Up jQuery

The first thing you need to do with jQuery is add it to the document you want to work with. Listing 5-1 shows the flower shop example document you first saw in Part 1, with the addition of the jQuery library.

Listing 5-1. The Flower Shop Example Document

```html
<!DOCTYPE html>
<html>
<head>
    <title>Example</title>
    <link rel="stylesheet" type="text/css" href="styles.css"/>
    <script src="jquery-2.0.2.js" type="text/javascript"></script>
</head>
<body>
    <h1>Jacqui's Flower Shop</h1>
    <form method="post">
        <div id="oblock">
            <div class="dtable">
                <div id="row1" class="drow">
                    <div class="dcell">
                        <img src="aster.png"/><label for="aster">Aster:</label>
                        <input name="aster" value="0" required>
                    </div>
                    <div class="dcell">
                        <img src="daffodil.png"/><label for="daffodil">Daffodil:</label>
                        <input name="daffodil" value="0" required >
                    </div>
                    <div class="dcell">
                        <img src="rose.png"/><label for="rose">Rose:</label>
                        <input name="rose" value="0" required>
                    </div>
                </div>
                <div id="row2" class="drow">
                    <div class="dcell">
                        <img src="peony.png"/><label for="peony">Peony:</label>
                        <input name="peony" value="0" required>
                    </div>
```

```
            <div class="dcell">
                <img src="primula.png"/><label for="primula">Primula:</label>
                <input name="primula" value="0" required>
            </div>
            <div class="dcell">
                <img src="snowdrop.png"/><label for="snowdrop">Snowdrop:</label>
                <input name="snowdrop" value="0" required>
            </div>
        </div>
    </div>
  </div>
  <div id="buttonDiv"><button type="submit">Place Order</button></div>
</form>
</body>
</html>
```

To help maintain focus on the content, I have moved the CSS styles to a separate style sheet called styles.css, as demonstrated in Chapter 3. You can see how I have added the jQuery library to the document, as follows:

```
...
<script src="jquery-2.0.2.js" type="text/javascript"></script>
...
```

Once you have selected the jQuery line that you will be using (the 1.x or 2.x line, as described in Chapter 3), you will have the choice of two files from jquery.com – one with a .js file extension and the other with .min.js. For version of the 2.x line that is current as I write this, the files are called jquery-2.0.2.js and jquery-2.0.2.min.js.

The jquery-2.0.2.js file is the one generally used during the development of a web site or application. This file is around 240KB and standard JavaScript code. You can open and read the file to learn about how jQuery implements its features and use the browser debugger to figure out what is going wrong if you encounter problems in your code.

■ **Tip** jQuery is actively developed, and so by the time you read this a later version will almost certainly have been released. But don't worry – despite all of the talk of deprecated methods and split development lines, the jQuery API is incredibly stable, and all of the techniques that I show you in this book will continue to work as jQuery 1.x and 2.x continue to mature.

The other file, jquery.2.0.2.min.js, is intended for use when you deploy your site or web application to users. It contains the same JavaScript code but has been *minified*, meaning that all of the whitespace characters have been removed, and the meaningful variable names have been replaced with single-character names to save space. The minified script is almost impossible to read for the purposes of debugging, but it is much smaller. The minification process reduces the size of the file to about 82KB and if you are serving up a lot of pages that rely on jQuery, then this difference can save you significant amounts of bandwidth.

■ **Tip** You can download a source map (which has the .min.map extension) from jquery.com. Source maps allow minified code to be more easily debugged. They are a new idea and are not that widely implemented as I write this. You can see a simple demonstration at http://www.html5rocks.com/en/tutorials/developertools/sourcemaps.

USING A CDN FOR JQUERY

An alternative to storing the jQuery library on your own web servers is to use a public *content delivery network* (CDN) that hosts jQuery. A CDN is a distributed network of servers that deliver files to the user using the server that is closest to them. There are a couple of benefits to using a CDN. The first is a faster experience to the user, because the jQuery library file is downloaded from the server closest to them, rather than from your servers. Often a download won't be required at all: jQuery is so popular that the user's browser may have already cached the library from another application or site that also uses jQuery. The second benefit is that none of your bandwidth is used delivering jQuery to the user. For high-traffic sites, this can be a significant cost savings.

When using a CDN, you must have confidence in the CDN operator. You want to be sure that the user receives the file they are supposed to and that service will always be available. Google and Microsoft both provide CDN services for jQuery (and other popular JavaScript libraries) free of charge. Both companies have good experience running highly available services and are unlikely to deliberately tamper with the jQuery library. You can learn about the Microsoft service at `www.asp.net/ajaxlibrary/cdn.ashx` and about the Google service at `http://code.google.com/apis/libraries/devguide.html`.

The CDN approach isn't suitable for applications that are delivered to users within an intranet because it causes all the browsers to go to the Internet to get the jQuery library, rather than access the local server, which is generally closer and faster and has lower bandwidth costs.

Using Conditional Comments

In Listing 5-1, I included only version 2.0.2 of the jQuery library. This version offers the best performance but it doesn't support older versions of Internet Explorer, as described in Chapter 1.

The good news is that you don't have to choose between performance and compatibility. There is a technique that dynamically selects between the 1.x and 2.x jQuery libraries automatically, using a feature called *conditional comments* that Microsoft created as a nonstandard enhancement to HTML for Internet Explorer 5. In Listing 5-2, you can see how I have applied the conditional comments feature to the example HTML document.

Listing 5-2. Using Conditional Comments to Dynamically Select between jQuery 1.x and 2.x

```
...
<head>
    <title>Example</title>
    <link rel="stylesheet" type="text/css" href="styles.css"/>
    <!--[if lt IE 9]>
        <script src="jquery-1.10.1.js" type="text/javascript"></script>
    <![endif]-->
    <!--[if gte IE 9]><!-->
        <script src="jquery-2.0.2.js" type="text/javascript"></script>
    <!--<![endif]-->
</head>
...
```

The conditional comments will load jQuery 1.10.1 for versions prior to Internet Explorer 9 and jQuery 2.0.2 for all other browsers. You should take care to copy these comments exactly – it is easy to make a mistake.

■ **Tip**   I am not going to go into conditional comments in this book, but you can learn more about them at
http://en.wikipedia.org/wiki/Conditional_comment.

A First jQuery Script

Now that I have added the jQuery library to the document, I can write some JavaScript that uses jQuery functionality.
Listing 5-3 contains a simple script element that shows off some of the basic jQuery features.

Listing 5-3. A First jQuery Script

```
<!DOCTYPE html>
<html>
<head>
    <title>Example</title>
    <link rel="stylesheet" type="text/css" href="styles.css"/>
    <script src="jquery-2.0.2.js" type="text/javascript"></script>
    <script type="text/javascript">
        $(document).ready(function () {
            $("img:odd").mouseenter(function (e) {
                $(this).css("opacity", 0.5);
            }).mouseout(function (e) {
                $(this).css("opacity", 1.0);
            });
        });
    </script>
</head>
<body>
    <h1>Jacqui's Flower Shop</h1>
    <form method="post">
        <div id="oblock">
            <div class="dtable">
                <div id="row1" class="drow">
                    <div class="dcell">
                        <img src="aster.png"/><label for="aster">Aster:</label>
                        <input name="aster" value="0" required>
                    </div>
                    <div class="dcell">
                        <img src="daffodil.png"/><label for="daffodil">Daffodil:</label>
                        <input name="daffodil" value="0" required >
                    </div>
                    <div class="dcell">
                        <img src="rose.png"/><label for="rose">Rose:</label>
                        <input name="rose" value="0" required>
                    </div>
                </div>
```

```
            <div id="row2" class="drow">
                <div class="dcell">
                    <img src="peony.png"/><label for="peony">Peony:</label>
                    <input name="peony" value="0" required>
                </div>
                <div class="dcell">
                    <img src="primula.png"/><label for="primula">Primula:</label>
                    <input name="primula" value="0" required>
                </div>
                <div class="dcell">
                    <img src="snowdrop.png"/><label for="snowdrop">Snowdrop:</label>
                    <input name="snowdrop" value="0" required>
                </div>
            </div>
        </div>
    </div>
    <div id="buttonDiv"><button type="submit">Place Order</button></div>
</form>
</body>
</html>
```

This is a short script, but it demonstrates some of the most important features and characteristics of jQuery. I'll break down the script line by line in this chapter, but it will take you the rest of the part of this book to fully understand all of the functional areas that this script touches upon. To start with, Figure 5-1 shows the effect that this script creates.

Figure 5-1. *Changing image opacity*

■ **Tip** You will notice that I have returned to the explicit use of jQuery 2.0.2 in the listing – which I will do for most of the rest of this book. I want to keep the examples clear and simple, but I recommend you use the conditional comments technique, which I find useful in my own projects.

The script changes the opacity of the daffodil, peony, and snowdrop images when the mouse is moved over them. This has the effect of making the image look a little brighter and washed out. When the mouse is moved away from the image, the opacity returns to its previous value. The images for the aster, rose, and primula are unaffected.

Understanding the jQuery $ Function

You access jQuery through the $(...) function, which I will refer to as the *$ function* for simplicity. The $ function is the entry point to the wonderful world of jQuery and is a shorthand for the jQuery function. You can rewrite the example script to use the full function name if you prefer, as shown in Listing 5-4.

Listing 5-4. Using the jQuery Function in Place of the Shorthand

```
...
<script type="text/javascript">
    jQuery(document).ready(function () {
        jQuery("img:odd").mouseenter(function(e) {
            jQuery(this).css("opacity", 0.5);
        }).mouseout(function(e) {
            jQuery(this).css("opacity", 1.0);
        });
    });
</script>
...
```

This script provides the same functionality as the previous example. It requires slightly more typing but has the advantage of making the use of jQuery explicit.

This can be useful because jQuery is not the only JavaScript library that uses the $ notation, which can cause problems when you use multiple libraries in the same document. You can make jQuery relinquish control of the $ by calling the jQuery.noConflict method, as shown in Listing 5-5.

Listing 5-5. Releasing jQuery's Control of $

```
...
<script type="text/javascript">
    jQuery.noConflict();
    jQuery(document).ready(function () {
        jQuery("img:odd").mouseenter(function(e) {
            jQuery(this).css("opacity", 0.5);
        }).mouseout(function(e) {
            jQuery(this).css("opacity", 1.0);
        });
    });
</script>
...
```

You can also define your own shorthand notation. You do this by assigning the result of the noConflict method to a variable, as shown in Listing 5-6.

Listing 5-6. Using an Alternative Shorthand

```
...
<script type="text/javascript">
    var jq = jQuery.noConflict();
    jq(document).ready(function () {
        jq("img:odd").mouseenter(function(e) {
            jq(this).css("opacity", 0.5);
        }).mouseout(function(e) {
            jq(this).css("opacity", 1.0);
        });
    });
</script>
...
```

In this example, I created my own shorthand, jq, and then used this shorthand throughout the rest of my script.

■ **Tip**   I will be using the $ notation throughout this book, since it is the normal convention for jQuery (and because I won't be using any other library that wants control of $).

Irrespective of how you refer to the main jQuery function, you can pass the same set of arguments, the most important of which I have described in Table 5-2. All of these arguments are described later in this chapter except the last one, which is described in Chapter 7.

Table 5-2. *Arguments to the Main jQuery Function*

Argument	Description
$(function)	Specifies a function to be executed when the DOM is ready.
$(selector) $(selector, context)	Selects elements from the document.
$(HTMLElement) $(HTMLElement[])	Creates a jQuery object from an HTMLElement or an array of HTMLElement objects.
$()	Creates an empty selection.
$(HTML) $(HTML, map)	Creates new elements from a fragment of HTML with an optional map object to define attributes. See Chapter 7 for details.

Waiting for the Document Object Model

In Chapter 2, I placed the script element at the end of the document so that the browser would create all of the objects in the DOM before executing my JavaScript code. You can neatly avoid this issue by using jQuery, by using the following technique:

```
...
<script type="text/javascript">
    $(document).ready(function () {
        // ...code to execute...
    });
</script>
...
```

Instead of putting the JavaScript statements directly in the script element, I have passed the document object (which I introduced in Chapter 1) to the $ function and called the ready method, passing in a function that I want to be executed only when the browser has loaded all of the content in the HTML document. Listing 5-7 shows how I applied this technique in the example HTML document.

Listing 5-7. Waiting for the DOM

```
...
<script type="text/javascript">
    $(document).ready(function () {
        $("img:odd").mouseenter(function (e) {
            $(this).css("opacity", 0.5);
        }).mouseout(function (e) {
            $(this).css("opacity", 1.0);
        });
    });
</script>
...
```

Using the ready function means I can place the script element wherever I want in the HTML document safe in the knowledge that jQuery will prevent the function from being executed prematurely. I like to put my script elements in the head element of the HTML document, but that's just my preference.

■ **Note** Passing a function to the ready method creates a handler for the jQuery ready event. I cover jQuery events fully in Chapter 9. For the moment, please accept that the function you pass to the ready method will be invoked when the document is loaded and the DOM is ready for use.

FORGETTING THE FUNCTION

A common error is to omit the `function` part of this incantation and just pass a series of JavaScript statements to the `ready` method. This doesn't work and the statements are executed by the browser immediately, rather than when the DOM is ready. Consider the following script:

```
...
<script type="text/javascript">

    function countImgElements() {
        return $("img").length;
    }

    $(document).ready(function() {
      console.log("Ready function invoked. IMG count: " + countImgElements());
    });

    $(document).ready(
      console.log("Ready statement invoked. IMG count: " + countImgElements())
    );
</script>
...
```

I call the `ready` method twice, once with a `function` and once just passing in a regular JavaScript statement. In both cases, I call the `countImgElements` function, which returns the number of `img` elements that are present in the DOM. (Don't worry about how this method works for the moment. I explain the call to the `length` property later in this chapter.) When I load the document, the script is executed, and the following output is written to the console:

```
Ready statement invoked. IMG count: 0
Ready function invoked. IMG count: 6
```

As you can see, the statement without the function is executed as the document is loaded and before the browser has discovered the `img` elements in the document and created the corresponding DOM objects.

Using the Alternative Notation

You can pass your function as the parameter to the jQuery $ function if you prefer. This has the same effect as using the `$(document).ready` approach. Listing 5-8 provides a demonstration.

Listing 5-8. Deferring Execution of a Function Until the DOM Is Ready

```
...
<script type="text/javascript">
    $(function() {
        $("img:odd").mouseenter(function(e) {
            $(this).css("opacity", 0.5);
        }).mouseout(function(e) {
            $(this).css("opacity", 1.0);
        })
    });
</script>
...
```

Deferring the ready Event

You can control when the ready event is triggered by using the holdReady method. This can be useful if you need to load external resources dynamically (an unusual and advanced technique). The holdReady method must be called before the ready event is triggered and can then be called again when you are ready. Listing 5-9 gives an example of using this method.

Listing 5-9. Using the holdReady Method

```
...
<script type="text/javascript">

    $.holdReady(true);

    $(document).ready(function() {
        console.log("Ready event triggered");
        $("img:odd").mouseenter(function(e) {
            $(this).css("opacity", 0.5);
        }).mouseout(function(e) {
            $(this).css("opacity", 1.0);
        })
    });

    setTimeout(function() {
        console.log("Releasing hold");
        $.holdReady(false);
    }, 5000);

</script>
...
```

I call the holdReady method at the start of the script element, passing in true as the argument that indicates that I want the ready event to be held. I then define the function I want to be called when the ready event is fired (this is the same set of statements that I opened the chapter with, which alter the opacity of some of the images).

Finally, I use the setTimeout method to invoke a function after five seconds. This function calls the holdReady method with an argument of false, which tells jQuery to trigger the ready event. The net effect is that I delay the ready event for five seconds. I have added some debug messages that write the following output to the console when the document is loaded into the browser:

```
Releasing hold
Ready event triggered
```

■ **Tip** You can call the holdReady method multiple times, but the number of calls to the holdReady method with true argument must be balanced by the same number of calls with the false argument before the ready event will be triggered.

Selecting Elements

One of the most important areas of jQuery functionality is how you select elements from the DOM. In the example script, I located all of the *odd* img elements, as shown in Listing 5-10.

Listing 5-10. Selecting Elements from the DOM

```
...
<script type="text/javascript">
    $(document).ready(function() {
        $("img:odd").mouseenter(function(e) {
            $(this).css("opacity", 0.5);
        }).mouseout(function(e) {
            $(this).css("opacity", 1.0);
        })
    });
</script>
...
```

To select elements, you simply pass a selector to the $ function. jQuery supports all of the CSS selectors I described in Chapter 3, plus some additional ones that give you some handy fine-grained control. In the example I used the :odd pseudo-selector, which selects the odd-numbered elements matched by the main part of the selector (img in this case, which selects all of the img elements, as described in Chapter 3). The :odd selector is zero-based, meaning that the first element is considered to be even. This can be a little confusing at first. Table 5-3 lists the most useful jQuery selectors.

Table 5-3. *jQuery Extension Selectors*

Selector	Description
:animated	Selects all elements that are being animated.
:contains(text)	Selects elements that contain the specified text.
:eq(n)	Selects the element at the nth index (zero-based).
:even	Selects all the event-numbered elements (zero-based).
:first	Selects the first matched element.
:gt(n)	Selects all of the elements with an index greater than n (zero-based).
:has(selector)	Selects elements that contain at least one element that matches the specified selector.
:last	Selects the last matched element.
:lt(n)	Selects all of the elements with an index smaller than n (zero-based).
:odd	Selects all the odd-numbered elements (zero-based).
:text	Selects all text elements.

■ **Tip** You can create an empty selection by calling the $ function without any arguments ($()). I mention this for completeness, but it is not a feature that I have ever had cause to use.

I have called these the most useful because they define functionality that would be difficult to re-create using CSS selectors. These selectors are used just like the CSS pseudo-selectors. They can be used on their own, in which case they are applied to all of the elements in the DOM, like this:

```
...
$(":even")
...
```

or combined with other selectors to narrow the selection, like this:

```
...
$("img:even")
...
```

jQuery also defines selectors that select elements based on type, as described in Table 5-4.

Table 5-4. *jQuery Type Extension Selectors*

Selector	Description
:button	Selects all buttons.
:checkbox	Selects all check boxes.
:file	Selects all file elements.
:header	Selects all header elements (h1, h2, and so on).
:hidden	Selects all hidden elements.
:image	Selects all image elements.
:input	Selects all input elements.
:last	Selects the last matched element.
:parent	Selects all of the elements that are parents to other elements.
:password	Selects all password elements.
:radio	Selects all radio elements.
:reset	Selects all elements that reset a form.
:selected	Selects all elements that are selected.
:submit	Selects all form submission elements.
:visible	Selects all visible elements.

CONSIDERING SELECTOR PERFORMANCE

If you spend any time reading about jQuery, you are sure to encounter a discussion about selector performance. A great many people spend a great deal of time comparing different ways of expressing selectors to squeeze the maximum performance out of jQuery.

My view is simple: it should not matter – and if it does matter, then it is a sign of some other problem. The performance of jQuery is pretty good, especially on the latest versions of the mainstream browsers that have fast JavaScript implementations. When I see project teams that are trying to optimize selector performance, it is usually because they are dealing with huge numbers of HTML elements where it can take hundreds of milliseconds to perform a selection – and when several such selections are required to perform an operation, we start to get into the length of delay that users notice.

The real problem isn't jQuery – it is the practice of sending more content to the browser than it can be reasonably expected to cope with. Browsers are increasingly powerful and capable, but there are limits to what they can be expected to do, especially older browsers and those running on mobile devices.

If you find yourself struggling to select elements quickly enough, don't try to optimize your use of selectors. Instead, reconsider your use of HTML elements: look for ways to minimize the content sent to the browser, take on some of the processing at the server and stop treating web applications as though they were desktop applications.

Narrowing the Selection with a Context

By default, jQuery searches the entire DOM for elements, but you can narrow the scope of a selection by providing an additional argument to the $ function. This gives the search a *context*, which is used as the starting point for matching elements, as shown in Listing 5-11.

Listing 5-11. Narrowing a Search with a Context

```
...
<script type="text/javascript">
    $(document).ready(function() {

        $("img:odd", $(".drow")).mouseenter(function(e) {
            $(this).css("opacity", 0.5);
        }).mouseout(function(e) {
            $(this).css("opacity", 1.0);
        })
    });
</script>
...
```

In this example, I use one jQuery selection as the context for another. The context is evaluated first, and it matches all of the elements that are members of the drow class. This set of elements is then used as the context for the img:odd selector.

When you supply a context that contains multiple elements, then each element is used as a starting point in the search. There is an interesting subtlety in this approach. The elements that match the context are gathered together, and then the main selection is performed. In the example, this means the img:odd selector is applied to the results of the drow selector, which means that the odd-numbered elements are not the same as when you search the entire document. The net result is that the opacity effect is applied to the odd-numbered img elements in each div element in the drow class, selecting the daffodil and primula images. When I omitted the context in the earlier example, the effect was applied to the daffodil, peony, and snowdrop images.

If you just want to match elements starting at a given point in the document, then you can use an HTMLElement object as the context. Listing 5-12 contains an example. I show you how to easily switch between the jQuery world and HTMLElement objects in the next section.

Listing 5-12. Using an HTMLElement as the Context

```
...
<script type="text/javascript">
    $(document).ready(function() {
        var elem = document.getElementById("oblock");

        $("img:odd", elem).mouseenter(function(e) {
            $(this).css("opacity", 0.5);
        }).mouseout(function(e) {
            $(this).css("opacity", 1.0);
        })
    });
</script>
...
```

The script in this example searches for odd-numbered img elements, limiting the search to those elements that are descended from the element whose id is oblock.

Of course, you could achieve the same effect using the descendant CSS selector. The benefit of this approach arises when you want to narrow a search programmatically, without having to construct a selector string. A good example of such a situation is when handling an event. You can learn more about events (and see how HTMLElement objects arise in this situation) in Chapter 9.

Understanding the Selection Result

When you use jQuery to select elements from the DOM, the result from the $ function is a confusingly named jQuery object, which represents zero or more DOM elements. In fact, when you perform a jQuery operation that modifies one or more elements, the result is likely to be a jQuery object, which is an important characteristic that I'll return to shortly.

The methods and properties that are defined by the jQuery object are essentially the contents for the rest of the book, but there are some basic members that I can cover in this chapter, as described in Table 5-5.

Table 5-5. *Basic jQuery Object Members*

Selector	Description	Returns
context	Returns the set of elements used as the search context.	HTMLElement
each(function)	Performs the function on each of the selected elements.	jQuery
get(index)	Gets the HTMLElement object at the specified index.	HTMLElement
index(HTMLElement)	Returns the index of the specified HTMLElement.	number
index(jQuery)	Returns the index of the first element in the jQuery object.	number
index(selector)	Returns the index of the first element in the jQuery object in the set of elements matched by the selector	number
length	Returns the number of elements contained by the jQuery object.	number
size()	Returns the number of elements in the jQuery object.	number
toArray()	Returns the HTMLElement objects contained by the jQuery object as an array.	HTMLElement[]

Determining the Context

The context property provides you with details of the context used when the jQuery was created. If a single HTMLElement object was used as the context, then the context property will return that HTMLElement. If no context was used or if multiple elements were used (as in the example I used earlier in the chapter), then the context property returns undefined instead. Listing 5-13 shows this property in use.

Listing 5-13. Determining the Context for a jQuery Object

```
...
<script type="text/javascript">
    $(document).ready(function() {
        var jq1 = $("img:odd");
        console.log("No context: " + jq1.context.tagName);

        var jq2 = $("img:odd", $(".drow"));
        console.log("Multiple context elements: " + jq2.context.tagName);

        var jq3 = $("img:odd", document.getElementById("oblock"));
        console.log("Single context element: " + jq3.context.tagName);
    });
</script>
...
```

This script selects elements using no context, multiple context objects, and a single context object. The output is as follows:

```
No context: undefined
Multiple context elements: undefined
Single context element: DIV
```

Dealing with DOM Objects

jQuery doesn't replace the DOM; it just makes it a lot easier to work with. The HTMLElement objects (which I introduced in Chapter 2) are still used, and the jQuery library makes it easy to switch between jQuery objects and DOM objects. The ease with which you can move from the traditional DOM to jQuery and back is part of the elegance of jQuery and helps you maintain compatibility with non-jQuery scripts and libraries.

Creating jQuery Objects from DOM Objects

You can create jQuery objects by passing an HTMLElement object or an array of HTMLElement objects as the argument to the $ function. This can be useful when dealing with JavaScript code that isn't written in jQuery or in situations where jQuery exposes the underlying DOM objects, such as event processing. Listing 5-14 contains an example.

Listing 5-14. Creating jQuery Objects from DOM Objects

```
...
<script type="text/javascript">
    $(document).ready(function() {

        var elems = document.getElementsByTagName("img");

        $(elems).mouseenter(function(e) {
            $(this).css("opacity", 0.5);
        }).mouseout(function(e) {
            $(this).css("opacity", 1.0);
        })
    });
</script>
...
```

In this example, I select the img elements in the document using the document.getElementsByTagName method, rather than using jQuery directly with a selector. I pass the results of this method (which is a collection of HTMLElement objects) to the $ function, which returns a regular jQuery object that I can use just as in the previous examples.

This script also demonstrates how you can create a jQuery object from a single HTMLElement object:

```
...
$(this).css("opacity", 1.0);
...
```

When you are handling events, jQuery sets the value of the this variable to the HTMLElement that is processing the event. I describe the jQuery event support in Chapter 9, so I don't want to get into the subject in this chapter (although I do mention the functions that contain these statements again a little later in this chapter).

Treating a jQuery Object as an Array

You can treat a jQuery object as an array of HTMLElement objects. This means you get to use the advanced features that jQuery provides but still access the DOM directly. You can use the length property or the size method to determine how many elements are collected in the jQuery object and access individual DOM objects by using an array-style index (using the [and] brackets).

■ **Tip**   You can use the `toArray` method to extract the `HTMLElement` objects from the `jQuery` object as an array. I like to use the `jQuery` object itself, but sometimes it is useful to work with the DOM objects, such as when dealing with legacy code that wasn't written using jQuery.

Listing 5-15 shows how you can enumerate the contents of a jQuery object to access the `HTMLElement` objects contained within.

Listing 5-15. Treating a jQuery Object as an Array

```
...
<script type="text/javascript">
    $(document).ready(function() {
        var elems = $("img:odd");
        for (var i = 0; i < elems.length; i++) {
            console.log("Element: " + elems[i].tagName + " " + elems[i].src);
        }
    });
</script>
...
```

In the listing, I use the $ function to select the odd-numbered `img` elements and enumerate the selected elements to print out the value of the `tagName` and `src` properties to the console. The results are as follows:

```
Element: IMG http://www.jacquisflowershop.com/jquery/daffodil.png
Element: IMG http://www.jacquisflowershop.com/jquery/peony.png
Element: IMG http://www.jacquisflowershop.com/jquery/snowdrop.png
```

Iterate a Function over DOM Objects

The `each` method lets you define a function that is performed for each DOM object in the jQuery object. Listing 5-16 gives a demonstration.

Listing 5-16. Using the each Method

```
...
<script type="text/javascript">
    $(document).ready(function() {
        $("img:odd").each(function(index, elem) {
            console.log("Element: " + elem.tagName + " " + elem.src);
        });
    });
</script>
...
```

jQuery passes two arguments to the specified function. The first is the index of the element in the collection, and the second is the element object itself. In this example, I write the tag name and the value of the `src` property to the console, producing the same results as the previous script:

```
Element: IMG http://www.jacquisflowershop.com/jquery/daffodil.png
Element: IMG http://www.jacquisflowershop.com/jquery/peony.png
Element: IMG http://www.jacquisflowershop.com/jquery/snowdrop.png
```

Finding Indices and Specific Elements

The index method lets you find the index of an HTMLElement in a jQuery object. You can pass the index that you want using either an HTMLElement or jQuery object as the argument. When you use a jQuery object, the first matched element is the one whose index is returned. Listing 5-17 gives a demonstration.

Listing 5-17. Locating the Index of an HTMLElement

```
...
<script type="text/javascript">
    $(document).ready(function() {

        var elems = $("body *");

        // find an index using the basic DOM API
        var index = elems.index(document.getElementById("oblock"));
        console.log("Index using DOM element is: " + index);

        // find an index using another jQuery object
        index = elems.index($("#oblock"));
        console.log("Index using jQuery object is: " + index);
    });
</script>
...
```

In this example, I locate a method using the DOM API's getElementById method to find a div element by the id attribute value. This returns an HTMLElement object. I then use the index method on a jQuery object to find the index of the object that represents the div element. I repeat the process using a jQuery object, which I obtain through the $ function. I write the results from both approaches to the console, which produces the following results:

```
Index using DOM element is: 2
Index using jQuery object is: 2
```

You can also pass a string to the index method. When you do this, the string is interpreted as a selector. However, this approach causes the index method to behave in a different way than the previous example. Listing 5-18 provides a demonstration.

Listing 5-18. Using the Selector Version of the index Method

```
...
<script type="text/javascript">
    $(document).ready(function() {

        var imgElems = $("img:odd");
        // find an index using a selector
```

```
        index = imgElems.index("body *");
        console.log("Index using selector is: " + index);

        // perform the same task using a jQuery object
        index = $("body *").index(imgElems);
        console.log("Index using jQuery object is: " + index);

    });
</script>
...
```

When you pass a `string` to the `index` method, the order in which the collection of elements is used changes. jQuery matches elements using the selector and then returns the index in the matched elements of the first element in the jQuery object on which you called the index method. This means that this statement:

```
...
index = imgElems.index("body *");
...
```

is equivalent to this statement:

```
...
index = $("body *").index(imgElems);
...
```

In essence, passing a string argument reverses the way in which the two sets of elements are considered. The listing produces the following result:

```
Index using selector is: 10
Index using jQuery object is: 10
```

■ **Tip** We can use the `index` method without an argument to get the position of an element relative to its siblings. This can be useful when using jQuery to explore the DOM, which is the topic of Chapter 7.

The get method is the complement to the `index` method, such that you specify an index and receive the `HTMLElement` object at that position in the jQuery object. This has the same effect as using the array-style index I described earlier in this chapter. Listing 5-19 provides a demonstration.

Listing 5-19. Getting the HTMLElement Object at a Given Index

```
...
<script type="text/javascript">
    $(document).ready(function() {
        var elem = $("img:odd").get(1);
        console.log("Element: " + elem.tagName + " " + elem.src);
    });
</script>
...
```

In this script, I select the odd-numbered img elements, use the get method to retrieve the HTMLElement object at index 1, and write the value of the tagName and src properties to the console. The output from this script is as follows:

```
Element: IMG http://www.jacquisflowershop.com/jquery/peony.png
```

Modifying Multiple Elements and Chaining Method Calls

One of the features that make jQuery so concise and expressive is that calling a method on a jQuery object usually modifies all of the elements that the object contains. I say *usually*, because some methods perform operations that don't apply to multiple elements, and you'll see examples of this in later chapters. Listing 5-20 shows how to perform an operation on multiple elements using the DOM API.

Listing 5-20. Operating on Multiple Elements Using the DOM API

```
...
<script type="text/javascript">
    $(document).ready(function() {

        var labelElems = document.getElementsByTagName("label");
        for (var i = 0; i < labelElems.length; i++) {
            labelElems[i].style.color = "blue";
        }
    });
</script>
...
```

The statements in the script element select all of the label elements and set the value of the CSS color property to blue. Listing 5-21 shows how to perform the same task using jQuery.

Listing 5-21. Operating on Multiple Elements Using the jQuery

```
...
<script type="text/javascript">
    $(document).ready(function () {
        $("label").css("color", "blue");
    });
</script>
...
```

I can perform the task using a single jQuery statement, which is less effort than using the DOM API—not a huge difference, I admit, but it mounts up in a complex web application. The jQuery statement is also easier to read and understand, which helps with the long-term maintenance of the JavaScript code.

Another nice feature of the jQuery object is that it implements a *fluent API*. This means that whenever you call a method that modifies the contents of the object, the result of the method is another jQuery object. This may seem simple, but it allows you to perform method chaining, as shown in Listing 5-22.

Listing 5-22. Method Chaining Method Calls On a jQuery Object

```
...
<script type="text/javascript">
    $(document).ready(function() {

        $("label").css("color", "blue").css("font-size", ".75em");

        var labelElems = document.getElementsByTagName("label");
        for (var i = 0; i < labelElems.length; i++) {
            labelElems[i].style.color = "blue";
            labelElems[i].style.fontSize = ".75em";
        }
    });
</script>
...
```

In this example, I create a jQuery object using the $ function, call the css method to set a value for the color property, and then call the css method again, this time to set the font-size property. I have also shown the equivalent addition using the basic DOM API. You can see that it doesn't require much work to achieve the same effect, because you already have a for loop that is enumerating the selected elements.

You start to get real benefit from the fluent API when chaining methods that make more substantial changes to the set of elements contained in the jQuery object. Listing 5-23 provides a demonstration.

Listing 5-23. A More Sophisticated Chaining Example

```
...
<script type="text/javascript">
    $(document).ready(function() {

        $("label").css("color", "blue").add("input[name!='rose']")
                    .filter("[for!='snowdrop']").css("font-size", ".75em");

        var elems = document.getElementsByTagName("label");
        for (var i = 0; i < elems.length; i++) {
            elems[i].style.color = "blue";
            if (elems[i].getAttribute("for") != "snowdrop") {
                elems[i].style.fontSize= ".75em";
            }
        }
        elems = document.getElementsByTagName("input");
        for (var i = 0; i < elems.length; i++) {
            if (elems[i].getAttribute("name") != "rose") {
                elems[i].style.fontSize= ".75em";
            }
        }
    });
</script>
...
```

This is an over-the-top example, but it demonstrates the flexibility that jQuery offers. Let's break down the chained methods to make sense of what is happening. I start with this:

```
...
$("label").css("color", "blue")
...
```

I have selected all of the label elements in the document and set the value of the CSS color property to be blue for all of them. The next step is as follows:

```
...
$("label").css("color", "blue").add("input[name!='rose']")
...
```

The add method adds the elements that match the specified selector to the jQuery object. In this case, I have selected the input elements that don't have a name attribute whose value is rose. These are combined with the previously matched elements to give me a jQuery objects that contains a mix of label and input elements. You'll see more of the add method in Chapter 6. Here is the next addition:

```
...
$("label").css("color", "blue").add("input[name!='rose']").filter("[for!='snowdrop']")
...
```

The filter method removes all of the elements in a jQuery object that don't meet a specified condition. I explain this method in more depth in Chapter 6, but for the moment it is enough to know that this allows me to remove any element from the jQuery object that has a for attribute whose value is snowdrop.

```
...
$("label").css("color", "blue").add("input[name!='rose']")
    .filter("[for!='snowdrop']").css("font-size", ".75em");
...
```

The final step is to call the css method again, this time setting the font-size property to .75em. The net result of this is as follows:

1. All label elements are assigned the value blue for the color CSS property.

2. All label elements except the one that has the for attribute value of snowdrop are assigned the value .75em for the CSS font-size property.

3. All input elements that don't have a name attribute value of rose are assigned the value of .75em for the CSS font-size property.

Achieving the same effect using the basic DOM API is a lot more complex, and I ran into some difficulties while writing this script. For example, I thought I could use the document.querySelectorAll method, described in Chapter 2, to select input elements using the selector input[name!='rose'], but it turns out that this kind of attribute filter doesn't work with that method. I then tried to avoid duplicating the call to set the font-size value by concatenating the results of two getElementsByTagName calls together, but that turns out to be a painful experience in its own right. I don't want to labor the point, especially since you must already have a certain commitment to jQuery to be reading this book, but jQuery provides a level of fluidity and expressiveness that is impossible to achieve using the basic DOM API.

Handling Events

Returning to the script I started the chapter with, you can see that I chained together two method calls, as highlighted in Listing 5-24.

Listing 5-24. Chained Method Calls in the Example Script

```
...
<script type="text/javascript">
    $(document).ready(function() {
        $("img:odd").mouseenter(function(e) {
            $(this).css("opacity", 0.5);
        }).mouseout(function(e) {
            $(this).css("opacity", 1.0);
        })
    });
</script>
...
```

The methods I chained were mouseenter and mouseout. These methods let me define handler functions for the mouseenter and mouseout events that I described in Chapter 2. I cover the jQuery support for events in Chapter 9, but I just wanted to show how you can use the behavior of the jQuery object to specify a single handler method for all of the elements that you have selected.

Summary

In this chapter, I introduced you to your first jQuery script and used it to demonstrate some of the key characteristics of the jQuery library: the $ function, the ready event, the jQuery result object, and how jQuery complements, rather than replaces, the built-in DOM API that is part of the HTML specification.

CHAPTER 6

■ ■ ■

Managing the Element Selection

Most of the time, the use of jQuery follows a distinctive two-step pattern. The first step is to select some elements, and the second step is to perform one or more operations on those elements. In this chapter, I focus on the first step, showing you how to take control of the jQuery selection and tailor it to your exact needs. I'll also show you how to use jQuery to navigate the DOM. In both cases, you start with one selection and perform operations on it until it contains just the elements you require. As you'll see, the correlation between the elements you start with and those you finish with can be as simple or as sophisticated as you like. Table 6-1 provides the summary for this chapter.

Table 6-1. *Chapter Summary*

Problem	Solution	Listing
Expand the selection.	Use the add method.	1
Reduce the selection to a single element.	Use the first, last, or eq method.	2
Reduce the selection to a range of elements.	Use the slice method.	3
Reduce the selection by applying a filter.	Use the filter or not method.	4, 5
Reduce the selection based on the descendants of the selected elements.	Use the has method.	6
Project a new selection from the existing selection.	Use the map method.	7
Check to see that at least one selected element meets a specific condition.	Use the is method.	8
Revert to the previous selection.	Use the end method.	9
Add the previous selection to the current selection.	Use the addBack method.	10
Navigate to the children and descendants of selected elements.	Use the children and find methods.	11–13
Navigate to the parents of selected elements.	Use the parent method.	14
Navigate to the ancestors or selected elements.	Use the parents method.	15
Navigate to the ancestors of elements until a specific element is encountered.	Use the parentsUntil method.	16, 17
Navigate to the nearest ancestor that matches a selector or that is a specific element.	Use the closest method.	18, 19
Navigate to the nearest positioned ancestor.	Use the offsetParent method.	20
Navigate to the siblings of the selected elements.	Use the siblings method.	21, 22
Navigate to the previous or next siblings for the selected elements.	Use the next, prev, nextAll, prevAll, nextUntil, or prevUntil method.	23

JQUERY CHANGES SINCE THE LAST EDITION

In jQuery 1.9, the addBack method has replaced the jQuery 1.8 addSelf method with the addBack method. These methods perform the same function, which is demonstrated in the "Changing and then Unwinding the Selection" section in this chapter.

Expanding the Selection

The add method allows you to expand the contents of a jQuery object by adding additional elements. Table 6-2 shows the different arguments you can use.

Table 6-2. *add Method Argument Types*

Arguments	Description
add(selector) add(selector, context)	Adds all of the elements that are matched by the selector, with or without a context.
add(HTMLElement) add(HTMLElement[])	Adds a single HTMLElement or an array of HTMLElement objects.
add(jQuery)	Adds the contents of the specified jQuery object.

Like many jQuery methods, the add method returns a jQuery object on which you can call other methods, including further calls to the add method. Listing 6-1 demonstrates the use of the add method to broaden a set of elements.

Listing 6-1. Using the add Method

```
<!DOCTYPE html>
<html>
<head>
    <title>Example</title>
    <script src="jquery-2.0.2.js" type="text/javascript"></script>
    <link rel="stylesheet" type="text/css" href="styles.css"/>
    <script type="text/javascript">
        $(document).ready(function () {

            var labelElems = document.getElementsByTagName("label");
            var jq = $("img[src*=daffodil]");

            $("img:even").add("img[src*=primula]").add(jq)
                .add(labelElems).css("border", "thick double red");

        });
    </script>
</head>
<body>
    <h1>Jacqui's Flower Shop</h1>
```

```
<form method="post">
    <div id="oblock">
        <div class="dtable">
            <div id="row1" class="drow">
                <div class="dcell">
                    <img src="aster.png"/><label for="aster">Aster:</label>
                    <input name="aster" value="0" required>
                </div>
                <div class="dcell">
                    <img src="daffodil.png"/><label for="daffodil">Daffodil:</label>
                    <input name="daffodil" value="0" required >
                </div>
                <div class="dcell">
                    <img src="rose.png"/><label for="rose">Rose:</label>
                    <input name="rose" value="0" required>
                </div>
            </div>
            <div id="row2"class="drow">
                <div class="dcell">
                    <img src="peony.png"/><label for="peony">Peony:</label>
                    <input name="peony" value="0" required>
                </div>
                <div class="dcell">
                    <img src="primula.png"/><label for="primula">Primula:</label>
                    <input name="primula" value="0" required>
                </div>
                <div class="dcell">
                    <img src="snowdrop.png"/><label for="snowdrop">Snowdrop:</label>
                    <input name="snowdrop" value="0" required>
                </div>
            </div>
        </div>
    </div>
    <div id="buttonDiv"><button type="submit">Place Order</button></div>
</form>
</body>
</html>
```

■ **Caution**   A common mistake is to assume that the remove method is the counterpart to the add method and will narrow the selection. In fact, the remove method changes the structure of the DOM, as I explain in Chapter 7. Use one of the methods I describe in the "Narrowing the Selection" section instead.

The script in this example uses all three approaches to add elements to the initial selection: with another selector, with some HTMLElement objects, and with another jQuery object. Once I have built up my set of objects, I call the css method to set a value for the border property, which has the effect of drawing a thick red border around the selected elements, as shown in Figure 6-1.

Figure 6-1. *Expanding the selection with the add method*

Narrowing the Selection

There are a number of methods that allow you to *remove* elements from the selection, as described in Table 6-3. In every case, the methods return a new jQuery object that contains the reduced element selection. The jQuery object on which the method was called remains unchanged.

Table 6-3. *Methods to Filter Elements*

Method	Description
eq(index)	Removes all of the elements except the one at the specified index.
filter(condition)	Removes elements that don't match the specified condition. See the later discussion for details of the arguments you can use with this method.
first()	Removes all of the elements except the first.
has(selector) has(jQuery) has(HTMLElement) has(HTMLElement[])	Removes elements that don't have a descendant matched by the specified selector or jQuery object or whose descendants don't include the specified HTMLElement objects.
last()	Removes all but the last element.
not(condition)	Removes all elements that match the condition. See the later discussion for details of how the condition can be specified.
slice(start, end)	Removes all elements outside the specified range of index values.

Reducing the Selection to a Specific Element

The three most basic narrowing methods are first, last, and eq. These three methods allow you to select a specific element based on its position in the jQuery object. Listing 6-2 provides a demonstration.

Listing 6-2. Reducing the Selection Based on Element Position

```
...
<script type="text/javascript">
    $(document).ready(function() {

        var jq = $("label");

        jq.first().css("border", "thick double red");
        jq.last().css("border", "thick double green");
        jq.eq(2).css("border", "thick double black");
        jq.eq(-2).css("border", "thick double black");

    });
</script>
...
```

The eq, first, and last methods are included for convenience. You can achieve the same effect using the basic array features that the jQuery object supports and the slice method that I described earlier in the chapter.

Notice that I call the eq method twice. When the argument to this method is positive, the index is counted from the first element in the jQuery object. When the argument is negative, the counting is done backward, starting from the last element. You can see the effect of this script in Figure 6-2.

Figure 6-2. *Reducing the selection to a specific element*

Reducing the Selection by Range

The `slice` method reduces the selection to a range of elements, as demonstrated by Listing 6-3.

Listing 6-3. Using the slice Method

```
...
<script type="text/javascript">
    $(document).ready(function() {

        var jq = $("label");

        jq.slice(0, 2).css("border", "thick double black");
        jq.slice(4).css("border", "thick solid red");

    });
</script>
...
```

The arguments to the `slice` method are the index to begin selection and the index to end selection. Indexes are zero-based, so the arguments I used in the example (0 and 2) select the first two elements. If the second argument is omitted, then the selection continues to the end of the set of elements. By specifying a single argument of 4 for a set of six elements, I selected the last two elements (which have the index values of 4 and 5). You can see the result of this script in Figure 6-3.

Figure 6-3. Reducing the selection by range

Filtering Elements

The `filter` method removes elements from the selection that don't meet a specified condition. Table 6-4 shows the different arguments that can be used to express the filtering condition.

Table 6-4. *filter Method Argument Types*

Arguments	Description
filter(selector)	Removes elements that don't match the selector.
filter(HTMLElement)	Removes all but the specified element.
filter(jQuery)	Removes elements that are not contained in the specified jQuery object.
filter(function(index))	The function is called for each element; those for which the function returns false are removed.

Listing 6-4 shows all four ways of specifying a filter.

Listing 6-4. Specifying a Filter

```
...
<script type="text/javascript">
    $(document).ready(function() {
        $("img").filter("[src*=s]").css("border", "thick double red");

        var jq = $("[for*=p]" );
        $("label").filter(jq).css("color", "blue");

        var elem = document.getElementsByTagName("label")[1];
        $("label").filter(elem).css("font-size", "1.5em");

        $("img").filter(function(index) {
            return this.getAttribute("src") == "peony.png" || index == 4;
        }).css("border", "thick solid red")
    });
</script>
...
```

The first three techniques are self-evident: you can filter based a selector, another jQuery object, or an HTMLElement object.

The fourth technique relies on a function and requires a little more explanation. jQuery calls the function once for every element contained by the jQuery object. If the function returns true then the element is retained, and it is removed if the function returns false.

There is one argument passed to the function, which is the index of the element for which the function is being called. In addition, the this variable is set to the HTMLElement object that you need to process. In the listing, I return true if the element has a particular value for the src attribute and for a specific index value. You can see the result in Figure 6-4.

Figure 6-4. *Using the filter method*

■ **Tip** You might be wondering why I have used the getAttribute method on the HTMLElement in the filter function, as opposed to calling the src property. The reason is that the getAttribute method will return the value that I set for the src *attribute* in the document (which is a relative URL), but the src *property* will return a fully qualified URL. For this example, the relative URL was simpler to work with.

The complement to the filter method is not, which works in much the same way but inverts the filtering process. Table 6-5 shows the different ways in which a condition can be applied using the not method.

Table 6-5. *not Method Argument Types*

Arguments	Description
not(selector)	Removes elements that match the selector.
not(HTMLElement[]) not(HTMLElement)	Removes the specified element or elements.
not(jQuery)	Removes elements that are contained in the specified jQuery object.
not(function(index))	The function is called for each element; those for which the function returns true are removed.

Listing 6-5 shows the use of the not method, based on the previous example.

Listing 6-5. Using the not Method

```
...
<script type="text/javascript">
    $(document).ready(function() {

        $("img").not("[src*=s]").css("border", "thick double red");

        var jq = $("[for*=p]");
        $("label").not(jq).css("color", "blue");

        var elem = document.getElementsByTagName("label")[1];
        $("label").not(elem).css("font-size", "1.5em");

        $("img").not(function(index) {
            return this.getAttribute("src") == "peony.png" || index == 4;
        }).css("border", "thick solid red")
    });
</script>
...
```

You can see the effect of this script in Figure 6-5. It is, of course, the inverse of the effect of the previous example.

Figure 6-5. Filtering elements using the not method

Reducing the Selection Based on Descendants

The has method reduces the selection to elements that have particular descendants, specified through a selector or one or more HTMLElement objects, as demonstrated in Listing 6-6.

125

Listing 6-6. Using the has Method

```
...
<script type="text/javascript">
    $(document).ready(function() {

        $("div.dcell").has("img[src*=aster]").css("border", "thick solid red");
        var jq = $("[for*=p]");
        $("div.dcell").has(jq).css("border", "thick solid blue");

    });
</script>
...
```

In the first case, where I use a selector, I reduce the selection to elements that have at least one descendant img element with a src attribute value that contains aster. In the second case, where I use a jQuery object, I reduce the selection to elements that have at least one descendant that has a for attribute with a value that contains the letter p. You can see the effect of this script in Figure 6-6.

Figure 6-6. *Using the has method to reduce the selection*

Mapping the Selection

The map method provides a flexible way to use one jQuery object as a means to create another, based on a function. The function is called for every element in the source jQuery object, and the HTMLElement objects that the function returns are included in the result jQuery object, as demonstrated by Listing 6-7.

Listing 6-7. Using the map Method

```
...
<script type="text/javascript">
    $(document).ready(function() {
```

```
$("div.dcell").map(function(index, elem) {
    return elem.getElementsByTagName("img")[0];
}).css("border", "thick solid red");

$("div.dcell").map(function(index, elem) {
    return $(elem).children()[1];
}).css("border", "thick solid blue");

});
</script>
...
```

In this script, I perform two mapping operations. The first uses the DOM API to return the first img element contained in each element, and the second uses jQuery to return the first item in the jQuery object returned by the children method (I'll explain this method fully later in this chapter, but as its name suggests, it returns the child nodes of each element in a jQuery object). You can see the result in Figure 6-7.

Figure 6-7. *Using the map method*

___

■ **Tip** You can return only one element each time the function is called. If you want to project multiple result elements for each source element, you can combine the each and add methods, which I describe in Chapter 8.

___

Testing the Selection

The is method determines whether one of more elements in a jQuery object meets a specific condition. Table 6-6 shows the arguments you can pass to the is method.

Table 6-6. *is Method Argument Types*

Arguments	Description
is(selector)	Returns true if the jQuery object contains at least one of the elements matched by the selector.
is(HTMLElement[]) is(HTMLElement)	Returns true if the jQuery object contains the specified element, or at least one of the elements in the specified array.
is(jQuery)	Returns true if the jQuery object contains at least one of the elements in the argument object.
is(function(index))	Returns true if the function returns true at least once.

When you specify a function as the condition, jQuery will invoke that function once for each element in the jQuery object, passing the index of the element as the function argument and setting the this variable to the element itself. Listing 6-8 shows the is method in use.

■ **Note**   This method returns a boolean value. As I mentioned in Chapter 5, not all jQuery methods return a jQuery object.

Listing 6-8. Using the is Method

```
...
<script type="text/javascript">
    $(document).ready(function() {

        var isResult = $("img").is(function(index) {
            return this.getAttribute("src") == "rose.png";
        });
        console.log("Result: " + isResult);

    });
</script>
...
```

This script tests to see whether the jQuery object contains an element whose src attribute value is rose.png and writes out the result to the console, as follows:

```
Result: true
```

Changing and Then Unwinding the Selection

jQuery preserves a history stack when you modify the selection by chaining methods together, and you can use a couple of methods to take advantage of this, as described in Table 6-7.

Table 6-7. *Methods to Unwind the Selection Stack*

Method	Description
end()	Pops the current selection off the stack and returns to the previous selection.
addBack() addBack(selector)	Adds the previous selection to the current selection, with an optional selector that filters the previous selection.

The end method returns to the previous selection, which allows you to select some elements, expand or reduce the selection, perform some operations, and then return to the original selection, as demonstrated by Listing 6-9.

Listing 6-9. Using the end Method

```
...
<script type="text/javascript">
    $(document).ready(function() {

        $("label").first().css("border", "thick solid blue")
            .end().css("font-size", "1.5em");

    });
</script>
...
```

In this script, I start by selecting all of the label elements in the document. I then reduce the selection by calling the first method (to get the first matched element) and then set a value for the CSS border property using the css method, which has the effect of only changing the CSS property for the first selected element.

I then call the end method to return to the previous selection (which moves the selection the first label element back to *all* of the label elements). I then call the css method again, this time to set a value for the font-size property. This CSS property is applied to all of the label elements, as illustrated in Figure 6-8.

Figure 6-8. *Using the end method*

The addBack method adds the contents of the previous selection on the stack to the current selection. Listing 6-10 shows the addBack method in use.

Listing 6-10. Using the andSelf Method

```
...
<script type="text/javascript">
    $(document).ready(function() {
        $("div.dcell").children("img").addBack().css("border", "thick solid blue");
    });
</script>
...
```

■ **Note**   The addBack method replaced the andSelf method in jQuery 1.9/2.0. The new method performs the same function and supports an additional selector argument to filter the selection.

In this example, I select all of the div elements that are members of the dcell class and then use the children method to select all of the img elements that are their children (I explain the children method fully in the *Navigating the DOM* section later in this chapter). I then call the addBack method, which combines the previous selection (the div element) with the current selection (the img elements) in a single jQuery object. Finally, I call use the css method to set a border for the selected elements. You can see the effect of this script in Figure 6-9.

Figure 6-9. Using the addBack method

Navigating the DOM

You can use a selection as the start point for navigating elsewhere in the DOM, using one selection as the start point for creating another. In the following sections, I'll describe and demonstrate the jQuery navigation methods. In this section I refer to the different kinds of relationships that can exist between elements that I introduced in Chapter 2.

■ **Tip** All of the methods that are described in the following sections return a jQuery object. This object will contain the matched elements if there are any and will be empty (i.e., the length property will be zero) if there are not.

Navigating Down the Hierarchy

When you navigate down the DOM hierarchy, you are selecting children and descendants of the elements contained in a jQuery object. Table 6-8 describes the relevant jQuery methods.

Table 6-8. *Methods to Navigate Down the DOM Hierarchy*

Method	Description
children()	Selects the children of all of the elements in the jQuery object.
children(selector)	Selects all of the elements that match the selector and that are children of the elements in the jQuery object.
contents()	Returns the children and text content of all the elements in the jQuery object.
find()	Selects the descendants of the elements in the jQuery object.
find(selector)	Selects the elements that match the selector and that are descendants of the elements in the jQuery object.
find(jQuery) find(HTMLElement) find(HTMLElement[])	Selects the intersection between the children of the elements in the jQuery object and the argument object.

The children method will select only those elements that are immediate descendants of each element in the jQuery object, optionally filtered by a selector. The find method will select all descendant elements, not just the immediate ones. The contents method will return the children elements, plus any text content. Listing 6-11 shows the children and find methods in use.

Listing 6-11. Using the children and find Methods

```
...
<script type="text/javascript">
    $(document).ready(function() {

        var childCount = $("div.drow").children().each(function(index, elem) {
            console.log("Child: " + elem.tagName + " " + elem.className);
        }).length;
        console.log("There are " + childCount + " children");

        var descCount = $("div.drow").find("img").each(function(index, elem) {
            console.log("Descendant: " + elem.tagName + " " + elem.src);
        }).length;
        console.log("There are " + descCount + " img descendants");

    });
</script>
...
```

In this example, I use the `children` method without a selector and the `find` method with one. I write the details of the selected elements to the console along with how many were selected. The console output from this script is as follows:

```
Child: DIV dcell
Child: DIV dcell
Child: DIV dcell
Child: DIV dcell
Child: DIV dcell
Child: DIV dcell
There are 6 children

Descendant: IMG http://www.jacquisflowershop.com/jquery/aster.png
Descendant: IMG http://www.jacquisflowershop.com/jquery/daffodil.png
Descendant: IMG http://www.jacquisflowershop.com/jquery/rose.png
Descendant: IMG http://www.jacquisflowershop.com/jquery/peony.png
Descendant: IMG http://www.jacquisflowershop.com/jquery/primula.png
Descendant: IMG http://www.jacquisflowershop.com/jquery/snowdrop.png
There are 6 img descendants
```

One of the nice features of the `children` and `find` methods is that you don't receive duplicate elements in the selection. Listing 6-12 provides a demonstration.

Listing 6-12. Generating a Selection with Overlapping Descendants

```
...
<script type="text/javascript">
    $(document).ready(function() {
        $("div.drow").add("div.dcell").find("img").each(function(index, elem) {
            console.log("Element: " + elem.tagName + " " + elem.src);
        });
    });
</script>
...
```

In this example, I start by creating a jQuery object that contains all of the `div` elements that are members of the `drow` class and all of the `div` elements that are members of the `dcell` class. Note is that all of the members of the `dcell` class are contained within members of the `drow` class, meaning that you have overlapping sets of descendants and the potential for duplication when I use the `find` method with the `img` selector, since the `img` elements are descendants of both classes of `div` elements. But jQuery ensures that there are no duplicates in the elements returned, as demonstrated in the console output that the listing produces:

```
Element: IMG http://www.jacquisflowershop.com/jquery/aster.png
Element: IMG http://www.jacquisflowershop.com/jquery/daffodil.png
Element: IMG http://www.jacquisflowershop.com/jquery/rose.png
Element: IMG http://www.jacquisflowershop.com/jquery/peony.png
Element: IMG http://www.jacquisflowershop.com/jquery/primula.png
Element: IMG http://www.jacquisflowershop.com/jquery/snowdrop.png
```

Using the find Method to Create an Intersection

You can pass a jQuery object, an HTMLElement object, or an array of HTMLElement objects as the argument to the find method. When you do this, you select the intersection between the descendants in the source jQuery object and the elements in the argument object. Listing 6-13 provides a demonstration.

Listing 6-13. Using the find Method to Create an Intersection

```
...
<script type="text/javascript">
    $(document).ready(function() {
        var jq = $("label").filter("[for*=p]").not("[for=peony]");
        $("div.drow").find(jq).css("border", "thick solid blue");
    });
</script>
...
```

As this script demonstrates, the advantage of this approach is that you can be specific about the elements that intersect with the descendants. I create a jQuery object that I then reduce using the filter and not methods. This object then becomes the argument to the find method on another jQuery object that contains all of the div elements in the drow class. The final selection is the intersection between the descendants of the div.drow elements and my reduced set of label elements. You can see the effect of the script in Figure 6-10.

Figure 6-10. *Using the find method to create an intersection*

Navigating Up the Hierarchy

When you navigate up the DOM hierarchy, you are interested in parents and ancestors of the elements contained in a jQuery object. Table 6-9 shows the methods you can use to navigate upward.

133

Table 6-9. *Methods to Navigate Up the DOM Hierarchy*

Method	Description
closest(selector) closest(selector, context)	Selects the nearest ancestor for each element in the jQuery object that intersects with the specified selector.
closest(jQuery) closest(HTMLElement)	Selects the nearest ancestor for each element in the jQuery object that intersects with the elements contained in the argument object.
offsetParent()	Finds the nearest ancestor that has a value for the CSS position property of fixed, absolute, or relative.
parent() parent(selector)	Selects the parent for each element in the jQuery object, optionally filtered by a selector.
parents() parents(selector)	Selects the ancestors for each element in the jQuery object, optionally filtered by a selector.
parentsUntil(selector) parentsUntil(selector, selector)	Selects the ancestors for each element in the jQuery object until a match for the selector is encountered. The results can be filtered using a second selector.
parentsUntil(HTMLElement) parentsUntil(HTMLElement, selector) parentsUntil(HTMLElement[]) parentsUntil(HTMLElement[], selector)	Selects the ancestors for each element in the jQuery object until one of the specified elements is encountered. The results can be filtered using a selector.

Selecting Parent Elements

The parent method selects the parent element for each of the elements in a jQuery object. If you provide a selector, then only parent elements that match the selector will be included in the result. Listing 6-14 shows the parent element in use.

Listing 6-14. Using the Parent Element

```
...
<script type="text/javascript">
    $(document).ready(function() {

        $("div.dcell").parent().each(function(index, elem) {
            console.log("Element: " + elem.tagName + " " + elem.id);
        });


        $("div.dcell").parent("#row1").each(function(index, elem) {
            console.log("Filtered Element: " + elem.tagName + " " + elem.id);
        });

    });
</script>
...
```

In this script, I select all of the div elements that are members of the dcell class and call the parent method to select the parent elements. I have also demonstrated using the parent method with a selector. I use the each method to write information about the selected parent elements to the console, which produces the following output:

```
Element: DIV row1
Element: DIV row2
Filtered Element: DIV row1
```

Selecting Ancestors

The parents method (note the final letter s) selects all of the ancestors of elements in a jQuery object, not just the immediate parents. Once again, you can pass a selector as a method to the argument to filter the results. Listing 6-15 demonstrates the parents method.

Listing 6-15. Using the parents Method

```
...
<script type="text/javascript">
    $(document).ready(function() {
        $("img[src*=peony], img[src*=rose]").parents().each(function(index, elem) {
            console.log("Element: " + elem.tagName + " " + elem.className + " "
                        + elem.id);
        });
    });
</script>
...
```

In this example, I selected two img elements and used the parents method to select their ancestors. I then write information about each ancestor to the console, to produce the following output:

```
Element: DIV dcell
Element: DIV drow row2
Element: DIV dcell
Element: DIV drow row1
Element: DIV dtable
Element: DIV  oblock
Element: FORM
Element: BODY
Element: HTML
```

A variation on selecting ancestors is presented by the parentsUntil method. For each element in the jQuery object, the parentsUntil method works its way up the DOM hierarchy, selecting ancestor elements until an element that matches the selector is encountered. Listing 6-16 provides a demonstration.

Listing 6-16. Using the parentsUntil Method

```
...
<script>
    $(document).ready(function() {
        $("img[src*=peony], img[src*=rose]").parentsUntil("form")
            .each(function(index, elem) {
                console.log("Element: " + elem.tagName + " " + elem.className
                    + " " + elem.id);
        });
    });
</script>
...
```

In this example, the ancestors for each element are selected until a form element is encountered. The output from the script is as follows:

```
Element: DIV dcell
Element: DIV drow row2
Element: DIV dcell
Element: DIV drow row1
Element: DIV dtable
Element: DIV  oblock
```

Notice that elements that match the selector are excluded from the selected ancestors. In this example, this means that the form element is excluded. You can filter the set of ancestors by providing a second selector argument, as shown in Listing 6-17.

Listing 6-17. Filtering the Set of Elements Selected by the parentsUntil Method

```
...
<script type="text/javascript">
    $(document).ready(function() {

        $("img[src*=peony], img[src*=rose]").parentsUntil("form", ":not(.dcell)")
            .each(function(index, elem) {
            console.log("Element: " + elem.tagName + " " + elem.className
                    + " " + elem.id);
        });

    });
</script>
...
```

In this example, I have added a selector that will filter out elements that belong to the dcell class. The output from this script is as follows:

```
Element: DIV drow row2
Element: DIV drow row1
Element: DIV dtable
Element: DIV  oblock
```

Selecting the First Matching Ancestor

The closest method selects the first ancestor that is matched by a selector for each element in a jQuery object. Listing 6-18 provides a demonstration.

Listing 6-18. Using the closest Method

```
...
<script type="text/javascript">
    $(document).ready(function() {

        $("img").closest(".drow").each(function(index, elem) {
            console.log("Element: " + elem.tagName + " " + elem.className
                        + " " + elem.id);
        });

        var contextElem = document.getElementById("row1");
        $("img").closest(".drow", contextElem).each(function(index, elem) {
            console.log("Context Element: " + elem.tagName + " " + elem.className
                        + " " + elem.id);
        });

    });
</script>
...
```

In this example, I select the img elements in the document and then use the closest method to find the nearest ancestor that belongs to the drow class. You can narrow the scope for selecting ancestors by specifying an HTMLElement object as the second argument to the method. Ancestors that are not the context object or are not descendants of the context object are excluded from the selection. The output from the script is as follows:

```
Element: DIV drow row1
Element: DIV drow row2
Context Element: DIV drow row2
```

When you specify a jQuery object or one or more HTMLElement objects as the argument to the closest method, jQuery works its way up the hierarchy for each element in the source jQuery object, matching the first argument object it finds. This is demonstrated by Listing 6-19.

Listing 6-19. Using the Closest Method with a Set of Reference Objects

```
...
<script type="text/javascript">
    $(document).ready(function() {

        var jq = $("#row1, #row2, form");

        $("img[src*=rose]").closest(jq).each(function(index, elem) {
            console.log("Context Element: " + elem.tagName + " " + elem.className
                        + " " + elem.id);
        });

    });
</script>
...
```

In this example, I select one of the img elements in the document and then use the closest method to select the ancestor elements. I have supplied a jQuery object containing the form element and the elements with the row1 and row2 ID as the argument to the closest method. jQuery will select whichever of the elements is the nearest ancestor to the img element. In other words, it will start to work its way up the hierarchy until it encounters one of the elements in the argument object. The output for this script is as follows:

```
Context Element: DIV drow row1
```

The offsetParent is a variation on the closest theme and funds the first ancestor that has a value for the position CSS property of relative, absolute, or fixed. Such an element is known as a *positioned ancestor*, and finding one can be useful when working with animation (see Chapter 10 for details of jQuery support for animation). Listing 6-20 contains a demonstration of this method.

Listing 6-20. Using the offsetParent Method

```html
<!DOCTYPE html>
<html>
<head>
    <title>Example</title>
    <script src="jquery-2.0.2.js" type="text/javascript"></script>
    <link rel="stylesheet" type="text/css" href="styles.css"/>
    <style type="text/css">
        #oblock {position: fixed; top: 120px; left: 50px}
    </style>
    <script type="text/javascript">
        $(document).ready(function() {
            $("img[src*=aster]").offsetParent().css("background-color", "lightgrey");
        });
    </script>
</head>
<body>
    <h1>Jacqui's Flower Shop</h1>
    <form method="post">
        <div id="oblock">
            <div class="dtable">
                <div id="row1" class="drow">
                    <div class="dcell">
                        <img src="aster.png"/><label for="aster">Aster:</label>
                        <input name="aster" value="0" required>
                    </div>
                    <div class="dcell">
                        <img src="daffodil.png"/><label for="daffodil">Daffodil:</label>
                        <input name="daffodil" value="0" required >
                    </div>
                    <div class="dcell">
                        <img src="rose.png"/><label for="rose">Rose:</label>
                        <input name="rose" value="0" required>
                    </div>
                </div>
            </div>
        </div>
```

```
        <div id="buttonDiv"><button type="submit">Place Order</button></div>
    </form>
</body>
</html>
```

In this cut-down version of the example document, I have used CSS to set a value for the position property for the element with the id of oblock. In the script, I use jQuery to select one of the img elements and then call the offsetParent method to find the closest positioned element. This method works its way up the hierarchy until it reaches an element with one of the required values. I use the css property to set a value for the background-color property for the selected element, as you can see in Figure 6-11.

Figure 6-11. *Finding the closest positioned ancestor*

Navigating Across the Hierarchy

The final form of DOM navigation deals with siblings. The methods that jQuery provides for this are described in Table 6-10.

Table 6-10. *Methods to Navigate Across the DOM Hierarchy*

Method	Description
next() next(selector)	Selects the immediate next sibling for each element in the jQuery object, optionally filtered by a selector.
nextAll() nextAll(selector)	Selects all of the next siblings for each element in the jQuery object, optionally filtered by a selector.
nextUntil((selector) nextUntil(selector, selector) nextUntil(jQuery) nextUntil(jQuery, selector) nextUntil(HTMLElement[]) nextUntil(HTMLElement[], selector)	Selects the next siblings for each element up to (and excluding) an element that matches the selector or an element in the jQuery object or the HTMLElement array. The results can optionally be filtered by a selector as the second argument to the method.
prev() prev(selector)	Selects the immediate previous sibling for each element in the jQuery object, optionally filtered by a selector.

(continued)

Table 6-10. (*continued*)

Method	Description
prevAll() prevAll(selector)	Selects all of the previous siblings for each element in the jQuery object, optionally filtered by a selector.
prevUntil(selector) prevUntil(selector, selector) prevUntil(jQuery) prevUntil(jQuery, selector) prevUntil(HTMLElement[]) prevUntil(HTMLElement[], selector)	Selects the previous siblings for each element up to (and excluding) an element that matches the selector or an element in the jQuery object or the HTMLElement array. The results can optionally be filtered by a selector as the second argument to the method.
siblings() siblings(selector)	Selects all of the siblings for each of the elements in the jQuery object, optionally filtered by a selector.

Selecting All Siblings

The siblings method selects all of the siblings for all of the elements in a jQuery object. Listing 6-21 shows this method in use. (For this listing, I have returned to the full flower shop document).

Listing 6-21. Using the siblings Method

```
<!DOCTYPE html>
<html>
<head>
    <title>Example</title>
    <script src="jquery-2.0.2.js" type="text/javascript"></script>
    <link rel="stylesheet" type="text/css" href="styles.css"/>
    <script type="text/javascript">
        $(document).ready(function () {
            $("img[src*=aster], img[src*=primula]")
                .parent().siblings().css("border", "thick solid blue");
        });
    </script>
</head>
<body>
    <h1>Jacqui's Flower Shop</h1>
    <form method="post">
        <div id="oblock">
            <div class="dtable">
                <div id="row1" class="drow">
                    <div class="dcell">
                        <img src="aster.png"/><label for="aster">Aster:</label>
                        <input name="aster" value="0" required>
                    </div>
                    <div class="dcell">
                        <img src="daffodil.png"/><label for="daffodil">Daffodil:</label>
                        <input name="daffodil" value="0" required >
                    </div>
```

```
                    <div class="dcell">
                        <img src="rose.png"/><label for="rose">Rose:</label>
                        <input name="rose" value="0" required>
                    </div>
                </div>
                <div id="row2"class="drow">
                    <div class="dcell">
                        <img src="peony.png"/><label for="peony">Peony:</label>
                        <input name="peony" value="0" required>
                    </div>
                    <div class="dcell">
                        <img src="primula.png"/><label for="primula">Primula:</label>
                        <input name="primula" value="0" required>
                    </div>
                    <div class="dcell">
                        <img src="snowdrop.png"/><label for="snowdrop">Snowdrop:</label>
                        <input name="snowdrop" value="0" required>
                    </div>
                </div>
            </div>
        </div>
        <div id="buttonDiv"><button type="submit">Place Order</button></div>
    </form>
</body>
</html>
```

In this example, I select two of the img elements, call the parent method to select their parent elements, and then call the siblings method to select their sibling elements. Both the previous and next siblings will be selected, and I use the css method to set a value for the border property. You can see the effect in Figure 6-12. (I used the parent method to make the effect of the CSS property clearer.)

Figure 6-12. *Selecting sibling elements*

Notice that only the siblings are selected, not the elements themselves. Of course, this changes if one element in the jQuery object is a sibling of another, as shown in Listing 6-22.

Listing 6-22. Overlapping Sets of Siblings

```
...
<script type="text/javascript">
    $(document).ready(function() {
        $("#row1 div.dcell").siblings().css("border", "thick solid blue");
    });
</script>
...
```

In this script, I start by selecting all of the div elements that are children of the row1 element and then call the siblings method. Each of the elements in the selection is the sibling to at least one of the other elements, as you can see in Figure 6-13.

Figure 6-13. Overlapping sibling elements

Selecting Next and Previous Siblings

I am not going to demonstrate all of the methods for selecting next and previous siblings, because they work in the same way as the other navigation methods. Listing 6-23 shows the nextAll and prevAll methods in use.

Listing 6-23. Using the nextAll and prevAll Methods

```
...
<script type="text/javascript">
    $(document).ready(function() {
        $("img[src*=aster]").parent().nextAll().css("border", "thick solid blue");
        $("img[src*=primula]").parent().prevAll().css("border", "thick double red");
    });
</script>
...
```

This script selects the next siblings for the parent of the aster image and the previous siblings for the primula image. You can see the effect of this script in Figure 6-14.

Figure 6-14. *Selecting next and previous siblings*

Summary

In this chapter, I showed you how to take control of the jQuery selection and tailor it to your exact needs, including adding elements, filtering elements, using mapping, and testing the selection to assess a condition. I also showed you how you can use a jQuery selection as the starting point to navigate the DOM, using one selection as the starting point for traversing the document in order to create another. In Chapter 7, I show you how to use a selection to manipulate the DOM, applying jQuery methods to create, remove, change, and create HTML elements.

CHAPTER 7

■ ■ ■

Manipulating the DOM

In the previous chapter, I showed you how to select elements. One of the most powerful things you can do with the selection is to change the structure of the HTML document itself, known as *manipulating the DOM*. In this chapter, I'll show you the different ways in which you can alter the structure, including inserting elements as children, parents, or siblings of other elements. I'll also show you how to create new elements, how to move elements from one part of the document to another, and how to remove elements entirely. Table 7-1 provides the summary for this chapter.

Table 7-1. *Chapter Summary*

Problem	Solution	Listing
Create new elements.	Pass an HTML fragment to the $ function, by using the clone method or by using the DOM API.	1–3
Insert elements as last children.	Use the append method.	4
Insert elements as first children.	Use the prepend method.	5, 6
Insert the same elements in different positions.	Clone the elements before inserting them.	7, 8
Insert the contents of a jQuery object as children of other elements.	Use the appendTo or prependTo methods.	9
Insert child elements dynamically.	Pass a function to the append or prepend methods.	10
Insert parent elements.	Use the wrap method.	11
Insert a common parent to several elements.	Use the wrapAll method.	12, 13
Wrap the contents of elements.	Use the wrapInner method.	14
Wrap elements dynamically.	Pass a function to the wrap or wrapInner method.	15
Insert sibling elements.	Use the after, before, insertAfter, or insertBefore method.	16, 17
Insert sibling elements dynamically.	Pass a function to the before or after method.	18
Replace elements with other elements.	Use the replaceWith or replaceAll method.	19
Replace elements dynamically.	Pass a function to the replaceWith method.	20
Remove elements from the DOM.	Use the remove or detach method.	21–23
Remove the contents of an element.	Use the empty method.	24
Remove the parents of elements.	Use the unwrap method.	25

JQUERY CHANGES SINCE THE LAST EDITION

For this chapter, the most important change in jQuery 1.9/2.0 is a stricter approach in interpreting HTML strings. However, this change was undone by the 1.10/2.0.1 releases and the old approach to HTML parsing was restored – see the *Changes to HTML Parsing* sidebar for details.

There are some behind-the-scenes changes to the way that the `after`, `before`, `replaceWith`, `appendTo`, `insertBefore`, `insertAfter`, and `replaceAll` methods to make the way that they handle jQuery objects consistent with the other DOM manipulation methods. These changes don't affect the techniques in this chapter.

Creating New Elements

When writing web applications, you will often need to create new elements and insert them into the DOM (although you can also insert existing elements, as I'll explain later in the chapter). In the sections that follow, I'll show you different ways that you can create content.

■ **Tip** It is important to understand that creating new elements doesn't automatically add them to the DOM. You need to explicitly tell jQuery where the new elements should be placed in the document, which I explain later in this chapter.

Creating Elements Using the $ Function

You can create new elements by passing an HTML fragment string to the $ function. jQuery parses the string and creates the corresponding DOM objects. Listing 7-1 contains an example.

Listing 7-1. Creating New Elements Using the $ Function

```
<!DOCTYPE html>
<html>
<head>
    <title>Example</title>
    <script src="jquery-2.0.2.js" type="text/javascript"></script>
    <link rel="stylesheet" type="text/css" href="styles.css"/>
    <script type="text/javascript">
        $(document).ready(function() {

            var newElems = $("<div class='dcell'><img src='lily.png'/></div>");

            newElems.each(function (index, elem) {
                console.log("New element: " + elem.tagName + " " + elem.className);
            });

            newElems.children().each(function(index, elem) {
                console.log("Child: " + elem.tagName + " " + elem.src);
            });
        });
    </script>
</head>
```

```
<body>
    <h1>Jacquils Flower Shop</h1>
    <form method="post">
        <div id="oblock">
            <div class="dtable">
                <div id="row1" class="drow">
                    <div class="dcell">
                        <img src="aster.png"/><label for="aster">Aster:</label>
                        <input name="aster" value="0" required>
                    </div>
                    <div class="dcell">
                        <img src="daffodil.png"/><label for="daffodil">Daffodil:</label>
                        <input name="daffodil" value="0" required >
                    </div>
                    <div class="dcell">
                        <img src="rose.png"/><label for="rose">Rose:</label>
                        <input name="rose" value="0" required>
                    </div>
                </div>
                <div id="row2"class="drow">
                    <div class="dcell">
                        <img src="peony.png"/><label for="peony">Peony:</label>
                        <input name="peony" value="0" required>
                    </div>
                    <div class="dcell">
                        <img src="primula.png"/><label for="primula">Primula:</label>
                        <input name="primula" value="0" required>
                    </div>
                    <div class="dcell">
                        <img src="snowdrop.png"/><label for="snowdrop">Snowdrop:</label>
                        <input name="snowdrop" value="0" required>
                    </div>
                </div>
            </div>
        </div>
        <div id="buttonDiv"><button type="submit">Place Order</button></div>
    </form>
</body>
</html>
```

In this example, I have created two new elements from an HTML fragment: a div element and an img element. Since you are dealing with HTML, you can use fragments that contain structure. In this case, the img element is a child of the div element.

```
╔══════════════════════════════════════════════════════════════════════════╗
║                        CHANGES TO HTML PARSING                             ║
╚══════════════════════════════════════════════════════════════════════════╝
```

When you pass a string to the $ function, jQuery has to decide whether it is a selector or an HTML string. Prior to version 1.9, the string was considered HTML if it has a tag anywhere within it (see Chapter 2 for details of tags). This presented some rare problems where complex selectors were being interpreted as HTML and so the policy was changed in jQuery 1.9/2.0 so that a string was only considered as HTML if it started with the < character.

That proved to be an unpopular change and so the policy was changed back in the jQuery 1.10/2.0.1 release – but with a warning that further changes can be expected in the way that HTML strings are detected. If you are working with strings that might be ambiguous, you can use the parseHTML method, which will process an HTML string without the risk of interpreting it as a selector.

The jQuery object that is returned by the $ function contains only the top-level elements from the HTML fragment. To demonstrate this, I have used the each function to write information about each element in the jQuery object to the console. jQuery doesn't discard the child elements. They are accessible via the usual navigation methods that I described in Chapter 6. To demonstrate this, I have called the children method on the jQuery object and printed information about each child element to the console as well. The output from this script is as follows:

```
New element: DIV dcell
Child: IMG http://www.jacquisflowershop.com/jquery/lily.png
```

■ **Tip**   You can also provide a map object that specifies attributes that should be applied to the HTML element. You can see this version of the $ function being used in Chapter 12.

Creating New Elements by Cloning Existing Elements

You can create new elements from existing elements by using the clone method. This duplicates all of the elements in a jQuery object, along with all of their descendants. Listing 7-2 gives an example.

Listing 7-2. Cloning Elements

```
...
<script type="text/javascript">
    $(document).ready(function() {

        var newElems = $("div.dcell").clone();

        newElems.each(function (index, elem) {
            console.log("New element: " + elem.tagName + " " + elem.className);
        });
```

```
        newElems.children("img").each(function(index, elem) {
            console.log("Child: " + elem.tagName + " " + elem.src);
        });

    });
</script>
...
```

In this script I have selected and cloned all of the div elements that are members of the dcell class. To demonstrate that the descendant elements are cloned as well, I have used the children method with a selector to obtain the cloned img elements. I have written details of the div and img elements to the console, producing the following output:

```
New element: DIV dcell
New element: DIV dcell
New element: DIV dcell
New element: DIV dcell
New element: DIV dcell
New element: DIV dcell
Child: IMG http://www.jacquisflowershop.com/jquery/aster.png
Child: IMG http://www.jacquisflowershop.com/jquery/daffodil.png
Child: IMG http://www.jacquisflowershop.com/jquery/rose.png
Child: IMG http://www.jacquisflowershop.com/jquery/peony.png
Child: IMG http://www.jacquisflowershop.com/jquery/primula.png
Child: IMG http://www.jacquisflowershop.com/jquery/snowdrop.png
```

■ **Tip** You can pass the value true as an argument to the clone method to include the event handlers and data associated with the elements in the copying process. Omitting this argument or specifying a value of false omits the event handlers and data. I explain the jQuery support for events in Chapter 9 and explain how to associate data with elements in Chapter 8.

Creating Elements Using the DOM API

You can use the DOM API directly to create new HTMLElement objects, which is essentially what jQuery is doing for you when you use the other techniques. I am not going to explain the details of the DOM API, but Listing 7-3 contains a simple example to give you a sense of how you can approach this technique.

Listing 7-3. Using the DOM API to Create New Elements

```
...
<script type="text/javascript">
    $(document).ready(function() {

        var divElem = document.createElement("div");
        divElem.classList.add("dcell");

        var imgElem = document.createElement("img");
        imgElem.src = "lily.png";
```

149

```
        divElem.appendChild(imgElem);

    var newElems = $(divElem);

    newElems.each(function (index, elem) {
        console.log("New element: " + elem.tagName + " " + elem.className);
    });

    newElems.children("img").each(function(index, elem) {
        console.log("Child: " + elem.tagName + " " + elem.src);
    });

    });
</script>
...
```

In this example, I create and configure a div HTMLElement and an img HTMLElement and assign the img as the child of the div, just as I did in the first example. There is nothing wrong with creating elements this way, but since this is a book about jQuery, I don't want to go off topic by straying too far into the DOM API.

I pass the div HTMLElement as an argument to the jQuery $ function so I can use the same each functions as for the other examples. The console output is as follows:

```
New element: DIV dcell
Child: IMG http://www.jacquisflowershop.com/jquery/lily.png
```

Inserting Child and Descendant Elements

Once I have created elements, I can start to insert them into the document. I start by looking at the methods that insert one element inside another in order to create child and descendant elements, as described by Table 7-2.

Table 7-2. *Methods for Inserting Child and Descendant Elements*

Method	Description
append(HTML) append(jQuery) append(HTMLElement[])	Inserts the specified elements as the last children of all of the elements in the DOM.
prepend(HTML) prepend(jQuery) prepend(HTMLElement[])	Inserts the specified elements as the first children of all of the elements in the DOM.
appendTo(jQuery) appendTo(HTMLElement[])	Inserts the elements in the jQuery object as the last children of the elements specified by the argument.
prependTo(HTML) prependTo(jQuery) prependTo(HTMLElement[])	Inserts the elements in the jQuery object as the first children of the elements specified by the argument.
append(function) prepend(function)	Appends or prepends the result of a function to the elements in the jQuery object.

■ **Tip**   You can also insert child elements using the `wrapInner` method, which I describe in the "Wrapping the Contents of Elements" section. This method inserts a new child between an element and its existing children. Another technique is to use the `html` method, which I describe in Chapter 8.

The elements passed as arguments to these methods are inserted as children to *every* element in the jQuery object, which makes it especially important to use the techniques I showed you in Chapter 6 to manage the selection so that it contains only the elements you want to work with. Listing 7-4 gives a demonstration of using the append method.

Listing 7-4. Using the append Method

```
...
<script type="text/javascript">
    $(document).ready(function() {
        var newElems = $("<div class='dcell'></div>")
            .append("<img src='lily.png'/>")
            .append("<label for='lily'>Lily:</label>")
            .append("<input name='lily' value='0' required />");

        newElems.css("border", "thick solid red");

        $("#row1").append(newElems);
    });
</script>
...
```

I use the append method in this script in two different ways: first to build up my set of new elements and then to insert those elements into the HTML document. Since this is the first DOM manipulation method that I have described, I am going to spend a moment demonstrating some behaviors that will help you avoid the most common DOM-related jQuery errors. But first, let's look at the effect of the script. You can see the result of adding the new elements in Figure 7-1.

Figure 7-1. *Inserting new elements into the document*

The first thing to look at is the way I built up my new elements using the append method:

```
...
var newElems = $("<div class='dcell'/>").append("<img src='lily.png'/>")
    .append("<label for='lily'>Lily:</label>")
    .append("<input name='lily' value='0' required />");
...
```

I could have just created a single, bigger block of HTML that contained all of the elements, but I wanted to show a key facet of the DOM manipulation methods, which is that the jQuery objects returned by these methods contain the same elements as the object on which the methods were called.

For example, I started with a jQuery object that contained a div element, and the result of each append method was a jQuery object that contained the same div element and not the element that I added. This means that chaining append calls together creates multiple new child elements for the originally selected elements.

The next behavior to point out was that newly created elements may not be attached to the document, but you can still use jQuery to navigate and modify them. I wanted to highlight the new elements with a border, so I made the following call:

```
...
newElems.css("border", "thick solid red");
...
```

This is a nice feature that allows you to create and manage complex sets of elements and prepare them fully before adding them to the document. Finally, I add the new elements to the document, like this:

```
...
$("#row1").append(newElems);
...
```

The new elements are added to each element in the selection. There is only one element in the selection in the example (the one with the id of row1) and so you have the new lily product added to the flower shop page.

Prepending Elements

The complement to the append method is prepend, which inserts the new elements as the first children of the elements in the jQuery object. Listing 7-5 contains an example.

Listing 7-5. Using the prepend Method

```
...
<script type="text/javascript">
    $(document).ready(function() {

        var orchidElems = $("<div class='dcell'/>")
            .append("<img src='orchid.png'/>")
            .append("<label for='orchid'>Orchid:</label>")
            .append("<input name='orchid' value='0' required />");

        var newElems = $("<div class='dcell'/>")
            .append("<img src='lily.png'/>")
```

```
        .append("<label for='lily'>Lily:</label>")
        .append("<input name='lily' value='0' required />").add(orchidElems);

    newElems.css("border", "thick solid red");

    $("#row1, #row2").prepend(newElems);
  });
</script>
...
```

In addition to the prepend method, this script demonstrates another jQuery DOM manipulation characteristic: *all* of the elements passed as an argument to one of these methods are added as children to *all* of the elements in the jQuery object. In this example, I create two div elements, one for lilies and one for orchids. I use the add method to bring both sets of elements together in a single jQuery object.

■ **Tip** The add method will also accept a string containing an HTML fragment. You can use this feature as an alternative to building up new elements using jQuery objects.

I then create another jQuery object that contains the elements with the row1 and row2 id values and use the prepend method to insert the orchid and lily elements into the document. You can see the effect in Figure 7-2. The new elements are highlighted with a red border. As the figure shows, the lily and orchid elements have been added to both row elements.

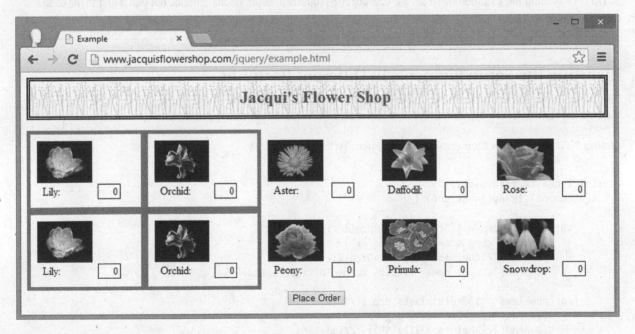

Figure 7-2. *Adding multiple new elements to multiple selected elements*

As an alternative to using the add method, you can pass multiple elements to the DOM modification methods, as shown in Listing 7-6. This listing produces the same results as shown in Figure 7-2.

Listing 7-6. Passing Multiple Arguments to the prepend Method

```
...
<script type="text/javascript">
    $(document).ready(function() {

        var orchidElems = $("<div class='dcell'/>")
            .append("<img src='orchid.png'/>")
            .append("<label for='orchid'>Orchid:</label>")
            .append("<input name='orchid' value='0' required />");

        var lilyElems = $("<div class='dcell'/>")
            .append("<img src='lily.png'/>")
            .append("<label for='lily'>Lily:</label>")
            .append("<input name='lily' value='0' required />");

        orchidElems.css("border", "thick solid red");
        lilyElems.css("border", "thick solid red");

        $("#row1, #row2").prepend(lilyElems, orchidElems);
    });
</script>
...
```

■ **Tip**   I am using the `css` method to set the CSS `border` property in separate statements, but that's just to make the example easier to follow. In fact, I can chain the call to the `css` method like any other jQuery method.

Inserting the Same Elements in Different Positions

You can add new elements to the document only once. At this point, using them as arguments to a DOM insertion method moves the elements, rather than duplicates them. Listing 7-7 shows the problem.

Listing 7-7. Adding New Elements to the Document Twice

```
...
<script type="text/javascript">
    $(document).ready(function() {

        var orchidElems = $("<div class='dcell'/>")
            .append("<img src='orchid.png'/>")
            .append("<label for='orchid'>Orchid:</label>")
            .append("<input name='orchid' value='0' required />");

        var newElems = $("<div class='dcell'/>")
            .append("<img src='lily.png'/>")
            .append("<label for='lily'>Lily:</label>")
            .append("<input name='lily' value='0' required />").add(orchidElems);
```

```
        newElems.css("border", "thick solid red");

        $("#row1").append(newElems);
        $("#row2").prepend(newElems);
    });
</script>
...
```

The intent in this script is clear: to append the new elements to row1 and prepend them to row2. Of course, this isn't what happens, as Figure 7-3 shows.

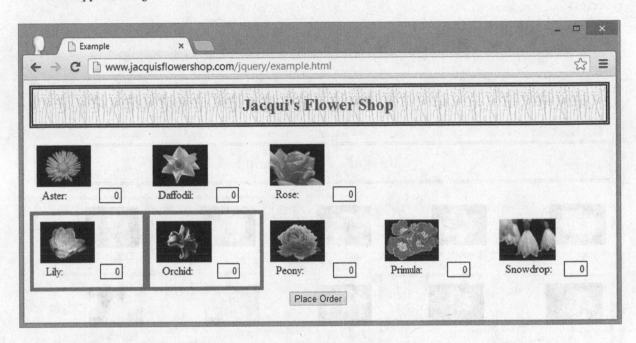

Figure 7-3. *Trying (and failing) to add new elements to the document twice*

The elements *were* appended to row1, but the call to prepend has the effect of moving the elements rather than adding them twice. To address this issue, you need to create copies of the elements you want to insert by using the clone method. Listing 7-8 shows the revised script.

Listing 7-8. Cloning Elements So They Can Be Added to the Document More Than Once

```
...
<script type="text/javascript">
    $(document).ready(function() {

        var orchidElems = $("<div class='dcell'/>")
            .append("<img src='orchid.png'/>")
            .append("<label for='orchid'>Orchid:</label>")
            .append("<input name='orchid' value='0' required />");
```

```
        var newElems = $("<div class='dcell'/>")
            .append("<img src='lily.png'/>")
            .append("<label for='lily'>Lily:</label>")
            .append("<input name='lily' value='0' required />").add(orchidElems);

        newElems.css("border", "thick solid red");

        $("#row1").append(newElems);
        $("#row2").prepend(newElems.clone());
    });
</script>
...
```

The elements are now copied and inserted in both locations, as shown in Figure 7-4.

Figure 7-4. *Cloning and inserting elements*

Inserting from a jQuery Object

You can use the appendTo and prependTo methods to change the relationship between elements, as shown in Listing 7-9.

Listing 7-9. Using the appendTo Method

```
...
<script type="text/javascript">
    $(document).ready(function() {

        var newElems = $("<div class='dcell'/>");
```

```
        $("img").appendTo(newElems);

        $("#row1").append(newElems);
    });
</script>
...
```

I create jQuery objects to contain a new div element and the img elements in the document. I then use the appendTo method to append the img elements as the children of the div element. You can see the result in Figure 7-5. As you can see, the effect of the script is to move the img elements to the new div element, which I appended to the row1 element.

Figure 7-5. *Using the appendTo method*

Inserting Elements Using a Function

You can pass a function to the append and prepend methods. This allows you to dynamically insert children for the elements selected by the jQuery object, as shown by Listing 7-10.

Listing 7-10. *Adding Child Elements Dynamically with a Function*

```
...
<script type="text/javascript">
    $(document).ready(function() {

        var orchidElems = $("<div class='dcell'/>")
            .append("<img src='orchid.png'/>")
            .append("<label for='orchid'>Orchid:</label>")
            .append("<input name='orchid' value='0' required />");
```

```
    var lilyElems = $("<div class='dcell'/>")
        .append("<img src='lily.png'/>")
        .append("<label for='lily'>Lily:</label>")
        .append("<input name='lily' value='0' required />");

    $(orchidElems).add(lilyElems).css("border", "thick solid red");

    $("div.drow").append(function(index, html) {
        if (this.id == "row1") {
            return orchidElems;
        } else {
            return lilyElems;
        }
    });
});
</script>
...
```

The function is invoked once for each element in the jQuery object. The arguments passed to the function are the index of the element in the selection and the HTML of the element that is being processed; the HTML is a string. In addition, the value of the this variable is set to the appropriate HTMLElement. The result from the function will be appended or prepended to the element being processed. You can return an HTML fragment, one or more HTMLElement objects, or a jQuery object.

In this example, I prepare by creating sets of elements for the lily and orchid products and then return them from the append function based on the value of the id property. You can see the result in Figure 7-6.

Figure 7-6. *Inserting elements dynamically based on a function*

Inserting Parent and Ancestor Elements

jQuery provides you with a set of methods for inserting elements as parents or ancestors of other elements. This is known as *wrapping* (because one element is wrapped by another). Table 7-3 describes these methods.

Table 7-3. Methods for Wrapping Elements

Method	Description
wrap(HTML) wrap(jQuery) wrap(HTMLElement[])	Wraps the specified elements around each of the elements in the jQuery object.
wrapAll(HTML) wrapAll(jQuery) wrapAll(HTMLElement[])	Wraps the specified elements around the set of elements in the jQuery object (as a single group).
wrapInner(HTML) wrapInner(jQuery) wrapInner(HTMLElement[])	Wraps the specified elements around the content of the elements in the jQuery object.
wrap(function) wrapInner(function)	Wraps elements dynamically using a function.

■ **Tip** The complement to the wrapping methods is unwrap, which I describe in the "Removing Elements" section later in this chapter.

When you perform wrapping, you can pass multiple elements as the argument, but you must make sure that there is only one inner element. Otherwise, jQuery can't figure out what to do. This means that each element in the argument must have at most one parent and at most one child. Listing 7-11 demonstrates the use of the wrap method.

Listing 7-11. Using the wrap Method

```
...
<script type="text/javascript">
    $(document).ready(function() {

        var newElem = $("<div/>").css("border", "thick solid red");
        $("div.drow").wrap(newElem);

    });
</script>
...
```

In this script, I create a new div element and use the css method to set a value for the CSS border property. I then use the wrap method to insert the div element as the parent to all of the label elements in the document. You can see the effect in Figure 7-7.

Figure 7-7. *Using the wrap method to add a parent to elements*

The elements passed as arguments to the wrap method are inserted between each element in the jQuery object and their current parents. So, for example, this fragment of HTML:

```
...
<div class="dtable">
    <div id="row1" class="drow">
        ...
    </div>
    <div id="row2" class="drow">
        ...
    </div>
</div>
...
```

is transformed like this:

```
...
<div class="dtable">
    <div style="...style properties...">
        <div id="row1" class="drow">
            ...
        </div>
    </div>
</div>
```

```
<div style="...style properties...">
    <div id="row2" class="drow">
        ...
    </div>
</div>
</div>
...
```

Wrapping Elements Together in a Single Parent

When you use the wrap method, the new elements are cloned, and each element in the jQuery object gets its own new parent element. You can insert a single parent for several elements by using the wrapAll method, as shown in Listing 7-12.

Listing 7-12. Using the wrapAll Method

```
...
<script type="text/javascript">
    $(document).ready(function() {

        var newElem = $("<div/>").css("border", "thick solid red");
        $("div.drow").wrapAll(newElem);

    });
</script>
...
```

The only change in this script is the use of the wrapAll method. You can see the effect in Figure 7-8.

Figure 7-8. Using the wrapAll method

161

The new element is used to insert a common parent to the selected elements, such that the HTML is transformed like this:

```
...
<div class="dtable">
    <div style="...style properties...">
        <div id="row1" class="drow">
            ...
        </div>
        <div id="row2" class="drow">
        </div>
    </div>
</div>
...
```

Be careful when using the `wrapAll` method. If the selected elements don't already share a common parent, then the new element is inserted as the parent to the first selected element. Then jQuery moves all of the other selected elements to be siblings of the first one. Listing 7-13 contains a script that demonstrates this behavior.

Listing 7-13. Using the wrapAll on Elements Without a Common Parent

```
...
<script type="text/javascript">
    $(document).ready(function() {

        var newElem = $("<div/>").css("border", "thick solid red");
        $("img").wrapAll(newElem);

    });
</script>
...
```

I have selected the `img` elements in the document, none of which share a common parent. You can see the effect of this script in Figure 7-9. The new `div` element has been inserted into the document as the parent to the aster image, and all of the other images have been inserted as siblings.

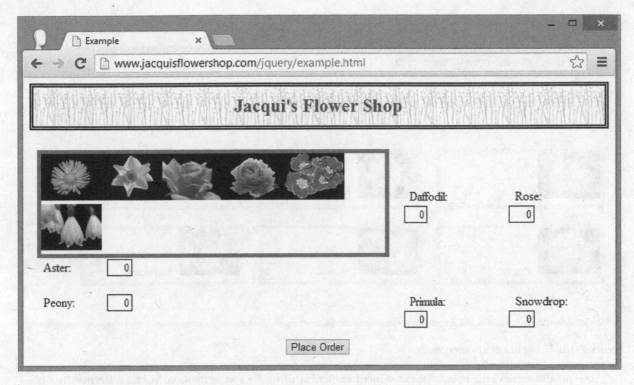

Figure 7-9. *Using wrapAll on elements that don't share a common parent*

Wrapping the Content of Elements

The wrapInner method wraps elements around the contents of the elements in a jQuery object, as demonstrated by Listing 7-14.

Listing 7-14. Using the wrapInner Method

```
...
<script type="text/javascript">
    $(document).ready(function() {

        var newElem = $("<div/>").css("border", "thick solid red");
        $(".dcell").wrapInner(newElem);

    });
</script>
...
```

The wrapInner method inserts new elements between the elements in the jQuery object and their immediate children. In the script, I select the elements that belong to the dcell class and wrap their contents with a new div element. You can see the effect in Figure 7-10.

Figure 7-10. *Using the wrapInner method*

You can also achieve the effect of the `wrapInner` method by using the `append` method. Just for reference, here is the equivalent script:

```
...
<script type="text/javascript">
    $(document).ready(function() {

        var newElem = $("<div/>").css("border", "thick solid red");
        $(".dcell").each(function(index, elem) {
            $(elem).append(newElem.clone().append($(elem).children()));
        });

    });
</script>
...
```

I am not suggesting you use this approach (the `wrapInner` method is easier to read and more convenient), but I think this is a good example of how you can use jQuery to perform the same task in different ways.

Wrapping Elements Using a Function

You can pass a function to the `wrap` and `wrapInner` methods to generate elements dynamically. The function is invoked for each of the selected elements and is passed the current element index. The special variable `this` is set to the element to be processed. The script in Listing 7-15 shows how you can wrap elements dynamically.

Listing 7-15. Wrapping Elements Dynamically

```
...
<script type="text/javascript">
    $(document).ready(function() {

        $(".drow").wrap(function(index) {
            if ($(this).has("img[src*=rose]").length > 0) {
                return $("<div/>").css("border", "thick solid blue");;
            } else {
                return $("<div/>").css("border", "thick solid red");;
            }
        });

    });
</script>
...
```

In this example, I use a function with the `wrap` method to tailor the new parent element based on the descendants of each of the selected elements. You can see the effect of this script in Figure 7-11.

Figure 7-11. Using the wrap method with a function to generate parent elements dynamically

Inserting Sibling Elements

jQuery also provides a set of methods that insert elements into the document as siblings of existing elements, as described in Table 7-4.

Table 7-4. *Methods for Inserting Sibling Elements*

Method	Description
after(HTML) after(jQuery) after(HTMLElement[])	Inserts the specified elements as next siblings to each element in the jQuery object.
before(HTML) before(jQuery) before(HTMLElement[])	Inserts the specified elements as previous siblings to each element in the jQuery object.
insertAfter(HTML) insertAfter(jQuery) insertAfter(HTMLElement[])	Inserts the elements in the jQuery object as the next siblings for each element specified in the argument.
insertBefore(HTML) insertBefore(jQuery) insertBefore(HTMLElement[])	Inserts the elements in the jQuery object as the previous siblings for each element specified in the argument.
after(function) before(function)	Inserts siblings dynamically using a function.

The before and after methods follow the same pattern you saw when inserting other kinds of element in the document. Listing 7-16 contains a demonstration of both methods.

Listing 7-16. Using the before and after Methods

```
...
<script type="text/javascript">
    $(document).ready(function() {

        var orchidElems = $("<div class='dcell'/>")
            .append("<img src='orchid.png'/>")
            .append("<label for='orchid'>Orchid:</label>")
            .append("<input name='orchid' value='0' required />");

        var lilyElems = $("<div class='dcell'/>")
            .append("<img src='lily.png'/>")
            .append("<label for='lily'>Lily:</label>")
            .append("<input name='lily' value='0' required />");

        $(orchidElems).add(lilyElems).css("border", "thick solid red");

        $("#row1 div.dcell").after(orchidElems);
        $("#row2 div.dcell").before(lilyElems);

    });
</script>
...
```

In this script, I create new sets of elements for orchids and lilies and use them with the `before` and `after` methods to insert them as siblings for each of the elements in the `dcell` class. The orchid elements are inserted as next siblings for all the elements in `row1`, and the lily elements are inserted as previous siblings for all of the elements in `row2`. You can see the effect of this script in Figure 7-12.

Figure 7-12. *Using the before and after elements to create siblings*

Inserting Siblings from a jQuery Object

The `insertAfter` and `insertBefore` methods insert the elements in the `jQuery` object as the next or previous siblings to the elements in the method argument. This is the same functionality as in the `after` and `before` methods, but the relationship between the `jQuery` object and the argument is reversed. Listing 7-17 shows the use of these methods. This script creates the same effect, as shown in Figure 7-12.

Listing 7-17. *Using the insertAfter and InsertBefore Methods*

```
...
<script type="text/javascript">
    $(document).ready(function() {

        var orchidElems = $("<div class='dcell'/>")
            .append("<img src='orchid.png'/>")
            .append("<label for='orchid'>Orchid:</label>")
            .append("<input name='orchid' value='0' required />");
```

```
            var lilyElems = $("<div class='dcell'/>")
                .append("<img src='lily.png'/>")
                .append("<label for='lily'>Lily:</label>")
                .append("<input name='lily' value='0' required />");

            $(orchidElems).add(lilyElems).css("border", "thick solid red");

            orchidElems.insertAfter("#row1 div.dcell");
            lilyElems.insertBefore("#row2 div.dcell");
        });
</script>
...
```

Inserting Siblings Using a Function

You can insert sibling elements dynamically using a function with the after and before methods, just as for parent and child elements. Listing 7-18 contains an example of dynamically generating sibling elements.

Listing 7-18. Generating Sibling Elements Dynamically with a Function

```
...
<script type="text/javascript">
    $(document).ready(function() {

        $("#row1 div.dcell").after(function(index, html) {
            if (index == 0) {
                return $("<div class='dcell'/>")
                    .append("<img src='orchid.png'/>")
                    .append("<label for='orchid'>Orchid:</label>")
                    .append("<input name='orchid' value='0' required />")
                    .css("border", "thick solid red");
            } else if (index == 1) {
                return $("<div class='dcell'/>")
                    .append("<img src='lily.png'/>")
                    .append("<label for='lily'>Lily:</label>")
                    .append("<input name='lily' value='0' required />")
                    .css("border", "thick solid red");
            }
        });

    });
</script>
...
```

In this script, I use the index argument to generate siblings when the index of the element being processed is 0 or 1. You can see the effect of this script in Figure 7-13.

Figure 7-13. *Adding sibling elements using a function*

Replacing Elements

You can replace one set of elements with another using the methods described in Table 7-5.

Table 7-5. *Methods for Wrapping Elements*

Method	Description
replaceWith(HTML) replaceWith(jQuery) replaceWith(HTMLElement[])	Replace the elements in the jQuery object with the specified content.
replaceAll(jQuery) replaceAll(HTMLElement[])	Replace the elements specified by the argument with the elements in the jQuery object.
replaceWith(function)	Replaces the elements in the jQuery object dynamically using a function.

The replaceWith and the replaceAll methods work in the same way, with the exception that the role of the jQuery object and the argument are reversed. Listing 7-19 demonstrates both methods.

Listing 7-19. *Using the replaceWith and replaceAll Methods*

```
...
<script type="text/javascript">
    $(document).ready(function() {

        var newElems = $("<div class='dcell'/>")
                    .append("<img src='orchid.png'/>")
                    .append("<label for='orchid'>Orchid:</label>")
                    .append("<input name='orchid' value='0' required />")
                    .css("border", "thick solid red");

        $("#row1").children().first().replaceWith(newElems);
```

```
        $("<img src='carnation.png'/>").replaceAll("#row2 img")
            .css("border", "thick solid red");

    });
</script>
...
```

In this script, I use the replaceWith method to replace the first child of the row1 div element with new content (this has the effect of replacing the aster with the orchid). I also use the replaceAll method to replace all of the img elements that are descendants of row2 with the image of a carnation. You can see the effect of this script in Figure 7-14.

Figure 7-14. *Replacing content with the replaceWith and replaceAll methods*

Replacing Elements Using a Function

You can replace elements dynamically by passing a function to the replaceWith method. This function is not passed any arguments, but the this variable is set to the element being processed. Listing 7-20 provides a demonstration.

Listing 7-20. Replacing Elements Using a Function

```
...
<script type="text/javascript">
    $(document).ready(function() {
        $("div.drow img").replaceWith(function() {
            if (this.src.indexOf("rose") > -1) {
                return $("<img src='carnation.png'/>").css("border", "thick solid red");
            } else if (this.src.indexOf("peony") > -1) {
                return $("<img src='lily.png'/>").css("border", "thick solid red");
```

```
        } else {
            return $(this).clone();
        }
    });
});
</script>
...
```

In this script, I replace img elements based on their src attribute. If the src attribute contains rose, then I replace the img element with one displaying carnation.png. If the src attribute contains peony, then I replace the element with one displaying lily.png. Both of the replacement elements have a red border to highlight their positions.

For all other elements, I return a clone of the element being processed, which has the effect of replacing the element with a copy of itself. You can see the effect in Figure 7-15.

Figure 7-15. *Replacing elements using a function*

■ **Tip** If you don't want to replace an element, then you can simply return a clone. If you don't clone the element, then jQuery ends up removing the element entirely. Of course, you could avoid this issue by narrowing your selection, but that isn't always an option.

Removing Elements

To complement inserting and replacing elements, jQuery provides a set of methods that to remove elements from the DOM, as described in Table 7-6.

Table 7-6. *Methods for Removing Elements*

Method	Description
detach() detach(selector)	Removes elements from the DOM. The data associated with the elements is preserved.
empty()	Removes all of the child nodes from each element in the jQuery object.
remove() remove(selector)	Removes elements from the DOM. As the elements are removed, the data associated with the elements is destroyed.
unwrap()	Removes the parent of each of the elements in the jQuery object.

Listing 7-21 shows how you can use the remove elements to remove elements from the DOM.

Listing 7-21. Removing Elements from the DOM with the remove Method

```
...
<script type="text/javascript">
    $(document).ready(function() {
        $("img[src*=daffodil], img[src*=snow]").parent().remove();
    });
</script>
...
```

This script selects the img elements whose src attributes contain daffodil and snow, gets their parent elements, and then removes them. You can filter the elements that you remove if you pass a selector to the remove method, as shown in Listing 7-22.

Listing 7-22. Filtering Elements to Remove Using a Selector

```
...
<script type="text/javascript">
    $(document).ready(function() {
        $("div.dcell").remove(":has(img[src*=snow], img[src*=daffodil])");
    });
</script>
...
```

Both of these scripts have the same effect, as shown in Figure 7-16.

Figure 7-16. *Removing elements from the DOM*

■ **Tip** The `jQuery` object returned from the `remove` method contains the original set of selected elements. In other words, the removal of elements is not reflected in the method result.

Detaching Elements

The `detach` method works in the same as the `remove` method, with the exception that data associated with the elements is preserved. I explain associating data with elements in Chapter 8, but for this chapter it is enough to know that this is usually the best method to use if you intend to insert the elements elsewhere in the document. Listing 7-23 shows the `detach` method in use.

Listing 7-23. *Using the detach Method to Remove Elements While Preserving the Associated Data*

```
...
<script type="text/javascript">
    $(document).ready(function() {
        $("#row2").append($("img[src*=aster]").parent().detach());
    });
</script>
...
```

This script detaches the parent element of the img element whose src attribute contains aster. The elements are then inserted back into the document using the append method, which I described earlier in the chapter. I tend not to use this method, because using append without detach has the same effect. You can rewrite the key statement in the listing as follows:

```
...
$("#row2").append($("img[src*=aster]").parent());
...
```

You can see the effect of the script in Figure 7-17.

Figure 7-17. *Using the detach element*

Empting Elements

The empty method removes any descendants and text from the elements in a jQuery object. The elements themselves are left in the document, as demonstrated by Listing 7-24.

Listing 7-24. *Using the empty Method*

```
...
<script type="text/javascript">
    $(document).ready(function() {
        $("#row1").children().eq(1).empty().css("border", "thick solid red");
    });
</script>
...
```

In this script, I select the child of the row1 element at index 1 and call the empty method. To make the change more evident, I added a border using the css method. You can see the effect in Figure 7-18.

Figure 7-18. *Using the empty method*

Unwrapping Elements

The unwrap method removes the parents of the elements in the jQuery object. The selected elements become children of their grandparent elements. Listing 7-25 shows the unwrap method in use.

Listing 7-25. *Using the unwrap Method*

```
...
<script type="text/javascript">
    $(document).ready(function () {
        $("div.dcell").unwrap();
    });
</script>
...
```

In this script, I select the div elements that are part of the dcell class and call the unwrap method. This has the effect of removing the row1 and row2 elements, as shown in Figure 7-19.

Figure 7-19. *Using the unwrap method*

Summary '

In this chapter, I showed you how to use jQuery in order to manipulate the DOM. I showed you how to create new elements and the many different ways in which elements (new or existing) can be inserted into the DOM as children, parents, and siblings. I also showed you how to move elements within the DOM and how to remove elements entirely. In Chapter 8, I show you how to use jQuery to manipulate the elements in the DOM.

CHAPTER 8

■ ■ ■

Manipulating Elements

In this chapter, I show you how to use jQuery manipulate elements, including how to get and set attributes, how to use the jQuery convenience methods for working with classes and CSS properties, and how to get and set HTML and text content. I also show you a nice feature that allows you to associate data with elements. Table 8-1 provides the summary for this chapter.

Table 8-1. *Chapter Summary*

Problem	Solution	Listing
Get the value of an attribute from the first element in a jQuery object	Use the attr method	1
Get the value of an attribute from every element in a jQuery object	Use the each and attr methods together	2
Set an attribute for all of the elements in a jQuery object	Use the attr method, optionally with a function	3
Set multiple attributes in a single operation	Use the attr method with a map object	4, 5
Unset an attribute	Use the removeAttr method	6
Get or set a property defined by the HTMLElement object	Use the prop counterparts to the attr methods	7
Control the classes that elements belong to	Use the addClass, hasClass, and removeClass methods, optionally with a function	8–10
Toggle the classes that elements belong to	Use the toggleClass method	11–16
Set the contents of the style attribute	Use the css method	17–21
Get details of the position of elements	Use the CSS property-specific methods	22–24
Get or set the text or HTML content of elements	Use the text or html method	25–27
Get or set the value of form elements	Use the val method	28–30
Associate data with elements	Use the data method	31

JQUERY CHANGES SINCE THE LAST EDITION

jQuery 1.9/2.0 introduced a new version of the css method that allows the values of multiple CSS properties to be obtained—see the section "Getting Multiple CSS Properties" for details.

jQuery 1.9/2.0 also enforces the separation between the roles of the attr and prop methods. In earlier versions, jQuery would allow the user of the attr method where the prop method should have been used in order to preserve backward compatibility with versions earlier than 1.6, which is when the prop method was added.

The final change is that the current versions of jQuery allow the use of the attr method to set the value of the type attribute on input elements when the browser supports it. Use this feature with caution because jQuery will throw an exception if the browser *doesn't* support it, and this includes the older versions of Internet Explorer. My advice is to replace elements when you need different types of input elements and avoid the issue entirely.

Working with Attributes and Properties

You can get and set the values of attributes for the elements in a jQuery object. Table 8-2 shows the methods that relate to attributes.

Table 8-2. *Methods for Working with Attributes*

Method	Description
attr(name)	Gets the value of the attribute with the specified name for the first element in the jQuery object
attr(name, value)	Sets the value of the attribute with the specified name to the specified value for all of the elements in the jQuery object
attr(map)	Sets the attributes specified in the map object for all of the elements in the jQuery object
attr(name, function)	Sets the specified attribute for all of the elements in the jQuery object using a function
removeAttr(name) removeAttr(name[])	Remove the attribute from all of the elements in the jQuery object
prop(name)	Returns the value of the specified property for the first element in the jQuery object
prop(name, value) prop(map)	Sets the value for one or more properties for all of the elements in the jQuery object
prop(name, function)	Sets the value of the specified property for all of the elements in the jQuery object using a function
removeProp(name)	Removes the specified property from all of the elements in the jQuery object

When the attr method is called with a single argument, jQuery returns the value of the specified attribute from the first element in the selection. Listing 8-1 contains a demonstration.

Listing 8-1. Reading the Value of an Attribute

```
<!DOCTYPE html>
<html>
<head>
    <title>Example</title>
    <script src="jquery-2.0.2.js" type="text/javascript"></script>
    <link rel="stylesheet" type="text/css" href="styles.css"/>
    <script type="text/javascript">
        $(document).ready(function() {
            var srcValue = $("img").attr("src");
            console.log("Attribute value: " + srcValue);
        });
    </script>
</head>
<body>
    <h1>Jacqui's Flower Shop</h1>
    <form method="post">
        <div id="oblock">
            <div class="dtable">
                <div id="row1" class="drow">
                    <div class="dcell">
                        <img src="aster.png"/><label for="aster">Aster:</label>
                        <input name="aster" value="0" required />
                    </div>
                    <div class="dcell">
                        <img src="daffodil.png"/><label for="daffodil">Daffodil:</label>
                        <input name="daffodil" value="0" required />
                    </div>
                    <div class="dcell">
                        <img src="rose.png"/><label for="rose">Rose:</label>
                        <input name="rose" value="0" required />
                    </div>
                </div>
                <div id="row2"class="drow">
                    <div class="dcell">
                        <img src="peony.png"/><label for="peony">Peony:</label>
                        <input name="peony" value="0" required />
                    </div>
                    <div class="dcell">
                        <img src="primula.png"/><label for="primula">Primula:</label>
                        <input name="primula" value="0" required />
                    </div>
                    <div class="dcell">
                        <img src="snowdrop.png"/><label for="snowdrop">Snowdrop:</label>
                        <input name="snowdrop" value="0" required />
                    </div>
                </div>
            </div>
        </div>
```

```
        <div id="buttonDiv"><button type="submit">Place Order</button></div>
    </form>
</body>
</html>
```

In this script, I select all of the img elements in the document and then use the attr method to get the value for the src attribute. The result from the attr method when you read an attribute value is a string, which I write out to the console. The console output from this script is as follows:

```
Attribute value: aster.png
```

The each method can be combined with attr to read the value of an attribute for all of the elements in a jQuery object. I described the each method in Chapter 5, and Listing 8-2 shows how you can use it in this situation.

Listing 8-2. Using the each and attr Methods to Read Attribute Values from Multiple Objects

```
...
<script type="text/javascript">
    $(document).ready(function() {
        $("img").each(function(index, elem) {
            var srcValue = $(elem).attr("src");
            console.log("Attribute value: " + srcValue);
        });
    });
</script>
...
```

In this script, I pass the HTMLElement object as the argument to the function to create a new jQuery object via the $ function. This object contains only one element, which is ideally suited to the attr method. The console output from this script is as follows:

```
Attribute value: aster.png
Attribute value: daffodil.png
Attribute value: rose.png
Attribute value: peony.png
Attribute value: primula.png
Attribute value: snowdrop.png
```

Setting an Attribute Value

When the attr method is used to set an attribute value, the change is applied to *all* of the elements in the jQuery object. This is in contrast to the read version of this method, which returns a value from only the *first* element. Listing 8-3 demonstrates how to set an attribute.

Listing 8-3. Setting an Attribute

```
...
<script type="text/javascript">
    $(document).ready(function() {
        $("img").attr("src", "lily.png");
    });
</script>
...
```

■ **Tip** When setting a value, the `attr` method returns a jQuery object, which means that you can perform method chaining.

I select all of the `img` elements and set the value of the `src` attribute to `lily.png`. This value is applied to the `src` attribute of all the selected elements, and you can see the effect in Figure 8-1.

Figure 8-1. *Setting an attribute to the same value for multiple elements*

Setting Multiple Attributes

You can set multiple attributes in a single method call by passing an object to the `attr` method. The properties of this object are interpreted as the attribute names, and the property values will be used as the attribute values. This is known as a *map object*. Listing 8-4 provides a demonstration.

Listing 8-4. Setting Multiple Elements Using a Map Object

```
...
<script type="text/javascript">
    $(document).ready(function() {
        var attrValues = {
            src: "lily.png",
            style: "border: thick solid red"
        };

        $("img").attr(attrValues);
    });
</script>
...
```

In this script I create a map object that has properties called src and style. I select the img elements in the document and pass the map object to the attr value. You can see the effect in Figure 8-2.

Figure 8-2. *Setting multiple attributes with the attr method*

■ **Tip**   Although I have set the style property explicitly in this example, jQuery provides some methods that simplify working with CSS. See the section "Working with CSS" for details.

Setting Attribute Values Dynamically

You can tailor the values that you assign to an attribute by passing a function to the `attr` method. Listing 8-5 provides a demonstration.

Listing 8-5. Setting Attribute Values with a Function

```
...
<script type="text/javascript">
    $(document).ready(function() {
        $("img").attr("src", function(index, oldVal) {
            if (oldVal.indexOf("rose") > -1) {
                return "lily.png";
            } else if ($(this).closest("#row2").length > 0) {
                return "carnation.png";
            }
        });
    });
</script>
...
```

The arguments passed to the function are the index of the element being processed and the old attribute value. The `this` variable is set to the `HTMLElement` being processed. If you want to change the attribute, then your function must return a string containing the new value. If you don't return a result, then the existing value is used. In Listing 8-5, I use the function to selectively change the images shown by the `img` elements. You can see the effect in Figure 8-3.

Figure 8-3. Changing attribute values with a function

Removing an Attribute

You can remove (unset) attributes by using the removeAttr method, as shown in Listing 8-6.

Listing 8-6. Removing Attribute Values

```
...
<script type="text/javascript">
    $(document).ready(function() {

        $("img").attr("style", "border: thick solid red");
        $("img:odd").removeAttr("style");

    });
</script>
...
```

I use the attr method to set the style attribute and then use the removeAttr method to remove the same attribute from the odd-numbered elements. You can see the effect in Figure 8-4.

Figure 8-4. Removing attributes from elements

Working with Properties

For each form of the attr method, there is a corresponding prop method. The difference is that the prop methods deal with properties defined by the HTMLElement object, rather than attribute values. Often, the attributes and properties are the same, but this isn't always the case. A simple example is the class attribute, which is represented in the HTMLElement object using the className property. Listing 8-7 shows the use of the prop method to read this property.

Listing 8-7. Using the prop Method to Read a Property Value

```
...
<script type="text/javascript">
    $(document).ready(function() {
        $("*[class]").each(function(index, elem) {
            console.log("Element:" + elem.tagName + " " + $(elem).prop("className"));
        });
    });
</script>
...
```

In this example, I select all of the elements that have a class attribute and use the each method to enumerate them. For each element, I print out the type and the value of the className property, producing the following console output:

```
Element:DIV dtable
Element:DIV drow
Element:DIV dcell
Element:DIV dcell
Element:DIV dcell
Element:DIV drow
Element:DIV dcell
Element:DIV dcell
Element:DIV dcell
```

Working with Classes

Although you can use the general attribute methods to manage classes, jQuery provides a set of much more convenient methods. Table 8-3 describes these methods. The most common use for classes in an HTML document is to cause the browser to apply a set of CSS properties defined in a style element. See Chapter 7 for details.

Table 8-3. Methods for Working with Classes

Method	Description
addClass(name name)	Adds all of the elements in a jQuery object to the specified class
addClass(function)	Assigns the elements in a jQuery object to classes dynamically
hasClass(name)	Returns true if at least one of the elements in the jQuery object is a member of the specified class
removeClass(name name)	Removes the elements in the jQuery object from the specified class
removeClass(function)	Removes the elements in a jQuery object from classes dynamically
toggleClass()	Toggles all of the classes that the elements in the jQuery object belong to
toggleClass(boolean)	Toggles all of the classes that the elements in the jQuery object belong to in one direction

(continued)

Table 8-3. (*continued*)

Method	Description
toggleClass(name) toggleClass(name name)	Toggles one or more named classes for all of the elements in the jQuery object
toggleClass(name, boolean)	Toggles a named class for all of the elements in the jQuery object in one direction
toggleClass(function, boolean)	Toggles classes dynamically for all of the elements in a jQuery object

Elements can be assigned to classes with the addClass method, removed from classes using the removeClass method, and you determine whether an element belongs to a class using the hasClass method. Listing 8-8 demonstrates all three methods in use.

Listing 8-8. Adding, Removing, and Testing for Class Membership

```
...
<style type="text/css">
    img.redBorder {border: thick solid red}
    img.blueBorder {border: thick solid blue}
</style>
<script type="text/javascript">
    $(document).ready(function() {

        $("img").addClass("redBorder");
        $("img:even").removeClass("redBorder").addClass("blueBorder");

        console.log("All elements: " + $("img").hasClass("redBorder"));
        $("img").each(function(index, elem) {
            console.log("Element: " + $(elem).hasClass("redBorder") + " " + elem.src);
        });

    });
</script>
...
```

To begin, I have used a style element to define two styles that will be applied based on class membership. Classes don't have to be used to manage CSS, but they make demonstrating the effect of changes easier in this chapter.

I select all of the img elements in the document and assign them to the redBorder class using the addClass method. I then select the even-numbered img elements, remove them from the redBorder class, and assign them to the blueBorder class using the removeClass method.

■ **Tip** The addClass method does not remove any existing classes from the elements; it just adds the new class in addition to those classes that have already been applied.

Finally, I use the hasClass method to test for the redBorder class on the set of all img elements (which returns true if at least one of the elements is a member of the class) and each element individually. You can see the effect of the class membership in Figure 8-5.

Figure 8-5. *Applying styles through class membership*

The output from the script, where I test for class membership, is as follows:

```
All elements: true
Element: false http://www.jacquisflowershop.com/jquery/aster.png
Element: true http://www.jacquisflowershop.com/jquery/daffodil.png
Element: false http://www.jacquisflowershop.com/jquery/rose.png
Element: true http://www.jacquisflowershop.com/jquery/peony.png
Element: false http://www.jacquisflowershop.com/jquery/primula.png
Element: true http://www.jacquisflowershop.com/jquery/snowdrop.png
```

Adding and Removing Classes Using a Function

You can decide dynamically which classes should be added or removed from a set of elements by passing a function to the addClass or removeClass method. Listing 8-9 shows the use of a function with the addClass method.

Listing 8-9. Using the addClass Method with a Function

```
...
<style type="text/css">
    img.redBorder {border: thick solid red}
    img.blueBorder {border: thick solid blue}
</style>
```

```
<script type="text/javascript">
    $(document).ready(function() {
        $("img").addClass(function(index, currentClasses) {
            if (index % 2 == 0) {
                return "blueBorder";
            } else {
                return "redBorder";
            }
        });
    });
</script>
...
```

The arguments to the function are the index of the element and the current set of classes for which the element is a member. As for similar functions, jQuery sets the this variable to the HTMLElement object of the element being processed. You return the class that you want the element to join. In this example, I use the index argument to assign alternate elements to either the blueBorder or redBorder class. The effect is the same as the one shown in Figure 8-5.

You take a similar approach to removing elements from classes. You pass a function to the removeClass method, as shown in Listing 8-10.

Listing 8-10. Removing Elements from Classes Using a Function

```
...
<style type="text/css">
    img.redBorder {border: thick solid red}
    img.blueBorder {border: thick solid blue}
</style>
<script type="text/javascript">
    $(document).ready(function() {

        $("img").filter(":odd").addClass("redBorder").end()
            .filter(":even").addClass("blueBorder");

        $("img").removeClass(function(index, currentClasses) {
            if ($(this).closest("#row2").length > 0
                && currentClasses.indexOf("redBorder") > -1) {
                    return "redBorder";
            } else {
                return "";
            }
        });
    });
</script>
...
```

In this script, the function I pass to the removeClass method uses the HTMLElement object and the current set of classes to remove the redBorder class from any img element that is a member and that is a descendant of the element with the ID of row2. You can see the effect of this script in Figure 8-6.

Figure 8-6. *Removing classes with a function*

■ **Tip** Notice that I return the empty string when I don't want to remove any classes. If you don't return a value, then jQuery removes *all* of the classes from the element.

Toggling Classes

In its most basic form, toggling a class means adding it to any element that is not a member and removing it from any element that is. You can achieve this effect by passing the name of the class you want to toggle to the `toggleClass` method, as shown in Listing 8-11.

Listing 8-11. Using the toggleClass Method

```
...
<style type="text/css">
    img.redBorder {border: thick solid red}
    img.blueBorder {border: thick solid blue}
</style>
<script type="text/javascript">
    $(document).ready(function() {

        $("img").filter(":odd").addClass("redBorder").end()
            .filter(":even").addClass("blueBorder");

        $("<button>Toggle</button>").appendTo("#buttonDiv").click(doToggle);
```

```
        function doToggle(e) {
            $("img").toggleClass("redBorder");
            e.preventDefault();
        };

    });
</script>
...
```

I start this script by applying the redBorder class to the odd-numbered img elements and the blueBorder class to the even-numbered ones. I then create a button element and append it to the element whose id is buttonDiv. This places my new button alongside the one that is already on the page. I have used the click method to specify a function that jQuery will invoke when the user clicks the button. This is part of the jQuery support for events, which I describe fully in Chapter 9.

The function that is executed when the button is clicked is called doToggle, and the key statement is

```
...
$("img").toggleClass("redBorder");
...
```

This statement selects all of the img elements in the document and toggles the redBorder class. The argument to the function and the call to the preventDefault method are not important in this chapter and I explain them in Chapter 9. You can see the effect of this script in Figure 8-7, although this kind of example makes most sense when you load the document into a browser and click the button yourself.

Figure 8-7. *Toggling class membership with the toggleClass method*

If you are especially observant, you will notice something a little odd in the figure. Those elements with red borders no longer have them, but the elements that started with blue borders still have blue borders. What happened was that jQuery removed the redBorder class from the odd-numbered img elements and added it to the even-numbered element, just as expected, but the element to which the redBorder class was added is also a member of blueBorder.

The blueBorder style is defined after redBorder in the style element, which means that its property values have higher precedence, as I explained in Chapter 3. So, the class toggling is working, but you have to take into account the subtleties of CSS as well. If you want the red borders to show through, then you can reverse the declaration order of the styles, as shown in Listing 8-12.

Listing 8-12. Matching Style Declaration to Suit Class Toggling

```
...
<style type="text/css">
    img.blueBorder {border: thick solid blue}
    img.redBorder {border: thick solid red}
</style>
<script type="text/javascript">
    $(document).ready(function() {
        $("img").filter(":odd").addClass("redBorder").end()
            .filter(":even").addClass("blueBorder");

        $("<button>Toggle</button>").appendTo("#buttonDiv").click(doToggle);

        function doToggle(e) {
            $("img").toggleClass("redBorder");
            e.preventDefault();
        };
    });
</script>
...
```

Now when an element belongs to both the blueBorder and redBorder classes, the redBorder setting for the border property will be used by the browser. You can see the effect of this change in Figure 8-8.

Figure 8-8. *The effect of coordinating the CSS declaration order with class toggling*

Toggling Multiple Classes

You can supply multiple class names, separated by a space, to the toggleClass method, and each will be toggled for the selected elements. Listing 8-13 shows a single example.

Listing 8-13. Toggling Multiple Classes

```
...
<style type="text/css">
    img.blueBorder {border: thick solid blue}
    img.redBorder {border: thick solid red}
</style>
<script type="text/javascript">
    $(document).ready(function() {

        $("img").filter(":odd").addClass("redBorder").end()
            .filter(":even").addClass("blueBorder");

        $("<button>Toggle</button>").appendTo("#buttonDiv").click(doToggle);

        function doToggle(e) {
            $("img").toggleClass("redBorder blueBorder");
            e.preventDefault();
        };

    });
</script>
...
```

In this example, I toggle the redBorder and blueBorder classes on all of the img elements. You can see the effect in Figure 8-9.

Figure 8-9. Toggling multiple elements

Toggling All Classes

You can toggle all of the classes that a set of elements belong to by calling the toggleClass method with no arguments. This is a clever technique because jQuery stores the classes that have been toggled so they are applied and removed correctly. Listing 8-14 contains an example of this use of the method.

Listing 8-14. Toggling All of the Classes for Selected Elements

```
...
<style type="text/css">
    img.blueBorder {border: thick solid blue}
    img.redBorder {border: thick solid red}
    label.bigFont {font-size: 1.5em}
</style>
<script type="text/javascript">
    $(document).ready(function() {

        $("img").filter(":odd").addClass("redBorder").end()
            .filter(":even").addClass("blueBorder");
        $("label").addClass("bigFont");

        $("<button>Toggle</button>").appendTo("#buttonDiv").click(doToggle);

        function doToggle(e) {
            $("img, label").toggleClass();
            e.preventDefault();
        };

    });
</script>
...
```

In this example, I used the addClass method to add classes to the img and label elements. When the Toggle button is clicked, I select those same elements and call the toggleClass method without any arguments. You get a specific effect, which is shown in Figure 8-10.

Figure 8-10. *Toggling all of the classes for an element*

When you first click the button, all of the classes are toggled off for the selected elements. jQuery makes a note of which classes were removed so that they can be reapplied when you click the button again.

Toggling Classes in One Direction

You can limit the way that toggling is performed by passing a boolean argument to the `toggleClass` method. If you pass `false`, the classes will only be removed, and if you pass `true`, the classes will only be added. Listing 8-15 gives an example.

Listing 8-15. *Restricting the Toggle Direction*

```
...
<style type="text/css">
    img.blueBorder {border: thick solid blue}
    img.redBorder {border: thick solid red}
</style>
<script type="text/javascript">
    $(document).ready(function() {

        $("img").filter(":odd").addClass("redBorder").end()
            .filter(":even").addClass("blueBorder");

        $("<button>Toggle On</button>").appendTo("#buttonDiv").click(doToggleOn);
        $("<button>Toggle Off</button>").appendTo("#buttonDiv").click(doToggleOff);

        function doToggleOff(e) {
            $("img, label").toggleClass("redBorder", false);
            e.preventDefault();
        };
```

```
    function doToggleOn(e) {
        $("img, label").toggleClass("redBorder", true);
        e.preventDefault();
    };
});
</script>
...
```

I have added two button elements to the document, each of which will toggle the redBorder class in only one direction. Once one of the button elements has been clicked, it will have no further effect until the other button is clicked too (because each button toggles classes in only one direction). You can see the effect in Figure 8-11.

Figure 8-11. *Toggling classes in one direction*

Toggling Classes Dynamically

You can decide which classes should be toggled for elements dynamically by passing a function to the toggleClass method. Listing 8-16 provides a simple demonstration.

Listing 8-16. Toggling Classes with a Function

```
...
<style type="text/css">
    img.blueBorder {border: thick solid blue}
    img.redBorder {border: thick solid red}
</style>
<script type="text/javascript">
    $(document).ready(function() {

        $("img").addClass("blueBorder");
        $("img:even").addClass("redBorder");

        $("<button>Toggle</button>").appendTo("#buttonDiv").click(doToggle);
```

```
        function doToggle(e) {
            $("img").toggleClass(function(index, currentClasses) {
                if (index % 2 == 0) {
                    return "redBorder";
                } else {
                    return "";
                }
            });
            e.preventDefault();
        };
    });
</script>
...
```

I apply the blueBorder class to all of the img elements and the redBorder class to the even-numbered img elements. The arguments to the function are the index of the element you are processing and the current set of classes it belongs to. In addition, the this variable is set to the HTMLElement object for the current element. The result from the function is the name of the classes that should be toggled. If you don't want to toggle any classes for the elements, then you return the empty string (not returning a result for an element toggles all of its classes). You can see the effect that the listing creates in Figure 8-12.

Figure 8-12. *Toggling classes dynamically*

Working with CSS

In an earlier example, I used the basic attribute methods to set the value of the style attribute to define values for a CSS property for a set of elements. jQuery provides a set of convenience elements that make dealing with CSS much easier. Table 8-4 describes css, the most broadly useful of these methods

Table 8-4. *The css Method*

Method	Description
css(name)	Gets the value of the specified property from the first element in the jQuery object
css(names)	Gets the value of multiple CSS properties, expressed as an array
css(name, value)	Sets the value of the specific property for all elements in the jQuery object
css(map)	Sets multiple properties for all of the elements in a jQuery object using a map object
css(name, function)	Sets values for the specified property for all of the elements in a jQuery object using a function

■ **Tip**   These methods operate on the `style` attribute of individual elements. If you want to work with styles defined in a `style` element, then you should use the class-related methods described earlier in this chapter.

Getting and Setting a Single CSS Value

To read the value of a CSS property, you pass the property name to the `css` method. What you receive is the value from the first element in the jQuery object only. However, when you set a property, the change is applied to all of the elements. Listing 8-17 shows the basic use of the `css` property.

Listing 8-17. Using the css Method to Get and Set CSS Property Values

```
...
<script type="text/javascript">
    $(document).ready(function() {
        var sizeVal = $("label").css("font-size");
        console.log("Size: " + sizeVal);
        $("label").css("font-size", "1.5em");
    });
</script>
...
```

■ **Tip**   Although I used the actual property name (`font-size`) and not the camel-case property name defined by the `HTMLElement` object (`fontSize`), jQuery happily supports both.

In this script, I select all of the `label` elements and use the `css` method to get the value of the `font-size` property and write it to the console. I then select all of the `label` elements again and apply a new value for the same property to all of them.

The output of the script is as follows:

```
Size: 16px
```

■ **Tip**   Setting a property to the empty string ("") has the effect of removing the property from the element's `style` attribute.

Getting Multiple CSS Properties

You can get the value of multiple CSS properties by passing an array of property names to the `css` method. This method returns an object that has properties for each of the names in the array and the value of each property in the object is set to the value of the corresponding CSS property for the first element in the selection. In Listing 8-18, you can see how I have used the `css` method to get values for three CSS properties.

Listing 8-18.   Using the css Method to Get Multiple CSS Property Values

```
...
<script type="text/javascript">
    $(document).ready(function () {
        var propertyNames = ["font-size", "color", "border"];
        var cssValues = $("label").css(propertyNames);
        for (var i = 0; i < propertyNames.length; i++) {
            console.log("Property: " + propertyNames[i]
                + " Value: " + cssValues[propertyNames[i]]);
        }
    });
</script>
...
```

■ **Note**   This version of the `css` method was introduced in jQuery 1.9/2.0.

I create an array that contains the names of the three CSS properties I am interested in: `font-size`, `color`, and `border`. I pass this array to the `css` method and I receive an object that contains the values I want. That object can be expressed as follows:

```
{font-size: "16px", color: "rgb(0, 0, 0)", border: "0px none rgb(0, 0, 0)"}
```

To process the object, I iterate through the array of property names and read the corresponding property value, producing the following console output:

```
Property: font-size Value: 16px
Property: color Value: rgb(0, 0, 0)
Property: border Value: 0px none rgb(0, 0, 0)
```

Setting Multiple CSS Properties

You can set multiple properties in two different ways. The first is simply by chaining calls to the `css` method, as shown in Listing 8-19.

Listing 8-19. Chaining Calls to the css Method

```
...
<script type="text/javascript">
    $(document).ready(function() {
        $("label").css("font-size", "1.5em").css("color", "blue");
    });
</script>
...
```

In this script, I set values for the font-size and color properties. You can achieve the same effect using a map object, as shown in Listing 8-20. The map object follows the same pattern as the object I received when I used the css method to get multiple property values in the previous section.

Listing 8-20. Setting Multiple Value Using a Map Object

```
...
<script type="text/javascript">
    $(document).ready(function() {
        var cssVals = {
            "font-size": "1.5em",
            "color": "blue"
        };

        $("label").css(cssVals);
    });
</script>
...
```

Both of these scripts create the effect shown in Figure 8-13.

Figure 8-13. Setting multiple properties

Setting Relative Values

The `css` method can accept relative values, which are numeric values that are preceded by += or -= and that are added to or subtracted from the current value. This technique can be used only with CSS properties that are expressed in numeric units. Listing 8-21 demonstrates.

Listing 8-21. Using Relative Values with the css Method

```
...
<script type="text/javascript">
    $(document).ready(function() {

        $("label:odd").css("font-size", "+=5")
        $("label:even").css("font-size", "-=5")

    });
</script>
...
```

These values are assumed to be in the same units that would be returned when the property value is read. In this case, I have increased the font size of the odd-numbered `label` elements by 5 pixels and decreased it for the even-numbered `label` elements by the same amount. You can see the effect in Figure 8-14.

Figure 8-14. Using relative values

Setting Properties Using a Function

You can set property values dynamically by passing a function to the `css` method, as demonstrated by Listing 8-22. The arguments passed to the function are the index of the element and the current value of the property. The `this` variable is set to the `HTMLElement` object for the element, and you return the value you want to set.

Listing 8-22. Setting CSS Values with a Function

```
...
<script type="text/javascript">
    $(document).ready(function() {
        $("label").css("border", function(index, currentValue) {
            if ($(this).closest("#row1").length > 0) {
                return "thick solid red";
            } else if (index % 2 == 1) {
                return "thick double blue";
            }
        });
    });
</script>
...
```

You can see the effect of this script in Figure 8-15.

Figure 8-15. Setting CSS property values with a function

Using the Property-Specific CSS Convenience Methods

In addition to the css method, jQuery defines a number of methods that can be used to get or set commonly used CSS properties and information derived from them. Table 8-5 describes these methods.

Table 8-5. *Methods for Working with Specific CSS Properties*

Method	Description
height()	Gets the height in pixels for the first element in the jQuery object
height(value)	Sets the height for all of the elements in the jQuery object
innerHeight()	Gets the inner height of the first element in the jQuery object (this is the height including padding but excluding the border and margin)
innerWidth()	Gets the inner width of the first element in the jQuery object (this is the width including padding but excluding the border and margin)
offset()	Returns the coordinates of the first element in the jQuery object relative to the document
outerHeight(boolean)	Gets the height of the first element in the jQuery object, including padding and border; the argument determines if the margin is included
outerWidth(boolean)	Gets the width of the first element in the jQuery object, including padding and border; the argument determines whether the margin is included
position()	Returns the coordinates of the first element in the jQuery object relative to the offset
scrollLeft() scrollTop()	Gets the horizontal or vertical position of the first element in the jQuery object
scrollLeft(value) scrollTop(value)	Sets the horizontal or vertical position of all the elements in a jQuery object
width()	Gets the width of the first element in a jQuery object
width(value)	Sets the width of all of the elements in a jQuery object
height(function) width(function)	Sets the width or height for all of the elements in the jQuery object using a function

Most of these methods are self-evident, but a couple warrant explanation. The result from the offset and position methods is an object that has top and left properties, indicating the location of the element. Listing 8-23 provides a demonstration using the position method.

Listing 8-23. Using the position Method

```
...
<script type="text/javascript">
    $(document).ready(function() {
        var pos = $("img").position();
        console.log("Position top: " + pos.top + " left: " + pos.left);
    });
</script>
...
```

This script writes out the value of the top and left properties of the object returned by the method. The result is as follows:

```
Position top: 108.078125 left: 18
```

Setting the Width and Height Using a Function

You can set the width and height for a set of elements dynamically by passing a function to the `width` or `height` method. The arguments to this method are the index of the element and the current property value. As you might expect by now, the `this` variable is set to the `HTMLElement` of the current element, and you return the value you want assigned. Listing 8-24 provides an example.

Listing 8-24. Setting the Height of Elements Using a Function

```
...
<script type="text/javascript">
    $(document).ready(function() {
        $("#row1 img").css("border", "thick solid red")
            .height(function(index, currentValue) {
                return (index + 1) * 25;
            });
    });
</script>
...
```

In this script, I use the index value as a multiplier for the height. You can see the effect in Figure 8-16.

Figure 8-16. *Using a function to set the height for elements*

Working with Element Content

The methods I have described so far in this chapter operate on the attributes that elements define, but jQuery also provides methods to work with the content of elements as well, as described in Table 8-6.

Table 8-6. *Methods for Working with Element Content*

Method	Description
text()	Gets the combined text contents of all the element in the jQuery object and their descendants
text(value)	Sets the content of each element in the jQuery object
html()	Gets the HTML contents of the first element in the jQuery object
html(value)	Sets the HTML content of each element in the jQuery object
text(function) html(function)	Sets the text or HTML content using a function

Unusually for jQuery, when you use the text method without arguments, the result that you receive is generated from *all* of the selected elements and not just the first one. The html method is more consistent with the rest of jQuery and returns just the content from the first element, as Listing 8-25 shows.

Listing 8-25. Using the html Method to Read Element Content

```
...
<script type="text/javascript">
    $(document).ready(function() {
        var html = $("div.dcell").html();
        console.log(html);
    });
</script>
...
```

This script uses the html method to read the HTML contents of the first element matched by the div.dcell selector. This is written to the console, producing the following results. Notice that the HTML of the element itself is not included.

```
<img src="aster.png">
<label for="aster">Aster:</label>
<input name="aster" value="0" required="">
```

Setting Element Content

You can set the content of elements using either the html or text method. My flower shop example document doesn't have any text content to speak of, so Listing 8-26 shows how to use the html method.

Listing 8-26. Using the html Method to Set Element Content

```
...
<script type="text/javascript">
    $(document).ready(function() {
        $("#row2 div.dcell").html($("div.dcell").html());
    });
</script>
...
```

This script sets the HTML contents of the div elements in the dcell class that are descendants of the row2 element. For the content I have used the html method to read the HTML from the first div.dcell element. This has the effect of setting the lower row of cells in the layout to have the aster content, as shown in Figure 8-17.

Figure 8-17. *Setting the content of elements with the html method*

Setting Element Content Using a Function

As with many of the other methods in this chapter, you can use the html and text methods with a function to set content dynamically. In both cases, the arguments are the index of the element in the jQuery object and the current text or HTML content. The this variable is set to the element's HTMLElement object, and you return the value you want to set as the result from the function. Listing 8-27 shows how you can use a function with the text method.

Listing 8-27. Setting Text Content Using a Function

```
...
<script type="text/javascript">
    $(document).ready(function() {
        $("label").css("border", "thick solid red").text(function(index, currentValue) {
            return "Index " + index;
        });
    });
</script>
...
```

In this script I set the text content of the label elements using the index value (I also use the css method to add a border to the elements I change). You can see the result in Figure 8-18.

Figure 8-18. *Setting text content using a function*

Working with Form Elements

You can get and set the value of form elements (such as input) using the val method, which is described in Table 8-7.

Table 8-7. *The val method*

Method	Description
val()	Returns the value of the first element in the jQuery object
val(value)	Sets the value of all of the elements in the jQuery object
val(function)	Sets the values for the elements in the jQuery object using a function

Listing 8-28 shows how you can use the val method to get the value from the first element in the jQuery object. In this script, I have used the each method so that I can enumerate the values of the set of input elements in the document.

Listing 8-28. *Using the val Method to Get the Value from an input Element*

```
...
<script type="text/javascript">
    $(document).ready(function() {
        $("input").each(function(index, elem) {
            console.log("Name: " + elem.name + " Val: " + $(elem).val());
        });
    });
</script>
...
```

I write the values to the console, which produces the following output:

```
Name: aster Val: 0
Name: daffodil Val: 0
Name: rose Val: 0
Name: peony Val: 0
Name: primula Val: 0
Name: snowdrop Val: 0
```

Setting Form Element Values

You can use the val method to set the value of all of the elements in a jQuery object by simply passing the value you want as an argument to the method. Listing 8-29 demonstrates.

Listing 8-29. Setting Element Values with the val Method

```
...
<script type="text/javascript">
    $(document).ready(function () {
        $("<button>Set Values</button>").appendTo("#buttonDiv")
            .click(function (e) {
                $("input").val(100);
                e.preventDefault();
            })
    });
</script>
...
```

In this script I have added a button element to the document and specified an inline function that is called when it is clicked. The function selects all of the input elements in the document and uses the val method to set their value to 100. You can see the effect in Figure 8-19. (The call to the preventDefault method stops the browser posting the HTML form back to the web server—I explain how jQuery supports events in detail in Chapter 9).

Figure 8-19. *Using the val method to set input element values*

Setting Form Element Values Using a Function

As you might expect by now, you can also use a function to set values with the val method. The arguments to the method are the index of the element and the element's current value. The this variable is set to the HTMLElement object representing the element being processed. By using the val method in this way, you can set new values dynamically, as demonstrated in Listing 8-30.

Listing 8-30. *Using the val Method with a Function*

```
...
<script type="text/javascript">
    $(document).ready(function() {
        $("input").val(function(index, currentVal) {
            return (index + 1) * 100;
        });
    });
</script>
...
```

In this example, I set the value based on the index argument. You can see the effect in Figure 8-20.

Figure 8-20. *Setting the values dynamically using the val method with a function*

Associating Data with Elements

jQuery allows you to associate arbitrary data with an element, which you can then test for and retrieve later. Table 8-8 describes the methods associated with this feature.

Table 8-8. *Methods for Working with Arbitrary Element Data*

Method	Description
data(key, value) data(map)	Associates one or more key/value pairs with the elements in a jQuery object
data(key)	Retrieves the value associated with the specified key from the first element in the jQuery object
data()	Retrieves the key/value pairs from the first element in the jQuery object
removeData(key)	Removes the data associated with the specified key from all of the elements in the jQuery object
removeData()	Removes all of the data items from all of the elements in the jQuery object

Listing 8-31 demonstrates setting, testing for, reading, and deleting data values.

Listing 8-31. Working with Element Data

```
...
<script type="text/javascript">
    $(document).ready(function() {
```

209

```
        // set the data
        $("img").each(function () {
            $(this).data("product", $(this). siblings("input[name]").attr("name"));
        });

        // find elements with the data and read the values
        $("*").filter(function() {
            return $(this).data("product") != null;
        }).each(function() {
            console.log("Elem: " + this.tagName + " " + $(this).data("product"));
        });

        // remove all data
        $("img").removeData();

    });
</script>
...
```

■ **Note**   When you use the clone method, the data you have associated with elements are removed from the newly copied elements unless you explicitly tell jQuery that you want to keep it. See Chapter 7 for details of the clone method and how to preserve the data.

There are three stages in this script. In the first, I use the data method to associate an item of data with the product key. I get the data by navigating from each img element to the input sibling that has a name attribute.

In the second stage, I select all of the elements in the document and then use the filter method to find those that have a value associated with the product key. I then use the each method to enumerate those elements and write the data values to the console. This is duplicative, but I wanted to demonstrate the best technique for selecting elements that have data. There is no dedicated selector or method, so you must make do with the filter method and a function.

Finally, I use the removeData to remove all data from all of the img elements. This script produces the following output on the console:

```
Elem: IMG aster
Elem: IMG daffodil
Elem: IMG rose
Elem: IMG peony
Elem: IMG primula
Elem: IMG snowdrop
```

Summary

In this chapter, I showed you the different ways that you can manipulate elements in the DOM. I showed you how to get and set attributes, including the jQuery convenience methods for working with classes and CSS properties. I also showed you how to get and set the text or HTML content of elements and how jQuery supports associated arbitrary data with elements.

CHAPTER 9

■ ■ ■

Working with Events

In this chapter, I describe the jQuery support for events. If you are unfamiliar with events, then I provided a brief overview of how they work and how they are propagated through the DOM (Domain Object Model) in Chapter 2. jQuery provides some useful event-related features, of which my favorite is the ability to automatically associate event handler functions with elements as they are added to the DOM. Table 9-1 provides the summary for this chapter.

Table 9-1. *Chapter Summary*

Problem	Solution	Listing
Register a function to handle one or more event	Use the bind method or one of the shorthand methods	1–4, 19, 20, 23
Suppress the default action for an event	Use the Event.preventDefault method or use the bind method without specifying a handler function	5–6
Remove an event handler function from an element	Use the unbind method	7–9
Create a handler function that is executed only once for each element it is associated with	Use the one method	10
Automatically apply an event handler function to elements as they are added to the document	Use the on method	11–13
Remove a handler created using the live method	Use the off method	14
Apply an automatically added handler to a specific element in the DOM	Use the delegate and undelegate methods	15
Manually invoke the event handler functions for an element	Use the trigger or triggerHandler method or one of the shorthand methods	16–18, 21, 22

JQUERY CHANGES SINCE THE LAST EDITION

jQuery 1.9/2.0 has removed the `live` and `die` methods. The same functionality is available through the `on` and `off` methods, which are described in the section "Performing Live Event Binding."

Some behind-the-scenes changes have been made to the order in which `focus` and `blur` events are sent when the `trigger` method is used so they better follow the sequence that would be seen had the events been triggered by the user. See the section "Manually Invoking Event Handlers" for details of how to use the `trigger` method.

A related change is that when you trigger the `click` event on a checkbox or radio button `input` element, the event handlers will receive the new state of the element, which is consistent with the effect caused by the user changing the state of the element. In previous versions of jQuery, the handlers would receive the old state.

I omitted some jQuery features in the last edition of this book because they were marked as deprecated. The resulting changes in the latest versions of jQuery don't affect the content in this chapter but are worth mentioning in case you have found references to them on `jquery.com` and started using them in your projects: the `attrChange`, `attrName`, `relatedNode`, and `srcElement` properties have been removed from the jQuery `Event` object; the `hover` pseudo-event is no longer supported (but the `hover` method I describe in the section "Using the Event Shorthand Methods" is unaffected); the `toggle` method, which alternated between two event handler functions for the same event, has been removed.

Handling Events

jQuery provides a set of methods that let you register functions that are called when specified events are triggered on elements you are interested in. Table 9-2 describes these methods.

Table 9-2. *Methods for Handling Events*

Method	Description
bind(eventType, function) bind(eventType, data, function)	Adds an event handler to the elements in a jQuery object with an optional data item
bind(eventType, boolean)	Creates a default handler that always returns false, preventing the default action; the boolean argument controls event bubbling
bind(map)	Adds a set of event handlers based on a map object to all elements in the jQuery object
one(eventType, function) one(eventType, data, function)	Adds an event handler to each element in a jQuery object with an optional data item; the handler will be unregistered from an element once it has been executed.
unbind()	Removes all event handlers on all elements in the jQuery object
unbind(eventType)	Removes a previously registered event handler from all elements in the jQuery object
unbind(eventType, boolean)	Removes a previously registered always-false handler from all elements in the jQuery object
unbind(Event)	Removes an event handler using an Event object

The various flavors of the bind method let you specify a function that will be invoked when an event is triggered, and since this is jQuery, the function is used for all of the elements in the jQuery object on which the bind method is called. Listing 9-1 shows a simple example.

Listing 9-1. Using the bind Method to Register an Event Handler Function

```html
<!DOCTYPE html>
<html>
<head>
    <title>Example</title>
    <script src="jquery-2.0.2.js" type="text/javascript"></script>
    <link rel="stylesheet" type="text/css" href="styles.css"/>
    <script type="text/javascript">
        $(document).ready(function() {
                function handleMouseEnter(e) {
            $(this).css({
                "border": "thick solid red",
                "opacity": "0.5"
            });
        };

        function handleMouseOut(e) {
            $(this).css({
                "border": "",
                "opacity": ""
            });
        }

        $("img").bind("mouseenter", handleMouseEnter)
            .bind("mouseout", handleMouseOut);
    });
    </script>
</head>
<body>
    <h1>Jacqui's Flower Shop</h1>
    <form method="post">
        <div id="oblock">
            <div class="dtable">
                <div id="row1" class="drow">
                    <div class="dcell">
                        <img src="aster.png"/><label for="aster">Aster:</label>
                        <input name="aster" value="0" required />
                    </div>
                    <div class="dcell">
                        <img src="daffodil.png"/><label for="daffodil">Daffodil:</label>
                        <input name="daffodil" value="0" required />
                    </div>
                    <div class="dcell">
                        <img src="rose.png"/><label for="rose">Rose:</label>
                        <input name="rose" value="0" required />
                    </div>
                </div>
</div>
```

```
                <div id="row2"class="drow">
                    <div class="dcell">
                        <img src="peony.png"/><label for="peony">Peony:</label>
                        <input name="peony" value="0" required />
                    </div>
                    <div class="dcell">
                        <img src="primula.png"/><label for="primula">Primula:</label>
                        <input name="primula" value="0" required />
                    </div>
                    <div class="dcell">
                        <img src="snowdrop.png"/><label for="snowdrop">Snowdrop:</label>
                        <input name="snowdrop" value="0" required />
                    </div>
                </div>
            </div>
        </div>
        <div id="buttonDiv"><button type="submit">Place Order</button></div>
    </form>
</body>
</html>
```

In Listing 9-1, I select all of the img elements in the document and use the bind method to register handler functions for the mouseenter and mouseout events. These handlers use the css method to set values for the border and opacity properties. When the user moves the mouse pointer over one of the img elements, the border is drawn and the image is made more transparent, returning to its previous state when the pointer is moved away.

When jQuery calls the handler function, the this variable is set to the element to which the handler is attached. The object passed to the handler function is jQuery's own Event object, which is different from the Event object defined by the DOM specification. Table 9-3 describes the properties and methods of the jQuery Event object.

Table 9-3. *Members of the jQuery Event Object*

Name	Description	Returns
currentTarget	Gets the element whose listeners are currently being invoked	HTMLElement
Data	Gets the optional data passed to the bind method when the handler was registered; see the section "Registering a Function to Handle Multiple Event Types" for details	Object
isDefaultPrevented()	Returns true if the preventDefault method has been called	Boolean
isImmediatePropagationStopped()	Returns true if the stopImmediatePropagation method has been called	Boolean
isPropagationStopped()	Returns true if the stopPropagation method has been called	Boolean
originalEvent	Returns the original DOM Event object	Event
pageX pageY	Returns the mouse position relative to the left edge of the document	number
preventDefault()	Prevents the default action associated with the event from being performed	void

(continued)

Table 9-3. (*continued*)

Name	Description	Returns
relatedTarget	For mouse events, returns the related element; this varies depending on which event has been triggered	HTMLElement
Result	Returns the result from the last event handler that processed this event	Object
stopImmediatePropagation()	Prevents any other event handlers being called for this event	void
stopPropagation()	Prevents the event from bubbling but allows handlers attached to the current target element to receive the event	void
Target	Gets the element that triggered the event	HTMLElement
timeStamp	Gets the time at which the event was triggered	number
Type	Gets the type of the event	string
Which	Returns the button or key that was pressed for mouse and keyboard events	number

The jQuery Event object also defines most of the properties from the standard DOM Event object. So, for almost all situations, you can treat the jQuery Event object as having a superset of the functionality defined by the DOM standard.

Registering a Function to Handle Multiple Event Types

A common technique is to use a single function to handle two or more kinds of event. These events are usually related in some way, such as the mouseenter and mouseout events. When using the bind method, you can specify multiple event types in the first argument, separated by a space. Listing 9-2 demonstrates this method.

Listing 9-2. Registering a Function to Handle Multiple Event Types

```
...
<script type="text/javascript">
    $(document).ready(function() {

        function handleMouse(e) {
            var cssData = {
                "border": "thick solid red",
                "opacity": "0.5"
            }
            if (event.type == "mouseout") {
                cssData.border = "";
                cssData.opacity = "";
            }
            $(this).css(cssData);
        }

        $("img").bind("mouseenter mouseout", handleMouse);

    });
</script>
...
```

In this script, I have used a single call to the `bind` method to specify that the `mouseenter` and `mouseout` events should be handled by the `handleMouse` function for all of the `img` elements in the document. Of course, you can also use a single function and chain the bind calls, as follows:

```
...
$("img").bind("mouseenter", handleMouse).bind("mouseout", handleMouse);
...
```

You can also register handlers using a map object. The properties of the object are the names of the events, and their values are the functions that will be invoked when the events are triggered. Listing 9-3 shows the use of a map object with the `bind` method.

Listing 9-3. Using a Map Object to Register Event Handlers

```
...
<script type="text/javascript">
    $(document).ready(function() {

        $("img").bind({
            mouseenter: function() {
                $(this).css("border", "thick solid red");
            },
            mouseout: function() {
                $(this).css("border", "");
            }
        });

    });
</script>
...
```

In Listing 9-3, I have defined the handler functions inline, as part of the map object. The `bind` method uses the functions I specify as handlers for the events that correspond to the property names in the map object.

Providing Data to the Event Handler Function

You can pass an object to the `bind` method, which jQuery will then make available to the handler function through the `Event.data` property. This can be useful when using a single function to handle events from different sets of elements. The `data` value can help determine what kind of response is required. Listing 9-4 shows how to define and use the data value.

Listing 9-4. Passing Data to the Event Handler Function via the bind Method

```
...
<script type="text/javascript">
    $(document).ready(function() {

        function handleMouse(e) {
            var cssData = {
                "border": "thick solid " + e.data,
            }
```

```
        if (event.type == "mouseout") {
            cssData.border = "";
        }
        $(this).css(cssData);

    }

    $("img:odd").bind("mouseenter mouseout", "red", handleMouse);
    $("img:even").bind("mouseenter mouseout", "blue", handleMouse);
});
</script>
...
```

I use the optional argument to the bind method to specify which color border should be displayed when the mouseenter event is triggered. For the odd-numbered img elements, the border will be red and for the even-numbered it will be blue. In the event handler function I use the Event.data property to read the data and use it to create the value for the CSS (Cascading Style Sheet) border property. You can see the effect in Figure 9-1.

Figure 9-1. *Passing data to the handler function via the bind method*

Suppressing the Default Action

As I mentioned in Chapter 2, some events have a default action when they are triggered on certain elements. A good example occurs when the user clicks a button whose type attribute is submit. If the button is contained in a form element, the default action is for the browser to submit the form. To prevent the default action from being performed, you can call the preventDefault method on the Event object, as shown in Listing 9-5.

Listing 9-5. Preventing the Default Action on an Event

```
...
<script type="text/javascript">
    $(document).ready(function() {

        $("button:submit").bind("click", function(e) {
            e.preventDefault();
        });

    });
</script>
...
```

This script sets up a handler function for the click event on all button elements whose type attribute is set to submit. The function only contains a call to the preventDefault method, which means that clicking the buttons won't do anything at all, since the default action is disabled and the handler function doesn't set up any alternatives.

Usually you want to suppress the default action so you can perform some other activity instead—for example, to stop the browser from submitting the form because you want to do it with Ajax (which is the topic of Chapters 14 and 15). Instead of writing a one-line function as I did in Listing 9-5, you can use a different version of the bind method, as shown in Listing 9-6.

Listing 9-6. Using the bind Method to Create a Handler That Prevents the Default Action

```
...
<script type="text/javascript">
    $(document).ready(function() {
        $("button:submit").bind("click", false);
    });
</script>
...
```

The first argument is the event or events whose default action you want to suppress, and the second argument allows you to specify whether the event should be prevented from bubbling up the DOM (I explain event bubbling in Chapter 2).

Removing Event Handler Functions

The unbind method removes a handler function from an element. You can unbind all of the handlers associated with all events for all elements in a jQuery object by calling the unbind method with no arguments, as shown in Listing 9-7.

Listing 9-7. Unbinding All Event Handlers

```
...
<script type="text/javascript">
    $(document).ready(function() {

        function handleMouse(e) {
            var cssData = {
                "border": "thick solid red",
                "opacity": "0.5"
            }
```

```
            if (event.type == "mouseout") {
                cssData.border = "";
                cssData.opacity = "";
            }
            $(this).css(cssData);
        }

        $("img").bind("mouseenter mouseout", handleMouse);

        $("img[src*=rose]").unbind();

    });
</script>
...
```

In Listing 9-7, I bind a handler for the mouseenter and mouseout events for all of the img elements and then use the unbind method to remove all of the handlers for the img element whose src attribute contains rose. You can be more selective by passing the events you want to unbind as an argument to the unbind method, as shown in Listing 9-8.

Listing 9-8. Selectively Unbinding Events

```
...
<script type="text/javascript">
    $(document).ready(function() {

        function handleMouse(e) {
            var cssData = {
                "border": "thick solid red",
                "opacity": "0.5"
            }
            if (event.type == "mouseout") {
                cssData.border = "";
                cssData.opacity = "";
            }
            $(this).css(cssData);
        }

        $("img").bind("mouseenter mouseout", handleMouse);

        $("img[src*=rose]").unbind("mouseout");

    });
</script>
...
```

In this script I unbind only the mouseout event, leaving the handler for the mouseenter event untouched.

Unbinding from Within the Event Handler Function

The final option for unbinding is to do so from within the event handler function. This can be useful if you want to handle an event a certain number of times, for example. Listing 9-9 contains a simple demonstration.

Listing 9-9. Unbinding from an Event Inside the Event Handler

```
...
<script type="text/javascript">
    $(document).ready(function() {

        var handledCount = 0;

        function handleMouseEnter(e) {
            $(this).css("border", "thick solid red");
        }
        function handleMouseExit(e) {
            $(this).css("border", "");
            handledCount ++;
            if (handledCount == 2) {
                $(this).unbind(e);
            }
        }
        $("img").bind("mouseenter", handleMouseEnter).bind("mouseout", handleMouseExit)
    });
</script>
...
```

In the handleMouseEvent function, I increment a counter each time that I handle the mouseout event. After I have handled the event twice, I pass the Event object to the unbind method to unregister the function as a handler. jQuery figures out the details it requires from the event object.

Executing a Handler Once

The one method lets you register an event handler that will be executed only once for an element and then removed. Listing 9-10 provides an example.

Listing 9-10. Using the one Method to Register a Single-Shot Event Handler Function

```
...
<script type="text/javascript">
    $(document).ready(function() {

        function handleMouseEnter(e) {
            $(this).css("border", "thick solid red");
        };

        function handleMouseOut(e) {
            $(this).css("border", "");
        };

        $("img").one("mouseenter", handleMouseEnter).one("mouseout", handleMouseOut);

    });
</script>
...
```

I have used the one method to register handlers for the mouseenter and mouseout events. The handler functions will be called when the user moves the mouse in and out of one of the img elements, and then the function will be unbound (but just for that element; the others will still have the handlers until the mouse is moved over them).

Performing Live Event Binding

One limitation of the bind method is that your event handler functions are not associated with any new element that you add to the DOM. Listing 9-11 contains an example.

Listing 9-11. Adding Elements After Setting Up the Event Handlers

```
...
<script type="text/javascript">
    $(document).ready(function() {
        $("img").bind({
            mouseenter: function() {
                $(this).css("border", "thick solid red");
            },
            mouseout: function() {
                $(this).css("border", "");
            }
        });

        $("#row1").append($("<div class='dcell'/>")
            .append("<img src='lily.png'/>")
            .append("<label for='lily'>Lily:</label>")
            .append("<input name='lily' value='0' required />"));
    });
</script>
...
```

In this script, I use the bind method to set up handlers for the mouseenter and mouseout events for all of the img elements. I then use the append methods to insert some new elements in the document, including another img element. This new img element didn't exist when I used the bind method, and my handler functions are not associated with it. The result of this is that I have six img elements that display a border when the mouse hovers over them and one that doesn't.

In an example as simple as the one in Listing 9-11, the easy answer is to call the bind method again, but it can be difficult to keep track of which handlers are required for different types of elements. Fortunately, jQuery makes this easy for you with a set of methods that automatically register event handlers when new elements that match a selector are added to the DOM. Table 9-4 describes these methods.

Table 9-4. Methods for Automatically Registering Event Handlers

Method	Description
on(events, selector, data, function) on (map, selector, data)	Defines handlers for events for elements that exist now or in the future
off(events, selector, function) off(map, selector)	Removes event handlers created using the on method
delegate(selector, eventType, function) delegate(selector, eventType, data, function) delegate(selector, map)	Adds an event handler to the elements that match the selector (now or in the future) attached to the elements in the jQuery object
undelegate() undelegate(selector, eventType)	Removes event handlers created with the delegate method for the specified event types

Listing 9-12 shows the previous example updated to use the on method. The changes are minor, but the effect is significant. Any elements that I add to the DOM that match the selector img will have the functions in the map object set up as handlers for the mouseenter and mouseout events.

Listing 9-12. Using the on Method

```
...
<script type="text/javascript">
    $(document).ready(function () {

        $(document).on({
            mouseenter: function () {
                $(this).css("border", "thick solid red");
            },
            mouseout: function () {
                $(this).css("border", "");
            }
        }, "img");

        $("#row1").append($("<div class='dcell'/>")
            .append("<img src='lily.png'/>")
            .append("<label for='lily'>Lily:</label>")
            .append("<input name='lily' value='0' required />"));
    });
</script>
...
```

Notice that I call the on method on a jQuery object that is created from document. This ensures that my event handlers are applied to any img element that is added anywhere in the DOM. I can narrow the focus by changing the initial selector—for example, if I only wanted my handler functions to be applied to img elements added to the row1 element, I could have used the following call instead:

```
...
$("#row1").on(...map..., "img");
...
```

■ **Tip** The on method doesn't need to add the handler functions directly to the element. In fact, it creates an event handler on the document object and looks for events that were triggered by elements that match the selector. When it sees such an event, it triggers the event handler. However, for all practical purposes, it is just easier to imagine the on method diligently adding handles to new elements.

Multiple events can be specified when using the on method. The event names are separated by space characters, either in the property names of the map object or in the first argument when the map isn't used, as illustrated by Listing 9-13.

Listing 9-13. Specifying Multiple Events Using the on Method

```
...
<script type="text/javascript">
    $(document).ready(function () {

        function handleMouse(event) {
            if (event.type == "mouseenter") {
                $(this).css("border", "thick solid red");
            } else if (event.type == "mouseout") {
                $(this).css("border", "");
            }
        }

        $("#row1").on("mouseenter mouseout", "img", handleMouse);

        $("#row1").append($("<div class='dcell'/>")
            .append("<img src='lily.png'/>")
            .append("<label for='lily'>Lily:</label>")
            .append("<input name='lily' value='0' required />"));
    });
</script>
...
```

In Listing 9-13 I have used the version of the on method that doesn't rely on a map object, specifying that the handleMouse function should be used for the mouseenter and mouseout events emitted by all img elements that are descendants of the row1 element.

The complement to the on method is off, which is used to remove the event handlers from existing elements and prevent them being used to respond to events from newly created elements. Listing 9-14 shows the use of the off method.

Listing 9-14. Using the off Method

```
...
<script type="text/javascript">
    $(document).ready(function () {

        function handleMouse(event) {
            if (event.type == "mouseenter") {
                $(this).css("border", "thick solid red");
```

```
            } else if (event.type == "mouseout") {
                $(this).css("border", "");
            }
        }

        $("#row1").on("mouseenter mouseout", "img", handleMouse);

        $("#row1").off("mouseout", "img");

        $("#row1").append($("<div class='dcell'/>")
            .append("<img src='lily.png'/>")
            .append("<label for='lily'>Lily:</label>")
            .append("<input name='lily' value='0' required />"));
    });
</script>
...
```

■ **Caution**   It is important to use the same selector with the on and off methods; otherwise, the off method won't undo the effect of on.

Limiting DOM Traversal for Live Event Handlers

One problem with the on method is that the events have to propagate all the way up to the document element before your handler functions are executed. You can take a more direct approach by using the delegate method, which allows you to specify where the event listener will be located in the document. Listing 9-15 provides an example.

Listing 9-15. Using the delegate Method

```
...
<script type="text/javascript">
    $(document).ready(function() {

        $("#row1").delegate("img", {
            mouseenter: function() {
                $(this).css("border", "thick solid red");
            },
            mouseout: function() {
                $(this).css("border", "");
            }
        });

        $("#row1").append($("<div class='dcell'/>")
            .append("<img src='carnation.png'/>")
            .append("<label for='carnation'>Carnation:</label>")
            .append("<input name='carnation' value='0' required />"));
```

```
        $("#row2").append($("<div class='dcell'/>")
            .append("<img src='lily.png'/>")
            .append("<label for='lily'>Lily:</label>")
            .append("<input name='lily' value='0' required />"));
    });

</script>
...
```

In Listing 9-15, I use the delegate method to add the listener to the element whose ID is #row1, and the selector I specified matches the img element. The effect of this is that my handler functions will be executed when a mouseenter or mouseout event that originated from an img element propagates to the row1 element. When I add another img element to row1, it is automatically covered by my call to the delegate method, which is not the case when I add elements to row2.

The main benefit of using the delegate method is speed, which can become an issue if you have a particularly large and complex document and a lot of event handlers. By pushing the point where the events are intercepted down into the documents, you reduce the distance that events have to travel in the DOM before they lead to the handler functions being invoked.

■ **Tip** To remove handlers added with the delegate method, you have to use undelegate. The off method works only with the on method.

Manually Invoking Event Handlers

You can manually invoke the event handling functions on elements using the methods described in Table 9-5.

Table 9-5. *Methods for Manually Invoking Event Handlers*

Method	Description
trigger(eventType)	Triggers the handler functions for the specified event types on all of the elements in a jQuery object
trigger(event)	Triggers the handler functions for the specified event on all of the elements in a jQuery object
triggerHandler(eventType)	Triggers the handler function on the first element in the jQuery object, without performing the default action or bubbling the event

Listing 9-16 shows how you can trigger the event handlers manually.

Listing 9-16. Triggering Event Handlers Manually

```
...
<script type="text/javascript">
    $(document).ready(function() {

        $("img").bind({mouseenter: function() {
                $(this).css("border", "thick solid red");
            },
```

```
        mouseout: function() {
            $(this).css("border", "");
        }
    });

    $("<button>Trigger</button>").appendTo("#buttonDiv").bind("click", function (e) {
        $("#row1 img").trigger("mouseenter");
        e.preventDefault();
    });

});
```

```
</script>
...
```

In this script, I use the `bind` method to set up a pair of event handler functions on the `img` elements in the document. I then use the `appendTo` method to insert a `button` element into the document method and the `bind` method to register a handler function for the `click` event.

When the button is pressed, the event handler function selects the `img` elements that are descendants of `row1` and uses the `trigger` method to invoke their handlers for the `mouseenter` button. The effect, which is shown in Figure 9-2, is as though the mouse were moved over all three `img` elements.

Figure 9-2. Manually triggering event handler functions

Using an Event Object

You can also use an Event object to trigger other elements' event handlers. This can be a convenient technique to use inside a handler, as demonstrated in Listing 9-17.

Listing 9-17. Manually Triggering Event Handles with an Event Object

```
...
<script type="text/javascript">
    $(document).ready(function() {

        $("#row1 img").bind("mouseenter", function() {
            $(this).css("border", "thick solid red");
        });

        $("#row2 img").bind("mouseenter", function(e) {
            $(this).css("border", "thick solid blue");
            $("#row1 img").trigger(e);
        });

    });

</script>
...
```

In Listing 9-17, I use the bind method to add a red border to the img descendants of the row1 element in response to the mouseenter event. I do the same with a blue border to the row2 img elements, but in the handler, I have added the following statement:

```
..
$("#row1 img").trigger(e);
...
```

The effect of this addition is that when the mouse enters one of the row2 img elements, the handler for the same event type is triggered on the row1 img elements as well. You can see the effect in Figure 9-3.

Figure 9-3. *Triggering event handlers using an event*

This approach is convenient when you want to trigger the handlers for the event type currently being processed, but you could as easily get the same effect by specifying the event type.

Using the triggerHandler Method

The triggerHandler method invokes the handler functions without performing the event's default action or allowing the event to bubble up through the DOM. And, unlike the trigger method, triggerHandler invokes the handler function only on the first element in a jQuery object. Listing 9-18 shows the use of this method.

Listing 9-18. Using the triggerHandler Method

```
...
<script type="text/javascript">
    $(document).ready(function() {
        $("#row1 img").bind("mouseenter", function() {
            $(this).css("border", "thick solid red");
        });

        $("#row2 img").bind("mouseenter", function(e) {
            $(this).css("border", "thick solid blue");
            $("#row1 img").triggerHandler("mouseenter");
        });
    });
</script>
...
```

228

■ **Tip** The result from the `triggerHandler` method is the result returned by the handler function, which means you cannot chain the `triggerHandler` method.

You can see the effect of this script in Figure 9-4.

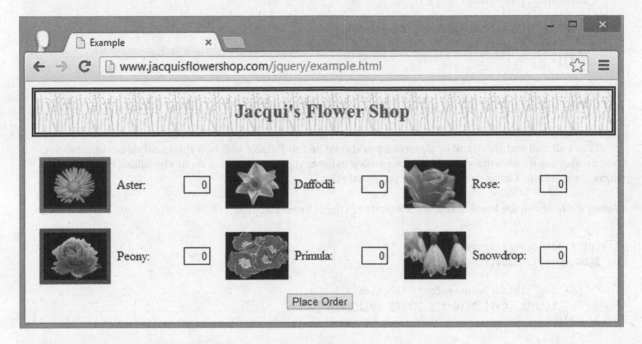

Figure 9-4. *Using the triggerHandler method*

Using the Event Shorthand Methods

jQuery defines some convenience methods that you can use as shorthand to register an event handler for commonly used events. In the tables that follow, I have shown these shorthand methods with a `function` argument. This is the most common use and is equivalent to calling the `bind` method, but these methods require less typing and (at least to my mind) make it more obvious which events you are binding to. Listing 9-19 shows how you can use a shorthand method in this way.

Listing 9-19. Using an Event Shorthand Method to Bind a Handler Function

```
...
<script type="text/javascript">
    $(document).ready(function() {

        $("img").mouseenter(function() {
            $(this).css("border", "thick solid red");
        });

    });
</script>
...
```

This is equivalent to using the bind event for the mouseenter event, which I have shown in Listing 9-20.

Listing 9-20. Using the bind Method for the mouseenter Event

```
...
<script type="text/javascript">
    $(document).ready(function() {

        $("img").bind("mouseenter", function() {
            $(this).css("border", "thick solid red");
        });

    });
</script>
...
```

That's all well and good, and by this point, you should be comfortable with how this example works. However, you can also use the shorthand methods as an analog to the trigger method. You do this by calling the method without arguments. Listing 9-21 shows how you can do this.

Listing 9-21. Using the Event Shorthand Methods to Trigger Event Handlers

```
...
<script type="text/javascript">
    $(document).ready(function() {

        $("img").bind("mouseenter", function() {
            $(this).css("border", "thick solid red");
        });

        $("<button>Trigger</button>").appendTo("#buttonDiv").click(function (e) {
            $("img").mouseenter();
            e.preventDefault();
        });
    });
</script>
...
```

I add a button to the document that, when clicked, selects the img elements and invokes their handlers for the mouseenter event. For completeness, Listing 9-22 shows the equivalent functionality written using the trigger method.

Listing 9-22. Using the trigger Method

```
...
<script type="text/javascript">
    $(document).ready(function() {

        $("img").bind("mouseenter", function() {
            $(this).css("border", "thick solid red");
        });
```

```
        $("<button>Trigger</button>").appendTo("#buttonDiv").click(function (e) {
            $("img").trigger("mouseenter");
            e.preventDefault();
        });
    });
</script>
...
```

In the sections that follow, I list the different categories of shorthand methods and the events they correspond to.

Using the Document Event Shorthand Methods

Table 9-6 describes the jQuery shorthand methods that apply to the document object.

Table 9-6. *Document Event Shorthand Methods*

Method	Description
load(function)	Corresponds to the load event, triggered when the elements and resources in the document have been loaded
ready(function)	Triggered when the elements in the document have been processed and the DOM is ready to use
unload(function)	Corresponds to the unload event, triggered when the user navigates away from the page

The ready method deserves special mention. It doesn't correspond directly to a DOM event but is incredibly useful when using jQuery. You can see the different ways you can use the ready method in Chapter 5, where I explain how to defer execution of a script until the DOM is ready and how you can control the execution of the ready event.

Using the Browser Event Shorthand Methods

Table 9-7 describes the browser events, which are usually targeted at the window object (although the error and scroll events are also used with elements as well).

Table 9-7. *Browser Event Shorthand Methods*

Method	Description
error(function)	Corresponds to the error event, triggered when there is a problem loading an external resource, such as an image
resize(function)	Corresponds to the resize event, triggered when the browser window is resized
scroll(function)	Corresponds to the scroll event, triggered when the scrollbars are used

Using the Mouse Event Shorthand Methods

Table 9-8 describes the set of shorthand methods that jQuery provides for dealing with mouse events.

Table 9-8. *Mouse Event Shorthand Methods*

Method	Description
click(function)	Corresponds to the click event, triggered when the user presses and releases the mouse
dblclick(function)	Corresponds to the dblclick event, triggered when the user presses and releases the mouse twice in quick succession
focusin(function)	Corresponds to the focusin event, triggered when the element gains the focus
focusout(function)	Corresponds to the focusout event, triggered when the element loses the focus
hover(function) hover(function, function)	Triggered when the mouse enters or leaves an element; when one function is specified, it is used for both enter and exit events
mousedown(function)	Corresponds to the mousedown event, triggered when the mouse button is pressed over an element
mouseenter(function)	Corresponds to the mouseenter event, triggered when the mouse enters the region of screen occupied by an element
mouseleave(function)	Corresponds to the mouseleave event, triggered when the mouse leaves the region of screen occupied by an element
mousemove(function)	Corresponds to the mousemouse event, triggered when the mouse is moved within the region of screen occupied by an element
mouseout(function)	Corresponds to the mouseout event, triggered when the mouse leaves the region of screen occupied by an element
mouseover(function)	Corresponds to the mouseover event, triggered when the mouse enters the region of screen occupied by an element
mouseup(function)	Corresponds to the mouseup event, triggered when the mouse button is pressed over an element

The hover method is a convenient way of binding a handler function to the mouseenter and mouseleave events. If you provide two functions as arguments, then the first is invoked in response to the mouseenter event and the second in response to mouseleave. If you specify only one function, it will be invoked for both events. Listing 9-23 shows the use of the hover method.

Listing 9-23. Using the hover Method

```
...
<script type="text/javascript">
    $(document).ready(function() {

        $("img").hover(handleMouseEnter, handleMouseLeave);

        function handleMouseEnter(e) {
            $(this).css("border", "thick solid red");
        };
```

```
        function handleMouseLeave(e) {
            $(this).css("border", "");
        }
    });
</script>
...
```

Using the Form Event Shorthand Methods

Table 9-9 describes the shorthand methods that jQuery provides for dealing with events that are usually associated with forms.

Table 9-9. *Form Event Shorthand Methods*

Method	Description
blur(function)	Corresponds to the blur event, triggered when an element loses the focus
change(function)	Corresponds to the change event, triggered when the value of an element changes
focus(function)	Corresponds to the focus event, triggered when an element gains the focus
select(function)	Corresponds to the select event, triggered when the user selects the element value
submit(function)	Corresponds to the submit event, triggered when the user submits a form

Using the Keyboard Event Shorthand Methods

Table 9-10 describes the shorthand methods that jQuery provides for dealing with keyboard events.

Table 9-10. *Keyboard Event Shorthand Methods*

Method	Description
keydown(function)	Corresponds to the keydown event, triggered when the user presses a key
keypress(function)	Corresponds to the keypress event, triggered when the user presses and releases a key
keyup(function)	Corresponds to the keyup event, triggered when the user releases a key

Summary

In this chapter, I showed you the jQuery support for events. As with much of jQuery, the benefit of the event functionality is simplicity and elegance. You can create and manage event handlers with little effort. I particularly like the support for creating live event handlers, such that elements that are added to the DOM that match a particular selector are automatically associated with event handlers. It significantly reduces the amount of time that I spend tracking down problems with event handling in my web applications. In Chapter 10, I describe the jQuery support for *effects*.

■ ■ ■

Using jQuery Effects

For the most part, jQuery UI contains the user interface (UI) functionality associated with jQuery, but the core library includes some basic effects and animations, and these are the topic of this chapter. Although I describe them as basic, they can be used to achieve some pretty sophisticated effects. The main focus is on animating the visibility of elements, but you can use these features to animate a range of CSS properties in a number of ways. Table 10-1 provides the summary for this chapter.

Table 10-1. *Chapter Summary*

Problem	Solution	Listing
Show or hide elements	Use the show or hide method	1
Toggle the visibility of elements	Use the toggle method	2, 3
Animate the visibility of elements	Provide a timespan argument to the show, hide, or toggle method	4
Call a function at the end of an animation	Provide a callback argument to the show, hide, or toggle method	5–7
Animate visibility along the vertically	Use the slideDown, slideUp, or slideToggle method	8
Animate visibility using opacity	Use the fadeIn, fadeOut, fadeToggle, or fadeTo method	9–11
Create a custom effect	Use the animate method	12–14
Inspect the queue of effects	Use the queue method	15, 16
Stop and clear the effect queue	Use the stop or finish methods	17, 18
Insert a delay into the effect queue	Use the delay method	19
Insert custom functions into the queue	Use the queue method with a function argument and ensure that the next function in the queue is executed	20, 21
Disable the animation of effects	Set the $.fx.off property to true	22

JQUERY CHANGES SINCE THE LAST EDITION

jQuery 1.9/2.0 defines a new finish method that is used to complete the current effect and clear the event queue. See the section "Stopping Effects and Clearing the Queue" for details.

Using the Basic Effects

The most basic effects are simply to show or hide elements. Table 10-2 describes the methods that you can use for this.

Table 10-2. *Basic Effects Methods*

Method	Description
hide()	Hides all of the elements in a jQuery object
hide(time) hide(time, easing)	Hides the elements in a jQuery object over the specified period of time with an optional easing style
hide(time, function) hide(time, easing, function)	Hides the elements in a jQuery object over the specified period of time with an optional easing style and a function that is called when the effect is complete
show()	Shows all of the elements in a jQuery object
show(time) show(time, easing)	Shows the elements in a jQuery object over the specified period of time with an optional easing style
show(time, function) show(time, easing, function)	Shows the elements in a jQuery object over the specified period of time with an optional easing style and a function that is called when the effect is complete
toggle()	Toggles the visibility of the elements in a jQuery object
toggle(time) toggle(time, easing)	Toggles the visibility of the elements in a jQuery object over the specified period of time with an optional easing style
toggle(time, function) toggle(time, easing, function)	Toggles the visibility of the elements in a jQuery object over the specified period of time with an optional easing style and a function that is called when the effect is complete
toggle(boolean)	Toggles the elements in a jQuery object in one direction

Listing 10-1 shows the simplest of these effects, which is to use the show and hide methods without any arguments.

Listing 10-1. *Using the Show and Hide Methods Without Arguments*

```
<!DOCTYPE html>
<html>
<head>
    <title>Example</title>
    <script src="jquery-2.0.2.js" type="text/javascript"></script>
    <link rel="stylesheet" type="text/css" href="styles.css"/>
    <script type="text/javascript">
        $(document).ready(function() {
            $("<button>Hide</button><button>Show</button>").appendTo("#buttonDiv")
                .click(function(e) {
                    if ($(e.target).text() == "Hide") {
                        $("#row1 div.dcell").hide();
                    } else {
                        $("#row1 div.dcell").show();
                    }
```

```
                        e.preventDefault();
                });

        });
    </script>
</head>
<body>
    <h1>Jacqui's Flower Shop</h1>
    <form method="post">
        <div id="oblock">
            <div class="dtable">
                <div id="row1" class="drow">
                    <div class="dcell">
                        <img src="aster.png"/><label for="aster">Aster:</label>
                        <input name="aster" value="0" required />
                    </div>
                    <div class="dcell">
                        <img src="daffodil.png"/><label for="daffodil">Daffodil:</label>
                        <input name="daffodil" value="0" required />
                    </div>
                    <div class="dcell">
                        <img src="rose.png"/><label for="rose">Rose:</label>
                        <input name="rose" value="0" required />
                    </div>
                </div>
                <div id="row2"class="drow">
                    <div class="dcell">
                        <img src="peony.png"/><label for="peony">Peony:</label>
                        <input name="peony" value="0" required />
                    </div>
                    <div class="dcell">
                        <img src="primula.png"/><label for="primula">Primula:</label>
                        <input name="primula" value="0" required />
                    </div>
                    <div class="dcell">
                        <img src="snowdrop.png"/><label for="snowdrop">Snowdrop:</label>
                        <input name="snowdrop" value="0" required />
                    </div>
                </div>
            </div>
        </div>
        <div id="buttonDiv"><button type="submit">Place Order</button></div>
    </form>
</body>
</html>
```

I manipulate the DOM (Domain Object Model) to add two button elements and provide a function to be called when either of them is clicked. This function uses the text method to figure out which button has been used and calls either the hide or show method. In both cases, I call this method on a jQuery object with the selector #row1 div.dcell, meaning that those div elements in the dcell class that are descendants of the element with the id of row1 will be made invisible or visible. Figure 10-1 illustrates what happens when I click the Hide button.

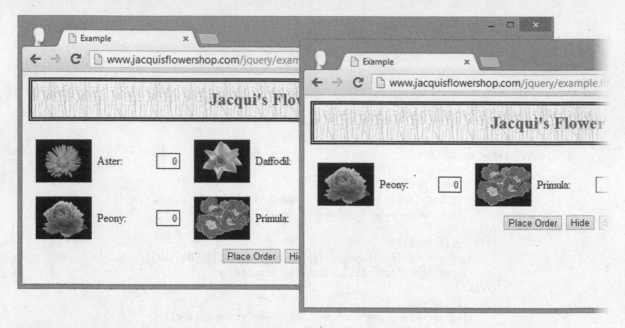

Figure 10-1. Hiding elements with the hide element

Clicking the Show button calls the show method, restoring the hidden elements, as Figure 10-2 shows.

Figure 10-2. Showing elements with the show method

It is hard to show transitions using figures, but there are a few points to note. The first is that the transition is immediate: there is no delay or effect, and the elements just appear and disappear. Second, calling hide on elements that are already hidden has no effect; nor does calling show on elements that are visible. Finally, when you hide or show an element, you also show or hide all of its descendants.

■ **Tip**   You can select elements using the :visible and :hidden selectors. See Chapter 5 for details of the jQuery extension CSS selectors.

Toggling Elements

You can flip elements from being visible or hidden and back using the toggle method. Listing 10-2 gives an example.

Listing 10-2.   Using the toggle Method to Switch Element Visibility

```
...
<script type="text/javascript">
    $(document).ready(function() {
        $("<button>Toggle</button>").appendTo("#buttonDiv")
            .click(function(e) {
                $("div.dcell:first-child").toggle();
                e.preventDefault();
            });
    });
</script>
...
```

In Listing 10-2 I add a single button to the document, and when it is clicked, I use the toggle element to change the visibility of the div.dcell elements that are the first children of their parents. You can see the effect in Figure 10-3.

Figure 10-3.   *Toggling the visibility of elements*

■ **Tip**   Notice that the structure of the document collapses around the hidden elements. If you want to hide the elements and leave space on the screen, then you can set the CSS `visibility` property to `hidden`.

Toggling in One Direction

You can pass a `boolean` argument to the `toggle` method to restrict the way that visibility is toggled. If you pass `true` as the argument, then only hidden elements will be shown (visible elements will not be hidden). If you pass `false` as the argument, then you get the opposite effect. Visible elements will be hidden, but hidden elements will not be made visible. Listing 10-3 shows the use of this flavor of the `toggle` method. The script in Listing 10-3 creates the effect shown in Figure 10-3.

Listing 10-3. Using the toggle Method in One Direction

```
...
<script type="text/javascript">
    $(document).ready(function() {
        $("<button>Toggle</button>").appendTo("#buttonDiv")
            .click(function(e) {
                $("div.dcell:first-child").toggle(false);
                e.preventDefault();
            });
    });
</script>
...
```

Animating the Visibility of Elements

You can animate the process of showing and hiding elements by passing a time span to the `show`, `hide`, or `toggle` methods. The process of showing and hiding elements is then performed gradually, over the specified period. Table 10-3 shows the different time span arguments you can use.

Table 10-3. *Time Span Arguments*

Method	Description
`<number>`	Specifies duration in milliseconds
`slow`	A shorthand equivalent to 600 milliseconds
`fast`	A shorthand equivalent to 200 milliseconds

Listing 10-4 shows how you can animate showing and hiding elements.

Listing 10-4. Animating the Visibility of Elements

```
...
<script type="text/javascript">
    $(document).ready(function() {
```

```
    $("<button>Toggle</button>").appendTo("#buttonDiv")
        .click(function(e) {
            $("img").toggle("fast", "linear");
            e.preventDefault();
        });

});
</script>
...
```

In Listing 10-4, I have used the `fast` value to specify that toggling the visibility of the `img` elements in the document should be done over a period of 600 milliseconds.

■ **Tip** When specifying a duration in milliseconds, be sure that the value is not quoted. That is, use `$("img").toggle(500)` and not `$("img").toggle("500")`. If you do use quotes, then the value will be ignored.

I have also provided an additional argument, which specifies the style of the animation, known as the *easing style* or *easing function*. Two easing styles are available, `swing` and `linear`. When animating with the `swing` style, the animation starts slowly, speeds up, and then slows down again as the animation reaches conclusion. The `linear` style maintains a constant pace throughout the animation. If you omit the argument, `swing` is used. You can see the effect of the animation as it hides elements in Figure 10-4. It is difficult to show animation in this way, but you'll get a sense of what happens.

Figure 10-4. *Animating hiding elements*

As the figure shows, the animation effect reduces the size of the image in both dimensions and decreases the opacity. At the end of the animation, the img elements are invisible. Figure 10-5 shows what happens if you click the Toggle button again to make the img elements visible.

Figure 10-5. *Animating showing elements*

Using Effect Callbacks

You can supply a function as an argument to the show, hide, and toggle methods, and the function will be called when these methods finish performing their effect. This can be useful for updating other elements to reflect the change in status, as shown in Listing 10-5.

Listing 10-5. Using an Event Callback

```
...
<script type="text/javascript">
    $(document).ready(function() {

        var hiddenRow = "#row2";
        var visibleRow = "#row1";

        $(hiddenRow).hide();

        function switchRowVariables() {
            var temp = hiddenRow;
            hiddenRow = visibleRow;
            visibleRow = temp;
        }
```

```
        function hideVisibleElement() {
            $(visibleRow).hide("fast", showHiddenElement);
        }

        function showHiddenElement() {
            $(hiddenRow).show("fast", switchRowVariables);
        }

        $("<button>Switch</button>").insertAfter("#buttonDiv button")
            .click(function(e) {
                hideVisibleElement();
                e.preventDefault();
            });
    });
</script>
...
```

■ **Tip**   If you want to perform multiple sequential effects on a single element, then you can use regular jQuery method chaining. See the section "Creating and Managing the Effect Queue" for details.

To make Listing 10-5 clearer, I have broken down the effect activities into separate functions. To get set up, I hide one of the div elements that acts as a row in my CSS table layout and define two variables that I use to track which row is visible and which row is not. I add a button element to the document, and when this is clicked I call the hideVisibleElement function, which uses the hide method to animate hiding the visible row.

```
...
$(visibleRow).hide("fast", showHiddenElement);
...
```

I specify the name of the function I want performed when the effect has completed, in this case showHiddenElement.

■ **Tip**   The callback function is not passed any arguments, but the this variable is set to the DOM element being animated. If multiple elements are being animated, then the callback function will be called once for each of them.

This function uses the show method to animate revealing the element, as follows:

```
...
$(hiddenRow).show("fast", switchRowVariables);
...
```

Once again, I specify a function to perform at the end of the effect. In this case, it is the switchRowVariables function, which shuffles the variables that track visibility so that you perform the effects on the right elements the next time the button is clicked. The result is that when the button is clicked, the current row is replaced by the hidden row, with a quick animation to make the transition less jarring to the user. Figure 10-6 shows the effect (although, once again, the true effect becomes apparent only when you load the example in the browser).

Figure 10-6. *Using callback functions to chain effects*

You wouldn't usually need to break out the individual functions as I did, so Listing 10-6 shows the same example rewritten using a terser set of inline functions.

Listing 10-6. Using Inline Callback Functions

```
...
<script type="text/javascript">
    $(document).ready(function() {

        var hiddenRow = "#row2";
        var visibleRow = "#row1";

        $(hiddenRow).hide();

        $("<button>Switch</button>").insertAfter("#buttonDiv button")
            .click(function(e) {
                $(visibleRow).hide("fast", function() {
                    $(hiddenRow).show("fast", function() {
                        var temp = hiddenRow;
                        hiddenRow = visibleRow;
                        visibleRow = temp;
                    });
                });

                e.preventDefault();
            });
    });
</script>
...
```

Creating Looping Effects

You can use the callback functions to produce effects that are performed in a loop. Listing 10-7 demonstrates.

Listing 10-7. Using Callback Functions to Create a Looping Effect

```
...
<script type="text/javascript">
    $(document).ready(function() {

        $("<button>Toggle</button>").insertAfter("#buttonDiv button")
            .click(function(e) {
                performEffect();
                e.preventDefault();
            });

        function performEffect() {
            $("h1").toggle("slow", performEffect)
        }
    });
</script>
...
```

In this example, clicking the button leads to the `performEffect` function being executed. This function uses the `toggle` method to change the visibility of the `h1` element in the document and passes itself as the callback argument. The result is that the `h1` element loops between being visible and hidden, as shown in Figure 10-7.

Figure 10-7. Performing an effect in a loop

245

■ **Tip** Some caution is required when using the current function as the callback function. Eventually you will exhaust the JavaScript call stack, and your script will stop working. The easiest way to solve this problem is with the `setTimeout` function, which will schedule a callback to your target function without nesting the function calls, like this: `$("h1").toggle("slow", setTimeout( performEffect, 1))`. It is actually pretty hard to exhaust the call stack, and it usually means leaving a page with animations running for a long time, but it is worth bearing in mind—however, it is something to be careful of when using the `finish` method, which I describe in the section "Stopping Effects and Clearing the Queue."

USING EFFECTS RESPONSIBLY

To my mind, loops like this should be used sparingly and only when they serve a purpose (and by that, I mean a purpose for the user and not to show off your excellent jQuery effect skills). In general, the impact of any kind of effect should be carefully considered. It may look great during development, but injudicious use of effects destroys the user's enjoyment of your web application, especially if it is an application he or she uses every day.

As a simple example, I am a keen runner (keen but not any good). I used to have a runner's wristwatch that collects data about my heart rate, speed, distance, calories burned, and 100 other data points. At the end of a run, I would upload the data to the manufacturer's web site for storage and analysis.

Here's where the pain started. Every time I clicked a button on the page, the content I wanted would be revealed through a long effect. I know the browser has received the data I want because I can see it being gradually revealed, but it is a couple of seconds before I can read it. A couple of seconds may not sound like a lot, but it is, especially when I want to look at between five and ten different data items at any time.

I am sure that the designer of the application thought the effects were nice and that they enhanced the experience. But they don't. They sucked so much that it made using the application a teeth-grinding experience—so much so that since the last edition of this book, I purchased a competitor product.

This web application for the (now discarded) watch had some useful data analysis tools, but I got to the point where it annoyed me so much that I was willing to pay several hundred dollars to get a replacement. I could be a champion marathon runner by now if not for those effects (and maybe the beer and pizza I find myself consuming with shocking frequency).

If you think I am exaggerating (about the effects . . . you can take my word about the pizza), then take one of the listings in this chapter and set the time span to two seconds. Then get a feel for how long that is when you are waiting for the effect to complete.

My advice is that *all* effects should be used sparingly. I tend to use them only when making a change to the DOM that would be jarring otherwise (elements suddenly disappearing from the page). When I do use them, I keep the time spans short, typically 200 milliseconds. I *never* employ endless loops. That's just a recipe for giving the user a headache. I urge you to take the time to think about how your users engage with your application or site and remove anything that doesn't make the tasks at hand easier to perform. Glossy sites are good, but glossy sites that are usable are *great*.

Using the Slide Effects

jQuery has a set of effects that slide elements on and off the screen. Table 10-4 describes the methods for this.

Table 10-4. *Slide Effects Methods*

Method	Description
slideDown() slideDown((time, function) slideDown(time, easing, function)	Show elements by sliding them down
slideUp() slideUp(time, function) slideUp(time, easing, function)	Hide elements by sliding them up
slideToggle() slideToggle(time, function) slideToggle(time, easing, function)	Toggle the visibility of elements by sliding them up and down

These methods animate an element in the vertical axis. The arguments to these methods are as for the basic effect. You can elect to provide a time span, an easing style, and a callback function. Listing 10-8 shows the slide effects in use.

Listing 10-8. Using the Slide Effects

```
...
<script type="text/javascript">
    $(document).ready(function() {
        $("<button>Toggle</button>").insertAfter("#buttonDiv button")
            .click(function(e) {
                $("h1").slideToggle("fast");
                e.preventDefault();
            });
    });
</script>
...
```

In this script, I use the slideToggle method to toggle the visibility of the h1 element. You can see the effect in Figure 10-8.

Figure 10-8. *Using the slide effect to reveal an element*

The figure shows the h1 element being made visible. The elements are clipped, rather than scaled, because jQuery creates the effect by manipulating the height of the element. You can see what I mean by this in Figure 10-9.

Figure 10-9. *jQuery creating an effect by manipulating the height of the elements*

This figure shows a close-up of the h1 element as it is made visible. You can see that the size of the text doesn't change, only the amount of it that is shown. However, this isn't true for images, because the browser scales them automatically. If you look really closely, you can see that the entire background image is always shown, but it is scaled down to fit the height.

Using the Fade Effects

The fade effect methods show and hide elements by reducing their opacity (or, if you prefer, increasing their transparency). Table 10-5 describes the fade effect methods.

Table 10-5. *Fade Effects Methods*

Method	Description
fadeOut() fadeOut(timespan) fadeOut(timespan, function) fadeOut(timespan, easing, function)	Hide elements by decreasing opacity
fadeIn() fadeIn(timespan) fadeIn(timespan, function) fadeIn(timespan, easing, function)	Show elements by increasing opacity
fadeTo(timespan, opacity) fadeTo(timespan, opacity, easing, function)	Change the opacity to the specified level
fadeToggle() fadeToggle(timespan) fadeToggle(timespan, function) fadeToggle(timespan, easing, function)	Toggle the visibility of elements using opacity

The fadeOut, fadeIn, and fadeToggle methods are consistent with the other effect methods. You can provide a time span, an easing style, and a callback function, just as in the previous listings. Listing 10-9 demonstrates how to use fading.

Listing 10-9. Showing and Hiding Elements by Fading

```
...
<script type="text/javascript">
    $(document).ready(function() {
        $("<button>Toggle</button>").insertAfter("#buttonDiv button")
            .click(function(e) {
                $("img").fadeToggle();
                e.preventDefault();
            });
    });
</script>
...
```

I have applied the fadeToggle method to the img elements in the document, in part to demonstrate one of the limitations of this effect. Figure 10-10 shows what happens when you hide the elements.

Figure 10-10. *Using the fade effect*

The fade effect operates only on opacity, unlike the other effects that change the size of the selected elements as well. This means you get a nice smooth fade effect until the elements are completely transparent, at which point jQuery hides them and the page snaps into a new layout. This last stage can be somewhat jarring if not used carefully.

Fading to a Specific Opacity

You can use the fadeTo method to fade elements to a particular opacity. The range of opacity values is a number within the range of 0 (completely transparent) to 1 (completely opaque). The visibility of the elements isn't changed, so you avoid the snap of the page layout I mentioned. Listing 10-10 shows the use of the fadeTo method.

Listing 10-10. Fading to a Specific Opacity

```
...
<script type="text/javascript">
    $(document).ready(function() {
        $("<button>Fade</button>").insertAfter("#buttonDiv button")
            .click(function(e) {
                $("img").fadeTo("fast", 0);
                e.preventDefault();
            });
    });
</script>
...
```

In this example, I have specified that the img elements should be faded until they are completely transparent. This has the same effect as the fadeOut method but doesn't hide the elements at the end of the transition. Figure 10-11 shows the effect.

Figure 10-11. *Fading out an element with the fadeTo method*

You don't have to fade elements to the extremes of the opacity range. You can specify intermediate values as well, as Listing 10-11 demonstrates.

Listing 10-11. Fading to a Specific Opacity

```
...
<script type="text/javascript">
    $(document).ready(function() {
        $("<button>Fade</button>").insertAfter("#buttonDiv button")
            .click(function(e) {
                $("img").fadeTo("fast", 0.4);
                e.preventDefault();
            });
    });
</script>
...
```

You can see the effect in Figure 10-12.

Figure 10-12. *Fading to a specific opacity*

Creating Custom Effects

jQuery doesn't limit you to the basic slide and fade effects. You can create your own as well. Table 10-6 shows the methods that you use for this process.

Table 10-6. *Custom Effects Methods*

Method	Description
animate(properties) animate(properties, time) animate(properties, time, function) animate(properties, time, easing, function)	Animates one or more CSS properties, with an optional time span, easing style, and callback function
animate(properties, options)	Animates one or more CSS properties, specifying the options as a map

jQuery can animate any property that accepts a simple numeric value (e.g., the height property).

■ **Note**   Being able to animate numeric CSS properties means you can't animate colors. There are a few ways to address this. The first (and to my mind best) solution is to use jQuery UI, which I describe in Part IV of this book. If you don't want to use jQuery UI, then you might like to consider using the native browser support for CSS animations. The performance of these is pretty good, but the support is patchy currently and nonexistent in older browser versions. For details of CSS animation, see my book The *Definitive Guide to HTML5*, which is also published by Apress. The approach that I like least is using a jQuery plug-in. Animating colors is difficult to get right, and I have yet to find a plug-in that I am entirely satisfied with, but the most reliable I have found is available from `https://github.com/jquery/jquery-color`.

You supply a set of properties that you want to animate as a map object, and, if you want, you can do the same for the options you want to set. Listing 10-12 shows a custom animation.

Listing 10-12. Using a Custom Animation

```
...
<script type="text/javascript">
    $(document).ready(function() {

        $("form").css({"position": "fixed", "top": "70px", "z-index": "2"});
        $("h1").css({"position": "fixed", "z-index": "1", "min-width": "0"});

        $("<button>Animate</button>").insertAfter("#buttonDiv button")
            .click(function(e) {

                $("h1").animate({
                    height: $("h1").height() + $("form").height() + 10,
                    width: ($("form").width())
                });

                e.preventDefault();
            });
    });
</script>
...
```

In Listing 10-12, I want to animate dimensions of the h1 element so that its background image extends behind the form element. Before I can do this, I need to make some changes to the CSS (Cascading Style Sheets) for the affected elements. I could do this using the style sheet I defined in Chapter 3, but since this is a book on jQuery, I have chosen to use JavaScript. To make the animation easier to manage, I have positioned both the form and h1 elements using the fixed mode and have used the z-index property to ensure that the h1 element is displayed below the form.

I have added a button to the document that calls the animate method when clicked. I have chosen to animate the height and width properties, using information obtained via other jQuery methods. You can see the effect of the animation in Figure 10-13.

Figure 10-13. *Performing a custom animation*

I have shown only the start and end states in the figure, but jQuery provides a smooth transition just like with the other effects, and you can exert control over the transition by specifying a time span and an easing style.

Using Absolute Target Property Values

Notice that you specify only the final values for the animation. The start point for jQuery custom animations is the current values of the properties being animated. I used values I derived from other jQuery methods, but you have some other choices. First, and most obvious, is that you can use absolute values, as shown in Listing 10-13.

Listing 10-13. Performing a Custom Animation Using Absolute Values

```
...
<script type="text/javascript">
    $(document).ready(function() {

        $("form").css({"position": "fixed", "top": "70px", "z-index": "2"});
        $("h1").css({"position": "fixed", "z-index": "1", "min-width": "0"});

        $("<button>Animate</button>").insertAfter("#buttonDiv button")
            .click(function(e) {
                $("h1").animate({
                    left: 50,
                    height: $("h1").height() + $("form").height() + 10,
                    width: ($("form").width())
                });

                e.preventDefault();
            });
    });
</script>
...
```

In Listing 10-13, I have added the `left` property to the animation, specifying an absolute value of 50 (which will be taken as 50 pixels). This shifts the h1 element to the right. Figure 10-14 shows the outcome of the animation.

Figure 10-14. *Creating a custom animation with a fixed final property value*

Using Relative Target Property Values

You can also specify your animation targets using relative values. You specify an increase by prefixing a value with += and a decrease with -=. Listing 10-14 shows the use of relative values.

Listing 10-14. Using Relative Values in a Custom Animation Effect

```
...
<script type="text/javascript">
    $(document).ready(function() {

        $("form").css({"position": "fixed", "top": "70px", "z-index": "2"});
        $("h1").css({"position": "fixed", "z-index": "1", "min-width": "0"});

        $("<button>Animate</button>").insertAfter("#buttonDiv button")
            .click(function(e) {
                $("h1").animate({
                    height: "+=100",
                    width: "-=700"
                });

                e.preventDefault();
            });
    });
</script>
...
```

255

Creating and Managing the Effect Queue

When you use effects, jQuery creates a queue of the animations that it has to perform and works its way through them. There are a set of methods you can use to get information about the queue or take control of it, as described in Table 10-7.

Table 10-7. *Effects Queue Methods*

Method	Description
queue()	Returns the queue of effects to be performed on the elements in the jQuery object
queue(function)	Adds a function to the end of the queue
dequeue()	Removes and executes the first item in the queue for the elements in the jQuery object
stop() stop(clear) stop(clear, jumpToEnd)	Stops the current animation
finish()	Stops the current animation and clears any queued animations
delay(time)	Inserts a delay between effects in the queue

You create a queue of effects by chaining together calls to effect-related methods, as shown in Listing 10-15.

Listing 10-15. Creating an Effect Queue

```
...
<script type="text/javascript">
    $(document).ready(function() {

        $("form").css({"position": "fixed", "top": "70px", "z-index": "2"});
        $("h1").css({"position": "fixed", "z-index": "1", "min-width": "0"});

        var timespan = "slow";

        cycleEffects();

        function cycleEffects() {
            $("h1")
            .animate({left: "+=100"}, timespan)
            .animate({left: "-=100"}, timespan)
            .animate({height: 223,width: 700}, timespan)
            .animate({height: 30,width: 500}, timespan)
            .slideUp(timespan)
            .slideDown(timespan, cycleEffects);
        }
    });
</script>
...
```

This script in Listing 10-15 uses regular jQuery method chaining to string together a series of effects on the h1 element. The last effect uses the cycleEffects function as the callback, which starts the process over again. This is a pretty annoying sequence. It is hypnotic for a moment and then a little irritating, and then it tips right over into the kind of effect that brings on a headache. But it does create a queue of effects, which is what I need to demonstrate the queue features.

■ **Note** I could have used the callback functions to achieve the same effect, but that doesn't create the effect queue, because the function that starts the next animation isn't executed until the previous animation has completed. When you use regular method chaining, as in this example, all of the methods are evaluated, and the animation effects are placed in the queue. The limitation of using method chaining is that you are limited to working with the current selection. When using callbacks, you can string together sequences that involve entirely unrelated elements.

Displaying the Items in the Effect Queue

You can use the queue method to inspect the contents of the effects queue. This is not entirely helpful because the queue contains one of two types of data object. If an effect is being executed, then the corresponding item in the queue is the string value inprogress. If the effect is not being executed, the item in the queue is the function that will be invoked (although the function doesn't reveal which animation function will be performed). That said, inspecting the content is a good place to start with the queue, and Listing 10-16 shows how it can be done.

Listing 10-16. Inspecting the Contents of the Effect Queue

```
...
<script type="text/javascript">
    $(document).ready(function () {

        $("h1").css({ "position": "fixed", "z-index": "1", "min-width": "0" });
        $("form").remove();
        $("<table border=1></table>")
            .appendTo("body").css({
                position: "fixed", "z-index": "2",
                "border-collapse": "collapse", top: 100
        });

        var timespan = "slow";

        cycleEffects();
        printQueue();

        function cycleEffects() {
            $("h1")
            .animate({ left: "+=100" }, timespan)
            .animate({ left: "-=100" }, timespan)
            .animate({ height: 223, width: 700 }, timespan)
            .animate({ height: 30, width: 500 }, timespan)
            .slideUp(timespan)
            .slideDown(timespan, cycleEffects);
        }
```

257

```
        function printQueue() {
            var q = $("h1").queue();
            var qtable = $("table");
            qtable.html("<tr><th>Queue Length:</th><td>" + q.length + "</td></tr>");
            for (var i = 0; i < q.length; i++) {
                var baseString = "<tr><th>" + i + ":</th><td>";
                if (q[i] == "inprogress") {
                    $("table").append(baseString + "In Progress</td></tr>");
                } else {
                    $("table").append(baseString + q[i] + "</td></tr>");
                }
            }
            setTimeout(printQueue, 500);
        }
    });
</script>
...
```

I don't need the form element in this example, so I have removed it from the DOM and replaced it with a simple table that I'll use to display the contents of the effect queue. I have added a repeating function called printQueue that calls the queue method and displays the number of items and a little detail about each of them in the table. As I say, the items in the queue are not especially useful in their own right, but they do give you an overall picture of what is going on. Figure 10-15 shows how jQuery progresses through the effects queue.

Figure 10-15. *Inspecting the contents of the queue*

Listing 10-16 is hard to portray in static images. I recommend you load the document into a browser to see for yourself. When the cycleEffects function is first called, there are six items in the effects queue, the first of which is shown as being in progress. The others are instances of an anonymous function that manages an animation. After each effect is completed, jQuery removes the item from the queue. At the end of the last effect, the cycleEffects function is called again, which puts six items in the queue again.

Stopping Effects and Clearing the Queue

You can use the stop and finish methods to interrupt the effect that jQuery is currently performing. For the stop method, you can provide two optional arguments to this method, both of which are boolean values. If you pass true as the first argument, then all of the other effects are removed from the queue and will not be performed. If you pass true as the second argument, then the CSS properties that are being animated by the current animation will be immediately set to their final values.

The default value for both arguments is false, which means that only the current effect is removed from the queue and that the properties that were being animated are left at the values they were set to at the moment the effect was interrupted. If you don't clear the queue, jQuery will move on to the next effect and begin executing it as normal. Listing 10-17 provides an example of using the stop method.

Listing 10-17. Using the stop Method

```
...
<script type="text/javascript">
    $(document).ready(function () {

        $("h1").css({ "position": "fixed", "z-index": "1", "min-width": "0" });
        $("form").remove();

        $("<table border=1></table>")
            .appendTo("body").css({
                position: "fixed", "z-index": "2",
                "border-collapse": "collapse", top: 100
            });

        $("<button>Stop</button><button>Start</button>")
          .appendTo($("<div/>").appendTo("body")
          .css({
                position: "fixed", "z-index": "2",
                "border-collapse": "collapse", top: 100, left: 200
          })).click(function (e) {
                $(this).text() == "Stop" ? $("h1").stop(true, true) : cycleEffects();
          });

        var timespan = "slow";

        cycleEffects();
        printQueue();

        function cycleEffects() {
            $("h1")
            .animate({ left: "+=100" }, timespan)
            .animate({ left: "-=100" }, timespan)
            .animate({ height: 223, width: 700 }, timespan)
            .animate({ height: 30, width: 500 }, timespan)
            .slideUp(timespan)
            .slideDown(timespan, cycleEffects);
        }
```

```
        function printQueue() {
            var q = $("h1").queue();
            var qtable = $("table");
            qtable.html("<tr><th>Queue Length:</th><td>" + q.length + "</td></tr>");

            for (var i = 0; i < q.length; i++) {
                var baseString = "<tr><th>" + i + ":</th><td>";
                if (q[i] == "inprogress") {
                    $("table").append(baseString + "In Progress</td></tr>");
                } else {
                    $("table").append(baseString + q[i] + "</td></tr>");
                }
            }
            setTimeout(printQueue, 500);
        }
    });
</script>
...
```

■ **Tip**   When you call the stop method, any callback associated with the current effect will not be executed. When you use the stop method to clear the queue, no callback associated with any of the effects in the queue will be executed.

To demonstrate the stop method, I have added two buttons to the document. When the Stop button is clicked, I call the stop method, passing in two true arguments. This has the effect of clearing the rest of the effect queue and snapping the element to the target values for the property that was being animated. Since callback functions are not invoked when the stop method is used, the loop of cycleEffects method calls is broken, and animation is brought to a halt. When the Start button is clicked, the cycleEffects method is called and the animation resumes.

■ **Tip**   Clicking the Start button when the animations are running doesn't confuse jQuery. It just adds the effects used by the cycleEffects method to the effects queue. The use of callbacks means that the size of the queue will jump around a little, but in terms of the animations, everything continues as normal.

The finish method has a similar effect to calling stop(true, true), but differs in the way that it handles the CSS properties that are being animated. When calling stop(true, true), the CSS properties that are being animated by the current effect jump to their final values, but when using the finish method, the CSS properties being animated by the current effect *and all of the queued effects* jump to their final values. You can see how I have applied the finish method in Listing 10-18.

Listing 10-18. Using the finish method

```
...
<script type="text/javascript">
    $(document).ready(function () {

        $("h1").css({ "position": "fixed", "z-index": "1", "min-width": "0" });
        $("form").remove();
```

```
$("<table border=1></table>")
    .appendTo("body").css({
        position: "fixed", "z-index": "2",
        "border-collapse": "collapse", top: 100
    });

var finishAnimations = false;

$("<button>Stop</button><button>Start</button>")
  .appendTo($("<div/>").appendTo("body")
    .css({
        position: "fixed", "z-index": "2",
        "border-collapse": "collapse", top: 100, left: 200
    })).click(function (e) {
        if ($(this).text() == "Stop") {
            finishAnimations = true;
            $("h1").finish();
        } else {
            finishAnimations = false;
            cycleEffects();
        }
    });

var timespan = "slow";

cycleEffects();
printQueue();

function cycleEffects() {
    $("h1")
    .animate({ left: "+=100" }, timespan)
    .animate({ left: "-=100" }, timespan)
    .animate({ height: 223, width: 700 }, timespan)
    .animate({ height: 30, width: 500 }, timespan)
    .slideUp(timespan)
    .slideDown(timespan, function () {
        if (!finishAnimations) {
            cycleEffects();
        }
    });
}

function printQueue() {
    var q = $("h1").queue();
    var qtable = $("table");
    qtable.html("<tr><th>Queue Length:</th><td>" + q.length + "</td></tr>");

    for (var i = 0; i < q.length; i++) {
        var baseString = "<tr><th>" + i + ":</th><td>";
        if (q[i] == "inprogress") {
            $("table").append(baseString + "In Progress</td></tr>");
```

```
                } else {
                    $("table").append(baseString + q[i] + "</td></tr>");
                }
            }
            setTimeout(printQueue, 500);
        }
    });
</script>
...
```

When using the `finish` method, care must be taken with effect loops, such as the one in Listing 10-18. In order to determine the final CSS values for all of the animated properties, the `finish` method needs to execute all of the effects—albeit without any time delays—and that means that any callback functions are executed as well.

In Listing 10-18, the last effect defined in the `cycleEffects` function sets up the next effect loop, as follows:

```
...
.slideDown(timespan, cycleEffects);
...
```

The `finish` method doesn't prevent new effects being added to the queue and it doesn't keep track of the state of the queue when it is called. This means that the `finish` method will call the `cycleEffects` method, which adds effects to the queue, which the `finish` method then executes, triggering the callback, which adds effects to the queue . . . and so on. The overall effect is to immediately exhaust the JavaScript call stack.

To avoid this, I have added a variable called `finishAnimations`, which I set in response to the `button` elements being clicked and I check before adding the next set of effects to the queue, as follows:

```
...
.slideDown(timespan, function () {
    if (!finishAnimations) {
        cycleEffects();
    }
});
...
```

Inserting a Delay into the Queue

You can use the `delay` method to introduce a pause between two effects in the queue. The argument to this method is the number of milliseconds that the delay should last for. Listing 10-19 shows the use of this method to introduce one-second delays into the effect queue.

Listing 10-19. Using the delay Method

```
...
function cycleEffects() {
    $("h1")
    .animate({ left: "+=100" }, timespan)
    .animate({ left: "-=100" }, timespan)
    .delay(1000)
    .animate({ height: 223, width: 700 }, timespan)
    .animate({ height: 30, width: 500 }, timespan)
    .delay(1000)
```

```
    .slideUp(timespan)
    .slideDown(timespan, function () {
        if (!finishAnimations) {
            cycleEffects();
        }
    });
}
...
```

Inserting Functions into the Queue

You can add your own functions into the queue using the queue method, and they will be executed just as the standard effect methods are. You can use this feature to start other animations, gracefully exit a chain of animations based on an external variable, or, well, do anything that you need. Listing 10-20 contains an example.

Listing 10-20. Inserting a Custom Function into the Queue

```
...
function cycleEffects() {
    $("h1")
    .animate({ left: "+=100" }, timespan)
    .animate({ left: "-=100" }, timespan)
    .queue(function () {
        $("body").fadeTo(timespan, 0).fadeTo(timespan, 1);
        $(this).dequeue();
    })
    .delay(1000)
    .animate({ height: 223, width: 700 }, timespan)
    .animate({ height: 30, width: 500 }, timespan)
    .delay(1000)
    .slideUp(timespan)
    .slideDown(timespan, function () {
        if (!finishAnimations) {
            cycleEffects();
        }
    });
}
...
```

The this variable is set to the jQuery object that the method was called on. This is useful because you must make sure to call the dequeue method at some point in your function in order to move the queue onto the next effect or function. In this example, I used the queue method to add a function that fades the body element to fully transparent and back.

■ **Tip** The effects I added in the custom function are added to the effect queues for the body element. Each element has its own queue, and you can manage them independently of one another. If you want to animate multiple properties on the same elements whose queue you are operating on, then you just use the animate method. Otherwise, your effects will just be added to the queue in sequence.

Alternatively, you can accept a single argument to the function, which is the next function in the queue. In this situation, you must invoke the function to move the queue to the next effect, as shown in Listing 10-21.

Listing 10-21. Using the Argument Passed to the Custom Function

```
...
function cycleEffects() {
    $("h1")
    .animate({ left: "+=100" }, timespan)
    .animate({ left: "-=100" }, timespan)
    .queue(function (nextFunction) {
        $("body").fadeTo(timespan, 0).fadeTo(timespan, 1);
        nextFunction();
    })
    .delay(1000)
    .animate({ height: 223, width: 700 }, timespan)
    .animate({ height: 30, width: 500 }, timespan)
    .delay(1000)
    .slideUp(timespan)
    .slideDown(timespan, function () {
        if (!finishAnimations) {
            cycleEffects();
        }
    });
}
...
```

■ **Caution**   The effect sequence will stall if you don't invoke the next function or call the dequeue method.

Enabling and Disabling Effect Animations

You can disable the animation of effects by setting the value of the $.fx.off property to true, as shown in Listing 10-22.

Listing 10-22. Disabling Animations

```
...
<script type="text/javascript">
    $(document).ready(function () {

        $.fx.off = true;

        $("h1").css({ "position": "fixed", "z-index": "1", "min-width": "0" });
        $("form").remove();

        // ...statements omitted for brevity...

    });
</script>
...
```

When animations are disabled, calls to effect methods cause the elements to snap to their target property values immediately. Time spans are ignored, and there are no intermediate animations. Looping sets of effects will quickly hit the call stack limit when animations are disabled. To avoid this, use the `setTimeout` method, as described earlier in this chapter.

Summary

In this chapter, I showed you how to use the jQuery effect features. The built-in effect methods are mostly for making elements visible and invisible in different ways, but you can go beyond this and animate any numeric CSS property. You can also dig into the effect queue and take more control over the sequence of effects that are applied to elements. In Chapter 11, I refactor the example document to show you how some of the basic jQuery features covered in this and earlier chapters can be combined.

■ ■ ■

Refactoring the Example: Part I

In the previous chapters, I showed you each functional area in isolation: how to deal with events, how to manipulate the DOM (Domain Object Model), and so on. The real power and flexibility of jQuery arise when you combine these features, and in this chapter, I am going to demonstrate the combination by refactoring the flower shop example document.

All of the changes that I make in this chapter are in the `script` element. I have not changed the underlying HTML of the example document. As with most jQuery features, there are many different routes to achieving the same result. The approaches I take in this chapter reflect the parts of jQuery that I like the most and the way that I tend to think about the DOM. You may have a different mental model and prefer different combinations of methods. It really doesn't matter, and there is no single correct way of using jQuery.

Reviewing the Example Document

I started this book with a simple example document, a basic flower shop page. In the chapters that followed, I used jQuery to select elements from the document, explore and rearrange its DOM, listen to events, and apply effects to its elements. Before I start to refactor the example, let's look back to where I started. Listing 11-1 shows the basic document.

Listing 11-1. The Basic Example Document

```
<!DOCTYPE html>
<html>
<head>
    <title>Example</title>
    <script src="jquery-2.0.2.js" type="text/javascript"></script>
    <link rel="stylesheet" type="text/css" href="styles.css"/>
    <script type="text/javascript">
        $(document).ready(function() {
            // jQuery statements will go here
        });
    </script>
</head>
<body>
    <h1>Jacqui's Flower Shop</h1>
    <form method="post">
        <div id="oblock">
            <div class="dtable">
                <div id="row1" class="drow">
                    <div class="dcell">
```

```
                        <img src="aster.png"/><label for="aster">Aster:</label>
                        <input name="aster" value="0" required />
                    </div>
                    <div class="dcell">
                        <img src="daffodil.png"/><label for="daffodil">Daffodil:</label>
                        <input name="daffodil" value="0" required />
                    </div>
                    <div class="dcell">
                        <img src="rose.png"/><label for="rose">Rose:</label>
                        <input name="rose" value="0" required />
                    </div>
                </div>
                <div id="row2"class="drow">
                    <div class="dcell">
                        <img src="peony.png"/><label for="peony">Peony:</label>
                        <input name="peony" value="0" required />
                    </div>
                    <div class="dcell">
                        <img src="primula.png"/><label for="primula">Primula:</label>
                        <input name="primula" value="0" required />
                    </div>
                    <div class="dcell">
                        <img src="snowdrop.png"/><label for="snowdrop">Snowdrop:</label>
                        <input name="snowdrop" value="0" required />
                    </div>
                </div>
            </div>
        </div>
        <div id="buttonDiv"><button type="submit">Place Order</button></div>
    </form>
</body>
</html>
```

I have highlighted the `script` element, because that's where you spend your time in this book. I have put in the ubiquitous jQuery handler for the ready event, but that's all. There are no other JavaScript statements. You can see how the unvarnished document appears in the browser in Figure 11-1.

Figure 11-1. *The basic example document*

Adding Additional Flower Products

The first change I make is to add some additional flowers to the shop. I want to do this to demonstrate how you can create elements in a loop. Listing 11-2 shows the `script` element with the additions.

Listing 11-2. Adding Products to the Page

```
...
<script type="text/javascript">
    $(document).ready(function() {
        var fNames = ["Carnation", "Lily", "Orchid"];
        var fRow = $("<div id=row3 class=drow/>").appendTo("div.dtable");
        var fTemplate = $("<div class=dcell><img/><label/><input/></div>");
        for (var i = 0; i < fNames.length; i++) {
            fTemplate.clone().appendTo(fRow).children()
                .filter("img").attr("src", fNames[i] + ".png").end()
                .filter("label").attr("for", fNames[i]).text(fNames[i]).end()
                .filter("input").attr({name: fNames[i], value: 0, required: "required"})
        }
    });
</script>
...
```

I have defined the three additional types of flower (`Carnation`, `Lily`, and `Orchid`) and created a new `div` element that is assigned to the `drow` class and that I append to the existing `div` element that acts as a table in the CSS (Cascading Style Sheet) table layout model.

```
...
var fNames = ["Carnation", "Lily", "Orchid"];
var fRow = $("<div id=row3 class=drow/>").appendTo("div.dtable");
...
```

I then define a skeletal set of elements; these describe the structure of elements that I want for each product but don't contain any of the attributes that distinguish one flower from another.

```
...
var fTemplate = $("<div class=dcell><img/><label/><input/></div>");
...
```

I use the skeletal elements as a simple template, cloning them for each of the flowers I want to add and using the name of the flower to add the attributes and values.

```
...
for (var i = 0; i < fNames.length; i++) {
    fTemplate.clone().appendTo(fRow).children()
        .filter("img").attr("src", fNames[i] + ".png").end()
        .filter("label").attr("for", fNames[i]).text(fNames[i]).end()
        .filter("input").attr({name: fNames[i], value: 0, required: "required"})
}
...
```

I use the filter and end methods to narrow and broaden the selection and the attr method to set the attribute values. I end up with a fully populated set of elements for each new flower, inserted into the row-level div element, which in turn is inserted into the table-level element. You can see the effect in Figure 11-2.

Figure 11-2. *Adding new flowers to the page*

One nice jQuery feature evident in this example is the way you can select and navigate around elements that are not attached to the main document. The template elements are not part of the document when I clone them, but I can still use the children and filter methods to narrow down the selection.

Adding the Carousel Buttons

I am going to create a simple carousel that will let the user page through sets of flowers. To begin with, I need left and right buttons for the pagination. Listing 11-3 shows how I added them to the document.

Listing 11-3. Adding the Carousel Buttons

```
...
<script type="text/javascript">
    $(document).ready(function() {

        var fNames = ["Carnation", "Lily", "Orchid"];
        var fRow = $("<div id=row3 class=drow/>").appendTo("div.dtable");
        var fTemplate = $("<div class=dcell><img/><label/><input/></div>");
        for (var i = 0; i < fNames.length; i++) {
            fTemplate.clone().appendTo(fRow).children()
                .filter("img").attr("src", fNames[i] + ".png").end()
                .filter("label").attr("for", fNames[i]).text(fNames[i]).end()
                .filter("input").attr({name: fNames[i], value: 0, required: "required"})
        }

        $("<a id=left></a><a id=right></a>").prependTo("form")
            .css({
                "background-image": "url(leftarrows.png)",
                "float": "left",
                "margin-top": "15px",
                display: "block", width: 50, height: 50
            }).click(handleArrowPress).hover(handleArrowMouse)

        $("#right").css("background-image", "url(rightarrows.png)").appendTo("form");

        $("#oblock").css({float: "left", display: "inline", border: "thin black solid"});
        $("form").css({"margin-left": "auto", "margin-right": "auto", width: 885});

        function handleArrowMouse(e) {
        }

        function handleArrowPress(e) {
        }
    });
</script>
...
```

I define a pair of a elements, prepend them to the form element, and use the css method to apply values for a number of different properties.

```
...
$("<a id=left></a><a id=right></a>").prependTo("form")
    .css({
        "background-image": "url(leftarrows.png)",
        "float": "left",
        "margin-top": "15px",
        display: "block", width: 50, height: 50
}).click(handleArrowPress).hover(handleArrowMouse)
...
```

The key property is background-image, which I set to leftarrows.png. You can see this image in Figure 11-3.

Figure 11-3. *The leftarrows.png image*

This image contains three different arrows in a combined image. Each individual arrow is 50 pixels wide, and by setting the width and height properties to 50, I make sure that only one of the individual arrows is showing at any time. I use the click and hover methods to define handler functions for the click, mouseenter, and mouseexit events.

```
...
$("<a id=left></a><a id=right></a>").prependTo("form")
    .css({
        "background-image": "url(leftarrows.png)",
        "float": "left",
        "margin-top": "15px",
        display: "block", width: 50, height: 50
}).click(handleArrowPress).hover(handleArrowMouse)
...
```

The handleArrowPress and handleArrowMouse functions are empty but I'll populate them in a moment. At this point, I have two a elements, both displaying left-facing arrows and both next to one another in the form element. I created and formatted the a elements together because most of the configuration is common, but now it is time to move and tailor the right button, which I do as follows:

```
...
$("#right").css("background-image", "url(rightarrows.png)").appendTo("form");
...
```

I use the append method to move the element to the end of the form element and use the css method to change the background-image property to use the rightarrows.png. You can see this image in Figure 11-4.

Figure 11-4. *The rightarrows.png image*

Using combined images like this is a common technique, because it avoids the browser having to incur the overhead of making three different requests to the server to get three closely related images. You'll see how you can use this kind of image when I fill in the handleArrowMouse function shortly. You can see how the page looks in Figure 11-5.

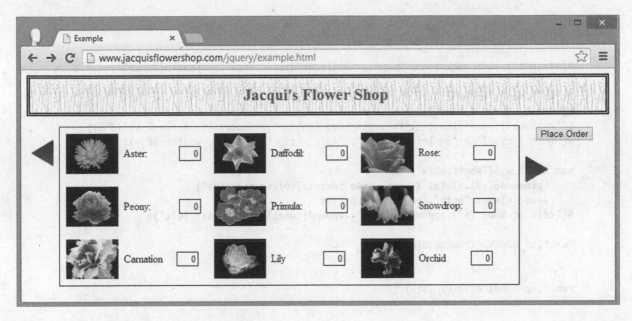

Figure 11-5. *The intermediate state for the example document*

Dealing with the Submit Button

As you can see from Figure 11-5, my example is in an intermediate state. New features have appeared, but I have not properly dealt with some of the existing elements. The most significant of these is the Place Order button that submits the form. Listing 11-4 shows the additions to the script to deal with this element (and add a new feature).

Listing 11-4. Dealing with the Submit Button

```
...
<script type="text/javascript">
    $(document).ready(function() {

        var fNames = ["Carnation", "Lily", "Orchid"];
        var fRow = $("<div id=row3 class=drow/>").appendTo("div.dtable");
        var fTemplate = $("<div class=dcell><img/><label/><input/></div>");
        for (var i = 0; i < fNames.length; i++) {
            fTemplate.clone().appendTo(fRow).children()
                .filter("img").attr("src", fNames[i] + ".png").end()
                .filter("label").attr("for", fNames[i]).text(fNames[i]).end()
                .filter("input").attr({name: fNames[i], value: 0, required: "required"})
        }
```

```
        $("<a id=left></a><a id=right></a>").prependTo("form")
            .css({
                "background-image": "url(leftarrows.png)",
                "float": "left",
                "margin-top": "15px",
                display: "block", width: 50, height: 50
            }).click(handleArrowPress).hover(handleArrowMouse)

        $("#right").css("background-image", "url(rightarrows.png)").appendTo("form");

        $("h1").css({"min-width": "0", width: "95%",});
        $("#row2, #row3").hide();
        $("#oblock").css({float: "left", display: "inline", border: "thin black solid"});
        $("form").css({"margin-left": "auto", "margin-right": "auto", width: 885});

        var total = $("#buttonDiv")
            .prepend("<div>Total Items: <span id=total>0</span></div>")
            .css({clear: "both", padding: "5px"});
        $("<div id=bbox />").appendTo("body").append(total).css("clear: left");

        function handleArrowMouse(e) {
        }

        function handleArrowPress(e) {

        }
    });
</script>
...
```

To accommodate the changes in the layout caused by the carousel buttons, I have moved the div that contains the button element (it has an id of buttonDiv) to be inside a new div element, which, in turn, I have appended to the body element. This moves the button to a position where it returns to the bottom of the page. I have also added a div and a span element. These will be used to display the total number of products that the user has selected.

```
...
var total = $("#buttonDiv")
    .prepend("<div>Total Items: <span id=total>0</span></div>")
    .css({clear: "both", padding: "5px"});
$("<div id=bbox />").appendTo("body").append(total).css("clear: left");
...
```

The next change for this section is to hide two of the rows of products. This is so that you can reveal them to the user when they click the carousel buttons.

```
...
$("#row2, #row3").hide();
...
```

I have also tweaked the style of the h1 element to match the revised layout style.

```
...
$("h1").css({"min-width": "0", width: "95%",});
...
```

You can see the effect of these changes in Figure 11-6.

Figure 11-6. *Dealing with the submit button and tidying the CSS*

Implementing the Carousel Event Handler Functions

The next step is to implement the functions that handle events for the carousel buttons. I am going to deal with the mouseenter and mouseexit events, which are handled by the handleArrowMouse function. Listing 11-5 shows the implementation of this function.

Listing 11-5. Handling the Arrow Button Mouse Events

```
...
function handleArrowMouse(e) {
    var propValue = e.type == "mouseenter" ? "-50px 0px" : "0px 0px";
    $(this).css("background-position", propValue);
}
...
```

The trick to dealing with combined images is to use the background-position property to shift the image so that only the part I want is visible. Although there are three images in my sets of arrows, I am going to use only two of them. The darkest image will be shown normally, and the middle image will be shown when the mouse is hovering over the element. You could use the remaining arrow to represent a button being clicked or being disabled, but I want to keep things simple. You can see the two states that the images represent in Figure 11-7.

Figure 11-7. *The two states of the arrow buttons*

The `handleArrowPress` function is responsible for creating the carousel effect, allowing the user to page through the rows of flowers. Listing 11-6 shows the implementation of this function.

Listing 11-6. Implementing the handleArrowPress Function

```
...
function handleArrowPress(e) {
    var elemSequence = ["row1", "row2", "row3"];
    var visibleRow = $("div.drow:visible");
    var visibleRowIndex = jQuery.inArray(visibleRow.attr("id"), elemSequence);

    var targetRowIndex;
    if (e.target.id == "left") {
        targetRowIndex = visibleRowIndex - 1;
        if (targetRowIndex < 0) {targetRowIndex = elemSequence.length -1};
    } else {
        targetRowIndex = (visibleRowIndex + 1) % elemSequence.length;
    }

    visibleRow.fadeOut("fast", function() {
        $("#" + elemSequence[targetRowIndex]).fadeIn("fast")});
}
...
```

The first three statements in this function set up the basic data you need.

```
...
var elemSequence = ["row1", "row2", "row3"];
var visibleRow = $("div.drow:visible");
var visibleRowIndex = jQuery.inArray(visibleRow.attr("id"), elemSequence);
...
```

The first statement defines the set of id attribute values for the row elements. The second statement uses jQuery to get the visible row, which I then use to determine the index of the visible row in the array of row id values. (I do this using the inArray utility method, which I explain in Chapter 34.) So, I know which row is visible and where in the sequence of rows I am. My next step is to figure out the index of the row that will be displayed next.

```
...
var targetRowIndex;
if (e.target.id == "left") {
    targetRowIndex = visibleRowIndex - 1;
    if (targetRowIndex < 0) {targetRowIndex = elemSequence.length -1};
} else {
    targetRowIndex = (visibleRowIndex + 1) % elemSequence.length;
}
...
```

In almost any other programming language, I could use the modulo operator to figure out the index of the next row to display, but the JavaScript implementation of modulo math doesn't support negative values properly. So, if the user clicks the left button, I check for array bounds manually; I do it using the % operator if the user clicks the right button. Once I have figured out the currently visible element and the element to display next, I use jQuery effects to animate a transition from one to the other.

```
...
visibleRow.fadeOut("fast", function() {
    $("#" + elemSequence[targetRowIndex]).fadeIn("fast")});
...
```

I have used the fadeOut and fadeIn methods because they work nicely with my CSS table-style layout. I use a callback in the first effect to trigger the second and perform both effects using the fast time span. There is no change in the static layout of the page, but the arrow buttons now take the user from one row of flowers to the next, as shown in Figure 11-8.

Figure 11-8. *Providing a carousel of product rows*

Totaling the Product Selection

The last change is to wire up the item total so that the total number of flowers selected in individual input fields is shown under the product carousel. Listing 11-7 shows the changes to the script.

Listing 11-7. Wiring Up the Product Total

```
...
<script type="text/javascript">
    $(document).ready(function() {

        var fNames = ["Carnation", "Lily", "Orchid"];
        var fRow = $("<div id=row3 class=drow/>").appendTo("div.dtable");
        var fTemplate = $("<div class=dcell><img/><label/><input/></div>");
        for (var i = 0; i < fNames.length; i++) {
            fTemplate.clone().appendTo(fRow).children()
                .filter("img").attr("src", fNames[i] + ".png").end()
                .filter("label").attr("for", fNames[i]).text(fNames[i]).end()
                .filter("input").attr({name: fNames[i], value: 0, required: "required"})
        }

        $("<a id=left></a><a id=right></a>").prependTo("form")
            .css({
                "background-image": "url(leftarrows.png)",
                "float": "left",
                "margin-top": "15px",
                display: "block", width: 50, height: 50
            }).click(handleArrowPress).hover(handleArrowMouse)

        $("#right").css("background-image", "url(rightarrows.png)").appendTo("form");

        $("h1").css({"min-width": "0", width: "95%",});
        $("#row2, #row3").hide();
        $("#oblock").css({float: "left", display: "inline", border: "thin black solid"});
        $("form").css({"margin-left": "auto", "margin-right": "auto", width: 885});

        var total = $("#buttonDiv")
            .prepend("<div>Total Items: <span id=total>0</span></div>")
            .css({clear: "both", padding: "5px"});
        $("<div id=bbox />").appendTo("body").append(total).css("clear: left");

        $("input").change(function(e) {
            var total = 0;
            $("input").each(function(index, elem) {
                total += Number($(elem).val());
            });
            $("#total").text(total);
        });
```

```
            function handleArrowMouse(e) {
                var propValue = e.type == "mouseenter" ? "-50px 0px" : "0px 0px";
                $(this).css("background-position", propValue);
            }

            function handleArrowPress(e) {
                var elemSequence = ["row1", "row2", "row3"];

                var visibleRow = $("div.drow:visible");
                var visibleRowIndex = jQuery.inArray(visibleRow.attr("id"), elemSequence);

                var targetRowIndex;

                if (e.target.id == "left") {
                    targetRowIndex = visibleRowIndex - 1;
                    if (targetRowIndex < 0) {targetRowIndex = elemSequence.length -1};
                } else {
                    targetRowIndex = (visibleRowIndex + 1) % elemSequence.length;
                }
                visibleRow.fadeOut("fast", function() {
                    $("#" + elemSequence[targetRowIndex]).fadeIn("fast")});
            }

        });
    </script>
    ...
```

In this addition, I select the input element in the document and register a handler function that gets the value from each, sums it, and sets it as the content for the span element I added earlier. You can see the effect in Figure 11-9.

Figure 11-9. Displaying the product selection total

The total shows the sum of all of the input elements and not just the ones that are currently visible (although it would be a simple matter to use the other approach).

Disabling JavaScript

I have made some sweeping changes to the example document, but all of them were made with jQuery. This means that I have effectively created two tiers of document, one for JavaScript-enabled browsers and one for non-JavaScript browsers, Figure 11-10 shows what happens when you disable JavaScript and view the example document.

Figure 11-10. *Disabling JavaScript and viewing the example document*

I am back where I started. With a little planning and forethought, I can offer non-JavaScript clients a set of functionality that still lets them interact with your page or application. This is generally a good idea; there are a lot of large corporations that manage IT (information technology) centrally and disable JavaScript as a security precaution. (Well, sort of. When working for such organizations for many years, I came to believe that these policies didn't actually stop staff from using JavaScript; they simply created incentives to find loopholes and workarounds.)

Summary

In this chapter, I showed you how to combine the techniques from previous chapters to refactor the example document. I added new content programmatically, created a simple carousel of products, and created a total that displays the overall number of selected items. Along the way, I tweaked the DOM and CSS to accommodate these changes, all in a way that lets non-JavaScript browsers fall back to a document that remains useful.

In the next part of this book, I'll continue to build on this example, bringing in ever more jQuery features to flesh out the functionality. For the most part, I'll apply these to the original example document so as to focus on each feature in turn, but in Chapter 16, I'll refactor the example again to bring in more features.

CHAPTER 12

■ ■ ■

Using Data Templates

In the previous edition of this book, I introduced data templates using the *jQuery Templates* plug-in. This history of this plug-in was rather odd. Microsoft and the jQuery team announced that three plug-ins developed by Microsoft had been accepted as "official" plug-ins, a status that had not been accorded to any other plug-in. A while later, the jQuery team announced that the plug-ins were deprecated, that the official status was removed, and that there were plans to replace them with other functionality. A replacement for the template plug-in would be created as part of jQuery UI (which I describe in Part IV of this book).

That was a while ago and the new official jQuery template engine that was announced, which was named *jsViews*, is still not finished. There is a beta version available, but it has rough edges and remains volatile. I am not a fan, but you can learn more and get the latest beta version of the library at https://github.com/BorisMoore/jsviews.

In the meantime, the deprecated jQuery Templates package I used in the last edition has not aged well. I stopped using it a while ago in my own projects and settled on an alternative called Handlebars, which is available from http://handlebarsjs.com. It doesn't come with any jQuery integration – in fact, it isn't a jQuery plug-in at all – but it is easy to write a small amount of code to support templates through the jQuery syntax, and I show you how this is done.

Handlebars – as did the jQuery Templates plug-in before it – supports *mustache templates*, which are expressed as HTML containing special *mustache directives*. I explain what these are, but the use of the term *mustache* comes from the fact that they are denoted using the brace characters ({ and }) which look a little like sideways mustaches. Table 12-1 provides the summary for this chapter.

Table 12-1. Chapter Summary

Problem	Solution	Listing
Generate elements using a template.	Install the Handlebars library, create a jQuery plug-in, and use the template method.	1–6
Assign the elements generated from a template to different parents.	Either split the source data and apply the template twice, or use the slice filter and end methods to divide up the generated elements.	7–10
Change the output of the template if a data property is defined and isn't null.	Use the built-in #if or #unless template helpers.	11, 12
Enumerate the contents of an array or the properties of an object.	Use the #each template helper.	13, 14
Refer to another part of the data object in a template.	Use the #with template helper, or use the ../ path.	15–17

(continued)

Table 12-1. (*continued*)

Problem	Solution	Listing
Create a custom template helper.	Use the Handlebars.registerHelper method to register the name of the helper and a helper function that returns template content.	18–22
Receive optional arguments in a template helper function.	Use the options.hash property.	23, 24
Define special properties that can be used within the block of a custom template helper.	Use the options.data property.	25, 26

Understanding the Problem That Templates Solve

Data templates solve a specific problem: they allow you to programmatically generate elements from the properties and values of JavaScript objects. This is something you can do in other ways, and, in fact, I did something similar in Chapter 11 when I created some elements to represent additional flowers in the example document. Listing 12-1 shows the relevant statements from that chapter.

Listing 12-1. Creating Elements Programmatically

```
...
<script type="text/javascript">
    $(document).ready(function() {
        var fNames = ["Carnation", "Lily", "Orchid"];
        var fRow = $("<div id=row3 class=drow/>").appendTo("div.dtable");
        var fTemplate = $("<div class=dcell><img/><label/><input/></div>");
        for (var i = 0; i < fNames.length; i++) {
            fTemplate.clone().appendTo(fRow).children()
                .filter("img").attr("src", fNames[i] + ".png").end()
                .filter("label").attr("for", fNames[i]).text(fNames[i]).end()
                .filter("input").attr({name: fNames[i], value: 0, required: "required"})
        }
    });
</script>
...
```

The statements in the listing are hard to read, and the difficulty increases sharply for more complex elements. Handily, as I'll explain, data templates put the emphasis back on HTML and minimize the amount of code needed to generate elements from data.

Taking a broader view, the need to integrate data into the document is a common issue to resolve. In my projects, it arises through two situations. The first is because I am working with some preexisting system that contains the data that drives my web application. I *could* obtain the data and integrate it into the document at the server – nd there are some great technologies available to do this – but it means that my server farm spends a lot of time doing work that I could get the browser to do for me. If you have ever built and operated a high-volume web application, you know that the costs are substantial and that any opportunity to reduce the amount of processing required is considered seriously.

The second reason I need to integrate data into a document is that my web application is sourcing the data via Ajax in response to a user action. I will explain the jQuery support for Ajax fully in Chapters 14 and 15, but the short version is that you can obtain and display data from a server without reloading the entire page in the browser. It is a powerful technique that is widely used, and the data templates work nicely with it.

Setting Up the Template Library

Before you can use templates, you must download the template library and link to it in your document. You can download the library from `http://handlebarsjs.com`, and I saved the JavaScript code to a file called `handlebars.js`, alongside the jQuery JavaScript file.

The handlebars library doesn't have any integration with jQuery, but it is a simple matter to create a jQuery plug-in that allows me to use jQuery syntax to generate templates. I created a file called `handlebars-jquery.js` and used it to define the code shown in Listing 12-2.

Listing 12-2. Adapting handlerbars.js to Use jQuery Syntax in the handlebars-jquery.js File

```
(function ($) {
    var compiled = {};
    $.fn.template = function (data) {
        var template = $.trim($(this).first().html());
        if (compiled[template] == undefined) {
            compiled[template] = Handlebars.compile(template);
        }
        return $(compiled[template](data));
    };
})(jQuery);
```

CREATING CUSTOM JQUERY PLUG-INS

As Listing 12-2 demonstrates, it is simple to create plug-ins for jQuery, especially if you are just creating a wrapper around an existing library. I don't describe how custom plug-ins work in this book because it is something that few developers need to do, but you can get full details at `http://learn.jquery.com/plugins`.

This code defines a method called `template` that can be called on jQuery objects to apply a template to a data object using handlebars. The result is a jQuery object containing the HTML elements generated from the template. In order to generate templates, I need to add `script` elements for the `handlebars.js` and `handlebars-jquery.js` files to the example document, as shown in Listing 12-3.

Listing 12-3. Adding the Library to the Example Document

```
<!DOCTYPE html>
<html>
<head>
    <title>Example</title>
    <script src="jquery-2.0.2.js" type="text/javascript"></script>
    <script src="handlebars.js" type="text/javascript"></script>
    <script src="handlebars-jquery.js" type="text/javascript"></script>
    <link rel="stylesheet" type="text/css" href="styles.css"/>
    <script type="text/javascript">
        $(document).ready(function () {
```

```
            // ...example code will go here...

        });
    </script>
</head>
<body>
    <h1>Jacqui's Flower Shop</h1>
    <form method="post">
        <div id="oblock">
            <div class="dtable">
                <div id="row1" class="drow"></div>
                <div id="row2"class="drow"></div>
            </div>
        </div>
        <div id="buttonDiv"><button type="submit">Place Order</button></div>
    </form>
</body>
</html>
```

I will use this listing as the example document for this chapter. Aside from the addition of the template library and my simple plug-in, you will notice that I have removed the elements that describe individual flowers – I have done this so that I can explore different techniques for adding them back in using templates. You can see how this initial HTML document appears in the browser in Figure 12-1.

Figure 12-1. *The starting example document*

A First Data Templates Example

The best way to start learning about data templates is to jump right in. Listing 12-4 demonstrates the basic template features. I have included the full HTML document in this listing because templates are expressed using a `script` element, but I'll just show the changes needed in subsequent listings.

Listing 12-4. A First Data Templates Example

```
<!DOCTYPE html>
<html>
<head>
    <title>Example</title>
    <script src="jquery-2.0.2.js" type="text/javascript"></script>
```

```html
<script src="handlebars.js" type="text/javascript"></script>
<script src="handlebars-jquery.js" type="text/javascript"></script>
<link rel="stylesheet" type="text/css" href="styles.css"/>
<script id="flowerTmpl" type="text/x-handlebars-template">
    {{#each flowers}}
        <div class="dcell">
        <img src="{{product}}.png"/>
        <label for="{{product}}">{{name}}:</label>
        <input name="{{product}}" data-price="{{price}}" data-stock="{{stock}}"
            value="0" required />
    </div>
    {{/each}}
</script>
<script type="text/javascript">
    $(document).ready(function () {
        var data = {
            flowers: [
            { name: "Aster", product: "aster", stock: "10", price: 2.99 },
            { name: "Daffodil", product: "daffodil", stock: "12", price: 1.99 },
            { name: "Rose", product: "rose", stock: "2", price: 4.99 },
            { name: "Peony", product: "peony", stock: "0", price: 1.50 },
            { name: "Primula", product: "primula", stock: "1", price: 3.12 },
            { name: "Snowdrop", product: "snowdrop", stock: "15", price: 0.99 }]
        };
        var template = $("#flowerTmpl").template(data).appendTo("#row1");
    });
</script>
</head>
<body>
    <h1>Jacqui's Flower Shop</h1>
    <form method="post">
        <div id="oblock">
            <div class="dtable">
                <div id="row1" class="drow"></div>
                <div id="row2"class="drow"></div>
            </div>
        </div>
        <div id="buttonDiv"><button type="submit">Place Order</button></div>
    </form>
</body>
</html>
```

In the sections that follow, I'll break down the example and explain each part.

■ **Tip** When the data is part of the document, it is known as *inline data*. The alternative is *remote data*, which is where you get the data from a server separately from the document. I'll demonstrate remote data later in the chapter, but it touches upon the jQuery support for Ajax, which is the topic of Chapters 14 and 15.

Defining the Data

The starting point for the example is the data, which in this case is an object with a single property that is set to an array of objects. Each object describes a single flower product, and Listing 12-5 shows the relevant statements from the example HTML document.

Listing 12-5. Defining the Flower Data

```
...
var data = {
    flowers: [
        { name: "Aster", product: "aster", stock: "10", price: 2.99 },
        { name: "Daffodil", product: "daffodil", stock: "12", price: 1.99 },
        { name: "Rose", product: "rose", stock: "2", price: 4.99 },
        { name: "Peony", product: "peony", stock: "0", price: 1.50 },
        { name: "Primula", product: "primula", stock: "1", price: 3.12 },
        { name: "Snowdrop", product: "snowdrop", stock: "15", price: 0.99 }]
};
...
```

Handlebars templates work on objects and properties, which is why I have to have an object wrapper around my array of flower objects. For this example, the array contains six objects, each of which has a set of properties that describe a flower shop product: the display name, the product name, the stock level, and the price.

Defining the Template

As you might imagine, at the heart of the data template library is the *data template*. This is a set of HTML elements containing placeholders that correspond to aspects of the data objects. Listing 12-6 shows the template for this example.

Listing 12-6. Defining the Data Template

```
...
<script id="flowerTmpl" type="text/x-handlebars-template">
    {{#flowers}}
    <div class="dcell">
        <img src="{{product}}.png"/>
        <label for="{{product}}">{{name}}:</label>
        <input name="{{product}}" data-price="{{price}}" data-stock="{{stock}}"
            value="0" required />
    </div>
    {{/flowers}}
</script>
...
```

The first point to note about the template is that it is contained within a script element with a type attribute of text/x-handlebars-template. This is to stop the browser from interpreting the contents of the template. The second point of note is that I have assigned a name to my script element using the id attribute: in this example, the template is called flowerTmpl. The name is important because I will need it to apply the template to the data.

The contents of the template will be applied to the objects in the data array in order to produce a set of HTML elements for each and every object. You can see that the structure of the template corresponds to the set of elements that I have used for the flower products in previous chapters.

The key difference, of course, is the parts I have emphasized in the listings. These are *double mustache directives* (so called because the brace characters used to denote them look like mustaches – hence the term *mustache template*). There are two kinds of directives in this example (and I'll introduce further types later in the chapter).

The first kind of directive is a *section*, which defines a region of the template that will be generated for each value of the property with the same name in the data object. Section directives start with a # character (`{{#flowers}}`, in this case) and end with a / character (`{{/flowers}}`). The section directive I used will generate the section of the template it contains for each of the objects assigned to the `flowers` property.

The other type of directive is a *variable*, which will be replaced with the corresponding property value from the data object. So, for example, when the template library encounters the `{{product}}` variable it replaces it with the value of the `product` property from the object that is being processed, meaning that the part of the template like this:

```
...
<img src="{{product}}.png"/>
...
```

is transformed into this:

```
...
<img src="aster.png"/>
...
```

Applying the Template

I apply the template to the data using the `template` method that I defined in my jQuery plug-in in Listing 12-2. Here is the call to the `template` method from the example HTML document:

```
...
var template = $("#flowerTmpl").template(data).appendTo("#row1");
...
```

I use the jQuery $ function to select the `script` element that contains the template and then call the `template` method on the resulting jQuery object, passing in the data that I want to process.

The `template` method returns a standard jQuery object that contains the elements produced from the template. In this case, I end up with a set of `div` elements, each of which contains an `img`, `label`, and `input` element that has been tailored for one of the objects in my data array. I use the `appendTo` method to insert the complete set as children to the `row1` element. You can see the result in Figure 12-2.

Figure 12-2. *Using data templates*

Tweaking the Result

I don't get exactly the result I wanted – all of the flowers are in a single row, rather than split over two rows as in previous chapters. But, since I am dealing with a jQuery object, I can slice and dice the elements using the techniques I described in Part 2. Listing 12-7 shows how you can do this by operating on the jQuery object that the template method returns.

Listing 12-7. Processing the Results from a Template

```
...
<script type="text/javascript">
    $(document).ready(function () {
        var data = {
            flowers: [
                { name: "Aster", product: "aster", stock: "10", price: 2.99 },
                { name: "Daffodil", product: "daffodil", stock: "12", price: 1.99 },
                { name: "Rose", product: "rose", stock: "2", price: 4.99 },
                { name: "Peony", product: "peony", stock: "0", price: 1.50 },
                { name: "Primula", product: "primula", stock: "1", price: 3.12 },
                { name: "Snowdrop", product: "snowdrop", stock: "15", price: 0.99 }]
        };

        $("#flowerTmpl").template(data)
            .slice(0, 3).appendTo("#row1").end().end().slice(3).appendTo("#row2")
    });
</script>
...
```

In this example, I use the slice and end methods to narrow and broaden the selection and the appendTo method to add subsets of the elements generated from the template to different rows.

Notice that I have to call the end method twice in succession to unwind the narrowing caused by the slide and appendTo methods. You can see the effect in Figure 12-3 – I am closer, but I still didn't get the result I had aimed for.

Figure 12-3. *Trying to adjust the layout of the HTML generated from the data*

The problem is that Handlebars adds text nodes to the HTML it generates at the point where the contents of my template are split across multiple lines – and since my use of the slice method applies to all of the elements that the template generates (including text nodes), I am splitting the content in the wrong place.

There are several ways of fixing this. The first is to adjust the template so that all of the content is on one line – but I don't like this approach, preferring to make templates as readable as possible.

Another approach is to adjust the indexes pass to the slice method to take the text nodes into account – but I don't like this either, because not all text editors represent new lines in a way that causes the text nodes to be created, and that means that editing the HTML file with a different editor can change the behavior of the JavaScript code, which is far from ideal.

My preferred approach is to use jQuery to remove the text nodes from the HTML generated by the template before adding it into the DOM. Unfortunately, jQuery doesn't include a useful method for this task and so the best approach is to use the filter method with the * selector, which matches all HTML tag types but excludes text nodes. You can see the addition of the filter method to my jQuery in Listing 12-8.

Listing 12-8. *Using the filter Method to Remove Text Nodes*

```
...
$("#flowerTmpl").template(data).filter("*")
    .slice(0, 3).appendTo("#row1").end().end().slice(3).appendTo("#row2")
...
```

You can see the result in Figure 12-4: the flowers are split properly across the two rows.

Figure 12-4. *Using the filter method to remove text nodes*

I am still not happy with the way that I handle the HTML generated by the template. I generally like using the end method to create single-statement operations, but I find the end().end() sequence dislikable. Instead, I would usually break down the steps into separate operations, as shown in Listing 12-9, which produces the same result as Listing 12-8, but is easier to read.

Listing 12-9. Splitting the Elements Using Multiple Statements

```
...
var templateHtml = $("#flowerTmpl").template(data).filter("*");
templateHtml.slice(0, 3).appendTo("#row1");
templateHtml.slice(3).appendTo("#row2");
...
```

Tweaking the Input

A different approach is to adjust the data that you pass to the template method. Listing 12-10 shows how this can be done.

Listing 12-10. Using the Data to Adjust the Output from the Template

```
...
<script type="text/javascript">
    $(document).ready(function () {
        var data = {
            flowers: [
            { name: "Aster", product: "aster", stock: "10", price: 2.99 },
            { name: "Daffodil", product: "daffodil", stock: "12", price: 1.99 },
            { name: "Rose", product: "rose", stock: "2", price: 4.99 },
```

```
            { name: "Peony", product: "peony", stock: "0", price: 1.50 },
            { name: "Primula", product: "primula", stock: "1", price: 3.12 },
            { name: "Snowdrop", product: "snowdrop", stock: "15", price: 0.99 }]
    };

    var tElem = $("#flowerTmpl");
    tElem.template({ flowers: data.flowers.slice(0, 3) }).appendTo("#row1");
    tElem.template({ flowers: data.flowers.slice(3) }).appendTo("#row2");
});
</script>
...
```

In this script, I solve the problem of allocating flowers to rows by using the template twice – once for each row. I used the split method so that I could feed a range of data objects to the template each time. The technique is different, but the result is the same, as shown in Figure 12-4. Notice that I have to take care to preserve the shape of the object that I pass to the template method so that it matches my section declarations – I must ensure that the object has a property called flowers that is set to the array of data objects that I want to process.

Using Template Logic

One of the ways you can differentiate between the huge varieties of JavaScript template engines is to look at how the output of the templates can be varied based on different data values.

At one end of the spectrum is the *logic-less template*, which contains no logic at all and varying the output from the template means careful preparation of the data before using the template engine. The other extreme is the *full-logic template*, which is like having a simple programming language dedicated to defining and executing templates, with built-in support for conditional statements, loops, array processing, and managing collections of data.

Opinions differ on just how much logic should be in a template and the whole topic is contentious. I like to be somewhere in the middle of the spectrum – I like to be able to use logic in my templates, but I want to keep it simple and not have add another language to my HTML documents. One of the reasons I chose the Handlebars library for this chapter is that it allows you to use as little or as much logic in a template as you like – and, as you'll see later in the chapter, makes it easy to define custom logic to solve specific problems. The Handlebars library contains some built-in *helpers*, described in Table 12-2, which are simple logic operators that can be used to vary the output from the template based on data values.

Table 12-2. The Built-in Handlebars Helpers

Helper	Description
#if	An if/then/else conditional, which evaluates to true if the specified property exists and is not null.
#unless	The inverse of the #if helper; evaluates to true if the specified property does *not* exist or is null.
#each	Iterates over an array of objects or the properties of an object.
#with	Sets the context for a section of the template.

Creating Conditional Content

To demonstrate how logic is used in Handlebars templates, I am going to set the value attribute of the input element in the template based on the value of the stock property of each object in the flowers array of the data object. My goal is to set the value to 1 when the corresponding stock property is greater than zero. You can see how I have done this by applying the #if helper in Listing 12-11.

Listing 12-11. Using Template Logic to Alter the Output from a Template

```
...
<script id="flowerTmpl" type="text/x-handlebars-template">
    {{#flowers}}
    <div class="dcell">
        <img src="{{product}}.png"/>
        <label for="{{product}}">{{name}}:</label>
        <input name="{{product}}" data-price="{{price}}" data-stock="{{stock}}"
            value="{{#if stock}}1{{else}}0{{/if}}" required />
    </div>
    {{/flowers}}
</script>
<script type="text/javascript">
    $(document).ready(function () {
        var data = {
            flowers: [
            { name: "Aster", product: "aster", stock: "10", price: 2.99 },
            { name: "Daffodil", product: "daffodil", stock: "12", price: 1.99 },
            { name: "Rose", product: "rose", stock: "2", price: 4.99 },
            { name: "Peony", product: "peony", stock: "0", price: 1.50 },
            { name: "Primula", product: "primula", stock: "1", price: 3.12 },
            { name: "Snowdrop", product: "snowdrop", stock: "15", price: 0.99 }]
        };
        for (var i = 0; i < data.flowers.length; i++) {
            if (data.flowers[i].stock == 0) {
                data.flowers[i].stock = null;
            }
        }
        var tElem = $("#flowerTmpl");
        tElem.template({ flowers: data.flowers.slice(0, 3) }).appendTo("#row1");
        tElem.template({ flowers: data.flowers.slice(3) }).appendTo("#row2");
    });
</script>
...
```

Each part of the helper is expressed using double mustaches: the first consists of #if followed by the property that I want to inspect, which is stock in this case. This will evaluate as true if the current object being processed by the #flowers section directive defines a stock property *and* that property is not null. If this is the case, the template engine will insert the value that follows the first part of the conditional into the HTML, which is 1 in this example.

The optional else section works just like it does in JavaScript and allows me to provide an alternative value that will be used if the current object doesn't have a stock property *or* if there is a stock property and it is null. In this case, the template engine will insert 0 into the HTML generated from the template. The final section is /if, which denotes the end of the conditional block.

The logic that is behind the #if helper is basic and returning true based on whether the property exists and is defined forces me to process my data before passing it to the template method. I use a JavaScript for loop to enumerate the flower objects and set any stock property that has a value of 0 to null. The result is that all of the input elements generated from the template will have a value of 1 except the one for the Peony, as shown in Figure 12-5.

Figure 12-5. *Using logic in a template to vary the generated HTML*

■ **Tip**   I am not fond of having to process the data to suit the limitations of the template engine, and I'll show you how to create custom logic that doesn't require data processing later in the chapter.

The #unless helper works in the same way as the #if helper, but will evaluate as true if the property it is applied to is doesn't exist or is null. In Listing 12-12, you can see how I have applied the #if and #unless helpers alongside each other without their optional else directives to set the value attribute of the input element in the template.

Listing 12-12. Applying the #if and #unless Helpers in the Template

```
...
<script id="flowerTmpl" type="text/x-handlebars-template">
    {{#flowers}}
    <div class="dcell">
        <img src="{{product}}.png"/>
        <label for="{{product}}">{{name}}:</label>
        <input name="{{product}}" data-price="{{price}}" data-stock="{{stock}}"
            value="{{#if stock}}1{{/if}}{{#unless stock}}0{{/unless}}" required />
    </div>
    {{/flowers}}
</script>
...
```

The #if and #unless helpers are completely independent of each other, but using them this way shows how you can test for the presence or the absence of a property without using an else directive. This listing produces the same result as Listing 12-11, which was illustrated by Figure 12-5.

Enumerating Arrays and Properties

The section directive that I used in Listing 12-12 is part of the Handlebars library's support for the more widely used mustache templates, and the #each helper is a more sophisticated alternative that provides some special properties that can be used within the template. These properties are described in Table 12-3.

Table 12-3. *The Special Properties Provided by the #each Helper*

Name	Description
this	Returns the object that is being processed.
@index	Returns the index of the current object when the #each helper is used on an array.
@key	Returns the name of the current property when used on an object.

In Listing 12-13, you can see how I have used the #each helper on the existing data, along with the @index property.

Listing 12-13. Using the #each Helper and the @index Property

```
...
<script id="flowerTmpl" type="text/x-handlebars-template">
    {{#each flowers}}
    <div class="dcell">
        <label>Position: {{@index}}</label>
        <img src="{{product}}.png"/>
        <label for="{{product}}">{{name}}:</label>
        <input name="{{product}}" data-price="{{price}}" data-stock="{{stock}}"
            value="{{#if stock}}1{{/if}}{{#unless stock}}0{{/unless}}" required />
    </div>
    {{/each}}
</script>
...
```

I specify the source of the objects to be enumerated as the argument to the #each helper, which is this case is the value of the flowers property of the data object passed to the template method. You can see the result in Figure 12-6 (the indexes restart for each row because I am splitting the data into two sections and calling the template method twice, as shown in Listing 12-11).

Figure 12-6. *Using the #each helper and the @index property*

The this and @key properties are useful when passing objects to the template method, rather than arrays. The Handlebars library will enumerate the properties of the object – the @key property is used to get the current property name and the this property is used to get the current value. You can see both properties used together in Listing 12-14.

Listing 12-14. Enumerating the Properties of an Object with the #each Helper

```html
<!DOCTYPE html>
<html>
<head>
    <title>Example</title>
    <script src="jquery-2.0.2.js" type="text/javascript"></script>
    <script src="handlebars.js" type="text/javascript"></script>
    <script src="handlebars-jquery.js" type="text/javascript"></script>
    <link rel="stylesheet" type="text/css" href="styles.css"/>
    <script id="flowerListTmpl" type="text/x-handlebars-template">
        <ul>
            {{#each stockData}}
                <li>{{@key}} ({{this}} in stock)</li>
            {{/each}}
        </ul>
    </script>
    <script type="text/javascript">
        $(document).ready(function () {

            var data = {
                stockData: {
                    Aster: 10, Daffodil: 12, Rose: 2,
                    Peony: 0, Primula: 1, Snowdrop: 15
                }
            };
            $("#flowerListTmpl").template(data).appendTo("form");
        });
    </script>
</head>
```

295

```
<body>
    <h1>Jacqui's Flower Shop</h1>
    <form method="post">
    </form>
</body>
</html>
```

I have replaced the data in this example with a simpler structure – the `data.stockData` property returns an object whose property names describe flowers and whose values describe the number in stock. For the template I use the `#each` helper on the `stockData` property (remember that I have to pass an object to the `template` method and apply the helpers and directives to its properties). The template in this example creates a list. I get the value of each property with the `this` property and the name of the property with the `@key` property, and you can see the result in Figure 12-7.

Figure 12-7. *Using the @key and this properties with the #each helper*

Changing the Data Context

The *data context* is the part of the data object that helpers and variables are applied to. When template processing begins, the context is the entire data object, but it is changed by helpers and section directives to make writing the template easier, as shown in the template I used in the last example:

```
...
{{#each stockData}}
    <li>{{@key}} ({{this}} in stock)</li>
{{/each}}
...
```

The #each helper shifts the context to each of the properties of the data object in turn – and that means that variables and helpers defined within the #each helper block will all be evaluated relative to the current object. You can see this more clearly in Listing 12-15, where I have changed the data and the template to make the effect of the context clearer.

Listing 12-15. Emphasizing the Role of the Context in a Template

```
...
<script id="flowerListTmpl" type="text/x-handlebars-template">
    <ul>
        <h3>{{title}}</h3>
        {{#each stockData}}
            <li>{{description.Name}} ({{description.Stock}} in stock)</li>
        {{/each}}
    </ul>
</script>
<script type="text/javascript">
    $(document).ready(function () {

        var data = {
            title: "Stock List",
            stockData: {
                aster: {
                    description: { Name: "Aster", Stock: 10 }
                },
                daffodil: {
                    description: { Name: "Daffodil", Stock: 12 }
                },
                rose: {
                    description: { Name: "Rose", Stock: 2 }
                }
            }
        };
        $("#flowerListTmpl").template(data).appendTo("form");
    });
</script>
...
```

I have added a `title` property to the data object and structure to the individual flowers. The first directive of the template relies on the default data context, which is the entire data object:

```
...
<h3>{{title}}</h3>
...
```

You can see what I mean about the directives being evaluated relative to the context – I just need to specify the property name without any qualification to get the value of the `title` property from the data object. The next directive in the template changes the context:

```
...
{{#each stockData}}
...
```

The #each helper enumerates the properties of the object returned by the stockData property and changes the context to be each property value in turn. You can see the effect in the next line of the template:

```
...
<li>{{description.Name}} ({{description.Stock}} in stock)</li>
...
```

I access the Name and Stock properties relative to the current context – and that means using a path to navigate through the description object, following the structure of the data object. The result is shown in Figure 12-8.

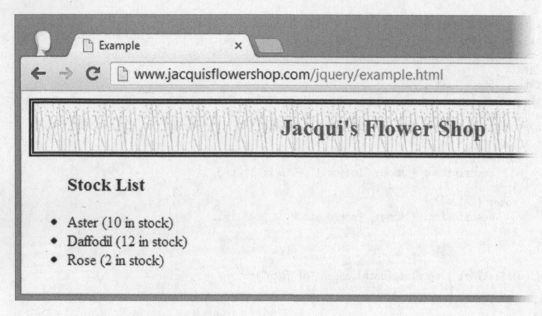

Figure 12-8. *Accessing properties relative to the context*

Using the #with Helper

In the previous example, I had to specify description.Name and description.Stock to access the property values I wanted for my template. The #with helper can eliminate the need to duplicate common property names by changing the data context for all of the directives that it contains, as shown in Listing 12-16.

Listing 12-16. Changing the Data Context with the #with Helper

```
...
<script id="flowerListTmpl" type="text/x-handlebars-template">
    <ul>
        <h3>{{title}}</h3>
        {{#each stockData}}
            {{#with description}}
                <li>{{Name}} ({{Stock}} in stock)</li>
```

```
            {{/with}}
        {{/each}}
    </ul>
</script>
...
```

Within the scope of the #with block the context is narrowed to the description property. When combined with the change in data context made by the #each helper, I am able to access the Name and Stock properties of each flower object without having to qualify the name.

Access Parent Data Contexts

Changes in data context are not always helpful, and you sometimes need to access another part of the data object to get a common property value. You can navigate to the parent context by prefixing variables with ../, as shown in Listing 12-17.

Listing 12-17. Accessing the Parent Data Context

```
...
<script id="flowerListTmpl" type="text/x-handlebars-template">
    <ul>
        <h3>{{title}}</h3>
        {{#each stockData}}
            {{#with description}}
                <li>{{Name}}{{../../prefix}}{{Stock}}{{../../suffix}}</li>
            {{/with}}
        {{/each}}
    </ul>
</script>
<script type="text/javascript">
    $(document).ready(function () {

        var data = {
            title: "Stock List",
            prefix: " (",
            suffix: " in stock)",
            stockData: {
                aster: {
                    description: { Name: "Aster", Stock: 10 }
                },
                daffodil: {
                    description: { Name: "Daffodil", Stock: 12 }
                },
                rose: {
                    description: { Name: "Rose", Stock: 2 }
                }
            }
        };
        $("#flowerListTmpl").template(data).appendTo("form");
    });
</script>
...
```

I have defined `prefix` and `suffix` properties at the top-level of the data object. To access these from the template, I need to navigate up two context levels, as follows:

```
...
{{../../prefix}}
...
```

This directive appears within the scope of the #with helper and so applying ../ once will change the context to the next level up in the template, which is the #each helper. The #each helper has set the context to be the contents of the stockData property, and so I need to up another level to get to the prefix property, meaning I must reference ../../prefix to get the value I want.

■ **Tip**   The ../ sequence navigates up one level in the *template* and not the data object.

Creating Custom Template Helpers

The logic in some of the helpers is pretty basic, and this means that processing the data to fit into the way the helpers work is often required. You can see an example of this in Listing 12-18, which repeats the example I used to demonstrate the #if helper earlier in the chapter.

Listing 12-18. Preparing Data for Use with a Template Helper

```html
<!DOCTYPE html>
<html>
<head>
    <title>Example</title>
    <script src="jquery-2.0.2.js" type="text/javascript"></script>
    <script src="handlebars.js" type="text/javascript"></script>
    <script src="handlebars-jquery.js" type="text/javascript"></script>
    <link rel="stylesheet" type="text/css" href="styles.css"/>

    <script id="flowerTmpl" type="text/x-handlebars-template">
        {{#flowers}}
        <div class="dcell">
            <img src="{{product}}.png"/>
            <label for="{{product}}">{{name}}:</label>
            <input name="{{product}}" data-price="{{price}}" data-stock="{{stock}}"
                value="{{#if stock}}1{{else}}0{{/if}}" required />
        </div>
        {{/flowers}}
    </script>
    <script type="text/javascript">
        $(document).ready(function () {
            var data = {
                flowers: [
                { name: "Aster", product: "aster", stock: "10", price: 2.99 },
                { name: "Daffodil", product: "daffodil", stock: "12", price: 1.99 },
                { name: "Rose", product: "rose", stock: "2", price: 4.99 },
                { name: "Peony", product: "peony", stock: "0", price: 1.50 },
```

```
                    { name: "Primula", product: "primula", stock: "1", price: 3.12 },
                    { name: "Snowdrop", product: "snowdrop", stock: "15", price: 0.99 }]
            };
            for (var i = 0; i < data.flowers.length; i++) {
                if (data.flowers[i].stock == 0) {
                    data.flowers[i].stock = null;
                }
            }
            var tElem = $("#flowerTmpl");
            tElem.template({ flowers: data.flowers.slice(0, 3) }).appendTo("#row1");
            tElem.template({ flowers: data.flowers.slice(3) }).appendTo("#row2");
        });
    </script>
</head>
<body>
    <h1>Jacqui's Flower Shop</h1>
    <form method="post">
        <div id="oblock">
            <div class="dtable">
                <div id="row1" class="drow"></div>
                <div id="row2"class="drow"></div>
            </div>
        </div>
        <div id="buttonDiv"><button type="submit">Place Order</button></div>
    </form>
</body>
</html>
```

I dislike having to process my data before passing it to the template engine because it means that I have logic for displaying my data in two places: the template and the `for` loop.

This is where the use of templates becomes contentious because there are two approaches to ensuring that the logic for generating content from the template is in just one place: remove the logic from the template and define it all in JavaScript or to remove the `for` loop and add extra logic to the template. There are lots of arguments to support both approaches, but it is essentially a personal choice driven by preference and the nature of the data that you are working with. I prefer to add logic to the template, which is something that the `Handlebars` library makes simple and easy.

Creating a Conditional Template Helper

In Listing 12-19, you can see the additions I made to the `handlebars-jquery.js` file to create a custom helper for my template.

■ **Tip**   You can define the custom logic in any script element or JavaScript file. I like to keep my additions to Handlebar.js in one place – but that's just personal preference.

301

Listing 12-19. Defining Custom Conditional Logic for Handlebars in the handlebars-jquery.js File

```
(function ($) {

    Handlebars.registerHelper('gt', function (a, b, options) {
        return (a > b) ? options.fn(this) : options.inverse(this);
    });

    var compiled = {};
    $.fn.template = function (data) {
        var template = $.trim($(this).first().html());
        if (compiled[template] == undefined) {
            compiled[template] = Handlebars.compile(template);
        }
        return $(compiled[template](data));
    };
})(jQuery);
```

The Handlebars library defines a global object called `Handlebars`, which in turn defines a method called `registerHelper`. The `registerHelper` takes two arguments – the name that you want to give your helper and a *helper function* that will be invoked when the helper is encountered in the template. I have called my custom helper gt (short for *greater than*), but the easiest way to demonstrate how the helper function works is to demonstrate my custom helper in action and then explain how its behavior relates to its definition. In Listing 12-20, you can see how I have applied my gt helper to the example HTML document.

Listing 12-20. Applying a Custom Template Helper

```
...
<script id="flowerTmpl" type="text/x-handlebars-template">
    {{#flowers}}
    <div class="dcell">
        <img src="{{product}}.png"/>
        <label for="{{product}}">{{name}}:</label>
        <input name="{{product}}" data-price="{{price}}" data-stock="{{stock}}"
            value="{{#gt stock 0}}1{{else}}0{{/gt}}" required />
    </div>
    {{/flowers}}
</script>
<script type="text/javascript">
    $(document).ready(function () {
        var data = {
            flowers: [
            { name: "Aster", product: "aster", stock: "10", price: 2.99 },
            { name: "Daffodil", product: "daffodil", stock: "12", price: 1.99 },
            { name: "Rose", product: "rose", stock: "2", price: 4.99 },
            { name: "Peony", product: "peony", stock: "0", price: 1.50 },
            { name: "Primula", product: "primula", stock: "1", price: 3.12 },
            { name: "Snowdrop", product: "snowdrop", stock: "15", price: 0.99 }]
        };
```

```
        var tElem = $("#flowerTmpl");
        tElem.template({ flowers: data.flowers.slice(0, 3) }).appendTo("#row1");
        tElem.template({ flowers: data.flowers.slice(3) }).appendTo("#row2");
    });
</script>
...
```

■ **Tip**   You may have to reload the web page in the browser to see the right effect. JavaScript files are sometimes aggressively cached, which can prevent changes from taking effect.

My #gt helper checks to see if the value of the stock property is greater than zero. If it is, then 1 is inserted into the template and 0 is inserted otherwise.

I have to call the Handlebars.registerHelper method before I generate content from the template so that the Handlebars library knows about the #gt helper. When the helper directive is encountered, Handlebars will pass all of the values that follow #gt in the directive as arguments to my function, after replacing any that can be resolved as variables in the current data context.

In the listing, I have placed the reference to the #gt helper inside of a section directive, which means that Handlebars will enumerate the data.flowers array, and the stock property will be replaced by the value for the current flower – this means that for the Aster, for example, the arguments passed to my helper function will be 10, the value of the Aster stock property, and 1, which cannot be resolved to a data value and is passed unchanged.

■ **Tip**   You can provide as many or as few arguments to your helper function as required. Two is just the number I need to perform a basic comparison.

These are the a and b values I receive in my helper function. I also receive an options object that is provided by Handlebars:

```
...
Handlebars.registerHelper('gt', function (a, b, options) {
    return (a > b) ? options.fn(this) : options.inverse(this);
});
...
```

The options object provides features that are useful for writing helpers, as described in Table 12-4.

Table 12-4. *The Properties and Methods eDfined by the Options Object*

Name	Description
fn(data)	Called to get the content that has been defined for the true outcome of a conditional helper, or the sole content for helpers that don't have an else directive.
inverse(data)	Called to get the content that has been defined in the else clause of a helper.
Hash	Used to receive optional arguments into the helper function.
Data	Used to provide templates with special properties.

In my #gt helper, I call the options.fn method to get the content that should be inserted into the HTML if a is greater than b (which in the example means that the value of the stock property of the current flower is greater than zero). I pass the this variable, which Handlebars sets to be the current data context. If a is not greater than b, then I call the options.inverse method instead. For this example, the options.fn method will return 1 and the options.inverse method will return 0.

Returning More Complex Content

The content inserted into the HTML is the result from the helper function, which means that I am free to increase the complexity of my helper functions to simplify my templates by inserting larger fragments of HTML. In Listing 12-21, you can see how I have defined a helper called #gtValAttr in the handlebars-jquery.js file.

Listing 12-21. Defining a More Complex Helper in the handlebars-jquery.js File

```
(function ($) {

    Handlebars.registerHelper('gt', function (a, b, options) {
        return (a > b) ? options.fn(this) : options.inverse(this);
    });

    Handlebars.registerHelper("gtValAttr", function () {
        return "value='" + (this.stock > 0 ? "1" : "0") + "'";
    });

    var compiled = {};
    $.fn.template = function (data) {
        var template = $.trim($(this).first().html());
        if (compiled[template] == undefined) {
            compiled[template] = Handlebars.compile(template);
        }
        return $(compiled[template](data));
    };
})(jQuery);
```

The new helper doesn't take any arguments at all – it gets the value it required through the this property (which, as I mentioned, is set to the current data context). The result from the helper function is a complete definition of the value attribute, tailored to the template in which it will be used. You can see how I have applied the #gtValAttr helper in the template in Listing 12-22.

Listing 12-22. Applying the #gtValAttr Helper in the Template

```
...
<script id="flowerTmpl" type="text/x-handlebars-template">
    {{#flowers}}
    <div class="dcell">
        <img src="{{product}}.png"/>
        <label for="{{product}}">{{name}}:</label>
        <input name="{{product}}" data-price="{{price}}" data-stock="{{stock}}"
            {{#gtValAttr}}{{/gtValAttr}} required />
    </div>
    {{/flowers}}
</script>
...
```

■ **Note**   I have shown you this helper to demonstrate the flexibility that the Handlebars library provides, but I don't use this kind of helper in real projects. It depends too much on the structure of the data and the template, and a change to either of them will break the code. I prefer to create small, focused helpers like #gt that can be used in any template and that generate the smallest amount of content possible, ideally provided through arguments.

Receiving Optional Arguments in the Helper Function

You can define arguments in the template that are passed to the helper function. The purpose of these optional arguments is entirely up to the creator of the helper, but the most common purpose is to pass attribute values to helpers that generate complete HTML elements. In Listing 12-23, you can see that I have defined a helper that creates complete input elements from a flower data object. Once again, this isn't how I like to use templates in my own projects, but readers may prefer complexity in the helpers to complexity in the template.

Listing 12-23. Defining a Helper That Takes Optional Arguments in the handlebars-jquery.js File

```
(function ($) {

    Handlebars.registerHelper('gt', function (a, b, options) {
        return (a > b) ? options.fn(this) : options.inverse(this);
    });

    Handlebars.registerHelper("gtValAttr", function () {
        return "value='" + (this.stock > 0 ? "1" : "0") + "'";
    });

    Handlebars.registerHelper("inputElem", function (product, stock, options) {
        options.hash.name = product;
        options.hash.value = stock > 0 ? "1" : "0";
        options.hash.required = "required";
        return $("<input>", options.hash)[0].outerHTML;
    });
```

```
        var compiled = {};
        $.fn.template = function (data) {
            var template = $.trim($(this).first().html());
            if (compiled[template] == undefined) {
                compiled[template] = Handlebars.compile(template);
            }
            return $(compiled[template](data));
        };
    })(jQuery);
```

The #inputElem helper generates a complete input element for a flower – but once again, it will be easier to understand how it works by seeing it applied in the template, as shown in Listing 12-24.

Listing 12-24. Applying the #inputElem Helper in the Template

```
...
<script id="flowerTmpl" type="text/x-handlebars-template">
    {{#flowers}}
    <div class="dcell">
        <img src="{{product}}.png"/>
        <label for="{{product}}">{{name}}:</label>
        {{#inputElem product stock data-stock=stock data-price=price}}{{/inputElem}}
    </div>
    {{/flowers}}
</script>
...
```

As you can see in Listing 12-23, the #inputElem helper function takes two arguments, and I use these to pass the value of the product and stock properties when I apply the helper in the template. The additional arguments are in the form key=value, and these are passed to the helper function via the options.hash property, having first being resolved against the current data context. For my example, this means that the options.hash property returns an object that looks like this for the Aster flower:

```
{"data-stock": 10, "data-price": 2.99}
```

In Part 2, I explained that there was a version of the jQuery $ function that generates a jQuery object from an HTML string and a map object of attributes, and the option.hash object is just the format I need to create the input element I desire. But it doesn't contain all of the attributes that I require, so I use the following statements to complete the set:

```
...
options.hash.name = product;
options.hash.value = stock > 0 ? "1" : "0";
options.hash.required = "required";
...
```

I can use the jQuery $ function to create my input element, apply the attributes, and return the HTML string that is required for the template, as follows:

```
...
return $("<input>", options.hash)[0].outerHTML;
...
```

To get the HTML string, I use an array indexer to get the `HTMLElement` object at index 0 and use the `outerHTML` property to get a string like this:

```
<input data-stock="10" data-price="2.99" name="aster" value="1" required="required">
```

Handlebars and jQuery work well together to make generating complete HTML elements from helpers easy – as the `#inputElem` helper demonstrates.

> ■ **Tip**   There is no convenient way to get the HTML of an element using jQuery, which is why I used the `outerHTML` property of the underlying `HTMLElement` object. The closest method is `html`, but that returns the HTML content of an element and not the HTML of the element itself, which means that I would have had to append my `input` element to another element before I could use the `html` method, like this: `$("<div />").append($("<input>", options.hash)).html();` I find that using the HTML element is simpler and easier to read.

Providing Custom Template Properties

I explained earlier in the chapter that the #each helper defines special properties that are available within the block it defines. This is something that you can do in custom helpers as well, and it can be a nice way to simplify the structure of a template. As a demonstration, I have created the #stockValue helper, shown in Listing 12-25.

Listing 12-25. Creating the #stockValue Helper in the handlebars-jquery.js File

```
(function ($) {

    Handlebars.registerHelper('gt', function (a, b, options) {
        return (a > b) ? options.fn(this) : options.inverse(this);
    });

    Handlebars.registerHelper("gtValAttr", function () {
        return "value='" + (this.stock > 0 ? "1" : "0") + "'";
    });

    Handlebars.registerHelper("inputElem", function (product, stock, options) {
        options.hash.name = product;
        options.hash.value = stock > 0 ? "1" : "0";
        options.hash.required = "required";
        return $("<input>", options.hash)[0].outerHTML;
    });

    Handlebars.registerHelper("stockValue", function (options) {
        options.data.attributeValue = this.stock > 0 ? "1" : "0";
        return options.fn(this);
    });

    var compiled = {};
    $.fn.template = function (data) {
        var template = $.trim($(this).first().html());
```

```
        if (compiled[template] == undefined) {
            compiled[template] = Handlebars.compile(template);
        }
        return $(compiled[template](data));
    };
})(jQuery);
```

This is a simple helper and all it does is create a property called `attributeValue` on the `options.data` object and assigns it the value that I want as the `value` attribute for the `input` element. I can access this value within the template block contained by the `#stockValue` helper in the template using the special property called `@attributeValue`, as shown in Listing 12-26.

Listing 12-26. Accessing the Special Property in the Template

```
...
<script id="flowerTmpl" type="text/x-handlebars-template">
    {{#flowers}}
    <div class="dcell">
        <img src="{{product}}.png"/>
        <label for="{{product}}">{{name}}:</label>
        {{#stockValue}}
            <input name="{{product}}" data-price="{{price}}" data-stock="{{stock}}"
                value="{{@attributeValue}}" required />
        {{/stockValue}}
    </div>
    {{/flowers}}
</script>
...
```

Summary

In this chapter, I introduced the Handlebars template library, which gives you a nice set of features for translating JavaScript data into HTML elements without getting bogged down in a mass of nasty code. The reason that I like using this library is that it provides flexibility as to how much logic is defined in the template, how much is handled by processing data, and how much is hidden away in handlers. In the next chapter, I show you how jQuery supports HTML forms and how to apply a widely used plug-in to validate the data that users enter into them.

CHAPTER 13

■■■

Working with Forms

In this chapter, I will show you the jQuery support for working with HTML forms. In part, I will recap the form-related events and the jQuery methods you can use to manage them, but most of this chapter is dedicated to a plug-in that provides a great mechanism for validating the values that users enter into a form before it is submitted to a server. If you have written any kind of form-based web application, you will have realized that users will enter all sorts of data into a form, so validation is an important process.

    I begin this chapter by introducing the Node.js server script that you will use in this part of the book. For this chapter, the script doesn't do a great deal other than show you the data values that were entered into the form, but in later chapters I'll start to rely on Node.js a little more. Table 13-1 provides the summary for this chapter.

Table 13-1. *Chapter Summary*

Problem	Solution	Listing
Set up the Node.js server.	Use the script listed in this chapter (and included in the source code that accompanies this book).	1, 2
Respond to the focus being gained or lost by a form element.	Use the focus and blur methods.	3
Respond to changes in the value that the user has entered into a form element.	Use the change method.	4
Respond to (and interrupt) the user submitting the form.	Use the submit method.	5, 6
Validate the values in a form.	Use the validation plug-in.	7
Configure the validation plug-in.	Pass a map object to the validate method.	8
Define and apply validation rules using a class.	Use the addClassRules and addClass methods.	9–12
Apply validation rules directly to elements.	Use the rules method.	13, 14
Apply validation rules using element names.	Add a rules property to the options object.	15
Apply validation rules using element attributes.	Define attributes that correspond to individual validation checks.	16
Define custom messages for rules applied via element names and attributes.	Add a message property to the options object, set to a map object that defines the custom messages.	17, 18
Define custom messages for rules applied directly to elements.	Include a map object defining the messages as an argument to the rules method.	19

(continued)

Table 13-1. (*continued*)

Problem	Solution	Listing
Create a custom validation check.	Use the addMethod method.	20, 21
Format the validation messages.	Use the highlight, unhighlight, errorElement, and errorClass properties of the options object.	22–26
Use a validation summary.	Use the errorContainer and errorLabelContainer properties.	27
Compose error messages using templates.	Use the $.validator.format method.	28

Preparing the Node.js Server

In this chapter, I will be using Node.js to receive and process form data from the browser. I don't want to get drawn into the details of how Node.js functions, but one of the reasons that I selected it for this book was because Node.js is built around JavaScript, which means you can use the same skills for server-side programming as you do for client-side programming.

■ **Tip** If you want to re-create the example in this chapter, see Chapter 1 for details of how to obtain Node.js. You can download the formserver.js server-side script along with all of the examples for this chapter from Apress.com.

Listing 13-1 shows the server-side script that you will use in this chapter, which I have saved in a file called formserver.js. I present this as a black box and explain only the inputs and output.

Listing 13-1. The formserver.js Node.js Script

```
var http = require("http");
var querystring = require("querystring");

var port = 80;

http.createServer(function (req, res) {
    console.log("[200 OK] " + req.method + " to " + req.url);

    if (req.method == "POST") {
        var dataObj = new Object();
        var cType = req.headers["content-type"];
        var fullBody = "";

        if (cType && cType.indexOf("application/x-www-form-urlencoded") > -1) {
            req.on("data", function(chunk) { fullBody += chunk.toString();});
            req.on("end", function() {
                res.writeHead(200, "OK", {"Content-Type": "text/html"});
                res.write("<html><head><title>Post data</title></head><body>");
                res.write("<style>th, td {text-align:left; padding:5px; color:black}\n");
```

```
            res.write("th {background-color:grey; color:white; min-width:10em}\n");
            res.write("td {background-color:lightgrey}\n");
            res.write("caption {font-weight:bold}</style>");
            res.write("<table border='1'><caption>Form Data</caption>");
            res.write("<tr><th>Name</th><th>Value</th>");
            var dBody = querystring.parse(fullBody);
            for (var prop in dBody) {
                res.write("<tr><td>" + prop + "</td><td>"
                    + dBody[prop] + "</td></tr>");
            }
            res.write("</table></body></html>");
            res.end();
        });
    }
}

}).listen(port);
console.log("Ready on port " + port);
```

To run this script, I enter the following at the command line:

```
node.exe formserver.js
```

The command will be different if you are using another operating system. See the Node.js documentation for details. To demonstrate the Node.js functionality I will use the example document shown in Listing 13-2, which I saved as example.html.

Listing 13-2. The Example Document for This Chapter

```
<!DOCTYPE html>
<html>
<head>
    <title>Example</title>
    <script src="jquery-2.0.2.js" type="text/javascript"></script>
    <script src="handlebars.js" type="text/javascript"></script>
    <script src="handlebars-jquery.js" type="text/javascript"></script>
    <link rel="stylesheet" type="text/css" href="styles.css"/>
    <script id="flowerTmpl" type="text/x-handlebars-template">
        {{#each flowers}}
        <div class="dcell">
            <img src="{{product}}.png"/>
            <label for="{{product}}">{{name}}: </label>
            <input name="{{product}}" value="0" required />
        </div>
        {{/each}}
    </script>
```

311

```
    <script type="text/javascript">
        $(document).ready(function () {

            var data = { flowers: [
                { name: "Aster", product: "aster", stock: "10", price: "2.99" },
                { name: "Daffodil", product: "daffodil", stock: "12", price: "1.99" },
                { name: "Rose", product: "rose", stock: "2", price: "4.99" },
                { name: "Peony", product: "peony", stock: "0", price: "1.50" },
                { name: "Primula", product: "primula", stock: "1", price: "3.12" },
                { name: "Snowdrop", product: "snowdrop", stock: "15", price: "0.99" }]
            };

            var templResult = $("#flowerTmpl").template(data).filter("*");
            templResult.slice(0, 3).appendTo("#row1");
            templResult.slice(3).appendTo("#row2");
        });
    </script>
</head>
<body>
    <h1>Jacqui's Flower Shop</h1>
    <form method="post" action="http://node.jacquisflowershop.com/order">
        <div id="oblock">
            <div class="dtable">
                <div id="row1" class="drow">
                </div>
                <div id="row2"class="drow">
                </div>
            </div>
        </div>
        <div id="buttonDiv"><button type="submit">Place Order</button></div>
    </form>
</body>
</html>
```

The individual product elements are generated using data templates (as described in Chapter 12). I have specified a value for the `action` attribute of the `form` element, which means it will post to the following URL:

```
http://node.jacquisflowershop.com/order
```

I am using two different servers. The first server (www.jacquisflowershop.com) is the one that has been serving up HTML content throughout this book. It delivers the static content such as HTML documents, scripts files, and images. For me, this is Microsoft's IIS, but you can use any server that appeals to you. (I use IIS because a lot of my books are about Microsoft web technologies, and I already have a server set up and ready to go.)

The second server (node.jacquisflowershop.com) runs Node.js (using the formserver.js script shown previously), and when you submit the form in the example document, this is where the data will be sent. In this chapter, I don't care a great deal about what the server does with the data it receives: I will be focused on the form itself. In Figure 13-1, you can see that I have entered some values into the input elements in the document.

Figure 13-1. *Entering data into the input elements*

When I click the Place Order button, the form is submitted to the Node.js server, and a simple response is sent back to the browser, as shown in Figure 13-2.

Name	Value
aster	1
daffodil	2
rose	3
peony	2
primula	4
snowdrop	7

Figure 13-2. *The response from the Node.js server*

I know this is not an interesting response, but I just need somewhere to send the data for now, and I don't want to get drawn off track into the world of server-side development.

313

Recapping the Form-Event Methods

jQuery includes a set of methods that deal with form-related events. It is worth recapping these now that you are specifically looking at forms. Table 13-2 describes the methods and the events to which they correspond.

Table 13-2. *The jQuery Form-Event Methods*

Method	Event	Description
blur(function)	Blur	Triggered when a form element loses the focus.
change(function)	Change	Triggered when the value of a form element changes.
focus(function)	Focus	Triggered when the focus is given to a form element.
select(function)	Select	Triggered when the user selects text within a form element.
submit(function)	Submit	Triggered when the user wants to submit the form.

■ **Tip** Don't forget that jQuery defines a set of extension selectors that match form elements. See Chapter 5 for details.

Dealing with Form Focus

The blur and focus methods allow you to respond to changes in the focus. A common use for these features is to help the user by emphasizing which element has the focus (and thus which element will receive input from the keyboard). Listing 13-3 provides a demonstration.

Listing 13-3. Managing Form Element Focus

```
...
<script type="text/javascript">
    $(document).ready(function () {

        var data = { flowers: [
            { name: "Aster", product: "aster", stock: "10", price: "2.99" },
            { name: "Daffodil", product: "daffodil", stock: "12", price: "1.99" },
            { name: "Rose", product: "rose", stock: "2", price: "4.99" },
            { name: "Peony", product: "peony", stock: "0", price: "1.50" },
            { name: "Primula", product: "primula", stock: "1", price: "3.12" },
            { name: "Snowdrop", product: "snowdrop", stock: "15", price: "0.99" }]
        };

        var templResult = $("#flowerTmpl").template(data).filter("*");
        templResult.slice(0, 3).appendTo("#row1");
        templResult.slice(3).appendTo("#row2");
```

```
        function handleFormFocus(e) {
            var borderVal = e.type == "focus" ? "medium solid green" : "";
            $(this).css("border", borderVal);
        }
        $("input").focus(handleFormFocus).blur(handleFormFocus);
    });
</script>
...
```

In this example, I select all of the input elements and register the handleFormFocus function as the handler for both the focus and blur events. The function applies a green border when an element gains the focus and removes it when the focus is lost. You can see the effect in Figure 13-3.

Figure 13-3. *Emphasizing the focused element*

Notice that I used the input selector. In other words, I selected the elements by tag. jQuery provides the extension selector :input (I described the extension selectors in Chapter 5), but the extension selector matches elements more broadly and will match button elements that are capable of submitting the form, which means if I had used use the extension selector, the border would have been applied to the button as well as the actual input elements. You can see the difference when the button is focused in Figure 13-4. Which selector you use is a matter for personal preference, but it is useful to be aware of the difference.

Figure 13-4. *The difference between the input and :input selectors*

Dealing with Value Changes

The change event is triggered when the user changes the value in a form element. This is a useful event if you are providing cumulative information based on the values in the form. Listing 13-4 shows how you can use this event to track the total number of items selected in the flower shop document. This is the same approach I took when I refactored the example at the end of Part II of this book.

Listing 13-4. *Responding to the Change Event*

```
...
<script type="text/javascript">
    $(document).ready(function () {

        var data = { flowers: [
            { name: "Aster", product: "aster", stock: "10", price: "2.99" },
            { name: "Daffodil", product: "daffodil", stock: "12", price: "1.99" },
            { name: "Rose", product: "rose", stock: "2", price: "4.99" },
            { name: "Peony", product: "peony", stock: "0", price: "1.50" },
            { name: "Primula", product: "primula", stock: "1", price: "3.12" },
            { name: "Snowdrop", product: "snowdrop", stock: "15", price: "0.99" }]
        };

        var templResult = $("#flowerTmpl").template(data).filter("*");
        templResult.slice(0, 3).appendTo("#row1");
        templResult.slice(3).appendTo("#row2");
```

```
        function handleFormFocus(e) {
            var borderVal = e.type == "focus" ? "medium solid green" : "";
            $(this).css("border", borderVal);
        }
        $("input").focus(handleFormFocus).blur(handleFormFocus);

        var total = $("#buttonDiv")
            .prepend("<div>Total Items: <span id=total>0</span></div>")
            .css({clear: "both", padding: "5px"});
        $("<div id=bbox />").appendTo("body").append(total).css("clear: left");

        $("input").change(function (e) {
            var total = 0;
            $("input").each(function (index, elem) {
                total += Number($(elem).val());
            });
            $("#total").text(total);
        });
    });
</script>
...
```

In this example, I respond to the change event by totaling the values in all of the input elements and displaying the result in the span element that I had previously added to the document.

■ **Tip**   Notice that I use the val method to get the value from the input elements.

Dealing with Form Submission

A lot of the more advanced activities you can perform with forms arise from the way you can prevent the browser's default form mechanism from working. Listing 13-5 provides a simple demonstration.

Listing 13-5. Intercepting the Form Submission

```
...
<script type="text/javascript">
    $(document).ready(function () {

        var data = { flowers: [
            { name: "Aster", product: "aster", stock: "10", price: "2.99" },
            { name: "Daffodil", product: "daffodil", stock: "12", price: "1.99" },
            { name: "Rose", product: "rose", stock: "2", price: "4.99" },
            { name: "Peony", product: "peony", stock: "0", price: "1.50" },
            { name: "Primula", product: "primula", stock: "1", price: "3.12" },
            { name: "Snowdrop", product: "snowdrop", stock: "15", price: "0.99" }]
        };
```

```
        var templResult = $("#flowerTmpl").template(data).filter("*");
        templResult.slice(0, 3).appendTo("#row1");
        templResult.slice(3).appendTo("#row2");

        $("form").submit(function (e) {
            if ($("input").val() == 0) {
                e.preventDefault();
            }
        });
    });
</script>
...
```

I register a handler function for the submit event. This event will be triggered when the user clicks the Place Order button. If the value of the first input element is 0, I call the preventDefault method to interrupt the default action of the form, which is to submit the data to the server. For any other value, the form is submitted.

■ **Tip** As an alternative, you can return false from the event handler function to achieve the same effect.

There are two different to submit a form programmatically. You can use the jQuery submit method without any arguments and you can use the submit method, which is defined for form elements by the HTML5 specification. Listing 13-6 shows both approaches in use.

Listing 13-6. Explicitly Submitting a Form

```
...
<script type="text/javascript">
    $(document).ready(function () {

        var data = { flowers: [
            { name: "Aster", product: "aster", stock: "10", price: "2.99" },
            { name: "Daffodil", product: "daffodil", stock: "12", price: "1.99" },
            { name: "Rose", product: "rose", stock: "2", price: "4.99" },
            { name: "Peony", product: "peony", stock: "0", price: "1.50" },
            { name: "Primula", product: "primula", stock: "1", price: "3.12" },
            { name: "Snowdrop", product: "snowdrop", stock: "15", price: "0.99" }]
        };

        var templResult = $("#flowerTmpl").template(data).filter("*");
        templResult.slice(0, 3).appendTo("#row1");
        templResult.slice(3).appendTo("#row2");

        $("form").submit(function (e) {
            if ($("input").val() == 0) {
                e.preventDefault();
            }
        });
```

```
$("<button>jQuery Method</button>").appendTo("#buttonDiv").click(function (e) {
    $("form").submit();
    e.preventDefault();
});

$("<button>DOM API</button>").appendTo("#buttonDiv").click(function (e) {
    document.getElementsByTagName("form")[0].submit();
    e.preventDefault();
});
  });
</script>
...
```

I have added two button elements to the document. The one that uses the jQuery submit method triggers the submit event, which I set up a handler function for in the last example. This means that if the value of the first input element is zero, the form won't be submitted.

The button elements that uses the DOM API and calls the submit method defined by the form element effectively bypasses the event handler because the submit event isn't triggered, and this means that the form will always be submitted, irrespective of the value of the first input element.

■ **Tip**   My advice is to stick to the jQuery methods, of course, but if you do use the DOM method, at least you will understand the results you get.

Validating Form Values

The main reason for interrupting and preventing the browser from submitting data to the server is that you want to *validate* the values that a user has entered into the form. At some point, every web programmer realizes that users will type anything at all into an input element, and it is unwise to assume that your users will provide useful and meaningful data. There are an infinite number of different values you might have to process, but in my experience there are only a few reasons why the user gives you something unexpected in a form.

The first reason is that the user doesn't understand what data you are after. You might have asked for the name on the credit card, but the user might have entered her card number, for example.

The second reason is that the user doesn't want to give you the information you have requested and is just trying to get through the form as quickly as possible. She'll enter anything that will move her to the next stage in the process. If you have a lot of new users whose e-mail address is a@a.com, then you know that this is the problem.

The third reason is that you are asking for information the user doesn't have, such as asking a U.K. resident which state he lives in. (We don't have states here. I am looking at you, NPR. No donation for you.)

The final reason is that the user has made a genuine mistake, typically a typo. For example, I am a quick but inaccurate typist, and I often type my surname as Freman instead of Freeman, missing out an e.

There is nothing you can do about typos, but the way that you deal with the other three reasons can make the difference between creating a smooth and seamless application and something that annoys and angers users.

I don't want to get into a long rant about the design of web forms, but I do want to say that the best way of approaching this issue is to focus on what the *user* is trying to achieve. And when things go wrong, try to see the problem (and the required resolution) the way the user sees it. Your users don't know about how you have built your systems, and they don't care about your business processes; they just want to get something done. Everyone can be happy if you keep the focus on the task the user is trying to complete and don't needlessly punish her when she don't give you the data you want.

jQuery provides you with all the tools you need to create your own system to validate data values, but I recommend a different approach. One of the most popular jQuery plug-ins is called Validation, and as you guess from the name, it handles form validation.

■ **Caution** What I am discussing in this chapter is *client-side validation*. This is a complement to rather than a replacement for *server-side validation*, where you check the data as it is received by the server. Client-side validation is for the benefit of the *user*: to stop him from having to make repeated submissions to the server to discover and correct data errors. Server-side validation is for the benefit of the *application* and ensures that bad data doesn't cause problems. You must use both: it is trivial to bypass client-side validation, and it does not provide reliable protection for your application.

You can download the validation plug-in from http://jqueryvalidation.org or use the version that I included in the source code download for this book (available at Apress.com). Listing 13-7 shows the use of this plug-in. (As I write this, the current version is 1.1.1.)

Listing 13-7. Using the Form Validation Plug-in

```
<!DOCTYPE html>
<html>
<head>
    <title>Example</title>
    <script src="jquery-2.0.2.js" type="text/javascript"></script>
    <script src="handlebars.js" type="text/javascript"></script>
    <script src="handlebars-jquery.js" type="text/javascript"></script>
    <script src="jquery.validate.js" type="text/javascript"></script>
    <link rel="stylesheet" type="text/css" href="styles.css"/>
    <style type="text/css">
        .errorMsg {color: red}
        .invalidElem {border: medium solid red}
    </style>
    <script id="flowerTmpl" type="text/x-handlebars-template">
        {{#each flowers}}
        <div class="dcell">
            <img src="{{product}}.png"/>
            <label for="{{product}}">{{name}}: </label>
            <input name="{{product}}" value="0" required />
        </div>
        {{/each}}
    </script>
    <script type="text/javascript">
        $(document).ready(function () {

            var data = { flowers: [
                { name: "Aster", product: "aster", stock: "10", price: "2.99" },
                { name: "Daffodil", product: "daffodil", stock: "12", price: "1.99" },
                { name: "Rose", product: "rose", stock: "2", price: "4.99" },
                { name: "Peony", product: "peony", stock: "0", price: "1.50" },
                { name: "Primula", product: "primula", stock: "1", price: "3.12" },
                { name: "Snowdrop", product: "snowdrop", stock: "15", price: "0.99" }]
            };
```

```
            var templResult = $("#flowerTmpl").template(data).filter("*");
            templResult.slice(0, 3).appendTo("#row1");
            templResult.slice(3).appendTo("#row2");


            $("form").validate({
                highlight: function (element, errorClass) {
                    $(element).add($(element).parent()).addClass("invalidElem");
                },
                unhighlight: function (element, errorClass) {
                    $(element).add($(element).parent()).removeClass("invalidElem");
                },
                errorElement: "div",
                errorClass: "errorMsg"
            });

            $.validator.addClassRules({
                flowerValidation: {
                    min: 0
                }
            })

            $("input").addClass("flowerValidation").change(function (e) {
                $("form").validate().element($(e.target));
            });
        });
    </script>
</head>
<body>
    <h1>Jacqui's Flower Shop</h1>
    <form method="post" action="http://node.jacquisflowershop.com/order">
        <div id="oblock">
            <div class="dtable">
                <div id="row1" class="drow">
                </div>
                <div id="row2"class="drow">
                </div>
            </div>
        </div>
        <div id="buttonDiv"><button type="submit">Place Order</button></div>
    </form>
</body>
</html>
```

The plug-in is distributed as a zip file, which you will need to decompress. Copy the jquery.validate.js file from the dist folder so that it is in the same directory as the example.html file.

___

■ **Tip** There are a lot of different configuration options for the validation plug-in. In this chapter, I have focused on those that are most frequently used and that cover the broadest range of situations. If they don't suit you, I suggest exploring some of the other options, which are described in the documentation available in the plug-in download.

___

■ **Note**   HTML5 includes support for some form validation. It is a good start, but it is pretty basic, and there are still significant differences in the way that browsers interpret the specification. Until the scope, richness, and consistency of the HTML5 features improve, I recommend sticking with jQuery for form validation.

Importing the JavaScript File

The first thing I have to do is bring the template plug-in JavaScript file into the document with a `script` element, as follows:

```
...
<script src="jquery-2.0.2.js" type="text/javascript"></script>
<script src="handlebars.js" type="text/javascript"></script>
<script src="handlebars-jquery.js" type="text/javascript"></script>
<script src="jquery.validate.js" type="text/javascript"></script>
...
```

■ **Tip**   I have used the debug version of the file, but there is a minimized version available, and some of the CDN services host this file because it is so popular.

Configuring the Validation

The next step is to configure the validation of the `form` element, which I do by calling the `validate` method on the `form` elements on which validation should be performed. The argument to the `validate` method is a map object that contains configuration settings, as shown in Listing 13-8.

Listing 13-8. Configuring the Validation

```
...
$("form").validate({
    highlight: function(element, errorClass) {
        $(element).add($(element).parent()).addClass("invalidElem");
    },
    unhighlight: function(element, errorClass) {
        $(element).add($(element).parent()).removeClass("invalidElem");
    },
    errorElement: "div",
    errorClass: "errorMsg"
});
...
```

I have specified values for four options (`highlight`, `unhighlight`, `errorElement`, and `errorClass`); I'll come back to these later in the chapter and explain their meaning.

Defining the Validation Rules

A lot of the flexibility of the validation plug-in comes from the way that rules to test for valid input can be quickly and easily defined. There are various ways of associating rules with elements and the one I tend to use works through classes. I define a set of rules and associate them with a class, and when the form is validated the rules are applied to any element contained with the form that is a member of the specified class. I created a single rule in the example, as shown in Listing 13-9.

Listing 13-9. Defining a Validation Rule

```
...
$.validator.addClassRules({
    flowerValidation: {
        min: 0
    }
})
...
```

In this case, I created a rule that will be applied to elements that are members of the flowerValidation class. The rule is that the value should be equal to or greater than zero. I have expressed the condition in the rule using min. This is just one of a number of convenient predefined checks that the validation plug-in provides, and I'll describe all of them later in the chapter.

Applying the Validation Rules

Validation rules are associated with the elements in the form by adding the element to the class specified in the previous step. This provides the ability to tailor the validation for different kinds of elements in a form. For this example, all of the elements are to be treated the same, so I use jQuery to select all of the input elements and add them to the flowerValidation class, as shown in Listing 13-10.

Listing 13-10. Adding the Input Elements to the Class Associated with Validation

```
...
$("input").addClass("flowerValidation").change(function(e) {
    $("form").validate().element($(e.target));
});
...
```

I have also set up a handler function for the change event to explicitly validate the element whose value has changed. This ensures that the user gets immediate feedback if he corrects an error. You can see the effect of the validation plug-in in Figure 13-5. To create this figure, I entered -1 in one of the input fields and clicked the Place Order button.

Figure 13-5. *Using the validation plug-in*

■ **Tip** The text of the message shown to the user is generated by the validation plug-in. I show you how to customize these messages later in the chapter.

The validation plug-in displays an error message, and the user is not able to submit the form until the problem has been resolved. The error message provides the user with guidance as to how the problems can be resolved. (The default messages, such as the one shown in the figure are a bit generic, but later in the chapter I'll show you how to change the text.)

Using the Validation Checks

The validation plug-in supports a wide range of checks that you can use to validate form values. You saw the min check in the previous example. This ensures that the value is greater to or equal to a specified numeric value. Table 13-3 describes the set of checks you can perform.

Table 13-3. *Validation Plug-in Checks*

Checks	Description
creditcard: true	The value must contain a credit card number.
date: true	The value must be a valid JavaScript date.
digits: true	The value must contain only digits.
email: true	The value must be a valid e-mail address.
max: maxVal	The value must be at least as large as maxVal.
maxlength: length	The value must contain no more than length characters.

(continued)

Table 13-3. (*continued*)

Checks	Description
min: minVal	The value must be at least as large as minVal.
minlength: length;	The value must contain at least length characters.
number: true	The value must be a decimal number.
range: [minVal, maxVal]	The value must be between minVal and maxVal.
rangelength: [minLen, maxLen]	The value must contain at least minLen and no more than maxLen characters.
required: true;	A value is required.
url: true	The value must be a URL.

You can associate multiple rules together in a single rule. This allows you to perform complex validations in a compact and expressive way.

■ **Tip**   Included in the validation plug-in distribution zip file is a file called additional-methods.js. This file defines some additional checks, including U.S. and U.K. phone numbers, IPv4 and IPv6 addresses, and some additional date, e-mail, and URL formats.

You can apply these checks to your elements in several ways. I describe each in the sections that follow.

■ **Note**   The Validation plug-in also supports *remote validation*, where the data the user has entered into a field is checked using a remote server. This is useful when you need to check with data that cannot be distributed to the client, because it would be either insecure or impractical (such as checking that a username hasn't already been used). I demonstrate remote validation in Chapter 16, after I introduce the features it relies on in Chapters 14 and 15.

Applying Validation Rules via Classes

As I explained earlier, the validation technique I use most frequently is to apply checks through classes and this is the approach I took in the example. I am not limited to a single check, however, and I can apply multiple checks together to validate different aspects of the value that the user provides, as demonstrated in Listing 13-11.

Listing 13-11. Combining Multiple Checks in a Single Rule

```
...
<script type="text/javascript">
    $(document).ready(function () {

        var data = { flowers: [
            { name: "Aster", product: "aster", stock: "10", price: "2.99" },
            { name: "Daffodil", product: "daffodil", stock: "12", price: "1.99" },
            { name: "Rose", product: "rose", stock: "2", price: "4.99" },
```

```
                { name: "Peony", product: "peony", stock: "0", price: "1.50" },
                { name: "Primula", product: "primula", stock: "1", price: "3.12" },
                { name: "Snowdrop", product: "snowdrop", stock: "15", price: "0.99" }]
        };

        var templResult = $("#flowerTmpl").template(data).filter("*");
        templResult.slice(0, 3).appendTo("#row1");
        templResult.slice(3).appendTo("#row2");

        $("form").validate({
            highlight: function (element, errorClass) {
                $(element).add($(element).parent()).addClass("invalidElem");
            },
            unhighlight: function (element, errorClass) {
                $(element).add($(element).parent()).removeClass("invalidElem");
            },
            errorElement: "div",
            errorClass: "errorMsg"
        });

        $.validator.addClassRules({
            flowerValidation: {
                required: true,
                digits: true,
                min: 0,
                max: 100
            }
        });

        $("input").addClass("flowerValidation").change(function (e) {
            $("form").validate().element($(e.target));
        });
    });
</script>
...
```

In this example, I have combined the required, digits, min, and max checks to ensure that the user provides a value that comprises only digits and that falls within the range of 0 to 100.

Notice that I associate the rule with the class using the addClassRules method. The argument to this method is one or more sets of checks and the class name they are to be applied to. As shown, you call the addClassRules method on the validator property of the main jQuery $ function.

Each validated form element is assessed individually, which means the user can be presented with different error messages for different problems, as shown in Figure 13-6.

Figure 13-6. *Applying multiple validation checks to form elements*

I have entered several values that will fail the checks. It is important to note that the checks are performed in the order they are defined in the rule. If you look at the error message for the Rose product, you will see that it has failed the `digits` check. If you rearrange the order of the checks, you can get a different error. Listing 13-12 shows the validation checks arranged in a different order.

Listing 13-12. *Changing the Order in Which Checks Are Applied*

```
...
$.validator.addClassRules({
    flowerValidation: {
        required: true,
        min: 0,
        max: 100,
        digits: true
    }
})
...
```

In this example, I have moved the digits check to the end of the rule. If I enter -1 into a form field now, it is the `min` check that will fail, as demonstrated by Figure 13-7.

Figure 13-7. Changing the order in which the checks are applied during validation

Applying Validation Rules Directly to Elements

The next technique allows you to apply rules to a single element, as shown in Listing 13-13.

Listing 13-13. Applying Validation Rules to the Elements in a Selection

```
...
<script type="text/javascript">
    $(document).ready(function () {

        var data = { flowers: [
            { name: "Aster", product: "aster", stock: "10", price: "2.99" },
            { name: "Daffodil", product: "daffodil", stock: "12", price: "1.99" },
            { name: "Rose", product: "rose", stock: "2", price: "4.99" },
            { name: "Peony", product: "peony", stock: "0", price: "1.50" },
            { name: "Primula", product: "primula", stock: "1", price: "3.12" },
            { name: "Snowdrop", product: "snowdrop", stock: "15", price: "0.99" }]
        };

        var templResult = $("#flowerTmpl").template(data).filter("*");
        templResult.slice(0, 3).appendTo("#row1");
        templResult.slice(3).appendTo("#row2");

        $("form").validate({
            highlight: function (element, errorClass) {
                $(element).add($(element).parent()).addClass("invalidElem");
            },
```

```
            unhighlight: function (element, errorClass) {
                $(element).add($(element).parent()).removeClass("invalidElem");
            },
            errorElement: "div",
            errorClass: "errorMsg"
        });

        $.validator.addClassRules({
            flowerValidation: {
                required: true,
                min: 0,
                max: 100,
                digits: true,
            }
        })

        $("#row1 input").each(function (index, elem) {
            $(elem).rules("add", {
                min: 10,
                max: 20
            })
        });

        $("input").addClass("flowerValidation").change(function (e) {
            $("form").validate().element($(e.target));
        });
    });
</script>
...
```

I call the rules method on a jQuery object, passing in the string add and a map object with the checks you want to perform and their arguments. The rules method operates on only the first element in the selection, so I have to use the each method to apply the rules more broadly. In this case, I selected all of the input elements that are descendants of the row1 element and applied the min and max checks to ensure that the user enters a value between 10 and 20.

■ **Tip**   You can remove rules from elements by replacing add with remove when you call the rules method.

Rules applied to elements using the rules methods are evaluated before those applied using a class. For my example, this means the input elements on the top row will be checked using a min value of 10 and a max value of 20, while the other input elements will use values of 0 and 100, respectively. You can see the effect of this in Figure 13-8.

Figure 13-8. *Applying rules directly to elements*

Because I am dealing with validation for each element individually, I can tailor the checks even further, as demonstrated by Listing 13-14.

Listing 13-14. Tailoring Checks for Elements

```
...
<script type="text/javascript">
    $(document).ready(function () {

        var data = { flowers: [
            { name: "Aster", product: "aster", stock: "10", price: "2.99" },
            { name: "Daffodil", product: "daffodil", stock: "12", price: "1.99" },
            { name: "Rose", product: "rose", stock: "2", price: "4.99" },
            { name: "Peony", product: "peony", stock: "0", price: "1.50" },
            { name: "Primula", product: "primula", stock: "1", price: "3.12" },
            { name: "Snowdrop", product: "snowdrop", stock: "15", price: "0.99" }]
        };

        var templResult = $("#flowerTmpl").template(data).filter("*");
        templResult.slice(0, 3).appendTo("#row1");
        templResult.slice(3).appendTo("#row2");

        $("form").validate({
            highlight: function (element, errorClass) {
                $(element).add($(element).parent()).addClass("invalidElem");
            },
            unhighlight: function (element, errorClass) {
                $(element).add($(element).parent()).removeClass("invalidElem");
            },
            errorElement: "div",
            errorClass: "errorMsg"
        });
```

```
        $("input").each(function (index, elem) {
            var rules = {
                required: true,
                min: 0,
                max: data.flowers[index].stock,
                digits: true
            }
            if (Number(data.flowers[index].price) > 3.00) {
                rules.max--;
            }
            $(elem).rules("add", rules);
        });

        $("input").addClass("flowerValidation").change(function (e) {
            $("form").validate().element($(e.target));
        });
    });
});
</script>
...
```

In this example, I tailor the value of the max check using the data object that I added to the document to generate elements using the template. The value for the max check is set based on the stock property and adjusted down if the price is greater than $3. When you have data like this, you are able to perform much more useful validation. You can see the effect of this change in Figure 13-9.

Figure 13-9. Setting different values for validation checks based on data

Applying Validation Rules via the Element Name Attribute

Validation rules can also be applied to elements based on the value of the name attribute. Nothing in the HTML specification requires the name attribute value to be unique, and a single value is often used to categorize a group of form elements. In my flower shop example document, each name is different and corresponds to a specific product. Either way, you can create rules that correspond to a name attribute value and rules that apply to all elements assigned that value. Listing 13-15 gives a demonstration.

Listing 13-15. Assigning Validation Rules Based on Element Name

```
...
<script type="text/javascript">
    $(document).ready(function () {

        var data = { flowers: [
            { name: "Aster", product: "aster", stock: "10", price: "2.99" },
            { name: "Daffodil", product: "daffodil", stock: "12", price: "1.99" },
            { name: "Rose", product: "rose", stock: "2", price: "4.99" },
            { name: "Peony", product: "peony", stock: "0", price: "1.50" },
            { name: "Primula", product: "primula", stock: "1", price: "3.12" },
            { name: "Snowdrop", product: "snowdrop", stock: "15", price: "0.99" }]
        };

        var templResult = $("#flowerTmpl").template(data).filter("*");
        templResult.slice(0, 3).appendTo("#row1");
        templResult.slice(3).appendTo("#row2");

        var rulesList = new Object();
        for (var i = 0; i < data.flowers.length; i++) {
            rulesList[data.flowers[i].product] = {
                min: 0,
                max: Number(data.flowers[i].stock),
            }
        }

        $("form").validate({
            highlight: function (element, errorClass) {
                $(element).add($(element).parent()).addClass("invalidElem");
            },
            unhighlight: function (element, errorClass) {
                $(element).add($(element).parent()).removeClass("invalidElem");
            },
            errorElement: "div",
            errorClass: "errorMsg",
            rules: rulesList
        });

        $("input").change(function (e) {
            $("form").validate().element($(e.target));
        });

    });
</script>
...
```

I added rules that rely on element names using the `rules` property of the configuration object I pass to the validate method when I set up form validation. Notice that I have used just the data object to create the set of rules and also that the product property in the data object is used to generate the name attribute on the input elements. Also notice that I have to use Number to convert the string data value so that it is processed correctly.

■ **Tip** I tend not to use this approach in my own projects, since I would rather work directly with the elements in the document, but this technique can be handy if you have a data object and want to set up validation before the form elements have been added to the document.

Applying Validation Rules Using Element Attributes

The final way to apply validation checks to elements is to use attributes. The validation plug-in examines form elements to see whether they define attributes that correspond to the name of the built-in checks, so an element that defines a required attribute is assumed to need the required check. Listing 13-16 provides a demonstration.

Listing 13-16. Performing Validation Using Element Attributes

```
...
<script id="flowerTmpl" type="text/x-handlebars-template">
    {{#each flowers}}
    <div class="dcell">
        <img src="{{product}}.png"/>
        <label for="{{product}}">{{name}}: </label>
        <input name="{{product}}" value="0" required min="0" max="{{stock}}"/>
    </div>
    {{/each}}
</script>
<script type="text/javascript">
    $(document).ready(function () {

        var data = { flowers: [
            { name: "Aster", product: "aster", stock: "10", price: "2.99" },
            { name: "Daffodil", product: "daffodil", stock: "12", price: "1.99" },
            { name: "Rose", product: "rose", stock: "2", price: "4.99" },
            { name: "Peony", product: "peony", stock: "0", price: "1.50" },
            { name: "Primula", product: "primula", stock: "1", price: "3.12" },
            { name: "Snowdrop", product: "snowdrop", stock: "15", price: "0.99" }]
        };

        var templResult = $("#flowerTmpl").template(data).filter("*");
        templResult.slice(0, 3).appendTo("#row1");
        templResult.slice(3).appendTo("#row2");

        $("form").validate({
            highlight: function (element, errorClass) {
                $(element).add($(element).parent()).addClass("invalidElem");
            },
```

```
            unhighlight: function (element, errorClass) {
                $(element).add($(element).parent()).removeClass("invalidElem");
            },
            errorElement: "div",
            errorClass: "errorMsg"
        });

        $("input").change(function (e) {
            $("form").validate().element($(e.target));
        });
    });
</script>
...
```

I like this technique when it is used in conjunction with a data template, but I find it clutters up a document when applied to statically defined elements because the same attributes are applied to elements over and over again.

Specifying Validation Messages

The validation plug-in defines a default error message for all of the built-in checks, but these are generic and not always useful to the user. As a simple example, if I set a max check with a value of 10 and the user enters 20 in the field, then the error message will be as follows:

```
Please enter a value less than or equal to 12
```

This message describes the constraint you have applied on a form element, but it doesn't provide any guidance to the user as to why there is a limit. Fortunately, you can change these messages to provide some additional context and tailor the message to your needs. The method used to change the messages depends on how you validation rule was created in the first place. It isn't possible to change the messages when you apply rules using a class, but in the following sections I describe how to define custom messages for the other techniques.

Specifying Messages for Attribute and Name Validation

When relying on the name attribute or on check attributes to associate rules with elements, you can change the messages displayed to the user by adding a messages property to the options object passed to the validate method. Listing 13-17 provides a demonstration.

Listing 13-17. Using the messages Property on the options Object

```
...
<script type="text/javascript">
    $(document).ready(function () {

        var data = { flowers: [
            { name: "Aster", product: "aster", stock: "10", price: "2.99" },
            { name: "Daffodil", product: "daffodil", stock: "12", price: "1.99" },
            { name: "Rose", product: "rose", stock: "2", price: "4.99" },
            { name: "Peony", product: "peony", stock: "0", price: "1.50" },
            { name: "Primula", product: "primula", stock: "1", price: "3.12" },
            { name: "Snowdrop", product: "snowdrop", stock: "15", price: "0.99" }]
        };
```

```
    var templResult = $("#flowerTmpl").template(data).filter("*");
    templResult.slice(0, 3).appendTo("#row1");
    templResult.slice(3).appendTo("#row2");

    $("form").validate({
        highlight: function (element, errorClass) {
            $(element).add($(element).parent()).addClass("invalidElem");
        },
        unhighlight: function (element, errorClass) {
            $(element).add($(element).parent()).removeClass("invalidElem");
        },
        errorElement: "div",
        errorClass: "errorMsg",
        messages: {
            rose: { max: "We don't have that many roses in stock!" },
            primula: { max: "We don't have that many primulas in stock!" }
        }
    });

    $("input").change(function (e) {
        $("form").validate().element($(e.target));
    });
});
</script>
...
```

The validation for this example is applied through the min and max attributes applied to the input element in the template, and you can see the structure of the object that sets out the values for the messages property in the JavaScript code.

Within the messages object, I define a property using the name of the element I am interested in and set the value of this property to be a map between the check and the new message you want to use. In this example, I have changed the message for the max check on the elements with the names rose and primula. You can see the effect in Figure 13-10, which illustrates how these custom messages are displayed.

Figure 13-10. *Changes messages via the options object*

The syntax for setting up these validation messages can be duplicative, so I tend to create an object with the messages I want programmatically, as shown in Listing 13-18.

Listing 13-18. Defining Custom Messages Programmatically

```
...
<script type="text/javascript">
    $(document).ready(function () {

        var data = { flowers: [
            { name: "Aster", product: "aster", stock: "10", price: "2.99" },
            { name: "Daffodil", product: "daffodil", stock: "12", price: "1.99" },
            { name: "Rose", product: "rose", stock: "2", price: "4.99" },
            { name: "Peony", product: "peony", stock: "0", price: "1.50" },
            { name: "Primula", product: "primula", stock: "1", price: "3.12" },
            { name: "Snowdrop", product: "snowdrop", stock: "15", price: "0.99" }]
        };

        var templResult = $("#flowerTmpl").template(data).filter("*");
        templResult.slice(0, 3).appendTo("#row1");
        templResult.slice(3).appendTo("#row2");

        var customMessages = new Object();
        for (var i = 0; i < data.flowers.length; i++) {
            customMessages[data.flowers[i].product] = {
                max: "We only have " + data.flowers[i].stock + " in stock"
            }
        }

        $("form").validate({
            highlight: function (element, errorClass) {
                $(element).add($(element).parent()).addClass("invalidElem");
            },
            unhighlight: function (element, errorClass) {
                $(element).add($(element).parent()).removeClass("invalidElem");
            },
            errorElement: "div",
            errorClass: "errorMsg",
            messages: customMessages
        });

        $("input").change(function (e) {
            $("form").validate().element($(e.target));
        });
    });
</script>
...
```

In this example, I incorporate the stock property from the data objects to give a more meaningful message to the user, as shown in Figure 13-11.

Figure 13-11. *Generating custom validation messages programmatically*

Specifying Messages for Per-Element Validation

When applying rules to individual elements, you pass in a `messages` object that defines the messages you want for your checks. Listing 13-19 shows how this is done.

Listing 13-19. Specifying Messages for Rules Applied on a Per-Element Basis

```
...
<script type="text/javascript">
    $(document).ready(function () {

        var data = { flowers: [
            { name: "Aster", product: "aster", stock: "10", price: "2.99" },
            { name: "Daffodil", product: "daffodil", stock: "12", price: "1.99" },
            { name: "Rose", product: "rose", stock: "2", price: "4.99" },
            { name: "Peony", product: "peony", stock: "0", price: "1.50" },
            { name: "Primula", product: "primula", stock: "1", price: "3.12" },
            { name: "Snowdrop", product: "snowdrop", stock: "15", price: "0.99" }]
        };

        var templResult = $("#flowerTmpl").template(data).filter("*");
        templResult.slice(0, 3).appendTo("#row1");
        templResult.slice(3).appendTo("#row2");

        $("form").validate({
            highlight: function (element, errorClass) {
                $(element).add($(element).parent()).addClass("invalidElem");
            },
```

337

```
            unhighlight: function (element, errorClass) {
                $(element).add($(element).parent()).removeClass("invalidElem");
            },
            errorElement: "div",
            errorClass: "errorMsg",
        });

        $("input").change(function (e) {
            $("form").validate().element($(e.target));
        }).each(function (index, elem) {
            $(elem).rules("add", {
                messages: {
                    max: "We only have " + data.flowers[index].stock + " in stock"
                }
            })
        });
    });
</script>
...
```

Once again, I have used the stock property from the corresponding flowers data object to define the message. For simplicity, I have assumed that the input elements are ordered in the same way that the data items are ordered. You can see the effect of these messages in Figure 13-12.

Figure 13-12. *Specifying messages that are derived from the data object*

■ **Tip**   I have only specified the messages using JavaScript. The min and max rules are still applied to the input elements via the template, as shown in Listing 13-17.

Creating a Custom Check

You can create a custom validation check if the built-in ones don't suit your needs. This is a simple process that means you can closely relate validation to the structure and nature of your web application. Listing 13-20 provides a demonstration.

Listing 13-20. Creating a Custom Validation Check

```
...
<script id="flowerTmpl" type="text/x-handlebars-template">
    {{#each flowers}}
    <div class="dcell">
        <img src="{{product}}.png"/>
        <label for="{{product}}">{{name}}: </label>
        <input name="{{product}}" value="0" required />
    </div>
    {{/each}}
</script>
<script type="text/javascript">
    $(document).ready(function () {

        var data = {
            flowers: [
                { name: "Aster", product: "aster", stock: "10", price: "2.99" },
                { name: "Daffodil", product: "daffodil", stock: "12", price: "1.99" },
                { name: "Rose", product: "rose", stock: "2", price: "4.99" },
                { name: "Peony", product: "peony", stock: "0", price: "1.50" },
                { name: "Primula", product: "primula", stock: "1", price: "3.12" },
                { name: "Snowdrop", product: "snowdrop", stock: "15", price: "0.99" }]
        };

        var templResult = $("#flowerTmpl").template(data).filter("*");
        templResult.slice(0, 3).appendTo("#row1");
        templResult.slice(3).appendTo("#row2");

        $("form").validate({
            highlight: function (element, errorClass) {
                $(element).add($(element).parent()).addClass("invalidElem");
            },
            unhighlight: function (element, errorClass) {
                $(element).add($(element).parent()).removeClass("invalidElem");
            },
            errorElement: "div",
            errorClass: "errorMsg"
        });

        $.validator.addMethod("stock", function (value, elem, args) {
            return Number(value) < Number(args);
        }, "We don't have that many in stock");
```

```
        $("input").each(function (index, elem) {
            $(elem).rules("add", {
                stock: data.flowers[index].stock
            })
        }).change(function (e) {
            $("form").validate().element($(e.target));
        });
    });
</script>
...
```

I have removed the min and max attributes from the input elements in the template and introduced a custom validation check in the JavaScript code. (You can mix and match custom and built-in validation freely, but the example in this listing duplicates the functionality of the max validator.)

Custom checks are created using the addMethod method, which is called on the validator property of the $ function. The arguments to this method are the name you want to assign the check, a function that is used to perform validation, and a message to show if validation fails. In this example, I have defined a check called stock, which I explain in the sections that follow.

Defining the Validation Function

The arguments to the custom validation function are the value entered by the user, the HTMLElement object representing the form element, and any arguments that were specified when the check is applied to an element for validation, like this:

```
...
$(elem).rules("add", {
    min: 0,
    stock: data.flowers[index].stock
})
...
```

When I applied the rule, I specified the value of a stock property from the flower data object that corresponds to the input element as the argument to the check. This is passed as is to the custom validation function:

```
...
function(value, elem, args) {
    return Number(value) <= Number(args);
}
...
```

The value and the arguments are presented as strings, and that means I have to use the Number type to ensure that JavaScript properly compares the values as numbers. The result of the validation function indicates if the value is valid – for an acceptable value, return true and return false for unacceptable values. For my function, a value is valid if it is smaller than or equal to the argument.

Defining the Validation Message

You can specify the message that is displayed in two ways. The first is as a string, which is what I used in the earlier example. The other way to specify a message is with a function, allowing you to create messages with a lot more context. Listing 13-21 provides a demonstration.

Listing 13-21. Creating a Message for a Custom Check Using a Function

```
...
<script type="text/javascript">
    $(document).ready(function () {

        var data = {
            flowers: [
                { name: "Aster", product: "aster", stock: "10", price: "2.99" },
                { name: "Daffodil", product: "daffodil", stock: "12", price: "1.99" },
                { name: "Rose", product: "rose", stock: "2", price: "4.99" },
                { name: "Peony", product: "peony", stock: "0", price: "1.50" },
                { name: "Primula", product: "primula", stock: "1", price: "3.12" },
                { name: "Snowdrop", product: "snowdrop", stock: "15", price: "0.99" }]
        };

        var templResult = $("#flowerTmpl").template(data).filter("*");
        templResult.slice(0, 3).appendTo("#row1");
        templResult.slice(3).appendTo("#row2");

        $("form").validate({
            highlight: function (element, errorClass) {
                $(element).add($(element).parent()).addClass("invalidElem");
            },
            unhighlight: function (element, errorClass) {
                $(element).add($(element).parent()).removeClass("invalidElem");
            },
            errorElement: "div",
            errorClass: "errorMsg"
        });

        $.validator.addMethod("stock", function (value, elem, args) {
            return Number(value) < Number(args);
        }, function(args) {
            return "We only have " + args + " in stock"
        });

        $("input").each(function (index, elem) {
            $(elem).rules("add", {
                stock: data.flowers[index].stock
            })
        }).change(function (e) {
            $("form").validate().element($(e.target));
        });
    });
</script>
...
```

The argument passed to the function is the argument you provided when applying the rule, which in this case is the stock property value from the data flower object. You can see the effect in Figure 13-13.

Figure 13-13. *Defining error messages for custom checks using a function*

Formatting the Validation Error Display

To my mind, one of the best features of the validation plug-in is the wide range of ways that you can configure how validation error messages are displayed to the user. In the examples so far in this chapter, I have relied on the configuration options highlighted in Listing 13-22.

Listing 13-22. The Configuration Options for Formatting the Validation Errors

```
...
<script type="text/javascript">
    $(document).ready(function () {

        var data = {
            flowers: [
                { name: "Aster", product: "aster", stock: "10", price: "2.99" },
                { name: "Daffodil", product: "daffodil", stock: "12", price: "1.99" },
                { name: "Rose", product: "rose", stock: "2", price: "4.99" },
                { name: "Peony", product: "peony", stock: "0", price: "1.50" },
                { name: "Primula", product: "primula", stock: "1", price: "3.12" },
                { name: "Snowdrop", product: "snowdrop", stock: "15", price: "0.99" }]
        };

        var templResult = $("#flowerTmpl").template(data).filter("*");
        templResult.slice(0, 3).appendTo("#row1");
        templResult.slice(3).appendTo("#row2");
```

```
        $("form").validate({
            highlight: function (element, errorClass) {
                $(element).add($(element).parent()).addClass("invalidElem");
            },
            unhighlight: function (element, errorClass) {
                $(element).add($(element).parent()).removeClass("invalidElem");
            },
            errorElement: "div",
            errorClass: "errorMsg"
        });

        $.validator.addMethod("stock", function (value, elem, args) {
            return Number(value) < Number(args);
        }, function(args) {
            return "We only have " + args + " in stock"
        });

        $("input").each(function (index, elem) {
            $(elem).rules("add", {
                stock: data.flowers[index].stock
            })
        }).change(function (e) {
            $("form").validate().element($(e.target));
        });
    });
</script>
...
```

I have relied on four different configuration options, but they are tightly coupled together. I explain the significance of each in the following sections.

Setting the Class for Invalid Elements

The errorClass option specifies a class that will be associated with invalid values. This class is applied to error message elements when they are added to the document. In my examples, I specify a class called errorMsg, for which there is a corresponding CSS style in the style element, as shown in Listing 13-23. The style sets the text color to red to emphasize the validation error.

Listing 13-23. The style Element for the Example Document

```
...
<style type="text/css">
    .errorMsg {color: red}
    .invalidElem {border: medium solid red}
</style>
...
```

Setting the Error Message Element

Error messages are inserted into the document as the immediate next sibling of the form element that contains the invalid value. By default, the error message text is contained within a label element. This didn't suit me in the examples, because the external style sheet already contains a selector that matches all label elements within the cell-level div elements in the CSS table layout and applied a style that prevented the text from displaying properly. To address this, I used the errorElement option to specify that a div element be used instead, as shown in Listing 13-24.

Listing 13-24. Specifying the Element That Will Be Used for the Error Message

```
...
$("form").validate({
    highlight: function(element, errorClass) {
        $(element).add($(element).parent()).addClass("invalidElem");
    },
    unhighlight: function(element, errorClass) {
        $(element).add($(element).parent()).removeClass("invalidElem");
    },
    errorElement: "div",
    errorClass: "errorMsg",

});
...
```

Setting the Highlighting for Invalid Elements

The highlight and unhighlight options specify functions that will be used to highlight elements that contain invalid values. The arguments to the functions are the HTMLElement object representing the invalid element and the class specified using the errorClass option.

As you can see in Listing 13-25, I ignore the second attribute but use the HTMLElement object to create a jQuery selection, navigate to the parent element, and add it to the invalidElem class.

Listing 13-25. Controlling the Element Highlight

```
...
$("form").validate({
    highlight: function(element, errorClass) {
        $(element).add($(element).parent()).addClass("invalidElem");
    },
    unhighlight: function(element, errorClass) {
        $(element).add($(element).parent()).removeClass("invalidElem");
    },
    errorElement: "div",
    errorClass: "errorMsg",

});
...
```

The function specified by the unhighlight option is called when the user has corrected the problem and the element contains a valid value. I use this opportunity to remove the class I added in the other function. The invalidElem class corresponds to a selector in the style element contained in the document, as shown in Listing 13-26.

Listing 13-26. The Style Used for Highlighting Element

```
...
<style type="text/css">
    .errorMsg {color: red}
    .invalidElem {border: medium solid red}
</style>
...
```

You can select and manipulate elements in these functions in any way you like. I have applied a border to the parent element, but I could have operated directly on the element itself or on another part of the document entirely had I preferred.

Using a Validation Summary

The validation plug-in can present the user with a single list of all the validation errors, rather than add individual messages next to each element. This can be useful if the structure or layout of your document can't easily flex to accommodate additional elements. Listing 13-27 shows how to create a validation summary.

Listing 13-27. Using a Validation Summary

```
...
<script type="text/javascript">
    $(document).ready(function () {

        var data = {
            flowers: [
                { name: "Aster", product: "aster", stock: "10", price: "2.99" },
                { name: "Daffodil", product: "daffodil", stock: "12", price: "1.99" },
                { name: "Rose", product: "rose", stock: "2", price: "4.99" },
                { name: "Peony", product: "peony", stock: "0", price: "1.50" },
                { name: "Primula", product: "primula", stock: "1", price: "3.12" },
                { name: "Snowdrop", product: "snowdrop", stock: "15", price: "0.99" }]
        };

        var plurals = {
            aster: "Asters", daffodil: "Daffodils", rose: "Roses",
            peony: "Peonies", primula: "Primulas", snowdrop: "Snowdrops"
        };

        var templResult = $("#flowerTmpl").template(data).filter("*");
        templResult.slice(0, 3).appendTo("#row1");
        templResult.slice(3).appendTo("#row2");

        $("<div id='errorSummary'>Please correct the following errors:</div>")
            .addClass("errorMsg invalidElem")
            .append("<ul id='errorsList'></ul>").hide().insertAfter("h1");
```

```
    $("form").validate({
        highlight: function (element, errorClass) {
            $(element).addClass("invalidElem");
        },
        unhighlight: function (element, errorClass) {
            $(element).removeClass("invalidElem");
        },
        errorContainer: "#errorSummary",
        errorLabelContainer: "#errorsList",
        wrapper: "li",
        errorElement: "div"
    });

    $.validator.addMethod("stock", function (value, elem, args) {
        return Number(value) <= Number(args.data.stock);
    }, function (args) {
        return "You requested " + $(args.element).val() + " "
            + plurals[args.data.product] + " but we only have "
            + args.data.stock + " in stock";
    });

    $("input").each(function (index, elem) {
        $(elem).rules("add", {
            stock: {
                index: index,
                data: data.flowers[index],
                element: elem
            }
        })
    }).change(function (e) {
        $("form").validate().element($(e.target));
    });

    });
</script>
...
```

For this example, I am going to work backward and show you the result before explaining how I get there. Figure 13-14 shows the validation summary being displayed.

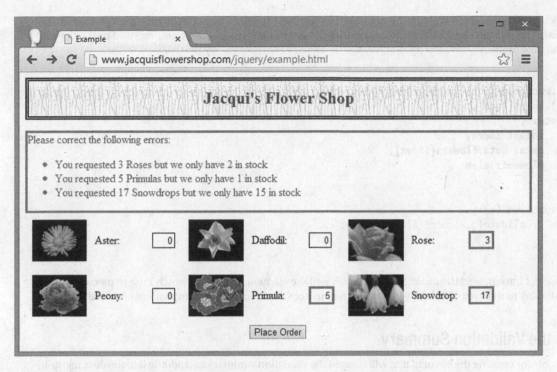

Figure 13-14. *Using a validation summary*

Preparing the Validation Messages

The first issue to solve when using a validation summary is that the context that is implied by placing an error message next to a form element is lost; I have to put some additional work into the error messages so that they make sense. To start with, I defined an object that contained the plurals of the flower names:

```
...
var plurals = {
    aster: "Asters", daffodil: "Daffodils", rose: "Roses",
    peony: "Peonies", primula: "Primulas", snowdrop: "Snowdrops"
}
...
```

I use these values to generate a specific error message using the function feature of the custom check, like this:

```
...
$.validator.addMethod("stock", function (value, elem, args) {
    return Number(value) <= Number(args.data.stock);
}, function (args) {
    return "You requested " + $(args.element).val() + " "
        + plurals[args.data.product] + " but we only have "
        + args.data.stock + " in stock";
});
...
```

The link between these two stages is the argument object that I specify when applying the custom check to the form elements. The built-in checks have simple arguments, but you can create complex objects and pass whatever data suits you, like this:

```
...
$("input").each(function (index, elem) {
    $(elem).rules("add", {
        stock: {
            index: index,
            data: data.flowers[index],
            element: elem
        }
    })
}).change(function (e) {
    $("form").validate().element($(e.target));
});
...
```

In this case, I have passed the index, the data array, and the element itself, all of which I use to piece together the message to display to the user. (I'll show you a useful feature for simplifying string composition later in the chapter.)

Creating the Validation Summary

I am responsible for creating the element that will contain the validation summary and adding it to the document. To that end, I added a div element that contains an ul element. My goal is to create an unnumbered list showing each error:

```
...
$("<div id='errorSummary'>Please correct the following errors:</div>")
    .addClass("errorMsg invalidElem").append("<ul id='errorsList'></ul>").hide().insertAfter("h1");
...
```

The text in the div element is displayed above the list of errors. Notice that I have used the hide method after appending these elements to the DOM. Not only am I responsible for creating the elements, but I am also responsible for ensuring that they are not visible when there are no errors. The hide method ensures that the validation summary isn't initially visible to the user – the validation plug-in will take care of the visibility once the validation process begins.

Now that I have all the pieces in place, I can configure the validation summary, as follows:

```
...
$("form").validate({
    highlight: function (element, errorClass) {
        $(element).addClass("invalidElem");
    },
    unhighlight: function (element, errorClass) {
        $(element).removeClass("invalidElem");
    },
    errorContainer: "#errorSummary",
    errorLabelContainer: "#errorsList",
    wrapper: "li",
    errorElement: "div"
});
...
```

I have changed the implementation of the `hightlight` and `unhighlight` functions to style just the `input` elements. The `errorContainer` option specifies a selector that will be made visible when there are validation errors to display. In my case, this is the element with the `errorSummary` ID (the `div` element). The `errorLabelContainer` option specifies the element into which the individual error messages will be inserted. For my example, this is the `ul` element, since I want my messages displayed as a list.

The `wrapper` option specifies an element into which the validation message will be inserted. This is useful only if you want a list display. Finally, the `errorElement` specifies the element that will contain the error text. This is the `label` element by default, but I have switched to `div` elements to make the formatting easier. The result of these options is the validation summary I showed you in Figure 13-14.

The validation plug-in removes messages from the summary when the user resolves an issue, and when there are no issues at all, the validation summary is entirely hidden and the user can submit the form. Figure 13-15 shows the validation summary after two of the three errors from the last figure have been resolved.

Figure 13-15. *A validation summary showing fewer error messages*

The choice between inline messages and validation summaries is a personal one and is usually driven by the structure of the document. The good news is that the validation plug-in is flexible, and it usually doesn't take much work to define and apply validation that is closely tailored to your needs.

349

Tidying Up the Error Message Composition

I am going to make one final change in this chapter, just to demonstrate a useful feature of the validation plug-in that is not directly related to validating data. In the previous example, when I wanted to create a contextual error message, I did so by concatenating strings and variables, like this:

```
...
$.validator.addMethod("stock", function (value, elem, args) {
    return Number(value) <= Number(args.data.stock);
}, function (args) {
    return "You requested " + $(args.element).val() + " "
        + plurals[args.data.product] + " but we only have "
        + args.data.stock + " in stock";
});
...
```

This works, but it is ugly and hard to read. The validation plug-in method provides a formatter than works in a way similar to string composition in languages like C#, and you can see how I have used this feature in Listing 13-28.

Listing 13-28. Using the jQuery Validator String Formatting Feature

```
...
$.validator.addMethod("stock", function (value, elem, args) {
    return Number(value) <= Number(args.data.stock);
}, function(args) {
    return $.validator.format("You requested {0} {1} but we only have {2} in stock",
        $(args.element).val(), plurals[args.data.product], args.data.stock )
});
...
```

The string composition is performed by the $.validator.format method, which takes a template string and a number of value arguments. The template string is parsed for occurrences of the brace characters surrounding an integer, such as {0}, and these are replaced with the corresponding value argument. The first value argument is referenced by {0}, the second by {1} and so on. The $.validator.format method returns a function that isn't evaluated until the error message is displayed, which ensures that the correct values are used when composing the string.

This can be an odd way of creating strings if you are not used to it, but a sorely missed feature if you are accustomed to a language like C# that frequently relies on this approach to string composition.

Summary

In this chapter, I showed you the support that jQuery provides for forms. I began by recapping the form-related event methods and explained the roles that the most important ones play in the life of an HTML form. Most of the chapter was spent covering the Validation plug-in, which provides flexible and extensible support for validating the values that users enter into a form and providing the means for resolving any problems before the data is submitted to the server. In Chapter 14, I begin the process of describing the support that jQuery provides for making Ajax requests.

CHAPTER 14

■ ■ ■

Using Ajax: Part I

Ajax stands for Asynchronous JavaScript and XML but is generally a word in its own right these days. Ajax allows you to make requests to the server asynchronously, meaning, in short, that your request happens in the background and doesn't prevent the user from interacting with the content in your HTML document. The most common use for Ajax is to submit data from a form element. The advantage of doing this is that the browser doesn't have to load a new document to display the server's response and you can use the standard jQuery functions to display the data within the document seamlessly.

The Ajax support that I use in this chapter is built into the core jQuery library, although I do briefly describe a useful plug-in at the end of the chapter. jQuery doesn't reinvent Ajax but, rather, makes the existing browser Ajax API (application programming interface) easier to use. In this chapter, I describe the *shorthand* and *convenience* Ajax methods. These are simpler methods that make using Ajax relatively quick and easy. In Chapter 15, I describe the low-level jQuery Ajax API on which these methods are based. However, as you'll see, the low-level API isn't *that* low level, and the main reason for its use is when the shorthand and convenience methods don't do quite what you want. Table 14-1 provides the summary for this chapter.

Table 14-1. Chapter Summary

Problem	Solution	Listing
Perform an asynchronous HTTP GET request	Use the get method	1–3
Process the data obtained from an Ajax GET request	Pass a function to the get method	4
Perform an Ajax request in response to a user action	Call the get method within an event handler	5
Request JSON data from the server	Use the get method and receive an object in the argument function	6, 7
Send data to the server as part of a GET request	Pass a JavaScript object as an argument to the get method	8
Perform an asynchronous HTTP POST request	Use the post method	9, 10
Send non-form data in a POST request	Pass any JavaScript object as an argument to the post method	11
Override the data type specified by the server in the response to an Ajax request	Pass the expected type as an argument to the get or post methods	12–13
Avoid the most common Ajax pitfall	Don't treat Ajax requests as though they were synchronous	14
Use the convenience methods to make GET requests for specific data types	Use the load, getScript, or getJSON method	15–22
Easily enable Ajax for form elements	Use the Ajax Forms plug-in	23

Using the Ajax Shorthand Methods

Although Ajax is usually associated with posting form data, it can be used a lot more widely. I am going to start introducing Ajax by performing some simple tasks, starting with ways that you can obtain data from the server without using forms at all.

jQuery defines a set of *Ajax shorthand methods*, which are convenient wrappers around the core Ajax functions and which allow you to easily perform common Ajax tasks. In the sections that follow, I introduce you to the shorthand methods for retrieving data from the server using HTTP GET requests. Table 14-2 summarizes these methods.

Table 14-2. *The jQuery Ajax Shorthand Methods*

Name	Description
$.get()	Performs an Ajax request using the HTTP GET method
$.post()	Performs an Ajax request using the HTTP POST method

(BRIEFLY) UNDERSTANDING ASYNCHRONOUS TASKS

For those of you who are new to Ajax, here's a simple explanation of asynchronous requests. This is important because these tasks are so central to Ajax that the first letter in the acronym stands for *asynchronous*. Most of the time, you are used to writing synchronous code. You define a block of statements that perform some task, and then you wait while the browser executes them. When the last statement has been executed, you know the task has been performed. During the execution, the browser doesn't let the user interact with the content in any way.

When you perform an asynchronous task, you are telling the browser that you want something done in the background. The phrase "in the background" is something of a catchall, but in essence you are saying, "Do this thing without preventing the user from interacting with the document and tell me when you have done it." In the case of Ajax, you are telling the browser to communicate with the server and notify you when the request has been completed. This notification is handled through *callback functions*. You give jQuery one or more functions that will be called when the task is complete. There will be a function to deal with a successful request, and there can be other functions for other outcomes, such as errors.

The advantage of asynchronous requests is that they allow you to create a rich HTML document that can be seamlessly updated using responses from the server without interrupting the user's interaction and without having to make the user wait while the browser loads a new document.

The disadvantage is that you have to think through your code carefully. You can't predict when an asynchronous request will be completed, and you can't make assumptions about the outcome. Further, the use of callback functions tends to create more complex code that can punish the unwary programmer who makes assumptions about the outcome or timeliness of a request.

Performing an Ajax GET Request

To begin, I am going to use Ajax to perform an HTTP GET request to load a fragment of HTML, which I will then add to the HTML document displayed by the browser. Listing 14-1 shows the example document that I will be working with.

Listing 14-1. The Example Document

```
<!DOCTYPE html>
<html>
<head>
    <title>Example</title>
    <script src="jquery-2.0.2.js" type="text/javascript"></script>
    <script src="handlebars.js" type="text/javascript"></script>
    <script src="handlebars-jquery.js" type="text/javascript"></script>
    <script src="jquery.validate.js" type="text/javascript"></script>
    <link rel="stylesheet" type="text/css" href="styles.css"/>
    <script type="text/javascript">
        $(document).ready(function() {
            // ...code will go here...
        });
    </script>
</head>
<body>
    <h1>Jacqui's Flower Shop</h1>
    <form method="post" action="http://node.jacquisflowershop.com/order">
        <div id="oblock">
            <div class="dtable">
                <div id="row1" class="drow">
                </div>
                <div id="row2"class="drow">
                </div>
            </div>
        </div>
        <div id="buttonDiv"><button type="submit">Place Order</button></div>
    </form>
</body>
</html>
```

This is similar to the examples I have used in earlier chapters but there are no elements to describe the products and no data item or templates to generate them. Instead, I have created a separate file called flowers.html, which I have placed next to the example document (which is called example.html and can be found in the Source Code/ Download area of the Apress web site [www.apress.com]). Listing 14-2 shows the content of flowers.html.

Listing 14-2. The Contents of the flowers.html File

```
<div>
    <img src="aster.png"/><label for="aster">Aster:</label>
    <input name="aster" value="0" required />
</div>
<div>
    <img src="daffodil.png"/><label for="daffodil">Daffodil:</label>
    <input name="daffodil" value="0" required />
</div>
<div>
    <img src="rose.png"/><label for="rose">Rose:</label>
    <input name="rose" value="0" required />
</div>
```

```
<div>
    <img src="peony.png"/><label for="peony">Peony:</label>
    <input name="peony" value="0" required />
</div>
<div>
    <img src="primula.png"/><label for="primula">Primula:</label>
    <input name="primula" value="0" required />
</div>
<div>
    <img src="snowdrop.png"/><label for="snowdrop">Snowdrop:</label>
    <input name="snowdrop" value="0" required />
</div>
```

These are the same elements I used in earlier chapters, except that they are not assigned to rows and I have removed the class attribute from the div elements. I have made these changes so that I can show you how to work with the elements once you load them. Notice that this isn't a complete HTML document, just a fragment—there are no html, head, or body elements, for example. At the moment, the flowers.html document is completely separate from the main example, and you can see this in Figure 14-1.

Figure 14-1. *The initial example document*

I am going to use the jQuery support for Ajax to bring the HTML fragment into the main HTML document. This might seem like an odd thing to do, but I am simulating a common situation where different pieces of content are produced by different systems and need to be stitched together to create a complex document or web application. I am using only one server in this example for simplicity, but it is easy to imagine that the information about the products is coming from elsewhere. In fact, in later examples, I introduce Node.js in order to show you how to deal with multiple servers. That is all to come. For the moment, let's look at the basic jQuery Ajax support and use it to deal with the flowers.html file. Listing 14-3 shows how I do this.

Listing 14-3. Using jQuery Ajax Support with an HTML Fragment

```
...
<script type="text/javascript">
    $(document).ready(function () {
        $.get("flowers.html", function (data) {
            var elems = $(data).filter("div").addClass("dcell");
            elems.slice(0, 3).appendTo("#row1");
            elems.slice(3).appendTo("#row2");
        });
    });
</script>
...
```

I used the jQuery get method and provided two arguments. The first argument is the URL that I want to load. In this case, I have specified flowers.html, which will be interpreted as being a URL that is relative to the URL from which the main document was loaded.

The second argument is a function that will be invoked if the request is successful. As I mentioned in the sidebar, Ajax relies on callback functions to provide notification because the requests are performed asynchronously. jQuery passes the data from the server response as the argument to the function.

When the document that contains this script is loaded into the browser, the script element is executed and my jQuery code loads the flowers.html from the server. Once the flowers.html document is loaded, the HTML fragment it contains is parsed into HTML elements that are then added to the document. Figure 14-2 shows the result.

Figure 14-2. *The effect of using Ajax*

OK, so I admit that I ended up with the same result as when the elements or data were inline, but the path I took to get there is worth exploring and in the sections that follow I dig into the detail.

■ **Tip**   Although I have used the get method to load HTML, it can be used to obtain any kind of data from the server.

Processing the Response Data

The argument passed to the success function is the data that the server has sent back in answer to my request. In this example, I get back the content of the flowers.html file, which is an HTML fragment. To make this into something I can use with jQuery, I passed the data into the jQuery $ function so that it is parsed into a hierarchy of HTMLElement objects, as shown in Listing 14-4.

Listing 14-4. Processing the Data Obtained from the Server

```
...
<script type="text/javascript">
    $(document).ready(function() {
```

```
        $.get("flowers.html", function(data) {
            var elems = $(data).filter("div").addClass("dcell");
            elems.slice(0, 3).appendTo("#row1");
            elems.slice(3).appendTo("#row2");
        });
    });
</script>
...
```

As I mentioned previously, I left out the class attributes from the div elements. You can see that I add them back in using the jQuery addClass method. Once the data has been passed to the $ function, I can use the jQuery object that is returned as I would any other. I add the elements to the document using the slice and appendTo methods, as I have in previous chapters.

■ **Tip**   Notice that I have used the filter method to select only the div elements generated from the data. When parsing the data, jQuery assumes that the carriage-return characters that I added between the div elements in the flowers.html file for structure are text content and creates text elements for them. To avoid this, you can either ensure that there are no carriage returns in the documents you request or use the filter method to remove then. This is similar to the issue I had with data templates in Chapter 13.

Making the Effect Easier to See

The statements that create the Ajax request are executed in response to the ready event (which I described in Chapter 5) and this makes it hard to visualize how using Ajax is any different from using inline data because the content of the flowers.html file is loaded and displayed automatically. To make the difference more obvious, I have added a button to the document and handle the click event it generates so that the Ajax request will be performed only when it is clicked. You can see the changes in Listing 14-5.

Listing 14-5. Making an Ajax Request in Response to a Button Press

```
...
<script type="text/javascript">
    $(document).ready(function () {
        $("<button>Ajax</button>").appendTo("#buttonDiv").click(function (e) {
            $.get("flowers.html",
                function (data) {
                    var elems = $(data).filter("div").addClass("dcell");
                    elems.slice(0, 3).appendTo("#row1");
                    elems.slice(3).appendTo("#row2");
                });
            e.preventDefault();
        });
    });
</script>
...
```

Now the `flowers.html` document isn't loaded until the button is clicked, and each time it is clicked, additional elements are added to the document, as shown in Figure 14-3.

Figure 14-3. *Using Ajax in response to a button press*

■ **Tip**   Notice that I have called the `preventDefault` method on the `Event` object that is passed to my event handler function. Since the `button` element is contained with a `form` element, the default action is to submit the form to the server.

Getting Other Kinds of Data

You are not limited to using the `get` method just for HTML—you can obtain any kind of data from the server. Of particular interest is JavaScript Object Notation (JSON) data, because of the way that jQuery helpfully processes the response from the server. Back when Ajax started to be widely adopted, XML was seen as the data format of choice, so much so that the *X* in Ajax stands for XML. I am not going to go into the details of XML, but XML tends to be verbose, hard to read, and relatively time- and resource-consuming to generate and process.

In recent years, XML has been largely replaced by the JSON, which is a simpler data format and is easy to work with in JavaScript code (as the name suggests). For this example, I have created a file called `mydata.json` and saved it alongside the `example.html` file on the web server. Listing 14-6 shows the contents of `mydata.json`.

Listing 14-6. The Contents of the mydata.json File

```
[{"name":"Aster","product":"aster","stock":"10","price":"2.99"},
 {"name":"Daffodil","product":"daffodil","stock":"12","price":"1.99"},
 {"name":"Rose","product":"rose","stock":"2","price":"4.99"},
 {"name":"Peony","product":"peony","stock":"0","price":"1.50"},
 {"name":"Primula","product":"primula","stock":"1","price":"3.12"},
 {"name":"Snowdrop","product":"snowdrop","stock":"15","price":"0.99"}]
```

The file contains the data for the flower products and as you can see, JSON data is almost identical to the way you represent data inline in JavaScript code. To load and process this data using Ajax, I can use the get method again, as shown in Listing 14-7.

Listing 14-7. Using the get Method to Obtain JSON Data

```
...
<script id="flowerTmpl" type="text/x-handlebars-template">
    {{#flowers}}
    <div class="dcell">
        <img src="{{product}}.png"/>
        <label for="{{product}}">{{name}}</label>
        <input name="{{product}}" data-price="{{price}}" data-stock="{{stock}}"
            value="0" required />
    </div>
    {{/flowers}}
</script>
<script type="text/javascript">
    $(document).ready(function () {
        $("<button>Ajax</button>").appendTo("#buttonDiv").click(function (e) {
            $.get("mydata.json", function (data) {
                var tmplData = $("#flowerTmpl").template({flowers: data}).filter("*");
                tmplData.slice(0, 3).appendTo("#row1");
                tmplData.slice(3).appendTo("#row2");
            });
            e.preventDefault();
        });
    });
</script>
...
```

In this example, I request the JSON data file in response to the button click. The data retrieved from the server is passed to a function, just as with the HTML fragment. I have used the Handlebars template plug-in (described in Chapter 12) to process the data and generate HTML elements from it and then the slice and appendTo method to insert the elements into the document. Notice that I didn't have to do anything to convert the JSON string to a JavaScript object: jQuery does this for me automatically.

■ **Tip**   Some web servers (and this includes some versions of Microsoft IIS, which I have used for this book) will not return content to browsers if they don't recognize the file extension or data format. To make this example work with IIS, I have to add a new mapping between the file extension (.json) and the MIME type for JSON data (application/json). Until I did this, IIS would return 404—Not Found errors when mydata.json was requested.

Providing Data to GET Requests

It is possible to send data to the server as part of a GET request, which is the kind of request made by the get method (as well as the load, getScript, and getJSON methods that I describe later in this chapter). To send data as part of the GET request, you pass a data object to the get method, as demonstrated by Listing 14-8.

Listing 14-8. Sending Data as Part of a GET Request

```
...
<script type="text/javascript">
    $(document).ready(function () {

        var requestData = {
            country: "US",
            state: "New York"
        };

        $("<button>Ajax</button>").appendTo("#buttonDiv").click(function (e) {
            $.get("mydata.json", requestData, function (data) {
                var tmplData = $("#flowerTmpl").template({flowers: data}).filter("*");
                tmplData.slice(0, 3).appendTo("#row1");
                tmplData.slice(3).appendTo("#row2");
            });
            e.preventDefault();
        });
    });
</script>
...
```

The data you provide is appended to the specified URL as a query string. For this example, this means you request the following:

```
http://www.jacquisflowershop.com/jquery/flowers.html?country=US&state=New+York
```

The server can use the data you provide to tailor the content that is returned. You might have different flower sections for different states, for example. You won't be able to see the URL used to make the Ajax request in the browser, but you can use the developer's tools (commonly known as the *F12 tools* because they are accessed via the F12 key) to see what requests are being made. For Google Chrome, press F12, click the Network tab in the window that appears, and click the *XHR* filter (XHR refers to the XmlHttpRequest object, which is the Document Object Model (DOM) object used by jQuery to make Ajax requests). Figure 14-4 illustrates how Chrome displays details of the Ajax request in the example.

Elements	Resources	Network	Sources	Timeline	Profiles	Audits	Console		
Name Path					**Method**	**Status** Text	**Type**		
mydata.json?country=US&state=New+York /jquery					GET	200 OK	application/json		

1 / 13 requests | 683 B / 3.0 KB transferred | 7.44 s (onload: 54 ms, DOMContentLoaded: 53 ms)

☐ ⊵ ⌕ ☰ ● ⊘ | All | Documents | Stylesheets | Images | Scripts | XHR

Figure 14-4. *Inspecting an Ajax request using the Google Chrome F12 tools*

```
┌────────────────────────────────────────────────────────────┐
│              GET AND POST: PICK THE RIGHT ONE                │
└────────────────────────────────────────────────────────────┘
```

You might be tempted to send form data using a GET request. Be careful. The rule of thumb is that GET requests should be used for read-only information retrieval, while POST requests should be used for any operation that changes the application state.

In standards-compliance terms, GET requests are for *safe* interactions (having no side effects besides information retrieval), and POST requests are for *unsafe* interactions (making a decision or changing something). These conventions are set by the World Wide Web Consortium (W3C), at www.w3.org/Provider/Style/URI.

So, you can use GET requests to send form data to the server, but not for operations that change state. Many web developers learned this the hard way in 2005 when Google Web Accelerator was released to the public. This application pre-fetched all the content linked from each page, which is legal within HTTP because GET requests should be safe. Unfortunately, many web developers had ignored the HTTP conventions and placed simple links to "delete item" or "add to shopping cart" in their applications. Chaos ensued.

One company believed its content management system was the target of repeated hostile attacks, because all its content kept getting deleted. The company later discovered that a search-engine crawler had hit upon the URL of an administrative page and was crawling all the delete links.

Performing an Ajax POST Request

Now that you have seen how to get data from the server, I can turn my attention to how you send it—that is, how to post form data to the server. Once again, there is a shorthand method: post, which makes posting a form simple. But before I demonstrate the use of the post method, I need to extend the code for the formserver.js file so that Node.js is able to receive and process the POST requests I use in the examples.

Preparing Node.js to Receive Form Data

I need a server script that will receive data sent from the browser using the HTTP POST method, perform some simple operation on the data that has been sent, and generate a response. Listing 14-9 shows the updated version of the formserver.js file that I first used in Chapter 13.

Listing 14-9. The Modified formserver.js File

```
var http = require("http");
var querystring = require("querystring");
var url = require("url");

var port = 80;

http.createServer(function (req, res) {
    console.log("[200 OK] " + req.method + " to " + req.url);

    if (req.method == "OPTIONS") {
        res.writeHead(200, "OK", {
            "Access-Control-Allow-Headers": "Content-Type",
            "Access-Control-Allow-Methods": "*",
            "Access-Control-Allow-Origin": "http://www.jacquisflowershop.com"
        });
        res.end();
```

```
} else if (req.method == "POST") {
    var dataObj = new Object();
    var contentType = req.headers["content-type"];
    var fullBody = "";

    if (contentType) {
        if (contentType.indexOf("application/x-www-form-urlencoded") > -1) {
            req.on("data", function (chunk) { fullBody += chunk.toString(); });
            req.on("end", function () {
                var dBody = querystring.parse(fullBody);
                writeResponse(req, res, dBody,
                    url.parse(req.url, true).query["callback"])
            });
        } else {
            req.on("data", function (chunk) { fullBody += chunk.toString(); });
            req.on("end", function () {
                dataObj = JSON.parse(fullBody);
                var dprops = new Object();
                for (var i = 0; i < dataObj.length; i++) {
                    dprops[dataObj[i].name] = dataObj[i].value;
                }
                writeResponse(req, res, dprops);
            });
        }
    }
} else if (req.method == "GET") {
    var data = url.parse(req.url, true).query;
    writeResponse(req, res, data, data["callback"])
}

function writeResponse(req, res, data, jsonp) {
    var total = 0;
    for (item in data) {
        if (item != "_" && data[item] > 0) {
            total += Number(data[item]);
        } else {
            delete data[item];
        }
    }
    data.total = total;
    jsonData = JSON.stringify(data);
    if (jsonp) {
        jsonData = jsonp + "(" + jsonData + ")";
    }

    res.writeHead(200, "OK", {
        "Content-Type": "application/json",
        "Access-Control-Allow-Origin": "*"
    });
```

```
        res.write(jsonData);
        res.end();
    }

}).listen(port);
console.log("Ready on port " + port);
```

■ **Tip** The easiest way to get this script is to download the source code that accompanies this book and that is freely available on the Apress web site at www.apress.com. I included details of obtaining Node.js in Chapter 1.

As before, I run the script by entering the following at the command prompt:

```
node.exe formserver.js
```

The revised Node.js script processes the data sent by the browser and creates a JSON response. I could have returned HTML from this script, but JSON is more compact and often simpler to work with. The JSON object I return is a simple object that contains the total number of products that the user has selected and the number of each of them for which a value was specified. So, for example, if I selected one aster, two daffodils, and three roses, the JSON response sent back by the Node.js script would be as follows:

```
{"aster":"1","daffodil":"2","rose":"2","total":5}
```

The previous JSON string I showed you represented an array of objects, but this server script returns just a single object whose properties correspond to the selected flowers. The total property contains the sum of the individual selections. I appreciate that this is hardly the most valuable activity a server can perform, but I want to focus on using Ajax rather than server-side development.

Understanding Cross-Origin Ajax Requests

If you look at the new formserver.js script, you will see that when I write the response to the browser, I set an HTTP header, as follows:

```
Access-Control-Allow-Origin: http://www.jacquisflowershop.com
```

By default, browsers limit scripts to making make Ajax requests within the same *origin* as the document that contains them. An origin is the combination of the protocol, hostname, and port components of a URL. If two URLs have the same protocol, hostname, and port, then they are within the same origin. If any of the three components is different, then they are in different origins.

■ **Tip** This policy is intended to reduce the risks of a *cross-site scripting* (CSS) attack, where the browser (or user) is tricked into executing a malicious script. CSS attacks are outside the scope of this book, but there is a useful Wikipedia article at http://en.wikipedia.org/wiki/Cross-site_scripting that provides a good introduction to the topic.

Table 14-3 shows how changes in URLs affect the origin when compared to the URL of the main example document, which is www.jacquisflowershop.com/jquery/example.html.

Table 14-3. Comparing URLs

URL	Origin Comparison
http://www.jacquisflowershop.com/apps/mydoc.html	Same origin
https://www.jacquisflowershop.com/apps/mydoc.html	Different origin; protocol differs
http://www.jacquisflowershop.com:81/apps/mydoc.html	Different origin; port differs
http://node.jacquisflowershop.com/order	Different origin; host differs

In my configuration, I have two servers. www.jacquisflowershop.com handles the static content, and node.jacquisflowershop.com runs Node.js. As you can see from the table, a document from the first server has a different origin from the second. When you want to make a request from one origin to another, it is known as a *cross-origin request*.

The problem with this policy is that it is a blanket ban; there are no cross-origin requests. This has led to the use of some ugly tricks to fool the browser into making requests that contravene the policy. Fortunately, there is now a legitimate means of making cross-origin requests, defined in the *Cross-Origin Resource Sharing* (CORS) specification. I am only going to describe CORS briefly. For complete details, see the full CORS standard at www.w3.org/TR/cors.

■ **Tip**   The CORS specification is reasonably recent. It is supported by the current generation of browsers, but older browsers will simply ignore cross-origin requests. A more established approach is to use JSONP, which I describe in the section "Working with JSONP."

The way that CORS works is that the browser contacts the second server (the Node.js server in this case) and includes an Origin header in the request. The value of this header is the origin of the document that has led to the request being made.

If the server recognizes the origin and wants to allow the browser to make a cross-origin request, then it adds the Access-Control-Allow-Origin header, setting the value to match the Origin header from the request. If the response doesn't contain this header, then the browser discards the response.

■ **Tip**   Supporting CORS means that the browser has to apply the cross-origin security policy after it has contacted the server and has obtained the response header, meaning that the request is made even if the response is discarded because the required header is missing or specified a different domain. This is a different approach from browsers that don't implement CORS and that simply block the request, never contacting the server.

In the formserver.js script, I set the Access-Control-Allow-Origin header to my trusted origin http://www.jacquisflowershop.com, but you could easily use the value of the Origin header in the request to follow a more sophisticated decision process. You can also set the Access-Control-Allow-Origin header to an asterisk (*), which means that cross-origin requests from *any* origin will be permitted. This is fine for the purposes of testing, but you should think carefully about the security implications before using this setting in a production application.

Using the post Method to Submit Form Data

So, now that I have prepared the server and understood CORS, I am in a position to use the post method to send form data to the server, as shown by Listing 14-10.

Listing 14-10. Sending Data with the post Method

```html
<!DOCTYPE html>
<html>
<head>
    <title>Example</title>
    <script src="jquery-2.0.2.js" type="text/javascript"></script>
    <script src="handlebars.js" type="text/javascript"></script>
    <script src="handlebars-jquery.js" type="text/javascript"></script>
    <script src="jquery.validate.js" type="text/javascript"></script>
    <link rel="stylesheet" type="text/css" href="styles.css"/>
    <script id="flowerTmpl" type="text/x-handlebars-template">
        {{#flowers}}
        <div class="dcell">
            <img src="{{product}}.png"/>
            <label for="{{product}}">{{name}}</label>
            <input name="{{product}}" data-price="{{price}}" data-stock="{{stock}}"
                value="0" required />
        </div>
        {{/flowers}}
    </script>
    <script id="totalTmpl" type="text/x-handlebars-template">
        <div id="totalDiv" style="clear: both; padding: 5px">
            <div style="text-align: center">Total Items:
                <span id=total>{{total}}</span></div>
        </div>
    </script>
    <script type="text/javascript">
        $(document).ready(function () {

            $.get("flowers.html", function (data) {
                var elems = $(data).filter("div").addClass("dcell");
                elems.slice(0, 3).appendTo("#row1");
                elems.slice(3).appendTo("#row2");
            });

            $("button").click(function (e) {
                var formData = $("form").serialize();
                $.post("http://node.jacquisflowershop.com/order",
                    formData, processServerResponse);
                e.preventDefault();
            });

            function processServerResponse(data) {
                var inputElems = $("div.dcell").hide();
                for (var prop in data) {
                    var filtered = inputElems.has("input[name=" + prop + "]")
                        .appendTo("#row1").show();
                }
```

```
                $("#buttonDiv").remove();
                $("#totalTmpl").template(data).appendTo("body");
            }
        });
    </script>
</head>
<body>
    <h1>Jacqui's Flower Shop</h1>
    <form method="post" action="http://node.jacquisflowershop.com/order">
        <div id="oblock">
            <div class="dtable">
                <div id="row1" class="drow">
                </div>
                <div id="row2"class="drow">
                </div>
            </div>
        </div>
        <div id="buttonDiv"><button type="submit">Place Order</button></div>
    </form>
</body>
</html>
```

This example looks more complicated than it really is. I start by using the getJSON method to obtain the mydata.json file that contains details of the flower products and then use a data template to generate elements and add them to the document. This gives me the starting point that you have come to know and love, as shown in Figure 14-5. You can see that I have entered some values into the input elements: 12 asters, 20 daffodils, 4 primula, and 4 snowdrops.

Figure 14-5. *The starting point for sending data to the server*

I use the `click` method to register a function that will be called when the `button` element is clicked, as follows:

```
...
$("button").click(function (e) {
    var formData = $("form").serialize();
    $.post("http://node.jacquisflowershop.com/order", formData, processServerResponse);
    e.preventDefault();
});
...
```

The first thing that I do is to call the `serialize` method on the `form` element. This is a helpful method that works its way through all of the `form` elements and creates a URL-encoded string that you can send to the server.

■ **Tip**   Notice that I call the `preventDefault` method on the `Event` object that is passed to my handler function for the `click` event. I need to do this to stop the browser posting the form in the regular way—that is, by sending the data and loading the response as a separate HTML document.

For the values I entered into the `input` elements, the `serialize` method generates a string as follows:

`aster=12&daffodil=20&rose=0&peony=0&primula=4&snowdrop=0`

I use the `serialize` method because the `post` method sends data in the URL-encoded format (although this can be changed by using the `ajaxSetup` global event handler method, which I describe in Chapter 15). Once I have the data from the input elements, I call the `post` method to initiate the Ajax request.

The arguments to the `post` method are the URL that I want to send the data to (which does not need to be the same as the URL specified by the `action` attribute of the `form` element), the data I want to send, and a function to call if the request is successful. In this example, I take the response from the server and pass it to the `processServerResponse` function, which is defined as follows:

```
...
function processServerResponse(data) {
    var inputElems = $("div.dcell").hide();
    for (var prop in data) {
        var filtered = inputElems.has("input[name=" + prop + "]")
            .appendTo("#row1").show();
    }
    $("#buttonDiv").remove();
    $("#totalTmpl").template(data).appendTo("body");
}
...
```

I hide all of the cell-level `div` elements in the CSS layout (which are members of the `dcell` class) and then display those that correspond to the properties in the JSON object from the server. I also use a new data template to generate a display for the total number of selected items. These are both activities you could have performed on the client, but the point here is that you obtained the data through an Ajax POST request. You can see the result in Figure 14-6.

Figure 14-6. *The effect of processing the data returned from the Ajax POST request*

You can see how easy it is to submit form data to the server (and, of course, how easy it is to process the response, especially if it is JSON).

■ **Tip** If you don't get the response shown in the figure, then the likely cause is that your CORS header isn't being set to the correct domain in the Node.js script. As a quick test, set it to * and see what happens.

Sending Other Data Using the post Method

Although the post method is usually used to submit form data, it can actually send any data to the server. I just create an object that contains your data, call the serialize method to format the data properly, and then pass it to the post method.

This can be a useful technique if you are collecting data from the user without using a form or if you want to be selective about the form elements that you include in the POST request. Listing 14-11 shows how you can use the post method in this way.

Listing 14-11. Using the post Method to Send Nonform Data to the Server

```
...
<script type="text/javascript">
    $(document).ready(function () {

        $("button").click(function (e) {
            var requestData = {
                apples: 2,
                oranges: 10
            };

            $.post("http://node.jacquisflowershop.com/order", requestData,
                function (responseData) {
                    console.log(JSON.stringify(responseData));
                })
            e.preventDefault();
        })
    });
</script>
...
```

367

In this script, I create an object and define properties explicitly. I pass this object to the post method and use the console.log method to write out the response from the server. (The formserver.js script doesn't really care what kind of data it gets from the browser; it will just try to add up the values and generate a total.) The script produces the following console output:

```
{"apples":"2","oranges":"10","total":12}
```

■ **Tip**   The JSON response from the server is automatically transformed into a JavaScript object by jQuery. I used the JSON.stringify method (which is supported by most browsers) to turn it back into a string so that I could display it on the console.

Specifying the Expected Data Type

When you use the get and post methods, jQuery has to figure out what kind of data the server is sending back in response to your request. It can be anything from HTML to a JavaScript file. To do this, jQuery relies on the information that the server provides in the response, particularly the Content-Type header. For the most part, this works well, but on occasion jQuery needs a little help. This is usually because the server is specifying the wrong MIME type for the data in the response.

You can override the information that the server provides and can tell jQuery what data you are expecting by passing an additional argument to the get or post methods. This argument can be one of the following values:

- xml
- json
- jsonp
- script
- html
- text

Listing 14-12 shows how you can specify the expected data type for the get method.

Listing 14-12. Specifying the Expected Data Type

```
...
<script type="text/javascript">
    $(document).ready(function () {
        $.get("mydata.json", function (responseData) {
            console.log(JSON.stringify(responseData));
        }, "json");
    });
</script>
...
```

You specify the data type as the last argument to the shorthand methods. In this example, I have told jQuery that I am expecting JSON data. It doesn't matter what the server says the content type is: jQuery will treat the response as JSON. This example produces the following console output:

```
[{"name":"Aster","product":"aster","stock":"10","price":"2.99"},
 {"name":"Daffodil","product":"daffodil","stock":"12","price":"1.99"},
 {"name":"Rose","product":"rose","stock":"2","price":"4.99"},
 {"name":"Peony","product":"peony","stock":"0","price":"1.50"},
 {"name":"Primula","product":"primula","stock":"1","price":"3.12"},
 {"name":"Snowdrop","product":"snowdrop","stock":"15","price":"0.99"}]
```

This is the same content that I put into the mydata.json file, which is, of course, what you would expect. The problem with specifying the data type is that you have to be right. If the data are actually of a different type, then you can have some problems, as demonstrated in Listing 14-13.

Listing 14-13. Specifying the Wrong Kind of Data

```
...
<script type="text/javascript">
    $(document).ready(function () {

        $.get("flowers.html", function (responseData) {
            console.log(JSON.stringify(responseData));
        }, "json");
    });
</script>
...
```

In this example, I have requested a file that contains HTML but told jQuery that it should treat it as JSON. The problem here is that when dealing with JSON, jQuery automatically creates a JavaScript object from the data, which it can't do with HTML.

■ **Tip** I'll show you how to detect Ajax errors in Chapter 15.

Avoiding the Most Common Ajax Pitfall

Before going any further, I want to show you the most common problem that web programmers make with Ajax, which is to treat the asynchronous request as though it were synchronous. Listing 14-14 gives an example of the problem.

Listing 14-14. A Common Ajax Mistake

```
...
<script type="text/javascript">
    $(document).ready(function () {

        var elems;

        $.get("flowers.html", function (data) {
            elems = $(data).filter("div").addClass("dcell");
        });
```

```
        elems.slice(0, 3).appendTo("#row1");
        elems.slice(3).appendTo("#row2");
    });
</script>
...
```

In this example, I have defined a variable called elems, which is then used by the Ajax callback function to assign the result of the server request. I use the slice and appendTo methods to add the elements that I have obtained from the server to the document. If you run this example, you will see that no elements are added to the document, and depending on your browser, you will see an error message displayed on the console. Following is the message shown by Google Chrome:

```
Uncaught TypeError: Cannot call method 'slice' of undefined
```

The issue here is that the statements in the script element are not executed in the order in which they are written. The code in the example assumes the following sequence will occur:

1. Define the elems variable.

2. Get the data from the server and assign it to the elems variable.

3. Slice the elements in the elems variable and add them to the document.

What really happens is this.

1. Define the elems variable.

2. Start the asynchronous request to the server.

3. Slice the elements in the elems variable and add them to the document.

And, at some point in the future, this happens.

1. Receive the request from the server.

2. Process the data and assign it to the elems variable.

In short, I get the error message because I called the slice method on a variable that doesn't contain any elements. The worst thing about this mistake is that sometimes the code actually works. This is because the Ajax response can complete so quickly that the variable contains the data before I come to process it (this is typically the case when the data is cached by the browser or you perform some complex operations between starting the Ajax request and trying to operate on the data). You now know what to look for whether you see this kind of behavior from your code.

Using the Type-Specific Convenience Methods

jQuery provides three convenience methods that make dealing with particular types of data a little easier. Table 14-4 summarizes these methods which are demonstrated in the sections that follow.

Table 14-4. *The jQuery Ajax Type-Specific Convenience Methods*

Name	Description
load()	Loads HTML elements and inserts them into the elements in the jQuery object on which the method has been called
$.getScript()	Gets and executes JavaScript code
$.getJSON()	Gets JSON data

Getting an HTML Fragment

The load method will *only* obtain HTML data, which allows you to request an HTML fragment, process the response to create a set of elements, and insert those elements in the document in a single step. Listing 14-15 shows how you can use the load method.

Listing 14-15. Using the Load Shorthand Method

```
...
<script type="text/javascript">
    $(document).ready(function () {
        $("#row1").load("flowers.html");
    });
</script>
...
```

You call the load method on the element in the document that you want to insert the new elements into and pass the URL as a method argument. If the request is successful and the response from the server contains valid HTML, then the elements will be inserted at the specified location, as shown in Figure 14-7.

Figure 14-7. Adding elements to the document using the load method

The elements from the `flower.html` file have all been added to the document, but because they lack the `class` attribute they are not properly added to the CSS table layout that the main document uses. For this reason, the `load` method is most useful when all of the elements are to be inserted in a single location and you don't need to modify them before they are added.

Manipulating the Elements Added by the load Method

The `load` method returns a jQuery object that contains the elements into which the loaded HTML content will be inserted. The key phrase is *will be* because the `load` method uses an asynchronous request to get the HTML from the server. This means that you have to be careful if you want to manipulate the elements that the `load` method adds to the DOM because normal jQuery techniques won't work. Listing 14-16 shows the most common problem I see when projects use the `load` method.

Listing 14-16. The Most Common Problem Code for the load Method

```
...
<script type="text/javascript">
    $(document).ready(function () {
        $("#row1").load("flowers.html").children().addClass("dcell");
    });
</script>
...
```

The objective of the code is obvious: to load the content of the flowers.html file into the row1 element, select the newly added elements, and add them to the dcell class (which will have the effect of laying them out horizontally as part of my CSS table layout).

But if you run this example, you will see that there is no change from the result shown in Figure 14-7. This is because the load method goes off and requests the flowers.html file asynchronously, leaving jQuery free to continue executing method calls. And so the child elements of the row1 element are selected and modified before the Ajax request has completed and the new elements are added to the document.

To address this, the load method has an optional argument that allows a callback function to be specified. The callback function won't be invoked until the Ajax elements have been added to the document and this ensures that I can sequence my manipulations correctly, as shown in Listing 14-17.

Listing 14-17. Using the Callback Argument of the load Method

```
...
<script type="text/javascript">
    $(document).ready(function () {
        var targetElems = $("#row1");
        targetElems.load("flowers.html", function () {
            targetElems.children().addClass("dcell");
        });
    });
</script>
...
```

The effect is that the calls to the children and addClass methods are not performed until after the content from the flowers.html file is added to the document, producing the effect shown in Figure 14-8.

Figure 14-8. Using a callback function to manipulate the elements added by the load method

Getting and Executing Scripts

The getScript method loads a JavaScript file and executes the statements it contains. To demonstrate this method, I have created a file called myscript.js and saved it alongside example.html on my web server. Listing 14-18 shows the contents of this file.

Listing 14-18. The Contents of the myscript.js File

```
var flowers = [
    ["Aster", "Daffodil", "Rose"],
    ["Peony", "Primula", "Snowdrop"],
    ["Carnation", "Lily", "Orchid"]
]

$("<div id=row3 class=drow/>").appendTo("div.dtable");

var fTemplate = $("<div class=dcell><img/><label/><input/></div>");

for (var row = 0; row < flowers.length; row++) {
    var fNames = flowers[row];

    for (var i = 0; i < fNames.length; i++) {
        fTemplate.clone().appendTo("#row" + (row + 1)).children()
            .filter("img").attr("src", fNames[i] + ".png").end()
            .filter("label").attr("for", fNames[i]).text(fNames[i]).end()
            .filter("input").attr({name: fNames[i], value: 0})
    }
}
```

These statements generate three rows of elements that describe flowers. I have generated these elements using loops so I don't have to get involved in defining templates (although, in general, I would much rather use data templates as described in Chapter 12). Listing 14-19 demonstrates the use of the getScript method to obtain and execute the contents of the myscript.js file.

Listing 14-19. Using the getScript Method

```
...
<script type="text/javascript">
    $(document).ready(function () {
        $.getScript("myscript.js");
    });
</script>
...
```

The getScript method is called when the DOM is ready. The execution of the myscript.js file leads to three rows of flowers elements, as shown by Figure 14-9.

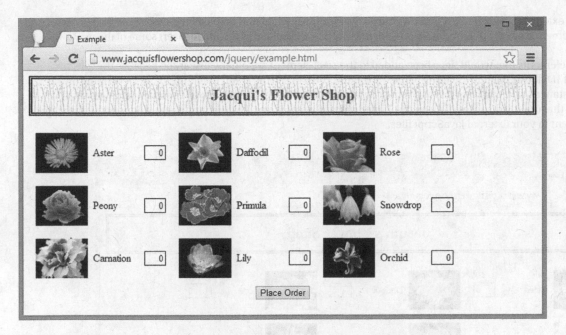

Figure 14-9. Using the getScript method to load and execute a JavaScript file

The most important thing to realize when dealing with scripts like this is that the state of the document may change between you initiating the Ajax request and the `script` statements being executed. Listing 14-20 contains a script from the main document that uses the `getScript` method but also modifies the DOM before the Ajax request can complete.

Listing 14-20. Requesting and Executing Scripts with the getScript Method

```
...
<script type="text/javascript">
    $(document).ready(function () {
        $.getScript("myscript.js");
        $("#row2").remove();
    });
</script>
...
```

■ **Tip** The `getScript` method can be used for any script file, but I find it especially useful for loading and executing scripts that are not central to a web application's functionality, like tracker or geolocation scripts. The user doesn't care if I am able to accurately locate his location for my site statistics, but he does care when loading and executing the script makes him wait. By using the `getScript` method, I can get the information I require without making it annoying. To be clear, I am not suggesting that you do anything that is hidden from the user, only that you defer loading and executing legitimate functionality that the user is unlikely to value more than his time.

In this example I start the Ajax request with the `getScript` method and then call the `remove` method to remove the row2 element from the document. This element is used by the `myscript.js` file to insert some of the new elements.

These elements that would have been added to the row2 element are quietly discarded because the selector for the row2 ID doesn't match anything in the document. You can see the result in Figure 14-10. Depending on the circumstances, you can view this as a robust design that does its best in the face of document changes or an annoyance that quietly disposes of elements. Either way, it pays not to make too many assumptions about the state of the document in your external JavaScript files.

Figure 14-10. *The effect of a document change during an Ajax request*

Getting JSON Data

The `getJSON` method obtains JSON data from the server and parses it to create JavaScript objects. This is perhaps the least useful of the three convenience methods because it doesn't do anything more with the data than the basic get method. Listing 14-21 shows the use of the `getJSON` method.

Listing 14-21. Using the getJSON Method

```
...
<script type="text/javascript">
    $(document).ready(function () {
        $.getJSON("mydata.json", function (data) {
            var tmplElems = $("#flowerTmpl").template({ flowers: data }).filter("*");
            tmplElems.slice(0, 3).appendTo("#row1");
            tmplElems.slice(3).appendTo("#row2");
        });
    });
</script>
...
```

The JSON data retrieved from the server is passed to a callback function, much as with the get method that I showed you earlier in the chapter. I have used a data template (described in Chapter 12) to process the data and generate HTML elements from it and then the `slice` and `appendTo` method to insert the elements into the document.

■ **Tip**   Notice that you are passed a JavaScript object as the argument to the function. You don't have to do anything to convert from the JSON format into an object because jQuery takes care of this for you.

Working with JSONP

JSONP is an alternative to CORS and works around the same-origin restriction on Ajax requests. It relies on the fact that the browser will allow you to load JavaScript code from any server, which is how the `script` element works when you specify a `src` attribute. To begin with, define a function in the document that will process the data, as follows:

```
...
function processJSONP(data) {
    //...do something with the data...
}
...
```

You then make a request to the server where the query string includes your form data and a `callback` property, set to the name of the function you just defined, as follows:

```
http://node.jacquisflowershop.com/order?callback=processJSONP&aster=1
    &daffodil=2&rose=2&peony=0&primula=0&snowdrop=0
```

The server, which needs to understand how JSONP works, generates the JSON data as normal and then creates a JavaScript statement that calls the function you created and passes in the data as an argument, as follows:

```
processJSONP({"aster":"1","daffodil":"2","rose":"2","total":5})
```

The server also sets the content type of the response to be `text/javascript`, which tells the browser that it has received some JavaScript statements and should execute them. This has the effect of invoking the method you defined earlier, passing in the data sent by the server. In this way, you neatly sidestep the same-domain issues without using CORS.

■ **Caution**   Cross-origin requests are restricted for good reason. Don't use JSONP casually. It can create some serious security problems.

jQuery has convenient support for JSONP. All you have to do is use the `getJSON` method and specify a URL that contains `callback=?` in the query string. jQuery creates a function with a random name and uses this when communicating to the server, meaning you don't have to modify your code at all. Listing 14-22 demonstrates how to make a JSONP request.

Listing 14-22. Making a JSONP Request Using the getJSON Method

```
...
<script type="text/javascript">
    $(document).ready(function () {
        $.getJSON("mydata.json", function (data) {
            var tmplElems = $("#flowerTmpl").template({ flowers: data }).filter("*");
            tmplElems.slice(0, 3).appendTo("#row1");
            tmplElems.slice(3).appendTo("#row2");

        });

        $("button").click(function (e) {
            var formData = $("form").serialize();
            $.getJSON("http://node.jacquisflowershop.com/order?callback=?",
                    formData, processServerResponse)
            e.preventDefault();
        })

        function processServerResponse(data) {
            var inputElems = $("div.dcell").hide();
            for (var prop in data) {
                var filtered = inputElems.has("input[name=' + prop + ']")
                    .appendTo("#row1").show();
            }
            $("#buttonDiv, #totalDiv").remove();
            $("#totalTmpl").template(data).appendTo("body");
        }
    });
</script>
...
```

Using the Ajax Forms Plug-in

So far, I have been using the built-in jQuery support for Ajax. As I mentioned previously, one of the strengths of jQuery is the ease with which it can be extended to add new functionality and the vibrant world of plug-ins that this leads to. To finish this chapter, I am going to briefly describe a useful form-related plug-in.

If you are interested in using Ajax solely to post form data to a server, then you might like the *jQuery Form* plug-in, which you can get from www.malsup.com/jquery/form and which I saved to a file called jquery.form.js. The jQuery Form plug-in makes using Ajax on forms extremely simple, as Listing 14-23 demonstrates.

Listing 14-23. Using the Ajax Forms Plug-in

```
<!DOCTYPE html>
<html>
<head>
    <title>Example</title>
    <script src="jquery-2.0.2.js" type="text/javascript"></script>
    <script src="handlebars.js" type="text/javascript"></script>
    <script src="handlebars-jquery.js" type="text/javascript"></script>
    <script src="jquery.validate.js" type="text/javascript"></script>
```

```
<script src="jquery.form.js" type="text/javascript"></script>
<link rel="stylesheet" type="text/css" href="styles.css"/>
<script id="flowerTmpl" type="text/x-handlebars-template">
    {{#flowers}}
    <div class="dcell">
        <img src="{{product}}.png"/>
        <label for="{{product}}">{{name}}</label>
        <input name="{{product}}" data-price="{{price}}" data-stock="{{stock}}"
            value="0" required />
    </div>
    {{/flowers}}
</script>
<script id="totalTmpl" type="text/x-handlebars-template">
    <div id="totalDiv" style="clear: both; padding: 5px">
        <div style="text-align: center">Total Items:
            <span id=total>{{total}}</span></div>
    </div>
</script>
<script type="text/javascript">
    $(document).ready(function () {

        $.getScript("myscript.js");

        $("form").ajaxForm(function (data) {
            var inputElems = $("div.dcell").hide();
            for (var prop in data) {
                var filtered = inputElems.has("input[name=' + prop + ']")
                    .appendTo("#row1").show();
            }
            $("#buttonDiv, #totalDiv").remove();
            $("#totalTmpl").template(data).appendTo("body");
        });
    });
</script>
</head>
<body>
    <h1>Jacqui's Flower Shop</h1>
    <form method="post" action="http://node.jacquisflowershop.com/order">
        <div id="oblock">
            <div class="dtable">
                <div id="row1" class="drow">
                </div>
                <div id="row2"class="drow">
                </div>
            </div>
        </div>
        <div id="buttonDiv"><button type="submit">Place Order</button></div>
    </form>
</body>
</html>
```

In this example, I have added the `jquery.form.js` script file to the document (this is included in the download for the plug-in) and, in the `script` element, called the `ajaxForm` method on the `form` element. The argument to the `ajaxForm` method is a callback function, and this provides me with access to the response from the server. This is a neat and simple approach to basic Ajax forms, right down to the fact that the URL to post the form to is taken from the `form` element itself.

This plug-in does a lot more, and it even includes some support for basic form validation, but if you get to the point where you want to start taking control of your Ajax requests, then I suggest using the low-level Ajax features that I describe in Chapter 15. But for quick and simple situations, this plug-in is convenient and well designed.

Summary

In this chapter, I introduced you to the shorthand and convenience methods that jQuery provides for Ajax. I have shown you how to use the `get` and `post` methods to make asynchronous HTTP GET and POST requests, how to work with JSON data, and how to use the convenience methods that deal with specific data types. Along the way, I have shown you the most common Ajax pitfall, explained cross-origin requests, and showed how to deal with them and briefly introduced a jQuery plug-in, which makes it even easier to use Ajax with forms that the shorthand methods. In the next chapter, I'll show you the low-level API, although you'll see that it isn't really that low level and is actually pleasant to use.

CHAPTER 15

■■■

Using Ajax: Part II

In this chapter, I show you how to use the low-level jQuery Ajax API (application programming interface). The term *low level* implies rooting around in the guts of the request, but that really isn't the case. The methods I describe in this chapter are not as convenient as those in Chapter 14, but with a little more effort you can configure the fine detail of the request when the configuration used by the shorthand and convenience methods doesn't quite do the job. Table 15-1 provides the summary for this chapter.

Table 15-1. *Chapter Summary*

Problem	Solution	Listing
Make an Ajax call with the low-level API	Use the ajax method	1
Get details of the request in a way that is similar to the native XMLHttpRequest object	Use the jqXHR method	2
Specify the URL for an Ajax request	Use the url setting	3
Specify the HTTP method for a request	Use the type setting	4
Respond to successful requests	Use the success setting	5
Respond to unsuccessful requests	Use the error setting	6
Respond to completed requests, regardless of success or errors	Use the complete setting	7, 8
Configure a request before it is sent	Use the beforeSend setting	9
Specify multiple functions to handle successful, unsuccessful, or completed requests	Specify an array of functions for the success, error, or complete setting	10
Specify the element that will be assigned to the this variable in the functions for the success, error, and complete settings	Use the context setting	11
Respond to events for all Ajax requests	Use the global event methods	12
Specify whether a request will lead to global events being triggered	Use the global setting	13
Set the timeout for a request	Use the timeout setting	14
Add headers to the request	Use the headers setting	14
Specify the content type being set to the server	Use the contentType header	15

(continued)

Table 15-1. (continued)

Problem	Solution	Listing
Specify whether a request will be performed synchronously or asynchronously	Use the `async` setting	16
Ignore data that has not been changed	Use the `ifModified` setting	17
Respond to the HTTP status code sent by the server	Use the `statusCode` setting	18
Clean up the response data	Use the `dataFilter` setting	19
Control how data is converted	Use the `converters` setting	20
Define a common configuration for all Ajax requests	Use the `ajaxSetup` method	21
Dynamically change the configuration for individual requests	Use the `ajaxPrefilter` method	22

JQUERY CHANGES SINCE THE LAST EDITION

As of jQuery 1.9/2.0, the methods that set up handlers for the Ajax global events can only be called on the `document` object (in earlier jQuery versions, these methods could be used on any element). See the section "Using the Global Ajax Events" for the details of these methods.

Making a Simple Ajax Request with the Low-Level API

Making a request with the low-level API isn't much more complicated than using the shorthand and convenience methods I showed you in Chapter 14. The difference is that you can configure many different aspects of the request and get a lot more information about the request as it is performed. The method that is at the heart of the low-level API is ajax, and Listing 15-1 provides a simple demonstration of its use.

Listing 15-1. Using the ajax Method

```
<!DOCTYPE html>
<html>
<head>
    <title>Example</title>
    <script src="jquery-2.0.2.js" type="text/javascript"></script>
    <script src="handlebars.js" type="text/javascript"></script>
    <script src="handlebars-jquery.js" type="text/javascript"></script>
    <script src="jquery.validate.js" type="text/javascript"></script>
    <link rel="stylesheet" type="text/css" href="styles.css"/>
    <script id="flowerTmpl" type="text/x-handlebars-template">
        {{#flowers}}
        <div class="dcell">
            <img src="{{product}}.png"/>
            <label for="{{product}}">{{name}}:</label>
            <input name="{{product}}" data-price="{{price}}" data-stock="{{stocklevel}}"
                value="0" required />
        </div>
```

```
            {{/flowers}}
        </script>
        <script type="text/javascript">
            $(document).ready(function () {
                $.ajax("mydata.json", {
                    success: function (data) {
                        var tmplElems = $("#flowerTmpl")
                            .template({flowers: data}).filter("*");
                        tmplElems.slice(0, 3).appendTo("#row1");
                        tmplElems.slice(3).appendTo("#row2");
                    }
                });
            });
        </script>
    </head>
    <body>
        <h1>Jacqui's Flower Shop</h1>
        <form method="post" action="http://node.jacquisflowershop.com/order">
            <div id="oblock">
                <div class="dtable">
                    <div id="row1" class="drow">
                    </div>
                    <div id="row2"class="drow">
                    </div>
                </div>
            </div>
            <div id="buttonDiv"><button type="submit">Place Order</button></div>
        </form>
    </body>
</html>
```

You use the ajax method by passing the URL that you want to request and a map object whose properties define a set of key/value pairs, each of which configures a setting for the request.

■ **Note**   This chapter relies on the same Node.js script used in Chapter 14.

In this example, my map object has one property—success—which specifies the function to call if the request is successful. I request the mydata.json file from the server and use it with a data template to create and insert elements into the document, just as I did in the previous chapter with the shorthand methods. By default, the ajax method makes an HTTP get request, which means that the example is equivalent to using the get or getJSON method, which I showed you in Chapter 14. (I'll show you how to create POST requests later in the section "Making a POST Request.")

Many settings are available and I explain them throughout the rest of the chapter, along with methods that jQuery provides to make Ajax easier to use.

Understanding the jqXHR Object

The result returned by the ajax method is a jqXHR object that you can use to get details about and interact with the Ajax request. The jqXHR object is a superset of the XMLHttpRequest object that is defined as part of the World Wide Web Consortium (W3C) standard that underpins browser support for Ajax, adapted to work with the jQuery *deferred object* features that I describe in Chapter 35.

You can simply ignore the jqXHR object for most Ajax requests, which is exactly what I suggest you do. The jqXHR object is useful when you need more information about the response from the server than would otherwise be available. Table 15-2 describes the members of the jqXHR object.

Table 15-2. *The jqXHR Members*

Member	Description
readyState	Returns the progress of the request through its life cycle from unsent (value 0) to complete (value 4)
status	Returns the HTTP status code sent back by the server
statusText	Returns the text description of the status code
responseXML	Returns the response if it is an XML document
responseText	Returns the response as a string
setRequestHeader(name, value)	Sets a header on the request
getAllResponseHeaders()	Returns all of the headers in the response as a single string
getResponseHeader(name)	Returns the value of the specified response header
abort()	Terminates the request

■ **Tip** The jqXHR object can be used to configure the Ajax request, but this is more easily done using the configuration options for the ajax method, which I explain in the section "...."

You will encounter the jqXHR object in several places when working with jQuery. The first is, as I say, as the result from the ajax method, as illustrated by Listing 15-2.

Listing 15-2. Using the jqXHR Object

```
...
<script type="text/javascript">
    $(document).ready(function () {
        var jqxhr = $.ajax("mydata.json", {
            success: function (data) {
                var tmplElems = $("#flowerTmpl").template({flowers: data}).filter("*");
                tmplElems.slice(0, 3).appendTo("#row1");
                tmplElems.slice(3).appendTo("#row2");
            }
        });
```

```
        var timerID = setInterval(function () {
            console.log("Status: " + jqxhr.status + " " + jqxhr.statusText);
            if (jqxhr.readyState == 4) {
                console.log("Request completed: " + jqxhr.responseText);
                clearInterval(timerID);
            }
        }, 100);

    });
</script>
...
```

In this listing, I assign the result from the ajax method to a variable called jqxhr and use the setInterval method to write information about the request to the console every 100 milliseconds. Using the result of the ajax method doesn't change the fact that the request is performed asynchronously, so caution is required when working with the jqXHR object. I use the readyState property to check the status of the request (the value of 4 indicates the request has completed) and write the response from the server to the console. This script produces the following console output (although you might see something slightly different based on your browser configuration):

```
Status: 200 OK

Request completed: [{"name":"Aster","product":"aster","stocklevel":"10","price":"2.99"},
{"name":"Daffodil","product":"daffodil","stocklevel":"12","price":"1.99"},
{"name":"Rose","product":"rose","stocklevel":"2","price":"4.99"},
{"name":"Peony","product":"peony","stocklevel":"0","price":"1.50"},
{"name":"Primula","product":"primula","stocklevel":"1","price":"3.12"},
{"name":"Snowdrop","product":"snowdrop","stocklevel":"15","price":"0.99"}]
```

■ **Tip**   I rarely use the jqXHR object and never when it is the result of the ajax method. If I want to work with the jqXHR object (typically to get additional information about the response from a server), then I usually do so through the event handler settings that I describe in the section "Handling Ajax Callbacks." They give me a context regarding the status of the request without making me poll for request status.

Setting the Request URL

As an alternative to passing the URL for the request as an argument to the ajax method, you can define a url property in the map object, as shown in Listing 15-3.

Listing 15-3. Using the url Property

```
...
<script type="text/javascript">
    $(document).ready(function () {
        $.ajax({
            url: "mydata.json",
```

```
            success: function (data) {
                var tmplElems = $("#flowerTmpl").template({flowers: data}).filter("*");
                tmplElems.slice(0, 3).appendTo("#row1");
                tmplElems.slice(3).appendTo("#row2");
            }
        });
    });
</script>
...
```

Making a POST Request

You set the HTTP method for requests using the type setting. The default is to make GET requests, as in the previous example. Listing 15-4 shows using the ajax method to create a POST request and submit form data to the server.

Listing 15-4. Creating a POST Request with the ajax Method

```
...
<script id="totalTmpl" type="text/x-handlebars-template">
    <div id="totalDiv" style="clear: both; padding: 5px">
        <div style="text-align: center">Total Items:
            <span id=total>{{total}}</span></div>
    </div>
</script>
<script type="text/javascript">
    $(document).ready(function () {
        $.ajax({
            url: "mydata.json",
            success: function (data) {
                var tmplElems = $("#flowerTmpl").template({flowers: data}).filter("*");
                tmplElems.slice(0, 3).appendTo("#row1");
                tmplElems.slice(3).appendTo("#row2");
            }
        });

        $("button").click(function (e) {
            $.ajax({
                url: $("form").attr("action"),
                data: $("form").serialize(),
                type: "post",
                success: processServerResponse
            })
            e.preventDefault();
        })

        function processServerResponse(data) {
            var inputElems = $("div.dcell").hide();
            for (var prop in data) {
                var filtered = inputElems.has("input[name='" + prop + "']")
                    .appendTo("#row1").show();
            }
```

```
        $("#buttonDiv").remove();
        $("#totalTmpl").template(data).appendTo("body");
    }
  });
</script>
...
```

I have used several settings in addition to `type`. To specify the target for the POST request, I used the `url` property, which I take from the target of the `form` element in the document. I specify the data to send using the `data` property, which I set by using the `serialize` method (described in Chapter 34).

GOING BEYOND GET AND POST

You can use the `type` property to specify any HTTP method, but you may have difficulty using anything other than GET or POST because many firewalls and application servers are configured to discard other kinds of request. If you want to use other HTTP methods, then you can make a POST request, but add the X-HTTP-Method-Override header, setting it to the method you want to use, as follows:

```
X-HTTP-Method-Override: PUT
```

This convention is widely supported by web application frameworks and is a common way of creating *RESTful web applications*, which you can learn more about at http://en.wikipedia.org/wiki/Representational_state_transfer. See the section "Setting Timeouts and Headers" for details of how to set a header on a jQuery Ajax request.

Handling Ajax Callbacks

Several properties let you specify callback functions for key points in the life of an Ajax request. You already saw one of these callbacks when I used the `success` property in Listing 15-4. Table 15-3 describes the property used to set up each of these callbacks.

Table 15-3. *The Ajax Event Properties*

Setting	Description
beforeSend	Specifies a function that will be called before the Ajax request is started
complete	Specifies a function that will be called when the Ajax request succeeds or fails
error	Specifies a function that will be called when the Ajax request fails
success	Specifies a function that will be called when the Ajax request succeeds

■ **Tip** The settings described in Table 15-3 are related to *local* callbacks, meaning that they deal with individual Ajax requests. You can also use a series of *global events*, which I describe in the section "Using the Global Ajax Events."

Dealing with Successful Requests

When I demonstrated the use of the `success` property, I omitted a couple of arguments from the function: a status message describing the result of the request and a jqXHR object. Listing 15-5 shows the use of a function that accepts these arguments.

Listing 15-5. Receiving All of the Arguments to a Success Function

```
...
<script type="text/javascript">
    $(document).ready(function () {
        $.ajax({
            url: "mydata.json",
            success: function (data, status, jqxhr) {

                console.log("Status: " + status);
                console.log("jqXHR Status: " + jqxhr.status + " " + jqxhr.statusText);
                console.log(jqxhr.getAllResponseHeaders());

                var tmplElems = $("#flowerTmpl").template({flowers: data}).filter("*");
                tmplElems.slice(0, 3).appendTo("#row1");
                tmplElems.slice(3).appendTo("#row2");
            }
        });
    });
</script>
...
```

The `status` argument is a string that describes the outcome of the request. The callback function specified by the `success` property is executed only for successful results and so this argument generally has the value `success`. The exception occurs when you use the `ifModified` setting, which I describe in the section "Ignoring Unmodified Data." The callback functions for the other Ajax events follow the same pattern, and this argument is more useful in some of the other events.

The final argument is a jqXHR object. You don't have to poll the status of the request before working with the jqXHR object since you know the function is executed only when the request has successfully completed. In Listing 15-5, I have used the jqXHR object to get the status information and the headers that the server has included in the response and write them to the console. This example produces the following result (although you will see a different set of headers depending on the web server you are using):

```
Status: success
jqXHR Status: 200 OK
Date: Thu, 20 Jun 2013 12:06:30 GMT
Last-Modified: Wed, 19 Jun 2013 16:29:49 GMT
Server: Microsoft-IIS/7.5
X-Powered-By: ASP.NET
ETag: "b680cf37a6dce1:0"
Content-Type: application/json
Cache-Control: no-cache
Accept-Ranges: bytes
Content-Length: 405
```

Dealing with Errors

The error property specifies a callback function to be called when a request fails. Listing 15-6 provides a demonstration.

Listing 15-6. Using the error Property

```
...
<style type="text/css">
    .error {color: red; border: medium solid red; padding: 4px;
            margin: auto; width: 200px; text-align: center}
</style>
<script type="text/javascript">
    $(document).ready(function () {
        $.ajax({
            url: "NoSuchFile.json",
            success: function (data, status, jqxhr) {
                var tmplElems = $("#flowerTmpl").template({flowers: data}).filter("*");
                tmplElems.slice(0, 3).appendTo("#row1");
                tmplElems.slice(3).appendTo("#row2");
            },
            error: function (jqxhr, status, errorMsg) {
                $("<div>").addClass("error")
                    .text("Status: " + status + " Error: " + errorMsg)
                    .insertAfter("h1");
            }
        });
    });
</script>
...
```

In Listing 15-6, I have requested a file called NoSuchFile.json, which doesn't exist on the web server. This ensures that the request will fail and the callback function I have specified with the error property will be invoked.

The arguments passed to the error callback function are a jqXHR object, a status message, and the error message from the server response. In the listing, I use the error callback to add a div element to the document showing the value of the status and errorMsg arguments, as shown in Figure 15-1.

Figure 15-1. Displaying an error message

The status argument can be one of the values shown in Table 15-4.

Table 15-4. *The Error Status Values*

Setting	Description
abort	Indicates that the request was aborted (using the jqXHR object)
error	Indicates a general error, usually reported by the server
parsererror	Indicates that the data returned by the server could not be parsed
timeout	Indicates that the request timed out before the server responded

The value of the errorMsg argument varies based on the status. When the status is error, then errorMsg will be set to the text portion of the response from the server. So, in this example, the response from the server was 404 Not Found, and so errorMsg is set to Not Found.

When the status is timeout, the value of errorMsg will also be timeout. You can specify the period before a request times out using the timeout setting, which I describe in the section "Setting Timeouts and Headers."

When the status is parsererror, then errorMsg will contain details of the problem. This error occurs when data is malformed or the server returns the wrong MIME type for the data. (You can override the data type using the dataType setting.) Finally, when the request is abort, both the status and the errorMsg values will be abort.

■ **Tip**   Although I have displayed the status and errorMsg values in the document, this is generally unhelpful to the user, since the messages require some understanding of what's happening inside the web application and they contain no instructions about how the problem might be resolved.

Dealing with Completed Requests

The complete property specifies a function that will be called when the Ajax request completes, irrespective of whether it succeeds or fails. Listing 15-7 provides a demonstration.

Listing 15-7. Using the Complete Property

```
...
<script type="text/javascript">
    $(document).ready(function () {
        $.ajax({
            url: "mydata.json",
            success: function (data, status, jqxhr) {
                var tmplElems = $("#flowerTmpl").template({flowers: data}).filter("*");
                tmplElems.slice(0, 3).appendTo("#row1");
                tmplElems.slice(3).appendTo("#row2");
            },
            error: function (jqxhr, status, errorMsg) {
                $("<div>").addClass("error")
                    .text("Status: " + status + " Error: " + errorMsg)
                    .insertAfter("h1");
            },
```

```
            complete: function (jqxhr, status) {
                console.log("Completed: " + status);
            }
        });
    });
</script>
...
```

The callback function specified by the complete property is called *after* the functions specified by the success and error properties. jQuery passes the jqXHR object and a status string to the callback function. The status string will be set to one of the values shown in Table 15-5.

Table 15-5. *The Ajax Event Settings*

Setting	Description
abort	Indicates that the request was aborted (using the jqXHR object)
error	Indicates a general error, usually reported by the server
notmodified	Indicates that the requested content has not been modified since it was last requested (see the section "Ignoring Unmodified Data" for more details)
parsererror	Indicates that the data returned by the server could not be parsed
success	Indicates that the request completed successfully
timeout	Indicates that the request timed out before the server responded

You might be tempted to use the complete setting to specify a single function that can handle all outcomes of a request, but doing so means you don't benefit from the way that jQuery processes data and errors. A better approach is to use the success and error settings and carefully organize the arguments on the common function, as shown in Listing 15-8.

Listing 15-8. Using a Single Function to Handle All Request Outcomes

```
...
<script type="text/javascript">
    $(document).ready(function () {
        $.ajax({
            url: "mydata.json",
            success: function (data, status, jqxhr) {
                handleResponse(status, data, null, jqxhr);
            },
            error: function (jqxhr, status, errorMsg) {
                handleResponse(status, null, errorMsg, jqxhr);
            }
        });

        function handleResponse(status, data, errorMsg, jqxhr) {
            if (status == "success") {
                var tmplElems = $("#flowerTmpl").template({ flowers: data }).filter("*");
                tmplElems.slice(0, 3).appendTo("#row1");
                tmplElems.slice(3).appendTo("#row2");
```

```
            } else {
                $("<div>").addClass("error")
                    .text("Status: " + status + " Error: " + errorMsg)
                    .insertAfter("h1");
            }
        }
    });
</script>
...
```

Configuring Requests Before They Are Sent

The beforeSend property lets you specify a function that will be called before the request is started. This gives you an opportunity to do last-minute configuration that supplements or overrides the settings you passed to the ajax method, which can be useful if you are using the same basic settings object for multiple requests. Listing 15-9 demonstrates the use of the beforeSend property.

Listing 15-9. Using the beforeSend Property

```
...
<script type="text/javascript">
    $(document).ready(function () {
        $.ajax({
            url: "NoSuchFile.json",
            success: function (data, status, jqxhr) {
                handleResponse(status, data, null, jqxhr);
            },
            error: function (jqxhr, status, errorMsg) {
                handleResponse(status, null, errorMsg, jqxhr);
            },
            beforeSend: function (jqxhr, settings) {
                settings.url = "mydata.json";
            }
        });

        function handleResponse(status, data, errorMsg, jqxhr) {
            if (status == "success") {
                var tmplElems = $("#flowerTmpl").template({ flowers: data }).filter("*");
                tmplElems.slice(0, 3).appendTo("#row1");
                tmplElems.slice(3).appendTo("#row2");
            } else {
                $("<div>").addClass("error")
                    .text("Status: " + status + " Error: " + errorMsg)
                    .insertAfter("h1");
            }
        }

    });
</script>
...
```

The arguments passed to the callback function are the jqXHR object and the settings object that you passed to the ajax method. In Listing 15-9, I used the url setting to specify the URL for the Ajax request, overriding the value of the url property.

Specifying Multiple Event Handler Functions

I have shown just one callback function to respond to the Ajax request, but you can set the success, error, complete, and beforeStart properties to an array of functions and each of them will be executed when the corresponding event is triggered. Listing 15-10 provides a demonstration.

Listing 15-10. Specifying Multiple Event Handling Functions

```
...
<script type="text/javascript">
    $(document).ready(function () {
        $.ajax({
            url: "mydata.json",
            success: [processData, reportStatus],
        });

        function processData(data, status, jqxhr) {
            var tmplElems = $("#flowerTmpl").template({ flowers: data }).filter("*");
            tmplElems.slice(0, 3).appendTo("#row1");
            tmplElems.slice(3).appendTo("#row2");
        }

        function reportStatus(data, status, jqxhr) {
            console.log("Status: " + status + " Result code: " + jqxhr.status);
        }
    });
</script>
...
```

In Listing 15-10, I have set the success property to an array containing two function names, one of which uses the data to add elements to the document and the other of which prints information to the console.

Setting the Context for Events

The context property lets you specify an element that will be assigned to the this variable when an event function is enabled. This can be useful for targeting elements in the document without having to select them in the handler function. Listing 15-11 gives a demonstration.

Listing 15-11. Using the context Property

```
...
<script type="text/javascript">
    $(document).ready(function () {
        $.ajax({
            url: "mydata.json",
            context: $("h1"),
            success: function (data, status, jqxhr) {
```

```
                var tmplElems = $("#flowerTmpl").template({ flowers: data }).filter("*");
                tmplElems.slice(0, 3).appendTo("#row1");
                tmplElems.slice(3).appendTo("#row2");
            },
            complete: function (jqxhr, status) {
                var color = status == "success" ? "green" : "red";
                this.css("border", "thick solid " + color);
            }
        });
    });
</script>
...
```

In Listing 15-11, I set the context property to the jQuery object containing the h1 elements in the document. In the complete callback function, I use the css method on the jQuery object (which I refer to via this) to set the border for the selected elements (or element, since there is only one in the document), varying the color based on the status of the request. You can see the result for successful and failed requests in Figure 15-2.

Figure 15-2. *Using the context property to indicate the outcome of an Ajax request*

■ **Tip** You can assign any object using the context property, and so you are responsible for ensuring that you do appropriate things with it. For example, if you set the context to be an HTMLElement object, then you must be sure to pass the object to the $ function before calling any jQuery methods on it.

Using the Global Ajax Events

In addition to the per-request callback functions that I described in the previous chapter, jQuery also defines a set of *global events*, which you can use to monitor all Ajax queries that are made by your application. Table 15-6 shows the methods available for global events.

Table 15-6. *jQuery Ajax Event Methods*

Method	Description
ajaxComplete(function)	Registers a function to be called when an Ajax request completes (irrespective of whether it was successful)
ajaxError(function)	Registers a function to be called when an Ajax requests encounters an error
ajaxSend(function)	Registers a function to be called before an Ajax request commences
ajaxStart(function)	Registers a function to be called when an Ajax request starts
ajaxStop(function)	Registers a function to be called when all Ajax requests complete
ajaxSuccess(function)	Registers a function to be called when an Ajax request succeeds

■ **Tip** Prior to jQuery 1.9, you could call the methods in the table on any element, but from jQuery 1.9/2.0 you can only call the methods in the table on the document element, as shown in the examples in this section.

These methods are used to register handler functions and must be applied to the document element (as I demonstrate shortly). The ajaxStart and ajaxStop methods do not pass any arguments to handler functions, but the other methods provide the following arguments:

- An Event object describing the event
- A jqXHR object describing the request
- The settings object that contains the configuration for the request

The ajaxError method passes an additional argument to the handler function, which is the description of the error that has occurred.

There are two important things to remember about these methods. The first is that the functions will be triggered for events from *all* Ajax requests, which means you have to be careful to ensure that you are not making assumptions that are true only for a specific request.

The second thing to remember is that you need to call these methods *before* you start making Ajax requests to ensure that the handler functions are properly triggered. If you call the global methods *after* calling the ajax method, you run the risk that the Ajax request will have finished before jQuery can properly register your handler function. Listing 15-12 provides a demonstration of using the global Ajax event methods.

Listing 15-12. *Using the Global Ajax Event Methods*

```
...
<script type="text/javascript">
    $(document).ready(function () {

        $("<div>").append("<label>Events:<label>")
        .append("<input type='checkbox' id='globalevents' name='globalevents' checked>")
            .insertAfter("h1");
        $("<ol id='info' class='ajaxinfo'>").insertAfter("h1").append("<li>Ready</li>");

        function displayMessage(msg) {
            $("#info").append($("<li>").text(msg));
        }
```

```
        $(document)
            .ajaxStart(function () {
                displayMessage("Ajax Start")
            })
            .ajaxSend(function (event, jqxhr, settings) {
                displayMessage("Ajax Send: " + settings.url)
            })
            .ajaxSuccess(function (event, jqxhr, settings) {
                displayMessage("Ajax Success: " + settings.url)
            })
            .ajaxError(function (event, jqxhr, settings, errorMsg) {
                displayMessage("Ajax Error: " + settings.url)
            })
            .ajaxComplete(function (event, jqxhr, settings) {
                displayMessage("Ajax Complete: " + settings.url)
            })
            .ajaxStop(function () {
                displayMessage("Ajax Stop")
            });

        $("button").click(function (e) {
            $("#row1, #row2, #info").empty();
            $.ajax({
                url: "mydata.json",
                global: $("#globalevents:checked").length > 0,
                success: function (data, status, jqxhr) {
                    var tmplElems = $("#flowerTmpl")
                        .template({ flowers: data }).filter("*");
                    tmplElems.slice(0, 3).appendTo("#row1");
                    tmplElems.slice(3).appendTo("#row2");
                }
            });
            e.preventDefault();
        });
    });
</script>
...
```

In Listing 15-12, I have registered functions for all of the global Ajax events. These functions call the displayMessage function to show which event has been triggered. Because Ajax requests can complete quickly, I use an ol element to display the messages as they arrive, building up a list of events.

I have added a handler function for the button element's click event that starts the Ajax request when the button is clicked. You can see the result in Figure 15-3, which shows the messages generated by the Ajax request once the button has been clicked.

Figure 15-3. *Displaying the global Ajax events*

Controlling Global Events

You will notice that I added a check box to the document. In the call to the ajax function, I use the check box to set the value of the global setting, as shown in Listing 15-13.

Listing 15-13. Using the global Property

```
...
$.ajax({
    url: "mydata.json",
    global: $("#globalevents:checked").length > 0,
    success: function (data, status, jqxhr) {
        var tmplElems = $("#flowerTmpl").template({ flowers: data }).filter("*");
        tmplElems.slice(0, 3).appendTo("#row1");
        tmplElems.slice(3).appendTo("#row2");
    }
})
...
```

When the global setting is false, the Ajax request doesn't generate the global Ajax events. You can try this yourself using the example. Uncheck the box and click the button and you will see that the Ajax request is performed without any status information being shown.

Configuring the Basic Settings for an Ajax Request

There are a group of settings that allow you to perform basic configuration of the Ajax request. These are the least interesting of the settings available, and they are largely self-evident. Table 15-7 describes these settings, and I demonstrate a small number of them in the sections that follow.

Table 15-7. *Basic Request Configuration Settings*

Setting	Description
accepts	Sets the value of the Accept request header, which specifies the MIME types that the browser will accept. By default, this is determined by the dataType setting.
cache	If set to false, the content from the request will not be cached by the server. By default, the script and jsonp data types are not cached, but everything else is.
contentType	Sets the Content-Type header for the request.
dataType	Specifies the data type that is expected from the server. When this setting is used, jQuery will ignore the information provided by the server about the response type. See Chapter 14 for details of how this works.
headers	Specifies additional headers and values to add to the request; see the following discussion for a demonstration.
jsonp	Specifies a string to use instead of a callback when making JSONP requests. This requires coordination with the server. See Chapter 14 for details about JSONP.
jsonpCallback	Specifies the name for the callback function, replacing the randomly generated name that jQuery uses by default. See Chapter 14 for details of JSONP.
password	Specifies a password to use in response to an authentication challenge.
scriptCharset	When requesting JavaScript content, tells jQuery that the script is encoded with the specified character set.
timeout	Specifies the timeout (in milliseconds) for the request. If the request times out, then the function specified by the error setting will be called with a status of timeout.
username	Specifies a username to use in response to an authentication challenge.

Setting Timeouts and Headers

Users are often not aware of Ajax requests happening, so setting a timeout period is a good way to avoid leaving the user hanging around waiting for a process they don't even know is occurring. Listing 15-14 shows how you can set a timeout on a request.

Listing 15-14. Setting Timeouts

```
...
<script type="text/javascript">
    $(document).ready(function() {

        $.ajax("mydata.json", {
            timeout: 5000,
            headers: { "X-HTTP-Method-Override": "PUT" },
```

```
        success: function(data, status, jqxhr) {
            var template = $("#flowerTmpl");
            template.tmpl(data.slice(0, 3)).appendTo("#row1");
            template.tmpl(data.slice(3)).appendTo("#row2");
        },
        error: function(jqxhr, status, errorMsg) {
            console.log("Error: " + status);
        }
    });
});
</script>
...
```

In Listing 15-14, I have used the `timeout` setting to specify a maximum duration for the request of five seconds. If the request hasn't completed in that time, then the function specified by the `error` setting will be executed, with a `status` value of `error`.

■ **Caution** The timer starts as soon as the request is passed to the browser, and most browsers put limits on the number of concurrent requests. This means you run the risk of timing out requests before they even start. To avoid this, you must have some awareness of the limits of the browser and the volume and expected duration of any other Ajax requests that are in progress.

In Listing 15-14, I also used the `headers` setting to add a header to the request, as follows:

```
...
headers: { "X-HTTP-Method-Override": "PUT" },
...
```

Additional headers are specified using a map object. The header in the example is the one I mentioned in a previous section "Making a POST Request." This header can be useful for creating a RESTful web application, as long as it is properly understood by the server.

Sending JSON Data to the Server

When you need to send data to the server, you can do so using the JSON format: it is a compact and expressive data format and easy to generate from JavaScript objects. The process for sending JSON is simple: just use the `contentType` property to set the `Content-Type` header in the request, which tells the server the kind of data being sent as demonstrated by Listing 15-15.

Listing 15-15. Sending JSON to the Server

```
...
<script type="text/javascript">
    $(document).ready(function () {
```

```
        $.ajax("mydata.json", {
            success: function (data, status, jqxhr) {
                var tmplElems = $("#flowerTmpl").template({ flowers: data }).filter("*");
                tmplElems.slice(0, 3).appendTo("#row1");
                tmplElems.slice(3).appendTo("#row2");
            }
        });

        $("button").click(function (e) {
            $.ajax({
                url: $("form").attr("action"),
                contentType: "application/json",
                data: JSON.stringify($("form").serializeArray()),
                type: "post",
                success: processServerResponse
            })
            e.preventDefault();
        })

        function processServerResponse(data) {
            var inputElems = $("div.dcell").hide();
            for (var prop in data) {
                var filtered = inputElems.has("input[name=" + prop + "]")
                    .appendTo("#row1").show();
            }
            $("#buttonDiv, #totalDiv").remove();
            $("#totalTmpl").template(data).appendTo("body");
        }
    });
</script>
...
```

I have used the contentType setting to specify a value of application/json, which is the MIME type for JSON. I could have sent any object to the server, but I wanted to demonstrate how you express form data as JSON, as follows:

```
...
data: JSON.stringify($("form").serializeArray()),
...
```

I select the form element and call the serializeArray method; this creates an array of objects, each of which has a name property and a value property representing one of the input elements in the form. I then use the JSON.stringify method to convert this into a string like the following:

```
[{"name":"aster","value":"1"}, {"name":"daffodil","value":"1"},
 {"name":"rose","value":"1"}, {"name":"peony","value":"1"},
 {"name":"primula","value":"1"},{"name":"snowdrop","value":"1"}]
```

And so I have a JSON string that describes an array of objects that I can send to the server. The Node.js script that I am using for this chapter is able to parse and process this object.

Using Advanced Configuration Settings

In the sections that follow, I describe the most interesting and useful of the advanced settings that you can apply to an Ajax request. I find that I don't use these often, but they are invaluable when required and they provide fine-grained control over how jQuery deals with Ajax.

Making the Request Synchronously

The `async` property specifies whether the request will be performed asynchronously. Setting this property to `true` (which is the default value used if the property isn't defined) means that it will performed asynchronously; a value of `false` means that the request will be performed synchronously.

When the request is performed synchronously, the `ajax` method behaves like a normal function, and the browser will wait for the request to complete before moving on to execute other statements in the script. Listing 15-16 gives an example.

Listing 15-16. Making a Synchronous Request

```
...
<script type="text/javascript">
    $(document).ready(function() {
        var elems;

        $.ajax("flowers.html", {
            async: false,
            success: function(data, status, jqxhr) {
                elems = $(data).filter("div").addClass("dcell");
            }
        });

        elems.slice(0, 3).appendTo("#row1");
        elems.slice(3).appendTo("#row2");
    });
</script>
...
```

This is the request that I showed in Chapter 14 to demonstrate the most common pitfall when using Ajax, updated to use the low-level API. The difference in this case is that the `async` setting is `false`, and so the browser won't get to the statements that call the `slice` and `appendTo` methods until the request has been completed and the results are assigned to the `elems` variable (assuming that the request completed successfully). Making synchronous calls using the Ajax method is an odd thing to do, and I recommend you consider why your web application needs to do this.

I often use this technique as a quick test when looking a troublesome Ajax code—not dealing with asynchronous requests properly is such a common problem that I start debugging with a quick synchronous test. If the code works, I know to start looking for bad assumptions about when data will arrive from the server.

■ **Tip** Do not use synchronous calls because you find making asynchronous calls arduous; I appreciate that using callbacks and making sure you don't make assumptions about the outcome of requests can be tiresome, but it really is worth the time to get your head around this approach to web programming.

401

Ignoring Unmodified Data

You can use the ifModified property to receive data only if the response has changed since the last time you queried it; this is determined by the Last-Modified header in the response. If you need to request the same data repeatedly in response to a user action, you often end up processing the server response and modifying the document just to present the user with whatever was already there. The default value for this setting is false, which tells jQuery to ignore the header and always return the data. Listing 15-17 provides a demonstration of using this property.

Listing 15-17. Using the ifModified property

```
...
<script type="text/javascript">
    $(document).ready(function () {

        $("button").click(function (e) {
            $.ajax("mydata.json", {
                ifModified: true,
                success: function (data, status) {
                    if (status == "success") {
                        $("#row1, #row2").children().remove();
                        var tmplElems = $("#flowerTmpl")
                            .template({ flowers: data }).filter("*");
                        tmplElems.slice(0, 3).appendTo("#row1");
                        tmplElems.slice(3).appendTo("#row2");
                    } else if (status == "notmodified") {
                        $("img").css("border", "thick solid green");
                    }
                }
            });
            e.preventDefault();
        })
    });
</script>
...
```

In Listing 15-17, the value of the ifModified setting is true. The success function is always called, but if the content has not been modified since I last requested it, then the data argument will be undefined and the status argument will be notmodified.

In this example, I perform different actions based on the status argument. If the argument is success, then I use the data argument to add elements to the document. If the argument is notmodified, then I use the css method to add a border to the img elements already in the document.

I make the call to the ajax method in response to the click event from the button element. This allows me to make the same request repeatedly to demonstrate the effect of the ifModified setting, which you can see in Figure 15-4.

Figure 15-4. *Using the ifModified setting*

■ **Caution**   This can be a useful setting but should be used with care. If you are making a request as a consequence of a user action (say, a button press), there is possibility that the user is pressing the button because the previous request didn't perform the way it was supposed to. Imagine that you request the data but the success method contains a bug that doesn't properly update the document with the content; the user is pressing the button to try to get the document to display properly. By using the ifModified setting unwisely, you can end up ignoring the user action, forcing the user to take more serious steps to resolve the problem.

Dealing with the Response Status Code

The statusCode property allows you to respond to the different status codes that can be returned in HTTP responses. You can use this feature as an alternative or complement to the success and error properties. Listing 15-18 shows how you can use the statusCode setting on its own.

Listing 15-18. Using the statusCode Property

```
...
<style type="text/css">
    .error {color: red; border: medium solid red; padding: 4px;
            margin: auto; width: 200px; text-align: center}
</style>
<script type="text/javascript">
    $(document).ready(function() {

        $.ajax({
            url: "mydata.json",
```

```
        statusCode: {
            200: handleSuccessfulRequest,
            404: handleFailedRequest,
            302: handleRedirect
        }
    });

    function handleSuccessfulRequest(data, status, jqxhr) {
        $("#row1, #row2").children().remove();
        var template = $("#flowerTmpl");
        template.tmpl(data.slice(0, 3)).appendTo("#row1");
        template.tmpl(data.slice(3)).appendTo("#row2");
    }

    function handleRedirect() {
        // this function will neber be called
    }

    function handleFailedRequest(jqxhr, status, errorMsg) {
        $("<div class=error>Code: " + jqxhr.status + " Message: "
            + errorMsg + "</div>").insertAfter("h1");
    }
    });
</script>
...
```

The statusCode property is assigned an object that maps between HTTP status codes and the functions you want executed when they are returned to the server. In Listing 15-18, I have defined three functions and associated them with the status codes 200, 404, and 302.

The arguments passed to the functions depend on whether the status code reflects a successful request or an error. If the code represents a success (such as 200) then the arguments are the same as for the success callback function. For failure status codes, such as the 404 code, which indicates the requested file can't be found, the arguments are the same as for the error callback function.

Notice that I have also added a map for the 302 code. This is sent back to the browser when the server wants to redirect you to another URL. jQuery automatically follows redirections until it receives some content or encounters an error. This means that my function for the 302 code won't ever be called.

■ **Tip**   The 304 code, indicating that content has not been modified since it was last requested, is generated only if the ifModified setting has been used. Otherwise, jQuery sends a 200 code. See the previous section "Ignoring Unmodified Data" for information about the ifModified setting.

I find this feature useful when I am debugging interactions between the browser and the server, typically to find out why jQuery isn't behaving quite the way I would like. When I do this, I use the statusCode setting to complement the success and error settings and print out information to the console.

■ **Tip**   The success or error callback function is executed before those specified by the statusCode setting.

Cleaning Up the Response Data

The dataFilter property specifies a function that will be called to process the data returned by the server. This is a useful feature when the server sends you data that aren't quite what you need, either because the formatting isn't perfect or because it contains data that you don't want processed. Listing 15-19 shows the use of the dataFilter property.

Listing 15-19. Using the dataFilter Property

```
...
<script type="text/javascript">
    $(document).ready(function () {

        $.ajax({
            url: "mydata.json",
            success: function (data, status, jqxhr) {
                $("#row1, #row2").children().remove();
                var tmplElems = $("#flowerTmpl").template({ flowers: data }).filter("*");
                tmplElems.slice(0, 3).appendTo("#row1");
                tmplElems.slice(3).appendTo("#row2");
            },
            dataType: "json",
            dataFilter: function (data, dataType) {
                if (dataType == "json") {
                    var filteredData = $.parseJSON(data);
                    filteredData.shift();
                    return JSON.stringify(filteredData.reverse());
                } else {
                    return data;
                }
            }
        });
    });
</script>
...
```

The function is passed the data received from the server and the value of the dataType setting. If the dataType setting has not been used, then the second function argument will be undefined. The purpose of the dataFilter function is to return the filtered data, and in Listing 15-19 I focus on the json data type, as follows:

```
...
var filteredData = $.parseJSON(data);
filteredData.shift();
return JSON.stringify(filteredData.reverse());
...
```

I convert the JSON data into a JavaScript array by using the jQuery parseJSON data (this is one of the jQuery utility methods I describe in Chapter 34). I then use the shift method to remove the first item in the array and use the reverse method to reverse the order of the remaining items.

The dataFilter callback function has to return a string, so I call the JSON.stringify method, even though I know that jQuery will convert the data back into a JavaScript object before calling the success function. That aside, you can see that I am able to remove an element from the array and reverse the remaining items—and while this is not the most useful transformation, it does demonstrate the filtering effect, which you can see in Figure 15-5.

Figure 15-5. *Removing an item and reversing the order of the data using the dataFilter setting*

Managing Data Conversion

I have saved one of my favorite properties until last. You will have noticed that jQuery does some handy conversions when it receives certain data types. As an example, when jQuery receives some JSON data, it presents the success function with a JavaScript object, rather than the raw JSON string.

You can control these conversions using the converters property. The value for this setting is an object that maps between data types and functions that are used to process them. Listing 15-20 shows how you can use this property to automatically parse HTML data into a jQuery object.

Listing 15-20. Using the converters Setting

```
...
<script type="text/javascript">
    $(document).ready(function() {

        $.ajax({
            url: "flowers.html",
            success: function(data, status, jqxhr) {
                var elems = data.filter("div").addClass("dcell");
                elems.slice(0, 3).appendTo("#row1");
                elems.slice(3).appendTo("#row2");
            },
            converters: {
                "text html": function(data) {
                    return $(data);
                }
            }
        });
    });
</script>
...
```

I registered a function for the `text html` type. Notice that you use a space between the components of the MIME type (as opposed to `text/html`). The function is passed the data that have been received from the server and returns the converted data. In this case, I pass the HTML fragment that is obtained from the `flowers.html` file to the jQuery `$` function and return the result. This means I can call all the usual jQuery methods on the object passed as the data argument to the `success` function.

■ **Tip** The data types don't always match the MIME types that are returned by the server. For example, `application/json` is usually presented as `"text json"` to the `converters` method.

It is easy to get carried away with these converters. I try to avoid the temptation to do more in these functions than I should. For example, I am sometimes tempted to take JSON data, apply a data template, and pass the resulting HTML elements back. And although this is a nice trick, it can trip you up if someone else tries to extend your code or you need to unwind heavy processing to get at the raw data later.

Setting Up and Filtering Ajax Requests

To finish this chapter, I am going to describe a couple of additional methods that jQuery provides to make configuring requests simpler.

Defining Default Settings

The `ajaxSetup` method specifies settings that will be used for every Ajax request, freeing you from having to define all of the settings you are interested in for each and every request. Listing 15-21 shows this method in use.

Listing 15-21. Using the ajaxSetup Method

```
...
<script type="text/javascript">
    $(document).ready(function() {

        $.ajaxSetup({
            timeout: 15000,
            global: false,
            error: function(jqxhr, status, errorMsg) {
                $("<div class=error/>")
                    .text("Status: " + status + " Error: " + errorMsg)
                    .insertAfter("h1");
            },
            converters: {
                "text html": function(data) {
                    return $(data);
                }
            }
        });
```

```
        $.ajax({
            url: "flowers.html",
            success: function(data, status, jqxhr) {
                var elems = data.filter("div").addClass("dcell");
                elems.slice(0, 3).appendTo("#row1");
                elems.slice(3).appendTo("#row2");
            },
        });
    });
</script>
...
```

You call the ajaxSetup method against the jQuery $ function, just as you do for the ajax method. The argument to the ajaxSetup is an object that contains the settings you want to use as the defaults for all your Ajax requests. In Listing 15-21, I define defaults for the timeout, global, error, and converters settings. Once I have called the ajaxSetup method, I only have to define values for those settings for which I haven't provided a default value or whose value I want to change. This can reduce code duplication when making a lot of Ajax requests that have similar configurations.

■ **Tip**   The settings specified by the ajaxSetup method also affect requests made by the convenience and shorthand methods I showed you in Chapter 14. This can be a nice way of combining the detailed control that comes with the low-level API with the simplicity of the convenience methods.

Filtering Requests

You can use the ajaxPrefilter method if you want to dynamically tailor the settings for individual requests, as shown in Listing 15-22.

Listing 15-22. Using the ajaxPrefilter Method

```
...
<script type="text/javascript">
    $(document).ready(function () {

        $.ajaxSetup({
            timeout: 15000,
            global: false,
            error: function (jqxhr, status, errorMsg) {
                $("<div class=error/>")
                    .text("Status: " + status + " Error: " + errorMsg)
                    .insertAfter("h1");
            },
            converters: {
                "text html": function (data) {
                    return $(data);
                }
            }
        });
```

```
$.ajaxPrefilter("json html", function (settings, originalSettings, jqxhr) {
    if (originalSettings.dataType == "html") {
        settings.timeout = 2000;
    } else {
        jqxhr.abort();
    }
});

$.ajax({
    url: "flowers.html",
    success: function (data, status, jqxhr) {
        var elems = data.filter("div").addClass("dcell");
        elems.slice(0, 3).appendTo("#row1");
        elems.slice(3).appendTo("#row2");
    },
});
});
</script>
...
```

The arguments to the ajaxPrefilter method are a set of data types and a callback function that will be executed when a request for those data types is made. If you omit the data type and just specify the function, it will be invoked for all requests.

The arguments passed to the callback function are the settings for the request (which includes any defaults you have set using the ajaxSetup method); the original settings passed to the Ajax method (which excludes any default values) and the jqXHR object for the request. You make changes to the object passed as the first argument, as shown in the example.

In Listing 15-22, I filter JSON and HTML requests so that if a dataType setting has been specified in the settings passed to the Ajax method, I set the timeout to be two seconds. For a request that doesn't have that setting, I call the abort method on the jqXHR object to prevent the request from being sent.

Summary

In this chapter, I showed you the low-level jQuery Ajax interface, which, as I hope you agree, isn't that much harder to work with than the convenience and shorthand methods I showed you in Chapter 14. For a modicum of additional effort, you can control many aspects of the way that the Ajax request is processed, giving you endless ways in which you can tweak the process to your needs and preferences. In Chapter 16, I refactor the example to incorporate the features and techniques that I described in this part of the book.

CHAPTER 16

Refactoring the Example: Part II

I introduced some rich features in this part of the book, and as I did in before in Chapter 11, I want to bring them together to give a broader view of jQuery.

■ Tip   I am not going to try to preserve a workable non-JavaScript structure in this chapter, since all of the features I am adding to the example rely heavily on JavaScript.

Reviewing the Refactored Example

In Chapter 11, I used the core jQuery features to refactor the example to include DOM (Domain Object Model) manipulation, effects, and events. Listing 16-1 shows the document I ended up with, which will be the starting point for this chapter as I integrate the features from this part of the book.

Listing 16-1. The Starting Point for This Chapter

```
<!DOCTYPE html>
<html>
<head>
    <title>Example</title>
    <script src="jquery-2.0.2.js" type="text/javascript"></script>
    <link rel="stylesheet" type="text/css" href="styles.css"/>
    <style type="text/css">
        a.arrowButton {
            background-image: url(leftarrows.png); float: left;
            margin-top: 15px; display: block; width: 50px; height: 50px;
        }
        #right {background-image: url(rightarrows.png)}
        h1 { min-width: 0px; width: 95%; }
        #oblock { float: left; display: inline; border: thin black solid; }
        form { margin-left: auto; margin-right: auto; width: 885px; }
        #bbox {clear: left}
    </style>
    <script type="text/javascript">
        $(document).ready(function() {
```

```
        var fNames = ["Carnation", "Lily", "Orchid"];
        var fRow = $("<div id=row3 class=drow/>").appendTo("div.dtable");
        var fTemplate = $("<div class=dcell><img/><label/><input/></div>");
        for (var i = 0; i < fNames.length; i++) {
            fTemplate.clone().appendTo(fRow).children()
                .filter("img").attr("src", fNames[i] + ".png").end()
                .filter("label").attr("for", fNames[i]).text(fNames[i]).end()
                .filter("input").attr({name: fNames[i],
                                        value: 0, required: "required"})
        }


        $("<a id=left></a><a id=right></a>").prependTo("form")
            .addClass("arrowButton").click(handleArrowPress).hover(handleArrowMouse);
        $("#right").appendTo("form");

        $("#row2, #row3").hide();

        var total = $("#buttonDiv")
            .prepend("<div>Total Items: <span id=total>0</span></div>")
            .css({clear: "both", padding: "5px"});
        $("<div id=bbox />").appendTo("body").append(total);


        $("input").change(function(e) {
            var total = 0;
            $("input").each(function(index, elem) {
                total += Number($(elem).val());
            });
            $("#total").text(total);
        });

        function handleArrowMouse(e) {
          var propValue = e.type == "mouseenter" ? "-50px 0px" : "0px 0px";
          $(this).css("background-position", propValue);
        }


        function handleArrowPress(e) {
            var elemSequence = ["row1", "row2", "row3"];

            var visibleRow = $("div.drow:visible");
            var visibleRowIndex = jQuery.inArray(visibleRow.attr("id"),elemSequence);

            var targetRowIndex;

            if (e.target.id == "left") {
                targetRowIndex = visibleRowIndex - 1;
                if (targetRowIndex < 0) {targetRowIndex = elemSequence.length -1};
            } else {
                targetRowIndex = (visibleRowIndex + 1) % elemSequence.length;
            }
```

```
                    visibleRow.fadeOut("fast", function() {
                        $("#" + elemSequence[targetRowIndex]).fadeIn("fast")});
                }
            });
    </script>
</head>
<body>
    <h1>Jacqui's Flower Shop</h1>
    <form method="post" action="http://node.jacquisflowershop.com/order">
        <div id="oblock">
            <div class="dtable">
                <div id="row1" class="drow">
                    <div class="dcell">
                        <img src="aster.png"/><label for="aster">Aster:</label>
                        <input name="aster" value="0" />
                    </div>
                    <div class="dcell">
                        <img src="daffodil.png"/><label for="daffodil">Daffodil:</label>
                        <input name="daffodil" value="0"/>
                    </div>
                    <div class="dcell">
                        <img src="rose.png"/><label for="rose">Rose:</label>
                        <input name="rose" value="0" />
                    </div>
                </div>
                <div id="row2"class="drow">
                    <div class="dcell">
                        <img src="peony.png"/><label for="peony">Peony:</label>
                        <input name="peony" value="0" />
                    </div>
                    <div class="dcell">
                        <img src="primula.png"/><label for="primula">Primula:</label>
                        <input name="primula" value="0" />
                    </div>
                    <div class="dcell">
                        <img src="snowdrop.png"/><label for="snowdrop">Snowdrop:</label>
                        <input name="snowdrop" value="0" />
                    </div>
                </div>
            </div>
        </div>
        <div id="buttonDiv"><button type="submit">Place Order</button></div>
    </form>
</body>
</html>
```

■ **Tip**   There are a number of points in the script where I insert elements dynamically. Rather than making these static, I am going to leave them as they are so that I can focus on adding the new features.

This isn't exactly the same document: I have tidied the Cascading Style Sheet (CSS) additions by adding a style element rather than using the css method on individual selections. You can see how this HTML document appears in the browser in Figure 16-1, and, of course, Chapter 11 breaks down the set of changes I applied to the document to get this far.

Figure 16-1. *The starting point for the example document in this chapter*

Updating the Node.js Script

I need to upgrade the formserver.js server-side script for this chapter. The changes, which are shown in Listing 16-2, are to enrich the data that is sent back when a form is submitted and to support a new validation feature. As with all of the examples in this book, you can download the revised formserver.js file from the Source Code/Download area of the Apress web site (www.apress.com).

Listing 16-2. The Revised Node.js Script

```
var http = require("http");
var querystring = require("querystring");
var url = require("url");

var port = 80;

http.createServer(function (req, res) {
    console.log("[200 OK] " + req.method + " to " + req.url);

    if (req.method == "OPTIONS") {
        res.writeHead(200, "OK", {
            "Access-Control-Allow-Headers": "Content-Type",
            "Access-Control-Allow-Methods": "*",
            "Access-Control-Allow-Origin": "http://www.jacquisflowershop.com"
        });
        res.end();

    } else if (req.method == "POST") {
        var dataObj = new Object();
        var contentType = req.headers["content-type"];
        var fullBody = "";
```

```javascript
        if (contentType) {
            if (contentType.indexOf("application/x-www-form-urlencoded") > -1) {
                req.on("data", function (chunk) { fullBody += chunk.toString(); });
                req.on("end", function () {
                    var dBody = querystring.parse(fullBody);
                    writeResponse(req, res, dBody,
                        url.parse(req.url, true).query["callback"])
                });
            } else {
                req.on("data", function (chunk) { fullBody += chunk.toString(); });
                req.on("end", function () {
                    dataObj = JSON.parse(fullBody);
                    var dprops = new Object();
                    for (var i = 0; i < dataObj.length; i++) {
                        dprops[dataObj[i].name] = dataObj[i].value;
                    }
                    writeResponse(req, res, dprops);
                });
            }
        }
    } else if (req.method == "GET") {
        var data = url.parse(req.url, true).query;
        writeResponse(req, res, data, data["callback"])
    }

var flowerData = {
    aster: { price: 2.99, stock: 10, plural: "Asters" },
    daffodil: { price: 1.99, stock: 10, plural: "Daffodils" },
    rose: { price: 4.99, stock: 2, plural: "Roses" },
    peony: { price: 1.50, stock: 3, plural: "Peonies" },
    primula: { price: 3.12, stock: 20, plural: "Primulas" },
    snowdrop: { price: 0.99, stock: 5, plural: "Snowdrops" },
    carnation: { price: 0.50, stock: 1, plural: "Carnations" },
    lily: { price: 1.20, stock: 2, plural: "Lillies" },
    orchid: { price: 10.99, stock: 5, plural: "Orchids" }
}

function writeResponse(req, res, data, jsonp) {
    var jsonData;
    if (req.url == "/stockcheck") {
        for (flower in data) {
            if (flowerData[flower].stock >= data[flower]) {
                jsonData = true;
            } else {
                jsonData = "We only have " + flowerData[flower].stock + " "
                    + flowerData[flower].plural + " in stock";
            }
            break;
        }
        jsonData = JSON.stringify(jsonData);
    } else {
        var totalCount = 0;
```

```
            var totalPrice = 0;
            for (item in data) {
                if (item != "_" && data[item] > 0) {
                    var itemNum = Number(data[item])
                    totalCount += itemNum;
                    totalPrice += (itemNum * flowerData[item].price);
                } else {
                    delete data[item];
                }
            }
            data.totalItems = totalCount;
            data.totalPrice = totalPrice.toFixed(2);

            jsonData = JSON.stringify(data);
            if (jsonp) {
                jsonData = jsonp + "(" + jsonData + ")";
            }
        }
        res.writeHead(200, "OK", {
            "Content-Type": jsonp ? "text/javascript" : "application/json",
            "Access-Control-Allow-Origin": "*"
        });
        res.write(jsonData);
        res.end();
    }

}).listen(port);
console.log("Ready on port " + port);
```

The response to the browser now includes the total prices for the items selected using the form elements and submitted to the server, returning a JSON result like the following:

```
{"aster":"1","daffodil":"2","rose":"4","totalItems":7,"totalPrice":"26.93"}
```

I run the script by entering the following at the command prompt:

```
node.exe formserver.js
```

Preparing for Ajax

To begin, I am going to add some basic elements and styles that I will use to display Ajax request errors and set up the basic configuration that will apply to all of my Ajax requests. Listing 16-3 shows the changes to the document.

Listing 16-3. Setting Up the Support for Ajax Requests and Error Handling

```
...
<style type="text/css">
    a.arrowButton {
```

```
            background-image: url(leftarrows.png); float: left;
            margin-top: 15px; display: block; width: 50px; height: 50px;
        }
        #right {background-image: url(rightarrows.png)}
        h1 { min-width: 0px; width: 95%; }
        #oblock { float: left; display: inline; border: thin black solid; }
        form { margin-left: auto; margin-right: auto; width: 885px; }
        #bbox {clear: left}
        #error {color: red; border: medium solid red; padding: 4px; margin: auto;
            width: 300px; text-align: center; margin-bottom: 5px}
    </style>
    <script type="text/javascript">
        $(document).ready(function () {

            $.ajaxSetup({
                timeout: 5000,
                converters: {"text html": function (data) { return $(data); }}
            });

            $(document).ajaxError(function (e, jqxhr, settings, errorMsg) {
                $("#error").remove();
                var msg = "An error occurred. Please try again"
                if (errorMsg == "timeout") {
                    msg = "The request timed out. Please try again"
                } else if (jqxhr.status == 404) {
                    msg = "The file could not be found";
                }
                $("<div id=error/>").text(msg).insertAfter("h1");
            }).ajaxSuccess(function () {
                $("#error").remove();
            });

            var fNames = ["Carnation", "Lily", "Orchid"];
            var fRow = $("<div id=row3 class=drow/>").appendTo("div.dtable");
            var fTemplate = $("<div class=dcell><img/><label/><input/></div>");
            for (var i = 0; i < fNames.length; i++) {
                fTemplate.clone().appendTo(fRow).children()
                    .filter("img").attr("src", fNames[i] + ".png").end()
                    .filter("label").attr("for", fNames[i]).text(fNames[i]).end()
                    .filter("input").attr({
                        name: fNames[i], value: 0, required: "required"
                    })
            };

            $("<a id=left></a><a id=right></a>").prependTo("form")
                .addClass("arrowButton").click(handleArrowPress).hover(handleArrowMouse);
            $("#right").appendTo("form");

            $("#row2, #row3").hide();

            var total = $("#buttonDiv")
                .prepend("<div>Total Items: <span id=total>0</span></div>")
```

417

```
            .css({ clear: "both", padding: "5px" });
        $("<div id=bbox />").appendTo("body").append(total).css("clear: left");

        $("input").change(function (e) {
            var total = 0;
            $("input").each(function (index, elem) {
                total += Number($(elem).val());
            });
            $("#total").text(total);
        });

        function handleArrowMouse(e) {
            var propValue = e.type == "mouseenter" ? "-50px 0px" : "0px 0px";
            $(this).css("background-position", propValue);
        }

        function handleArrowPress(e) {
            var elemSequence = ["row1", "row2", "row3"];
            var visibleRow = $("div.drow:visible");
            var visibleRowIndex =
                jQuery.inArray(visibleRow.attr("id"), elemSequence);

            var targetRowIndex;
            if (e.target.id == "left") {
                targetRowIndex = visibleRowIndex - 1;
                if (targetRowIndex < 0) { targetRowIndex = elemSequence.length - 1 };
            } else {
                targetRowIndex = (visibleRowIndex + 1) % elemSequence.length;
            }

            visibleRow.fadeOut("fast", function () {
                $("#" + elemSequence[targetRowIndex]).fadeIn("fast")
            });
        }
    });
</script>
...
```

I have used the global Ajax events to set up a simple display for errors. When an error occurs, new elements are created to provide a description of the problem. The simple error messages that I show are derived from the information I get from jQuery, but in a real web application, these messages should be more descriptive and provide suggestions for resolution. You can see an example of an error being shown to the user in Figure 16-2.

Figure 16-2. *Displaying an error message for Ajax*

The error is displayed until a successful request is made or another error occurs, at which point the elements are removed from the document. In addition to the global events, I used the `ajaxSetup` method to define values for the `timeout` setting and to provide a converter for HTML fragments so that they are automatically processed by jQuery.

Sourcing the Product Information

The next change is to remove the existing product elements and the loop that adds three additional flowers to the list, replacing them with a pair of Ajax calls and a data template. First, however, I created a file called `additionalflowers.json` and placed it in the same directory as the other example files. Listing 16-4 shows the contents of the `additionalflowers.json` file.

Listing 16-4. The Contents of the Additionalflowers.json File

```
[{"name":"Carnation","product":"carnation"},
 {"name":"Lily","product":"lily"},
 {"name":"Orchid","product":"orchid"}]
```

This file contains a JSON description of the additional products I want to display. I am going to get the main set of products as an HTML fragment and then add to the set by processing the JSON data. Listing 16-5 shows the changes.

Listing 16-5. Setting Up the Products via HTML and JSON Obtained via Ajax

```html
<!DOCTYPE html>
<html>
<head>
    <title>Example</title>
    <script src="jquery-2.0.2.js" type="text/javascript"></script>
    <script src="handlebars.js" type="text/javascript"></script>
    <script src="handlebars-jquery.js" type="text/javascript"></script>
    <link rel="stylesheet" type="text/css" href="styles.css"/>
    <style type="text/css">
        a.arrowButton {
            background-image: url(leftarrows.png); float: left;
```

```css
        margin-top: 15px; display: block; width: 50px; height: 50px;
    }
    #right {background-image: url(rightarrows.png)}
    h1 { min-width: 0px; width: 95%; }
    #oblock { float: left; display: inline; border: thin black solid; }
    form { margin-left: auto; margin-right: auto; width: 885px; }
    #bbox {clear: left}
    #error {color: red; border: medium solid red; padding: 4px; margin: auto;
        width: 300px; text-align: center; margin-bottom: 5px}
</style>
<script id="flowerTmpl" type="text/x-handlebars-template">
    {{#flowers}}
    <div class="dcell">
        <img src="{{product}}.png"/>
        <label for="{{product}}">{{name}}:</label>
        <input name="{{product}}" value="0" />
    </div>
    {{/flowers}}
</script>
<script type="text/javascript">
    $(document).ready(function () {

        $.ajaxSetup({
            timeout: 5000,
            converters: {"text html": function (data) { return $(data); }}
        });

        $(document).ajaxError(function (e, jqxhr, settings, errorMsg) {
            $("#error").remove();
            var msg = "An error occurred. Please try again"
            if (errorMsg == "timeout") {
                msg = "The request timed out. Please try again"
            } else if (jqxhr.status == 404) {
                msg = "The file could not be found";
            }
            $("<div id=error/>").text(msg).insertAfter("h1");
        }).ajaxSuccess(function () {
            $("#error").remove();
        });

        $("<a id=left></a><a id=right></a>").prependTo("form")
            .addClass("arrowButton").click(handleArrowPress).hover(handleArrowMouse);
        $("#right").appendTo("form");

        $("#row2, #row3").hide();

        $.get("flowers.html", function (data) {
            var elems = data.filter("div").addClass("dcell");
            elems.slice(0, 3).appendTo("#row1");
            elems.slice(3).appendTo("#row2");
        })
```

```
        $.getJSON("additionalflowers.json", function (data) {
            $("#flowerTmpl").template({ flowers: data }).appendTo("#row3");
        })


        var total = $("#buttonDiv")
            .prepend("<div>Total Items: <span id=total>0</span></div>")
            .css({ clear: "both", padding: "5px" });
        $("<div id=bbox />").appendTo("body").append(total).css("clear: left");

        $("input").change(function (e) {
            var total = 0;
            $("input").each(function (index, elem) {
                total += Number($(elem).val());
            });
            $("#total").text(total);
        });

        function handleArrowMouse(e) {
            var propValue = e.type == "mouseenter" ? "-50px 0px" : "0px 0px";
            $(this).css("background-position", propValue);
        }


        function handleArrowPress(e) {
            var elemSequence = ["row1", "row2", "row3"];
            var visibleRow = $("div.drow:visible");
            var visibleRowIndex =
                jQuery.inArray(visibleRow.attr("id"), elemSequence);

            var targetRowIndex;
            if (e.target.id == "left") {
                targetRowIndex = visibleRowIndex - 1;
                if (targetRowIndex < 0) { targetRowIndex = elemSequence.length - 1 };
            } else {
                targetRowIndex = (visibleRowIndex + 1) % elemSequence.length;
            }

            visibleRow.fadeOut("fast", function () {
                $("#" + elemSequence[targetRowIndex]).fadeIn("fast")
            });
        }
    });
    </script>
</head>
<body>
    <h1>Jacqui's Flower Shop</h1>
    <form method="post" action="http://node.jacquisflowershop.com/order">
        <div id="oblock">
            <div class="dtable">
                <div id="row1" class="drow"></div>
                <div id="row2" class="drow"></div>
                <div id="row3" class="drow"></div>
```

```
        </div>
    </div>
    <div id="buttonDiv"><button type="submit">Place Order</button></div>
  </form>
</body>
</html>
```

I have used the Ajax shorthand methods to get the HTML fragment and the JSON data I need to create the rows. It may not be obvious from the script, but one of the nice things about the shorthand methods is that they are just wrappers around calls to the low-level API—and this means that the settings you apply via the ajaxSetup method work just as they do when you use the ajax method directly. In addition to the calls to the get and getJSON methods, I have added a data template so I can process the JSON easily. There is no change to the appearance of the document, but the source of the content has changed.

Adding Form Validation

The next stage is to add validation to the input elements. Listing 16-6 shows the additions that are required.

Listing 16-6. Adding Form Validation

```
<!DOCTYPE html>
<html>
<head>
    <title>Example</title>
    <script src="jquery-2.0.2.js" type="text/javascript"></script>
    <script src="handlebars.js" type="text/javascript"></script>
    <script src="handlebars-jquery.js" type="text/javascript"></script>
    <script src="jquery.validate.js" type="text/javascript"></script>
    <link rel="stylesheet" type="text/css" href="styles.css"/>
    <style type="text/css">
        a.arrowButton {
            background-image: url(leftarrows.png); float: left;
            margin-top: 15px; display: block; width: 50px; height: 50px;
        }
        #right {background-image: url(rightarrows.png)}
        h1 { min-width: 0px; width: 95%; }
        #oblock { float: left; display: inline; border: thin black solid; }
        form { margin-left: auto; margin-right: auto; width: 885px; }
        #bbox {clear: left}
        #error {color: red; border: medium solid red; padding: 4px; margin: auto;
            width: 300px; text-align: center; margin-bottom: 5px}
        .invalidElem {border: medium solid red}
        #errorSummary {border: thick solid red; color: red; width: 350px; margin: auto;
            padding: 4px; margin-bottom: 5px}
    </style>
    <script id="flowerTmpl" type="text/x-handlebars-template">
        {{#flowers}}
        <div class="dcell">
            <img src="{{product}}.png"/>
            <label for="{{product}}">{{name}}:</label>
            <input name="{{product}}" value="0" />
```

```
    </div>
    {{/flowers}}
</script>
<script type="text/javascript">
    $(document).ready(function () {

        $.ajaxSetup({
            timeout: 5000,
            converters: {"text html": function (data) { return $(data); }}
        });

        $(document).ajaxError(function (e, jqxhr, settings, errorMsg) {
            $("#error").remove();
            var msg = "An error occurred. Please try again"
            if (errorMsg == "timeout") {
                msg = "The request timed out. Please try again"
            } else if (jqxhr.status == 404) {
                msg = "The file could not be found";
            }
            $("<div id=error/>").text(msg).insertAfter("h1");
        }).ajaxSuccess(function () {
            $("#error").remove();
        });

        $("<a id=left></a><a id=right></a>").prependTo("form")
            .addClass("arrowButton").click(handleArrowPress).hover(handleArrowMouse);
        $("#right").appendTo("form");

        $("#row2, #row3").hide();

        var flowerReq = $.get("flowers.html", function (data) {
            var elems = data.filter("div").addClass("dcell");
            elems.slice(0, 3).appendTo("#row1");
            elems.slice(3).appendTo("#row2");
        });

        var jsonReq = $.getJSON("additionalflowers.json", function (data) {
            $("#flowerTmpl").template({ flowers: data }).appendTo("#row3");
        });

        $("<div id=errorSummary>").text("Please correct the following errors:")
            .append("<ul id='errorsList'></ul>").hide().insertAfter("h1");

        $("form").validate({
            highlight: function(element, errorClass) {
                $(element).addClass("invalidElem");
            },
            unhighlight: function(element, errorClass) {
                $(element).removeClass("invalidElem");
            },
            errorContainer: "#errorSummary",
```

423

```javascript
            errorLabelContainer: "#errorsList",
            wrapper: "li",
            errorElement: "div"
    });


    var plurals = {
        aster: "Asters", daffodil: "Daffodils", rose: "Roses",
        peony: "Peonies", primula: "Primulas", snowdrop: "Snowdrops",
        carnation: "Carnations", lily: "Lillies", orchid: "Orchids"
    };


    $.when(flowerReq, jsonReq).then(function() {
        $("input").each(function(index, elem) {
            $(elem).rules("add", {
                required: true,
                min: 0,
                digits: true,
                messages: {
                    required: "Please enter a number of " + plurals[elem.name],
                    digits: "Please enter a number of" + plurals[elem.name],
                    min: "Please enter a positive number of "
                            + plurals[elem.name]
                }
            })
        }).change(function(e) {
            if ($("form").validate().element($(e.target))) {
                var total = 0;
                $("input").each(function(index, elem) {
                    total += Number($(elem).val());
                });
                $("#total").text(total);
            }
        });
    });

    var total = $("#buttonDiv")
        .prepend("<div>Total Items: <span id=total>0</span></div>")
        .css({ clear: "both", padding: "5px" });
    $("<div id=bbox />").appendTo("body").append(total).css("clear: left");


    $("input").change(function (e) {
        var total = 0;
        $("input").each(function (index, elem) {
            total += Number($(elem).val());
        });
        $("#total").text(total);
    });

    function handleArrowMouse(e) {
        var propValue = e.type == "mouseenter" ? "-50px 0px" : "0px 0px";
        $(this).css("background-position", propValue);
    }
```

```
        function handleArrowPress(e) {
            var elemSequence = ["row1", "row2", "row3"];
            var visibleRow = $("div.drow:visible");
            var visibleRowIndex =
                jQuery.inArray(visibleRow.attr("id"), elemSequence);

            var targetRowIndex;
            if (e.target.id == "left") {
                targetRowIndex = visibleRowIndex - 1;
                if (targetRowIndex < 0) { targetRowIndex = elemSequence.length - 1 };
            } else {
                targetRowIndex = (visibleRowIndex + 1) % elemSequence.length;
            }

            visibleRow.fadeOut("fast", function () {
                $("#" + elemSequence[targetRowIndex]).fadeIn("fast")
            });
        }
    });
    </script>
</head>
<body>
    <h1>Jacqui's Flower Shop</h1>
    <form method="post" action="http://node.jacquisflowershop.com/order">
        <div id="oblock">
            <div class="dtable">
                <div id="row1" class="drow"></div>
                <div id="row2" class="drow"></div>
                <div id="row3" class="drow"></div>
            </div>
        </div>
        <div id="buttonDiv"><button type="submit">Place Order</button></div>
    </form>
</body>
</html>
```

In this listing, I imported the validation plug-in and defined some CSS that will be used to style validation errors. I call the validate method on the form element to set up form validation, specifying a single validation summary, just as I did in Chapter 13.

The fact that I am using Ajax to generate elements for the flower products gives me a problem to solve. These are, of course, asynchronous calls, so I can't make assumptions about the presence of the input elements in the document in the statements that follow the Ajax calls. This is the common pitfall I described in Chapter 14, and if the browser executes my selection of the input elements before both Ajax requests are complete, I won't match any elements (because they have yet to be created and added to the document), and my validation setup will fail.

To solve this problem, I have used the when and then methods, which are part of the jQuery *deferred objects* feature that I describe in Chapter 35. Following are the relevant statements:

```
...
$.when(flowerReq, jsonReq).then(function() {
    $("input").each(function(index, elem) {
        $(elem).rules("add", {
            required: true,
```

```
                min: 0,
                digits: true,
                messages: {
                    required: "Please enter a number of " + plurals[elem.name],
                    digits: "Please enter a number of" + plurals[elem.name],
                    min: "Please enter a positive number of "
                        + plurals[elem.name]
                }
            })
        }).change(function(e) {
            if ($("form").validate().element($(e.target))) {
                var total = 0;
                $("input").each(function(index, elem) {
                    total += Number($(elem).val());
                });
                $("#total").text(total);
            }
        });
    })
...
```

I don't want to get ahead of myself, but the jqXHR objects that are returned by all of the Ajax methods can be passed as arguments to the when method, and if both requests are successful, the function passed to the then method will be executed.

I set up my form validation in the function I pass to the then method, selecting the input elements and adding the validation rules I require to each of them. I have specified that values are required, that they must be digits, and that the minimum acceptable value is zero. I have defined custom messages for each validation check and these refer to an array of plural flower names to help them make sense to the user.

Since I have the input elements selected, I take the opportunity to provide a handler function for the change event, which is triggered when the value entered into the field changes. Notice that I call the element method, as follows:

```
...
if ($("form").validate().element($(e.target))) {
...
```

This triggers validation on the changed element, and the result from the method is a Boolean indicating the validity of the entered value. By using an if block, I avoid adding invalid values to my running total of selected items.

Adding Remote Validation

The validation I performed in the Listing 16-6 and that I described in Chapter 13 are examples of *local validation*, which is to say that the rules and the data required to enforce them are part of the HTML document.

The validation plug-in also supports *remote validation*, where the value entered by the user is sent to the server and the rules are applied there. This is useful when you don't want to send the validation rules to the browser because it would require too much data (e.g., you might validate a user name for a new account by checking that it has not already been used—something that would require all account names to be sent to the client for local validation).

■ **Caution**   Some caution is required when using remote validation because the load it can place on a server is significant. In this example, I perform a remote validation every time the user changes the value of an `input` element and this is likely to generate a lot of requests in a real application. A more sensible approach is usually to perform remote validation only as a precursor to submitting the form.

I didn't explain remote validation in Chapter 13 because it relies on JSON and Ajax, and I didn't want to get into those topics too early. Listing 16-7 shows how I set up remote validation, which I use to ensure that the user cannot order more items than are in stock.

Listing 16-7. Performing Remote Validation

```
...
$.when(flowerReq, jsonReq).then(function() {
    $("input").each(function(index, elem) {
        $(elem).rules("add", {
            required: true,
            min: 0,
            digits: true,
            remote: {
                url: "http://node.jacquisflowershop.com/stockcheck",
                type: "post",
                global: false
            },
            messages: {
                required: "Please enter a number of " + plurals[elem.name],
                digits: "Please enter a number of" + plurals[elem.name],
                min: "Please enter a positive number of "
                    + plurals[elem.name]
            }
        })
    }).change(function(e) {
        if ($("form").validate().element($(e.target))) {
            var total = 0;
            $("input").each(function(index, elem) {
                total += Number($(elem).val());
            });
            $("#total").text(total);
        }
    });
});
...
```

Setting remote validation is easy: I specify the validation check by setting the `remote` property to a map object that configures the Ajax request the validation plug-in will make to the user. In this example, I have used the `url` setting to specify the URL that will be called to perform the remote validation, the `type` setting to specify that I want a POST request, and the `global` setting to disable global events.

427

I have disabled global events because I don't want errors that arise when making the remote validation Ajax request to be treated as general errors that the user can do something about. Instead, I want them to fail quietly, on the basis that the server will perform further validation when the form is submitted (the formserver.js script doesn't perform any validation, but it is important that real web applications do, as I explained in Chapter 13).

The validation plug-in uses the standard jQuery Ajax settings to make a request to the specified remote validation URL, sending the name of the input element and the value that the user has entered. If I enter 22 into the Aster input element and then navigate away to trigger the change event, the validation plug-in will make an HTTP POST request to the server that contains the following information:

```
aster=22
```

The response that the server sends is simple. If the response is the word true, then the value is valid. Any other response is considered to be an error message that will be displayed to the user. My formserver.js script will send back an error message such as the following:

```
We only have 10 Asters in stock
```

This message is treated just like a local validation message, as illustrated in Figure 16-3.

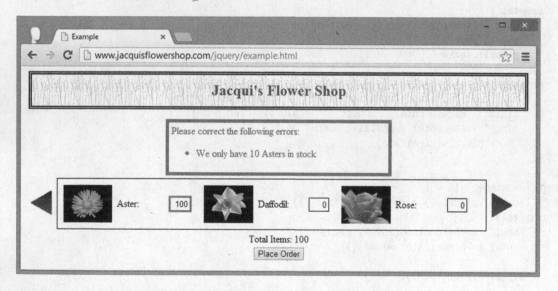

Figure 16-3. *Displaying remote validation messages*

Submitting the Form Data Using Ajax

Submitting the values in the form is exceptionally simple, and Listing 16-8 shows the technique I used in Chapter 15.

Listing 16-8. Submitting the Form Using Ajax

```
<!DOCTYPE html>
<html>
<head>
```

```
<title>Example</title>
<script src="jquery-2.0.2.js" type="text/javascript"></script>
<script src="handlebars.js" type="text/javascript"></script>
<script src="handlebars-jquery.js" type="text/javascript"></script>
<script src="jquery.validate.js" type="text/javascript"></script>
<link rel="stylesheet" type="text/css" href="styles.css"/>
<style type="text/css">
    a.arrowButton {
        background-image: url(leftarrows.png); float: left;
        margin-top: 15px; display: block; width: 50px; height: 50px;
    }
    #right {background-image: url(rightarrows.png)}
    h1 { min-width: 0px; width: 95%; }
    #oblock { float: left; display: inline; border: thin black solid; }
    form { margin-left: auto; margin-right: auto; width: 885px; }
    #bbox {clear: left}
    #error {color: red; border: medium solid red; padding: 4px; margin: auto;
        width: 300px; text-align: center; margin-bottom: 5px}
    .invalidElem {border: medium solid red}
    #errorSummary {border: thick solid red; color: red; width: 350px; margin: auto;
        padding: 4px; margin-bottom: 5px}
    #popup {
        text-align: center; position: absolute; top: 100px;
        left: 0px; width: 100%; height: 1px; overflow: visible; visibility: visible;
        display: block }
    #popupContent { color: white; background-color: black; font-size: 14px;
        font-weight: bold; margin-left: -75px; position: absolute; top: -55px;
        left: 50%; width: 150px; height: 60px; padding-top: 10px; z-index: 2; }
</style>
<script id="flowerTmpl" type="text/x-handlebars-template">
    {{#flowers}}
    <div class="dcell">
        <img src="{{product}}.png"/>
        <label for="{{product}}">{{name}}:</label>
        <input name="{{product}}" value="0" />
    </div>
    {{/flowers}}
</script>
<script type="text/javascript">
    $(document).ready(function () {

        $("<div id='popup'><div id='popupContent'><img src='progress.gif'"
            + "alt='progress'/><div>Placing Order</div></div></div>")
        .appendTo("body");

        $.ajaxSetup({
            timeout: 5000,
            converters: {"text html": function (data) { return $(data); }}
        });

        $(document).ajaxError(function (e, jqxhr, settings, errorMsg) {
            $("#error").remove();
```

```
            var msg = "An error occurred. Please try again"
            if (errorMsg == "timeout") {
                msg = "The request timed out. Please try again"
            } else if (jqxhr.status == 404) {
                msg = "The file could not be found";
            }
            $("<div id=error/>").text(msg).insertAfter("h1");
        }).ajaxSuccess(function () {
            $("#error").remove();
        });

        $("<a id=left></a><a id=right></a>").prependTo("form")
            .addClass("arrowButton").click(handleArrowPress).hover(handleArrowMouse);
        $("#right").appendTo("form");

        $("#row2, #row3, #popup").hide();

        var flowerReq = $.get("flowers.html", function (data) {
            var elems = data.filter("div").addClass("dcell");
            elems.slice(0, 3).appendTo("#row1");
            elems.slice(3).appendTo("#row2");
        });

        var jsonReq = $.getJSON("additionalflowers.json", function (data) {
            $("#flowerTmpl").template({ flowers: data }).appendTo("#row3");
        });

        $("<div id=errorSummary>").text("Please correct the following errors:")
            .append("<ul id='errorsList'></ul>").hide().insertAfter("h1");

        $("form").validate({
            highlight: function(element, errorClass) {
                $(element).addClass("invalidElem");
            },
            unhighlight: function(element, errorClass) {
                $(element).removeClass("invalidElem");
            },
            errorContainer: "#errorSummary",
            errorLabelContainer: "#errorsList",
            wrapper: "li",
            errorElement: "div"
        });

        var plurals = {
            aster: "Asters", daffodil: "Daffodils", rose: "Roses",
            peony: "Peonies", primula: "Primulas", snowdrop: "Snowdrops",
            carnation: "Carnations", lily: "Lillies", orchid: "Orchids"
        };

        $.when(flowerReq, jsonReq).then(function() {
            $("input").each(function(index, elem) {
                $(elem).rules("add", {
```

```
                        required: true,
                        min: 0,
                        digits: true,
                        remote: {
                            url: "http://node.jacquisflowershop.com/stockcheck",
                            type: "post",
                            global: false
                        },
                        messages: {
                            required: "Please enter a number of " + plurals[elem.name],
                            digits: "Please enter a number of" + plurals[elem.name],
                            min: "Please enter a positive number of "
                                + plurals[elem.name]
                        }
                    })
            }).change(function(e) {
                if ($("form").validate().element($(e.target))) {
                    var total = 0;
                    $("input").each(function(index, elem) {
                        total += Number($(elem).val());
                    });
                    $("#total").text(total);
                }
            });
        });

$("button").click(function (e) {
    e.preventDefault();
    var formData = $("form").serialize();
    $("body *").not("#popup, #popup *").css("opacity", 0.5);
    $("input").attr("disabled", "disabled");
    $("#popup").show();
    $.ajax({
        url: "http://node.jacquisflowershop.com/order",
        type: "post",
        data: formData,
        complete: function () {
            setTimeout(function () {
                $("body *").not("#popup, #popup *").css("opacity", 1);
                $("input").removeAttr("disabled");
                $("#popup").hide();
            }, 1500);
        }
    })
});

var total = $("#buttonDiv")
    .prepend("<div>Total Items: <span id=total>0</span></div>")
    .css({ clear: "both", padding: "5px" });
$("<div id=bbox />").appendTo("body").append(total).css("clear: left");
```

```javascript
        $("input").change(function (e) {
            var total = 0;
            $("input").each(function (index, elem) {
                total += Number($(elem).val());
            });
            $("#total").text(total);
        });

        function handleArrowMouse(e) {
            var propValue = e.type == "mouseenter" ? "-50px 0px" : "0px 0px";
            $(this).css("background-position", propValue);
        }

        function handleArrowPress(e) {
            var elemSequence = ["row1", "row2", "row3"];
            var visibleRow = $("div.drow:visible");
            var visibleRowIndex =
                jQuery.inArray(visibleRow.attr("id"), elemSequence);

            var targetRowIndex;
            if (e.target.id == "left") {
                targetRowIndex = visibleRowIndex - 1;
                if (targetRowIndex < 0) { targetRowIndex = elemSequence.length - 1 };
            } else {
                targetRowIndex = (visibleRowIndex + 1) % elemSequence.length;
            }

            visibleRow.fadeOut("fast", function () {
                $("#" + elemSequence[targetRowIndex]).fadeIn("fast")
            });
        }
    });
    </script>
</head>
<body>
    <h1>Jacqui's Flower Shop</h1>
    <form method="post" action="http://node.jacquisflowershop.com/order">
        <div id="oblock">
            <div class="dtable">
                <div id="row1" class="drow"></div>
                <div id="row2" class="drow"></div>
                <div id="row3" class="drow"></div>
            </div>
        </div>
        <div id="buttonDiv"><button type="submit">Place Order</button></div>
    </form>
</body>
</html>
```

I have gone beyond just making an Ajax POST request because I want to provide some additional context for how these requests can be handled in real projects. To start with, I have added an element that is positioned above all of the other elements in the document and tells the user that her order is being placed. Following is the statement that creates these elements:

```
...
$("<div id='popup'><div id='popupContent'><img src='progress.gif'"
    + "alt='progress'/><div>Placing Order</div></div></div>").appendTo("body");
...
```

I also added some CSS to the style element for these new elements.

```
...
#popup {
    text-align: center; position: absolute; top: 100px;
    left: 0px; width: 100%; height: 1px; overflow: visible; visibility: visible;
    display: block }
#popupContent { color: white; background-color: black; font-size: 14px;
    font-weight: bold; margin-left: -75px; position: absolute; top: -55px;
    left: 50%; width: 150px; height: 60px; padding-top: 10px; z-index: 2; }
...
```

It is hard to create an element that looks like a pop-up and that is properly positioned on the screen, and you can see that the amount of CSS required to make it work is substantial. The HTML elements themselves are simple by comparison and the HTML that is generated from the jQuery statement looks like the following:

```
...
<div id="popup" style="display: none;">
    <div id="popupContent">
        <img src="progress.gif" alt="progress">
        <div>Placing Order</div>
    </div>
</div>
...
```

The img element I have specified (progress.gif) is an animated GIF image. There are a number of web sites that will generate progress images to your specification, and I used one of them. If you don't want to create your own, then use the one from this example, which is included in the Source Code/Download area for this book (freely available from the Apress web site [www.apress.com]). You can see how the progress elements appear in Figure 16-4 (I have removed the other elements for clarity).

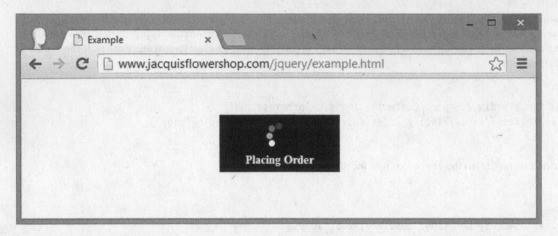

Figure 16-4. *Showing progress to the user*

I hide these elements initially because it makes no sense to show the user a progress display until he actually places the order.

```
...
$("#row2, #row3, #popup").hide();
...
```

With these elements in place and hidden, I turn to the form submission. I register a handler function for the click event for the button element, as follows:

```
...
$("button").click(function (e) {
    e.preventDefault();
    var formData = $("form").serialize();
    $("body *").not("#popup, #popup *").css("opacity", 0.5);
    $("input").attr("disabled", "disabled");
    $("#popup").show();
    $.ajax({
        url: "http://node.jacquisflowershop.com/order",
        type: "post",
        data: formData,
        complete: function () {
            setTimeout(function () {
                $("body *").not("#popup, #popup *").css("opacity", 1);
                $("input").removeAttr("disabled");
                $("#popup").hide();
            }, 1500);
        }
    })
});
...
```

Before starting the Ajax request, I show the pop-up elements and make all of the other elements partially transparent. I disable the input elements by adding the disabled attribute because I don't want the user to be able to change the value of any of the input elements while I am sending the data to the user.

```
...
$("body *").not("#popup, #popup *").css("opacity", 0.5);
$("input").attr("disabled", "disabled");
$("#popup').show();
...
```

The problem with disabling the input elements is that their values won't be included in the data sent to the server. The serialize method will include values only from input elements that are considered *successful controls*, as defined by the HTML specification; this excludes those elements that are disabled or don't have a name attribute. I could iterate through the input elements myself and get the values anyway, but it is simpler to gather the data to send before disabling the elements, as follows:

```
...
var formData = $("form").serialize();
...
```

I have used the complete setting to restore the interface to its normal state by making all of the elements opaque, removing the disabled attribute from the input elements, and hiding the pop-up elements. I have introduced an artificial 1.5-second delay after the request has completed before restoring the interface, as follows:

```
...
complete: function() {
    setTimeout(function() {
        $("body *").not("#popup, #popup *").css("opacity", 1);
        $("input").removeAttr("disabled");
        $("#popup").hide();
    }, 1500);
}
...
```

I would not do this in a real web application, but for demonstration purposes when the development machine and the server are on the same local network, this is useful to emphasize the transition. You can see how the browser appears during the Ajax request in Figure 16-5.

Figure 16-5. The browser during the form submission request

Processing the Server Response

All that remains is to do something useful with the data that I get back from the server. For this chapter, I am going to use a simple table. You will learn about creating rich user interfaces with jQuery UI in the next part of this book, and I don't want to have to do by hand what I can do much more elegantly with the UI widgets. Figure 16-6 shows the finished result.

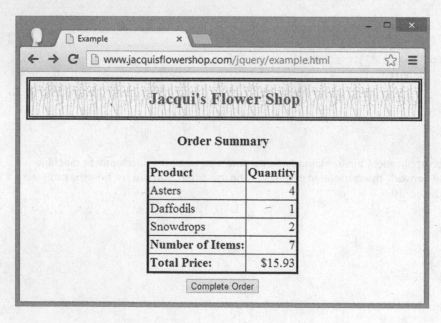

Figure 16-6. Displaying the order summary

Listing 16-9 shows the changes to the HTML document that support this enhancement. I'll break down the changes I made step by step in the sections that follow.

Listing 16-9. Processing the Response from the Server

```html
<!DOCTYPE html>
<html>
<head>
    <title>Example</title>
    <script src="jquery-2.0.2.js" type="text/javascript"></script>
    <script src="handlebars.js" type="text/javascript"></script>
    <script src="handlebars-jquery.js" type="text/javascript"></script>
    <script src="jquery.validate.js" type="text/javascript"></script>
    <link rel="stylesheet" type="text/css" href="styles.css"/>
    <style type="text/css">
        a.arrowButton {
            background-image: url(leftarrows.png); float: left;
            margin-top: 15px; display: block; width: 50px; height: 50px;
        }
        #right {background-image: url(rightarrows.png)}
        h1 { min-width: 0px; width: 95%; }
        #oblock { float: left; display: inline; border: thin black solid; }
        #orderForm { margin-left: auto; margin-right: auto; width: 885px; }
        #bbox {clear: left}
        #error {color: red; border: medium solid red; padding: 4px; margin: auto;
            width: 300px; text-align: center; margin-bottom: 5px}
        .invalidElem {border: medium solid red}
        #errorSummary {border: thick solid red; color: red; width: 350px; margin: auto;
            padding: 4px; margin-bottom: 5px}
        #popup {
            text-align: center; position: absolute; top: 100px;
            left: 0px; width: 100%; height: 1px; overflow: visible; visibility: visible;
            display: block }
        #popupContent { color: white; background-color: black; font-size: 14px;
            font-weight: bold; margin-left: -75px; position: absolute; top: -55px;
            left: 50%; width: 150px; height: 60px; padding-top: 10px; z-index: 2; }
        #summary {text-align: center}
        table {border-collapse: collapse; border: medium solid black; font-size: 18px;
            margin: auto; margin-bottom: 5px;}
        th {text-align: left}
        th, td {padding: 2px}
        tr > td:nth-child(1) {text-align: left}
        tr > td:nth-child(2) {text-align: right}
    </style>
    <script id="flowerTmpl" type="text/x-handlebars-template">
        {{#flowers}}
        <div class="dcell">
            <img src="{{product}}.png"/>
            <label for="{{product}}">{{name}}:</label>
            <input name="{{product}}" value="0" />
        </div>
        {{/flowers}}
```

```
    </script>
    <script id="productRowTmpl" type="text/x-handlebars-template">
        {{#rows}}
            <tr><td>{{name}}</td><td>{{quantity}}</td></tr>
        {{/rows}}
    </script>
    <script type="text/javascript">
        $(document).ready(function () {

            $("<div id='popup'><div id='popupContent'><img src='progress.gif'"
                + "alt='progress'/><div>Placing Order</div></div></div>")
            .appendTo("body");

            $.ajaxSetup({
                timeout: 5000,
                converters: {"text html": function (data) { return $(data); }}
            });

            $(document).ajaxError(function (e, jqxhr, settings, errorMsg) {
                $("#error").remove();
                var msg = "An error occurred. Please try again"
                if (errorMsg == "timeout") {
                    msg = "The request timed out. Please try again"
                } else if (jqxhr.status == 404) {
                    msg = "The file could not be found";
                }
                $("<div id=error/>").text(msg).insertAfter("h1");
            }).ajaxSuccess(function () {
                $("#error").remove();
            });

            $("<a id=left></a><a id=right></a>").prependTo("#orderForm")
                .addClass("arrowButton").click(handleArrowPress).hover(handleArrowMouse);
            $("#right").appendTo("#orderForm");

            $("#row2, #row3, #popup, #summaryForm").hide();

            var flowerReq = $.get("flowers.html", function (data) {
                var elems = data.filter("div").addClass("dcell");
                elems.slice(0, 3).appendTo("#row1");
                elems.slice(3).appendTo("#row2");
            });

            var jsonReq = $.getJSON("additionalflowers.json", function (data) {
                $("#flowerTmpl").template({ flowers: data }).appendTo("#row3");
            });

            $("<div id=errorSummary>").text("Please correct the following errors:")
                .append("<ul id='errorsList'></ul>").hide().insertAfter("h1");

            $("#orderForm").validate({
                highlight: function(element, errorClass) {
```

```
                $(element).addClass("invalidElem");
        },
        unhighlight: function(element, errorClass) {
            $(element).removeClass("invalidElem");
        },
        errorContainer: "#errorSummary",
        errorLabelContainer: "#errorsList",
        wrapper: "li",
        errorElement: "div"
});

var plurals = {
    aster: "Asters", daffodil: "Daffodils", rose: "Roses",
    peony: "Peonies", primula: "Primulas", snowdrop: "Snowdrops",
    carnation: "Carnations", lily: "Lillies", orchid: "Orchids"
};

$.when(flowerReq, jsonReq).then(function() {
    $("input").each(function(index, elem) {
        $(elem).rules("add", {
            required: true,
            min: 0,
            digits: true,
            remote: {
                url: "http://node.jacquisflowershop.com/stockcheck",
                type: "post",
                global: false
            },
            messages: {
                required: "Please enter a number of " + plurals[elem.name],
                digits: "Please enter a number of" + plurals[elem.name],
                min: "Please enter a positive number of "
                    + plurals[elem.name]
            }
        })
    }).change(function(e) {
        if ($("#orderForm").validate().element($(e.target))) {
            var total = 0;
            $("input").each(function(index, elem) {
                total += Number($(elem).val());
            });
            $("#total").text(total);
        }
    });
});

$("#orderForm button").click(function (e) {
    e.preventDefault();
    var formData = $("#orderForm").serialize();
    $("body *").not("#popup, #popup *").css("opacity", 0.5);
    $("input").attr("disabled", "disabled");
    $("#popup").show();
```

```javascript
        $.ajax({
            url: "http://node.jacquisflowershop.com/order",
            type: "post",
            data: formData,
            dataType: "json",
            dataFilter: function (data, dataType) {
                data = $.parseJSON(data);
                var cleanData = {
                    totalItems: data.totalItems,
                    totalPrice: data.totalPrice
                };
                delete data.totalPrice; delete data.totalItems;
                cleanData.products = [];
                for (prop in data) {
                    cleanData.products.push({
                        name: plurals[prop],
                        quantity: data[prop]
                    })
                }
                return cleanData;
            },
            converters: { "text json": function (data) { return data; } },
            success: function (data) {
                processServerResponse(data);
            },
            complete: function () {
                $("body *").not("#popup, #popup *").css("opacity", 1);
                $("input").removeAttr("disabled");
                $("#popup").hide();
            }
        })
    });

    function processServerResponse(data) {
        if (data.products.length > 0) {
            $("body > *:not(h1)").hide();
            $("#summaryForm").show();
            $("#productRowTmpl")
                .template({ rows: data.products }).appendTo("tbody");
            $("#totalitems").text(data.totalItems);
            $("#totalprice").text("$" + data.totalPrice);
        } else {
            var elem = $("input").get(0);
            var err = new Object();
            err[elem.name] = "No products selected";
            $("#orderForm").validate().showErrors(err);
            $(elem).removeClass("invalidElem");
        }
    }

    var total = $("#buttonDiv")
        .prepend("<div>Total Items: <span id=total>0</span></div>")
```

```
            .css({ clear: "both", padding: "5px" });
        $("<div id=bbox />").appendTo("body").append(total).css("clear: left");

        $("input").change(function (e) {
            var total = 0;
            $("input").each(function (index, elem) {
                total += Number($(elem).val());
            });
            $("#total").text(total);
        });

        function handleArrowMouse(e) {
            var propValue = e.type == "mouseenter" ? "-50px 0px" : "0px 0px";
            $(this).css("background-position", propValue);
        }

        function handleArrowPress(e) {
            var elemSequence = ["row1", "row2", "row3"];
            var visibleRow = $("div.drow:visible");
            var visibleRowIndex =
                jQuery.inArray(visibleRow.attr("id"), elemSequence);

            var targetRowIndex;
            if (e.target.id == "left") {
                targetRowIndex = visibleRowIndex - 1;
                if (targetRowIndex < 0) { targetRowIndex = elemSequence.length - 1 };
            } else {
                targetRowIndex = (visibleRowIndex + 1) % elemSequence.length;
            }

            visibleRow.fadeOut("fast", function () {
                $("#" + elemSequence[targetRowIndex]).fadeIn("fast")
            });
        }
    });
    </script>
</head>
<body>
    <h1>Jacqui's Flower Shop</h1>
    <form id="orderForm" method="post" action="http://node.jacquisflowershop.com/order">
        <div id="oblock">
        <div class="dtable">
            <div id="row1" class="drow"></div>
            <div id="row2" class="drow"></div>
            <div id="row3" class="drow"></div>
        </div>
        </div>
        <div id="buttonDiv"><button type="submit">Place Order</button></div>
    </form>
    <form id="summaryForm" method="post" action="">
        <div id="summary">
        <h3>Order Summary</h3>
```

```
            <table border="1">
                <thead>
                    <tr><th>Product</th><th>Quantity</th>
                </thead>
                <tbody>
                </tbody>
                <tfoot>
                    <tr><th>Number of Items:</th><td id="totalitems"></td></tr>
                    <tr><th>Total Price:</th><td id="totalprice"></td></tr>
                </tfoot>
            </table>
            <div id="buttonDiv2"><button type="submit">Complete Order</button></div>
        </div>
    </form>
</body>
</html>
```

Adding the New Form

The first thing that I did was add a new form to the static HTML part of the document, as follows:

```
...
<form id="summaryForm" method="post" action="">
    <div id="summary">
        <h3>Order Summary</h3>
        <table border="1">
            <thead>
                <tr><th>Product</th><th>Quantity</th>
            </thead>
            <tbody>
            </tbody>
            <tfoot>
                <tr><th>Number of Items:</th><td id="totalitems"></td></tr>
                <tr><th>Total Price:</th><td id="totalprice"></td></tr>
            </tfoot>
        </table>
        <div id="buttonDiv2"><button type="submit">Complete Order</button></div>
    </div>
</form>
...
```

This is the heart of the new functionality. When the user submits his product selection to the server, the `table` in this `form` will be used to display the data I get back from the Ajax request.

■ **Tip** I had been using the `$("form")` selector in previous examples, but since they are two forms in the document now, I have gone through and switched these references to the use the `form` elements' `id` attribute values.

I don't want to display the new form immediately, so I added it to the list of elements that I hide in the script, as follows:

```
...
$("#row2, #row3, #popup, #summaryForm").hide();
...
```

And, as you might expect by now, where there are new elements there is new CSS to style them, as follows:

```
...
#summary {text-align: center}
table {border-collapse: collapse; border: medium solid black; font-size: 18px;
    margin: auto; margin-bottom: 5px;}
th {text-align: left}
th, td {padding: 2px}
tr > td:nth-child(1) {text-align: left}
tr > td:nth-child(2) {text-align: right}
...
```

These styles ensure that the table is displayed in the middle of the browser window and the text in the table columns is aligned to the correct edge.

Completing the Ajax Request

The next step is to complete the call to the ajax request.

```
...
$("#orderForm button").click(function (e) {
    e.preventDefault();
    var formData = $("#orderForm").serialize();
    $("body *").not("#popup, #popup *").css("opacity", 0.5);
    $("input").attr("disabled", "disabled");
    $("#popup").show();
    $.ajax({
        url: "http://node.jacquisflowershop.com/order",
        type: "post",
        data: formData,
        dataType: "json",
        dataFilter: function (data, dataType) {
            data = $.parseJSON(data);
            var cleanData = {
                totalItems: data.totalItems,
                totalPrice: data.totalPrice
            };
            delete data.totalPrice; delete data.totalItems;
            cleanData.products = [];
            for (prop in data) {
```

```
            cleanData.products.push({
                name: plurals[prop],
                quantity: data[prop]
            })
        }
        return cleanData;
    },
    converters: { "text json": function (data) { return data; } },
    success: function (data) {
        processServerResponse(data);
    },
    complete: function () {
        $("body *").not("#popup, #popup *").css("opacity", 1);
        $("input").removeAttr("disabled");
        $("#popup").hide();
    }
})
});
...
```

I removed the explicit delay in the `complete` function and added the `dataFilter`, `converters`, and `success` settings to the request. I use the `dataFilters` setting to provide a function that transforms the JSON data from the server into something more useful. The server sends me a JSON string like the following:

```
{"aster":"4","daffodil":"1","snowdrop":"2","totalItems":7,"totalPrice":"15.93"}
```

I parse the JSON data and restructure it so that I get the following:

```
{"totalItems":7,"totalPrice":"15.93",
    "products":[{"name":"Asters","quantity":"4"}, {"name":"Daffodils","quantity":"1"},
        {"name":"Snowdrops","quantity":"2"}]
}
```

This format gives me two advantages. The first is that it is better suited for use with data templates because I can pass the `products` property to the `template` method. The second is that I can check whether the user has selected any elements with `products.length`. These are two quite minor advantages, but I wanted to integrate as many of the features from the earlier chapters as possible. Notice that I have also replaced the name of the product (orchid, for example) with the plural name (ochids).

Having already parsed the JSON data into a JavaScript object (using the `parseJSON` method, which I describe in Chapter 34), I want to disable the built-in converter, which will try to do the same thing. To that end, I have defined a custom converter for JSON, which just passes the data through without modification.

```
...
converters: {"text json": function(data) { return data;}}
...
```

Processing the Data

For the ajax method success callback, I specified the processServerResponse function, which I defined as follows:

```
...
function processServerResponse(data) {
    if (data.products.length > 0) {
        $("body > *:not(h1)").hide();
        $("#summaryForm").show();
        $("#productRowTmpl").template({ rows: data.products }).appendTo("tbody");
        $("#totalitems").text(data.totalItems);
        $("#totalprice").text("$" + data.totalPrice);
    } else {
        var elem = $("input").get(0);
        var err = new Object();
        err[elem.name] = "No products selected";
        $("#orderForm").validate().showErrors(err);
        $(elem).removeClass("invalidElem");
    }
}
...
```

If the data from the server contain product information, then I hide all of the elements in the document that I don't want (including the original form element and the additions I made in the script) and show the new form. I populate the table using the following data template:

```
...
<script id="productRowTmpl" type="text/x-handlebars-template">
    {{#rows}}
        <tr><td>{{name}}</td><td>{{quantity}}</td></tr>
    {{/rows}}
</script>
...
```

This template produces a table row for each selected product. Finally, I set contents of the cells that display the total price and item count using the text method.

```
...
$("#totalitems").text(data.totalItems);
$("#totalprice").text("$" + data.totalPrice);
...
```

However, if the data from the server don't contain any product information (which indicates that the user has left all of the input element values as zero), then I do something different. First I select the first of the input elements, as follows:

```
...
var elem = $("input").get(0);
...
```

445

I then create an object that contains a property whose name is the name value of the input element and whose value is a message to the user. I then call the validate method on the form element and the showErrors method on the result, as follows:

```
...
var err = new Object();
err[elem.name] = "No products selected";
$("#orderForm").validate().showErrors(err);
...
```

This allows me to manually inject an error into the validation system and take advantage of the structure and formatting that I put in place earlier. I have to provide the name of an element so that the validation plug-in can highlight where the error occurs, which is not ideal, as you can see in Figure 16-7.

Figure 16-7. *Display the selection error*

I am displaying a general message, but the highlighting is applied to just one input element, which will be confusing to the user. To deal with this, I remove the class that the validation plug-in uses for highlighting, as follows:

```
...
$(elem).removeClass("invalidElem");
...
```

This produces the effect shown in Figure 16-8.

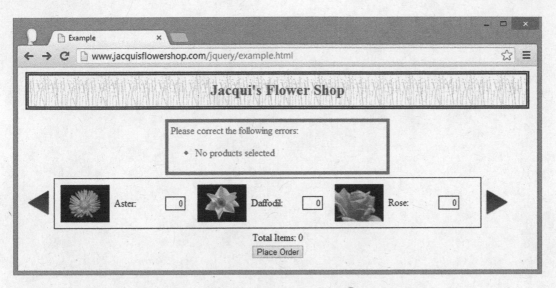

Figure 16-8. *Removing the highlighting from the element associated with the error*

Summary

In this chapter, I refactored the example to bring together the themes and features covered in this part of the book. I used Ajax widely (using both the shorthand and low-level methods), applied a pair of data templates, and used the validation plug-in to check values locally and remotely (and to display an error manually). In the next part of the book, I turn to jQuery UI and the next time that I refactor the example document, it will have a very different appearance.

CHAPTER 17

▨ ▨ ▨

Setting Up jQuery UI

Downloading and installing jQuery UI is more complicated than for other JavaScript libraries. It is not burdensome, but it requires some explanation, which I provide in this chapter. You only need to get set up for development for this book, but I have also included details of how to install the minimized files that are suitable for production deployment and how to use jQuery UI through a content distribution network (CDN).

▨ **Note** As I explained in Chapter 1, the jQuery UI API changed with the release of version 1.10, and I highlight these changes in the chapters that follow.

Obtaining jQuery UI

There are four main areas of functionality in jQuery UI and you create a custom download that includes and configures each of them. In this part of the book, I show you all the jQuery UI features, but for a real web application you can omit the parts you don't need and create a smaller library for browsers to download.

▨ **Tip** jQuery UI isn't the only UI toolkit that is based on jQuery, although it is by far the most popular. An alternative is jQuery Tools, which is open source and can be downloaded without any license or restrictions from http://flowplayer.org/tools. There are also some commercial alternatives such as jQWidgets (www.jqwidgets.com) and Wijmo (http://wijmo.com). And, of course, there is jQuery Mobile, which I describe in Part 5 of this book.

Deciding on a Theme

Before you build your custom jQuery UI library, you need to select a theme. jQuery UI is endlessly configurable and you can change the appearance of every aspect of every feature that you use. In fact, there are so many choices that it can be somewhat overwhelming. The jQuery UI web site includes a tool for creating custom themes, but there is also a gallery of predefined themes that you can choose to make life easier.

To start, go to http://jqueryui.com and click the Themes button. This loads the *ThemeRoller* page, which consists of a display of jQuery UI widgets and a panel on the left that lets you configure the theme settings, as shown in Figure 17-1.

Figure 17-1. *The jQuery UI web site theme page*

Use the Roll Your Own tab (which is selected by default) if you have a certain visual style that you need to follow to make jQuery UI fit in with the rest of a site or application. You can change every aspect of the theme used by jQuery UI.

The predefined themes are available on the Gallery tab. As I write this, 24 themes are available in the gallery and they range from the understated and subtle to the bright and garish. As you click each gallery theme, the widgets in the rest of the page are updated to show you what your application will look like, as shown in Figure 17-2.

Figure 17-2. *The gallery showing the Sunny theme*

The default theme for jQuery UI is called *UI lightness*, but it doesn't have enough contrast to show up well on a book page, so I will be using the *Sunny* theme, which shows up a little better. You don't need to do anything with the theme at the moment, other than to remember which one you want to use. The themes don't look that good when printed, but they have a better appearance on the screen and I recommend you look through the list until you find one you like.

■ **Tip**   You don't have to select the same theme that I will be using, but if you pick a different one, you will obviously get results that look different from mine.

Creating the jQuery UI Custom Download

Now that you have a theme in mind, you can create your jQuery UI download. Click the Download button at the top of the page to move to the Build Your Download page.

The first step is to select the version of jQuery UI that you want to download. As I write this, the latest version is 1.10.3 and that is the version I will be using in this book.

In addition to specifying the jQuery UI version, this page has a list of jQuery UI components, broken into four functional groups: *UI Core*, *Interactions*, *Widgets*, and *Effects*.

By selecting only the features that you require for a project, you can create a set of smaller files for the browser to download. I think this a nice idea, but it is something that I tend not to use as I prefer to reduce the bandwidth required to deliver jQuery UI by using a CDN, which I show you how to do in the section "Using jQuery UI via a Content Distribution Network."

For this chapter, you will need all of the components, so make sure that all four options are checked.

■ **Tip**   Some of the components in the list depend on others, but you don't have to worry about this when you build a custom jQuery UI library. When you enable a component, any other component it depends on is also loaded.

The next step is to select the theme you want. The selector for this is at the bottom of the page, just above the Download button, as shown in Figure 17-3.

Figure 17-3. *Selecting the theme*

Once you have selected all of the components, the theme you want, and the stable version, click the `Download` button to download the customized jQuery UI library.

Installing jQuery UI for Development

The jQuery UI download is a zip file that contains all the files that you need for development and production. For this book, you will use the development files that include the unminified source code. This makes it easy to look into the internals of jQuery UI if you have a problem. You need to copy the following into the folder that contains your example files:

- The `js\jquery-ui-1.10.3.custom.js` file
- The `themes\sunny\jquery-ui-1.10.3.custom.css` file
- The `themes\sunny\images` folder

You will notice that there are JavaScript and Cascading Style Sheets (CSS) files for individual components and features in the ui and themes folders. You don't need to use them, but they can be helpful if you need to work with only a limited set of jQuery UI features.

■ **Tip**   The name of the JavaScript and CSS files include the version number of the release that was downloaded. For me, this is version 1.10.3. jQuery UI is actively developed and you may have downloaded a later release. If so, you'll need to change the references to the jQuery UI files in the HTML examples.

Adding jQuery UI to an HTML Document

All that remains is to add jQuery UI to an example HTML document, which is done through script and link elements that refer to the JavaScript and CSS files that I listed in the previous section, as shown in Listing 17-1.

Listing 17-1. Adding jQuery UI to an HTML Document

```
<!DOCTYPE html>
<html>
<head>
    <title>Example</title>
    <script src="jquery-2.0.2.js" type="text/javascript"></script>
    <script src="jquery-ui-1.8.16.custom.js" type="text/javascript"></script>
    <link rel="stylesheet" type="text/css" href="styles.css"/>
    <link rel="stylesheet" type="text/css" href="jquery-ui-1.8.16.custom.css"/>
    <script type="text/javascript">
        $(document).ready(function() {
            $("a").button();
        });
    </script>
</head>
<body>
    <a href="http://apress.com">Visit Apress</a>
</body>
</html>
```

■ **Tip**   You don't need to refer directly to the images directory. As long as the images directory and the CSS file are in the same place, jQuery UI will be able to find the resources it needs.

■ **Tip**   jQuery UI depends on jQuery. You must have added jQuery to a document in order to use jQuery UI.

The document shown in the listing includes a simple test that allows you to check that jQuery UI has been added properly. If you view this in the browser, you should see a button like the one in Figure 17-4. Don't worry about the call to the button method in the script element in the listing. I'll explain what this does and how it works in Chapter 18.

Figure 17-4. *Checking that jQuery UI has been added to the document correctly*

If you have not properly specified the path to either of the two files, then you will see a simple a element instead, as illustrated by Figure 17-5.

Figure 17-5. *Identifying a problem importing jQuery UI into a document*

Installing jQuery UI for Production

When you have finished developing your web application and are ready to deploy it, you can use the minified file that is included in the jQuery UI download. This file is smaller but harder to read for debugging purposes. To use the production files, you must copy the following into your web server directory:

- The `js\jquery-ui-1.10.3.custom.min.js` file
- The `themes\sunny\jquery-ui-1.10.3.custom.css` file
- The `themes\sunny\images` folder

The `images` directory and CSS file are the same as for the development version; only the JavaScript file changes.

Using jQuery UI via a Content Distribution Network

I touched upon using a CDN for jQuery in Chapter 5. If this is an approach that appeals to you, you will be pleased to learn that you can do the same with jQuery UI. Both Google and Microsoft host the jQuery UI files on their CDNs. For this example, I'll use the Microsoft service, because it hosts the standard themes as well as the jQuery UI JavaScript.

To use a CDN, you just need the URLs to the files you want. For the Microsoft service, go to `www.asp.net/ajaxlibrary/cdn.ashx` to get started. If you scroll down the page, you will see a section for jQuery UI releases, broken down by version. Click the link for the version you are using. You will see the URLs for the regular and minimized version of the jQuery UI library file. For the version that is current as I write this, the URL for the minimized file is as follows:

```
http://ajax.aspnetcdn.com/ajax/jquery.ui/1.10.3/jquery-ui.min.js
```

The rest of the page shows each of the predefined jQuery UI themes, with the URL for the theme CSS shown underneath. The URL for the *Sunny* theme is as follows:

```
http://ajax.aspnetcdn.com/ajax/jquery.ui/1.10.3/themes/sunny/jquery-ui.css
```

To use these files on the CDN, you simply place the URLs in the `script` and `link` elements that refer to the local jQuery UI files, as shown in Listing 17-2.

Listing 17-2. Using jQuery UI via a CDN

```html
<!DOCTYPE html>
<html>
<head>
    <title>Example</title>
    <script src="jquery-2.0.2.js" type="text/javascript"></script>
    <script src="http://ajax.aspnetcdn.com/ajax/jquery.ui/1.10.3/jquery-ui.min.js"
        type="text/javascript"></script>
    <link
    href="http://ajax.aspnetcdn.com/ajax/jquery.ui/1.10.3/themes/sunny/jquery-ui.css"
        rel="stylesheet" />
    <link rel="stylesheet" type="text/css" href="styles.css"/>
    <script type="text/javascript">
        $(document).ready(function () {
            $("a").button();
        });
    </script>
</head>
<body>
    <a href="http://apress.com">Visit Apress</a>
</body>
</html>
```

Once again, you can tell whether you have the correct URLs by loading the document and seeing whether the browser displays a button similar to the one in Figure 17-4.

Summary

In this chapter, I showed you the steps required to create and prepare a jQuery UI download. There is a lot of flexibility in the features you include and the default appearance jQuery UI imparts on your web application. I particularly like the ThemeRoller application. It is an elegant way of creating a completely customized theme to fit into an existing visual scheme, which is ideal for adding jQuery UI to corporate-branded sites. In the next chapter, you'll start to look at the different jQuery UI features, starting with the most popular functional area: widgets.

CHAPTER 18

∎∎∎

Using the Button, Progress Bar, and Slider Widgets

Now that you have configured, downloaded, and installed jQuery UI, you can start to look at the widgets it contains. These are the major functional blocks of jQuery UI, and although there are other features (such as effects, which I describe in Chapter 35), jQuery UI is known for the widgets.

In this chapter, I describe the three simplest widgets: the button, the progress bar, and the slider. All jQuery UI widgets have common characteristics: settings, methods, and events. Mastering one widget provides a solid foundation for working with all of them, so I spend some time at the start of this chapter providing overall context.

It is hard to tie all of the widgets into the flower shop example, so you will find that many of the examples in this part of the book are small, self-contained HTML documents that demonstrate a single widget. I return to the flower shop example in Chapter 26 when I refactor it to include jQuery UI. Table 18-1 provides the summary for this chapter.

Table 18-1. *Chapter Summary*

Problem	Solution	Listing
Create a jQuery UI button	Select an element and use the button method	1
Configure a button element	Pass a map object to the button method or use the option method	2, 3
Use icons in jQuery UI buttons	Use the icons setting	4
Use a custom image in a jQuery UI button	Set the content of the button to be an img element	5
Remove the jQuery UI button widget	Use the destroy method	6
Enable or disable the jQuery UI button	Use the enable or disable method	7
Refresh the state of a jQuery UI button to reflect a programmatic change to the underlying element	Use the refresh method	8
Respond to a jQuery UI button being created	Specify a function for the create event	9
Create uniform buttons from different kinds of element	Create jQuery UI buttons from input, button, or a element	10
Create a toggle button	Create a jQuery UI from a check box	11
Create a button set	Use the buttonset method	12, 13
Create a jQuery UI progress bar	Use the progressbar method	14, 15

(*continued*)

Table 18-1. (*continued*)

Problem	Solution	Listing
Get or set the progress shown to the user	Use the value method	16
Respond to changes in the progress bar	Specify functions for the create, change, or complete event	17
Create a jQuery UI slider	Use the slider method	18
Change the orientation of a jQuery UI slider	Use the orientation setting	19, 20
Animate the movement of the handle when the user clicks the slider	Use the animate setting	21
Create a jQuery UI slider that allows the user to specify a range of values	Use the range and values settings	22
Control a jQuery UI slider programmatically	Use the value or values methods	23
Respond to changes in the slider handle positions	Handle the start, stop, change, or slide event	24

JQUERY UI CHANGES SINCE THE LAST EDITION

As of jQuery UI 1.10, the progress widget can be used to display indeterminate tasks. See the section "Using the jQuery UI Progress Bar" for details and an example.

Using the jQuery UI Button

The first widget I look at provides a good introduction into the world of jQuery UI. The button widget is simple but has a transformational effect on HTML documents. The button widget applies the jQuery UI theme to button and a elements. This means that the size, shape, font, and color of the element are transformed to match the theme I selected when I created my custom jQuery UI download in Chapter 17. Applying jQuery UI widgets is simple, as Listing 18-1 shows.

Listing 18-1. A Simple HTML Document

```
<!DOCTYPE html>
<html>
<head>
    <title>Example</title>
    <script src="jquery-2.0.2.js"></script>
    <script src="handlebars.js"></script>
    <script src="handlebars-jquery.js"></script>
    <script src="jquery-ui-1.10.3.custom.js"></script>
    <link href="jquery-ui-1.10.3.custom.css" rel="stylesheet" />
    <link rel="stylesheet" type="text/css" href="styles.css"/>

    <script id="flowerTmpl" type="text/x-handlebars-template">
        {{#flowers}}
        <div class="dcell">
            <img src="{{product}}.png"/>
```

```
                <label for="{{product}}">{{name}}:</label>
                <input name="{{product}}" data-price="{{price}}" data-stock="{{stocklevel}}"
                    value="0" required />
            </div>
            {{/flowers}}
    </script>

    <script type="text/javascript">
        $(document).ready(function () {
            $.ajax("mydata.json", {
                success: function (data) {
                    var tmplData = $("#flowerTmpl")
                        .template({ flowers: data }).filter("*");
                    tmplData.slice(0, 3).appendTo("#row1");
                    tmplData.slice(3).appendTo("#row2");
                }
            });

            $("button").button();
        });
    </script>
</head>
<body>
    <h1>Jacqui's Flower Shop</h1>
    <form method="post" action="http://node.jacquisflowershop.com/order">
        <div id="oblock">
            <div class="dtable">
                <div id="row1" class="drow">
                </div>
                <div id="row2"class="drow">
                </div>
            </div>
        </div>
        <div id="buttonDiv"><button type="submit">Place Order</button></div>
    </form>
</body>
</html>
```

To apply the button widget, I use jQuery to select the elements I want to transform and call the button method; jQuery UI takes care of the rest. You can see the effect in Figure 18-1.

Figure 18-1. *Applying the Button widget*

■ **Tip**   Notice that I apply the button method to a jQuery selection object. The integration between jQuery and jQuery UI is close, and it means that using jQuery UI is generally a natural extension of using the core jQuery techniques that I showed you earlier in this book.

Like all of the jQuery UI widgets, the button shown in the figure is a series of CSS styles applied to the existing HTML elements. The button method transforms an element like this

```
<button type="submit">Place Order</button>
```

to this

```
<button type="submit" class="ui-button ui-widget ui-state-default ui-corner-all
    ui-button-text-only" role="button" aria-disabled="false">
        <span class="ui-button-text">Place Order</span>
</button>
```

This is a nice approach because it works around the standard HTML elements, meaning that you don't have to make any special provision for jQuery UI when you create HTML content.

Configuring the Button

The jQuery UI button widget can be configured via settings properties, allowing control over the way that you create the button. Table 18-2 describes these properties.

Table 18-2. *The Settings Properties for the Button Widget*

Property	Description
disabled	Gets or sets the disabled state of the button. A true value indicates that the button is disabled. jQuery UI doesn't take into account the state of the underlying HTML element.
text	Gets or sets whether the button will display text. This setting is ignored if the icons property is false.
icons	Gets or sets whether the button will display an icon.
label	Gets or sets the text that is displayed by the button.

These settings can be applied in two ways. The first is using a map object when calling the button method, as highlighted in Listing 18-2.

Listing 18-2. Configuring the Button Widget Using a Map Object

```
...
<script type="text/javascript">
    $(document).ready(function () {
        $.ajax("mydata.json", {
            success: function (data) {
                var tmplData = $("#flowerTmpl")
                    .template({ flowers: data }).filter("*");
                tmplData.slice(0, 3).appendTo("#row1");
                tmplData.slice(3).appendTo("#row2");
            }
        });

        $("button").button({
            label: "Place Your Order",
            disabled: true
        });

        $("button").button("option", "disabled", false);
    });
</script>
...
```

I have set the text that the button displays with the label property and used the disabled property to disable the button. Using a map object is the approach for defining the initial configuration for a widget and follows the style you saw most recently in Chapter 15 for configuring Ajax requests.

Listing 18-2 also shows the technique used to change the value for a settings property after the widget has been created, as follows:

```
...
$("button").button("option", "disabled", false);
...
```

I call the button method again, but with three arguments this time. The first argument is the string option and tells jQuery UI that I want to change a setting. The second argument is the setting I want to change and the third argument is the new value for the setting. This statement sets the disabled setting to false, enabling the button and changing the value I set with the map object when I created the widget.

461

You can combine these techniques so that you call the `button` method with a first argument of `option` and a map object as the second argument. This allows you to change multiple settings in one go, as shown in Listing 18-3.

Listing 18-3. Using the Option Argument with a Map Object

```
...
<script type="text/javascript">
    $(document).ready(function () {
        $.ajax("mydata.json", {
            success: function (data) {
                var tmplData = $("#flowerTmpl")
                    .template({ flowers: data }).filter("*");
                tmplData.slice(0, 3).appendTo("#row1");
                tmplData.slice(3).appendTo("#row2");
            }
        });

        $("button").button();

        $("button").button("option", {
            label: "Place Your Order",
            disabled: false
        });

        console.log("Disabled: " + $("button").button("option", "disabled"));
    });
</script>
...
```

You can use the same technique to *read* the value of a setting as well. In this case, you call the `button` method with just two arguments. The first is the string `option` and the second is the name of the setting whose value you want to read, as the following statement from the listing demonstrates:

```
...
console.log("Disabled: " + $("button").button("option", "disabled"));
...
```

When used this way, the `button` method returns the current setting value. The example statement reads the value of the `disabled` setting and writes it to the console, producing the following output:

```
Disabled: false
```

Using jQuery UI Icons in Buttons

The jQuery UI themes include a set of icons that you can use for any purpose, including displaying them in buttons. Listing 18-4 shows the use of icons in a jQuery UI button.

Listing 18-4. Displaying an Icon in a Button

```
...
<script type="text/javascript">
    $(document).ready(function () {
        $.ajax("mydata.json", {
            success: function (data) {
                var tmplData = $("#flowerTmpl")
                    .template({ flowers: data }).filter("*");
                tmplData.slice(0, 3).appendTo("#row1");
                tmplData.slice(3).appendTo("#row2");
            }
        });

        $("button").button({
            icons: {
                primary: "ui-icon-star",
                secondary: "ui-icon-circle-arrow-e"
            }
        });
    });
</script>
...
```

The `icons` property specifies which icons will be displayed. The button widget has two positions for icons. The `primary` icon is displayed to the left of the text and the `secondary` icon is displayed to the right of the text and both are specified with a map object. You can omit either property to display an icon in just one of the positions. The icons themselves are quite small, as you can see in Figure 18-2.

Figure 18-2. Displaying icons in a button

Icons are specified using classes that are defined in the jQuery UI CSS file. There are 173 different icons available, which is too many to list here. The easiest way to figure out the name of the icon you want is to go to http://jqueryui.com, select the Themes page and scroll down the page. You will see all of the icons listed in a grid, and moving the mouse button over each icon reveals the class name to use for the icon, as shown in Figure 18-3.

Figure 18-3. *The jQuery UI icon grid*

■ **Tip**   The name that pops up on the web page has a leading period that must be omitted to be used with the icons setting. So, for example, if the mouse hovers over the first icon in the grid, `.ui-icon-caret-1-n` will pop up. To use this icon with a button, set the primary or secondary property to `ui-icon-caret-1-n`.

Using a Custom Image

I don't find the jQuery UI icons all that useful because they are usually too small for my needs. Fortunately, there is a pair of alternate techniques to display a custom image in a jQuery UI button.

The first is to insert an `img` element inside the `button` element to which you intend to apply the jQuery UI button widget. The jQuery UI button widget respects the content of the underlying `button` element and—as long as you use an image with a transparent background—you don't have to worry about making the image match the theme. Listing 18-5 gives a simple demonstration.

Listing 18-5. *Using a Custom Image with a jQuery UI Button*

```
...
<script type="text/javascript">
    $(document).ready(function () {
        $.ajax("mydata.json", {
            success: function (data) {
                var tmplData = $("#flowerTmpl")
                    .template({ flowers: data }).filter("*");
                tmplData.slice(0, 3).appendTo("#row1");
                tmplData.slice(3).appendTo("#row2");
            }
        });

        $("button")
            .text("")
            .append("<img src=rightarrows.png width=100 height=30 />")
```

```
        .button();
    });
</script>
...
```

Since I want neither text *nor* a jQuery UI icon, I use the jQuery text method to set the content to an empty string. I then use the append method to insert an img element into the button element and finally call the button method to apply jQuery UI. You can see the result in Figure 18-4.

Figure 18-4. *Showing a custom image in a button*

Using the Button Methods

The jQuery UI widgets also define methods that you use to control the widget once it has been created. These methods are a little odd because you call the same JavaScript method but pass in different argument values to change the jQuery UI behavior. These are, however, still called methods by the jQuery UI team and I will refer to them as such. Table 18-3 shows the different jQuery UI methods you can use on the button widget and the effect each has.

Table 18-3. *Button Methods*

Method	Description
button("destroy")	Returns the HTML element to its original state
button("disable")	Disables the button
button("enable")	Enables the button
button("option")	Sets one or more options; see the section "Configuring the Button"
button("refresh")	Refreshes the button; see the section "Refreshing the State of a jQuery UI Button"

Removing the Widget

The destroy method removes the jQuery UI button widget from the HTML button element, returning it to its original state, as shown in Listing 18-6.

Listing 18-6. *Using the destroy Method*

```
...
<script type="text/javascript">
    $(document).ready(function () {
        $.ajax("mydata.json", {
            success: function (data) {
                var tmplData = $("#flowerTmpl")
```

465

```
                .template({ flowers: data }).filter("*");
            tmplData.slice(0, 3).appendTo("#row1");
            tmplData.slice(3).appendTo("#row2");
        }
    });

    $("button").button().click(function (e) {
        $("button").button("destroy");
        e.preventDefault();
    });
    });
});
</script>
...
```

In Listing 18-6, I have used the standard jQuery click method to register a handler function for the button element. This is the technique I demonstrated for handling events in Chapter 9 and requires no adjustment to support jQuery UI. The click handler function in the listing means that clicking the button removes the jQuery UI widget from the button element, as illustrated by Figure 18-5.

Figure 18-5. *Destroying the jQuery UI button widget*

Enabling and Disabling the Button

The enable and disable methods change the state of the jQuery UI button, as shown in Listing 18-7.

Listing 18-7. Enabling and Disabling a Button

```
...
<script type="text/javascript">
    $(document).ready(function () {
        $.ajax("mydata.json", {
            success: function (data) {
                var tmplData = $("#flowerTmpl")
                    .template({ flowers: data }).filter("*");
                tmplData.slice(0, 3).appendTo("#row1");
                tmplData.slice(3).appendTo("#row2");
            }
        });
```

```
$("<span>Enabled:<span><input type=checkbox checked />").prependTo("#buttonDiv");
$(":checkbox").change(function (e) {
    $("button").button(
        $(":checked").length == 1 ? "enable" : "disable"
    )
});

$("button").button();
    });
</script>
...
```

I have inserted a check box into the document and used the change method to register a function that will be called when the box is checked or unchecked. I call the enable and disable methods to change the state of the button to match the check box. You can see the effect in Figure 18-6.

Figure 18-6. *Enabling and disabling a jQuery UI button*

Refreshing the State of a jQuery UI Button

The refresh method updates the state of the jQuery UI button widget to reflect changes in the underlying HTML element. This can be useful when you modify elements elsewhere in the code as shown in Listing 18-8.

Listing 18-8. *Refreshing the jQuery UI Button*

```
...
<script type="text/javascript">
    $(document).ready(function () {
        $.ajax("mydata.json", {
            success: function (data) {
                var tmplData = $("#flowerTmpl")
                    .template({ flowers: data }).filter("*");
                tmplData.slice(0, 3).appendTo("#row1");
                tmplData.slice(3).appendTo("#row2");
            }
        });

        $("<span>Enabled:<span><input type=checkbox checked />").prependTo("#buttonDiv");
        $(":checkbox").change(function (e) {
```

```
            var buttons = $("button");
            if ($(":checked").length == 1) {
                buttons.removeAttr("disabled");
            } else {
                buttons.attr("disabled", "disabled");
            }
            buttons.button("refresh");
        });

        $("button").button();
    });
</script>
...
```

In this example, I use the check box to trigger adding and removing the `disabled` attribute from the HTML `button` element that underpins the button widget. This change isn't automatically detected by jQuery UI, so I call the `refresh` method to bring everything back in sync.

■ **Tip**   You might be wondering why I would not just use the jQuery UI `enable` and `disable` methods, but the scenario in Listing 18-8 is surprisingly common because jQuery UI is often applied to HTML content late in the development process, frequently to give a face-lift to an existing web application. In this situation, HTML elements will be generated and manipulated by code which predates the user of jQuery UI and doesn't know that a button widget will be used—and so being able to update the state of the widget to reflect the state of the underlying HTML element can be an important feature.

Using the Button Event

The jQuery UI widgets define events in addition to those of the underlying HTML elements. The `button` widget defines a single event called `create`, which is triggered when you create a jQuery UI button widget. Handlers for jQuery UI events are defined by passing a JavaScript map object to the jQuery UI method for the widget, which is `button` in this case, as illustrated by Listing 18-9.

Listing 18-9. Using the jQuery UI Button create Event

```
...
<script type="text/javascript">
    $(document).ready(function () {
        $.ajax("mydata.json", {
            success: function (data) {
                var tmplData = $("#flowerTmpl")
                    .template({ flowers: data }).filter("*");
                tmplData.slice(0, 3).appendTo("#row1");
                tmplData.slice(3).appendTo("#row2");
            }
        });

        $("button").button({
            create: function (e) {
```

```
            $(e.target).click(function (e) {
                alert("Button was pressed");
                e.preventDefault();
            })
        }
    });
});
</script>
...
```

In Listing 18-9, I use the `create` event to set up a function to respond to the `click` event on the `button`. I don't find the `create` event useful and generally find that anything that can be done in response to this event can be done in a way that is more in keeping with the broader jQuery approach.

Creating Different Types of Button

The jQuery UI button widget is sensitive to the kind of element it is applied to. The basic behavior, a regular button, is created when you call the `button` method on `button` elements, or on a elements, or on `input` elements whose types are set to `submit`, `reset`, or `button`. Listing 18-10 shows all of these elements being transformed into jQuery UI buttons.

Listing 18-10. Creating Standard Buttons

```
<!DOCTYPE html>
<html>
<head>
    <title>Example</title>
    <script src="jquery-1.7.js" type="text/javascript"></script>
    <script src="jquery-ui-1.8.16.custom.js" type="text/javascript"></script>
    <link rel="stylesheet" type="text/css" href="jquery-ui-1.8.16.custom.css"/>
    <script type="text/javascript">
        $(document).ready(function() {
            $(".jqButton").click(function(e) {
                e.preventDefault();
                $(this).button();
            });
        });
    </script>
</head>
<body>
    <form>
        <input class="jqButton" type="submit" id="inputSubmit" value="Submit">
        <input class="jqButton" type="reset" id="inputReset" value="Reset">
        <input class="jqButton" type="button" id="inputButton" value="Input Button">
        <button class="jqButton">Button Element</button>
        <a class="jqButton" href="http://apress.com">A Element</a>
    </form>
</body>
</html>
```

I have defined one of each type of the HTML elements I have described. I have used the `click` method so that each element is transformed into a jQuery UI button widget when it is clicked. You can see the transformation in Figure 18-7.

Figure 18-7. *Creating standard jQuery UI buttons*

Creating a Toggle Button

If you call the button method on an input element whose type is set to checkbox, you get a toggle button widget. A toggle button is switched on or off when you click it, following the checked and unchecked states of the underlying HTML element. Listing 18-11 provides a demonstration.

Listing 18-11. Applying jQuery UI to a Check Box

```
<!DOCTYPE html>
<html>
<head>
    <title>Example</title>
    <script src="jquery-2.0.2.js"></script>
    <script src="jquery-ui-1.10.3.custom.js"></script>
    <link href="jquery-ui-1.10.3.custom.css" rel="stylesheet" />
    <script type="text/javascript">
        $(document).ready(function () {
            $(".jqButton").button();
        });
    </script>
</head>
<body>
    <form>
        <input class="jqButton" type="checkbox" id="toggle">
        <label for="toggle">Toggle Me</label>
    </form>
</body>
</html>
```

To create a jQuery UI button from a check box, you must have an input element and a matching label element, as shown in the listing. jQuery UI creates a button that has the same appearance as a basic button but that toggles its state when clicked. You can see the effect in Figure 18-8.

Figure 18-8. *Creating a toggle button from a check box*

Remember that jQuery UI doesn't change the underlying HTML element, so the check box is still treated the same way by the browser when included in forms. The change of state is reflected using the checked attribute, just as it would be without jQuery UI.

Creating a Button Set

You can use the buttonset method to create jQuery UI buttons from radio button elements, as shown in Listing 18-12.

Listing 18-12. Creating a Button Set

```
<!DOCTYPE html>
<html>
<head>
    <title>Example</title>
    <script src="jquery-2.0.2.js"></script>
    <script src="jquery-ui-1.10.3.custom.js"></script>
    <link href="jquery-ui-1.10.3.custom.css" rel="stylesheet" />
    <script type="text/javascript">
        $(document).ready(function () {
            $("#radioDiv").buttonset();
        });
    </script>
</head>
<body>
    <form>
        <div id="radioDiv">
            <input type="radio" name="flower" id="rose" checked />
            <label for="rose">Rose</label>
            <input type="radio" name="flower" id="lily"/><label for="lily">Lily</label>
            <input type="radio" name="flower" id="iris"/><label for="iris">Iris</label>
        </div>
    </form>
</body>
</html>
```

Notice that I have selected the div element that contains the radio buttons in order to call the buttonset method: you don't call the button method on the individual input elements. You can see the effect of the buttonset method in Figure 18-9.

Figure 18-9. *Creating a button set*

At most, one of the buttons in the set can be selected, allowing you to provide the user with a fixed set of choices in a way that is visually consistent with other jQuery UI buttons. Notice that jQuery UI emphasizes the relationship between the buttons in a set by applying different styling to the edges where buttons meet. This is shown more clearly in Figure 18-10.

Figure 18-10. *The jQuery UI styling for button sets*

Creating Button Sets from Regular Buttons

You can use the buttonset method on any element that can be used with the regular button method. This has the effect of applying the *style* of a set of radio buttons but *not* the behavior, so that each button works individually. Listing 18-13 shows this use of the buttonset method.

Listing 18-13. Creating a Button Set from Regular Buttons

```
<!DOCTYPE html>
<html>
<head>
    <title>Example</title>
    <script src="jquery-2.0.2.js"></script>
    <script src="jquery-ui-1.10.3.custom.js"></script>
    <link href="jquery-ui-1.10.3.custom.css" rel="stylesheet" />
    <script type="text/javascript">
```

```
        $(document).ready(function () {
            $("#radioDiv").buttonset();
        });
    </script>
</head>
<body>
    <form>
        <div id="radioDiv">
            <input type="submit" value="Submit"/>
            <input type="reset" value="Reset"/>
            <input type="button" value="Press Me"/>
            <a href="http://apress.com">Visit Apress</a>
        </div>
    </form>
</body>
</html>
```

Any suitable element in the div container will be transformed into a button, and the adjoining edges will be styled just as with the radio button, as you can see in Figure 18-11.

Figure 18-11. *Creating a button set from regular buttons*

■ **Tip** Be careful when using this technique. It can be confusing to the user, especially if you are using radio buttons elsewhere in the same document or web application.

Using the jQuery UI Progress Bar

Now that I have used the button to explore the basic structure of a jQuery UI widget, I will look at the other widgets that jQuery UI supports, starting with the progress bar.

The progress bar allows you to show the user progress in completing a task. The progress bar is designed to show *determinate tasks*, where you can give the user an accurate indication of how far you are through the task as a percentage, and *indeterminate tasks*, where the percentage of progress is currently unknown.

■ **Tip** The support for displaying indeterminate tasks was added to jQuery UI in version 1.10. See the section "Creating an Indeterminate Progress Bar" for details of this feature.

SHOWING USEFUL PROGRESS INFORMATION

There are no rules for the way widgets should be used in web applications, but the user expectations of controls such as progress bars are informed by the standards set by operating systems such as Windows and Mac OS. To help the user make sense of your progress bar, there are a couple of rules to follow.

First, only increment the progress. Don't be tempted to reduce the progress when the task has more steps than initially expected. The progress bar shows the percentage of a task that been completed and is not an estimate of the remaining time. If there are different possible paths for a task to follow, then show the most pessimistic progress. It is better to take a giant leap in progress than to confuse the user.

Second, don't loop around the progress bar more than once. If you have enough information to show the user reasonably accurate completion information, then you should be using an indeterminate progress indicator. When the progress nears 100%, the user expects the task to complete. If the progress bar then resets and starts to build up again, you have simply confused the user and made the use of the progress bar meaningless.

Creating the Progress Bar

You create a progress bar by selecting a div element and calling the progressbar method, as shown in Listing 18-14.

Listing 18-14. Creating a Progress Bar

```
<!DOCTYPE html>
<html>
<head>
    <title>Example</title>
    <script src="jquery-2.0.2.js"></script>
    <script src="jquery-ui-1.10.3.custom.js"></script>
    <link href="jquery-ui-1.10.3.custom.css" rel="stylesheet" />
    <script type="text/javascript">
        $(document).ready(function () {
            $("#progressDiv").progressbar({
                value: 21
            });
        });
    </script>
</head>
<body>
    <div id="progressDiv"></div>
</body>
</html>
```

The document contains a div element with an id of progressDiv. To create a progress bar, I must use an empty div element–if the div element has any content, it will affect the layout of the progress bar. I use jQuery to select the progressDiv element and call the jQuery UI progressbar method, passing in a map object to provide the initial configuration. The progress bar supports three settings, which I have described in Table 18-4.

Table 18-4. *The Settings for the Progress Bar Widget*

Setting	Description
disabled	If true, the progress bar will be disabled. The default value is false.
value	Sets the percentage complete displayed to the user. The default is zero. Set the property to false to display an indeterminate progress bar, as described in the section "Creating an Indeterminate Progress Bar."
max	Sets the maximum value that the progress bar will display. The default is 100.

In the example, I specified an initial value of 21 (which will be equivalent to 21% since I have not changed the value of the max setting), and you can see the effect in Figure 18-12.

Figure 18-12. *Creating a progress bar*

Creating an Indeterminate Progress Bar

As of jQuery UI 1.10, the jQuery UI progress bar widget supports displaying progress for indeterminate tasks, which is configured by setting the value configuration property to false rather than specifying a numeric value, as shown in Listing 18-15.

Listing 18-15. Creating an Indeterminate Progress Bar

```
<!DOCTYPE html>
<html>
<head>
    <title>Example</title>
    <script src="jquery-2.0.2.js"></script>
    <script src="jquery-ui-1.10.3.custom.js"></script>
    <link href="jquery-ui-1.10.3.custom.css" rel="stylesheet" />
    <script type="text/javascript">
        $(document).ready(function () {
            $("#progressDiv").progressbar({
                value: false
            });
        });
    </script>
</head>
<body>
    <div id="progressDiv"></div>
</body>
</html>
```

jQuery UI displays an indeterminate progress with a simple animation applied to the entire bar. You need to run the example to see the effect of the animation, but Figure 18-13 shows one frame.

Figure 18-13. *Creating an indeterminate progress bar*

Using the Progress Bar Methods

The progress bar widget defines a number of methods, which are in the same style as for the button. In other words, you call the JavaScript progressbar method, and the first argument specifies the jQuery UI widget method you want. Table 18-5 describes the available methods.

Table 18-5. *Progress Bar Methods*

Method	Description
progressbar("destroy")	Returns the div element to its original state
progressbar("disable")	Disables the progress bar
progressbar("enable")	Enables the progress bar
progressbar("option")	Sets one or more options; see the section "Configuring the Button" for details of configuring a jQuery UI widget
progressbar("value", value)	Gets and sets the value displayed by the progress bar and switches between an indeterminate and determinate progress bar

Most of these methods work in the same way as for the button widget, so I am not going to demonstrate them again. The exception is the value method, which lets you get and set the value that is displayed by the progress bar and switch between the determinate and indeterminate states. Listing 18-16 demonstrates the use of the value method.

Listing 18-16. *Using the Progress Bar Value Method*

```
<!DOCTYPE html>
<html>
<head>
    <title>Example</title>
    <script src="jquery-2.0.2.js"></script>
    <script src="jquery-ui-1.10.3.custom.js"></script>
    <link href="jquery-ui-1.10.3.custom.css" rel="stylesheet" />
    <script type="text/javascript">
        $(document).ready(function () {
```

```
        $("#progressDiv").progressbar({
            value: 21
        });

        $("button").click(function (e) {
            var divElem = $("#progressDiv");
            if (this.id == "mode") {
                divElem.progressbar("value", false);
            } else {
                var currentProgress = divElem.progressbar("value");
                if (!currentProgress) {
                    divElem.progressbar("value", 21);
                } else {
                    divElem.progressbar("value",
                        this.id == "decr" ? currentProgress - 10 :
                                            currentProgress + 10)
                }
            }
        });
    });
</script>
</head>
<body>
    <div id="progressDiv"></div>
    <button id="decr">Decrease</button>
    <button id="incr">Increase</button>
    <button id="mode">Indeterminate</button>
</body>
</html>
```

I have added button elements to this example. I use them to increase or decrease the value displayed by the progress bar and switch between the determinate and indeterminate modes. Each press of the Decrease or Increase button changes the value by 10% as shown in Figure 18-14.

Figure 18-14. *Using the value method to change the progress displayed*

The Indeterminate button calls the value method to switch the progress bar to its intermediate mode. Clicking either of the other buttons will set a numeric value, which will put the progress bar back to its determinate mode, as shown in Figure 18-15.

Figure 18-15. *Changing the Mode of the Progress Bar*

Using the Progress Bar Events

The jQuery UI progress bar widget defines three events, as described in Table 18-6.

Table 18-6. *Progress Bar Events*

Event	Description
create	Triggered when the progress bar is created
change	Triggered when the value of the progress bar changes
complete	Triggered when the value of the progress bar is set to 100

Listing 18-17 shows the events in use.

Listing 18-17. Using the Progress Bar Events

```
<!DOCTYPE html>
<html>
<head>
    <title>Example</title>
    <script src="jquery-2.0.2.js"></script>
    <script src="jquery-ui-1.10.3.custom.js"></script>
    <link href="jquery-ui-1.10.3.custom.css" rel="stylesheet" />
     <script type="text/javascript">
        $(document).ready(function () {

            $("button").button();

            $("#progressDiv").progressbar({
                value: 21,
                create: function (e) {
                    $("#progVal").text($("#progressDiv").progressbar("value"));
                },
                complete: function (e) {
                    $("#incr").button("disable")
                },
                change: function (e) {
```

```
                    var currentValue = $("#progressDiv").progressbar("value");
                    if (!currentValue) {
                        $("#progWrapper").hide();
                    } else {
                        if ($(this).progressbar("value") < 100) {
                            $("#incr").button("enable")
                        }
                        $("#progVal").text(currentValue);
                        $("#progWrapper").show();
                    }
                }
            });

            $("button").click(function (e) {
                var divElem = $("#progressDiv");
                if (this.id == "mode") {
                    divElem.progressbar("value", false);
                } else {
                    var currentProgress = divElem.progressbar("value");
                    if (!currentProgress) {
                        divElem.progressbar("value", 21);
                    } else {
                        divElem.progressbar("value",
                            this.id == "decr" ? currentProgress - 10 :
                                                currentProgress + 10)
                    }
                }
            });
        });
    </script>
</head>
<body>
    <div id="progressDiv"></div>
    <button id="decr">Decrease</button>
    <button id="incr">Increase</button>
    <button id="mode">Indeterminate</button>
    <span id="progWrapper">Progress: <span id="progVal"></span>%</span>
</body>
</html>
```

In Listing 18-17, I use span elements to display the numeric progress value while the progress bar is in the determinate mode. I use the create event to display the initial value, which is set using the value configuration property.

■ **Tip**   Notice that I have used the same map object for the settings and events of the progress bar. This isn't required, but it does allow me to create and configure a widget in a single method call.

I use the complete event to disable the Increase button when the progress reaches 100% and the change event to ensure that the button is enabled for other values, to display the current value and to switch between the determinate and indeterminate modes. You can see the effect in Figure 18-16.

Figure 18-16. *Responding to progress bar events*

■ **Tip** There are a couple of things to remember when using the events. First, the complete event fires every time the value is set to 100 or greater. This means the event can fire multiple times if you repeatedly set the value to 100, for example. Second, both the change and complete events are triggered for values of 100 or more, so you have to be able to deal with both when you complete the progress update.

Using the jQuery UI Slider

As its name suggests, the slider widget creates a slider out of an element in the HTML document and allows the user to select a value without having to enter text into an input element. The slider widget is applied to HTML elements using the slider method, as shown in Listing 18-18.

Listing 18-18. Creating a Slider

```
<!DOCTYPE html>
<html>
<head>
    <title>Example</title>
    <script src="jquery-2.0.2.js"></script>
    <script src="jquery-ui-1.10.3.custom.js"></script>
    <link href="jquery-ui-1.10.3.custom.css" rel="stylesheet" />
    <style>
        #slider { margin: 10px; }
    </style>
    <script type="text/javascript">
        $(document).ready(function () {
            $("#slider").slider();
        });
    </script>
</head>
<body>
    <div id="slider"></div>
</body>
</html>
```

The slider is themed consistently with the other jQuery UI widgets and allows the user to use the mouse or arrow keys to move the slider handle up and down the scale. You can see how the basic slider appears in Figure 18-17. (Notice that I defined a CSS style for the element that underpins the slider in this example—without this, the slider is displayed right up against the edges of its parent element.)

Figure 18-17. *A basic jQuery UI slider*

Configuring the Slider

A with all jQuery UI widgets, the slider widget defines a number of settings that you can use to configure the appearance and behavior of sliders. Table 18-7 describes these settings, and I show you how to use these settings to configure the widget in the sections that follow.

Table 18-7. *The Settings for the Slider Widget*

Setting	Description
animate	When true, animates the slider when the user clicks a position outside the handle. The default is false.
disabled	Disables the slider when set to true. The default is false.
max	Defines the maximum value for the slider. The default is 100.
min	Defines the minimum value for the slider. The default is 0.
orientation	Defines the orientation for the slider; see Listing 18-19 for details.
range	Used with the values setting to create a multihandle slider.
step	Defines the interval that the slider moves between the min and max values.
value	Defines the value that the slider represents.
values	Used with the range setting to create a multihandle slider.

■ **Tip** The min and max values are *exclusive*, meaning that if you set a min value of 0 and a max value of 100, the user can select values between 1 and 99.

Changing the Slider Orientation

By default, sliders are horizontal, but you can use the orientation setting to create vertical sliders as well, as shown by Listing 18-19.

Listing 18-19. Using the orientation Setting

```html
<!DOCTYPE html>
<html>
<head>
    <title>Example</title>
    <script src="jquery-2.0.2.js"></script>
    <script src="jquery-ui-1.10.3.custom.js"></script>
    <link href="jquery-ui-1.10.3.custom.css" rel="stylesheet" />
    <style>
        #hslider, #vslider { margin: 10px }
    </style>
     <script type="text/javascript">
         $(document).ready(function () {
             $("#hslider").slider({
                 value: 35
             });

             $("#vslider").slider({
                 orientation: "vertical",
                 value: 35
             });
         });
    </script>
</head>
<body>
    <div id="hslider"></div>
    <div id="vslider"></div>
</body>
</html>
```

I created two sliders, one of which has the orientation setting of vertical. I have also changed the style element so that I can apply a margin to the slider elements to keep them apart. You control the size and position of sliders (and any jQuery UI widget) by styling the underlying element (which is why div elements work best; they can be readily manipulated with CSS). You can see the sliders in Figure 18-18. Notice that I used the value setting to set the initial position of the handle.

Figure 18-18. Creating vertical and horizontal sliders

Although I am keeping the options and methods separate, I could have written Listing 18-19 differently to make better use of the underlying jQuery functionality, as shown in Listing 18-20.

Listing 18-20. Making Better Use of jQuery

```
<!DOCTYPE html>
<html>
<head>
    <title>Example</title>
    <script src="jquery-2.0.2.js"></script>
    <script src="jquery-ui-1.10.3.custom.js"></script>
    <link href="jquery-ui-1.10.3.custom.css" rel="stylesheet" />
    <style>
        #hslider, #vslider { margin: 10px}
    </style>
     <script type="text/javascript">
        $(document).ready(function () {
            $("#hslider, #vslider").slider({
                value: 35,
                orientation: "vertical"
            }).filter("#hslider").slider("option", "orientation", "horizontal");
        });
    </script>
</head>
<body>
    <div id="hslider"></div>
    <div id="vslider"></div>
</body>
</html>
```

It is a minor point but I don't want you to forget that jQuery UI is built on and tightly integrated with jQuery and that you can use all of the selections and manipulations you saw earlier in the book.

■ **Tip** Notice that I set the initial orientation to vertical and then changed it to horizontal. There is a bug with the slider where changing the orientation to vertical after the slider has been created causes the handle to be misaligned.

Animating the Slider

The animate setting enables smooth handle movement when the user clicks the slider at the point he wants the handle to move to (as opposed to setting a value by dragging the slider). You can enable the default animation by setting animate to true, set a speed for the animation by using fast or slow, or specify the number of milliseconds that the animation should last for. Listing 18-21 shows the use of the animate setting.

Listing 18-21. Using the animate Setting

```
<!DOCTYPE html>
<html>
<head>
    <title>Example</title>
    <script src="jquery-1.7.js" type="text/javascript"></script>
```

```
<script src="jquery-ui-1.8.16.custom.js" type="text/javascript"></script>
<link rel="stylesheet" type="text/css" href="jquery-ui-1.8.16.custom.css"/>
<style type="text/css">
    #slider {margin: 10px}
</style>
<script type="text/javascript">
    $(document).ready(function() {
        $("#slider").slider({
            animate: "fast"
        });
    });
</script>
</head>
<body>
    <div id="slider"></div>
</body>
</html>
```

I have set the animate setting to fast. It is hard to show animations in a screenshot, but Figure 18-19 shows what the animate setting does.

Figure 18-19. *Animating the movement of the handle*

This screenshot shows the slider just before I clicked the mouse button. If I had not enabled animations, then the handle would snap to the location I clicked, immediately setting the new value for the slider. But since I have enabled animations, the slider will gracefully move to its new position in a less jarring way. However, like any effect or animation, I don't want to overdo the effect, which is why I have selected the fast option.

■ **Tip** This is an example that you need to play with to see the full result. If you don't want to type in the code and HTML, you can find the code samples for this chapter in the Source Code/Download area of the Apress web site at www.apress.com. It is freely available from apress.com and contains all of the examples in this book.

Creating a Range Slider

A range slider has two handles and lets the user specify a range of values rather than a single value. For example, you might want to let the user express the price range she is willing to pay for products so that you can filter anything else out. Listing 18-22 demonstrates creating a range slider.

Listing 18-22. Creating a Range Slider

```
<!DOCTYPE html>
<html>
<head>
    <title>Example</title>
    <script src="jquery-2.0.2.js"></script>
    <script src="jquery-ui-1.10.3.custom.js"></script>
    <link href="jquery-ui-1.10.3.custom.css" rel="stylesheet" />
    <style>
        #slider {margin: 20px}
    </style>
    <script type="text/javascript">
        $(document).ready(function () {
            $("#slider").slider({
                values: [35, 65],
                range: true,
                create: displaySliderValues,
                slide: displaySliderValues
            });

            function displaySliderValues() {
                $("#lower").text($("#slider").slider("values", 0));
                $("#upper").text($("#slider").slider("values", 1));
            }
        });
    </script>
</head>
<body>
    <div id="slider"></div>
    <div>Lower Value: <span id="lower">
    </span> Upper Value: <span id="upper"></span></div>
</body>
</html>
```

To create a range slider, you must set the range setting to true and set the value setting to an array that contains the initial lower and upper bounds of the range. (When using a regular slider, you use the value setting, and when using a range slider, you use the values setting.) In this example, I have set the bounds to 35 and 65. You can see the effect in Figure 18-20.

Figure 18-20. *Creating a range slider*

I have added a handler function for the `create` and `slide` events. I'll get to the events supported by the slider in the section "Using Slider Events," but I want to demonstrate how to obtain the position of the handles in a range slider. You do this through the `values` method, specifying the index of the slider you are interested in, as follows:

```
...
$("#slider").slider("values", 0);
...
```

The index is zero based, so this statement gets the value for the handle that represents the lower bound of the range. I have used the events to set the contents of two span elements.

Using the Slider Methods

The slider defines the same set of basic methods that all jQuery UI widgets define, plus a couple that let you set either a single value or the range of values to be shown. Table 18-8 describes the methods.

Table 18-8. *Slider Methods*

Method	Description
`slider("destroy")`	Returns the underlying element to its original state
`slider("disable")`	Disables the slider
`slider("enable")`	Enables the slider
`slider("option")`	Sets one or more options; see the section "Configuring the Button" for details of configuring a jQuery UI widget
`slider("value", value)`	Gets or sets the value for a regular slider
`slider("values", [values])`	Gets or sets the values for a range slider

Listing 18-23 shows how you can use the `value` and `values` methods to control a slider programmatically.

Listing 18-23. Controlling Sliders Programmatically

```
<!DOCTYPE html>
<html>
<head>
    <title>Example</title>
    <script src="jquery-2.0.2.js"></script>
```

```
<script src="jquery-ui-1.10.3.custom.js"></script>
<link href="jquery-ui-1.10.3.custom.css" rel="stylesheet" />
<style>
    #slider, #rangeslider, *.inputDiv { margin: 10px }
    label {width: 80px; display: inline-block; margin: 4px}
</style>
 <script type="text/javascript">
     $(document).ready(function () {

         $("#slider").slider({
             value: 50,
             create: function () {
                 $("#slideVal").val($("#slider").slider("value"));
             }
         });

         $("#rangeslider").slider({
             values: [35, 65],
             range: true,
             create: function () {
                 $("#rangeMin").val($("#rangeslider").slider("values", 0));
                 $("#rangeMax").val($("#rangeslider").slider("values", 1));
             }
         })

         $("input").change(function (e) {
             switch (this.id) {
                 case "rangeMin":
                 case "rangeMax":
                     var index = (this.id == "rangeMax") ? 1 : 0;
                     $("#rangeslider").slider("values", index, $(this).val())
                     break;
                 case "slideVal":
                     $("#slider").slider("value", $(this).val())
                     break;
             }
         })
     });
 </script>
</head>
<body>
    <div id="rangeslider"></div>
    <div class="inputDiv">
        <label for="rangeMin">Range Min: </label><input id="rangeMin" />
        <label for="rangeMax">Range Max: </label><input id="rangeMax" />
    </div>
    <div id="slider"></div>
    <div class="inputDiv">
        <label for="slideVal">Slide Val: </label><input id="slideVal" />
    </div>
</body>
</html>
```

This document contains two sliders and three `input` elements that allow the values for the handles to be specified without moving the handles themselves. You can see the layout of the elements in Figure 18-21.

Figure 18-21. *Controlling sliders programmatically*

I used jQuery to select the `input` elements and called the `change` method to set up a handler for the change event, meaning that the function is invoked whenever the value of one of the `input` elements is changed.

Within the handler function, I use the `id` attribute of the element that triggered the event to figure out which slider I need to manipulate and call the `value` or `values` methods to set the handle positions. The relationship between the `input` elements and the sliders is one-way, meaning that moving the handles doesn't update the `input` elements. I'll show you how to create a two-way relationship in the next section.

Using Slider Events

Table 18-9 shows the events that the slider supports. The best feature of these events is the support for both `change` and `stop`, which allows you to differentiate between new values created by the user moving the handle and values that you set programmatically.

Table 18-9. *Slider Events*

Event	Description
create	Triggered when the slider is created
start	Triggered when the user starts sliding the handle
slide	Triggered for every mouse move while the handle is sliding
change	Triggered when the user stops sliding the handle or when the value is changed programmatically
stop	Triggered when the user stops sliding the handle

Listing 18-24 shows the use of slider events to create a two-way (bidirectional) relationship between sliders and `input` elements, similar to the example in the previous section, albeit I have removed one of the sliders to keep the example simple. The two-way relationship allows me to tie together programmatic support and user interaction to manage the sliders.

Listing 18-24. Using Slider Events to Create a Bidirectional Relationship Between Sliders and Inputs

```html
<!DOCTYPE html>
<html>
<head>
    <title>Example</title>
    <script src="jquery-2.0.2.js"></script>
    <script src="jquery-ui-1.10.3.custom.js"></script>
    <link href="jquery-ui-1.10.3.custom.css" rel="stylesheet" />
    <style>
        #rangeslider, *.inputDiv { margin: 10px }
        label {width: 80px; display: inline-block; margin: 4px}
    </style>
     <script type="text/javascript">
        $(document).ready(function () {
            $("#rangeslider").slider({
                values: [35, 65],
                range: true,
                create: setInputsFromSlider,
                slide: setInputsFromSlider,
                stop: setInputsFromSlider
            });

            function setInputsFromSlider() {
                $("#rangeMin").val($("#rangeslider").slider("values", 0));
                $("#rangeMax").val($("#rangeslider").slider("values", 1));
            }

            $("input").change(function (e) {
                var index = (this.id == "rangeMax") ? 1 : 0;
                $("#rangeslider").slider("values", index, $(this).val())
            });
        });
    </script>
</head>
<body>
    <div id="rangeslider"></div>
    <div class="inputDiv">
        <label for="rangeMin">Range Min: </label><input id="rangeMin" />
        <label for="rangeMax">Range Max: </label><input id="rangeMax" />
    </div>
</body>
</html>
```

I handle the create, slide, and stop events in this example. Now the slider handles are moved when new values are entered into the input elements, and the values in the input elements are updated when the slider is moved. You can see how the document appears in Figure 18-22, but this is an example that requires interaction to see the full effect.

Figure 18-22. *Responding to slider events*

Summary

In this chapter, I introduced you to the first three jQuery UI widgets: the button, the progress bar, and the slider. Each widget follows the same basic structure: there is a single method that creates and configures the widget as well as letting you supply functions that will respond to its events. Some methods and events are common to each widget, but there are unique additions as well that expose the special functionality that some widgets offer. Now that I have the basics out of the way, I'll show you some more flexible and complex widgets in the chapters that follow. In Chapter 19, I show you the autocomplete and accordion widgets.

CHAPTER 19

■ ■ ■

Using the Autocomplete and Accordion Widgets

In this chapter, I describe the jQuery UI autocomplete and accordion widgets. They are more complex than the widgets I showed you in Chapter 18, but they follow the same pattern of settings, methods, and events. These are highly configurable, flexible, and clever user interface controls, and used wisely they can significantly enhance the appearance and usability of your documents and web applications. Table 19-1 provides the summary for this chapter.

Table 19-1. *Chapter Summary*

Problem	Solution	Listing
Add the jQuery UI autocomplete feature to an input element	Use the autocomplete method	1, 2
Obtain autocomplete suggestions from a remote server	Set the source setting to a URL	3–5
Generate autocomplete suggestions dynamically	Specify a function for the source setting	6
Return autocomplete results from an asynchronous task	Call the response function	7
Control the placement of the autocomplete pop-up	Use the position property	8
Control the autocomplete feature programmatically	Use the search and close methods	9
Receive notification of the selected autocomplete item	Use the focus, select, and change events	10
Modify the autocomplete results shown to the user	Handle the response event	11
Override the default autocomplete action	Override the default action for the select event	12
Create a jQuery UI accordion widget	Use the accordion method	13
Set the height of the accordion and its content panels	Use the heightStyle setting	14–16
Change the action that the user has to perform to activate a content element	Use the event setting	17
Set the active content element in a jQuery UI accordion	Use the active and collapsible settings	18, 19
Change the icons used by an accordion	Use the icons setting	20
Receive notifications when the active element in an accordion changes	Handle the activate or beforeactivate events	21

491

JQUERY UI CHANGES SINCE THE LAST EDITION

There have been a number of API changes to the accordion widget in the jQuery UI 1.10 release: the configuration options, methods, and events have all changed. I have listed the changes in the relevant sections throughout this chapter.

The autocomplete widget, which I also describe in this chapter, has a useful new feature: you can control how the pop-up that offers completion choices to the user is positioned (see the section "Positioning the Pop-up").

Using jQuery UI Autocomplete

The autocomplete widget provides suggestions to the user as she enters values into an input element. Used well, this widget can be a helpful time-saver to the user, speeding up data entry and reducing errors. In the sections that follow, I show you how to create, configure, and use the jQuery UI autocomplete widget.

Creating the Autocomplete Element

You use the autocomplete method on an input element to create an autocomplete widget. Listing 19-1 demonstrates how to set up basic autocompletion.

Listing 19-1. Creating an Autocompleting Input Element

```
<!DOCTYPE html>
<html>
<head>
    <title>Example</title>
    <script src="jquery-2.0.2.js" type="text/javascript"></script>
    <script src="jquery-ui-1.10.3.custom.js" type="text/javascript"></script>
    <link rel="stylesheet" type="text/css" href="jquery-ui-1.10.3.custom.css"/>
    <script type="text/javascript">
        $(document).ready(function() {

            var flowers = ["Aster", "Daffodil", "Rose", "Peony", "Primula", "Snowdrop",
                            "Poppy", "Primrose", "Petuna", "Pansy"];

            $("#acInput").autocomplete({
                source: flowers
            })
        });
    </script>
</head>
<body>
    <form>
        <div class="ui-widget">
            <label for="acInput">Flower Name: </label><input id="acInput"/>
        </div>
    </form>
</body>
</html>
```

The autocomplete method is applied to HTML elements just like the other jQuery UI methods you have seen and is configured with a map object that defines a source property. This property specifies where the autocomplete entries will come from.

You can use a range of different data sources for the autocomplete values, which I demonstrate later in this chapter. In Listing 19-1, I have used a simple array of values. Figure 19-1 illustrates the way that the autocomplete feature is presented to the user.

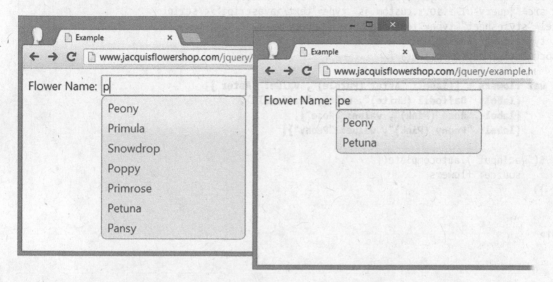

Figure 19-1. *A basic jQuery UI autocomplete element*

■ **Caution** The autocomplete feature doesn't enforce any kind of validation, and the user can enter any value into the input element, not just those that are defined by the source setting.

There are two screenshots in Figure 19-1. The first shows what happens when I type the letter *P*. As you can see, the first screenshot shows a list of the data items that contain the letter *P*. This list includes the flower names that start with *P*, but it also includes Snowdrop as well (because it contains the letter *p*). In the second screenshot, I have typed *Pe*, and jQuery UI shows only the items that contain that combination of letters. The user can continue to type his entry or select one from the autocomplete list.

■ **Tip** In the document, I put the input element and its label inside a div element that belongs to the ui-widget class. This sets the CSS font properties for the label and input elements to match those used by the autocomplete pop-up. I explain more about how you can use the jQuery UI CSS classes in Chapter 35.

Using an Object Array as the Data Source

An alternative approach is to use an array of objects, rather than strings. This allows me to separate the label that is displayed in the pop-up menu from the value inserted into the input element, as demonstrated by Listing 19-2.

Listing 19-2. Using an Array of Objects for Autocompletion

```
<!DOCTYPE html>
<html>
<head>
    <title>Example</title>
    <script src="jquery-2.0.2.js" type="text/javascript"></script>
    <script src="jquery-ui-1.10.3.custom.js" type="text/javascript"></script>
    <link rel="stylesheet" type="text/css" href="jquery-ui-1.10.3.custom.css"/>
    <script type="text/javascript">
        $(document).ready(function() {

            var flowers = [{label: "Aster (Purple)", value: "Aster"},
                {label: "Daffodil (White)", value: "Daffodil"},
                {label: "Rose (Pink)", value: "Rose"},
                {label: "Peony (Pink)", value: "Peony"}]

            $("#acInput").autocomplete({
                source: flowers
            })

        });
    </script>
</head>
<body>
    <form>
        <div class="ui-widget">
            <label for="acInput">Flower Name: </label><input id="acInput"/>
        </div>
    </form>
</body>
</html>
```

When using an array of objects, the autocomplete feature looks for properties called label and value. The label property is used to create the pop-up list, and the value entry is inserted into the input element if the item is selected. In Listing 19-2, I have added some color information to the labels that is not included in the values when they are selected, as shown in Figure 19-2.

Figure 19-2. Using an array of objects to separate labels from values

Configuring Autocomplete

The autocomplete feature supports a number of settings that let you control different aspects of its functionality, as described by Table 19-2. In the sections that follow, I show you how to use these settings to configure the widget.

Table 19-2. *Autocomplete Settings*

Setting	Description
appendTo	Specifies the element that the pop-up menu should be appended to. The default is the body element.
autoFocus	If set to true, the first item in the list will be given the focus, meaning that the user can select this item by pressing the Return key. The default is false.
delay	Specifies the delay (in milliseconds) after a keystroke after which the autocomplete data are updated. The default is 300.
disabled	Disables the autocomplete feature when set to true. This setting does not affect the underlying input element. The default is false.
minLength	Specifies the minimum number of characters that the user has to type before the autocomplete menu is displayed. The default is 1.
position	Sets the position of the pop-up menu relative to the input element.
source	Specifies the source of items to be added to the autocomplete menu. There is no default for this setting, which must be specified when calling the autocomplete method.

Using a Remote Data Source

The most interesting autocomplete setting is source because you can use it to work with a wide range of different kinds of data to populate the pop-up menu. I used a JavaScript array in Listing 19-2, which is fine for simple static lists of data. For more complex situations, you can get the list of matching items from a server. All you have to do is specify the URL that will generate the data, as shown in Listing 19-3.

Listing 19-3. Using a Remote Data Source

```
<!DOCTYPE html>
<html>
<head>
    <title>Example</title>
    <script src="jquery-2.0.2.js" type="text/javascript"></script>
    <script src="jquery-ui-1.10.3.custom.js" type="text/javascript"></script>
    <link rel="stylesheet" type="text/css" href="jquery-ui-1.10.3.custom.css"/>
    <script type="text/javascript">
        $(document).ready(function() {

            $("#acInput").autocomplete({
                source: "http://node.jacquisflowershop.com/auto"
            })
        });
    </script>
</head>
```

```
<body>
    <form>
        <div class="ui-widget">
            <label for="acInput">Flower Name: </label><input id="acInput"/>
        </div>
    </form>
</body>
</html>
```

When jQuery UI needs the list of items for the pop-up autocomplete menu, it will make an HTTP GET request to the specified URL. The characters that the user has typed so far are included in the request query string using the key term. So, for example, if the user has typed the letter *s*, then jQuery UI will request the following URL:

```
http://node.jacquisflowershop.com/auto?term=s
```

If the user then types the letter *n*, jQuery UI will request the following:

```
http://node.jacquisflowershop.com/auto?term=sn
```

This technique is useful when there are a lot of data items and you don't want to send them all to the client. It can also be useful when the list of items changes dynamically and you want to make sure the user benefits from the latest data available.

The server is responsible for taking the term value from the query string and returning a JSON string representing the array of items to display to the user. Listing 19-4 shows how I have updated the formserver.js script for Node.js script to do just that. (See Chapter 1 for details of obtaining and installing Node.js.)

Listing 19-4. The Node.js Script to Support Remote Autocompletion

```
var http = require("http");
var querystring = require("querystring");
var url = require("url");

var port = 80;

http.createServer(function (req, res) {
    console.log("[200 OK] " + req.method + " to " + req.url);

    var flowers = ["Aster", "Daffodil", "Rose", "Peony", "Primula", "Snowdrop",
                   "Poppy", "Primrose", "Petuna", "Pansy"];

    var matches = [];
    var term = url.parse(req.url, true).query["term"];

    if (term) {
        var pattern = new RegExp("^" + term, "i");
        for (var i = 0; i < flowers.length; i++) {
            if (pattern.test(flowers[i])) {
                matches.push(flowers[i]);
            }
        }
    }
```

```
    } else {
        matches = flowers;
    }

    res.writeHead(200, "OK", {
        "Content-Type": "application/json",
        "Access-Control-Allow-Origin": "*"
    });
    res.write(JSON.stringify(matches));
    res.end();
}).listen(port);
console.log("Ready on port " + port);
```

This Node.js script uses the same set of flower names as in Listing 19-2 and returns those that match the term sent by the browser. I have changed the search slightly so that only those names that start with the term are returned. For example, if jQuery UI sends a request like the following:

```
http://node.jacquisflowershop.com/auto?term=p
```

then the Node.js server will return the following JSON:

```
["Peony","Primula","Poppy","Primrose","Petuna","Pansy"]
```

Because I am matching at the start of the flower name, Snowdrop is omitted from the list, as you can see in Figure 19-3.

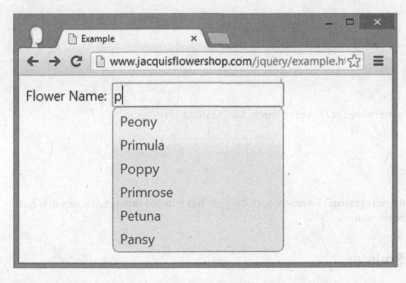

Figure 19-3. *Obtaining autocomplete entries from a remote server*

This is a nice technique but it can generate a lot of requests to the server. This isn't a problem in my example because I am performing a simple search and my server and browser are on the same network. But for complex searches, across a wide-area network that can suffer delays, the load on the server can become an issue.

The best way to manage the rate at which autocomplete requests are made is to use the minLength and delay settings. The minLength setting specifies the number of characters that the user has to type before jQuery UI makes an autocomplete request to the server. You can use this setting such that you only request data from the server after several characters have been entered, by which time you have enough information to narrow the scope of the search.

The delay setting specifies the amount of time after a key press that the autocomplete information will be requested. You can use this setting to prevent requests from being made when the user is typing quickly. So, if the user types *s* and *n*, you can avoid hitting the server for the s list and then immediately doing so again for the sn list. By combining these settings, you can reduce the number of requests and still provide the user with guidance when it is needed. Listing 19-5 shows the uses of these settings.

Listing 19-5. Using the delay and minLength Settings to Reduce Server Requests

```
<!DOCTYPE html>
<html>
<head>
    <title>Example</title>
    <script src="jquery-2.0.2.js" type="text/javascript"></script>
    <script src="jquery-ui-1.10.3.custom.js" type="text/javascript"></script>
    <link rel="stylesheet" type="text/css" href="jquery-ui-1.10.3.custom.css"/>
    <script type="text/javascript">
        $(document).ready(function() {

            $("#acInput").autocomplete({
                source: "http://node.jacquisflowershop.com/auto",
                minLength: 3,
                delay: 1000
            })
        });
    </script>
</head>
<body>
    <form>
        <div class="ui-widget">
            <label for="acInput">Flower Name: </label><input id="acInput"/>
        </div>
    </form>
</body>
</html>
```

In Listing 19-5, the initial request to the server won't be made until the user has entered three characters *and* has not typed any additional characters for one second.

Using a Function as the Data Source

You can use a function to create a truly customized source for autocomplete entries. You assign the function to the source setting, and it is called each time the autocomplete feature needs to display items to the user. Listing 19-6 demonstrates.

Listing 19-6. *Using a Function to Generate Autocomplete Items*

```
<!DOCTYPE html>
<html>
<head>
    <title>Example</title>
    <script src="jquery-2.0.2.js" type="text/javascript"></script>
    <script src="jquery-ui-1.10.3.custom.js" type="text/javascript"></script>
    <link rel="stylesheet" type="text/css" href="jquery-ui-1.10.3.custom.css"/>
    <script type="text/javascript">
        $(document).ready(function() {

            var flowers = ["Aster", "Daffodil", "Rose", "Peony", "Primula", "Snowdrop",
                           "Poppy", "Primrose", "Petuna", "Pansy"];

            $("#acInput").autocomplete({
                source: function(request, response) {
                    var term = request.term;
                    var pattern = new RegExp("^" + term, "i");

                    var results = $.map(flowers, function(elem) {
                        if (pattern.test(elem)) {
                            return elem;
                        }
                    })
                    response(results);
                }
            })
        });
    </script>
</head>
<body>
    <form>
        <div class="ui-widget">
            <label for="acInput">Flower Name: </label><input id="acInput"/>
        </div>
    </form>
</body>
</html>
```

Two arguments are passed to the function. The first argument is an object that has a single property called `term`. The value of this property is the string of characters that the user has entered into the `input` element. The second argument is a function that you call when you have generated the list of autocomplete items that you want to show to the user. The argument to this function is an array of strings or objects.

In Listing 19-6, I have reproduced the server-side functionality from Listing 19-5, and I generate an array containing those items that start with the specified term.

■ **Tip**   I processed the contents of the array using the jQuery `map` utility method, which I describe in Chapter 34.

I then pass the results back to jQuery UI by passing the array as an argument to the response function, as follows:

```
...
response(results);
...
```

This seems like an odd way to process the results, but it means that you can call the function after an asynchronous task has completed. In Listing 19-7, you can see how I have used a function that makes an Ajax request to get details of the flowers, performs a local search of the content that is returned, and then calls the response function to give the final result to jQuery UI.

Listing 19-7. Using a Custom Data Source Function That Performs an Asynchronous Task

```
<!DOCTYPE html>
<html>
<head>
    <title>Example</title>
    <script src="jquery-2.0.2.js" type="text/javascript"></script>
    <script src="jquery-ui-1.10.3.custom.js" type="text/javascript"></script>
    <link rel="stylesheet" type="text/css" href="jquery-ui-1.10.3.custom.css"/>
    <style type="text/css">
        button {margin-bottom: 5px}
    </style>
    <script type="text/javascript">
        $(document).ready(function () {
            $("#acInput").autocomplete({
                source: function (request, response) {
                    $.getJSON("http://node.jacquisflowershop.com/auto",
                        function(flowers) {
                            var term = request.term;
                            var pattern = new RegExp("^" + term, "i");

                            var results = $.map(flowers, function (elem) {
                                if (pattern.test(elem)) {
                                    return elem;
                                }
                            })
                            response(results);
                        });
                }
            })
        });
    </script>
</head>
<body>
    <form>
        <div class="ui-widget">
            <label for="acInput">Flower Name: </label><input id="acInput"/>
        </div>

    </form>
</body>
</html>
```

In this example, I use the getJSON method to get the complete set of flower values from the Node.js server. I search for matches locally and call the response function when I have a set of suggestions to present to jQuery UI.

Positioning the Pop-up

By default, the pop-up that allows the user to select a value will appear beneath the input element, but you can change this by setting the position property—although the syntax for doing so is a little awkward. Listing 19-8 shows an example that changes the position.

Listing 19-8. Changing the Position of the Pop-up

```
<!DOCTYPE html>
<html>
<head>
    <title>Example</title>
    <script src="jquery-2.0.2.js" type="text/javascript"></script>
    <script src="jquery-ui-1.10.3.custom.js" type="text/javascript"></script>
    <link rel="stylesheet" type="text/css" href="jquery-ui-1.10.3.custom.css"/>
    <style>
        #target { margin-top: 40px; display:inline-block }
    </style>
    <script type="text/javascript">
        $(document).ready(function () {

            var flowers = [{ label: "Aster (Purple)", value: "Aster" },
                { label: "Daffodil (White)", value: "Daffodil" },
                { label: "Rose (Pink)", value: "Rose" },
                { label: "Peony (Pink)", value: "Peony" }]

            $("#acInput").autocomplete({
                source: flowers,
                position: {
                    my: "left top",
                    at: "right bottom+20",
                    of: "#target",
                    collision: "fit"
                }
            })

        });
    </script>
</head>
<body>
    <form>
        <div class="ui-widget">
            <label for="acInput">Flower Name: </label><input id="acInput"/>
        </div>
    </form>
    <span id="target">Target</span>
</body>
</html>
```

The `position` property is configured with an object that specifies properties for different aspects of the policy for placing the pop-up and I have described the four properties I used in the listing in Table 19-3.

Table 19-3. *Autocomplete Position Properties*

Name	Description
my	Specifies the part of the pop-up that will be used to determine placement (see below for details of the range of values that can be used)
at	Specifies the part of the target element that the pop-up will be positioned relative to (see below for details of the range of values that can be used)
of	Specifies the target element that the pop-up will be positioned relative to; this is the input element if omitted, but can be specified as an HTMLElement, a selector, or a jQuery object
collision	Specifies how the placement of the pop-up should be adjusted if it overflows the window (Table 19-4 shows the values for this property)

Table 19-4. *Autocomplete Position Properties*

Name	Description
flip	jQuery UI checks to see if more of the pop-up can be displayed on the opposite side of the element specified by the of property; the side that will display the greatest amount of the pop-up will be selected
fit	jQuery UI moves the pop-up away from the edge of the window
flipfit	Combines the behavior of both the flip and fit values
none	Tells jQuery UI not to adjust the position of the pop-up

■ **Tip** The autocomplete pop-up is placed using the jQuery UI *position* utility feature, which has more configuration options than the ones I use in this chapter. See `http://api.jqueryui.com/position` for further details.

The `my` and `at` properties are set using values that specify horizontal and vertical positions, separated by a space. The horizontal values are `left`, `right`, and `center` and the vertical values are `top`, `bottom`, and `center`. You can also specify offsets from a position, either as a percentage or as a number of pixels. In the listing, you can see that I have set the `my`, `at`, and `of` properties as follows:

```
...
my: "left top",
at: "right bottom+20",
of: "#target",
...
```

This combination means the following: position the top-left corner of the autocomplete pop-up against the point which is 20 pixels below the bottom-right corner of the element whose id is `target`. You would not commonly specify an element using the `of` property because it breaks the visual association between the pop-up menu and the `input` element, but I wanted to demonstrate that there is a lot of flexibility in how the pop-up is placed and you can see the effect of these configuration properties in Figure 19-4.

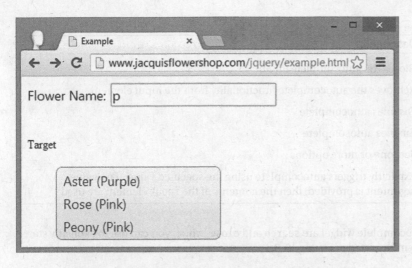

Figure 19-4. *Configuring the placement of the autocomplete pop-up*

The collision property specifies what happens if the pop-up won't fit in the space available. Table 19-4 describes the supported values for this property.

I selected the fit value for the collision property and this means that jQuery UI will move the pop-up to fit it inside the browser window, as shown in Figure 19-5.

Figure 19-5. *Moving the autocomplete pop-up to accommodate the edge of the browser window*

Using the Autocomplete Methods

The jQuery UI autocomplete feature supports a number of methods that you can use to manipulate the autocomplete process. Table 19-5 describes these methods.

Table 19-5. *Autocomplete Methods*

Method	Description
autocomplete("close")	Closes the autocomplete menu
autocomplete("destroy")	Removes the autocomplete functionality from the input element
autocomplete("disable")	Disables autocomplete
autocomplete("enable")	Enables autocomplete
autocomplete("option")	Sets one or more options
autocomplete("search", value)	Explicitly triggers autocomplete using the specified value; if no value argument is provided, then the contents of the input element are used

The two methods unique to the autocomplete widget are search and close, which you can use to explicitly start and end the autocomplete process, as demonstrated in Listing 19-9.

Listing 19-9. Using the search and close Methods

```
<!DOCTYPE html>
<html>
<head>
    <title>Example</title>
    <script src="jquery-2.0.2.js" type="text/javascript"></script>
    <script src="jquery-ui-1.10.3.custom.js" type="text/javascript"></script>
    <link rel="stylesheet" type="text/css" href="jquery-ui-1.10.3.custom.css"/>
    <style type="text/css">
        button {margin-bottom: 5px}
    </style>
    <script type="text/javascript">
        $(document).ready(function() {

            var flowers = ["Aster", "Daffodil", "Rose", "Peony", "Primula", "Snowdrop",
                           "Poppy", "Primrose", "Petuna", "Pansy"];

        $("#acInput").autocomplete({
            source: flowers
        });

        $("button").click(function(e) {
            e.preventDefault();
            switch (this.id) {
                case "close":
                    $("#acInput").autocomplete("close");
                    break;
                case "input":
                    $("#acInput").autocomplete("search");
                    break;
```

```
                    default:
                        $("#acInput").autocomplete("search", this.id);
                        break;
                }
            });
        });
    </script>
</head>
<body>
    <form>
        <button id="s">S</button>
        <button id="p">P</button>
        <button id="input">Input Content</button>
        <button id="close">Close</button>
        <div class="ui-widget">
            <label for="acInput">Flower Name: </label><input id="acInput"/>
        </div>
    </form>
</body>
</html>
```

I added button elements and used the jQuery click method to set up different autocomplete method calls. When the buttons marked *S* or *P* are pressed, I call the search method, passing in the selected letter as the search value. This triggers the autocomplete feature using the selected letter, irrespective of the contents of the input element, as shown in Figure 19-6.

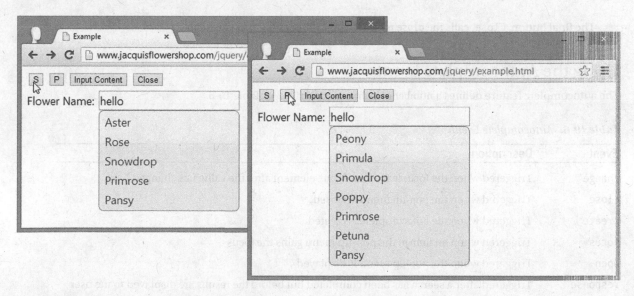

Figure 19-6. *Using the search method with a search term*

As you can see in the figure, the pop-up menu displays the entries that contain the letter from the button even though the input element contains the word hello.

The Input Content button triggers the autocomplete feature using whatever characters are contained in the input element, as shown in Figure 19-7.

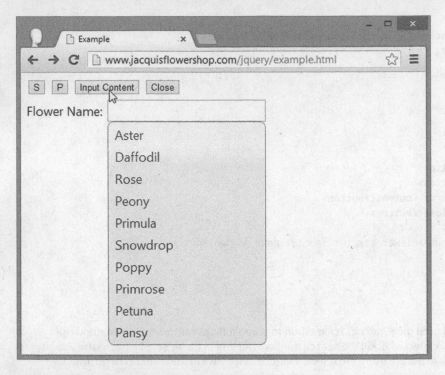

Figure 19-7. Searching using the contents of the input element

The final button, Close, calls the close method that dismisses the pop-up menu.

Using the Autocomplete Events

The autocomplete feature defines a number of events, as described in Table 19-6.

Table 19-6. Autocomplete Events

Event	Description
change	Triggered when the focus leaves the input element after the value has changed
close	Triggered when the pop-up menu is closed
create	Triggered when the autocomplete is created
focus	Triggered when an item in the pop-up menu gains the focus
open	Triggered when the pop-up menu is displayed
response	Triggered after a search has been completed but before the results are displayed to the user
search	Triggered before the list of autocomplete items is generated or requested
select	Triggered when an item is selected from the menu

Getting Details of the Selected Item

jQuery UI provides additional information about an event through a second argument, typically called ui. For the change, focus, and select events, jQuery UI gives the ui object an item property that returns an object describing the selected or focused item from the pop-up menu. Listing 19-10 shows how you can use this feature to get information about the item.

Listing 19-10. Using the ui Object in Event Handlers

```html
<!DOCTYPE html>
<html>
<head>
    <title>Example</title>
    <script src="jquery-2.0.2.js" type="text/javascript"></script>
    <script src="jquery-ui-1.10.3.custom.js" type="text/javascript"></script>
    <link rel="stylesheet" type="text/css" href="jquery-ui-1.10.3.custom.css"/>
    <script type="text/javascript">
        $(document).ready(function() {

            var flowers = ["Aster", "Daffodil", "Rose", "Peony", "Primula", "Snowdrop",
                            "Poppy", "Primrose", "Petuna", "Pansy"];

            $("#acInput").autocomplete({
                source: flowers,
                focus: displayItem,
                select: displayItem,
                change: displayItem
            })

            function displayItem(event, ui) {
                $("#itemLabel").text(ui.item.label)
            }
        });
    </script>
</head>
<body>
    <form>
        <div class="ui-widget">
            <label for="acInput">Flower Name: </label><input id="acInput"/>
            Item Label: <span id="itemLabel"></span>
        </div>
    </form>
</body>
</html>
```

I have added a span element that I use to display the label property of the selected object. jQuery UI creates objects with label and value properties even when you use a simple string array for the source setting, so you always need to read one of these properties from the ui.item object. In this example, I use the same function to display the item from the focus, select, and change events. You can see the effect in Figure 19-8.

Figure 19-8. *Getting the details of the selected item*

Modifying Search Results

The response event provides an opportunity to modify the results before they are shown to the user. In Listing 19-11, you can see how I handle the response event to prevent the Peony value from being shown.

Listing 19-11. Handling the response Event

```
<!DOCTYPE html>
<html>
<head>
    <title>Example</title>
    <script src="jquery-2.0.2.js" type="text/javascript"></script>
    <script src="jquery-ui-1.10.3.custom.js" type="text/javascript"></script>
    <link rel="stylesheet" type="text/css" href="jquery-ui-1.10.3.custom.css"/>
    <script type="text/javascript">
        $(document).ready(function () {

            var flowers = ["Aster", "Daffodil", "Rose", "Peony", "Primula", "Snowdrop",
                           "Poppy", "Primrose", "Petuna", "Pansy"];

            $("#acInput").autocomplete({
                source: flowers,
                response: filterResults
            });

            function filterResults(event, ui) {
                for (var i = 0; i < ui.content.length; i++) {
                    if (ui.content[i].label == "Peony") {
                        ui.content.splice(i, 1);
                    }
                }
            }
        });
    </script>
</head>
```

```
<body>
    <form>
        <div class="ui-widget">
            <label for="acInput">Flower Name: </label><input id="acInput"/>
        </div>
    </form>
</body>
</html>
```

I have defined a function called `filterResults` to handle the `response` event. Within the function, I enumerate the results that will be presented to the user, which are available as an array accessed through the `ui.content` property. The handler function for the `response` event must modify the array directly and so I use the `splice` method to remove the Peony entry from the `ui.content` array.

Overriding the Default Select Action

The `select` event has a default action, which is to replace the contents of the `input` element with the contents of the value property of the item selected from the pop-up menu. This is exactly what is required most of the time, but this event can be used to supplement the default action or prevent it and do something entirely different. Listing 19-12 contains an example of supplementing the default by setting the value of a related field.

Listing 19-12. Overriding the Default Action of the select Event

```
<!DOCTYPE html>
<html>
<head>
    <title>Example</title>
    <script src="jquery-2.0.2.js" type="text/javascript"></script>
    <script src="jquery-ui-1.10.3.custom.js" type="text/javascript"></script>
    <link rel="stylesheet" type="text/css" href="jquery-ui-1.10.3.custom.css"/>
    <script type="text/javascript">
        $(document).ready(function() {

            var flowers = ["Aster", "Daffodil", "Rose"];

            var skus = { Aster: 100, Daffodil: 101, Rose: 102};

            $("#acInput").autocomplete({
                source: flowers,
                select: function(event, ui) {
                    $("#sku").val(skus[ui.item.value]);
                }
            })
        });
    </script>
</head>
<body>
    <form>
        <div class="ui-widget">
            <label for="acInput">Flower Name: </label><input id="acInput"/>
```

```
            <label for="sku">Stock Keeping Unit: </label><input id="sku"/>
        </div>
    </form>
</body>
</html>
```

■ **Tip**   I described default actions for events in Chapter 9.

When the `select` event is triggered, my handler function uses the `ui` argument to get the value of the selected item and set the value of a related field—in this case, the stock keeping unit, which is obtained from the `skus` object. In this way, I can help the user by providing default values for other fields based on the initial selection. This can be helpful in lots of situations, especially when selecting items such as shipping addresses. You can see the result in Figure 19-9, although this is an example where you should load a browser to get the full effect. The HTML for this document and all of the other examples in this book are freely available in the Source Code/Download area of the Apress web site (`www.apress.com`).

Figure 19-9. *Using the select event to populate another field*

Using the jQuery UI Accordion

The accordion widget takes a set of content elements and presents them so that at most one is visible to the user. The visible content is hidden when the user selects another, creating an effect that is reminiscent of the bellows in the musical instrument of the same name.

Accordions are great for presenting content that can be broken into discrete sections when you don't want to overwhelm the user by displaying it all at once. Ideally, the individual content sections share some overarching theme that can be expressed using simple headers.

Creating the Accordion

The jQuery UI accordion widget is applied using the `accordion` method, as shown in Listing 19-13.

Listing 19-13. Creating an Accordion

```
<!DOCTYPE html>
<html>
<head>
    <title>Example</title>
    <script src="jquery-2.0.2.js" type="text/javascript"></script>
    <script src="handlebars.js"></script>
```

```
<script src="handlebars-jquery.js"></script>
<script src="jquery-ui-1.10.3.custom.js" type="text/javascript"></script>
<link rel="stylesheet" type="text/css" href="jquery-ui-1.10.3.custom.css"/>
<link rel="stylesheet" type="text/css" href="styles.css"/>
<style type="text/css">
    #accordion {margin: 5px}
    .dcell img {height: 60px}
</style>
<script id="flowerTmpl" type="text/x-jquery-tmpl">
    {{#flowers}}
    <div class="dcell">
        <img src="{{product}}.png"/>
        <label for="{{product}}">{{name}}:</label>
        <input name="{{product}}" value="0" />
    </div>
    {{/flowers}}
</script>
<script type="text/javascript">
    $(document).ready(function () {
        var data = {
            flowers: [{ "name": "Aster", "product": "aster" },
            { "name": "Daffodil", "product": "daffodil" },
            { "name": "Rose", "product": "rose" },
            { "name": "Peony", "product": "peony" },
            { "name": "Primula", "product": "primula" },
            { "name": "Snowdrop", "product": "snowdrop" },
            { "name": "Carnation", "product": "carnation" },
            { "name": "Lily", "product": "lily" },
            { "name": "Orchid", "product": "orchid" }]
        };

        var elems = $("#flowerTmpl").template(data).filter("*");
        elems.slice(0, 3).appendTo("#row1");
        elems.slice(3, 6).appendTo("#row2");
        elems.slice(6).appendTo("#row3");

        $("#accordion").accordion();

        $("button").button();
    });
</script>
</head>
<body>
    <h1>Jacqui's Flower Shop</h1>
    <form method="post" action="http://node.jacquisflowershop.com/order">
        <div id="accordion">
            <h2><a href="#">Row 1</a></h2>
            <div id="row1"></div>
            <h2><a href="#">Row 2</a></h2>
            <div id="row2"></div>
```

```
        <h2><a href="#">Row 3</a></h2>
        <div id="row3"></div>
    </div>
    <div id="buttonDiv"><button type="submit">Place Order</button></div>
</form>
</body>
</html>
```

The most important part of this example is the content of the div element whose id is accordion.

```
...
<div id="accordion">
    <h2><a href="#">Row 1</a></h2>
    <div id="row1"></div>

    <h2><a href="#">Row 2</a></h2>
    <div id="row2"></div>

    <h2><a href="#">Row 3</a></h2>
    <div id="row3"></div>
</div>
...
```

I have changed the formatting to make the structure more obvious. The top-level div element is the one that is targeted with the accordion method. jQuery UI looks at the contents of the div for header elements (the h1 to h6 elements) and breaks up the content so that each header is associated with the element that follows it. In this case, I have used h2 elements as headers, each of which is followed by a div element. I use data templates to populate these div elements with details of the products offered by the flower shop.

Notice that I have added an a element within each h2 element. This is the means by which the title for each content section is specified. You can see how jQuery UI transforms the top-level div element and its contents in Figure 19-10.

Figure 19-10. *A jQuery UI accordion*

■ **Tip** Setting the href attribute to # is a common technique when defining a elements that are going to be used solely for JavaScript. I have used this approach because it makes the example simpler, but I generally recommend using jQuery to insert the a elements dynamically so that they don't interfere with non-JavaScript users.

When the accordion is created, the first content section is displayed while the others are hidden. The content of the a elements are used as the labels for each section, and clicking a label closes the current section and opens the selected one (there is a nice animation effect during the transition that I can't show using screenshots). You can see the effect of clicking the headers in Figure 19-11.

Figure 19-11. The accordion transitions

Configuring the Accordion

The accordion supports a number of configuration settings that can be used to fine-tune its behavior. Table 19-7 describes these settings, and I show you how to use these settings to configure the widget in the sections that follow.

Table 19-7. Accordion Settings

Setting	Description
active	Gets or sets the content element to be displayed. The default is to initially display the first content element.
animate	Specifies the animation that will be used during the transition from one content element to another. See Chapter 35 for details of the jQuery UI animations.
collapsible	When true, all of the content sections can be collapsed. The default is false.
disabled	When true, the accordion is disabled. The default is false.
event	Specifies the event from the header element that triggers the transition to another content element. The default is click.
header	Specifies which elements will be used as headers.
heightStyle	Controls the height of the accordion and its panels.
icons	Specifies the icons used in the accordion.

■ **Tip**   In jQuery UI 1.10, the animate setting replaces the animated setting; the heightStyle option replaces the autoHeight, clearStyle, and fillSpace settings; and a new property name is used to specify the icons used for the selected content panels (activeHeader) when using the icons property.

Setting the Height of the Accordion

The heightStyle property controls the height of the accordion and its panels. There are three supported values, which I have described in Table 19-8.

Table 19-8. *The Values for the heightStyle*

Name	Description
auto	All of the panels will be set to the height of the tallest panel
fill	Expands the accordion to fill the parent element's height
content	Each panel will be as high as its content

You can set the height of the accordion based on either the height of the content elements or the height of the parent element. The most common technique is to rely on the auto value, which is the default, and which sets all of the content elements to be the same height (the height of the tallest content element) and sizes the accordion based on that height.

This is the approach I used in the previous example, although some caution is required when using content elements that contain images, especially when the img elements are inserted into the document using jQuery. The problem is that the call to the accordion method can be made before all of the images are loaded, which causes jQuery UI to get misleading information from the browser about the height of the content elements. In my example document, the height of the content div elements is 55 pixels before the images are loaded and 79 pixels when they are loaded. You can tell whether you have hit this problem when the accordion shows unexpected scrollbars to display the content, as shown in Figure 19-12.

Figure 19-12. *Problems caused by incorrect height information*

515

jQuery UI doesn't detect the change in the content element's height when the images are loaded and ends up displaying the content incorrectly. To address this, you need to provide information about the height that the content elements will be once you load all of the external resources. There are lots of ways of doing this, and in the example, I chose to set the CSS height property for the img elements in a style element, as follows:

```
...
<style type="text/css">
    #accordion {margin: 5px}
    .dcell img {height: 60px}
</style>
...
```

Image issues aside, the auto value is useful when you want consistent heights for each of the content elements, but it can lead to some unappealing visuals when there is a large disparity between the sizes of the content elements. Listing 19-14 shows a script element that inserts the product information elements in a different way.

Listing 19-14. An Accordion with a Large Height Differential

```
...
<script type="text/javascript">
    $(document).ready(function () {

        var data = {
            flowers: [{ "name": "Aster", "product": "aster" },
            { "name": "Daffodil", "product": "daffodil" },
            { "name": "Rose", "product": "rose" },
            { "name": "Peony", "product": "peony" },
            { "name": "Primula", "product": "primula" },
            { "name": "Snowdrop", "product": "snowdrop" },
            { "name": "Carnation", "product": "carnation" },
            { "name": "Lily", "product": "lily" },
            { "name": "Orchid", "product": "orchid" }]
        };

        var elems = $("#flowerTmpl").template(data).filter("*");
        elems.slice(0, 3).appendTo("#row1");
        elems.slice(3, 6).appendTo("#row2");
        elems.slice(6).appendTo("#row3");

        $("<h2><a href=#>All</a></h2><div id=row0></div>").prependTo("#accordion")
            .filter("div").append($("#row1, #row2, #row3").clone());

        $("#accordion").accordion();

        $("button").button();
    });
</script>
...
```

To create an extra-high content element, I have used jQuery to clone the existing content `div` elements and insert them into a new content element, creating a panel that displays all of the products. This new panel is three times the height of the others, which causes the accordion to display a lot of empty space when the smaller content elements are displayed, as shown in Figure 19-13.

Figure 19-13. *The effect of the auto setting with a large height difference*

If a large expanse of empty space doesn't suit your application, then you can simple change the `heightStyle` property to `content`, as shown in Listing 19-15.

Listing 19-15. Changing the heightStyle Setting

```
...
$("#accordion").accordion({
    heightStyle: "content"
});
...
```

The accordion will now change its height as part of the transition between content elements, as shown in Figure 19-14.

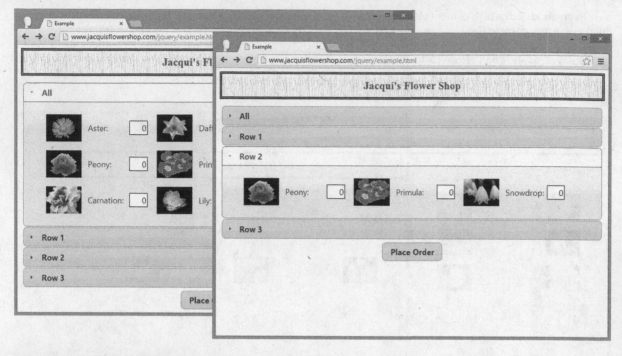

Figure 19-14. *The accordion resizing itself to accomodate different content heights*

This is a neater approach to displaying the content, but it does mean that the layout of the page changes as the accordion resizes itself. This can be annoying to users if key controls are constantly moving around the screen.

Using the Parent to Determine the Height of the Accordion

An entirely different approach is to set the size of the accordion so that it simply fills its parent element. I find this most useful when I am working with content that is generated dynamically such that I don't have a good handle on the size and I don't want the layout to be adjusted. You can size the accordion this way through the fill setting, as shown in Listing 19-16.

Listing 19-16. Sizing the Accordion to Fill the Parent Element

```
...
<script type="text/javascript">
    $(document).ready(function () {

        var data = {
            flowers: [{ "name": "Aster", "product": "aster" },
            { "name": "Daffodil", "product": "daffodil" },
            { "name": "Rose", "product": "rose" },
            { "name": "Peony", "product": "peony" },
            { "name": "Primula", "product": "primula" },
            { "name": "Snowdrop", "product": "snowdrop" },
            { "name": "Carnation", "product": "carnation" },
            { "name": "Lily", "product": "lily" },
            { "name": "Orchid", "product": "orchid" }]
        };
```

```
        var elems = $("#flowerTmpl").template(data).filter("*");
        elems.slice(0, 3).appendTo("#row1");
        elems.slice(3, 6).appendTo("#row2");
        elems.slice(6).appendTo("#row3");

        $("<h2><a href=#>All</a></h2><div id=row0></div>").prependTo("#accordion")
            .filter("div").append($("#row1, #row2, #row3").clone());

        $("#accordion").wrap("<div style='height:300px'></div>");

        $("#accordion").accordion({
            heightStyle: "fill"
        });

        $("button").button();
    });
</script>
...
```

In this example, I have wrapped the accordion element in a new parent div element that has a fixed size of 300 pixels. When I call the accordion method, I set heightStyle to fill. If the parent is smaller than a content element, then the accordion adds a scrollbar. If the parent is larger than a content element, then padding is added. You can see the application of the scrollbar in Figure 19-15. This arises because the content element that displays all of the flowers is taller than the 300 pixels of the parent element.

Figure 19-15. *Using the accordion to fill the height of the parent*

Changing the Event Type

By default, the user opens and closes content elements by clicking them. You can change this behavior through the event setting, as shown in Listing 19-17.

Listing 19-17. Using the event Setting

```
...
<script type="text/javascript">
    $(document).ready(function () {

        var data = {
            flowers: [{ "name": "Aster", "product": "aster" },
            { "name": "Daffodil", "product": "daffodil" },
            { "name": "Rose", "product": "rose" },
            { "name": "Peony", "product": "peony" },
            { "name": "Primula", "product": "primula" },
            { "name": "Snowdrop", "product": "snowdrop" },
            { "name": "Carnation", "product": "carnation" },
            { "name": "Lily", "product": "lily" },
            { "name": "Orchid", "product": "orchid" }]
        };

        var elems = $("#flowerTmpl").template(data).filter("*");
        elems.slice(0, 3).appendTo("#row1");
        elems.slice(3, 6).appendTo("#row2");
        elems.slice(6).appendTo("#row3");

        $("#accordion").accordion({
            event: "mouseover"
        });

        $("button").button();
    });
</script>
...
```

In Listing 19-17, I have used the event setting to specify that content elements should be opened in response to the mouseover event (which I described in Chapter 9). The effect of this change is that as soon as the mouse pointer enters the label for a content element, jQuery UI opens the element and displays its content. I can't show this effect in a screenshot, but I recommend you load this example to see how it works. It is a neat feature, but I recommend that you use it carefully. Users are generally quick to grasp the idea of clicking the icon to open a section of content, but responding to mouse events can make for a twitchy and surprising user experience.

Selecting the Active Header

The default behavior of the accordion is initially to show the first content element to the user. You can change this behavior using the active property. You set active to the index of the content element you want to display as shown in Listing 19-18.

Listing 19-18. Using the Active Property

```
...
<script type="text/javascript">
    $(document).ready(function () {

        var data = {
            flowers: [{ "name": "Aster", "product": "aster" },
            { "name": "Daffodil", "product": "daffodil" },
            { "name": "Rose", "product": "rose" },
            { "name": "Peony", "product": "peony" },
            { "name": "Primula", "product": "primula" },
            { "name": "Snowdrop", "product": "snowdrop" },
            { "name": "Carnation", "product": "carnation" },
            { "name": "Lily", "product": "lily" },
            { "name": "Orchid", "product": "orchid" }]
        };

        var elems = $("#flowerTmpl").template(data).filter("*");
        elems.slice(0, 3).appendTo("#row1");
        elems.slice(3, 6).appendTo("#row2");
        elems.slice(6).appendTo("#row3");

        $("#accordion").accordion({
            active: 1
        });

        $("button").button();
    });
</script>
...
```

The effect is that the accordion opens the row at index 1 (the indexes are zero based, so this is the second content element) initially, as shown in Figure 19-16.

521

Figure 19-16. *Selecting the initial content element to display*

You can also have no content initially active by setting `active` to `false`. If you do this, you must also set the collapsible setting to `true`. This disables the default policy that one content element must always be visible. Listing 19-19 shows the application of these settings.

Listing 19-19. Disabling the Initially Active Content Element

```
...
$("#accordion").accordion({
    active: false,
    collapsible: true
});
...
```

You can see the effect of these settings in Figure 19-17.

Figure 19-17. *The accordion with no initially active content element*

The accordion works as before, with the exception that there is no initially active content element and that all of the content elements can be closed. This is a useful technique when screen estate is limited and the content in the accordion is not of primary interest to the user.

Changing the Accordion Icons

You can use the icons setting to change the icons used in the accordion content headers. Listing 19-20 provides an example.

Listing 19-20. Changing the Icons Used by the Accordion

```
...
$("#accordion").accordion({
    collapsible: true,
    icons: {
        header: "ui-icon-zoomin",
        activeHeader: "ui-icon-zoomout"
    }
});
...
```

■ **Tip** In jQuery UI 1.10, the activeHeader property replaced the headerSelected property.

You set icons to be an object that has header and activeHeader properties. The first property specifies the icon to use when the content element is closed, and the second specifies the icon to use when it is open. I tend to use this feature in conjunction with the collapsible setting because it gives a more natural feel when using icons that suggest that user can perform an action. You can see how these icons appear in Figure 19-18.

Figure 19-18. *Using custom icons for the accordion section headers*

Using the Accordion Methods

The jQuery UI accordion defines a number of methods, as described in Table 19-9.

Table 19-9. *Accordion Methods*

Method	Description
accordion("destroy")	Removes the accordion functionality from the input element
accordion("disable")	Disables the accordion
accordion("enable")	Enables the accordion
accordion("option")	Sets one or more options
accordion("refresh")	Refreshes the size of the widget panels.

■ **Tip** The activate method was removed in jQuery UI 1.10. Use the active option I described in the previous section instead. The resize method has been replaced with the refresh method.

The refresh method updates the sizes of the accordion panels to reflect changes in the content elements. The effect of size changes depends on the value used for the heightStyle option I described in the previous section. The other methods are those which jQuery UI provides for all elements.

■ **Tip** As of jQuery UI 1.10, calling the refresh method will also update the set of panels to reflect changes in the content elements, allowing elements to be added or removed.

Using the Accordion Events

The jQuery UI accordion widget supports the three events shown in Table 19-10.

Table 19-10. *Accordion Events*

Event	Description
activate	Triggered when a content panel is activated
beforeActivate	Triggered just before a content panel is activated
create	Triggered when the accordion is created

■ **Tip** The events defined by the accordion widget have changed in jQuery UI 1.10. The changestart event has been replaced by beforeActivate and the change event has been replaced with activate. The additional ui object passed to handler functions for these events use different property names from the old events, as described in Table 19-11.

Table 19-11. *The Properties of the ui Object for the change and changestart Events*

Name	Description
newHeader	The header element for the newly active content element
oldHeader	The header element for the previously active content element
newPanel	The newly active content element
oldPanel	The previously active content element

You can use the beforeActivate and active events to monitor the transition between content elements, as shown in Listing 19-21.

Listing 19-21. Using the change Event

```
...
<script type="text/javascript">
    $(document).ready(function () {

        var data = {
            flowers: [{ "name": "Aster", "product": "aster" },
            { "name": "Daffodil", "product": "daffodil" },
            { "name": "Rose", "product": "rose" },
            { "name": "Peony", "product": "peony" },
            { "name": "Primula", "product": "primula" },
            { "name": "Snowdrop", "product": "snowdrop" },
            { "name": "Carnation", "product": "carnation" },
            { "name": "Lily", "product": "lily" },
            { "name": "Orchid", "product": "orchid" }]
        };
```

```
        var elems = $("#flowerTmpl").template(data).filter("*");
        elems.slice(0, 3).appendTo("#row1");
        elems.slice(3, 6).appendTo("#row2");
        elems.slice(6).appendTo("#row3");

        $("#accordion").accordion({
            active: false,
            collapsible: true,
            activate: handleAccordionChange
        })

        function handleAccordionChange(event, ui) {
            if (ui.oldHeader.length) {
                console.log("Old header: " + ui.oldHeader[0].innerText);
            }
            if (ui.newHeader.length) {
                console.log("New header: " + ui.newHeader[0].innerText);
            }
        }

        $("button").button();
    });
</script>
...
```

I use the `activate` event to respond to the content element being changed. jQuery UI passes information to the event handler function about the active elements via an additional argument to the handler function, just as for the autocomplete widget. This additional argument, usually given the name `ui`, defines the properties shown in Table 19-11.

These properties are arrays, which is why I test for the `length` property before getting the `HTMLElement` object at the first index and writing the value of the `innerText` property to the console.

Summary

In this chapter, I showed you the jQuery UI autocomplete and accordion widgets. These follow the same basic pattern I used in Chapter 18 but offer richer functionality and a wider range of configuration options to customize the widgets so that they fit neatly into your web application model. In Chapter 20, I show you the tabs widget.

CHAPTER 20

■ ■ ■

Using the Tabs Widget

The tabs widget is superficially similar to the accordion that I described in Chapter 19 but offers more functionality and opportunities for customization. In common with the earlier widget chapters, I start with details of how to create the widget and then show you the settings, methods, and events that the widgets support. I finish this chapter with an example of how you can use the tabs widget to present forms to users in sections, which is a useful technique for dealing with long forms that require a lot of data input. Table 20-1 provides the summary for this chapter.

Table 20-1. *Chapter Summary*

Problem	Solution	Listing
Create a tabs widget	Define a label and content element structure and call the tabs method	1
Get the content for a tab via Ajax	Set the href attribute for the tab a element to the HTML document that should be displayed in the content panel	2, 3
Get or set the active tab	Use the active setting	4
Disable individual tabs	Use the disabled setting	5
Change the event that activates a tab	Use the event setting	6
Allow all of the tabs to be deactivated	Use the collapsible setting	7
Add or remove tabs	Change the underlying HTML elements and then call the refresh method	8
Force remote content to be loaded	Use the load method	9
Configure Ajax requests before they are made and modify the remote content when it is loaded	Handle the beforeLoad and load events	10, 11
Display a form across multiple tabs	Partition the form using div elements, add a label structure, and call the tabs method	12–14
Validate the content of a form displayed in multiple tabs	Handle the beforeActivate and activate events	15

JQUERY UI CHANGES SINCE THE LAST EDITION

The tabs widget underwent a significant API change in jQuery UI 1.10. There are fewer methods and configuration options and, in keeping with changes to other widgets, there is more reliance on directly manipulating the elements to which the widget has been applied when making changes.

The following options have been removed: fx, ajaxOptions, cache, spinner, selected, idPrefix, tabTemplate, panelTemplate, and cookie. The following methods have been removed: url, abort, select, add, remove, and length. The set of events that the tabs widget defines has been simplified. See the section "Using the Tabs Events" for details of the new events.

The changes may seem drastic, but the result is a widget which is simpler and easier to work with. All of the functionality provided by the methods and options remains available by using jQuery to manipulate the underlying HTML elements and then using the new refresh method to update the state of the widget, as demonstrated by the listings in this chapter.

Creating the Tabs

You create jQuery UI tabs using the tabs method. As with the accordion widget, the tab widget requires a specific HTML element structure to work, as shown in Listing 20-1.

Listing 20-1. Creating jQuery UI Tabs

```
<!DOCTYPE html>
<html>
<head>
    <title>Example</title>
    <script src="jquery-2.0.2.js" type="text/javascript"></script>
    <script src="handlebars.js"></script>
    <script src="handlebars-jquery.js"></script>
    <script src="jquery-ui-1.10.3.custom.js" type="text/javascript"></script>
    <link rel="stylesheet" type="text/css" href="jquery-ui-1.10.3.custom.css"/>
    <link rel="stylesheet" type="text/css" href="styles.css"/>
    <script id="flowerTmpl" type="text/x-jquery-tmpl">
        {{#flowers}}
        <div class="dcell">
            <img src="{{product}}.png"/>
            <label for="{{product}}">{{name}}:</label>
            <input name="{{product}}" value="0" />
        </div>
        {{/flowers}}
    </script>
    <script type="text/javascript">
        $(document).ready(function () {
            var data = {
                flowers: [{ "name": "Aster", "product": "aster" },
                { "name": "Daffodil", "product": "daffodil" },
                { "name": "Rose", "product": "rose" },
                { "name": "Peony", "product": "peony" },
```

```
                { "name": "Primula", "product": "primula" },
                { "name": "Snowdrop", "product": "snowdrop" },
                { "name": "Carnation", "product": "carnation" },
                { "name": "Lily", "product": "lily" },
                { "name": "Orchid", "product": "orchid" }]
        };

        var elems = $("#flowerTmpl").template(data).filter("*");
        elems.slice(0, 3).appendTo("#tab1");
        elems.slice(3, 6).appendTo("#tab2");
        elems.slice(6).appendTo("#tab3");

        $("#tabs").tabs();
        $("button").button();
    });
    </script>
</head>
<body>
    <h1>Jacqui's Flower Shop</h1>
    <form method="post" action="http://node.jacquisflowershop.com/order">
        <div id="tabs">
            <ul>
                <li><a href="#tab1">Row 1</a>
                <li><a href="#tab2">Row 2</a>
                <li><a href="#tab3">Row 3</a>
            </ul>
            <div id="tab1"></div>
            <div id="tab2"></div>
            <div id="tab3"></div>
        </div>
        <div id="buttonDiv"><button type="submit">Place Order</button></div>
    </form>
</body>
</html>
```

The element that the `tabs` method is applied to must contain two kinds of element. The first is the *content elements*, which are those elements whose contents should appear inside the tabs. The second kind of element is the *structure elements*, which give the jQuery UI tab widget the information it needs to create the tab structure.

I use `div` elements to provide the structure. In the following example, I have used three `div` elements, each of which will hold one row of flower product information, just as in earlier examples:

```
...
<div id="tab1"></div>
<div id="tab2"></div>
<div id="tab3"></div>
...
```

It is important that each content element has an `id` attribute so that the jQuery UI tab widget can find the right element to display. For the structure, I use `li` elements, each of which contains an a element, as follows:

```
...
<ul>
    <li><a href="#tab1">Row 1</a>
    <li><a href="#tab2">Row 2</a>
    <li><a href="#tab3">Row 3</a>
</ul>
...
```

The number of `li` items defines the number of tabs. The content of the a element is used as the tab label, and the `href` attribute specifies which content element the tab relates to.

■ **Tip**   I used data templates to generate the tab content dynamically because it lets me show the required structure more clearly. The content can be defined statically or, as I explain in the next section, obtained dynamically from the server.

You can see how the structure in the example is transformed into a set of tabs in Figure 20-1.

Figure 20-1. *Creating jQuery UI tabs*

Tabs are a familiar user interface metaphor. Clicking a tab causes jQuery UI to display the corresponding content element. As with the accordion, the tabs widget lets you present a lot of content in a relatively compact manner, allowing the user to focus on what is important to him. This means you have to think carefully about how the tabs and their content relate to one another. The goal should be to group your content to minimize the amount of switching the user has to do between tabs to find what she is looking for, while preserving the natural grouping of the content elements. As with any user interface, this requires a solid understanding of the task that the user is performing and how her workflow (and not your systems) operates.

Getting Tab Content with Ajax

One of the nice features of the tab widget is the ability to obtain tab content via Ajax. To do this, you simply specify a URL as the `href` attribute for the appropriate a element. A tab that gets its content via Ajax is known as a *remote tab*. To demonstrate this feature, I have created an HTML document called `tabflowers.html`, the contents of which are shown in Listing 20-2.

Listing 20-2. The Contents of the tabflowers.html File

```
<div>
    <div class="dcell">
        <img src="aster.png"/><label for="aster">Aster:</label>
        <input name="aster" value="0" />
    </div>
    <div class="dcell">
        <img src="daffodil.png"/><label for="daffodil">Daffodil:</label>
        <input name="daffodil" value="0" />
    </div>
    <div class="dcell">
        <img src="rose.png"/><label for="rose">Rose:</label>
        <input name="rose" value="0" />
    </div>
</div>
<div>
    <div class="dcell">
        <img src="peony.png"/><label for="peony">Peony:</label>
        <input name="peony" value="0" />
    </div>
    <div class="dcell">
        <img src="primula.png"/><label for="primula">Primula:</label>
        <input name="primula" value="0" />
    </div>
    <div class="dcell">
        <img src="snowdrop.png"/><label for="snowdrop">Snowdrop:</label>
        <input name="snowdrop" value="0" />
    </div>
</div>
```

I have used the same structure and content as for the generated content elements in order to keep the example simple. Listing 20-3 shows how I can use the `tabflowers.html` file as the content for a tab.

Listing 20-3. Obtaining the Content of a Tab via Ajax

```
...
<body>
    <h1>Jacqui's Flower Shop</h1>
    <form method="post" action="http://node.jacquisflowershop.com/order">
        <div id="tabs">
            <ul>
                <li><a href="tabflowers.html">Ajax Content</a>
                <li><a href="#tab1">Row 1</a>
```

```
                <li><a href="#tab2">Row 2</a>
                <li><a href="#tab3">Row 3</a>
            </ul>
            <div id="tab1"></div>
            <div id="tab2"></div>
            <div id="tab3"></div>
        </div>
        <div id="buttonDiv"><button type="submit">Place Order</button></div>
    </form>
</body>
...
```

In Listing 20-2, I have added a new tab called Ajax Content and specified the URL of the content that should be loaded. You can see the effect in Figure 20-2.

Figure 20-2. *Getting the contents of a tab via Ajax*

■ **Tip** You don't need to create a content element for a remote tab. This is done for you automatically by the tabs widget.

Configuring the Tabs Widget

At first glance, the tabs widget may look like a vertical variation of the accordion widget that I showed you in Chapter 19. There are some common characteristics, but there is a wider set of configuration options and settings when you use tabs. Table 20-2 describes the settings that are supported by the jQuery UI tabs widget. In the sections that follow, I show you how to use these settings to configure the widget.

Table 20-2. *Tabs Settings*

Setting	Description
active	Gets or sets the currently displayed tab; individual panels are specified using a zero-based index and all panels can be closed by specifying false (but this only works if collapsible is set to true)
collapsible	When set to true, all of the tabs are closed
disabled	Used to enable/disable individual tabs
event	Used to set the event that triggers transition between tabs
heightStyle	Specifies how the height of the widget and its tabs is determined
hide	Specifies how tabs are animated when they are closed—I describe the jQuery UI animations in Chapter 35.
show	Specifies how tabs are animated when they are opened—I describe the jQuery UI animations in Chapter 35.

■ **Tip**   The set of configuration options for the tabs widget changed substantially in the jQuery UI 1.10 release. See the note at the start of this chapter for full details, but the new set of options—as shown in Table 20-2—are simpler and more consistent with those of the other jQuery UI widgets.

Selecting the Active Tab

The active setting provides support for determining and changing the tab that is currently shown, as demonstrated by Listing 20-4.

Listing 20-4. Using the active Option to Get and Set the Displayed Tab

```
<!DOCTYPE html>
<html>
<head>
    <title>Example</title>
    <script src="jquery-2.0.2.js" type="text/javascript"></script>
    <script src="handlebars.js"></script>
    <script src="handlebars-jquery.js"></script>
    <script src="jquery-ui-1.10.3.custom.js" type="text/javascript"></script>
    <link rel="stylesheet" type="text/css" href="jquery-ui-1.10.3.custom.css"/>
    <link rel="stylesheet" type="text/css" href="styles.css"/>
    <style>
        #radioDiv { text-align: center; margin-top: 10px;}
    </style>
```

```
<script id="flowerTmpl" type="text/x-jquery-tmpl">
    {{#flowers}}
    <div class="dcell">
        <img src="{{product}}.png"/>
        <label for="{{product}}">{{name}}:</label>
        <input name="{{product}}" value="0" />
    </div>
    {{/flowers}}
</script>
<script type="text/javascript">
    $(document).ready(function () {
        var data = {
            flowers: [{ "name": "Aster", "product": "aster" },
            { "name": "Daffodil", "product": "daffodil" },
            { "name": "Rose", "product": "rose" },
            { "name": "Peony", "product": "peony" },
            { "name": "Primula", "product": "primula" },
            { "name": "Snowdrop", "product": "snowdrop" },
            { "name": "Carnation", "product": "carnation" },
            { "name": "Lily", "product": "lily" },
            { "name": "Orchid", "product": "orchid" }]
        };

        var elems = $("#flowerTmpl").template(data).filter("*");
        elems.slice(0, 3).appendTo("#tab1");
        elems.slice(3, 6).appendTo("#tab2");
        elems.slice(6).appendTo("#tab3");

        $("#tabs").tabs();

        $("#radioDiv").buttonset().change(function (e) {
            $("#tabs").tabs("option", "active", e.target.value);
        });
    });
</script>
</head>
<body>
    <h1>Jacqui's Flower Shop</h1>
    <form method="post" action="http://node.jacquisflowershop.com/order">
        <div id="tabs">
            <ul>
                <li><a href="tabflowers.html">Ajax Content</a>
                <li><a href="#tab1">Row 1</a>
                <li><a href="#tab2">Row 2</a>
                <li><a href="#tab3">Row 3</a>
            </ul>
            <div id="tab1"></div>
            <div id="tab2"></div>
            <div id="tab3"></div>
        </div>
        <div id="radioDiv">
            <input type="radio" name="tabNo" id="one" value="1" />
```

```
            <label for="one">1</label>
        <input type="radio" name="tabNo" id="two" value="2"/>
            <label for="two">2</label>
        <input type="radio" name="tabNo" id="three" value="3"/>
            <label for="three">3</label>
    </div>
</form>
</body>
</html>
```

I have added a jQuery UI button set to the document, as described in Chapter 18. I use the jQuery change method to register a handler function that is called when one of the buttons in the set is clicked. The handler function uses the option method to set the active property, producing the effect shown in Figure 20-3.

Figure 20-3. *Using the active setting to change the active tab*

Disabling Individual Tabs

The disabled setting changes the state of the tabs widget if you use boolean values, but it can also be employed to enable and disable individual tabs by using an array of numbers. Listing 20-5 demonstrates.

Listing 20-5. Enabling and Disabling Individual Tabs

```
<!DOCTYPE html>
<html>
<head>
    <title>Example</title>
    <script src="jquery-2.0.2.js" type="text/javascript"></script>
    <script src="jquery-ui-1.10.3.custom.js" type="text/javascript"></script>
    <link rel="stylesheet" type="text/css" href="jquery-ui-1.10.3.custom.css"/>
    <link rel="stylesheet" type="text/css" href="styles.css"/>
    <style type="text/css">
        #buttonDiv {margin: 5px}
    </style>
```

```
<script type="text/javascript">
    $(document).ready(function () {

        $("#tabs").tabs();

        $("input:checkbox").button().click(function () {
            var disabledPositions = [];
            $("input:checked").each(function (index, elem) {
                disabledPositions.push(Number(elem.value));
            })

            $("#tabs").tabs("option", "disabled", disabledPositions)
        });
    });
</script>
</head>
<body>
    <h1>Jacqui's Flower Shop</h1>
    <form method="post" action="http://node.jacquisflowershop.com/order">
        <div id="tabs">
            <ul>
                <li><a href="#tab1">Tab 1</a>
                <li><a href="#tab2">Tab 2</a>
                <li><a href="#tab3">Tab 3</a>
            </ul>
            <div id="tab1">This is the content for tab 1</div>
            <div id="tab2">This is the content for tab 2</div>
            <div id="tab3">This is the content for tab 3</div>
        </div>
        <div id="buttonDiv">
            <label for="cb0">Tab 1</label><input type="checkbox" id="cb0" value=0>
            <label for="cb1">Tab 2</label><input type="checkbox" id="cb1" value="1">
            <label for="cb2">Tab 3</label><input type="checkbox" id="cb2" value="2">
        </div>
    </form>
</body>
</html>
```

I have created a tabs widget with static content and added a set of check boxes that I have transformed into jQuery UI toggle buttons. When one of the buttons is clicked, the corresponding tab is enabled or disabled, as shown in Figure 20-4.

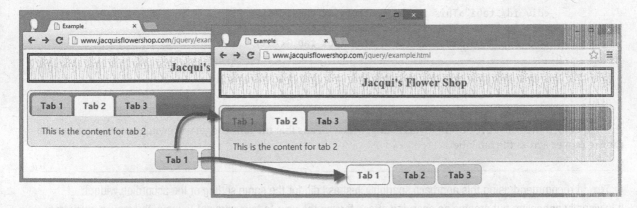

Figure 20-4. *Disabling and enabling tabs in response to button clicks*

Changing the Event Trigger

The tabs widget responds to the click event by default, meaning that users must click a tab to activate it. You can use the event setting to specify a different event to respond to. This is most useful for responding to mouse events, as shown in Listing 20-6.

Listing 20-6. Changing the Event That Activates a Tab

```
<!DOCTYPE html>
<html>
<head>
    <title>Example</title>
    <script src="jquery-2.0.2.js" type="text/javascript"></script>
    <script src="jquery-ui-1.10.3.custom.js" type="text/javascript"></script>
    <link rel="stylesheet" type="text/css" href="styles.css"/>
    <link rel="stylesheet" type="text/css" href="jquery-ui-1.10.3.custom.css"/>
    <style type="text/css"> #buttonDiv {margin: 5px}</style>
    <script type="text/javascript">
        $(document).ready(function() {

            $("#tabs").tabs({
                event: "mouseover"
            });
        });
    </script>
</head>
<body>
    <h1>Jacqui's Flower Shop</h1>
    <form method="post" action="http://node.jacquisflowershop.com/order">
        <div id="tabs">
            <ul>
                <li><a href="#tab1">Tab 1</a>
                <li><a href="#tab2">Tab 2</a>
                <li><a href="#tab3">Tab 3</a>
            </ul>
```

```
            <div id="tab1">This is the content for tab 1</div>
            <div id="tab2">This is the content for tab 2</div>
            <div id="tab3">This is the content for tab 3</div>
        </div>
    </form>
</body>
</html>
```

I specified the mouseover event in this listing, which means that the tabs widget will switch between tabs as the mouse moves across the tab labels.

■ **Tip**   I recommend using this approach sparingly, just as I did for the same setting of the accordion widget. It is visually appealing but creates an annoying effect, forcing the user to take care not to move the mouse away from the label of the tab he wants to interact with.

Using Collapsible Tabs

You can create a sort of hybrid between tabs and accordions by using the collapsible setting, as shown in Listing 20-7.

Listing 20-7. Using the collapsible Setting

```
...
<script type="text/javascript">
    $(document).ready(function() {
        $("#tabs").tabs({
            collapsible: true
        });
    });
</script>
...
```

When the collapsible setting is true, clicking the active tab collapses it just like an accordion content element. You can see the transition in Figure 20-5.

Figure 20-5. *Collapsing the active tab*

■ **Tip** I have included this setting for completeness, but it is one that I never use in my own projects because the result is confusing to users.

Using the Tabs Methods

Table 20-3 shows the methods that are supported by the jQuery UI tabs widget.

Table 20-3. Tabs Methods

Method	Description
tabs("destroy")	Removes the tab widget from the underlying HTML element
tabs("disable")	Disables the entire widget or individual tabs (see the section "Using Collapsible Tabs" for an example of using the corresponding setting)
tabs("enable")	Enables the entire widget or an individual tab
tabs("option")	Changes one or more settings (see the section "Configuring the Button" in Chapter 18 for details of configuring a jQuery UI widget)
tabs("load")	Explicitly loads the contents of a tab using an Ajax request
tabs("refresh")	Updates the widget to reflect changes in the underlying HTML elements

■ **Tip** The set of methods supported by the tabs widget changed in version 1.10. The following methods have been removed: add, remove, select, url, length, and abort. The add and remove methods have been replaced by a new method called refresh; the functionality of the select method is available through the active setting; you can implement the functionality abort method using the new beforeActivate event. There is no alternative functionality for the length method.

Adding and Removing Tabs

I use the jQuery UI tabs widget to define add and remove methods for manipulating the set of tabs that were displayed to the user. These methods were removed in jQuery UI 1.10 and replaced with the refresh method, which updates the tabs based on changes to the underlying HTML elements that the widget has been applied to. In Listing 20-8, you can see how to use the refresh method.

Listing 20-8. Using the refresh Method to Update the Tabs Widget

```
<!DOCTYPE html>
<html>
<head>
    <title>Example</title>
    <script src="jquery-2.0.2.js" type="text/javascript"></script>
    <script src="jquery-ui-1.10.3.custom.js" type="text/javascript"></script>
    <link rel="stylesheet" type="text/css" href="jquery-ui-1.10.3.custom.css"/>
```

```
<link rel="stylesheet" type="text/css" href="styles.css"/>
<style type="text/css">
    #buttons {margin: 5px 0}
</style>
<script type="text/javascript">
    $(document).ready(function () {

        $("#tabs").tabs();

        $("button").button().click(function (e) {
            var tabsElem = $("#tabs");
            if (this.id == "add") {
                var tabID = tabsElem.children("div").length + 1;
                tabsElem.children("ul").append($("<li>").append($("<a>")
                    .attr("href", "#tab" + tabID).text("Tab " + tabID)));
                $("<div>").attr("id", "tab" + tabID)
                    .text("This is the content for tab " + tabID).appendTo(tabsElem);
            } else {
                tabsElem.find("li").first().remove();
                tabsElem.children("div").first().remove();
            }
            tabsElem.tabs("refresh");
        })
    });
</script>
</head>
<body>
    <h1>Jacqui's Flower Shop</h1>
    <div id="buttons" class="ui-widget">
        <button id="add">Add Tab</button>
        <button id="remove">Remove Tab</button>
    </div>
    <div id="tabs">
        <ul>
            <li><a href="#tab1">Tab 1</a>
            <li><a href="#tab2">Tab 2</a>
            <li><a href="#tab3">Tab 3</a>
        </ul>
        <div id="tab1">This is the content for tab 1</div>
        <div id="tab2">This is the content for tab 2</div>
        <div id="tab3">This is the content for tab 3</div>
    </div>
</body>
</html>
```

I have added a pair of button elements that add and remove the li and div elements used by the tabs widget. When the Add Tab button is clicked I generate new elements and add them to the Document Object Model (DOM). When the Remove Tab button is clicked I remove the first li and div element I can find.

I call the refresh method after making these changes, notifying the tabs widget that it should update itself to reflect the changes I have made, creating the effect shown in Figure 20-6.

Figure 20-6. *Adding and removing tabs*

Triggering Tab Ajax Requests

By default, the tabs widget will only make Ajax requests for tabs that have remote content when the user opens that tab. This approach prevents requesting content that may never be displayed, but it can lead to delays when the user opens a tab. You can tell the tabs widget to explicitly load the contents of a remote tab using the load method, as demonstrated in Listing 20-9.

Listing 20-9. *Using the load Method to Explicitly Obtain Remote Content*

```
<!DOCTYPE html>
<html>
<head>
    <title>Example</title>
    <script src="jquery-2.0.2.js" type="text/javascript"></script>
    <script src="jquery-ui-1.10.3.custom.js" type="text/javascript"></script>
    <link rel="stylesheet" type="text/css" href="jquery-ui-1.10.3.custom.css"/>
    <link rel="stylesheet" type="text/css" href="styles.css"/>
    <style type="text/css">
        #buttons {margin: 5px 0}
    </style>
    <script type="text/javascript">
        $(document).ready(function () {

            $("#tabs").tabs();

            $("#load").button().click(function (e) {
                var tabsElem = $("#tabs");
```

```
            tabsElem.find("a").each(function (index, elem) {
                if (elem.href.indexOf("example.html") == -1) {
                    tabsElem.tabs("load", index);
                }
            });
        });
    });
    </script>
</head>
<body>
    <h1>Jacqui's Flower Shop</h1>

    <div id="buttons" class="ui-widget">
        <button id="load">Load</button>
    </div>

    <div id="tabs">
        <ul>
            <li><a href="#tab1">Tab 1</a>
            <li><a href="#tab2">Tab 2</a>
            <li><a href="#tab3">Tab 3</a>
            <li><a href="tabflowers.html">Ajax Content</a>
        </ul>
        <div id="tab1">This is the content for tab 1</div>
        <div id="tab2">This is the content for tab 2</div>
        <div id="tab3">This is the content for tab 3</div>
    </div>
</body>
</html>
```

The argument to the load method is the index of the remote tab you want to load content for. In this case, I have used the load method in response to a button being clicked.

Using the Tabs Events

The set of events supported by the jQuery UI tabs widget is described in Table 20-4 and I describe them in the sections that follow.

Table 20-4. *Tabs Events*

Event	Description
create	Triggered when the tabs widget is applied to an underlying HTML element
beforeActivate	Triggered before a tab panel is shown to the user
activate	Triggered after a tab panel is shown to the user
beforeLoad	Triggered when the contents of a remote tab are about to be loaded
load	Triggered when the contents of a remote tab have been loaded

■ **Tip** The set of events supported by the tabs widget changed in jQuery UI version 1.10, removing the select, show, add, remove, enable, and disable events and adding the beforeActivate, activate, and beforeLoad events. The events that are removed are moot either because the tabs widget now relies on the state of the underlying HTML elements (and the refresh method) or because the functionality can be recreated using the new events.

Intercepting Ajax Requests

The beforeLoad event is triggered before a request for the contents of a remote tab is made. Handler functions are passed a jQuery event object and an additional object—usually assigned the name ui in the handler function—that defines the properties shown in Table 20-5.

Table 20-5. *The Properties of the Additional Object Passed to beforeLoad Event Handler Functions*

Name	Description
tab	Returns a jQuery object containing the tab element for the remote tab
panel	Returns a jQuery object containing the panel element for the remote tab
jqXHR	Returns the jqXHR object that will be used to make the Ajax request
ajaxSettings	Returns a map object that will be passed to the $.ajax method to make the request

These properties reveal the close integration between jQuery UI and jQuery, by building on the jQuery Ajax functionality that I described in Chapters 14 and 15. In Listing 20-10, you can see how I handle the beforeLoad event to adjust the settings of the Ajax request.

Listing 20-10. Handling the beforeLoad Event

```
<!DOCTYPE html>
<html>
<head>
    <title>Example</title>
    <script src="jquery-2.0.2.js" type="text/javascript"></script>
    <script src="jquery-ui-1.10.3.custom.js" type="text/javascript"></script>
    <link rel="stylesheet" type="text/css" href="jquery-ui-1.10.3.custom.css"/>
    <link rel="stylesheet" type="text/css" href="styles.css"/>
    <script type="text/javascript">
        $(document).ready(function () {
            $("#tabs").tabs({
                beforeLoad: function (e, ui) {
                    ui.ajaxSettings.url = "flowers.html";
                }
            });
        });
    </script>
</head>
<body>
    <h1>Jacqui's Flower Shop</h1>
    <div id="tabs">
```

```
        <ul>
            <li><a href="#tab1">Tab 1</a>
            <li><a href="#tab2">Tab 2</a>
            <li><a href="#tab3">Tab 3</a>
            <li><a href="tabflowers.html">Ajax Content</a>
        </ul>
        <div id="tab1">This is the content for tab 1</div>
        <div id="tab2">This is the content for tab 2</div>
        <div id="tab3">This is the content for tab 3</div>
    </div>
</body>
</html>
```

The handler function that I registered for the beforeLoad event sets the url property on the ui.ajaxSettings object to change the source of the content that will be displayed by the remote tab. Instead of the tabflowers.html file specified by the HTML elements, the flowers.html file will be loaded instead.

Manipulating Remote Tab Data

The load event is triggered when the data for a remote tab have been loaded from the server and can be used to manipulate the content before it is shown to the user. The handler function is passed a jQuery event object and an additional ui object that defines the properties shown in Table 20-6.

Table 20-6. *The Properties of the Additional Object Passed to load Event Handler Functions*

Name	Description
tab	Returns a jQuery object that contains the tab element that was loaded
panel	Returns a jQuery object that contains the element into which the content was loaded

Notice that neither of the properties returned by the ui object directly refers to the content that was loaded from the server. Instead, the handler function has access to the elements that are used by the tabs widget for the tab header and the content panel. In Listing 20-11, you can see how I use these elements to change the title of the tab and manipulate the content loaded from the server.

Listing 20-11. Handling the Tabs load Event

```
...
<script type="text/javascript">
    $(document).ready(function () {
        $("#tabs").tabs({
            load: function (e, ui) {
                ui.tab.find("a").text("Loaded!");
                ui.panel.children().first().remove();
            }
        });
    });
</script>
...
```

I use the `ui.tab` property to locate the a element used for the tab and call the jQuery text method to change the title. I use the `ui.panel` property to locate the first child content element loaded from the server and remove it from the DOM. You can see the effect in Figure 20-7.

Figure 20-7. *Handling the load event*

> ■ **Tip**   Notice that I don't have to call the `refresh` method, even though I am modifying the DOM elements on which the tabs widget relies. The refresh is applied automatically after the load event has been triggered.

Using Tabs to Display a Form

This is a useful technique for making a long form more approachable while giving the user a sense of how far she has progressed through the form. To begin, Listing 20-12 shows the document that contains the form that I will use.

Listing 20-12. The Document That Contains a Form

```
<!DOCTYPE html>
<html>
<head>
    <title>Example</title>
    <script src="jquery-2.0.2.js" type="text/javascript"></script>
    <script src="handlebars.js"></script>
    <script src="handlebars-jquery.js"></script>
    <script src="jquery-ui-1.10.3.custom.js" type="text/javascript"></script>
    <link rel="stylesheet" type="text/css" href="styles.css"/>
    <link rel="stylesheet" type="text/css" href="jquery-ui-1.10.3.custom.css"/>
    <style type="text/css">
        #tab2 input, #tab3 input {width: 200px; text-align: left}
        #tab1, #tab2, #tab3 {padding: 10px}
```

```
        .fl {float: left}
        #buttonDiv {clear: both}
        #tabs, h1 {margin: 10px}
        .regLabel {width: auto}
    </style>
    <script id="flowerTmpl" type="text/x-jquery-tmpl">
        {{#flowers}}
            <div class="dcell ui-widget">
                <img src="{{product}}.png"/>
                <label for="{{product}}">{{name}}:</label>
                <input name="{{product}}" value="0"/>
            </div>
        {{/flowers}}
    </script>
    <script id="detailsTmpl" type="text/x-jquery-tmpl">
        {{#details}}
            <div class="ui-widget">
                <label for="{{name}}">{{name}}:</label>
                <input name="{{name}}" placeholder="{{hint}}"/>
            </div>
        {{/details}}
    </script>
    <script type="text/javascript">
        $(document).ready(function () {

            var data = [{ "name": "Aster", "product": "aster" },
                        { "name": "Daffodil", "product": "daffodil" },
                        { "name": "Rose", "product": "rose" },
                        { "name": "Peony", "product": "peony" }];

            var elems = $("#flowerTmpl").template({ flowers: data }).filter("*");
            elems.slice(0, 2).appendTo("#row1");
            elems.slice(2, 4).appendTo("#row2");

            var detailsData = [{ name: "Name", hint: "Enter your name" },
                    { name: "Street", hint: "Enter your street" },
                    { name: "City", hint: "Enter your city" },
                    { name: "State", hint: "Enter your state" },
                    { name: "Zip", hint: "Enter your zip code" }];

            $("#detailsTmpl").template({ details: detailsData }).filter("*")
                .appendTo("#tab2").clone().appendTo("#tab3")

            $("button").button();
        });
    </script>
</head>
<body>
    <h1>Jacqui's Flower Shop</h1>
    <form method="post" action="http://node.jacquisflowershop.com/order">
        <div id="tabs" class="ui-widget">
            <ul>
```

```
            <li><a href="#tab1">1. Select Products</a>
            <li><a href="#tab2">2. Your Details</a>
            <li><a href="#tab3">3. Your Shipping Address</a>
        </ul>
        <div id="tab1">
            <h2>1. Select Products</h2>
            <div id="row1"></div>
            <div id="row2"></div>
        </div>
        <div id="tab2" class="fl">
            <h2>2. Your Details</h2>
        </div>
        <div id="tab3" class="fl">
            <h2>3. Your Shipping Address</h2>
        </div>
    </div>
    <div id="buttonDiv"><button type="submit">Place Order</button></div>
  </form>
</body>
</html>
```

I have added some extra content and structure to the document to flesh out earlier examples. There are fewer flower products, but I have added regions of the document to capture the user's personal and shipping details. You can see the basic form in Figure 20-8.

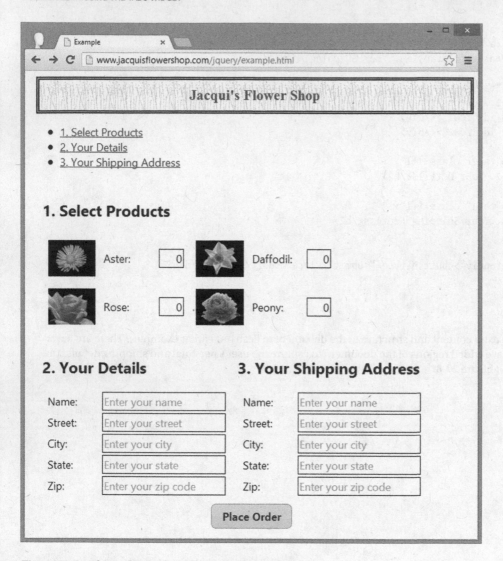

Figure 20-8. *The multipart form for use with the tabs widget*

There is nothing special about the form, other than being well-suited for use with the jQuery UI tabs widget because it is neatly divided into distinct regions, each of which can be displayed in a tab.

I have added most of the content programmatically using data templates and you can see how I use the jQuery functionality I demonstrated in earlier chapters to generate elements from the data, clone them as required, and then add the results to the document. This isn't a requirement for using tabs to display forms, but in a book about jQuery, I like to use the core features as much as possible.

You can also see the ul element in the figure and the links that it contains that point to the content elements. I would usually hide this element, but I wanted to show you a nice side effect of the structure that the tabs widget uses for the labels. Creating a list where each list item contains a link means that clicking that link will jump to that part of the document, and, if the link is to another file, then the browser will navigate to that document. This will help me get the behavior I want from the tab headers.

Applying the Tabs

I am ready to apply the tabs widget to the example. Listing 20-13 shows the changes that are required in the `script` element. No changes are required anywhere else in the document.

Listing 20-13. Creating the Tabs Widget

```
...
<script type="text/javascript">

    $(document).ready(function () {

        var data = [{ "name": "Aster", "product": "aster" },
                    { "name": "Daffodil", "product": "daffodil" },
                    { "name": "Rose", "product": "rose" },
                    { "name": "Peony", "product": "peony" }];

        var elems = $("#flowerTmpl").template({ flowers: data }).filter("*");
        elems.slice(0, 2).appendTo("#row1");
        elems.slice(2, 4).appendTo("#row2");

        var detailsData = [{ name: "Name", hint: "Enter your name" },
                { name: "Street", hint: "Enter your street" },
                { name: "City", hint: "Enter your city" },
                { name: "State", hint: "Enter your state" },
                { name: "Zip", hint: "Enter your zip code" }];

        $("#detailsTmpl").template({ details: detailsData }).filter("*")
            .appendTo("#tab2").clone().appendTo("#tab3")

        $(".fl").removeClass("fl");
        $("#tabs").tabs().find("h2").remove();

        $("button").button();
    });
</script>
...
```

I remove the fl class that I used to position the content for the details and shipping address regions and remove the h2 elements that I was using for section headers. I then call the tabs method, which uses the content elements as the basis for the tabs, as you can see in Figure 20-9.

Figure 20-9. *Applying tabs to the form*

Handling the Button Presses

To make the form easier to fill in using the tabs, I have registered a handler for the click event of the button element. In this handler, I suppress the default action for the event and move to the next tab in the sequence until the last tab is reached. At this point, clicking the button submits the form to the server. Listing 20-14 shows the additions I have made to the script element.

Listing 20-14. *Progressing Through the Form Using the Submit Button*

```
...
<script type="text/javascript">

    $(document).ready(function () {

        var data = [{ "name": "Aster", "product": "aster" },
                    { "name": "Daffodil", "product": "daffodil" },
                    { "name": "Rose", "product": "rose" },
                    { "name": "Peony", "product": "peony" }];

        var elems = $("#flowerTmpl").template({ flowers: data }).filter("*");
        elems.slice(0, 2).appendTo("#row1");
        elems.slice(2, 4).appendTo("#row2");

        var detailsData = [{ name: "Name", hint: "Enter your name" },
                { name: "Street", hint: "Enter your street" },
                { name: "City", hint: "Enter your city" },
                { name: "State", hint: "Enter your state" },
                { name: "Zip", hint: "Enter your zip code" }];

        $("#detailsTmpl").template({ details: detailsData }).filter("*")
            .appendTo("#tab2").clone().appendTo("#tab3")
```

```
        $(".fl").removeClass("fl");
        $("#tabs").tabs().find("h2").remove();

        $("button").button().click(function (e) {
            var tabsElem = $("#tabs");
            var activeTab = tabsElem.tabs("option", "active");
            if (activeTab < tabsElem.find("ul > li").length -1) {
                tabsElem.tabs("option", "active", activeTab + 1)
                e.preventDefault();
            }
        });
    });
</script>
...
```

I use the `active` option to get the index of the active tab and use a jQuery selector to get the set of tab header elements and work out how many there are. If the user has not reached the last tab, then I set the `active` option to advance to the next tab in the sequence. I call the `preventDefault` method only when the user isn't on the final tab, which allows the form to be submitted at the end of the tab sequence.

Performing Validation

At the moment, the user can just jump to the last page and submit the form. To prevent this, I am going to apply some basic form validation. To keep this example simple, I am going to handle the validation manually, but for real projects I recommend using the validation plug-in and the techniques I described in Chapter 13. Listing 20-15 shows the changes to the `script` element to implement some basic validation and stop the user from jumping to the end of the tab sequence prematurely.

Listing 20-15. Preventing the User from Skipping Through the Tabs with Some Basic Validation

```
...
<script type="text/javascript">

    $(document).ready(function () {

        var data = [{ "name": "Aster", "product": "aster" },
                    { "name": "Daffodil", "product": "daffodil" },
                    { "name": "Rose", "product": "rose" },
                    { "name": "Peony", "product": "peony" }];

        var elems = $("#flowerTmpl").template({ flowers: data }).filter("*");
        elems.slice(0, 2).appendTo("#row1");
        elems.slice(2, 4).appendTo("#row2");

        var detailsData = [{ name: "Name", hint: "Enter your name" },
                { name: "Street", hint: "Enter your street" },
                { name: "City", hint: "Enter your city" },
                { name: "State", hint: "Enter your state" },
                { name: "Zip", hint: "Enter your zip code" }];
```

```
$("#detailsTmpl").template({ details: detailsData }).filter("*")
    .appendTo("#tab2").clone().appendTo("#tab3")

var activePanel;

$(".fl").removeClass("fl");
$("#tabs").tabs({
    beforeActivate: function (e, ui) {
        validatePanel(e, ui.oldPanel);
    },
    activate: function (e, ui) {
        activePanel = ui.newPanel;
    }
}).find("h2").remove();


function validatePanel(e, panelElem) {
    var inputElems = panelElem.find("input");
    if (panelElem.attr("id") == "tab1" ?
        sumInputElems(inputElems) : countEmptyOrZeroValues(inputElems)) {
        alert("Validation Problem!");
        e.preventDefault();
    }
}

function sumInputElems(inputs) {
    var total = 0;
    inputs.each(function (index, elem) {
        total+= Number($(elem).val());
    });
    return total == 0;
}

function countEmptyOrZeroValues(inputs) {
    var count = 0;
    inputs.each(function (index, elem) {
        if (elem.value == null || elem.value == "") {
            count++;
        }
    });
    return count > 0;
}

$("button").button().click(function (e) {
    var tabsElem = $("#tabs");
    var activeTab = tabsElem.tabs("option", "active");
    if (activeTab < tabsElem.find("ul > li").length - 1) {
        tabsElem.tabs("option", "active", activeTab + 1)
        e.preventDefault();
```

```
        } else {
            validatePanel(e, activePanel);
        }
    });
});
</script>
...
```

I use two of the tabs events to get the effect I want. The beforeActivated event is useful when the user is navigating from one tab to the next because it provides me with a reference to the content panel of the tab that is about to be closed, which I access through the properties of the second argument passed to my handler function—the ui object—as described in Table 20-7.

Table 20-7. *The Properties of the Additional Object Passed to beforeActivate and activate Event Handlers*

Name	Description
newHeader	The header element for the newly active tab
oldHeader	The header element for the previously active tab
newPanel	The newly active content panel
oldPanel	The previously active content panel

I use the oldPanel reference to perform validation and stop the transition to another tab by calling the preventDefaultAction method on the event object (as described in Chapter 9).

There is a wrinkle with this approach, which is that the beforeActivate event isn't triggered when the user clicks the button element after completing the last tab because the form is submitted to the server. For this reason, I also handle the activate event and store a reference to the new tab that is displayed (which I access through the newPanel property of the ui object, which also defines the properties shown in Table 20-7). I use this reference to perform validation before allowing the form to be submitted to the server.

My approach to telling the user about a validation error is to call the alert function and display a message in a dialog box, as shown in Figure 20-10. Obviously, in a real project, you could use the summary features of the validation plug-in, as I described in Chapter 13.

Figure 20-10. The alert box shown in response to a validation error

Summary

In this chapter, I showed you the jQuery UI tabs widget. This widget offers rich and complex functionality and can be used in a wide range of situations. I find myself using this widget a lot. It is flexible and completely customizable, and users are generally familiar with the idea of selectively revealing content contained in individual tabs, something that is not always the case with other widgets such as the accordion. In Chapter 21, I show you the datepicker widget.

■ ■ ■

Using the Datepicker Widget

This chapter focuses on the jQuery UI datepicker widget, which provides a convenient mechanism for helping users select dates. Getting date information from users is notoriously problematic because of the wide range of formats in which dates can be expressed. The datepicker widget can make it easier for the user to select a date in a way that is more consistent and less prone to errors and using a regular text input element. Table 21-1 provides the summary for this chapter.

Table 21-1. Chapter Summary

Problem	Solution	Listing
Create a pop-up jQuery UI datepicker	Use the datepicker method on an input element	1
Create an inline datepicker	Use the datepicker method on a span or div element	2
Specify the date displayed by the datepicker	Use the defaultDate setting	3
Specify an additional element that will be updated when the user selects a date	Use the altField setting	4
Change the action that causes a pop-up datepicker to appear	Use the showOn setting	5
Specify the text displayed in the datepicker trigger button	Use the buttonText setting	6
Show an image in place of the trigger button	Use the buttonImage and buttonImageOnly settings	7
Restrict the date selection	Use the constrainInput, minDate, and maxDate settings	8, 9
Display several months in the datepicker	Use the numberOfMonths setting	10–12
Enable drop-down menus to aid navigation to months and years	Use the changeMonth and changeYear settings	13
Show week information in the datepicker	Use the showWeek and weekHeader settings	14
Fill the date grid with dates from the previous and subsequent months	Use the showOtherMonths and selectOtherMonths settings	15
Display a button bar at the base of the datepicker	Use the showButtonBar and gotoCurrent settings	16
Show a formatting hint to the user	Use the appendText setting (or the HTML5 placeholder feature)	17, 18
Get or set the date programmatically	Use the getDate and setDate methods	19

(continued)

Table 21-1. (*continued*)

Problem	Solution	Listing
Show or hide a pop-up datepicker programmatically	Use the show and hide methods	20
Respond to the user navigating to a new month or year	Use the onChangeMonthYear event	21
Respond to a pop-up datepicker closing	Use the onClose event	22
Localize the datepicker	Use the jQuery UI i8n support	23

Creating the Datepicker

You can use the datepicker in two ways. The most common is to attach the widget to an input element, using the datapicker method. There is no immediate visual change to the input, but when the element gains the focus (because the user either tabs from other elements or clicks the input field), the datepicker pops up to help the user select a date. Listing 21-1 demonstrates this *pop-up* datepicker.

Listing 21-1. Creating a Pop-up Datepicker

```
<!DOCTYPE html>
<html>
<head>
    <title>Example</title>
    <script src="jquery-2.0.2.js" type="text/javascript"></script>
    <script src="jquery-ui-1.10.3.custom.js" type="text/javascript"></script>
    <link rel="stylesheet" type="text/css" href="styles.css"/>
    <link rel="stylesheet" type="text/css" href="jquery-ui-1.10.3.custom.css"/>
    <style type="text/css">
        input {width: 200px; text-align: left}
    </style>
    <script type="text/javascript">
        $(document).ready(function() {
            $("#datep").datepicker();
        });
    </script>
</head>
<body>
    <h1>Jacqui's Flower Shop</h1>
    <form method="post" action="http://node.jacquisflowershop.com/order">
      <div class="ui-widget">
        <label for="datep">Date: </label><input id="datep"/>
      </div>
    </form>
</body>
</html>
```

You can see how focusing on the input element displays the datepicker in Figure 21-1.

Figure 21-1. *The datepicker pop ups up when the input element gains the focus*

When the datepicker pop-up is displayed, the user can choose to enter a date manually or use the datepicker window to select a date. The datepicker pop-up disappears when the input element loses the focus or when the user hits the Enter or Escape keys.

Creating an Inline Datepicker

The other way to use the datepicker is to use it *inline*. To achieve this, you select a div or span element using jQuery and then call the datepicker method. An inline datepicker is visible whenever the underlying element is visible. Listing 21-2 demonstrates the creation of an inline datepicker.

Listing 21-2. Creating an Inline Datepicker

```
<!DOCTYPE html>
<html>
<head>
    <title>Example</title>
    <script src="jquery-2.0.2.js" type="text/javascript"></script>
    <script src="jquery-ui-1.10.3.custom.js" type="text/javascript"></script>
    <link rel="stylesheet" type="text/css" href="styles.css"/>
    <link rel="stylesheet" type="text/css" href="jquery-ui-1.10.3.custom.css"/>
```

```
    <style type="text/css">
        input {width: 200px; text-align: left; margin-right: 10px}
        #wrapper > * {float: left}
    </style>
    <script type="text/javascript">
        $(document).ready(function () {
            $("#inline").datepicker();
        });
    </script>
</head>
<body>
    <h1>Jacqui's Flower Shop</h1>
    <form method="post" action="http://node.jacquisflowershop.com/order">
        <div id="wrapper" class="ui-widget">
            <label for="datep">Date: </label>
            <input id="datep"/>
            <span id="inline"></span>
        </div>
    </form>
</body>
</html>
```

In this example, I have added a span element and used it as the target of the datepicker method. You can see the effect in Figure 21-2.

Figure 21-2. An inline datepicker

An inline datepicker can be useful when you don't want to work with pop-ups. In some applications dates are so important that it makes sense to display the datepicker all of the time, but in most cases hiding the pop-up until it is required is more sensible. The problem with hiding and showing an inline datepicker is that the layout of the document has to flex to accommodate the datepicker, which can cause presentation problems. For almost all situations, I find the pop-up datepicker to be more useful.

Configuring the Datepicker

If you have done any work with dates before, you will understand that they are complicated to deal with. You see this complexity reflected in the large number of settings supported by the datepicker widget. In the following sections, I describe groups of related settings that can be used to configure the datepicker.

Performing Basic Configuration

Table 21-2 describes the settings that perform the basic configuration for the datepicker widget. I show you how to use these settings in the sections that follow.

Table 21-2. *Basic Datepicker Settings*

Setting	Description
altField	Specifies an additional field that will be updated with the data selection.
buttonImageOnly	Specifies that the image specified by buttonImage should be contained in an img element rather than a button. The default is false.
buttonImage	Specifies the URL of an image to use for the pop-up trigger button. Not used by default.
buttonText	Specifies the text for the pop-up trigger button. The default is an ellipsis (...).
defaultDate	Sets the date to highlight when the datepicker is displayed.
disabled	Specifies whether the datepicker widget is initially disabled. The default is false.
showOn	Specifies the trigger for displaying a pop-up datepicker. The default is focus.

Specifying the Default Date

The most basic setting is also one of the most useful. The defaultDate setting specifies the date that will be shown when the datepicker is displayed. If you don't provide a value for the defaultDate setting, then the current date will be used. (This is, of course, the date as defined by the user's system. Time zones, date lines, and misconfiguration can all present the user with a different date from the one you might be expecting to appear.)

■ **Tip** This setting is used only if there isn't a value attribute for the input element. If there is, either because you have included the value attribute in the document or because the user has previously made a selection, then the datepicker ignores the setting.

If you don't want today's date, then you can choose from several different formats to express the date you want to start with. Table 21-3 shows the range of formats and values you can use.

Table 21-3. *Formats and Values for the defaultDate Setting*

Value/Format	Description
null	Use the current system date.
Date object	Use the value represented by the Date object.
+days, -days	Use the date that is the specified number of days from today. For example, +3 means show three days from today, and -2 means show the date two days ago.
+1d +7w -1m +1y	Use a date that is relative to today, expressed as a number of days (d), weeks (w), months (m), and years (y) in the future (+) or in the past (-). Positive and negative values can be mixed in a single date so that a value of -1d +1m used on November 12, 2011, selects the date December 11, 2011.

Listing 21-3 shows the use of the defaultDate setting to specify a date five years in the future.

Listing 21-3. Using the defaultDate Setting

```
...
<script type="text/javascript">
    $(document).ready(function() {
        $("#datep").datepicker({
            defaultDate: "+5y"
        });
    });
</script>
...
```

I am writing this chapter in June 2013, and you can see in Figure 21-3 that the +5y value for the defaultDate setting focuses the datepicker on June 2018.

Figure 21-3. *Displaying a future date using the defaultDate setting*

As in the example, you can omit any interval that you don't want to change such that you can use +5y rather than +0d +0w +0m +5y. You can mix and match negative and positive values for different intervals to zero in on the date you want.

Specifying the Alternate Element

The altField setting specifies an input element that will be updated when you make a date selection. This is the easiest way of linking an input element with an inline datepicker. Listing 21-4 shows the use of the altField setting as a means of displaying the selection from an inline datepicker.

Listing 21-4. *Using the altField Setting with an Inline Datepicker*

```
...
<script type="text/javascript">
    $(document).ready(function() {
        $("#inline").datepicker({
            altField: "#datep"
        });
    });
</script>
...
```

In Listing 21-4, I have used a selector string to identify the element I want to use, but the altField setting will also accept a jQuery object or a Document Object Model (DOM) HTMLElement object. The effect of this example is that the input element displays the date each time I make a selection using the datepicker, as shown in Figure 21-4.

Figure 21-4. *Specifying the input element that the datepicker will update*

Managing the Pop-up Trigger

The showOn setting controls what causes a pop-up datepicker to be shown to the user. There are three allowed values for this setting.

- focus: The pop-up is shown when the input element gains the focus. This is the default.

- button: The pop-up is shown when a button is clicked.

- both: The pop-up is shown when a button is clicked or when the input gains focus.

When you use the button or both value, the datepicker widget creates a button element and adds it to the document immediately after the input element. Listing 21-5 shows the use of the showOn setting.

Listing 21-5. Using the showOn Setting

```
...
<script type="text/javascript">
    $(document).ready(function() {
        $("#datep").datepicker({
            showOn: "both"
        });
    });
</script>
...
```

You can see the button element created by the widget in Figure 21-5. Since I used the both value in this example, the pop-up will be displayed when the user either clicks the button or focuses on the input element.

Figure 21-5. *The button added in response to the showOn setting*

■ **Tip** The button that the datepicker widget adds is not a jQuery UI button widget. If you want to keep your buttons consistent, then you will need to select the `button` element and call the jQuery UI `button` method, as described in Chapter 18.

You can format the button element using the `buttonImage` or `buttonText` setting. If you set `buttonImage` to a URL, the datepicker widget will use the image in the button. Alternatively, you can use the `buttonText` setting to set a phrase to replace the default content (which is . . .). Listing 21-6 shows the use of the `buttonText` setting.

Listing 21-6. Using the buttonText Setting

```
...
<script type="text/javascript">
    $(document).ready(function() {
        $("#datep").datepicker({
            showOn: "both",
            buttonText: "Select"
        });
    });
</script>
...
```

You can do away with the button text entirely if you use the `buttonImage` and `buttonTextOnly` settings together. This causes the datepicker to add an `img` element to the document rather than a button. Listing 21-7 provides a demonstration.

Listing 21-7. Using an Image Rather Than a Button

```
<!DOCTYPE html>
<html>
<head>
    <title>Example</title>
    <script src="jquery-2.0.2.js" type="text/javascript"></script>
    <script src="jquery-ui-1.10.3.custom.js" type="text/javascript"></script>
    <link rel="stylesheet" type="text/css" href="styles.css"/>
```

```
<link rel="stylesheet" type="text/css" href="jquery-ui-1.10.3.custom.css"/>
<style type="text/css">
    input {width: 200px; text-align: left}
    #dpcontainer * {vertical-align: middle}
    #dpcontainer img {width: 35px;}
</style>
<script type="text/javascript">
    $(document).ready(function() {
        $("#datep").datepicker({
            showOn: "both",
            buttonImage: "right.png",
            buttonImageOnly: true
        });
    });
</script>
</head>
<body>
    <h1>Jacqui's Flower Shop</h1>
    <form method="post" action="http://node.jacquisflowershop.com/order">
      <div id="dpcontainer" class="ui-widget">
        <label for="datep">Date: </label><input id="datep"/>
      </div>
    </form>
</body>
</html>
```

I have specified an image called right.png and set buttonImageOnly to true. I have also added some CSS styles to the document to control the appearance of the image relative to the label and input elements. The datepicker widget isn't particularly smart about how it creates the img element, so I need to compensate to bring the style of the image in line with the rest of the document. You can see the effect of having an image rather than a button in Figure 21-6.

Figure 21-6. *Using an image instead of a button with a pop-up datepicker*

Managing the Date Selection

You will often want to apply constraints to the range of dates that the user can select using the datepicker widget. Table 21-4 describes the settings that allow you to apply selection constraints to guide the user to a date you can work with.

Table 21-4. Datepicker Settings for Managing Date Selection

Setting	Description
changeMonth	When true, the datepicker displays a drop-down menu that allows direct navigation to a month. The default is false.
changeYear	When true, the datepicker displays a drop-down menu that allows direct navigation to a year. The default is false.
constrainInput	When true, limits the characters in the input element to those contained in a valid date. The default is true.
hideIfNoPrevNext	When true, the previous and next buttons are hidden, rather than disabled, when there are no selectable dates in the past or future relative to the displayed period. The default is false.
maxDate	Specifies the latest date that the user can select. The default is to allow the user to select any date.
minDate	Specifies the earliest date that the user can select. The default is to allow the user to select any date.
numberOfMonths	Specifies the number of months displayed by the datepicker. The default is 1.
showCurrentAtPos	Specifies where the current or default month is displayed in a multimonth datepicker. The default is 0.
stepMonths	Specifies the number of months that the display jumps when the previous and next buttons are clicked. The default is 1.
yearRange	Specifies the range of years that can be selected in the drop-down list that is enabled by the changeYear setting. The default is to display ten years before and ten years after the present year.

Limiting the Input Character and Date Range

When set to true, the constrainInput setting restricts the characters that can be entered into the input element to those that are contained in a valid date. The set of characters is dependent on the *localization configuration* you are using, which I talk more about in the section "Localizing Date Selection." If you have not localized the datepicker widget, then you can expect the input element to be restricted so that the user can enter only numbers and the / character.

This setting doesn't mean that the user can only enter valid dates because a value like 99/99/99 can be entered, but it can help reduce errors. The importance of this setting increases when the showOn setting is set to button because the pop-up won't automatically appear when the input element gains the focus. Users will typically select from the datepicker when it is presented to them but won't always realize that a button will display a picker. Every opportunity you give the user to enter a date directly increases the chances you have to process a badly formatted value. Listing 21-8 shows the use of the constrainInput setting.

Listing 21-8. Applying Basic Constraints to the Date Selection

```
<!DOCTYPE html>
<html>
<head>
    <title>Example</title>
    <script src="jquery-2.0.2.js" type="text/javascript"></script>
    <script src="jquery-ui-1.10.3.custom.js" type="text/javascript"></script>
    <link rel="stylesheet" type="text/css" href="styles.css"/>
    <link rel="stylesheet" type="text/css" href="jquery-ui-1.10.3.custom.css"/>
    <style type="text/css">
        input {width: 200px; text-align: left; margin-right: 10px}
        #wrapper > * {float: left}
    </style>
    <script type="text/javascript">
        $(document).ready(function() {
            $("#datep").datepicker({
                constrainInput: true,
                minDate: "-3",
                maxDate: "+5"
            });
        });
    </script>
</head>
<body>
    <h1>Jacqui's Flower Shop</h1>
    <form method="post" action="http://node.jacquisflowershop.com/order">
      <div id="wrapper" class="ui-widget">
        <label for="datep">Date: </label><input id="datep"/><span id="inline"></span>
      </div>
    </form>
</body>
</html>
```

The constrainInput setting is true by default, so I have added values for the minDate and maxDate settings as well, just to make the example a little more interesting. These settings allow me to specify the earliest and latest dates that the user can select. As with the defaultDate setting I showed you in section "Specifying the Default Date," I can specify the dates for the minDate and maxDate settings as null (no date), a Date object, a number of days, or a relative date string. In Listing 21-8, I used the number option that specifies the number of days relative to today. In Figure 21-7, you can see that the datepicker widget disables any date that the user cannot select.

Figure 21-7. *Restricting the dates that the user can select*

■ **Tip**   Notice that the previous and next buttons are disabled automatically when they are not required. These are
the buttons at the top left and top right of the datepicker that allow the user to move to the previous and next months.
In Figure 21-7, all of the dates that the user can select are in the current or previous month, so the next button is
disabled. You can hide, rather than disable, buttons in this situation by setting hideIfNoPrevNext to true.

The minDate need not be in past, the maxDate need not be in the future, and you don't have to provide values for
both settings. If you need the user to pick a date for which there is some kind of lead time, you can specify a future
date for the minDate setting to prevent dates from being selected that are inside the period you need to prepare,
as shown in Listing 21-9.

Listing 21-9. Providing One Date Restriction to Create a Delay Window

```
...
<script type="text/javascript">
    $(document).ready(function() {
        $("#datep").datepicker({
            minDate: "+7"
        });
    });
</script>
...
```

In this example, I have specified that the user cannot select any date that occurs sooner than a week from today. There is no maxDate value, meaning that any future date after a week from now can be selected. You can see the result in Figure 21-8. Notice that the next button (which allows the user to navigate to the next month) is enabled in this figure, but the previous button is disabled (since there are no dates in the past that the user is allowed to select).

Figure 21-8. *Creating an open-ended date selection range*

■ **Tip** The minDate and maxDate settings work in conjunction with the defaultDate setting, meaning that you can specify ranges of dates relative to a date that is not today.

Creating a Multimonth Display

The datepicker allows you to specify how many months are displayed to the user through the numberOfMonths setting. You can specify either a number of months or a two-element array, which specifies the size of a grid of months. Listing 21-10 shows the array-based approach, which I find is most suited to inline datepickers because the grid is often too big to use as a pop-up (I'll explain why in a moment).

Listing 21-10. Using the numberofMonths Setting

```
...
<script type="text/javascript">
    $(document).ready(function() {
        $("#inline").datepicker({
            numberOfMonths: [1, 3]
        });
    });
</script>
...
```

In this example, I have specified a grid of one month high and three months wide. You can see the effect in Figure 21-9.

Figure 21-9. Displaying a grid of months

■ **Tip** The two-element array [1, 3] is equivalent to the numeric value 3. When you provide a number for the numberOfMonths setting, the datepicker displays the specified number of months in a single row.

The reason that I rarely use this feature with pop-up datepickers is that a large grid requires assumptions about the size of the user's browser window and display. The datepicker pop-up isn't an operating system dialog box. It is a carefully formatted HTML element that is displayed as part of the HTML document. This means that when a large datepicker is displayed on a small screen or in a small browser window, much of the detail is displaced off the edge of the screen. Listing 21-11 shows a grid of months applied to a pop-up datepicker.

Listing 21-11. Using the numberOfMonths Setting with a Pop-up Datepicker

```
...
<script type="text/javascript">
    $(document).ready(function() {
        $("#datep").datepicker({
            numberOfMonths: [1, 3]
        });
    });
</script>
...
```

You can see the result in Figure 21-10. Not only are many of the available dates hidden from the user, but the next button (which allows the user to advance the displayed months) is off the screen as well.

Figure 21-10. Displaying a large pop-up datepicker

You can change the position of the selected date in a multimonth datepicker using the showCurrentAtPos setting. As you can see in Figures 21-9 and 21-10, the default is to display the current month first, followed by the next two months in the future. The showCurrentAtPos setting takes a zero-based index value that specifies the location where the current month should be displayed. This is a handy feature if you need to allow the user to select dates on either side of today. Listing 21-12 shows the use of this setting.

Listing 21-12. Using the showCurrentAtPos Setting

```
...
<script type="text/javascript">
    $(document).ready(function() {
        $("#inline").datepicker({
            numberOfMonths: 3,
            showCurrentAtPos: 1
        });
    });
</script>
...
```

I have specified that the current date should be shown in the middle of the three months shown by the datepicker. You can see the result in Figure 21-11.

Figure 21-11. *Specifying the location of the current month in a multimonth datepicker*

Providing Direct Access to Months and Years

You can replace the month and year in the header of the datepicker header with drop-down menus that provide direct access to months and years. This can be a useful shortcut for users when there is a large date range to select from. The settings that control these features are changeMonth and changeYear. A true value for these settings enables the corresponding menu, and the menus can be enabled independently of one another. Listing 21-13 shows the use of these settings.

Listing 21-13. Providing Direct Access to Months and Years Through Drop-Down Menus

```
...
<script type="text/javascript">
    $(document).ready(function() {
        $("#datep").datepicker({
            changeMonth: true,
            changeYear: true,
            yearRange: "-1:+2"

        });
    });
</script>
...
```

In this listing, I have enabled both drop-down menus. I have also used the yearRange setting to limit the range of years that the user can navigate to. I specified a value of -1:+2, which means that the user can select one year back from today through to two years into the future. Since I am writing this chapter in 2013, the range of years that the user is presented with is 2012 to 2015. You can see how the menus are displayed (and how the year range appears) in Figure 21-12.

Figure 21-12. Providing the user with direct access to months and years

■ **Tip** You can also supply a range of actual years for the yearRange setting. I could have achieved the same result in Figure 21-12 with a value of 2012:2015.

Managing the Appearance of the Datepicker

You can use a number of settings to tailor the appearance of the datepicker when it is displayed to the user. For general date selection purposes, the default appearance that you have seen in earlier examples is usually suitable, but the ability to tweak the appearance to suit the requirements of a web application is extremely useful. Table 21-5 describes the appearance-related settings.

Table 21-5. Datepicker Settings for Controlling Appearance

Setting	Description
appendText	Specifies a formatting hint that will be inserted into the document after the input element.
closeText	Specifies the text to use for the button in the button bar that dismisses a pop-up datepicker. The default is Done.
currentText	Specifies the text to use for the button in the button bar that returns to the current date. The default is Today.
duration	Specifies the speed or duration for the animation specified by the showAnim setting is performed. The default is normal. I described the jQuery UI animation effects in Chapter 35.
gotoCurrent	When true, the Today button in the button bar will return to the selected date rather than today's date. The default is false.
selectOtherMonths	When true, the dates shown as a result of the showOtherMonths setting can be selected. The default is false.
showAnim	Specifies the animation used to show and hide pop-up datepickers. I describe the jQuery UI animation effects in Chapter 35. The default is show.
showButtonPanel	When true, the datepicker displays a button bar allowing the user to jump to the current date and (when used with a pop-up) to dismiss the datepicker. The default is false.
showOptions	Specifies the options for the animation defined by the showAnim setting. I describe the jQuery UI animation effects in Chapter 35.
showOtherMonths	When true, the datepicker fills blanks in the date grid with dates from the previous and subsequent months. The default is false.
showWeek	When true, the datepicker displays a column showing week information. The default is true.
weekHeader	Sets the header for the week column enabled through the showWeek setting. The default is Wk.

Displaying Weeks

For some applications, knowing which week of the year a date falls in is essential. This is often the case in budget management applications, for example. The jQuery UI datepicker can display week information, configured through the showWeek and weekHeader settings, as shown in Listing 21-14.

Listing 21-14. Displaying Week Information in the Datepicker

```
...
<script type="text/javascript">
    $(document).ready(function() {
        $("#datep").datepicker({
            showWeek: true,
            weekHeader: "Week"
        });
    });
</script>
...
```

When the showWeek setting is true, the datepicker displays a column that shows week numbers. You can use the weekHeader setting to change the title of the week column from the default, Wk. In the example, I have enabled the week column and changed the title to Week. You can see the result in Figure 21-13.

Figure 21-13. Showing week information in the datepicker

Allowing Bleed Between Months

The datepicker displays only the dates in the current month by default. This means there are blank entries in the date grid before and after the range of dates. You can show dates from the previous and next months by using a value of true for the showOtherMonth setting, as shown in Listing 21-15.

Listing 21-15. Allowing Months to Bleed into One Another

```
...
<script type="text/javascript">
    $(document).ready(function() {
        $("#datep").datepicker({
            showOtherMonths: true
        });
    });
</script>
...
```

You can see the result in Figure 21-14. The dates from the other months cannot be selected unless
selectOtherMonths is set to true.

Figure 21-14. Showing dates from previous and subsequent months

Using the Button Bar

When true, the showButtonBar setting enables a button bar at the bottom of the datepicker window. When using a
pop-up datepicker, the button bar contains Today and Done buttons. The Today button jumps back to the current date,
and the Done button dismisses the pop-up. You can see the buttons in Figure 21-15. When part of an inline datepicker,
only the Today button is shown.

Figure 21-15. *Showing the button bar*

■ **Tip**   You can change the text used for the Today and Done buttons using the currentText and closeText settings.

When true, the gotoCurrent setting will return the datepicker to the currently selected date rather than today's date. This is useful when you have configured the datepicker with the defaultDate setting. It doesn't always make sense to return to the current date if the purpose of the date selection is related to historical or future events. Listing 21-16 contains an example.

Listing 21-16. Using the gotoCurrent Setting

```
...
<script type="text/javascript">
    $(document).ready(function() {
        $("#datep").datepicker({
            showButtonPanel: true,
            gotoCurrent: true,
            defaultDate: "+1m +1y"
        }).val("12/25/2012");
    });
</script>
...
```

Note that the gotoCurrent setting causes the button to go to the selected date. In Listing 21-16, the date will be taken from the value attribute of the input element, but if the user selects another date and later opens the datepicker again, the button will return to the date the user selected rather than the dates you specified.

Providing a Format Hint to the User

You can use the appendText setting to provide the user with a hint about the date format that you are expecting. Listing 21-17 demonstrates.

Listing 21-17. Using the appendText Setting to Provide a Format Hint

```
...
<script type="text/javascript">
    $(document).ready(function() {
        $("#datep").datepicker({
            appendText: "(mm/dd/yyyy)"
        });
    });
</script>
...
```

The datepicker inserts the text you specify into the document, as shown in Figure 21-16.

Figure 21-16. Using the appendText setting to provide a format hint to the user

This setting is most useful when you rely on a button to make the pop-up datepicker appear. When the user is free to enter the text without the datepicker, then the hint you give her about the format can significantly reduce the errors you have to deal with (which is good for you and less frustrating for the user). Recently, I have started using the HTML5 placeholder attribute for input elements as a neater alternative to the datepicker appendTo setting. Listing 21-18 demonstrates.

Listing 21-18. Providing a Formatting Hint Using the HTML5 Placeholder Attribute

```
...
<script type="text/javascript">
    $(document).ready(function() {
        $("#datep").attr("placeholder", "mm/dd/yyyy").datepicker();
    });
</script>
...
```

Obviously, this requires the user to have an HTML5-enabled browser, but the effect is more elegant. The user is presented with the hint in grayed-out text that disappears as soon as he starts typing. I prefer this because it is more closely associated the formatting hint with the input element, and it doesn't require space in the document layout. You can see how the placeholder is displayed in Google Chrome in Figure 21-17.

Figure 21-17. Using an HTML5 placeholder as a formatting hint

Using the Datepicker Methods

The datepicker widget supports the methods that are shown in Table 21-6.

Table 21-6. Accordion Methods

Method	Description
datepicker("destroy")	Removes the datepicker from the underlying element
datepicker("disable")	Disables the datepicker
datepicker("enable")	Enables the datepicker
datepicker("option")	Sets one or more options for the datepicker
datepicker("isDisabled")	Returns true if the datepicker is disabled
datepicker("hide")	Hides a pop-up datepicker
datepicker("show")	Shows a pop-up datepicker
datepicker("refresh")	Refreshes a datepicker to reflects changes in the underlying element
datepicker("getDate")	Gets the selected date from the datepicker
datepicker("setDate", date)	Sets the selected date for the datepicker

Getting and Setting the Date Programmatically

I find the getDate and setDate methods most useful when I am using multiple inline date pickers to allow the user to select a date range. In this situation, I don't want to display the selected dates in input elements. I want to display just the number of days between the first and second dates. Listing 21-19 demonstrates.

Listing 21-19. Using Two Datepickers to Select a Date Range

```
<!DOCTYPE html>
<html>
<head>
    <title>Example</title>
    <script src="jquery-2.0.2.js" type="text/javascript"></script>
```

```
<script src="jquery-ui-1.10.3.custom.js" type="text/javascript"></script>
<link rel="stylesheet" type="text/css" href="styles.css"/>
<link rel="stylesheet" type="text/css" href="jquery-ui-1.10.3.custom.css"/>
<style type="text/css">
    input {width: 200px; text-align: left; margin-right: 10px}
    #wrapper > * {float: left}
    #result {margin: auto; padding: 10px; width: 200px; clear: left}
</style>
<script type="text/javascript">
    $(document).ready(function() {

        $("#result").hide();

        $("#dateStart, #dateEnd").datepicker({
            minDate: "-7d",
            maxDate: "+7d",
            onSelect: function(date, datepicker) {
                if (datepicker.id == "dateStart") {
                    $("#dateEnd").datepicker("setDate", date)
                        .datepicker("enable").datepicker("option", "minDate", date)
                }

                if (!$("#dateEnd").datepicker("isDisabled")) {
                    var startDate = $("#dateStart").datepicker("getDate");
                    var endDate = $("#dateEnd").datepicker("getDate");
                    var diff = endDate.getDate() - startDate.getDate();
                    $("#dayCount").text(diff).parent().show();
                }
            }
        }).filter("#dateEnd").datepicker("disable");
    });
</script>
</head>
<body>
    <h1>Jacqui's Flower Shop</h1>
    <form method="post" action="http://node.jacquisflowershop.com/order">
      <div id="wrapper" class="ui-widget">
        <label for="dateStart">Start: </label><span id="dateStart"></span>
        <label for="dateEnd">End: </label><span id="dateEnd"></span>
      </div>
      <div id="result" class="ui-widget">
        Number of Days: <span id="dayCount"></span>
      </div>
    </form>
</body>
</html>
```

There are two datepickers in Listing 21-19, the second of which is disabled when the document is first loaded. I use the onSelect event (which is triggered when a date is selected) to respond to the user making date selections. When the user makes a selection in the first datepicker, I use the setDate method to prepare the second datepicker and the getDate method to get the dates from both datepicker in order to work out the number of days between the first and second selected dates (to keep this example simple, I have done a comparison that assumes that both dates are in the same month). You can see how this document is displayed in the browser in Figure 21-18.

Figure 21-18. *Using the getDate and setDate methods*

Showing and Hiding Pop-up Datepickers Programmatically

You can use the show and hide methods to programmatically control the presence of a pop-up datepicker on the screen. This can be useful if you want to associate the datepicker with something other than the focus of the input element or the button that the datepicker widget creates. I am not much of a fan of letting the datepicker create a button in the document, so I occasionally find myself using these methods to control the datepicker from a button I have added myself, as demonstrated in Listing 21-20.

Listing 21-20. Using the show and hide Methods

```
<!DOCTYPE html>
<html>
<head>
    <title>Example</title>
    <script src="jquery-2.0.2.js" type="text/javascript"></script>
    <script src="jquery-ui-1.10.3.custom.js" type="text/javascript"></script>
    <link rel="stylesheet" type="text/css" href="styles.css"/>
    <link rel="stylesheet" type="text/css" href="jquery-ui-1.10.3.custom.css"/>
    <style type="text/css">
        input {width: 200px; text-align: left; margin-right: 10px}
        #wrapper > * {float: left}
        label {padding: 4px; text-align: right; width: auto}
    </style>
```

```
<script type="text/javascript">
    $(document).ready(function() {

        $("#datep").datepicker();

        $("button").click(function(e) {
            e.preventDefault();
            $("#datep").datepicker("show");
            setTimeout(function() {
                $("#datep").datepicker("hide");
            }, 5000)
        })

    });
</script>
</head>
<body>
    <h1>Jacqui's Flower Shop</h1>
    <form method="post" action="http://node.jacquisflowershop.com/order">
      <div id="wrapper" class="ui-widget">
        <label for="datep">Date: </label><input id="datep"/><span id="inline"></span>
        <button>Datepicker</button>
      </div>
    </form>
</body>
</html>
```

I call the datepicker show method when the button is clicked. I don't often use the hide method because I want the user to be able to dismiss the pop-up when he has made a selection, but for completeness, I have used the setTimeout function so that the pop-up is dismissed five seconds after the button has been pressed.

Using the Datepicker Events

Like all jQuery UI widgets, the datepicker supports a set of events that allow you to receive notifications of important changes. Table 21-7 describes these events.

Table 21-7. Datepicker Events

Event	Description
create	Triggered when the datepicker is created
onChangeMonthYear	Triggered when the user moves to a different month or year
onClose	Triggered when a pop-up datepicker is closed
onSelect	Triggered when the user selects a date

I am not going to demonstrate the onSelect method again because I have already used it in a couple of examples, including the one in the section "Getting and Setting the Date Programmatically." The arguments passed to the handler function for this event are a string representation of the selected date and the datepicker that has triggered the event.

Responding to a Month or Year Change

The onChangeMonthYear event allows you to respond when the user selects a new month or year, either from the drop-down menus enabled by the changeMonth and changeYear settings or through the previous and next buttons. Listing 21-21 shows how you can use this event to keep two datepickers consistent.

Listing 21-21. Using the onChangeMonthYear Event

```html
<!DOCTYPE html>
<html>
<head>
    <title>Example</title>
    <script src="jquery-2.0.2.js" type="text/javascript"></script>
    <script src="jquery-ui-1.10.3.custom.js" type="text/javascript"></script>
    <link rel="stylesheet" type="text/css" href="styles.css"/>
    <link rel="stylesheet" type="text/css" href="jquery-ui-1.10.3.custom.css"/>
    <style type="text/css">
        input {width: 200px; text-align: left; margin-right: 10px}
        #wrapper > * {float: left}
    </style>
    <script type="text/javascript">
        $(document).ready(function() {

            $("#dateStart, #dateEnd").datepicker({
                onSelect: function(date, datepicker) {
                    if (datepicker.id == "dateStart") {
                        $("#dateEnd").datepicker("setDate", date)
                    }
                },
                onChangeMonthYear: function(year, month, datepicker) {
                    if (datepicker.id == "dateStart") {
                        var newDate = new Date();
                        newDate.setMonth(month -1);
                        newDate.setYear(year);
                        $("#dateEnd").datepicker("setDate", newDate);
                    }
                }
            })
        });
    </script>
</head>
<body>
    <h1>Jacqui's Flower Shop</h1>
    <form method="post" action="http://node.jacquisflowershop.com/order">
      <div id="wrapper" class="ui-widget">
        <label for="dateStart">Start: </label><span id="dateStart"></span>
        <label for="dateEnd">End: </label><span id="dateEnd"></span>
      </div>
    </form>
</body>
</html>
```

The three arguments to the function for this event are the displayed year, the displayed month, and the datepicker that triggered the event. The `this` variable is set to the `input` element for pop-up datepickers. When the user navigates to a new month or year on the first datepicker, I set the date on the second datepicker to keep them in sync.

Notice that the datepicker widget represents January as month 1 while the JavaScript `Date` object uses 0. This is why I have to make an ugly adjustment like this

```
...
newDate.setMonth(month -1);
...
```

when I am creating the date I want displayed in the second datepicker.

Responding to the Pop-up Closing

You can use the `onClose` method to respond to the pop-up datepicker being closed. This event is triggered even when the user has not made a date selection. The arguments to the handler function are a string representation of the date (or the empty string if the user dismissed the datepicker without making a selection) and the datepicker that triggered the event. Listing 21-22 shows a simple response to this event.

Listing 21-22. Using the onClose Event

```html
<!DOCTYPE html>
<html>
<head>
    <title>Example</title>
    <script src="jquery-2.0.2.js" type="text/javascript"></script>
    <script src="jquery-ui-1.10.3.custom.js" type="text/javascript"></script>
    <link rel="stylesheet" type="text/css" href="styles.css"/>
    <link rel="stylesheet" type="text/css" href="jquery-ui-1.10.3.custom.css"/>
    <style type="text/css">
        input {width: 200px; text-align: left; margin-right: 10px}
        #wrapper > * {float: left}
    </style>
    <script type="text/javascript">
        $(document).ready(function() {
            $("#datep").datepicker({
                onClose: function(date, datepicker) {
                    if (date != "") {
                        alert("Selected: " + date);
                    }
                }
            });
        });
    </script>
</head>
```

```
<body>
    <h1>Jacqui's Flower Shop</h1>
    <form method="post" action="http://node.jacquisflowershop.com/order">
      <div id="wrapper" class="ui-widget">
        <label for="datep">Date: </label><input id="datep"/>
      </div>
    </form>
</body>
</html>
```

In Listing 21-22, I display an alert box to the user displaying the selection, if one has been made. I must admit that I have never found myself using this event in a real project; the onSelect event is the one that I find most useful.

Localizing Date Selection

The jQuery UI datepicker has comprehensive support for the different date formats used around the world. To use them, you need to import an additional JavaScript file into your document and tell the datepicker which locale you want to use. Listing 21-23 provides an example.

Listing 21-23. Using the Localized Datepicker

```
<!DOCTYPE html>
<html>
<head>
    <title>Example</title>
    <script src="jquery-2.0.2.js" type="text/javascript"></script>
    <script src="jquery-ui-1.10.3.custom.js" type="text/javascript"></script>
    <script src="jquery-ui-i18n.js" type="text/javascript"></script>
    <link rel="stylesheet" type="text/css" href="styles.css"/>
    <link rel="stylesheet" type="text/css" href="jquery-ui-1.10.3.custom.css"/>
    <style type="text/css">
        input {width: 200px; text-align: left; margin-right: 10px}
        #wrapper > * {float: left}
    </style>
    <script type="text/javascript">
        $(document).ready(function() {
            $("#inline").datepicker($.datepicker.regional["es"]);
        });
    </script>
</head>
<body>
    <h1>Jacqui's Flower Shop</h1>
    <form method="post" action="http://node.jacquisflowershop.com/order">
      <div id="wrapper" class="ui-widget">
        <label for="datep">Date: </label><input id="datep"/><span id="inline"></span>
      </div>
    </form>
</body>
</html>
```

The `jquery-ui-i18n.js` file can be found in the `development-bundle/ui/i18n` folder of the customized jQuery UI download you created in Chapter 17. Copy this file into place alongside the main jQuery and jQuery UI script files and add the following to your document:

```
...
<script src="jquery-ui-i18n.js" type="text/javascript"></script>
...
```

You can specify the locale to use for the datepicker when you create it, as follows:

```
...
$("#inline").datepicker($.datepicker.regional["es"]);
...
```

This is a messy syntax, but it allows you to specify the localized formats you want. In this example, I have specified `es`, which means that I will be using the Spanish date formats. You can see the result in Figure 21-19.

Figure 21-19. *Localizing the date display*

My advice for localization is that it should be done properly or not at all. This means going far beyond just date formats and presenting the user with an interface that fully follows language, address, gender, currency, time, and every other local convention. Users find it jarring if you localize only part of a web application or following conventions inconsistently. To properly localize an application, you should hire an individual or a company that specializes in such work. There are so many ways to go wrong that you are doomed to fail without professional support.

If you find yourself trying to localize an application using Google Translate (which is not uncommon), then I recommend you just deliver the application using US English and US localization conventions. This limits your customer base to those who are familiar with US variants on spelling, dates, currency, and so on, but at least you will avoid the train wreck that almost always arises when ad hoc localization is attempted.

Summary

In this chapter, I showed you the workings of the jQuery UI datepicker widget, which you can use to assist the user in selecting dates. The datepicker is a flexible widget that allows you to tailor the way that date selections are made and the appearance of the datepicker. My own experience with datepickers is that they are invaluable for reducing the number of formatting problems I have to deal with when requesting date information from users. In Chapter 22, I show you the jQuery UI dialog and spinner widgets.

CHAPTER 22

■ ■ ■

Using the Dialog and Spinner Widgets

In this chapter, I describe the jQuery UI dialog and spinner widgets. Table 22-1 provides the summary for this chapter.

Table 22-1. *Chapter Summary*

Problem	Solution	Listing
Create a jQuery UI dialog	Select a div element with a title attribute and call the dialog method	1
Prevent a dialog from being displayed as soon as it is created	Set the autoOpen setting to false	2
Prevent the user from resizing a dialog	Set the resizable setting to false	3
Focus on an element in the dialog	Set the autofocus attribute	4
Change the initial position of a dialog	Use the position setting	5
Add one or more buttons to a dialog	Use the buttons setting	6
Display icons on the dialog buttons	Use the icons setting	7
Allow the user to move the dialog	Use the draggable setting	8
Create a model dialog	Set the modal setting to true	9, 10
Programmatically open and close a dialog	Use the open, close, and isOpen methods	11
Prevent a dialog from closing	Return false in the handler function for the beforeClose event	12
Respond to the user moving or changing the size of a dialog	Respond to the dragStart, dragStop, drag, resizeStart, resizeStop, and resize events	13
Create a jQuery UI spinner	Select an input element and call the spinner method	14–16
Configure the basic spinner behavior	Use the min, max, step and page settings	17
Change the icons used for the spinner buttons	Use the icons property	18
Control the rate of change when the spin buttons are held down	Use the incremental setting	19
Change the format of the spinner number	Use the culture and numberFormat settings	20
Change the spinner value programmatically	Call the pageDown, pageUp, stepDown, and stepUp methods	21
Respond to changes in the spinner value	Handle the spinner events	22

JQUERY UI CHANGES SINCE THE LAST EDITION

The spinner widget didn't exist when I wrote the first edition of this book. The dialog widget *did* exist and the API (application programming interface) has been updated in jQuery UI version 1.10. There are some new dialog features: an appendTo setting which specifies where in the DOM (Document Object Model) the dialog elements will be located; support for setting focus on dialog elements; the position option has changed to use the format I described in Chapter 19; and there is support for displaying icons in the dialog buttons. Some features have been removed as well: the stack and zIndex settings.

Using the jQuery UI Dialog Widget

The jQuery UI dialog widget creates a floating window with a title and content area, similar to the kind of dialog you might see from a native application. Dialogs are useful for focusing the user's attention on an important event or message. As with any element that can obscure the document content, the dialog must be used sparingly and only when displaying the content inside the document layout isn't feasible.

Creating the Dialog

The dialog widget is created by selecting a div element and then calling the dialog method on the resulting jQuery object. The dialog widget requires a specific structure of HTML elements in order to operate, although the structure is simpler than the tabs widget requires, for example. Listing 22-1 shows a document that contains the required elements and that creates a dialog box.

Listing 22-1. Creating a Dialog Box Using jQuery UI

```
<!DOCTYPE html>
<html>
<head>
    <title>Example</title>
    <script src="jquery-2.0.2.js" type="text/javascript"></script>
    <script src="jquery-ui-1.10.3.custom.js" type="text/javascript"></script>
    <link rel="stylesheet" type="text/css" href="styles.css"/>
    <link rel="stylesheet" type="text/css" href="jquery-ui-1.10.3.custom.css"/>
    <script type="text/javascript">
        $(document).ready(function() {
            $("#dialog").dialog();
        });
    </script>
</head>
<body>
    <h1>Jacqui's Flower Shop</h1>
    <div id="dialog" title="Dialog Box">
        This is the content that will be displayed in the dialog box. This <b>content</b>
        can be <em>styled</em>.
    </div>
</body>
</html>
```

The dialog widget requires a `div` element that has a `title` attribute. The value of this attribute is used as the title bar of the dialog box. The content of the `div` element is used as the content for the dialog box, and, as Listing 22-1 shows, this content can contain other elements. When you call the `dialog` method with no settings, as I have done in the listing, the dialog box appears immediately. Figure 22-1 shows how the browser presents the dialog.

Figure 22-1. *A simple dialog box*

The dialog widget is created through the clever use of HTML elements and not through the operating system. This means a jQuery UI dialog doesn't behave in quite the same way as a native dialog box does. For example, it doesn't show up in the operating system's list of open windows and it is possible to resize the browser window so that you obscure part (or all) of the jQuery UI dialog.

That being said, the jQuery UI team has done a good job of making the dialog as fully featured as possible. By clicking the title and dragging, the user can reposition the dialog within the browser window. The dialog can be resized and can be dismissed by clicking the close button at the top right. And, since the jQuery UI dialog widget is constructed from HTML, it is styled using the jQuery UI theme I selected in Chapter 17 and can display complex and styled HTML content.

I want to demonstrate a common usage of the dialog before I get into the details of the settings, methods, and events that the widget supports. When you call the `dialog` method with no arguments, as I did in the first example, the dialog appears immediately, but this isn't usually convenient. A more common scenario is that you want to create the dialog box when the document loads (so that the element structure isn't visible to the user) and then display the dialog box later in response to an event. Listing 22-2 shows how you can do this.

Listing 22-2. Deferring the Appearance of a jQuery UI Dialog Box

```
<!DOCTYPE html>
<html>
<head>
    <title>Example</title>
    <script src="jquery-2.0.2.js" type="text/javascript"></script>
    <script src="jquery-ui-1.10.3.custom.js" type="text/javascript"></script>
    <link rel="stylesheet" type="text/css" href="styles.css"/>
    <link rel="stylesheet" type="text/css" href="jquery-ui-1.10.3.custom.css"/>
    <script type="text/javascript">
```

```
        $(document).ready(function() {
            $("#dialog").dialog({
                autoOpen: false
            });

            $("button").button().click(function(e) {
                $("#dialog").dialog("open")
            })
        });
    </script>
</head>
<body>
    <h1>Jacqui's Flower Shop</h1>
    <div id="dialog" title="Dialog Box">
      This is the content that will be displayed in the dialog box. This <b>content</b>
      can be <em>styled</em>.
    </div>
    <button>Show Dialog</button>
</body>
</html>
```

You use the autoOpen setting to prevent the dialog from appearing immediately. When this setting is false, the HTML element structure is hidden from the user, but the dialog isn't displayed. When you are ready to display the dialog, you can call the open method. You can see how this works in Figure 22-2.

Figure 22-2. *Deferring the appearance of a dialog box*

Configuring the Dialog

The dialog widget supports a range of settings that allow you to customize the way that you present the dialog to the user. I showed you the autoOpen setting in the previous section, but there other settings, as described in Table 22-2.

Table 22-2. *Dialog Settings*

Setting	Description
appendTo	Specifies the element that the dialog should be appended to.
autoOpen	When true, the dialog is displayed as soon as it is created with the dialog method. The default is true.
buttons	Specifies the set of buttons to add to the dialog and the functions that will be invoked when those buttons are clicked. The default is to use no buttons.
closeOnEscape	When true, pressing the Escape key dismisses the dialog. The default is true.
draggable	When true, the user can click the dialog title and drag to move the dialog within the browser. The default is true.
height	Specifies the initial height of the dialog in pixels. The default is auto, which allows the dialog to size itself.
hide	Specifies the animation effect that is used to hide the dialog. See Chapter 35 for details of the jQuery UI effects.
maxHeight	Specifies the maximum height (in pixels) of the dialog. The default is false, which means that there is no size limit.
maxWidth	Specifies the maximum width (in pixels) of the dialog. The default is false, which means that there is no size limit.
minHeight	Specifies the minimum height (in pixels) of the dialog. The default is false, which means that there is no minimum size limit.
minWidth	Specifies the minimum width (in pixels) of the dialog. The default is false, which means that there is no minimum size limit.
modal	When true, the dialog is modal and the user cannot interact with the document until the dialog is dismissed. The default is false.
position	Specifies the initial position of the dialog.
resizable	When true, the dialog is displayed with a drag handle that allows the user to resize the dialog. The default is true.
show	Specifies the animation effect that is used to show the dialog. See Chapter 35 for details of the jQuery UI effects.
title	Specifies the title of the dialog.
width	Specifies the initial width of the dialog in pixels. The default is auto, which allows the dialog to size itself.

▪ **Tip** jQuery UI 1.10 added the appendTo option, which allows the element to which the dialog will be appended to be specified. Another new feature is that dialog will also focus automatically on content elements. (I demonstrate these features later in this part of the chapter). Other changes include a change in the way that the value of the position setting is specified and the removal of the stack and zIndex configuration options.

Configuring the Basic Dialog Appearance

The `title` setting allows you to create a dialog from a `div` element that doesn't have a `title` attribute. This can be useful if you are unable to control the generation of the elements that you want to use in the dialog. Listing 22-3 shows the application of the `title` setting.

Listing 22-3. Using the title Setting

```
<!DOCTYPE html>
<html>
<head>
    <title>Example</title>
    <script src="jquery-2.0.2.js" type="text/javascript"></script>
    <script src="jquery-ui-1.10.3.custom.js" type="text/javascript"></script>
    <link rel="stylesheet" type="text/css" href="styles.css"/>
    <link rel="stylesheet" type="text/css" href="jquery-ui-1.10.3.custom.css"/>
    <script type="text/javascript">
        $(document).ready(function() {
            $("#dialog").dialog({
                title: "Hello",
                resizable: false
            });
        });
    </script>
</head>
<body>
    <h1>Jacqui's Flower Shop</h1>
    <div id="dialog">
      This is the content that will be displayed in the dialog box. This <b>content</b>
      can be <em>styled</em>.
    </div>
</body>
</html>
```

I have also applied the `resizable` setting in this example. This setting prevents the user from resizing the dialog. I usually leave the `resizable` setting set to `true` because I like to leave the user with the opportunity to resize the dialog to accommodate the content. You can see how the browser shows the dialog in the example in Figure 22-3.

Figure 22-3. *A dialog box with a custom title and no resize drag handle*

The dialog will automatically focus on the first content element it finds that has the autofocus attribute, which can be useful when using the dialog widget to solicit input from the user, as shown in Listing 22-4.

Listing 22-4. Using the autofocus Attribute on a Content Element

```
<!DOCTYPE html>
<html>
<head>
    <title>Example</title>
    <script src="jquery-2.0.2.js" type="text/javascript"></script>
    <script src="jquery-ui-1.10.3.custom.js" type="text/javascript"></script>
    <link rel="stylesheet" type="text/css" href="styles.css"/>
    <link rel="stylesheet" type="text/css" href="jquery-ui-1.10.3.custom.css"/>
    <script type="text/javascript">
        $(document).ready(function () {
            $("#dialog").dialog({
                title: "Hello",
                resizable: false
            });
        });
    </script>
</head>
<body>
    <h1>Jacqui's Flower Shop</h1>
    <div id="dialog">
      This is the content that will be displayed in the dialog box. This <b>content</b>
      can be <em>styled</em>.
        <p>Name: <input id="name"/> City: <input id="city" autofocus="autofocus" /></p>
    </div>
</body>
</html>
```

I have added input elements to the content for the dialog, the second of which has the autofocus attribute. You can see how the dialog widget focuses on this element in Figure 22-4.

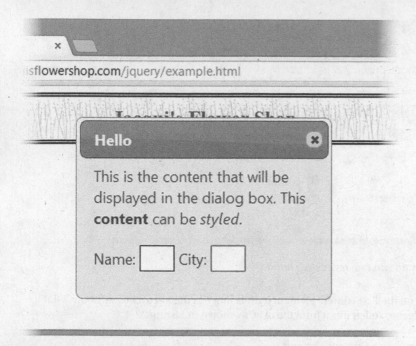

Figure 22-4. *The effect of the autofocus attribute*

Setting the Location of the Dialog

The position setting allows you to specify where the dialog will be displayed in the browser window. The position is expressed using the same properties and values that I described in Chapter 19 for the autocomplete pop-up, which I have repeated in Table 22-3.

Table 22-3. *Position Properties*

Name	Description
my	Specifies the part of the dialog that will be used to determine placement
at	Specifies the part of the target element that the dialog will be positioned relative to
of	Specifies the target element that the dialog will be positioned relative to; this is the body element if omitted
collision	Specifies how the placement of the dialog should be adjusted if it overflows the window

The my and at properties are set using values that specify horizontal and vertical positions, separated by a space. The horizontal values are left, right, and center and the vertical values are top, bottom, and center. You can see how I have set these properties in Listing 22-5. (You can learn about the other position properties in Chapter 19.)

Listing 22-5. Positioning the Dialog

```
<!DOCTYPE html>
<html>
<head>
    <title>Example</title>
    <script src="jquery-2.0.2.js" type="text/javascript"></script>
    <script src="jquery-ui-1.10.3.custom.js" type="text/javascript"></script>
    <link rel="stylesheet" type="text/css" href="styles.css"/>
    <link rel="stylesheet" type="text/css" href="jquery-ui-1.10.3.custom.css"/>
    <script type="text/javascript">
        $(document).ready(function () {
            $("#dialog").dialog({
                title: "Positioned Dialog",
                position: {
                    my: "left top",
                    at: "left top"
                }
            });
        });
    </script>
</head>
<body>
    <h1>Jacqui's Flower Shop</h1>
    <div id="dialog">
    This is the content that will be displayed in the dialog box. This <b>content</b>
    can be <em>styled</em>.
    </div>
</body>
</html>
```

I have positioned the dialog so that the top-left edge is positioned with the top-left edge of its parent element, which is the body element by default. You can see how the dialog is positioned in Figure 22-5.

Figure 22-5. Specifying the position of the dialog

Adding Buttons to a Dialog

You can add buttons to a jQuery UI dialog using the buttons setting. The value of this setting is an array of objects, each of which has text and click properties. The value of the text property is used as the label for the button, and you provide a function as the value of click property, which will be invoked when the button is clicked. Listing 22-6 shows the use of this setting.

Listing 22-6. Adding Buttons to a Dialog

```
...
<script type="text/javascript">
    $(document).ready(function() {
        $("#dialog").dialog({
            title: "Dialog",
            buttons: [{text: "OK", click: function() {/* do something */}},
                      {text: "Cancel", click: function() {$(this).dialog("close")}}]

        });
    });
</script>
...
```

In this script, I have added two buttons. The function for the OK button doesn't do anything, but for the Cancel button, I close the dialog. Notice that I use the this variable in the jQuery selector within the Cancel function. This is set to the div element that was used to create the dialog. You can see how the buttons are displayed in Figure 22-6. This example uses the close method, which dismisses the dialog. I describe the dialog methods later in this chapter.

Figure 22-6. Adding buttons to a jQuery UI dialog

As of jQuery UI version 1.10, you can specify icons for buttons in a dialog by adding an `icons` property to the objects that define each button, as shown in Listing 22-7.

Listing 22-7. Adding Icons to the Buttons in a Dialog Widget

```
...
<script type="text/javascript">
    $(document).ready(function () {
        $("#dialog").dialog({
            title: "Dialog",
            buttons: [{
                text: "OK",
                click: function () {/* do something */ },
                icons: {
                    primary: "ui-icon-star",
                    secondary: "ui-icon-circle-arrow-e"
                }
            },{ text: "Cancel", click: function () { $(this).dialog("close") }}]
        });
    });
</script>
...
```

The `icons` property is set to an object that defines properties named `primary` and `secondary`, which define icons to the left and right of the button text. These properties are used to specify icons in the same way as for the button widget, as described in Chapter 18. You can see the effect of the additions to the listing in Figure 22-7.

Figure 22-7. Using icons in dialog buttons

■ **Tip** You can disable the text in a dialog button by defining a property called `showText` on the object that defines the button (not the `icons` object) and setting it to `false`.

Dragging Dialogs

The `draggable` setting determines whether the user can drag the dialog box within the browser window. This setting is `true` by default, and I recommend that you leave the setting unchanged. It allows the user to see the underlying content. This can be particularly important if you are showing a dialog to express some kind of error or problem. If the `draggable` setting is `false`, then the user won't be able to reposition the dialog box.

The `draggable` setting can also be important when you are using multiple dialogs in the same window. This is not something I recommend, but if you must display dialog boxes, you need to make sure the user can arrange them so that they can all be read. On small screens, they tend to pile up on top of each other, as shown in Listing 22-8.

Listing 22-8. Using the draggable Setting

```html
<!DOCTYPE html>
<html>
<head>
    <title>Example</title>
    <script src="jquery-2.0.2.js" type="text/javascript"></script>
    <script src="jquery-ui-1.10.3.custom.js" type="text/javascript"></script>
    <link rel="stylesheet" type="text/css" href="styles.css"/>
    <link rel="stylesheet" type="text/css" href="jquery-ui-1.10.3.custom.css"/>
    <script type="text/javascript">
        $(document).ready(function () {
            $(".dialog").dialog({
                draggable: true
            });
        });
    </script>
</head>
<body>
    <h1>Jacqui's Flower Shop</h1>
    <div id="d1" class="dialog" title="First Dialog">
      This is the first dialog
    </div>
    <div id="d2" class="dialog" title="Second Dialog">
      This is the second dialog
    </div>
    <div id="d3" class="dialog" title="Third Dialog">
      This is the third dialog
    </div>
</body>
</html>
```

I create three dialogs in this document and the default positioning stacks them up. Setting the `draggable` setting to `true` allows me to move the dialogs, as shown in Figure 22-8.

Figure 22-8. *Dragging dialogs*

Creating Modal Dialogs

A modal dialog prevents the user from interacting with the elements in the document until the dialog has been dismissed. A value of true for the modal setting creates a modal dialog, as shown in Listing 22-9.

Listing 22-9. Creating a Modal Dialog

```
<!DOCTYPE html>
<html>
<head>
    <title>Example</title>
    <script src="jquery-2.0.2.js" type="text/javascript"></script>
    <script src="jquery-ui-1.10.3.custom.js" type="text/javascript"></script>
    <link rel="stylesheet" type="text/css" href="styles.css"/>
    <link rel="stylesheet" type="text/css" href="jquery-ui-1.10.3.custom.css"/>
    <script type="text/javascript">
        $(document).ready(function() {
            $("#dialog").dialog({
                buttons: [{text: "OK", click: function() {$(this).dialog("close")}}],
                modal: true,
                autoOpen: false
            })

            $("#show").button().click(function() {
                $("#dialog").dialog("open");
            })
        });
    </script>
</head>
<body>
    <h1>Jacqui's Flower Shop</h1>
    <div id="dialog" title="Modal Dialog">
```

599

```
        This is a modal dialog. Press OK to continue.
    </div>
    <button id="show">Show Dialog</button>
</body>
</html>
```

In Listing 22-9, I have created a modal dialog that is not initially visible to the user. The dialog is shown in response to a button being clicked and you can see the effect in Figure 22-9. This example relies on the open and close methods, which show and dismiss the dialog. I explain all of the methods that the dialog widget supports later in this chapter.

Figure 22-9. Displaying a modal dialog

When showing a modal dialog, jQuery UI places a dark layer behind the dialog but in front of the rest of the document. The document doesn't return to its original state until the dialog is dismissed. In this example, I have provided the user with an OK button that does this.

■ **Tip** When selecting the button you have added to the document to show the dialog, be careful not to use $("button") if you are also adding buttons to the dialog itself. This selector matches the buttons that you have added *and* those that are created by the dialog method, which means that the dialog buttons will end up with the same click handler as the button in the document, rather than the handlers specified by the buttons setting.

Showing a Form in a Modal Dialog

The benefit of a modal dialog is that it focuses the user's attention. You can use this to your advantage by displaying forms in modal dialogs, as shown in Listing 22-10.

Listing 22-10. Displaying a Form in a Model Dialog

```html
<!DOCTYPE html>
<html>
<head>
    <title>Example</title>
    <script src="jquery-2.0.2.js" type="text/javascript"></script>
    <script src="jquery-ui-1.10.3.custom.js" type="text/javascript"></script>
    <script src="handlebars.js"></script>
    <script src="handlebars-jquery.js"></script>
    <link rel="stylesheet" type="text/css" href="jquery-ui-1.10.3.custom.css"/>
    <link rel="stylesheet" type="text/css" href="styles.css"/>
    <style type="text/css">
        #dialog input {width: 150px; margin: 5px; text-align: left}
        #dialog label {width: 100px}
        table {border-collapse: collapse; border: thin solid black; margin: 10px}
        #placeholder {text-align: center}
        #show {margin: 10px}
        td, th {padding: 5px; width: 100px}
    </style>
    <script id="rowTmpl" type="text/x-handlebars-template">
        <tr><td>{{product}}</td><td>{{color}}</td><td>{{count}}</td></tr>
    </script>
    <script type="text/javascript">
        $(document).ready(function () {
            $("#dialog").dialog({
                buttons: [{ text: "OK", click: addDataToTable }],
                modal: true,
                autoOpen: false,
                width: 340
            })

            $("#show").button().click(function () {
                $("#dialog").dialog("open");
            })

            function addDataToTable() {
                var data = {
                    product: $("#product").val(),
                    color: $("#color").val(),
                    count: $("#count").val()
                }
                $("#placeholder").hide();
                $("#rowTmpl").template(data).filter("*").appendTo("#prods tbody");
                $("#dialog").dialog("close");
            }
        });
    </script>
</head>
<body>
    <h1>Jacqui"s Flower Shop</h1>
    <div id="dialog" title="Enter Details" class="ui-widget">
```

601

```
        <div><label for="product">Product: </label><input id="product" /></div>
        <div><label for="color">Color: </label><input id="color" /></div>
        <div><label for="count">Quantity: </label><input id="count" /></div>
    </div>
    <table id="prods" class="ui-widget" border="1">
        <tr><th>Product</th><th>Color</th><th>Quantity</th></tr>
        <tr id="placeholder"><td colspan=3>No Products Selected</td></tr>
    </table>
    <button id="show">Add Product</button>
</body>
</html>
```

In Listing 22-10, I have defined a set of input elements inside the div element that I use to create the modal dialog. When the user clicks the button in the document, the dialog is shown and gathers data from the user. When the user clicks the OK button (which I defined using the buttons setting), I collect the values from the input elements and use a data template to generate a new row for an HTML table. You can see the sequence in Figure 22-10.

Figure 22-10. *Using a modal dialog to capture input from the user*

I have tried to keep this example simple, but you can readily apply the validation techniques I showed you in Chapter 13 to reduce the risk of data errors, and you can use the Ajax techniques I showed in Chapters 14 and 15 to submit the data entered by the user to a remote server.

■ **Caution**   Showing a form inside a modal dialog is a useful technique for simple forms only. You are at risk of confusing and annoying the user if you find yourself trying to combine tabs or accordions with a modal dialog. If a form represents a substantial effort to fill in, then it warrants being properly integrated into the document itself.

Using the Dialog Methods

The jQuery UI dialog widget supports the methods described in Table 22-4.

Table 22-4. *Dialog Methods*

Method	Description
dialog("destroy")	Removes the dialog widget from the underlying element
dialog("option")	Changes one or more settings
dialog("close")	Dismisses the dialog
dialog("isOpen")	Returns true if the dialog is visible
dialog("moveToTop")	Moves the dialog to the top of the stack
dialog("open")	Displays the dialog to the user

As you might expect, most of these methods allow you to manage a dialog programmatically. The methods that I find myself using most frequently are open and close, of course. Listing 22-11 shows these methods.

Listing 22-11. Using the Dialog Methods

```
<!DOCTYPE html>
<html>
<head>
    <title>Example</title>
    <script src="jquery-2.0.2.js" type="text/javascript"></script>
    <script src="jquery-ui-1.10.3.custom.js" type="text/javascript"></script>
    <link rel="stylesheet" type="text/css" href="styles.css"/>
    <link rel="stylesheet" type="text/css" href="jquery-ui-1.10.3.custom.css"/>
    <script type="text/javascript">
        $(document).ready(function () {
            $("#d1, #d2").dialog({
                autoOpen: false,
            });

            $("#t1, #t2").button().click(function (e) {
                var target = this.id == "t1" ? "#d1" : "#d2";
                if ($(target).dialog("isOpen")) {
                    $(target).dialog("close")
                } else {
                    $(target).dialog("open")
                }
            })
        });
    </script>
</head>
<body>
    <h1>Jacqui's Flower Shop</h1>
    <div id="d1" class="dialog" title="First Dialog" class="ui-widget">
        This is the first dialog
    </div>
    <div id="d2" class="dialog" title="Second Dialog" class="ui-widget">
        This is the second dialog
    </div>
```

```
    <div>
        <button id="t1">Toggle Dialog 1</button>
    </div>
    <button id="t2">Toggle Dialog 2</button>
</body>
</html>
```

This document includes two button elements that toggle the visibility of two dialogs. The visibility of each dialog is assessed using the isOpen method. Figure 22-11 shows the document displayed in the browser with both dialogs visible.

Figure 22-11. *Toggling the visibility of dialogs using widget methods*

Using the Dialog Events

The jQuery UI dialog widget supports the events described in Table 22-5. I describe some of the more useful events in the sections that follow.

Table 22-5. *Dialog Events*

Event	Description
create	Triggered when the dialog widget is applied to an underlying HTML element
beforeClose	Triggered when the dialog is about to close; returning false from the handler function forces the dialog to remain open
open	Triggered when the dialog is opened
focus	Triggered when the dialog gains the focus
dragStart	Triggered when the user starts to drag a dialog
drag	Triggered for every mouse movement while a dialog is being dragged

(continued)

Table 22-5. (*continued*)

Event	Description
dragStop	Triggered when the user finishes dragging a dialog
resizeStart	Triggered when the user beings resizing a dialog
resize	Triggered for every mouse movement while a dialog is being resized
resizeStop	Triggered when the user finishes resizing a dialog
close	Triggered when a dialog is closed

Keeping the Dialog Open

The beforeClose event allows you to receive notification that the user has requested that the dialog be closed. This can be because the user pressed the Escape key (if the closeOnEscape setting is true), clicked the close icon at the top-right of the dialog, or clicked a button you have added through the buttons setting.

Most of the time, you should respect the user's wishes and allow the dialog to close, but there are rare occasions when you require the user to perform some action using the dialog first, or, as Listing 22-12 demonstrates, you require the dialog to be displayed for a certain period before allowing the user to continue.

Listing 22-12. Preventing a Dialog from Closing

```
<!DOCTYPE html>
<html>
<head>
    <title>Example</title>
    <script src="jquery-2.0.2.js" type="text/javascript"></script>
    <script src="jquery-ui-1.10.3.custom.js" type="text/javascript"></script>
    <link rel="stylesheet" type="text/css" href="styles.css"/>
    <link rel="stylesheet" type="text/css" href="jquery-ui-1.10.3.custom.css"/>
    <style type="text/css">
        input {width: 150px}
    </style>
    <script type="text/javascript">
        $(document).ready(function() {

            var canClose = false;
            var delay = 15;

            $("#dialog").dialog({
                modal: true,
                autoOpen: false,
                beforeClose: function() {
                    return canClose;
                },
                open: function() {
                    var count = delay;
                    var intID = setInterval(function() {
                        count--;
                        $("#time").text(count);
                        if (count == 0) {
```

```
                            clearInterval(intID)
                            canClose = true;
                            $("#dialog").dialog("close")
                        }
                    }, 1000)
                }
            })

            $("button").click(function(e) {
                $("#dialog").dialog("open")
            })

        });
    </script>
</head>
<body>
    <h1>Jacqui's Flower Shop</h1>

    <div class="ui-widget">
        <label for="user">Username: </label><input id="user"/>
        <label for="pass">Password: </label><input id="pass"/>
        <button id="send">Login</button>
    </div>
    <div id="dialog" title="Wrong Password">
        The password you entered was incorrect. Please try again in
        <span id="time">15</span> seconds.
    </div>
</body>
</html>
```

In Listing 22-12, I have defined a pair of input elements to collect a username and password from the user. It doesn't matter what the user enters, however, because I respond to the Login button being clicked by displaying a Wrong Password modal dialog.

I respond to the open event by starting a repeating function that counts down from 15 seconds. During this period, I use the beforeClose event to prevent the user from closing the dialog. At the end of the 15 seconds, I call the close method and dismiss the dialog. By combining the open and beforeClose events, I can ensure that the user cannot immediately try other username or password combinations (well, at least not without reloading the HTML document, anyway).

Responding to Changing Sizes and Positions

The dialog widget provides a comprehensive set of events for tracking the dialog as it is resized or dragged. These are events that are usually not required but are handy to have in those rare situations where being able to track the changes becomes important. Listing 22-13 demonstrates using the dragStart and dragStop events to disable the input and button elements in a document while a dialog is being dragged.

Listing 22-13. Responding to a Dialog Being Dragged

```
<!DOCTYPE html>
<html>
<head>
    <title>Example</title>
    <script src="jquery-2.0.2.js" type="text/javascript"></script>
```

```
<script src="jquery-ui-1.10.3.custom.js" type="text/javascript"></script>
<link rel="stylesheet" type="text/css" href="styles.css"/>
<link rel="stylesheet" type="text/css" href="jquery-ui-1.10.3.custom.css"/>
<style type="text/css">
    input {width: 150px; text-align: left}
</style>
<script type="text/javascript">
    $(document).ready(function() {

        $("#dialog").dialog({
            autoOpen: true,
            dragStart: function() {
                $("input, #send").attr("disabled", "disabled")
            },
            dragStop: function() {
                $("input, #send").removeAttr("disabled")
            }
        })

        $("button").click(function(e) {
            $("#dialog").dialog("open")
        })
    });
</script>
</head>
<body>
    <h1>Jacqui's Flower Shop</h1>

    <div class="ui-widget">
        <label for="user">Username: </label><input id="user"/>
        <label for="pass">Password: </label><input id="pass"/>
        <button id="send">Login</button>
    </div>
    <div id="dialog" title="Wrong Password">
        The password you entered was incorrect. Please try again in
        <span id="time">15</span> seconds.
    </div>
</body>
</html>
```

Using the jQuery UI Spinner Widget

The spinner widget was added to jQuery UI in version 1.9 and enhances an input element with up and down buttons so that the user can *spin* through a range of values. The spinner widget is applied using the spinner method, as shown in Listing 22-14.

Listing 22-14. Creating a Basic Spinner Widget

```
<!DOCTYPE html>
<html>
<head>
    <title>Example</title>
    <script src="jquery-2.0.2.js" type="text/javascript"></script>
    <script src="jquery-ui-1.10.3.custom.js" type="text/javascript"></script>
    <link rel="stylesheet" type="text/css" href="jquery-ui-1.10.3.custom.css"/>
    <link rel="stylesheet" type="text/css" href="styles.css"/>
    <style type="text/css">
        input {width: 150px;}
    </style>
    <script type="text/javascript">
        $(document).ready(function () {
            $("#entry").spinner();
        });
    </script>
</head>
<body>
    <h1>Jacqui's Flower Shop</h1>
    <div class="ui-widget">
        Enter value: <input id="entry" value="0" />
    </div>
</body>
</html>
```

You can see the way in which the `input` element is transformed in Figure 22-12, as well as the effect of clicking on the buttons that jQuery UI adds to the element.

Figure 22-12. Creating and using a spinner

Using the Spinner Widget with the HTML5 Input Element Types

HTML5 supports some new values for the type attribute of the input element, one of which has a similar effect to using the spinner widget: the number type. You can see how I have used this type in Listing 22-15.

Listing 22-15. Using the HTML5 Number Input Element

```
<!DOCTYPE html>
<html>
<head>
    <title>Example</title>
    <link rel="stylesheet" type="text/css" href="jquery-ui-1.10.3.custom.css"/>
    <link rel="stylesheet" type="text/css" href="styles.css"/>
    <style type="text/css">
        input {width: 150px;}
    </style>
</head>
<body>
    <h1>Jacqui's Flower Shop</h1>
    <div class="ui-widget">
        Enter value: <input id="entry" value="0" type="number" />
    </div>
</body>
</html>
```

I have taken out all of the JavaScript libraries and code from this example to emphasize the built-in browser support for the new type of input element. Figure 22-13 shows you how Google Chrome displays this listing.

Figure 22-13. *Using the number type input element in Google Chrome*

This approach has some advantages over the jQuery UI spinner because the implementation of the controls that change the value is not part in the HTML5 standard—this allows browsers to present the user with device-specific navigation. jQuery UI spinners always use the up and down buttons, which can be hard to use on small touch screen devices like smartphones.

The biggest problem with the new number type is that most browsers just ignore it, even those that implement other HTML5 features. And it is hard to mix and match the native HTML5 spinner with jQuery UI because the spinner widget doesn't check the type of the input element when the spinner method is called. Listing 22-16 shows an example HTML document that applies the spinner widget to an input element whose type is number.

Listing 22-16. Mixing jQuery UI Widgets and HTML5 input Element Types

```
<!DOCTYPE html>
<html>
<head>
    <title>Example</title>
    <script src="jquery-2.0.2.js" type="text/javascript"></script>
    <script src="jquery-ui-1.10.3.custom.js" type="text/javascript"></script>
    <link rel="stylesheet" type="text/css" href="jquery-ui-1.10.3.custom.css"/>
    <link rel="stylesheet" type="text/css" href="styles.css"/>
    <style type="text/css">
        input {width: 150px;}
    </style>
    <script type="text/javascript">
        $(document).ready(function () {
            $("#entry").spinner();
        });
    </script>
</head>
<body>
    <h1>Jacqui's Flower Shop</h1>
    <div class="ui-widget">
        Enter value: <input id="entry" value="0" type="number" />
    </div>
</body>
</html>
```

I have restored the JavaScript libraries and code and you can see the effect in Figure 22-14—two sets of buttons to change the value in the input element. The browser implementation of the new input element types and the jQuery UI handling of them are not yet mature enough to be reliable and I recommend avoiding them, especially in combination.

Figure 22-14. *Combining the HTML5 number input element and the jQuery UI spinner*

Configuring the Spinner Widget

The spinner widget supports a range of settings that allow you to customize the way that it operates, as described in Table 22-6 and as demonstrated in the sections that follow.

Table 22-6. *Spinner Settings*

Setting	Description
culture	Specifies the locale setting for parsing and formatting the data value.
disabled	Disables the spinner when set to true.
icons	Specifies the icons used for the spinner buttons (the default icons are up and down arrows).
incremental	Specifies how the value is incremented when one of the buttons is held down. When set to true, the rate of change will increase the longer the button is held. When set to false, the rate of change will remain constant. You can also specify a function to customize the rate change.
max	Specifies the largest allowed value.
min	Specifies the smallest allowed value.
numberFormat	Specifies the format of the number that the spinner displays.
page	Specifies the size of a page, which is the amount the value changes when the pageUp and pageDown method (described later in the chapter).
step	Specifies the amount by which the value will change when the up and down buttons are clicked.

Configuring the Basic Spinner Behavior

The basic behavior of the spinner widget is controlled by four settings: min, max, step, and page. In Listing 22-17, you can see how I have used these properties to constrain the values the spinner will support and how they are incremented and decremented.

Listing 22-17. Configuring the Basic Spinner Behavior

```
<!DOCTYPE html>
<html>
<head>
    <title>Example</title>
    <script src="jquery-2.0.2.js" type="text/javascript"></script>
    <script src="jquery-ui-1.10.3.custom.js" type="text/javascript"></script>
    <link rel="stylesheet" type="text/css" href="jquery-ui-1.10.3.custom.css"/>
    <link rel="stylesheet" type="text/css" href="styles.css"/>
    <style type="text/css">
        input {width: 150px;}
    </style>
    <script type="text/javascript">
        $(document).ready(function () {
            $("#entry").spinner({
                min: 2,
                max: 100,
                step: 2,
                page: 5
```

```
                });
            });
        </script>
    </head>
    <body>
        <h1>Jacqui's Flower Shop</h1>
        <div class="ui-widget">
            Enter value: <input id="entry" value="0" />
        </div>
    </body>
</html>
```

The min and max properties don't enforce validation on the input element—they only control the range of values that will be used by the up and down buttons. Once the limit defined by the max property has been reached (e.g., pressing the up button won't increment the value any further), the user can still edit the contents of the input element directly and insert a larger value (or a non-numeric value).

■ **Tip**   See Chapter 13 for details of how you can perform validation on input elements

---

The step and page properties control how the spinner widget increments and decrements the numeric value. The step property specifies the amount by which the value is changed when the user presses one of the buttons added by the widget; the page property specifies the amount by which the value is changed when the pageUp and pageDown methods are called (I describe these methods later in the chapter).

In the listing, I have specified a minimum value of 2 and a maximum value of 100. I used the step property to tell jQuery UI that the up and down buttons should change the value by 2 and the page property to tells jQuery UI to respond to the pageUp and pageDown methods by incrementing or decrementing the value by 5. You can see the effect in Figure 22-15.

Figure 22-15. *Controlling the basic behavior of the spinner widget*

■ **Tip**   Notice that the min value doesn't affect the initial value displayed by the input element. I have set the value attribute on the input element to zero, which is less than the min value I used when setting up the spinner.

The spinner widget will reset the contents of the `input` element to the smallest allowed value if the user enters a value which is outside the allowed range and then clicks the up or down buttons. You can see the effect in Figure 22-16.

Figure 22-16. *The spinner resetting the input element value*

Changing the Spinner Button Icons

The icons displayed by the up and down buttons are set using the `icons` property. The default icons are up and down arrows, but they can be set to any of the jQuery UI icons (which I described in Chapter 18) as shown in Listing 22-18.

Listing 22-18. Changing the Spinner Button Icons

```
<!DOCTYPE html>
<html>
<head>
    <title>Example</title>
    <script src="jquery-2.0.2.js" type="text/javascript"></script>
    <script src="jquery-ui-1.10.3.custom.js" type="text/javascript"></script>
    <link rel="stylesheet" type="text/css" href="jquery-ui-1.10.3.custom.css"/>
    <link rel="stylesheet" type="text/css" href="styles.css"/>
    <style type="text/css">
        input {width: 150px;}
    </style>
    <script type="text/javascript">
        $(document).ready(function () {
            $("#entry").spinner({
                min: 2,
                max: 100,
                step: 2,
                page: 5,
```

```
                icons: {
                    up: "ui-icon-circle-plus",
                    down: "ui-icon-circle-minus",
                }
            });
        });
    </script>
</head>
<body>
    <h1>Jacqui's Flower Shop</h1>
    <div class="ui-widget">
        Enter value: <input id="entry" value="0" />
    </div>
</body>
</html>
```

The icons property is set with an object that has up and down properties, which define the icon that will be used for the corresponding button. I specified plus and minus icons and you can see the result in Figure 22-17.

Figure 22-17. *Changing the icons used by the spinner widget*

Controlling the Change Rate

The incremental property is used to set the rate at which the value is changed when the user holds the up or down button. Setting this property to true will gradually increase the rate at which the value is changed the longer the button is held for; a value of false keeps the rate of change constant. The third option is to specify a function that customizes the rate of change, which Listing 22-19 demonstrates.

Listing 22-19. Specifying a Function for the incremental Setting Property

```
<!DOCTYPE html>
<html>
<head>
    <title>Example</title>
    <script src="jquery-2.0.2.js" type="text/javascript"></script>
    <script src="jquery-ui-1.10.3.custom.js" type="text/javascript"></script>
    <link rel="stylesheet" type="text/css" href="jquery-ui-1.10.3.custom.css"/>
    <link rel="stylesheet" type="text/css" href="styles.css"/>
```

```
<style type="text/css">
    input {width: 150px;}
</style>
<script type="text/javascript">
    $(document).ready(function () {
        $("#entry").spinner({
            incremental: function (spins) {
                return Math.pow(spins, 2);
            }
        });
    });
</script>
</head>
<body>
    <h1>Jacqui's Flower Shop</h1>
    <div class="ui-widget">
        Enter value: <input id="entry" value="0" />
    </div>
</body>
</html>
```

The argument passed to the function is the number of spins that the duration for which the button has been held is equivalent to. The function returns the value that should be displayed and my example returns the square of the spin count.

Setting the Number Format

The format of the number which is displayed by the spinner is controlled by the numberFormat and culture properties and is dependent on an external library called *Globalize*.

You can get the Globalize files from https://github.com/jquery/globalize. Click the Releases link, select the version you want (as I write this, the latest version is 0.1.1), and download either a zip or tar.gz archive. Extract the files from the archive and copy the following files to the folder that contains example.html and the JavaScript library files.

- lib/globalize.js
- lib/cultures/globalize.cultures.js

The first file contains the JavaScript code for dealing with localization and the second file contains a complete set of the locales that the Globalize library comes with.

■ **Tip** There are other, smaller, files in the lib/cultures folder that deal with a single locale and which you can use if you are only working with a limited set of regions.

The numberFormat property for the spinner widget specifies the format for the number, and the culture property specifies the locale whose formatting conventions will be used. In Listing 22-20, you can see both properties in use.

Listing 22-20. Using the numberFormat and culture Properties

```
<!DOCTYPE html>
<html>
<head>
    <title>Example</title>
    <script src="jquery-2.0.2.js" type="text/javascript"></script>
    <script src="jquery-ui-1.10.3.custom.js" type="text/javascript"></script>
    <link rel="stylesheet" type="text/css" href="jquery-ui-1.10.3.custom.css"/>
    <script src="globalize.js"></script>
    <script charset="utf-8" src="globalize.cultures.js"></script>
    <link rel="stylesheet" type="text/css" href="styles.css"/>
    <style type="text/css">
        input {width: 150px;}
    </style>
    <script type="text/javascript">
        $(document).ready(function () {
            $("#entry").spinner({
                culture: "fr-FR",
                numberFormat: "C"
            });
        });
    </script>
</head>
<body>
    <h1>Jacqui's Flower Shop</h1>
    <div class="ui-widget">
        Enter value: <input id="entry" value="5.00"/>
    </div>
</body>
</html>
```

The globalize.js file must be imported before the globalize.cultures.js file so that the locale information can be registered with the main library. When configuring the spinner, I have set the culture to fr-FR (which is the locale designator for French-speaking France) and the numberFormat to C, which specifies a currency. You can see the result in Figure 22-18.

Figure 22-18. *Setting the culture and format for the spinner widget*

■ **Tip** If you omit the culture setting, the locale defaults to the settings for the United States.

France uses the euro as its currency, places the symbol after the number, and separates the whole and fractional parts of a number with a comma.

Notice that I set the charset attribute of the script element for the local information, as follows:

```
...
<script charset="utf-8" src="globalize.cultures.js"></script>
...
```

You can set the character set for an HTML document using a meta element, but if you have not done so—and I have not in the example document—then you should set the character set explicitly for the script element that contains the locale information. Without this, most browsers have problems displaying currency symbols of other locales, as shown in Figure 22-19, which should display the euro symbol, but it gets interpreted as nonsense.

Figure 22-19. *The effect of omitting the charset attribute from the locale script element*

Using the Spinner Methods

The jQuery UI spinner widget supports the methods described in Table 22-7.

Table 22-7. *Spinner Methods*

Method	Description
spinner("destroy")	Removes the dialog widget from the underlying element
spinner("disable")	Disables the spinner widget
spinner("enable")	Enables the spinner widget
spinner("option")	Gets or sets settings
spinner("pageDown", count)	Decrements the spinner value by the specified number of pages
spinner("pageUp", count)	Increments the spinner value by the specified number of pages
spinner("stepDown", count)	Decrements the spinner value by the specified number of steps
spinner("stepUp", count)	Increments the spinner value by the specified number of steps
spinner("value")	Gets or sets the current value of the spinner

In Listing 22-21, you can see how I have applied the spinner-specific methods to the example.

Listing 22-21. Using the Spinner Methods

```html
<!DOCTYPE html>
<html>
<head>
    <title>Example</title>
    <script src="jquery-2.0.2.js" type="text/javascript"></script>
    <script src="jquery-ui-1.10.3.custom.js" type="text/javascript"></script>
    <link rel="stylesheet" type="text/css" href="jquery-ui-1.10.3.custom.css"/>
    <script src="globalize.js"></script>
    <script src="globalize.cultures.js"></script>
    <link rel="stylesheet" type="text/css" href="styles.css"/>
    <style type="text/css">
        input {width: 150px;}
        button { margin-top: 10px; }
    </style>
    <script type="text/javascript">
        $(document).ready(function () {

            $("#entry").spinner({
                culture: "en-US",
                numberFormat: "C",
                step: 2,
                page: 10
            });

            $("button").button().click(function () {
                $("#entry").spinner(this.id);
                console.log("Value: " + $("#entry").spinner("value"));
            });

        });
    </script>
</head>
<body>
    <h1>Jacqui's Flower Shop</h1>
    <div class="ui-widget">
        Enter value: <input id="entry" value="5.00"/>
    </div>
    <div>
        <button id="pageDown">Page Down</button>
        <button id="stepDown">Step Down</button>
        <button id="stepUp">Step Up</button>
        <button id="pageUp">Page Up</button>
    </div>
</body>
</html>
```

I have added button elements which I use to call the methods on the spinner control, incrementing and decrementing the value based on the step and page values. You can see the result in Figure 22-20.

Figure 22-20. *Controlling the value of the spinner programmatically*

If you look at the browser console, you will see output like the following:

```
Value: 8
Value: 10
Value: 12
```

The spinner value method returns the unformatted value, without the effect of the culture and numberFormat settings. You'll get the formatted value if you use jQuery to select the underlying input element and use the val method.

Using the Spinner Events

The jQuery UI spinner widget supports the events described in Table 22-8.

Table 22-8. *Dialog Events*

Event	Description
create	Triggered when the widget is created
change	Triggered when the value of the spinner changes and the underlying input element has lost the focus
spin	Triggered when the value is incremented or decremented
start	Triggered before the value is incremented or decremented
stop	Triggered after the value is incremented or decremented

In Listing 22-22, you can see how I have updated the previous example to write out the value of the spinner in response to the stop event.

Listing 22-22. Using the stop Event

```
...
<script type="text/javascript">
    $(document).ready(function () {
        $("#entry").spinner({
            culture: "en-US",
            numberFormat: "C",
            step: 2,
            page: 10,
            stop: function () {
                console.log("Value: " + $("#entry").spinner("value"));
            }
        });

        $("button").button().click(function () {
            $("#entry").spinner(this.id);
            //console.log("Value: " + $("#entry").spinner("value"));
        });

    });
</script>
...
```

■ **Tip** You can stop the value from changing by canceling the spin or start events. See Chapter 9 for details of the jQuery support for events.

Summary

In this chapter, I showed you the jQuery UI dialog and spinner widgets. Following the same format as the other widget chapters, I focused on the settings, methods, and events that the dialog and spinner widgets support. In Chapter 23, I show you the menu and tooltip widgets.

CHAPTER 23

■ ■ ■

Using the Menu and Tooltip Widgets

In this chapter, I describe the jQuery UI menu and tooltip widgets. Table 23-1 provides the summary for this chapter.

Table 23-1. *Chapter Summary*

Problem	Solution	Listing
Create a menu widget	Select an element structure and call the menu method; the structure is usually created using ul, li, and a elements	1
Add separators and disabled menu items	Add elements that contain only dashes or spaces and apply the ui-state-disabled class	2
Perform basic navigation	Add href attributes to a elements in the menu element structure	3
Use custom element structures	Use the menus setting	4, 5
Add custom icons to submenus	Use the icons setting	6
Add icons to menu items	Add span elements that are assigned to the ui-icon class and that specify the jQuery UI icon.	7
Set the location of submenus	Use the position setting	8
Receive notifications when menu items are active and selected	Handle the blur, focus, and select events	9
Create a tooltip widget	Select an element with a title attribute and call the tooltip menu	10, 11
Set the content of tooltips	Use the content and items settings	12–15
Add custom styles to tooltips	Use the tooltipClass setting and the ui-tooltip-content class	16, 17
Move the tooltip to follow the mouse	Use the track setting	18
Set the location of the tooltip	Use the position setting	19
Control the tooltips programmatically	Call the open and close methods	20
Receive notifications when tooltips are shown and hidden	Handle the open and close events	21

Using the jQuery UI Menu Widget

The menu widget—as its name suggests—provides a menu that allows the user to navigate through a tree of options. This widget is useful when presenting the user with content that has a deep structure, such as product categories for an online store.

Creating the Menu

The menu widget relies on the menu structure being expressed as a structure of HTML elements, which are selected and transformed with the menu method, as shown in Listing 23-1.

Listing 23-1. Creating a Menu Widget

```html
<!DOCTYPE html>
<html>
<head>
    <title>Example</title>
    <script src="jquery-2.0.2.js" type="text/javascript"></script>
    <script src="jquery-ui-1.10.3.custom.js" type="text/javascript"></script>
    <link rel="stylesheet" type="text/css" href="jquery-ui-1.10.3.custom.css"/>
    <link rel="stylesheet" type="text/css" href="styles.css"/>
    <style>
        .ui-menu { width: 200px; }
    </style>
    <script type="text/javascript">
        $(document).ready(function () {
            $("#menu").menu();
        });
    </script>

</head>
<body>
    <h1>Jacqui's Flower Shop</h1>

    <ul id="menu">
        <li><a>Bouquets</a></li>
        <li><a>Heirloom Blooms</a></li>
        <li><a>Summer Color</a>
            <ul>
                <li><a>Aster</a></li>
                <li><a>Rose</a></li>
                <li><a>Orchid</a></li>
            </ul>
```

```
        </li>
        <li><a>Wedding Classics</a></li>
        <li><a>Exotica</a></li>
    </ul>
</body>
</html>
```

The structure of the menu is defined using an `ul` element, where individual menu items are `li` elements that contain an `a` element and the label for menu items is taken from the text of the `a` element. Nested submenus can be created by defining a `ul` element within an `li` element and you can see the effect of applying the `menu` method to the structure in the listing in Figure 23-1.

Figure 23-1. *Creating a simple menu widget*

In the figure, you can see how I have opened a submenu and have positioned my mouse over one of the items that have been revealed. This example demonstrates two key characteristics of the menu widget. First of all, the menu is always visible—it isn't a pop-up menu and is intended to be a permanent feature in a web page, similar to the way that Amazon presents its top-level product categories.

Second, the menu widget preserves the structure of the elements that it is applied to—the menu items are not sorted by name or any other characteristic. You can see in Figure 23-1 that ordering has been preserved, including the position of the submenu.

■ **Tip** Notice that I have set the width of the top-level `ul` element to 200 pixels using CSS). By default, the menu widget will fill all of the available horizontal space.

Formatting Menu Items

In addition to nesting submenus, the element structure can also be used to format menu items, creating disabled items and separators between groups of related items. Listing 23-2 shows both types of formatting.

Listing 23-2. Formatting the Menu via the Element Structure

```
...
<body>
    <h1>Jacqui's Flower Shop</h1>
    <ul id="menu">
        <li><a>Bouquets</a></li>
        <li><a>Heirloom Blooms</a></li>
        <li>-</li>
        <li><a>Summer Color</a>
            <ul>
                <li><a>Aster</a></li>
                <li><a>Rose</a></li>
                <li><a>Orchid</a></li>
            </ul>
        </li>
        <li><a>Wedding Classics</a></li>
        <li>-</li>
        <li class="ui-state-disabled"><a>Exotica</a></li>
    </ul>
</body>
...
```

Any element with content that is all spaces or dashes is interpreted as a menu divider—I have added two such elements in the listing. Assigning an element to the ui-state-disabled class tells the menu widget that the corresponding menu item should be disabled. You can see the result of these additions in Figure 23-2.

Figure 23-2. Adding separators and disabling menu items

Performing Basic Navigation

One common use for the menu widget is to provide navigation between the web pages that make up a web application and the simplest way to perform this task is to define the href attribute on the a elements in the HTML element structure that underpins the menu widget. When the user selects a menu item that corresponds to an a element with an href attribute, the browser will navigate to the specified URL. In Listing 23-3, you can see how I have added an href attribute to one of the menu item elements.

Listing 23-3. Adding an href Attribute to a Menu Element

```
...
<body>
    <h1>Jacqui's Flower Shop</h1>

    <ul id="menu">
        <li><a>Bouquets</a></li>
        <li><a>Heirloom Blooms</a></li>
        <li>-</li>
        <li><a>Summer Color</a>
            <ul>
                <li><a href="http://apress.com">Aster</a></li>
                <li><a>Rose</a></li>
                <li><a>Orchid</a></li>
            </ul>
        </li>
        <li><a>Wedding Classics</a></li>
        <li>-</li>
        <li class="ui-state-disabled"><a>Exotica</a></li>
    </ul>
</body>
...
```

I added an href attribute to one of the menu items, meaning that selecting the Summer Color ➤ Aster menu item will cause the browser to navigate to Apress.com.

■ **Tip**   Not all menus are used to navigate between web pages. You can perform arbitrary actions when the user selects a menu item by handling the select event, which I describe in the *Using the Menu Events* section later in this chapter.

Configuring the Menu

The menu widget supports a range of settings that allow you to customize the way that the menu is presented to the user, as described in Table 23-2.

Table 23-2. *Menu Settings*

Setting	Description
disabled	Disables the entire menu when set to true
icons	Specifies icons to be used on submenus
menus	Specifies the elements to be used for the menu structure
position	Specifies the position of the submenus relative to the main widget
role	Sets a custom ARIA role for accessibility

Using a Different Element Structure

Although the use of ul, li, and a elements to define menus is the standard technique, the menu widget can work with any element structure where there is a clearly defined parent-child relationship. In Listing 23-4, you can see how I have redefined the example menu using div elements.

Listing 23-4. Using a Different Element Type for the Menu Structure

```
<!DOCTYPE html>
<html>
<head>
    <title>Example</title>
    <script src="jquery-2.0.2.js" type="text/javascript"></script>
    <script src="jquery-ui-1.10.3.custom.js" type="text/javascript"></script>
    <link rel="stylesheet" type="text/css" href="jquery-ui-1.10.3.custom.css"/>
    <link rel="stylesheet" type="text/css" href="styles.css"/>
    <style>
        .ui-menu { width: 200px; }
    </style>
    <script type="text/javascript">
        $(document).ready(function () {
            $("#menu").menu();
        });
    </script>
</head>
<body>
    <h1>Jacqui's Flower Shop</h1>
    <div id="menu">
        <div><a>Bouquets</a></div>
        <div><a>Heirloom Blooms</a></div>
        <div>-</div>
        <div><a>Summer Color</a>
            <div>
                <div><a>Aster</a></div>
                <div><a>Rose</a></div>
                <div><a>Orchid</a></div>
            </div>
        </div>
```

```
        <div><a>Wedding Classics</a></div>
        <div>-</div>
        <div><a>Exotica</a></div>
    </div>
</body>
</html>
```

This is most useful when you want to make a menu out of existing HTML elements, typically those which are generated from a template or obtained from a remote server via Ajax. The problem is that the menu widget doesn't know which of my div elements represents submenus and so all of my div elements are treated as top-level menu items, as shown in Figure 23-3.

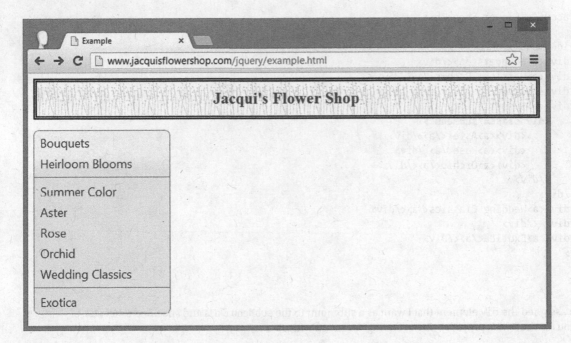

Figure 23-3. *The menu widget treating all elements as menu items*

I can give the menu widget information about the elements through the menus property, which is set to a selector that matches the elements I want for my submenus, as shown in Listing 23-5.

Listing 23-5. Using the Menus Configuration Property

```
<!DOCTYPE html>
<html>
<head>
    <title>Example</title>
    <script src="jquery-2.0.2.js" type="text/javascript"></script>
    <script src="jquery-ui-1.10.3.custom.js" type="text/javascript"></script>
    <link rel="stylesheet" type="text/css" href="jquery-ui-1.10.3.custom.css"/>
    <link rel="stylesheet" type="text/css" href="styles.css"/>
```

```
<style>
    .ui-menu { width: 200px; }
</style>
<script type="text/javascript">
    $(document).ready(function () {
        $("#menu").menu({
            menus: "div.subMenu"
        });
    });
</script>
</head>
<body>
    <h1>Jacqui's Flower Shop</h1>

    <div id="menu">
        <div><a>Bouquets</a></div>
        <div><a>Heirloom Blooms</a></div>
        <div>-</div>
        <div><a>Summer Color</a>
            <div class="subMenu">
                <div><a>Aster</a></div>
                <div><a>Rose</a></div>
                <div><a>Orchid</a></div>
            </div>
        </div>
        <div><a>Wedding Classics</a></div>
        <div>-</div>
        <div><a>Exotica</a></div>
    </div>
</body>
</html>
```

I have assigned the div element that I want as a submenu to the subMenu class and specified a selector of div.subMenu for the menus property when creating the menu widget.

■ **Tip**   You don't have to use a class and—if you do—it doesn't have to be called subMenu. Any selector that matches your elements will work.

Using Icons in Menus

The icons setting specifies the icons that the menu widget uses for submenus and is set to the name of one of the icons that I described in Chapter 18. Listing 23-6 shows the use of the icons setting.

Listing 23-6. Setting the Icons Used in Submenus

```
...
<script type="text/javascript">
    $(document).ready(function () {
        $("#menu").menu({
            menus: "div.subMenu",
            icons: { submenu: "ui-icon-circle-plus" }
        });
    });
</script>
...
```

The icons property is set using an object that defines a submenu property which, in turn, is set to the name of the icon you want to use. In the listing, I have specified the icon which shows a plus symbol in a circle and you can see the effect in Figure 23-4.

Figure 23-4. *Changing the icon used for submenus*

You can specify icons for individual menu items by adding span elements to the menu structure and using the class attribute to specify the icon name, as shown in Listing 23-7.

Listing 23-7. Adding Icons to Menu Items

```
<!DOCTYPE html>
<html>
<head>
    <title>Example</title>
    <script src="jquery-2.0.2.js" type="text/javascript"></script>
    <script src="jquery-ui-1.10.3.custom.js" type="text/javascript"></script>
    <link rel="stylesheet" type="text/css" href="jquery-ui-1.10.3.custom.css"/>
    <link rel="stylesheet" type="text/css" href="styles.css"/>
    <style>
        .ui-menu { width: 200px; }
    </style>
```

```
<script type="text/javascript">
    $(document).ready(function () {
        $("#menu").menu({
            icons: { submenu: "ui-icon-circle-plus" }
        });
    });
</script>
</head>
<body>
    <h1>Jacqui's Flower Shop</h1>

    <ul id="menu">
        <li><a>Bouquets</a></li>
        <li><a>Heirloom Blooms</a></li>
        <li>-</li>
        <li><a>Summer Color</a>
            <ul>
                <li><a>Aster</a></li>
                <li><a>Rose</a></li>
                <li><a>Orchid</a></li>
            </ul>
        </li>
        <li>
            <a><span class="ui-icon ui-icon-circle-check"></span>Wedding Classics</a>
        </li>
        <li>-</li>
        <li class="ui-state-disabled"><a>Exotica</a></li>
    </ul>
</body>
</html>
```

The span element must appear within the a element and be assigned to the ui-icon class *and* the class that represents the icon to display, which is ui-icon-circle-check in this example. You can see the effect of this change in Figure 23-5.

Figure 23-5. *Adding icons to menu items*

Positioning Submenu Pop-ups

The position setting determines where the pop-up appears for submenus and uses the same position format that I described in Chapter 19. My advice is to allow the menu widget to position submenus automatically, not least because the pop-ups for submenus are transparent and you can see the underlying menu structure when the pop-up is positioned over the parent widget. In Listing 23-8, you can see the position setting used to display submenus so that they are centered over the menu widget.

Listing 23-8. Positioning the Pop-ups for Submenus

```
...
<script type="text/javascript">
    $(document).ready(function () {
        $("#menu").menu({
            icons: { submenu: "ui-icon-circle-plus" },
            position: {
                my: "left center",
                at: "center center"
            }
        });
    });
</script>
...
```

The effect can be seen in Figure 23-6, with the underlying menu items visible through the pop-up.

Figure 23-6. *Positioning a submenu pop-up over the menu widget*

Using the Menu Methods

The jQuery UI menu widget supports the methods described in Table 23-3. I don't find these methods useful because they mainly provide the means to drive navigation in the menu widget, something that is best left to the user. These methods make it easy to create a jarring user experience and I recommend against using them.

Table 23-3. Menu Methods

Method	Description
menu("blur")	Removes the focus from the menu – triggers the blur event (described later in the chapter)
menu("collapse")	Closes the currently active submenu
menu("collapseAll")	Closes all open submenus
menu("destroy")	Removes the menu widget from the underlying element
menu("disable")	Disables the menu
menu("enable")	Enables the menu
menu("expand")	Opens the submenu associated with the currently selected menu item
menu("focus")	Focuses on a menu item
menu("isFirstItem")	Returns true if the currently selected item is the first in the menu
menu("isLastItem")	Returns true if the currently selected item is the last in the menu
menu("next")	Moves the focus to the next menu item
menu("option")	Changes one or more settings
menu("previous")	Moves the focus to the previous menu item
menu("refresh")	Updates the menu to reflect changes in the underlying HTML elements
menu("select")	Selects the active menu item, closes all open submenus, and triggers the select event (described later in the chapter)

It is difficult to demonstrate these methods because the behavior of the menu widget is tied closely to the currently selected menu items. Trying to control a menu with buttons, for example, doesn't work because clicking the button takes the focus away from the menu. My advice is to avoid using these methods and rely on standard user interaction, handling the events that I describe in the next section.

■ **Note** The menu widget also defines methods for navigating through menus that can scroll, but this feature doesn't work reliably at the time of this writing and so I have omitted the methods from the table.

Using the Menu Events

The jQuery UI menu widget supports the events described in Table 23-4.

Table 23-4. Menu Events

Event	Description
blur	Triggered when the menu loses focus (this event can be explicitly triggered by calling the blur method)
create	Triggered when the widget is created
focus	Triggered when the menu gains the focus and when a menu item is activated (this event can be explicitly triggered by calling the focus method)
select	Triggered when menu item is selected, either by the user or because the select method has been called

In Listing 23-9, you can see how I have used the blur and focus events to keep track of which menu items are activated by the user and the select event to respond when the user clicks on a menu item.

Listing 23-9. Handling the Blur, Focus, and Select Events from the Menu Widget

```
<!DOCTYPE html>
<html>
<head>
    <title>Example</title>
    <script src="jquery-2.0.2.js" type="text/javascript"></script>
    <script src="jquery-ui-1.10.3.custom.js" type="text/javascript"></script>
    <link rel="stylesheet" type="text/css" href="jquery-ui-1.10.3.custom.css"/>
    <link rel="stylesheet" type="text/css" href="styles.css"/>
    <style>
        .ui-menu { width: 200px; }
    </style>
    <script type="text/javascript">
        $(document).ready(function () {
            $("#menu").menu({
                focus: function (e, ui) {
                    console.log("Focus: " + ui.item.find("a").first().text());
                },
                blur: function () {
                    console.log("Blur");
                },
                select: function (e, ui) {
                    console.log("Select: " + ui.item.find("a").first().text());
                    e.preventDefault();
                }
            });
        });
    </script>
</head>
<body>
    <h1>Jacqui's Flower Shop</h1>

    <ul id="menu">
        <li><a>Bouquets</a></li>
        <li><a>Heirloom Blooms</a></li>
        <li>-</li>
        <li><a>Summer Color</a>
            <ul>
                <li><a href="http://apress.com">Aster</a></li>
                <li><a>Rose</a></li>
                <li><a>Orchid</a></li>
            </ul>
        </li>
        <li><a>Wedding Classics</a></li>
        <li>-</li>
        <li class="ui-state-disabled"><a>Exotica</a></li>
    </ul>
</body>
</html>
```

The handler functions for all three events are passed a jQuery event object (which I described in Chapter 9) and an additional `ui` object whose `item` property returns a jQuery object. The jQuery object is meant to contain the HTML element that the event corresponds to, but as I write this, the value of this property isn't set properly for the `blur` event.

With this in mind, I handle the `focus` and `select` events by writing the text content of the first `a` element contained by the element that the event relates to and simply note that the `blur` event has been triggered. If you run this example and navigate around the menu, you will see output similar to the following:

```
Focus: Bouquets
Blur
Focus: Heirloom Blooms
Blur
Focus: Summer Color
Select: Summer Color
Blur
Focus: Aster
Blur
Focus: Aster
Select: Aster
Blur
Focus: Aster
Blur
```

I have highlighted one of the statements written to the console because it demonstrates that items which contain submenus can themselves be selected—in this case, I was able to click on the Summer Color menu item even though it contains a submenu. This can lead to unexpected behavior when the handler for the `select` method doesn't take this into account.

■ **Tip**   Notice that I call the `preventDefault` method when handling the `select` event to prevent the browser from navigating to the URL specified by the `href` attribute of the `a` elements.

Using the jQuery UI Tooltip Widget

The tooltip widget provides small pop-ups that can be used to provide the user with helpful context information. Tooltips can be a force for good or evil. When used carefully, tooltips can help users navigate a complex process, but more often they are misused and become a distraction or an annoyance.

The most common pitfall is telling the user something she already knows and, in doing so, missing an opportunity to provide something more useful—this happens most frequently in web forms which require complex data. A recent example I saw came in an online tax form. Taxes are naturally complex and the developers felt it would be helpful to provide tooltips to give users information about the data required for each field. This was a noble gesture, but each tooltip simply restated information that was already evident from the form labels. So, for example, the tooltip for the form labeled Birth Date told me to "Enter your date of birth." What wasn't provided was the format I had to use—*month/day/year, day/month/year, year/month/day,* and so on. You can see examples of this problem all over the web and each one represents a lost opportunity to provide the user with a helpful insight. A related problem is tooltips preventing the user from completing a task. Each time I made another wrong guess in the tax form at the required format for key fields, I would be presented with a tooltip that obscured the `input` element, slowing down my attempts to get through the process.

My advice is to use tooltips sparingly and to think carefully about what value they offer to the user. If you are simply restating information that the user already has, then reconsider your goals.

Creating the Tooltip

The jQuery UI tooltip widget can be applied to any HTML element with the `tooltip` method and, by default, displays the contents of the `title` attribute, as shown in Listing 23-10.

■ **Tip** The mainstream browsers will use the `title` attribute to display tooltips anyway, without needing to use jQuery UI. The advantage of the tooltip widget is that it allows you to style the tooltip consistently with the rest of the application, take control of how the tooltip is used, and use a wider range of content.

Listing 23-10. Creating a Tooltip Widget

```
<!DOCTYPE html>
<html>
<head>
    <title>Example</title>
    <script src="jquery-2.0.2.js" type="text/javascript"></script>
    <script src="jquery-ui-1.10.3.custom.js" type="text/javascript"></script>
    <link rel="stylesheet" type="text/css" href="jquery-ui-1.10.3.custom.css"/>
    <link rel="stylesheet" type="text/css" href="styles.css"/>
    <style>
        [title] { font-weight: bold; font-style:italic }
    </style>
    <script type="text/javascript">
        $(document).ready(function () {
            $("[title]").tooltip();
        });
    </script>
</head>
<body class="ui-widget">
    <h1>Jacqui's Flower Shop</h1>

    <h3>Color and Beauty to Your Door</h3>
    <p>We are pleased to announce that we are starting a home delivery service for
    your flower needs. We will deliver within a
    <span title="We are at 200 Main St">20 mile radius</span>
    of the store for free and $1/mile thereafter.</p>
</body>
</html>
```

In this example I have defined a span element that has a `title` attribute. I select any element that has a `title` attribute and call the `tooltip` method and—to emphasize which elements have tooltips—I have defined a CSS style that uses the same selector. The result is that jQuery UI creates a tooltip widget which is shown when the mouse hovers over the span element, as shown in Figure 23-7.

Figure 23-7. *A jQuery UI tooltip*

Using Tooltips with Input Elements

Tooltips are also shown when the element they relate to has the focus—something that can be useful when working with input elements because the tooltips will appear for each element as the user tabs through the form. Applying tooltips to an input element is just the same as for other elements, as demonstrated in Listing 23-11.

Listing 23-11. Applying Tooltips to Input Elements

```
<!DOCTYPE html>
<html>
<head>
    <title>Example</title>
    <script src="jquery-2.0.2.js" type="text/javascript"></script>
    <script src="jquery-ui-1.10.3.custom.js" type="text/javascript"></script>
    <link rel="stylesheet" type="text/css" href="jquery-ui-1.10.3.custom.css"/>
    <link rel="stylesheet" type="text/css" href="styles.css"/>
    <style>
        input { width: 150px; }
    </style>
    <script type="text/javascript">
        $(document).ready(function () {
            $("input").tooltip();
        });
    </script>
</head>
<body class="ui-widget">
    <h1>Jacqui's Flower Shop</h1>
    <div><label>Name:</label><input title="Use lastname, firstname" /></div>
    <div><label>City:</label><input title="Don't include your state" /></div>
</body>
</html>
```

There are two input elements with `title` attributes in this listing and you can see the effect of tabbing through the elements in Figure 23-8.

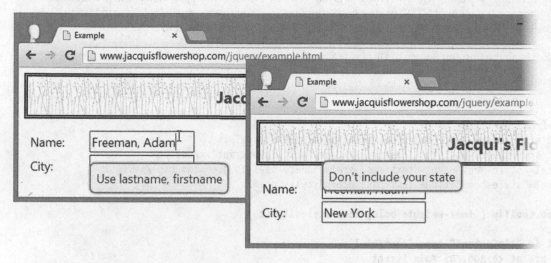

Figure 23-8. *Using tooltips with input elements*

Configuring the Tooltip

The tooltip widget supports a range of settings that allow you to customize the way that the widget is presented to the user, as described in Table 23-5 and demonstrated in the sections that follow.

Table 23-5. *Tooltip Settings*

Setting	Description
content	Sets the content for the tooltip, which can be expressed as a string of HTML or as a function
disabled	Disables the tooltip when set to `true`
hide	Specifies how the tooltip is animated when it is hidden—see Chapter 34 for details of the jQuery UI animation support
items	Specifies a selector that can narrow the set of elements for which tooltips are created
position	Specifies the position of the tooltip in relation to the element it corresponds to
show	Specifies how the tooltip is animated when it is shown—see Chapter 34 for details of the jQuery UI animation support
tooltipClass	Specifies an additional class that the tooltip element will be added to, allowing styling for different types of tooltip (errors, for example)
track	When set to `true`, the position of the tooltip will change to track the position of the mouse as it moves over the underlying HTML element

Setting the Tooltip Content

One of the big advantages of using jQuery UI tooltips is that you can use them to display rich content, which can be specified either as a fragment of HTML or via a JavaScript function. You can see the first of these in Listing 23-12, where I use the content property to specify a fragment of HTML that contains formatting.

Listing 23-12. Using the Content Setting to Display Formatted Content

```
<!DOCTYPE html>
<html>
<head>
    <title>Example</title>
    <script src="jquery-2.0.2.js" type="text/javascript"></script>
    <script src="jquery-ui-1.10.3.custom.js" type="text/javascript"></script>
    <link rel="stylesheet" type="text/css" href="jquery-ui-1.10.3.custom.css"/>
    <link rel="stylesheet" type="text/css" href="styles.css"/>
    <style>
        span.toolTip { font-weight: bold; font-style:italic }
    </style>
    <script id="tipContent" type="text/html">
        We are at <b>200</b> Main Street
    </script>
    <script type="text/javascript">
        $(document).ready(function () {
            $("span.toolTip").tooltip({
                content: $("#tipContent").html(),
                items: "span.toolTip"
            });
        });
    </script>
</head>
<body class="ui-widget">
    <h1>Jacqui's Flower Shop</h1>

    <h3>Color and Beauty to Your Door</h3>
    <p>We are pleased to announce that we are starting a home delivery service for
    your flower needs. We will deliver within a
    <span class="toolTip">20 mile radius</span>
    of the store for free and $1/mile thereafter.</p>
</body>
</html>
```

I have defined a new script element but set the type attribute to be text/html—this has the effect of preventing the browser from treating the contents of the script element as JavaScript or as part of the HTML content. This is the same technique that is used for data templates (as described in Chapter 12), but my goal is just to stash an HTML fragment out of the main part of the document until I need it.

I use the content setting to pass the HTML fragment to the tooltip widget. Notice that I have to select the script element that contains the fragment using jQuery and then call the html method to get its content—the tooltip widget isn't nicely integrated into jQuery and will only take HTML as a string.

I have had to use the items setting as well—and that's because I am no longer using the title attribute, which the tooltip widget looks for by default. Without this change, the call to the tooltip method will ignore my span element. I have added the span element to a class called toolTip and used this as the basis for the selector I provided for the items setting.

The HTML fragment contained in the script element is used as the content for the tooltip and the effect is shown in Figure 23-9, including the modest styling I added through a b element.

Figure 23-9. *Styling the content in a tooltip*

■ **Tip** I have shown formatted text in this example, but you can use a jQuery UI tooltip to display any HTML content, including images.

Generating Tooltip Content with a Function

I can also specify content using a function. For locally generated tooltip content, I can simply return an HTML fragment directly from the function, as shown in Listing 23-13.

Listing 23-13. Generating Tooltip Content from a Function

```html
<!DOCTYPE html>
<html>
<head>
    <title>Example</title>
    <script src="jquery-2.0.2.js" type="text/javascript"></script>
    <script src="jquery-ui-1.10.3.custom.js" type="text/javascript"></script>
    <link rel="stylesheet" type="text/css" href="jquery-ui-1.10.3.custom.css"/>
    <link rel="stylesheet" type="text/css" href="styles.css"/>
    <style>
        span.toolTip { font-weight: bold; font-style:italic }
    </style>
    <script type="text/javascript">
        $(document).ready(function () {
            $("span.toolTip").tooltip({
                content: function () {
                    if (this.id == "address") {
                        return "We are at <b>200</b> Main Street";
```

639

```
                    } else {
                        return "Fee capped at <i>$20</i> during June!"
                    }
                },
                items: "span.toolTip"
            });
        });
    </script>
</head>
<body class="ui-widget">
    <h1>Jacqui's Flower Shop</h1>

    <h3>Color and Beauty to Your Door</h3>
    <p>We are pleased to announce that we are starting a home delivery service for
    your flower needs. We will deliver within a
    <span id="address" class="toolTip">20 mile radius</span> of the store for free and
    <span id="maxPrice" class="toolTip">$1/mile thereafter.</span></p>
</body>
</html>
```

I have defined two span elements that have tooltips in this example and I use the function I provided to the content setting to give unique content to each tooltip. When the function is called, the value of the this variable is set to the element that has triggered the need for tooltip content. I use the id property to get the value of the id attribute and return different HTML fragments based on the element. You can see the result in Figure 23-10.

Figure 23-10. *Generating tooltip content using a function*

Getting Remote Tooltip Content

You can also obtain tooltip content asynchronously using Ajax and provide the fragment you want to display to jQuery UI via a callback. To demonstrate how this works, I have created a new JSON file called tooltips.json and placed it in the same directory as the other files in the example. You can see the content of the tooltips.json file in Listing 23-14.

Listing 23-14. The Contents of the tooltips.json File

```
{"address": "We are at <b>200</b> Main Street",
 "maxPrice": "Fee capped at <i>$20</i> during June!"}
```

In a real application, the server would usually send back a specific message for a given element, but for simplicity my JSON file contains all of the tooltip content that my example requires. You can see how I can obtain this data and use it to provide tooltip content in Listing 23-15.

Listing 23-15. Obtaining Remote Tooltip Content

```
...
<script type="text/javascript">
    $(document).ready(function () {

        var tooltipData;

        $("span.toolTip").tooltip({
            content: function (callback) {
                if (tooltipData != null) {
                    console.log("Requested serviced locally: " + this.id);
                    return tooltipData[this.id];
                } else {
                    var elemID = this.id;
                    $.getJSON("tooltips.json", function (data) {
                        tooltipData = data;
                        console.log("Requested serviced remotely: " + elemID);
                        callback(tooltipData[elemID]);
                    });
                }
            },
            items: "span.toolTip"
        });
    });
</script>
...
```

Given that the JSON file contains all of the values I require, I can make one request to the server and then store the data I retrieve for subsequent tooltips—and that's what most of the code in the example relates to. The key point in this example is that the callback that I pass to the getJSON method (which I described in Chapter 14) won't be executed until *after* the function used for the content setting has completed, meaning that I can't simply return the HTML fragment for the tooltip as the result.

Instead, my content function is passed an argument, which is a function to invoke when I have prepared the HTML fragment.

```
...
content: function (callback) {
...
```

When my Ajax request completes, I call this function with the data I want to display:

```
...
callback(tooltipData[elemID]);
...
```

The resulting tooltips are indistinguishable from the earlier examples, but the content that is displayed has been obtained via an Ajax request.

■ **Tip**   I have included this feature for completeness, but you should use it with caution. Tooltips work best when they provide immediate feedback to the user and this may not happen if your Ajax request takes a while to complete.

Adding Extra CSS Classes to Tooltips

The `tooltipClass` setting lets you specify one or more CSS classes that will be applied to tooltips for custom styling. Listing 23-16 provides an example.

Listing 23-16. Using the tooltipClass Setting

```
<!DOCTYPE html>
<html>
<head>
    <title>Example</title>
    <script src="jquery-2.0.2.js" type="text/javascript"></script>
    <script src="jquery-ui-1.10.3.custom.js" type="text/javascript"></script>
    <link rel="stylesheet" type="text/css" href="jquery-ui-1.10.3.custom.css"/>
    <link rel="stylesheet" type="text/css" href="styles.css"/>
    <style>
        span.toolTip { font-weight: bold; font-style:italic }
        *.customTip { border-color: red; }
    </style>
    <script type="text/javascript">
        $(document).ready(function () {
            $("span.toolTip").tooltip({
                content: function () {
                    if (this.id == "address") {
                        return "We are at <b>200</b> Main Street";
                    } else {
                        return "Fee capped at <i>$20</i> during June!"
                    }
                },
                items: "span.toolTip",
                tooltipClass: "customTip"
            });
        });
    </script>
</head>
```

```
<body class="ui-widget">
    <h1>Jacqui's Flower Shop</h1>
    <h3>Color and Beauty to Your Door</h3>
    <p>We are pleased to announce that we are starting a home delivery service for
    your flower needs. We will deliver within a
    <span id="address" class="toolTip">20 mile radius</span> of the store for free and
    <span id="maxPrice" class="toolTip">$1/mile thereafter.</span></p>
</body>
</html>
```

I have defined a CSS style for a class called `customTip` and applied this class to the tooltips using the `tooltipClass` setting. My style sets the color of the border, which produces the result shown in Figure 23-11.

Figure 23-11. *Applying a custom class to tooltips*

The HTML generated by jQuery UI for tooltips includes another class that can be useful for styling. Following is an example of the HTML generated for one of the widgets in the example:

```
...
<div id="ui-tooltip-3" role="tooltip" class="ui-tooltip ui-widget ui-corner-all
    ui-widget-content customTip" style="top: 210.15625px; left: 161px; display: block;">
    <div class="ui-tooltip-content">We are at <b>200</b> Main Street</div>
</div>
...
```

There is an outer div element to which the class specified by the `tooltipClass` setting is applied, but the content displayed by the tooltip is contained within an inner div element, which belongs to the `ui-tooltip-content` class. For advanced styling, you can use both classes to target the widget and its content separately, as shown in Listing 23-17.

■ **Tip** The other classes applied to the tooltip, such as `ui-widget` and `ui-corner-all`, are part of the jQuery UI CSS framework, which I describe in Chapter 35.

Listing 23-17. Styling the Widget and Its Content Separately

```
...
<style>
    span.toolTip { font-weight: bold; font-style:italic }
    *.customTip { border-color: red; }
    *.ui-tooltip-content { border: thick solid black; margin: 10px; padding: 10px;
                           background-color: white; }
</style>
...
```

You can see the effect of this change in Figure 23-12.

Figure 23-12. *Changing the style of the tooltip content independently from the tooltip itself*

■ **Tip**   If you want to change the background color of a tooltip, you will need to set the `background-image` property to `none` in the class that is specified with the `tooltipClass` setting. jQuery UI widget backgrounds are generated using images from the theme rather than colors.

Tracking the Mouse

When the `track` setting is `true`, the tooltip will follow the movements of the mouse over the HTML element that the tooltip corresponds to. This is useful when you want to change the content of the tooltip based on the position of the mouse, reflecting different regions of the underlying HTML element, as shown in Listing 23-18.

Listing 23-18. Tracking the Position of the Mouse with the Tooltip

```
<!DOCTYPE html>
<html>
<head>
    <title>Example</title>
    <script src="jquery-2.0.2.js" type="text/javascript"></script>
    <script src="jquery-ui-1.10.3.custom.js" type="text/javascript"></script>
    <link rel="stylesheet" type="text/css" href="jquery-ui-1.10.3.custom.css"/>
    <link rel="stylesheet" type="text/css" href="styles.css"/>
```

```
<style>
    span.toolTip { font-weight: bold; font-style:italic }
</style>
<script type="text/javascript">
    $(document).ready(function () {
        $("span.toolTip").tooltip({
            content: "Move the mouse",
            items: "span.toolTip",
            track: true
        }).mousemove(function(e) {
            $(this).tooltip("option", "content",
                "X: " + e.pageX + " Y: " + e.pageY);
        });
    });
</script>
</head>
<body class="ui-widget">
    <h1>Jacqui's Flower Shop</h1>
    <h3>Color and Beauty to Your Door</h3>
    <p>We are pleased to announce that we are starting a home delivery service for
    your flower needs. We will deliver within a
    <span id="address" class="toolTip">20 mile radius</span> of the store for free and
    <span id="maxPrice" class="toolTip">$1/mile thereafter.</span></p>
</body>
</html>
```

I enable tracking the mouse with the track setting and set up a handler function for the mousemove event (as described in Chapter 9) which uses the option method to update the content that the tooltip displays. This is an example that you need to experience firsthand to see the updates being performed, but Figure 23-13 shows a snapshot of the new behavior.

Figure 23-13. Tracking the position of the mouse with the tooltip

Positioning the Tooltip

The position setting specifies how the tooltip will be positioned relative to the element it corresponds to, using the same format I described in Chapter 19. You can see an example in Listing 23-19.

Listing 23-19. Positioning the Tooltip

```html
<!DOCTYPE html>
<html>
<head>
    <title>Example</title>
    <script src="jquery-2.0.2.js" type="text/javascript"></script>
    <script src="jquery-ui-1.10.3.custom.js" type="text/javascript"></script>
    <link rel="stylesheet" type="text/css" href="jquery-ui-1.10.3.custom.css"/>
    <link rel="stylesheet" type="text/css" href="styles.css"/>
    <style>
        span.toolTip { font-weight: bold; font-style:italic }
    </style>
    <script type="text/javascript">
        $(document).ready(function () {
            $("span.toolTip").tooltip({
                content: function () {
                    if (this.id == "address") {
                        return "We are at <b>200</b> Main Street";
                    } else {
                        return "Fee capped at <i>$20</i> during June!"
                    }
                },
                items: "span.toolTip",
                position: {
                    my: "center bottom",
                    at: "center top"
                }
            });
        });
    </script>
</head>
<body class="ui-widget">
    <h1>Jacqui's Flower Shop</h1>
    <h3>Color and Beauty to Your Door</h3>
    <p>We are pleased to announce that we are starting a home delivery service for
    your flower needs. We will deliver within a
    <span id="address" class="toolTip">20 mile radius</span> of the store for free and
    <span id="maxPrice" class="toolTip">$1/mile thereafter.</span></p>
</body>
</html>
```

I have used the position setting to specify that the tooltip should be positioned directly above the element it relates to, as shown in Figure 23-14.

Figure 23-14. *Positioning the tooltip*

Using the Tooltip Methods

The jQuery UI tooltip widget supports the methods described in Table 23-6.

Table 23-6. *Tooltip Methods*

Method	Description
tooltip("close")	Closes the tooltip if it is open
tooltip("destroy")	Removes the tooltip widget from the underlying HTML element
tooltip("disable")	Disables the tooltip, preventing it from being shown
tooltip("enable")	Enables the tooltip, allowing it to be shown
tooltip("open")	Opens the tooltip if it is closed
tooltip("option")	Sets a configuration option

The methods of note are open and close, which allow programmatic control over the tooltips. In Listing 23-20, you can see how I have used these methods to show and hide all of the tooltips contained in the HTML document using buttons.

Listing 23-20. Using the open and close Methods

```
<!DOCTYPE html>
<html>
<head>
    <title>Example</title>
    <script src="jquery-2.0.2.js" type="text/javascript"></script>
    <script src="jquery-ui-1.10.3.custom.js" type="text/javascript"></script>
    <link rel="stylesheet" type="text/css" href="jquery-ui-1.10.3.custom.css"/>
    <link rel="stylesheet" type="text/css" href="styles.css"/>
    <style>
        span.toolTip { font-weight: bold; font-style:italic }
    </style>
```

647

```
<script type="text/javascript">
    $(document).ready(function () {
        $("span.toolTip").tooltip({
            content: function () {
                if (this.id == "address") {
                    return "We are at <b>200</b> Main Street";
                } else {
                    return "Fee capped at <i>$20</i> during June!"
                }
            },
            items: "span.toolTip",
            position: {
                my: "center bottom",
                at: "center top"
            }
        });
        $("button").button().click(function (e) {
            $("span.toolTip").tooltip(this.id);
        });
    });
</script>
</head>
<body class="ui-widget">
    <h1>Jacqui's Flower Shop</h1>
    <h3>Color and Beauty to Your Door</h3>
    <p>We are pleased to announce that we are starting a home delivery service for
    your flower needs. We will deliver within a
    <span id="address" class="toolTip">20 mile radius</span> of the store for free and
    <span id="maxPrice" class="toolTip">$1/mile thereafter.</span></p>
    <div>
        <button id="open">Open</button>
        <button id="close">Close</button>
    </div>
</body>
</html>
```

You can see the effect in Figure 23-15.

Figure 23-15. *Showing and hiding the tooltips programmatically*

Using the Tooltip Events

The jQuery UI tooltip widget supports the events described in Table 23-7.

Table 23-7. *Tooltip Events*

Event	Description
close	Triggered when the tooltip is closed
create	Triggered when the widget is applied
open	Triggered when the tooltip is shown

I have demonstrated the open and close events in Listing 23-21. The handler function is passed a jQuery event object (as described in Chapter 9) and an additional ui object whose tooltip property returns a jQuery object that contains the tooltip element.

Listing 23-21. Handling the open and close Events

```
<!DOCTYPE html>
<html>
<head>
    <title>Example</title>
    <script src="jquery-2.0.2.js" type="text/javascript"></script>
    <script src="jquery-ui-1.10.3.custom.js" type="text/javascript"></script>
    <link rel="stylesheet" type="text/css" href="jquery-ui-1.10.3.custom.css"/>
    <link rel="stylesheet" type="text/css" href="styles.css"/>
    <style>
        span.toolTip { font-weight: bold; font-style:italic }
        span.active { border: medium solid red; padding: 10px; background-color: white }
    </style>
```

```
<script type="text/javascript">
    $(document).ready(function () {
        $("span.toolTip").tooltip({
            content: function () {
                if (this.id == "address") {
                    return "We are at <b>200</b> Main Street";
                } else {
                    return "Fee capped at <i>$20</i> during June!"
                }
            },
            items: "span.toolTip",
            open: function (e, ui) {
                $(this).toggleClass("active");
            },
            close: function (e, ui) {
                $(this).toggleClass("active");
            }
        });
    });
</script>
</head>
<body class="ui-widget">
    <h1>Jacqui's Flower Shop</h1>
    <h3>Color and Beauty to Your Door</h3>
    <p>We are pleased to announce that we are starting a home delivery service for
    your flower needs. We will deliver within a
    <span id="address" class="toolTip">20 mile radius</span> of the store for free and
    <span id="maxPrice" class="toolTip">$1/mile thereafter.</span></p>
</body>
</html>
```

In this example I handle the open and close events by toggling a CSS class called active on the element that the tooltip relates to (which is available via the this variable). The effect is that the element is highlighted when the tooltip is shown, as illustrated by Figure 23-16.

Figure 23-16. *Handling the open and close events*

Summary

In this chapter, I have shown you how the jQuery UI menu and tooltip widgets work. Following the same format as the other widget chapters, I focused on the settings, methods, and events that these widgets support. In Chapter 24, I describe the first of the jQuery UI interactions.

CHAPTER 24

■ ■ ■

Using the Drag-and-Drop Interactions

In addition to the widgets I showed you in Chapters 18–23, jQuery UI includes a set of *interactions*. These are lower-level building blocks that allow you to add functionality to your web application interface. In this chapter, I describe the *draggable* and *droppable* interactions, which you can use to add drag and drop to an HTML document.

The interactions follow the same basic structure as the widgets. They have settings, methods, and events. I will follow the same pattern in describing the interactions, but I'll be jumping around a little to accommodate the unique nature of some of the interactions.

It is hard to show the effect of applying the interactions using screenshots. They are, as the name suggests, dependent on interaction. I tried to give you the essence of what is happening, but to truly understand interactions you should experiment with them in the browser. All of the examples in this chapter (and every other chapter for that matter) are included in the free Source Code/Download area of the Apress web site (`www.apress.com`). Table 24-1 provides the summary for this chapter.

Table 24-1. *Chapter Summary*

Problem	Solution	Listing
Apply the draggable interaction	Use the draggable method	1
Constrain the direction in which an element can be dragged	Use the axis setting	2
Limit the area in which the element can be dragged	Use the containment setting	3
Constrain dragging to the cells in a grid	Use the grid setting	4
Delay dragging for a period of time or for a number of pixels	Use the delay and distance settings	5
Respond to an element being dragged	Use the start, drag, and stop events	6
Apply the droppable interaction	Use the droppable method	7
Highlight a droppable element when an element is being dragged	Use the activate and deactivate events	8
Respond when a draggable element overlaps with a droppable element	Use the over and out events	9
Specify which draggable elements a droppable element will accept	Use the accept setting	10
Automatically apply CSS classes to a droppable element when dragging starts or overlaps	Use the activeClass and hoverClass settings	11

(continued)

Table 24-1. (*continued*)

Problem	Solution	Listing
Changing the amount of overlap that will trigger the over event	Use the tolerance setting	12
Create groups of compatible draggable and droppable elements	Use the scope setting	13
Leave the draggable element in place during and after dragging	Use the helper setting	14, 15
Manipulate the helper element in response to a droppable event	Use the ui.helper property	16
Force the draggable element to snap to the edge of other elements	Use the snap, snapMode, and snapTolerance settings	17

Creating the Draggable Interaction

An element to which you apply the draggable interaction can be moved (dragged) around the browser window. The element appears in the initial document layout as it would normally, but the element's position changes if the user holds down the pointer over the draggable element and moves the mouse. Listing 24-1 provides a demonstration of the draggable interaction.

Listing 24-1. Using the Draggable Interaction

```
<!DOCTYPE html>
<html>
<head>
    <title>Example</title>
    <script src="jquery-2.0.2.js" type="text/javascript"></script>
    <script src="jquery-ui-1.10.3.custom.js" type="text/javascript"></script>
    <link rel="stylesheet" type="text/css" href="styles.css"/>
    <link rel="stylesheet" type="text/css" href="jquery-ui-1.10.3.custom.css"/>
    <style type="text/css">
        #draggable {font-size: x-large; border: thin solid black;
            width: 5em; text-align: center}
    </style>
    <script type="text/javascript">
        $(document).ready(function() {
            $("#draggable").draggable();
        });
    </script>
</head>
<body>
    <h1>Jacqui's Flower Shop</h1>
    <div id="draggable">
        Drag me
    </div>
</body>
</html>
```

In Listing 24-1, I selected a div element and called the draggable method to create a draggable element. As Figure 24-1 shows, the element starts in its regular position but can be dragged anywhere in the browser window. Note that the other element in the document, the h1, is not affected by the draggable method.

Figure 24-1. *Dragging an element around the browser window*

■ **Tip** Being able to drag elements can be useful in its own right, but it becomes much more powerful when combined with the droppable interaction, which I describe in later in this chapter.

The draggable interaction is performed using some clever HTML and CSS. This means that it works in almost any browser—but it also means draggable elements are not able to interact with the native drag and drop implemented by the user's operating system.

■ **Tip** HTML5 includes support for drag and drop that is usually implemented using the native operating system mechanisms. I provide details and examples of HTML5 drag and drop in my book *The Definitive Guide to HTML5*, also published by Apress. If you are using the jQuery UI drag-and-drop mechanism, I recommend disabling the HTML5 equivalent to avoid confusion. To do this, set the draggable attribute to false on the body element in your document.

Configuring the Draggable Interaction

There are lots of ways you can configure the draggable interaction. Table 24-2 summarizes the most important settings available, which I demonstrate in the sections that follow.

Table 24-2. *Draggable Settings*

Setting	Description
axis	Restricts the drag to a particular direction. The default is false, meaning no restriction, but you can also specify x (for the x-axis) and y (for the y-axis).
containment	Restricts the draggable element to a region of the screen. See Table 24-3 for details of the supported range of values. The default is false, meaning no restriction.
delay	Specifies a duration for which the user must drag the element before it moves. The default is 0, meaning no delay.
distance	Specifies a distance that the user must drag the element from its initial position before it moves. The default is 1 pixel.
grid	Forces the draggable element to snap to a grid. The default is false, meaning no grid will be used.

■ **Tip** In the *Tuning Drag & Drop* section later in the chapter, I describe some additional settings that change the relationship between the draggable and droppable elements.

Constraining the Drag Axis

There are several ways in which you can constrain the way an element can be dragged. The first is to use the axis setting, which allows you to limit dragging to the x-axis or y-axis. Listing 24-2 provides an example.

Listing 24-2. Using the axis Setting to Constrain Dragging

```
<!DOCTYPE html>
<html>
<head>
    <title>Example</title>
    <script src="jquery-2.0.2.js" type="text/javascript"></script>
    <script src="jquery-ui-1.10.3.custom.js" type="text/javascript"></script>
    <link rel="stylesheet" type="text/css" href="styles.css"/>
    <link rel="stylesheet" type="text/css" href="jquery-ui-1.10.3.custom.css"/>
    <style type="text/css">
        div.dragElement {font-size: large; border: thin solid black;
            width: 5em; text-align: center; background-color: lightgray; margin: 4px }
    </style>
    <script type="text/javascript">
        $(document).ready(function() {

            $(".dragElement").draggable({
                axis: "x"
            }).filter("#dragV").draggable("option", "axis", "y");

        });
    </script>
</head>
```

```
<body>
    <h1>Jacqui's Flower Shop</h1>
    <div id="dragV" class="dragElement">
        Drag Vertically
    </div>
    <div id="dragH" class="dragElement">
        Drag Horizontally
    </div>
</body>
</html>
```

In Listing 24-2, I defined two div elements, selected them with jQuery, and called the draggable method. I use the settings object to define a value of x for both div elements initially, and then use the jQuery filter method to select the dragV element so that I can change the y setting without having to make jQuery search the entire document again. The result is one div element that can be dragged vertically and another that can be dragged horizontally. You can see the effect in Figure 24-2.

Figure 24-2. *Constraining the direction in which an element can be dragged*

Constraining the Drag Region

You can limit the region of the screen in which an element can be dragged. You do this through the containment setting. This setting can be set using several formats, as described in Table 24-3.

Table 24-3. *Values for the Containment Setting*

Value	Description
Selector	When you specify a selector string, the draggable element is constrained to the area occupied by the first matching element
HTMLElement	The draggable element is constrained to the area occupied by the specified element
string	You can specify the values parent, document, and window to restrict dragging
Number Array	You can use a number array in the format [x1, y1, x2, y2] to restrict dragging to a region

Listing 24-3 shows the use of the containment setting.

Listing 24-3. Using the containment Setting

```
<!DOCTYPE html>
<html>
<head>
    <title>Example</title>
    <script src="jquery-2.0.2.js" type="text/javascript"></script>
    <script src="jquery-ui-1.10.3.custom.js" type="text/javascript"></script>
    <link rel="stylesheet" type="text/css" href="styles.css"/>
    <link rel="stylesheet" type="text/css" href="jquery-ui-1.10.3.custom.css"/>
    <style type="text/css">
        div.dragElement {font-size: large; border: thin solid black; padding: 4px;
            width: 5em; text-align: center; background-color: lightgray; margin: 4px }
        #container { border: medium double black; width: 400px; height: 150px}
    </style>
    <script type="text/javascript">
        $(document).ready(function() {
            $(".dragElement").draggable({
                containment: "parent"
            }).filter("#dragH").draggable("option", "axis", "x");

        });
    </script>
</head>
<body>
    <h1>Jacqui's Flower Shop</h1>
    <div id="container">
        <div id="dragH" class="dragElement">
            Drag Horizontally
        </div>
        <div class="dragElement">
            Drag within Parent
        </div>
    </div>
</body>
</html>
```

In Listing 24-3, I constrained both div elements such that they can be dragged only within their parent element, which is a fixed-size div element. For one of the draggable div elements, I also applied the axis setting, meaning that it can be dragged only horizontally within the parent element. You can see the result in Figure 24-3.

Figure 24-3. *Restricting dragging to the parent element*

Constraining Dragging to a Grid

The grid setting can be used to make a draggable element snap to a grid as it is dragged. The value for this setting is a two-element array specifying the width and the height of the grid in pixels. Listing 24-4 shows the grid setting in use.

Listing 24-4. Using the Grid Setting

```html
<!DOCTYPE html>
<html>
<head>
    <title>Example</title>
    <script src="jquery-2.0.2.js" type="text/javascript"></script>
    <script src="jquery-ui-1.10.3.custom.js" type="text/javascript"></script>
    <link rel="stylesheet" type="text/css" href="styles.css"/>
    <link rel="stylesheet" type="text/css" href="jquery-ui-1.10.3.custom.css"/>
    <style type="text/css">
        #draggable {font-size: large; border: thin solid black; padding: 4px;
            width: 100px; text-align: center; background-color: lightgray; margin: 4px; }
    </style>
    <script type="text/javascript">
        $(document).ready(function() {
            $("#draggable").draggable({
                grid: [100, 50]
            })
        });
    </script>
</head>
```

```
<body>
    <h1>Jacqui's Flower Shop</h1>
    <div id="draggable">
        Drag Me
    </div>
</body>
</html>
```

In Listing 24-4, I specified a grid in which the cells are 100 pixels wide and 50 pixels high. As you drag the element, it snaps from one (invisible) cell to the next, as shown in Figure 24-4.

Figure 24-4. *Dragging an element with a grid*

The snapping effect is hard to represent in a screenshot and this is an example that particularly benefits from interaction.

■ **Tip**   You can snap-to-grid in one direction only by specifying a value of 1 for the free-movement axis. For example, setting a value of [100, 1] forces the draggable element to snap to 100 pixel cells along the x-axis but allows free movement along the y-axis.

Delaying Dragging

There are two settings that allow you to delay the dragging action. You can use the delay setting to specify a time span so that the user has to drag the element for a number of milliseconds before the element starts to move. You can also use the distance setting, which forces the user make the drag motion for a certain number of pixels before the element begins to follow the mouse. Listing 24-5 shows both settings in use.

Listing 24-5. Using the delay and distance Settings

```
<!DOCTYPE html>
<html>
<head>
    <title>Example</title>
    <script src="jquery-2.0.2.js" type="text/javascript"></script>
    <script src="jquery-ui-1.10.3.custom.js" type="text/javascript"></script>
    <link rel="stylesheet" type="text/css" href="styles.css"/>
    <link rel="stylesheet" type="text/css" href="jquery-ui-1.10.3.custom.css"/>
    <style type="text/css">
```

```
    #time, #distance {font-size: large; border: thin solid black; padding: 4px;
        width: 100px; text-align: center; background-color: lightgray; margin: 4px; }
    </style>
    <script type="text/javascript">
        $(document).ready(function() {
            $("#time").draggable({
                delay: 1000
            })

            $("#distance").draggable({
                distance: 150
            })
        });
    </script>
</head>
<body>
    <h1>Jacqui's Flower Shop</h1>
    <div id="time">Time Delay</div>
    <div id="distance">Distance</div>
</body>
</html>
```

I have two draggable div elements in Listing 24-5, one of which I configured with the delay setting and the other with the distance setting. When using the delay, the user has to continue dragging for the specified number of milliseconds before the element will begin to move. This is 1,000 milliseconds in the example. The user doesn't have to keep the mouse moving for this duration, but the mouse button has to be held down for the entire period and the mouse has to have been moved to start the dragging process. When the time span has elapsed, the draggable element will snap to the location of the mouse pointer, subject to the grid, region, and axis constraints I showed you earlier.

The distance setting has a similar effect, but the user has to have moved the mouse pointer at least the specified number of pixels in any direction from the element's starting point. When the mouse has moved that far, the draggable element will snap to the current mouse location.

■ **Tip**   If you apply both settings to a single element, the draggable element won't move until both conditions have been met—that is, the user has to have been dragging for the specified time span *and* moved the mouse the specified number of pixels.

Using the Draggable Methods

The draggable interaction defines only the set of core methods you saw implemented by the widgets. There are no draggable-specific methods. Table 24-4 describes those that are available.

Table 24-4. *Draggable Methods*

Method	Description
draggable("destroy")	Removes the interaction from the element
draggable("disable")	Disables the draggable interaction
draggable("enable")	Enables the draggable interaction
draggable("option")	Changes one or more settings

Using the Draggable Events

The draggable interaction supports a simple set of events that notify you when an element is dragged. Table 24-5 describes the events.

Table 24-5. *Draggable Events*

Event	Description
create	Triggered when the draggable interaction is applied to an element
start	Triggered when dragging starts
drag	Triggered as the mouse moves during dragging
stop	Triggered when dragging stops

You respond to interaction events just as you do for widget events. Listing 24-6 demonstrates handling the start and stop events.

Listing 24-6. Using the Draggable start and stop Events

```html
<!DOCTYPE html>
<html>
<head>
    <title>Example</title>
    <script src="jquery-2.0.2.js" type="text/javascript"></script>
    <script src="jquery-ui-1.10.3.custom.js" type="text/javascript"></script>
    <link rel="stylesheet" type="text/css" href="styles.css"/>
    <link rel="stylesheet" type="text/css" href="jquery-ui-1.10.3.custom.css"/>
    <style type="text/css">
        #draggable {font-size: large; border: thin solid black; padding: 4px;
            width: 100px; text-align: center; background-color: lightgray; margin: 4px; }
    </style>
    <script type="text/javascript">
        $(document).ready(function() {
            $("#draggable").draggable({
                start: function() {
                    $("#draggable").text("Dragging...")
                },
```

```
            stop: function() {
                $("#draggable").text("Drag Me")
            }
        })
    });
    </script>
</head>
<body>
    <h1>Jacqui's Flower Shop</h1>
    <div id="draggable">
        Drag Me
    </div>
</body>
</html>
```

In Listing 24-6, I use the `start` and `stop` events to change the contents of the element while it is being dragged. This is a benefit of the way that the draggable interaction (and all of the other jQuery UI interactions, for that matter) is implemented using HTML and CSS: you can use jQuery to modify the draggable element even when it is being moved around the screen. You can see the effect that this example creates in Figure 24-5.

Figure 24-5. *Using the draggable events to modify an element while it is being dragged*

Using the Droppable Interaction

The real utility of the draggable interaction arises when you combine it with the *droppable* interaction. You create droppable elements using the `droppable` method, but to get any real functionality you need to provide handler functions for the events that the interaction defines. Table 24-6 describes the events that are available.

Table 24-6. *Droppable Events*

Event	Description
create	Triggered when the droppable interaction is applied
activate	Triggered when the user starts to drag a draggable element
deactivate	Triggered when the user stops dragging a draggable element
over	Triggered when the user drags a draggable element over the droppable element (but has not yet released the mouse button)
out	Triggered when the user drags a draggable element out of the droppable element
drop	Triggered when the user drops a draggable element on the droppable element

You can create a basic droppable element with just the drop event, as shown in Listing 24-7.

Listing 24-7. Creating a Basic Droppable Interaction

```
<!DOCTYPE html>
<html>
<head>
    <title>Example</title>
    <script src="jquery-2.0.2.js" type="text/javascript"></script>
    <script src="jquery-ui-1.10.3.custom.js" type="text/javascript"></script>
    <link rel="stylesheet" type="text/css" href="styles.css"/>
    <link rel="stylesheet" type="text/css" href="jquery-ui-1.10.3.custom.css"/>
    <style type="text/css">
        #draggable, #droppable {font-size: large; border: thin solid black; padding: 4px;
            width: 100px; text-align: center; background-color: lightgray; margin: 4px;}
        #droppable {padding: 20px; position: absolute; left: 5px; bottom: 5px}
    </style>
    <script type="text/javascript">
        $(document).ready(function() {
            $("#draggable").draggable();

            $("#droppable").droppable({
                drop: function() {
                    $("#draggable").text("Dropped")
                }
            });
        });
    </script>
</head>
<body>
    <h1>Jacqui's Flower Shop</h1>
    <div id="droppable">
        Drop Here
    </div>
```

```
    <div id="draggable">
        Drag Me
    </div>
</body>
</html>
```

I added a div element whose text content is Drop Here. I use jQuery to select this element and call the droppable method, passing in a settings object that defines a handler for the drop event. In response to this method, I change the text of the draggable element using the text method. Listing 24-7 creates the dullest possible drag-and-drop interaction, but it also provides a useful foundation to explain the way that the draggable and droppable interactions can be used together. You can see the different stages of the example in Figure 24-6.

Figure 24-6. *Using simple drag and drop*

This is pretty basic stuff. I drag the draggable element over the droppable element and let go. The draggable element stays where I left it, and its text content is changed in response to the drop event. In the sections that follow, I'll show you how to use the other droppable events to improve the experience.

Highlighting a Drop Target

You can use the activate and deactivate events to highlight the drop target when the user starts the drag motion. This is usually a good idea, because it gives the user a clear signal regarding which elements are part of the drag-and-drop model. Listing 24-8 provides an example.

Listing 24-8. Responding to the activate and deactivate Events

```
...
<script type="text/javascript">
    $(document).ready(function() {
        $("#draggable").draggable();

        $("#droppable").droppable({
            drop: function() {
                $("#draggable").text("Dropped");
            },
            activate: function() {
                $("#droppable").css({
                    border: "medium double green",
                    backgroundColor: "lightGreen"
                });
            },
            deactivate: function() {
                $("#droppable").css("border", "").css("background-color", "");
            }
        });
    });
</script>
...
```

When the user starts dragging an element, my droppable element triggers the activate event and my handler function uses the css method to apply new values for the CSS border and background-color properties. This causes the drop target to light up, indicating to the user that the droppable element has a relationship to the element being dragged. I use the deactivate event to remove the CSS property values and return the droppable element to its original state when the user releases the mouse button. (This event is triggered whenever dragging stops, regardless of whether the user has dropped the draggable element on a droppable element.) You can see the effect in Figure 24-7.

Figure 24-7. Using the activate and deactivate events

Dealing with Overlapping Elements

You can refine your drag-and-drop technique by handling the over and out events. The over event is triggered when 50% of a draggable element is over any part of the droppable element. The out event is triggered when the elements no longer overlap. Listing 24-9 shows how you can respond to these events.

Listing 24-9. Using the over and out Events

```
...
<script type="text/javascript">
    $(document).ready(function() {
        $("#draggable").draggable();

        $("#droppable").droppable({
            drop: function() {
                $("#draggable").text("Dropped");
            },
            over: function() {
                $("#droppable").css({
                    border: "medium double green",
                    backgroundColor: "lightGreen"
                });
            },
            out: function() {
                $("#droppable").css("border", "").css("background-color", "");
            }
        });
    });
</script>
...
```

I used the same event handler functions as in the previous example, but I associated them with the over and out events. The droppable element will show the border and background color when at least 50% of the draggable element overlaps with it, as shown in Figure 24-8.

Figure 24-8. *Responding to the over and out events*

■ **Tip** The 50% limit is known as the *tolerance*, and you can configure the droppable element with different tolerances, as I demonstrate in the section "Changing the Overlap Tolerance."

Configuring the Droppable Interaction

I broke away from the usual pattern in this part of the book because the events are so central to the droppable interaction. Of course, this interaction does have a number of settings you can use to change the way that it behaves and these are described in Table 24-7.

Table 24-7. *Droppable Settings*

Setting	Description
disabled	When true, the interaction is disabled initially. The default is false.
accept	Narrows the draggable elements that the droppable element will respond to. The default is *, which matches all elements.
activeClass	Specifies a class that will be applied in response to the activate event and removed in response to the deactivate event.
hoverClass	Specifies a class that will be applied in response to the over event and removed in response to the out event.
tolerance	Specifies the amount of overlap that has to occur before the on event is triggered.

■ **Tip** In the section "Tuning Drag and Drop," I describe some additional settings that change the relationship between the draggable and droppable elements.

Restricting Acceptable Draggable Elements

You can restrict the set of elements you are willing to receive with your droppable interaction by applying the accept setting. You use the accept setting by providing a selector as the value. This has the effect of triggering only the droppable events when a draggable element matches the selector. Listing 24-10 provides an example.

Listing 24-10. Restricting the Acceptable Elements

```
<!DOCTYPE html>
<html>
<head>
    <title>Example</title>
    <script src="jquery-2.0.2.js" type="text/javascript"></script>
    <script src="jquery-ui-1.10.3.custom.js" type="text/javascript"></script>
    <link rel="stylesheet" type="text/css" href="styles.css"/>
    <link rel="stylesheet" type="text/css" href="jquery-ui-1.10.3.custom.css"/>
    <style type="text/css">
```

```
        .draggable, #droppable {font-size: large; border: thin solid black; padding: 4px;
            width: 100px; text-align: center; background-color: lightgray; margin: 4px;}
        #droppable {padding: 20px; position: absolute; left: 5px; bottom: 5px}
    </style>
    <script type="text/javascript">
        $(document).ready(function() {
            $(".draggable").draggable();

            $("#droppable").droppable({
                drop: function(event, ui) {
                    ui.draggable.text("Dropped");
                },
                activate: function() {
                    $("#droppable").css({
                        border: "medium double green",
                        backgroundColor: "lightGreen"
                    });
                },
                deactivate : function() {
                    $("#droppable").css("border", "").css("background-color", "");
                },
                accept: "#drag1"
            });
        });
    </script>
</head>
<body>
    <h1>Jacqui's Flower Shop</h1>
    <div id="droppable">
        Drop Here
    </div>
    <div id="drag1" class="draggable">
        Drag 1
    </div>
    <div id="drag2" class="draggable">
        Drag 2
    </div>
</body>
</html>
```

There are two draggable elements in this example, with the IDs drag1 and drag2. When creating the droppable element, I used the accept setting to specify that only the drag1 element should be accepted. When the drag1 element is dragged, you see the same effect as in the previous example. The activate, deactivate, over, out, and drop events are all fired at the appropriate moments. However, when you drag the drag2 element, it fails to match the selector I specified for the accept setting and those events don't fire. I can still drag the element around, but I can no longer drop it on the droppable element. You can see the effect in Figure 24-9.

Figure 24-9. *Using the accept setting*

Notice that I changed the way I select the dropped element so that I can call the text method. When there was only one draggable element in the document, I just used the id attribute, as follows:

```
...
$("#draggable").text("Dropped");
...
```

In this example, there are multiple draggable elements, so selecting by id won't work because I'll always be changing the text on the same element, regardless of which one was dropped. Instead, I use the ui object, which jQuery UI provides as an additional argument to the event handling functions. The draggable property of the ui object returns a jQuery object that contains the element that the user is dragging or has dropped, allowing me to target that element as follows:

```
...
ui.draggable.text("Dropped");
...
```

Highlighting the Droppable Using Classes

You can use the activeClass and hoverClass settings to change the appearance of the droppable element without using the activate, deactivate, over, and out events. Listing 24-11 provides a demonstration.

Listing 24-11. Using the activeClass and hoverClass Settings

```html
<!DOCTYPE html>
<html>
<head>
    <title>Example</title>
    <script src="jquery-2.0.2.js" type="text/javascript"></script>
    <script src="jquery-ui-1.10.3.custom.js" type="text/javascript"></script>
    <link rel="stylesheet" type="text/css" href="styles.css"/>
    <link rel="stylesheet" type="text/css" href="jquery-ui-1.10.3.custom.css"/>
    <style type="text/css">
        .draggable, #droppable {font-size: large; border: thin solid black; padding: 4px;
            width: 100px; text-align: center; background-color: lightgray; margin: 4px;}
        #droppable {padding: 20px; position: absolute; left: 5px; bottom: 5px}
        #droppable.active {border: thick solid green}
        #droppable.hover {background-color: lightgreen}
    </style>
    <script type="text/javascript">
        $(document).ready(function() {
            $(".draggable").draggable();

            $("#droppable").droppable({
                drop: function(event, ui) {
                    ui.draggable.text("Dropped");
                },
                activeClass: "active",
                hoverClass: "hover"
            });
        });
    </script>
</head>
<body>
    <h1>Jacqui's Flower Shop</h1>
    <div id="droppable">
        Drop Here
    </div>
    <div class="draggable">
        Drag Me
    </div>
</body>
</html>
```

I defined two new CSS styles, which I have highlighted in the listing. I created classes that are specific to the id of the draggable element (e.g., #draggable.active) so that they are more specific than the other styles I have been using (e.g., #droppable) and so that they take precedence. See Chapter 3 for details of the rules by which CSS styles are applied to elements.

Having defined these styles, I then name them as the values to the activeClass and hoverClass settings. The droppable interaction takes care of adding and removing these classes from the droppable elements in response to the events. You can see the result in Figure 24-10.

Figure 24-10. *Using the activeClass and hoverClass Settings*

Changing the Overlap Tolerance

By default, the over event will trigger only when at least 50% of the draggable element overlaps with the droppable element. You can change this using the `tolerance` setting, which accepts the values shown in Table 24-8.

Table 24-8. *Tolerance Values*

Value	Description
fit	The dragged element must completely overlap the droppable element.
intersect	At least 50% of the dragged element must overlap the droppable element. This is the default.
pointer	The mouse pointer must be over the droppable element, regardless of where the user has grabbed the draggable element.
touch	The dragged element must overlap the droppable element by any amount.

The two values I use most frequently are `fit` and `touch`, because these represent the most readily understood approaches to the user. I use `fit` when I preserve the location of the dropped item and `touch` when I have the dropped item revert to its original location (something I demonstrate later in the chapter). Listing 24-12 shows the use of the `fit` and `touch` settings. ·

Listing 24-12. Changing the Tolerance for Draggable Elements

```
<!DOCTYPE html>
<html>
<head>
    <title>Example</title>
    <script src="jquery-2.0.2.js" type="text/javascript"></script>
```

```
<script src="jquery-ui-1.10.3.custom.js" type="text/javascript"></script>
<link rel="stylesheet" type="text/css" href="styles.css"/>
<link rel="stylesheet" type="text/css" href="jquery-ui-1.10.3.custom.css"/>
<style type="text/css">
    .draggable, .droppable {font-size: large; border: thin solid black; padding: 4px;
        width: 100px; text-align: center; background-color: lightgray;}
    .droppable {margin-bottom: 10px; margin-right: 5px; height: 50px; width: 120px}
    #dropContainer {position: absolute; right: 5px;}
    div span {position: relative; top: 25%}
    .droppable.active {border: thick solid green}
    .droppable.hover {background-color: lightgreen}
</style>
<script type="text/javascript">
    $(document).ready(function() {

        $(".draggable").draggable();

        $("div.droppable").droppable({
            drop: function(event, ui) {
                ui.draggable.text("Dropped");
            },
            activeClass: "active",
            hoverClass: "hover",
            tolerance: "fit"
        });

        $("#touchDrop").droppable("option", "tolerance", "touch");
    });
</script>
</head>
<body>
    <h1>Jacqui's Flower Shop</h1>
    <div id="dropContainer">
        <div id="fitDrop" class="droppable">
            <span>Fit</span>
        </div>
        <div id="touchDrop" class="droppable">
            <span>Touch</span>
        </div>
    </div>
    <div class="draggable">
        <span>Drag Me</span>
    </div>
</body>
</html>
```

In Listing 24-12, I created two droppable elements, one of which is configured with the fit value for the tolerance setting and the other with the touch value. There is a single draggable element, and Figure 24-11 shows the effect that the different values create. I took each screenshot at the moment that the over event triggered. Notice that the border I applied to the droppable elements is included when the tolerance setting is used to determine overlap.

Figure 24-11. *Using the fit and touch values for the tolerance setting*

Using the Droppable Methods

The droppable interaction defines only the set of core methods you saw implemented by the widgets. There are no interaction-specific methods. Table 24-9 describes those that are available.

Table 24-9. *Droppable Methods*

Method	Description
droppable("destroy")	Removes the interaction from the element
droppable("disable")	Disables the droppable interaction
droppable("enable")	Enables the droppable interaction
droppable("option")	Changes one or more settings

Tuning Drag and Drop

There are some additional settings you can use to fine-tune the way jQuery UI drag and drop works. In this section, I describe the settings and demonstrate their use.

Using Element Scope

Earlier in the chapter, I showed how the droppable accept setting can be used to filter the elements that will activate the drop zone. Using selectors works just fine for simple projects, but the selectors can become overly complex and error prone if you have a lot of draggable elements to manage.

An alternative is to apply the scope setting on both the draggable and droppable elements. A draggable element will activate droppable elements with the same scope value. Listing 24-13 shows the scope setting in use.

■ **Tip** The `scope` setting can be combined with the `accept` setting in droppable elements. The droppable element will be activated only if the draggable element shares the same `scope` and matches the selector defined by the `accept` setting.

Listing 24-13. Using the scope Setting

```html
<!DOCTYPE html>
<html>
<head>
    <title>Example</title>
    <script src="jquery-2.0.2.js" type="text/javascript"></script>
    <script src="jquery-ui-1.10.3.custom.js" type="text/javascript"></script>
    <link rel="stylesheet" type="text/css" href="styles.css"/>
    <link rel="stylesheet" type="text/css" href="jquery-ui-1.10.3.custom.css"/>
    <style type="text/css">
        .draggable, .droppable {font-size: large; border: medium solid black;
            padding: 4px; width: 100px; text-align: center;
            background-color: lightgray; margin-bottom: 10px;}
        .droppable {margin-right: 5px; height: 50px; width: 120px}
        #dropContainer {position: absolute; right: 5px;}
        div span {position: relative; top: 25%}
        .droppable.active {border: medium solid green}
        .droppable.hover {background-color: lightgreen}
    </style>
    <script type="text/javascript">
        $(document).ready(function() {

            $("#apple").draggable({
                scope: "fruit"
            });
            $("#orchid").draggable({
                scope: "flower"
            });

            $("#flowerDrop").droppable({
                activeClass: "active",
                hoverClass: "hover",
                scope: "flower"
            });

            $("#fruitDrop").droppable({
                activeClass: "active",
                hoverClass: "hover",
                scope: "fruit"
            });
        });
    </script>
</head>
```

675

```
<body>
    <h1>Jacqui's Flower Shop</h1>
    <div id="dropContainer">
        <div id="flowerDrop" class="droppable">
            <span>Flowers</span>
        </div>
        <div id="fruitDrop" class="droppable">
            <span>Fruit</span>
        </div>
    </div>
    <div id="orchid" class="draggable">
        <span>Orchid</span>
    </div>
    <div id="apple" class="draggable">
        <span>Apple</span>
    </div>
</body>
</html>
```

In Listing 24-13, I created two draggable elements and two droppable elements. When creating these elements, I assigned them to one of two scope values: fruit and flower. The result is that each draggable element will activate and be accepted only by the droppable element with the same scope, as shown in Figure 24-12.

Figure 24-12. *Grouping draggable and droppable elements by scope*

■ **Caution** Notice that I defined the scope for each element in the initial call to the draggable and droppable methods, rather than using the option method. As I write this, there is a bug in jQuery UI where assigning a scope after the interaction has been created doesn't work.

Using a Helper Element

The helper setting allows you to specify an element that will be dragged in place of the draggable element, leaving the original draggable element in place. This is an entirely different effect from previous examples, where the draggable element has been moved from its original position. Listing 24-14 shows an example of using a helper element.

Listing 24-14. Using a Large Draggable Element

```
<!DOCTYPE html>
<html>
<head>
    <title>Example</title>
    <script src="jquery-2.0.2.js" type="text/javascript"></script>
    <script src="jquery-ui-1.10.3.custom.js" type="text/javascript"></script>
    <link rel="stylesheet" type="text/css" href="styles.css"/>
    <link rel="stylesheet" type="text/css" href="jquery-ui-1.10.3.custom.css"/>
    <style type="text/css">
        .draggable, .droppable {font-size: large; border: medium solid black;
            padding: 4px; width: 150px; text-align: center;
            background-color: lightgray; margin-bottom: 10px;}
        .droppable {margin-right: 5px; height: 50px; width: 120px}
        #dropContainer {position: absolute; right: 5px;}
        div span {position: relative; top: 25%;}
        .droppable.active {border: medium solid green}
        .droppable.hover {background-color: lightgreen}
    </style>
    <script type="text/javascript">
        $(document).ready(function() {

            $("div.draggable").draggable({
                helper: "clone"
            });

            $("#basket").droppable({
                activeClass: "active",
                hoverClass: "hover"
            });
        });
    </script>
</head>
<body>
    <h1>Jacqui's Flower Shop</h1>
    <div id="dropContainer">
        <div id="basket" class="droppable">
            <span>Basket</span>
        </div>
    </div>
    <div class="draggable">
        <img src="lily.png"/><label for="lily">Lily</label>
    </div>
</body>
</html>
```

The value clone tells jQuery UI to make a copy of the draggable element and all of its contents and use the result as the helper element. You can see the effect in Figure 24-13. The helper element is removed when the user drops it, leaving the draggable and droppable elements in their original positions.

Figure 24-13. *A large draggable element*

As the figure shows, the original draggable element remains in position and only the helper is moved across the screen to follow the user's mouse. Large draggable elements like the one in this example make it difficult for the user to see the underlying elements in the document, including the position of the droppable element. You can address this issue by providing a function as the value for the helper setting, as shown in Listing 24-15.

Listing 24-15. Using the helper Setting

```
...
<script type="text/javascript">
    $(document).ready(function() {

        $("div.draggable").draggable({
            helper: function() {
                return $("<img src=lily.png />")
            }
        });

        $("#basket").droppable({
            activeClass: "active",
            hoverClass: "hover"
        });
    });
</script>
...
```

When the user starts to drag the element, jQuery UI calls the helper function and uses the element that it returns as the draggable item. In this case, I use jQuery to create an img element. You can see the effect in Figure 24-14.

Figure 24-14. *Using a helper*

The smaller image acts as a more compact stand-in for the draggable element, making it easier to see the rest of the document while dragging.

Manipulating the Helper Element

The ui object that jQuery UI passes to the droppable events contains a helper property, which you can use to manipulate the helper element as it is being dragged. Listing 24-16 shows the use of this property, tied to the over and out events.

Listing 24-16. Using the ui.helper Property

```
...
<script type="text/javascript">
    $(document).ready(function() {

        $("div.draggable").draggable({
            helper: function() {
                return $("<img src=lily.png />")
            }
        });

        $("#basket").droppable({
            over: function(event, ui) {
                ui.helper.css("border", "thick solid green")
            },
            out: function(event, ui) {
                ui.helper.css("border", "")
            }
        });
    });
</script>
...
```

I use the over and out events and the ui.helper property to display a border on the helper element when it overlaps the droppable element. You can see the result in Figure 24-15.

Figure 24-15. *Manipulating the helper element*

Snapping to the Edges of Elements

You can make the draggable element snap to the edges of the elements that it passes over using the snap setting. The value for this setting is a selector. The draggable will snap to the edges of any element that it is near that matches the selector. Listing 24-17 shows the use of the snap setting.

Listing 24-17. Using the snap Setting

```
<!DOCTYPE html>
<html>
<head>
    <title>Example</title>
    <script src="jquery-2.0.2.js" type="text/javascript"></script>
    <script src="jquery-ui-1.10.3.custom.js" type="text/javascript"></script>
    <link rel="stylesheet" type="text/css" href="styles.css"/>
    <link rel="stylesheet" type="text/css" href="jquery-ui-1.10.3.custom.css"/>
    <style type="text/css">
        #snapper, .draggable, .droppable {font-size: large; border: medium solid black;
            padding: 4px; width: 150px; text-align: center;
            background-color: lightgray; margin-bottom: 10px;}
        .droppable {margin-right: 5px; height: 50px; width: 120px}
        #dropContainer {position: absolute; right: 5px;}
        div span {position: relative; top: 25%}
        .droppable.active {border: medium solid green}
        .droppable.hover {background-color: lightgreen}
        #snapper {position: absolute; left: 35%; border: medium solid black;
            width: 180px; height: 50px}
    </style>
    <script type="text/javascript">
        $(document).ready(function() {

            $("div.draggable").draggable({
                snap: "#snapper, .droppable",
                snapMode: "both",
                snapTolerance: 50
            });
```

```
            $("#basket").droppable({
                activeClass: "active",
                hoverClass: "hover"
            });
        });
    </script>
</head>
<body>
    <h1>Jacqui's Flower Shop</h1>
    <div id="dropContainer">
        <div id="basket" class="droppable">
            <span>Basket</span>
        </div>
    </div>
    <div id="snapper"><span>Snap Here</span></div>
    <div class="draggable">
        <span>Drag Me</span>
    </div>
</body>
</html>
```

As the draggable element nears one of the matching elements, it jumps (snaps) so that the two closest edges touch. You can select any element to snap to, not just droppable elements. In Listing 24-17, I added a div element and defined a value for the snap setting, which selects it and the droppable element in the document. It is pretty much impossible to show the effect of snapping using a screenshot, so I encourage you to experiment with this example in the browser.

There are a couple of supporting settings you can use to tweak the snapping behavior. The first is snapMode. This setting lets you specify which edges the draggable will snap to. The accepted values are inner (snap to the inner edges of the underlying element), outer (snap to the outer edges), and both (snap to all edges, which is the default value).

You use the snapTolerance setting to specify how far the draggable element has to be away from the target before it snaps into position. The default is 20, meaning 20 pixels. In Listing 24-17, I specified a value of 50, which makes snapping occur from further away. Getting the right value for this setting is important. The user won't notice the snapping effect if the snapTolerance value is too small, and if the value is too large the draggable element starts leaping unexpectedly across the screen to snap to faraway elements

Summary

In this chapter, I introduced you to the two most important and useful of the jQuery UI interactions: draggable and droppable. I showed you how to apply and configure these interactions individually, how to respond to their events, and how to tune the way that they work together to get fine-grained control over the drag-and-drop experience you provide to your web application users. In Chapter 25, I show you the other jQuery UI interactions.

CHAPTER 25

■ ■ ■

Using the Other Interactions

In this chapter, I describe the three remaining jQuery UI interactions: *sortable*, *selectable*, and *resizable*. These interactions are less used (and less useful) than draggable and droppable, which I described in Chapter 24. The interactions in this chapter can be useful, but they use models that are hard to highlight to the user. Because of that, they perform best as supplements to other, more conventional, approaches. Table 25-1 provides the summary for this chapter.

Table 25-1. *Chapter Summary*

Problem	Solution	Listing
Apply the sortable interaction	Select the container element, and call the sortable method	1
Obtain the order that the user created with a sortable interaction	Call the toArray or serialize method	2, 3
Enable dragging elements from one sortable item to another	Use the connectWith setting	4
Connect a draggable element with a sortable item	Use the connectToSortable setting on the draggable element	5
Specify which elements are sortable	Use the items setting	6
Style the empty space created while a sortable item is being dragged	Use the placeholder setting	7
Ignore a change in order	Use the cancel method	8
Refresh the set of elements in a sortable item	Use the refresh method	9
Get information about the sort operation in progress	Use the ui object provided to event handler functions	10
Apply the selectable interaction	Select the container element, and call the selectable method	11, 12
Prevent an element from being selected	Use the cancel method	13
Apply the resizable interaction	Use the resizable method	14
Resize multiple elements	Use the alsoResize setting	15, 16
Limit the size of a resizable element	Use the maxHeight, maxWidth, minHeight, and minWidth settings	17
Select the draggable edges and corners for a resizable element	Use the handles setting	18

Using the Sortable Interaction

The sortable interaction lets the user change the order of a set of elements by dragging them around. You apply the sortable interaction by selecting the element that contains the individual items that you want to sort and then calling the sortable method, as shown in Listing 25-1.

Listing 25-1. Using the sortable Interaction

```html
<!DOCTYPE html>
<html>
<head>
    <title>Example</title>
    <script src="jquery-2.0.2.js" type="text/javascript"></script>
    <script src="jquery-ui-1.10.3.custom.js" type="text/javascript"></script>
    <link rel="stylesheet" type="text/css" href="styles.css"/>
    <link rel="stylesheet" type="text/css" href="jquery-ui-1.10.3.custom.css"/>
    <style type="text/css">
        div.sortable { width: 100px; background-color: lightgrey; font-size: large;
            float: left; margin: 4px; text-align: center; border: medium solid black;
            padding: 4px;}
    </style>
    <script type="text/javascript">
        $(document).ready(function() {
            $("#sortContainer").sortable();
        });
    </script>
</head>
<body>
    <h1>Jacqui's Flower Shop</h1>
    <div id="sortContainer">
        <div id="item1" class="sortable">Item 1</div>
        <div id="item2" class="sortable">Item 2</div>
        <div id="item3" class="sortable">Item 3</div>
    </div>
</body>
</html>
```

In Listing 25-1, I created a number of div elements and assigned them to the sortable class. This class has no effect on the interaction: I use it only to style the elements. To create the interaction, I select the parent div element (the one whose id is sortContainer) and call the sortable method. The result is that I can change the order of my three div elements simply by dragging them into a new position. You can see the effect in Figure 25-1 (although, like all the examples in this chapter, you will get a better sense of what is happening by running the example in the browser).

Figure 25-1. *Sorting items by dragging them*

To demonstrate the `sortable` interaction, I dragged the element labeled Item 2 to the right of the browser window. Once I drag the element past the one labeled Item 3, jQuery UI rearranges the items so that they are in a new order. I only dragged an element one position, but you can move them around several positions at a time.

Getting the Sortable Order

At some point, you need to know the order that the user created by moving the elements around. To get this information, you can call the `toArray` method, which returns a JavaScript array of the `id` attribute values for the sorted elements. Listing 25-2 shows the addition of a button to the example that writes the current order to the console.

Listing 25-2. Obtaining the Sorted Element Order

```
...
<script type="text/javascript">
    $(document).ready(function() {
        $("#sortContainer").sortable();

        $("<div id=buttonDiv><button>Get Order</button></div>").appendTo("body");
        $("button").button().click(function() {
            var order = $("#sortContainer").sortable("toArray");
            for (var i = 0; i < order.length; i++) {
                console.log("Position: " + i + " ID: " + order[i]);
            }
        });
    });
</script>
...
```

You can see the effect in Figure 25-2. When the button is pressed, I call the `toArray` method and enumerate the contents of the resulting array to the console.

Figure 25-2. *Adding a button to write out the sort order*

For the order in the figure, pressing the button produces the following output:

```
Position: 0 ID: item2
Position: 1 ID: item3
Position: 2 ID: item1
```

You can also use the `serialize` method to generate a string that can easily be used with a form. Listing 25-3 provides an example.

Listing 25-3. Using the serialize Method

```html
<!DOCTYPE html>
<html>
<head>
    <title>Example</title>
    <script src="jquery-2.0.2.js" type="text/javascript"></script>
    <script src="jquery-ui-1.10.3.custom.js" type="text/javascript"></script>
    <link rel="stylesheet" type="text/css" href="styles.css"/>
    <link rel="stylesheet" type="text/css" href="jquery-ui-1.10.3.custom.css"/>
    <style type="text/css">
        div.sortable { width: 100px; background-color: lightgrey; font-size: large;
            float: left; margin: 4px; text-align: center; border: medium solid black;
            padding: 4px;}
        #buttonDiv {clear: both}
    </style>
    <script type="text/javascript">
        $(document).ready(function() {
            $("#sortContainer").sortable();
```

```
            $("<div id=buttonDiv><button>Get Order</button></div>").appendTo("body");
            $("button").button().click(function() {
                var formstring = $("#sortContainer").sortable("serialize");
                console.log(formstring);
            })
        });
    </script>
</head>
<body>
    <h1>Jacqui's Flower Shop</h1>
    <div id="sortContainer">
        <div id="item_1" class="sortable">Item 1</div>
        <div id="item_2" class="sortable">Item 2</div>
        <div id="item_3" class="sortable">Item 3</div>
    </div>
</body>
</html>
```

Notice that I had to change the id values of the sortable elements. The serialize method looks for a pattern of <key>_<index> when generating its string. The output for the order shown in Figure 25-2 is as follows:

```
item[]=2&item[]=3&item[]=1
```

Configuring the Sortable Interaction

The sortable interaction relies on the draggable interaction I described in Chapter 24. This means that the options I described for that interaction (such as axis and tolerance) can be applied with the same effect to configure sortable interactions. I won't describe those settings again. Instead, Table 25-2 shows the settings that are unique to the sortable interaction and the most useful. I describe these settings in the sections that follow.

Table 25-2. Sortable Settings

Setting	Description
connectWith	Specifies another sortable element to connect to so that items can be dragged between them. The default is false, meaning that there is no connection.
dropOnEmpty	When false, items cannot be dropped on a connected sortable interaction that contains no items. The default is true.
items	Specifies the items that will be sortable through a selector. The default is > *, which selects any descendant of the element on which the sortable method has been called.
placeholder	Specifies a class that will be assigned to the element that is created to preserve space while a sortable item is being dragged to a new location.

Connecting Sortable Interactions

The sortable feature I like most is the ability to connect two sortable interactions, allowing items to be dragged between them. You achieve this using the connectWith setting, specifying a selector that matches the element you want to connect with. You can create a bidirectional connection by using the connectWith setting on both sortable elements, as shown in Listing 25-4.

Listing 25-4. Connecting Sortable Interactions

```
<!DOCTYPE html>
<html>
<head>
    <title>Example</title>
    <script src="jquery-2.0.2.js" type="text/javascript"></script>
    <script src="jquery-ui-1.10.3.custom.js" type="text/javascript"></script>
    <link rel="stylesheet" type="text/css" href="styles.css"/>
    <link rel="stylesheet" type="text/css" href="jquery-ui-1.10.3.custom.css"/>
    <style type="text/css">
        div.sortable { width: 100px; background-color: lightgrey; font-size: large;
            margin: 4px; text-align: center; border: medium solid black; padding: 4px;}
        #fruitContainer {position: absolute; right:50px}
        #flowerContainer {position: absolute; left:50px}
        div.flower {background-color: lightgreen}
    </style>
    <script type="text/javascript">
        $(document).ready(function() {
            $("#fruitContainer").sortable({
                connectWith: "#flowerContainer"
            });
            $("#flowerContainer").sortable({
                connectWith: "#fruitContainer"
            });
        });
    </script>
</head>
<body>
    <h1>Jacqui's Flower Shop</h1>
    <div id="fruitContainer" class="sortContainer">
        <div id="fruit_1" class="sortable fruit">Apple</div>
        <div id="fruit_2" class="sortable fruit">Orange</div>
        <div id="fruit_3" class="sortable fruit">Banana</div>
        <div id="fruit_4" class="sortable fruit">Pear</div>
    </div>
    <div id="flowerContainer" class="sortContainer">
        <div id="flower_1" class="sortable flower">Aster</div>
        <div id="flower_2" class="sortable flower">Peony</div>
        <div id="flower_3" class="sortable flower">Lily</div>
        <div id="flower_4" class="sortable flower">Orchid</div>
    </div>
</body>
</html>
```

In Listing 25-4, I created two groups of items and called the `sortable` method on their container element. I used the `connectwith` setting to associate each sortable with the other, and Figure 25-3 shows the result.

Figure 25-3. *Dragging elements between connected sortable interactions*

Connecting a Draggable Element with a Sortable Element

You can also connect a draggable element with a sortable one. You do this by applying the `connectToSortable` setting on the draggable element, specifying a selector that matches the draggable element you want to connect to. Listing 25-5 shows how this is done.

Listing 25-5. Connecting a Draggable Element and a Sortable Element

```html
<!DOCTYPE html>
<html>
<head>
    <title>Example</title>
    <script src="jquery-2.0.2.js" type="text/javascript"></script>
    <script src="jquery-ui-1.10.3.custom.js" type="text/javascript"></script>
    <link rel="stylesheet" type="text/css" href="styles.css"/>
    <link rel="stylesheet" type="text/css" href="jquery-ui-1.10.3.custom.css"/>
    <style type="text/css">
        div.sortable { width: 100px; background-color: lightgrey; font-size: large;
            margin: 4px; text-align: center; border: medium solid black; padding: 4px;}
        #fruitContainer {position: absolute; right:50px}
        #flowerContainer {position: absolute; left:50px}
        div.flower {background-color: lightgreen}
    </style>
    <script type="text/javascript">
        $(document).ready(function() {
            $("#fruit_1").draggable({
                connectToSortable: "#flowerContainer",
                helper: "clone"
            });
            $("#flowerContainer").sortable();
        });
    </script>
</head>
```

```
<body>
    <h1>Jacqui's Flower Shop</h1>
    <div id="fruitContainer" class="sortContainer">
        <div id="fruit_1" class="sortable fruit">Apple</div>
    </div>
    <div id="flowerContainer" class="sortContainer">
        <div id="flower_1" class="sortable flower">Aster</div>
        <div id="flower_2" class="sortable flower">Peony</div>
        <div id="flower_3" class="sortable flower">Lily</div>
        <div id="flower_4" class="sortable flower">Orchid</div>
    </div>
</body>
</html>
```

In Listing 25-5, I reduced the number of fruit items to one and made it draggable, connecting to the sortable list of flowers. The result is that the draggable item can be added to the sortable list, as shown in Figure 25-4. This setting works best when the helper setting for the draggable item is clone. It will work for other values, but an error will be reported.

Figure 25-4. *Connecting a sortable item and a draggable item*

Selecting the Sortable Items

You can be selective about which items in the container are sortable. You do this through the items setting, the value of which is a selector that matches the elements you want to enable sorting for. Elements that do not match the selector cannot be rearranged. Listing 25-6 demonstrates.

Listing 25-6. Selecting Specific Elements to Be Sortable

```
<!DOCTYPE html>
<html>
<head>
    <title>Example</title>
    <script src="jquery-2.0.2.js" type="text/javascript"></script>
    <script src="jquery-ui-1.10.3.custom.js" type="text/javascript"></script>
    <link rel="stylesheet" type="text/css" href="styles.css"/>
    <link rel="stylesheet" type="text/css" href="jquery-ui-1.10.3.custom.css"/>
```

```
    <style type="text/css">
        div.sortable { width: 100px; background-color: lightgrey; font-size: large;
            margin: 4px; text-align: center; border: medium solid black; padding: 4px;}
        #fruitContainer {position: absolute; right:50px}
        #flowerContainer {position: absolute; left:50px}
    </style>
    <script type="text/javascript">
        $(document).ready(function() {
            $("div.flower:even").css("background-color", "lightgreen")
            $("#flowerContainer").sortable({
                items: ".flower:even"
            });
        });
    </script>
</head>
<body>
    <h1>Jacqui's Flower Shop</h1>
    <div id="flowerContainer" class="sortContainer">
        <div id="flower_1" class="sortable flower">Aster</div>
        <div id="flower_2" class="sortable flower">Peony</div>
        <div id="flower_3" class="sortable flower">Lily</div>
        <div id="flower_4" class="sortable flower">Orchid</div>
    </div>
</body>
</html>
```

In Listing 25-6, I used the items setting to specify that only the even-numbered elements in the container should be sortable. In Figure 25-5, the Aster and Lily elements can be sorted, but the Peony and Orchid elements won't respond to being dragged and remain in position.

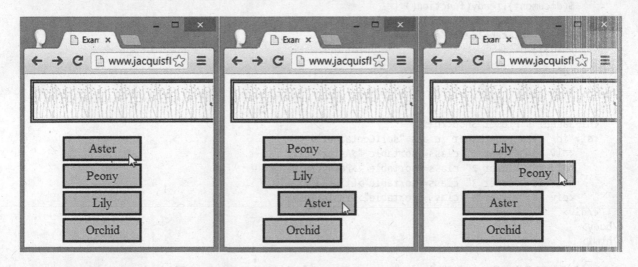

Figure 25-5. Selecting the items that can be sorted

There is an oddity you should be aware of when using the items setting, and I have shown it in the last frame of the figure. An element that doesn't match the selector cannot be dragged into a new position unless it has been dislodged by another element. So in the figure, I dragged the Aster element to a new position, which forces the Peony element to move. Once it is moved, the Peony element will respond to being dragged and sorted as though it matches the items selector.

Styling the Empty Space

While you are dragging an item into a new position, the space it leaves behind remains empty. You can apply a CSS class to this space through the placeholder setting. This can be a useful way to emphasize that the empty space is a drop target. Listing 25-7 shows the use of the placeholder setting.

Listing 25-7. Using the placeholder Setting

```
<!DOCTYPE html>
<html>
<head>
    <title>Example</title>
    <script src="jquery-2.0.2.js" type="text/javascript"></script>
    <script src="jquery-ui-1.10.3.custom.js" type="text/javascript"></script>
    <link rel="stylesheet" type="text/css" href="styles.css"/>
    <link rel="stylesheet" type="text/css" href="jquery-ui-1.10.3.custom.css"/>
    <style type="text/css">
        div.sortable {width: 100px; background-color: lightgrey; font-size: large;
            margin: 4px; text-align: center; border: medium solid black; padding: 4px;}
        #flowerContainer {position: absolute; left:25%}
        .emptySpace {border: medium dotted red; height: 25px; margin: 4px}
    </style>
    <script type="text/javascript">
        $(document).ready(function() {
            $("#flowerContainer").sortable({
                placeholder: "emptySpace"
            });
        });
    </script>
</head>
<body>
    <h1>Jacqui's Flower Shop</h1>
    <div id="flowerContainer" class="sortContainer">
        <div id="flower_1" class="sortable ">Aster</div>
        <div id="flower_2" class="sortable ">Peony</div>
        <div id="flower_3" class="sortable">Lily</div>
        <div id="flower_4" class="sortable">Orchid</div>
    </div>
</body>
</html>
```

In Listing 25-7, I defined a CSS class called emptySpace, which defines sizes for the height and margin properties and defines a red dotted border. I specify this class using the placeholder setting and, as Figure 25-6 shows, when I drag an element to sort it, the space that it leaves behind is assigned to the emptySpace class.

Figure 25-6. *Using the placeholder setting*

Using the Sortable Methods

The sortable interaction defines all of the standard jQuery UI methods, plus a few that are specific to working with sortable elements. Table 25-3 describes these methods.

Table 25-3. *Sortable Methods*

Method	Description
sortable("destroy")	Removes the interaction from the element
sortable("disable")	Disables the sortable interaction
sortable("enable")	Enables the sortable interaction
sortable("option")	Changes one or more settings
sortable("toArray")	Returns an array containing the sorted set of id attribute values (see the section "Getting the Sortable Order" for an example)
sortable("refresh")	Refreshes the sortable interaction
sortable("cancel")	Cancels a sort operation

Cancelling a Sort

You can use the cancel method to prevent elements from being sorted. This is something that should be done sparingly because it effectively ignores the actions that the user has taken. If you *do* cancel a sort, you should make sure the user knows why this happened. Listing 25-8 provides an example of using the cancel method in conjunction with the update event. The update event is triggered when the user releases the mouse button after having dragged an element to create a new sorted order. I describe the sortable events in the section "Using the Sortable Events."

Listing 25-8. Using the cancel Method

```html
<!DOCTYPE html>
<html>
<head>
    <title>Example</title>
    <script src="jquery-2.0.2.js" type="text/javascript"></script>
    <script src="jquery-ui-1.10.3.custom.js" type="text/javascript"></script>
    <link rel="stylesheet" type="text/css" href="styles.css"/>
    <link rel="stylesheet" type="text/css" href="jquery-ui-1.10.3.custom.css"/>
    <style type="text/css">
        div.sortable {width: 100px; background-color: lightgrey; font-size: large;
            margin: 4px; text-align: center; border: medium solid black; padding: 4px;}
    </style>
    <script type="text/javascript">
        $(document).ready(function() {
            $("#error").dialog({autoOpen: false, modal: true})

            $("#flowerContainer").sortable({
                update: function() {
                    var sortedItems = $("#flowerContainer").sortable("toArray");
                    if (sortedItems[0] != "item_1") {
                        $("#error").dialog("open")
                        $("#flowerContainer").sortable("cancel")
                    }
                }
            });
        });
    </script>
</head>
<body>
    <div id="error">The King must be first</div>
    <h1>Jacqui's Flower Shop</h1>
    <div id="flowerContainer" class="sortContainer">
        <div id="item_1" class="sortable ">King</div>
        <div id="item_2" class="sortable ">Queen</div>
        <div id="item_3" class="sortable ">Jack</div>
        <div id="item_4" class="sortable">10</div>
    </div>
</body>
</html>
```

In Listing 25-8, I call the cancel method if the new sorted order that the user has created means that the King element isn't in the first place in the list. I use the dialog widget, described in Chapter 22, to alert the user to the problem. Changes that affect the other sortable elements are allowed to continue.

Refreshing the Sortable Elements

The `refresh` method causes the sortable interaction to refresh its cache of the elements in the sortable container. Listing 25-9 shows how you can use this feature to add new sortable elements.

Listing 25-9. Adding New Sortable Elements

```
<!DOCTYPE html>
<html>
<head>
    <title>Example</title>
    <script src="jquery-2.0.2.js" type="text/javascript"></script>
    <script src="jquery-ui-1.10.3.custom.js" type="text/javascript"></script>
    <link rel="stylesheet" type="text/css" href="styles.css"/>
    <link rel="stylesheet" type="text/css" href="jquery-ui-1.10.3.custom.css"/>
    <style type="text/css">
        div.sortable {width: 100px; background-color: lightgrey; font-size: large;
            margin: 4px; text-align: center; border: medium solid black; padding: 4px;}
    </style>
    <script type="text/javascript">
        $(document).ready(function() {
            $("#flowerContainer").sortable();

            var itemCount = 2;

            $("button").click(function() {
                $("<div id=flower_" + (itemCount++) + " class=sortable>Item " +
                  itemCount + "</div>").appendTo("#flowerContainer");
                $("#flowerContainer").sortable("refresh");
            })
        });
    </script>
</head>
<body>
    <h1>Jacqui's Flower Shop</h1>
    <button>Add Sortable Item</button>
    <div id="flowerContainer" class="sortContainer">
        <div id="flower_1" class="sortable">Aster</div>
        <div id="flower_2" class="sortable">Peony</div>
    </div>
</body>
</html>
```

In Listing 25-9, I added a `button` to the document that adds new items to the sortable container and calls the `refresh` method to make sure that the items are properly sortable.

Using the Sortable Events

The sortable interaction supports all of the events defined by the draggable interaction, which I described in Chapter 24. Table 25-4 describes the events that are unique to the sortable interaction.

Table 25-4. *Sortable Events*

Event	Description
change	Triggered when positions change while an element is being sorted by the user
receive	Triggered when an item is dragged to this sortable item from a connected one
remove	Triggered when an item is dragged from this sortable item to a connected one
sort	Triggered for each mouse move during a sort
update	Triggered when the user stops dragging an item and the order of items has changed

When triggering these events, jQuery UI provides additional information via a ui object argument, which has the properties shown in Table 25-5.

Table 25-5. *Sortable ui Object Properties*

Property	Description
helper	Returns the helper element
position	Returns the current position of the helper as an object with top and left properties
item	Returns a jQuery object containing the currently dragged item
placeholder	Returns a jQuery object containing the placeholder element
sender	Returns a jQuery object containing the connected sortable from which the element originates (this property is null when there is no connected sortable)

Listing 25-10 shows the use of the ui object with the sort and change events.

Listing 25-10. Using the change and sort Events

```
<!DOCTYPE html>
<html>
<head>
    <title>Example</title>
    <script src="jquery-2.0.2.js" type="text/javascript"></script>
    <script src="jquery-ui-1.10.3.custom.js" type="text/javascript"></script>
    <link rel="stylesheet" type="text/css" href="styles.css"/>
    <link rel="stylesheet" type="text/css" href="jquery-ui-1.10.3.custom.css"/>
    <style type="text/css">
        div.sortable {width: 100px; background-color: lightgrey; font-size: large;
            margin: 4px; text-align: center; border: medium solid black; padding: 4px;}
        #flowerContainer {position: absolute; left:10px}
        #info {position: absolute; right: 10px; border: medium solid black; padding: 4px}
    </style>
    <script type="text/javascript">
        $(document).ready(function() {
            $("#flowerContainer").sortable({
                sort: function(event, ui) {
                    $("#itemId").text(ui.item.attr("id"))
                },
```

```
                change: function(event, ui) {
                    $("#pos").text($("#flowerContainer *").index(ui.placeholder))
                }
            });
        });
    </script>
</head>
<body>
    <h1>Jacqui's Flower Shop</h1>
    <div id="flowerContainer" class="sortContainer">
        <div id="flower_1" class="sortable ">Aster</div>
        <div id="flower_2" class="sortable ">Peony</div>
        <div id="flower_3" class="sortable">Lily</div>
        <div id="flower_4" class="sortable">Orchid</div>
    </div>
    <div id="info" class="ui-widget">
        <div>Item ID: <span id="itemId">None</span></div>
        <div>Pos: <span id="pos">None</span></div>
    </div>
</body>
</html>
```

I use the events to display information about the sorting operation. For the sort event, I read the `ui.item` property and get the `id` attribute of the element being dragged. For the change event, I use the `ui.placeholder` property, and I use the `index` method to figure out its position among the sortable elements.

Using the Selectable Interaction

The selectable interaction allows the user to select one or more elements, either by dragging the mouse or by clicking individual elements. You apply the interaction through the `selectable` method as demonstrated in Listing 25-11.

Listing 25-11. Applying the Selectable Interaction

```
<!DOCTYPE html>
<html>
<head>
    <title>Example</title>
    <script src="jquery-2.0.2.js" type="text/javascript"></script>
    <script src="jquery-ui-1.10.3.custom.js" type="text/javascript"></script>
    <link rel="stylesheet" type="text/css" href="styles.css"/>
    <link rel="stylesheet" type="text/css" href="jquery-ui-1.10.3.custom.css"/>
    <style type="text/css">
        div.flower {width: 200px; background-color: lightgrey; font-size: large;
            margin: 4px; text-align: center; border: medium solid black; padding: 4px;}
        #flowerContainer {position: absolute; left:10px}
        div.ui-selected {border: medium solid green; background-color: lightgreen}
        div.ui-selecting {border: medium solid green}
    </style>
```

```
    <script type="text/javascript">
        $(document).ready(function() {
            $("#flowerContainer").selectable();
        });
    </script>
</head>
<body>
    <h1>Jacqui's Flower Shop</h1>
    <div id="flowerContainer">
        <div id="flower_1" class="flower">Aster</div>
        <div id="flower_2" class="flower">Peony</div>
        <div id="flower_3" class="flower">Lily</div>
        <div id="flower_4" class="flower">Orchid</div>
    </div>
</body>
</html>
```

You apply the selectable interaction to the element that contains the elements you want the user to be able to select. In this case, I use the same div elements I used for the sortable interaction earlier in the chapter. I select the container and call the selectable method as follows:

```
...
$("#flowerContainer").selectable();
...
```

Although I have now applied the selectable interaction to my container, I need to define a pair of CSS styles for specific classes to give the user visual feedback. Here are the styles I associated with these classes:

```
...
div.ui-selected {border: medium solid green; background-color: lightgreen}
div.ui-selecting {border: medium solid green}
...
```

The selectable interaction applies these classes to my elements to reflect their selection status. The ui.selecting class is applied when the user is dragging the mouse to select the elements in a specific area, and the ui-selected class is applied when an element has been selected (either because the user has clicked the element or because it was in the area covered by a mouse drag). I used simple styles that just apply green borders and backgrounds. You can see the effect of selecting elements by dragging the mouse in Figure 25-7.

Figure 25-7. *Selecting elements with a mouse*

The user must start dragging the mouse within the container element to start the selection process. You can see the outline of the area that has been selected (known as the *marquee*) in the middle frame of the figure—at that point, jQuery UI has applied the `ui-selecting` class. When the mouse is released, the elements that the marquee overlaps are selected and the `ui-selected` class is applied, as shown in the last frame of the figure.

The user can also select elements by clicking on them. Multiple elements can be selected, and holding the Control/Meta key allows for noncontiguous selections. If you find that clicking causes a single selected element to toggle, you need the addition shown in Listing 25-12.

Listing 25-12. Enabling Multiple Element Selection for the Selectable Interaction

```
...
<script type="text/javascript">
    $(document).ready(function() {
        $("#flowerContainer")
            .bind("mousedown", function(e) {e.metaKey = true;})
            .selectable();
    });
</script>
...
```

When the user presses the mouse button, the `ui-selecting` class is applied. The `ui-selected` class is applied when the mouse button is released.

Configuring the Selectable Interaction

You can configure the selectable interaction using the settings described in Table 25-6.

Table 25-6. *Selectable Settings*

Setting	Description
disabled	When `true`, the interaction is initially disabled. The default is `false`.
autoRefresh	When `true`, the interaction refreshes the size and position of each of the selectable elements at the start of each select operation. The default is `true`.
cancel	A selector string that prevents matching elements from being selected.
delay	See the `delay` setting on the draggable interaction in Chapter 24.
distance	See the `distance` setting on the draggable interaction in Chapter 24.
filter	A selector used to match selectable elements in the container. The default is *, which matches all elements.

Most of these settings are self-evident or are the same as for other interactions. Of particular interest, though, is the `cancel` setting, which you can use to make elements unselectable by the user. Listing 25-13 demonstrates.

Listing 25-13. Using the cancel Setting

```
...
<script type="text/javascript">
    $(document).ready(function() {
        $("#flowerContainer")
            .bind("mousedown", function(e) {e.metaKey = true;})
            .selectable({
                cancel: "#flower_3"
            });
    });
</script>
...
```

In this script, I use a selector that prevents the element with the ID of `flower_3` from being selected. This works well when the user is selecting elements by clicking on them, but it doesn't prevent selection by dragging. For this reason, use the `cancel` setting with care.

Using the Selectable Interaction Methods

The selectable interaction defines only one unique method, as described in Table 25-7. The other methods are those that are common to all widgets and interactions.

Table 25-7. *Selectable Methods*

Method	Description
selectable("destroy")	Removes the interaction from the element
selectable("disable")	Disables the selectable interaction
selectable("enable")	Enables the selectable interaction
selectable("option")	Changes one or more settings
selectable("refresh")	Refreshes the selectable interaction; this is the manual alternative to using false for the value of the autoRefresh setting

Using the Selectable Interaction Events

The selectable interaction defines the events shown in Table 25-8.

Table 25-8. *Selectable Methods*

Event	Description
create	Triggered when the interaction is applied to an element.
selected	Triggered when an item has been selected. If multiple items have been selected, this event will be triggered once for each of them.
selecting	Triggered when the user has started the selection process (by pressing the mouse button or by dragging the mouse).
unselected	Triggered when an item has been unselected. If multiple items have been unselected, this event will be triggered once for each of them.
unselecting	Triggered when the user has started the unselection process by pressing the mouse button.

jQuery UI provides additional information for most of these events through a ui object. For the selected and selecting events, the ui object has a property called selected, which contains the HTMLElement corresponding to the element that has been (or is about to be) selected. For the unselected and unselecting events, the ui object has an unselected property that performs the same purpose.

Using the Resizable Interaction

The resizable interaction adds drag handles to elements that allow them to be resized by the user. Some browsers do this automatically with text areas, but the resizable interaction lets us apply this feature to any element in a document. Listing 25-14 shows the application of the resizable interaction that you perform using the resizable method.

Listing 25-14. Applying the resizable Interaction

```
<!DOCTYPE html>
<html>
<head>
    <title>Example</title>
    <script src="jquery-2.0.2.js" type="text/javascript"></script>
    <script src="jquery-ui-1.10.3.custom.js" type="text/javascript"></script>
```

```
<link rel="stylesheet" type="text/css" href="styles.css"/>
<link rel="stylesheet" type="text/css" href="jquery-ui-1.10.3.custom.css"/>
<style type="text/css">
    #aster, #lily {text-align: center; width: 150px; border: thin solid black;
        padding: 5px; float: left; margin: 20px}
    #aster img, #lily img {display: block; margin: auto}
</style>
<script type="text/javascript">
    $(document).ready(function() {
        $("#aster").resizable({
            alsoResize: "#aster img"
        });
    });
</script>
</head>
<body>
    <h1>Jacqui's Flower Shop</h1>
    <div id="aster" class="ui-widget">
        <img src="aster.png" />
        Aster
    </div>
    <div id="lily" class="ui-widget">
        <img src="lily.png" />
        Lilly
    </div>
</body>
</html>
```

In Listing 25-14, I created two div elements whose contents are an img and some text. I select one of these in the script and apply the resizable method (using the alsoResize setting, which I'll describe later in this chapter). jQuery UI adds a drag handle to the selected element, allowing me to resize it vertically and horizontally, as shown in Figure 25-8. In the figure, I increased the height of the element and reduced the width.

Figure 25-8. Using the drag handle to change the dimensions of a resizable element

Configuring the Resizable Interaction

You can configure the resizable interaction using the settings described in Table 25-9. The resizable interaction relies on the draggable interaction I described in Chapter 24. This means that, in addition to the settings described in the table, you can configure the resizable interaction using the draggable settings as well, including delay, distance, grid, and containment.

Table 25-9. *Resizable Settings*

Setting	Description
alsoResize	A selector used to match elements that should be resized at the same time as the resizable element. The default is false, meaning no other elements are resized.
aspectRatio	When true, the element's aspect ratio is preserved when resized. The default is false.
autoHide	When true, the drag handles are visible only when the mouse hovers over the resizable element. The default is false.
ghost	When true, a semitransparent helper element is drawn to show the user what the new size of the element will be. The default is true.
handles	Specifies where the drag handles will be placed on the resizable element. See later in this chapter for a list of supported values.
maxHeight	Specifies the maximum height that the element can be resized to. The default is null, meaning no limit.
maxWidth	Specifies the maximum width that the element can be resized to. The default is null, meaning no limit.
minHeight	Specifies the minimum height that the element can be resized to. The default is 10 pixels.
minWidth	Specifies the minimum width that the element can be resized to. The default is 10 pixels.

Resizing Related Elements

To my mind, alsoResize is the most useful setting for configuring the resizable interaction. It allows you to specify additional elements that will be resized along with the element to which you applied the resizable method. I use this mainly to ensure that content elements are resized in sync with their parent, as I demonstrated earlier in the chapter when I selected the img element to be resized with the div. First of all, it helps to understand what happens when you have content elements and don't use the alsoResize setting. Listing 25-15 sets the scene.

Listing 25-15. Resizing an Element with Content Without the alsoResize Setting

```
...
<script type="text/javascript">
    $(document).ready(function() {
        $("#aster").resizable();
    });
</script>
...
```

Without the alsoResize setting, only the div element will change size. The content elements will be left as they are. You can see what happens in Figure 25-9.

Figure 25-9. *Resizing an element, but not its content*

There are times when this is useful, but I find myself using the alsoResize setting almost every time I use the resizable interaction. For me, the neat thing about the alsoResize setting is that the matched elements are not limited to the contents of the element you are resizing. You can specify any element, as Listing 25-16 shows.

Listing 25-16. *Resizing Additional Elements with the alsoResize Setting*

```
...
<script type="text/javascript">
    $(document).ready(function() {
        $("#aster").resizable({
            alsoResize: "#aster img, #lily, #lily img"
        });
    });
</script>
...
```

In this script, I broadened the selection to include the other div and img elements in the document. This means that when I resize the resizable div element, jQuery UI resizes four elements simultaneously. You can see the effect in Figure 25-10.

Figure 25-10. Resizing multiple elements

Constraining the Resizable Element Size

You can limit the size of resizable elements by applying the maxHeight, maxWidth, minHeight, and minWidth settings. The value for all four settings is a number of pixels or null, meaning that there is no limit. Listing 25-17 shows how you can use these settings.

■ **Tip**   The default values for the minWidth and minHeight settings are 10 pixels. If the value is any smaller, jQuery UI cannot display the drag handles, which means the user would be unable to increase the size again. Use smaller values with caution.

Listing 25-17. Limiting the Size of a Resizable Element

```
...
<script type="text/javascript">
    $(document).ready(function() {
        $("#aster").resizable({
            alsoResize: "#aster img",
            maxWidth: 200,
            maxHeight: 150
        });
    });
</script>
...
```

■ **Tip**   You can also use the containment setting that is defined by the draggable interaction, which I described in
Chapter 24. This allows you to limit the maximum size of a resizable element to the size of another element.

Positioning the Drag Handles

You can specify which edges and corners can be dragged through the handles setting. The value for this setting is
either all (meaning that all edges and corners are draggable) or a combination of compass points (n, e, s, w, ne, se, nw, sw)
to specify individual corners and edges.

You can specify multiple values, separated by commas. The default value for this setting is e, s, se, which means
that the lower-right corner (se) and the right (e) and bottom (s) edges will be draggable. jQuery UI draws a diagonal
drag handle only in the lower-right corner and only if you have specified se as part of the handles value.
For all other edges and corners, the cursor will change to indicate that dragging is possible when the mouse hovers
above the edge or corner. Listing 25-18 shows the use of the handles setting.

Listing 25-18. Using the handles Setting

```
...
<script type="text/javascript">
    $(document).ready(function() {
        $("#aster").resizable({
            alsoResize: "#aster img"
        });

        $("#lily").resizable({
            alsoResize: "#lilyimg",
            handles: "n, s, e, w"

        });
    });
</script>
...
```

In this script, I made both div elements resizable and applied a custom set of drag handles to one of them.
You can see how jQuery UI handles the visible drag handles and the cursor change in Figure 25-11.

Figure 25-11. *Using the handles setting*

Summary

In this chapter, I explained and demonstrated three of the jQuery UI interactions: sortable, selectable, and resizable. These are less commonly used than the draggable and droppable interactions I described in Chapter 24, but they can still be useful if applied carefully. As with all of the interactions, the main challenge is in making the user aware that he or she can drag, select, sort, or resize an element when there are no standardized visual cues in web applications. For that reason, the interactions should be used as supplements to other mechanisms for interacting with your application or document. This allows advanced users to discover the advantages of the interactions, while other users rely on more obvious and conventional techniques.

■ ■ ■

Refactoring the Example: Part III

In this part of the book, I introduced you to the jQuery UI widgets and interactions. These allow you to create rich web applications that are consistently themed and that can be endlessly configured and tweaked to meet your needs. In this chapter, I'll add some of these features to the example to demonstrate how they can fit together.

Reviewing the Refactored Example

When you last refactored the example, you were at the verge of re-creating some of the jQuery UI functionality that uses the core jQuery library. You can see where I got to in Figure 26-1.

Figure 26-1. *The previously refactored example document*

The additions in the previous part of the book included data templates, form validation, and Ajax, but I also added a simple product carousel that displayed the available products in a single row. I am going to use some of these features in this chapter, but my emphasis will be on applying jQuery UI. Listing 26-1 shows the starting point for this chapter.

Listing 26-1. The Starting Document for This Chapter

```html
<!DOCTYPE html>
<html>
<head>
    <title>Example</title>
    <script src="jquery-2.0.2.js" type="text/javascript"></script>
    <script src="jquery-ui-1.10.3.custom.js" type="text/javascript"></script>
    <script src="handlebars.js"></script>
    <script src="handlebars-jquery.js"></script>
    <link rel="stylesheet" type="text/css" href="jquery-ui-1.10.3.custom.css"/>
    <link rel="stylesheet" type="text/css" href="styles.css"/>
    <script id="flowerTmpl" type="text/x-handlebars-template">
        {{#flowers}}
        <div class="dcell">
            <img src="{{product}}.png"/>
            <label for="{{product}}">{{name}}:</label>
            <input name="{{product}}" value="0" />
        </div>
        {{/flowers}}
    </script>
    <script type="text/javascript">
        $(document).ready(function () {
            $.getJSON("mydata.json", function (data) {
                $("#flowerTmpl").template({ flowers: data })
                    .filter("*").appendTo("#products");
            });
        });
    </script>
</head>
<body>
    <h1>Jacqui's Flower Shop</h1>
    <form method="post" action="http://node.jacquisflowershop.com/order">
        <div id="products"></div>
        <div id="buttonDiv"><button type="submit">Place Order</button></div>
    </form>
</body>
</html>
```

I use the getJSON method to get the details of the products from a JSON file and generate elements using a data template. I add the product elements to a single div element, which has an id of products. You can see the result in Figure 26-2.

Figure 26-2. *The starting document for this chapter*

Displaying the Products

I am going to use an accordion to display products to the user. I have only six products to deal with, but I am going to break them into groups of two and use jQuery to create the structure of elements that the accordion requires. Listing 26-2 shows the changes to the document.

Listing 26-2. *Sorting and Structuring the Flower Elements*

```
<!DOCTYPE html>
<html>
<head>
    <title>Example</title>
    <script src="jquery-2.0.2.js" type="text/javascript"></script>
    <script src="jquery-ui-1.10.3.custom.js" type="text/javascript"></script>
    <script src="handlebars.js"></script>
    <script src="handlebars-jquery.js"></script>
    <link rel="stylesheet" type="text/css" href="jquery-ui-1.10.3.custom.css"/>
    <link rel="stylesheet" type="text/css" href="styles.css"/>
    <style type="text/css">
        .dcell img {height: 60px}
    </style>
    <script id="flowerTmpl" type="text/x-handlebars-template">
        {{#flowers}}
            <div class="dcell">
                <img src="{{product}}.png"/>
                <label for="{{product}}">{{name}}:</label>
                <input name="{{product}}" value="0" />
            </div>
        {{/flowers}}
    </script>
    <script type="text/javascript">
        $(document).ready(function () {
            $.getJSON("mydata.json", function (data) {
```

```
            var flowers = $("#flowerTmpl").template({ flowers: data }).filter("*");

            var rowCount = 1;
            for (var i = 0; i < flowers.length; i += 2) {

                $("<a>").text(data[i].name + " & " + data[i + 1].name)
                    .appendTo("<h2>").parent().appendTo("#products");

                $("<div>").attr("id", "row" + (rowCount++))
                    .appendTo("#products")
                    .append(flowers.slice(i, i + 2))
            }
            $("#products").accordion();
        });
    });
    </script>
</head>
<body>
    <h1>Jacqui's Flower Shop</h1>
    <form method="post" action="http://node.jacquisflowershop.com/order">
        <div id="products"></div>
        <div id="buttonDiv"><button type="submit">Place Order</button></div>
    </form>
</body>
</html>
```

I have rewritten the function passed to the getJSON method to create the accordion, including constructing the element structure and calling the accordion method. The new implementation uses the JSON data object to extract the names of the flowers for the section titles but still uses the data template to generate the HTML elements, which are sliced and placed into wrapper div elements to suit the accordion widget. You can see how the document appears before and after the addition of the call to the accordion method in Figure 26-3.

Figure 26-3. *Creating the element structure and calling the accordion method*

Adding the Shopping Basket

The next step is to add a simple shopping basket to show the user the selections she has made. Listing 26-3 shows the additions to the example document.

Listing 26-3. Adding the Shopping Basket

```html
<!DOCTYPE html>
<html>
<head>
    <title>Example</title>
    <script src="jquery-2.0.2.js" type="text/javascript"></script>
    <script src="jquery-ui-1.10.3.custom.js" type="text/javascript"></script>
    <script src="handlebars.js"></script>
    <script src="handlebars-jquery.js"></script>
    <link rel="stylesheet" type="text/css" href="jquery-ui-1.10.3.custom.css"/>
    <link rel="stylesheet" type="text/css" href="styles.css"/>
    <style type="text/css">
        .dcell img {height: 60px}
        #basketTable {border: thin solid black; border-collapse: collapse}
        th, td {padding: 4px; width: 50px}
        td:first-child, th:first-child {width: 150px}
        #placeholder {text-align: center}
        #productWrapper {float: left; width: 65%}
        #basket {width: 30%; text-align: left; float: left; margin-left: 10px}
        #buttonDiv {clear: both}
    </style>
    <script id="flowerTmpl" type="text/x-handlebars-template">
        {{#flowers}}
            <div class="dcell">
                <img src="{{product}}.png"/>
                <label for="{{product}}">{{name}}:</label>
                <input name="{{product}}" value="0" />
            </div>
        {{/flowers}}
    </script>
    <script id="rowTmpl" type="text/x-handlebars-template">
        <tr id="{{name}}"><td>{{product}}</td><td>{{val}}</td>
            <td><a href="#">Remove</a></td>
        </tr>
    </script>
    <script type="text/javascript">
        $(document).ready(function () {

            $.getJSON("mydata.json", function (data) {

                var flowers = $("#flowerTmpl").template({ flowers: data }).filter("*");

                var rowCount = 1;
                for (var i = 0; i < flowers.length; i += 2) {
                    $("<a>").text(data[i].name + " & " + data[i + 1].name)
                        .appendTo("<h2>").parent().appendTo("#products");
```

```
                    $("<div>").attr("id", "row" + (rowCount++))
                        .appendTo("#products")
                        .append(flowers.slice(i, i + 2));
                }
                $("#products").accordion();

                $("input").change(function (event) {
                    $("#placeholder").hide();
                    var fname = $(this).attr("name");
                    var row = $("tr[id=" + fname + "]");

                    if (row.length == 0) {
                        $("#rowTmpl").template({
                            name: fname,
                            val: $(this).val(),
                            product: $(this).siblings("label").text()
                        }).appendTo("#basketTable").find("a").click(function () {
                            removeTableRow($(this).closest("tr"));
                            var iElem = $("#products").find("input[name=" + fname + "]");
                            $("#products").accordion("option", "active",
                                iElem.closest("div[id^=row]").index("div[id^=row]"));
                            iElem.val(0).select();
                        });
                    } else if ($(this).val() != "0") {
                        row.children().eq(1).text($(this).val());
                    } else {
                        removeTableRow(row);
                    }
                });
            });

            function removeTableRow(row) {
                row.remove();
                if ($("#basketTable tbody").children(":visible").length == 1) {
                    $("#placeholder").show();
                }
            }
        });
    </script>
</head>
<body>
    <h1>Jacqui's Flower Shop</h1>
    <form method="post" action="http://node.jacquisflowershop.com/order">
        <div id="productWrapper">
            <div id="products"></div>
        </div>
        <div id="basket" class="ui-widget">
            <table border=1 id="basketTable">
                <tr><th>Product</th><th>Quantity</th><th>Remove</th></tr>
                <tr id="placeholder"><td colspan=3>No Products</td></tr>
```

```
        </table>
      </div>
      <div id="buttonDiv"><button type="submit">Place Order</button></div>
    </form>
</body>
</html>
```

Wrapping the Accordion

I want to display the basket alongside the accordion. To do this, I have wrapped the element that I select for the accordion method in another div element, like this:

```
...
<div id="productWrapper">
    <div id="products"></div>
</div>
...
```

The accordion widget gets confused if it isn't set to occupy 100 percent of the parent element's width, so I add the wrapper element and then use the CSS width property to fix its size, as follows:

```
...
#productWrapper {float: left; width: 65%}
...
```

The accordion widget happily occupies 100 percent of the wrapper div element, which occupies only 65 percent of its parent element.

Adding the Table

I decided to display the basket using a table element, which I have added to the static elements in the document, as follows:

```
...
<div id="basket" class="ui-widget">
    <table border=1 id="basketTable">
        <tr><th>Product</th><th>Quantity</th><th>Remove</th></tr>
        <tr id="placeholder"><td colspan=3>No Products</td></tr>
    </table>
</div>
...
```

Just as for the accordion, I have put the table element inside a wrapper whose width I set using CSS:

```
...
#basket {width: 30%; text-align: left; float: left; margin-left: 10px}
...
```

The table element contains a header row and a placeholder that spans the entire table. You can see the effect that is created in Figure 26-4.

715

Figure 26-4. *Adding the table to the document*

Handling Input Value Changes

To link the table to the accordion, I listen to the change event on the input elements that I create in the getJSON function, like this:

```
...
$("input").change(function (event) {
    $("#placeholder").hide();
    var fname = $(this).attr("name");
    var row = $("tr[id=" + fname + "]");

    if (row.length == 0) {
        $("#rowTmpl").template({
            name: fname,
            val: $(this).val(),
            product: $(this).siblings("label").text()
        }).appendTo("#basketTable").find("a").click(function () {
            removeTableRow($(this).closest("tr"));
            var iElem = $("#products").find("input[name=" + fname + "]");
            $("#products").accordion("option", "active",
                iElem.closest("div[id^=row]").index("div[id^=row]"));
            iElem.val(0).select();
        });
    } else if ($(this).val() != "0") {
        row.children().eq(1).text($(this).val());
    } else {
        removeTableRow(row);
    }
});
...
```

A lot is going on in this function. When the user changes a value, I check to see whether there is already a row in the table for the corresponding product. If there is not, then I use the following template to create a new row:

```
...
<script id="rowTmpl" type="text/x-handlebars-template">
    <tr id="{{name}}"><td>{{product}}</td><td>{{val}}</td>
        <td><a href=#>Remove</a></td>
    </tr>
</script>
...
```

To get the values for this template, I use core jQuery methods to get information from the input element that triggered the event. I also want the display name for the product, which I obtain by navigating the DOM to find the nearby label element and reading its content, like this:

```
...
$(this).siblings("label").text()
...
```

I append the new row to the table. The placeholder row has already been hidden, back at the start of the function:

```
...
$("#placeholder").hide();
...
```

You can see how newly added rows appear in Figure 26-5. The user enters a value in an input element, and a new row appears in the basket table when the focus changes.

Figure 26-5. Adding rows to the basket table

Deleting Rows

You can see that I have added an a element to the table row as part of the data template. I register a handler for this element when I create the row from the data template, as follows:

```
...
}).appendTo("#basketTable").find("a").click(function () {
    removeTableRow($(this).closest("tr"));
    var iElem = $("#products").find("input[name=" + fname + "]");
    $("#products").accordion("option", "active",
        iElem.closest("div[id^=row]").index("div[id^=row]"));
    iElem.val(0).select();
});
...
```

The first thing I do is call the removeTableRow function, passing in the closest ancestor tr element to the a element. The removeTableRow function uses the remove method to remove the specified element from the document. It also restores the placeholder row in the table if there are no product-related rows, like this:

```
...
function removeTableRow(row) {
    row.remove();
    if ($("#basketTable tbody").children(":visible").length == 1) {
        $("#placeholder").show();
    }
}
...
```

Once the row has been deleted, I find the input element that is associated with the row in the product. I then navigate through the DOM to find the accordion panel element that is the parent to the input element, get its index among its peers, and set this as the active option for the accordion widget. This has the effect of opening the part of the accordion that contains the product that the user has just deleted from the basket. Finally, I set the value of the input element to zero and call the select method so that it is focused and the value is selected. You can see the effect in Figure 26-6 (although this is something that you really need to see in the browser to appreciate).

Figure 26-6. *Focusing on an input element in the accordion when a table row is deleted*

■ **Tip**   I also delete rows when the user enters a value of zero in an `input` element for which there is a row in the table. I do this using the `removeTableRow` function so that the placeholder is shown if needed.

Updating Existing Rows

If there is already a row for the product, then the user is effectively changing the quantity that she wants to order. Rather than remove and replace the row, I find it in the `table` and update the contents of the cell:

```
...
row.children().eq(1).text($(this).val())
...
```

The `row` variable is a jQuery object containing the `tr` element for the product in the table. I access the `td` element by position (using the `index` method) and then set its content using the `text` method.

Applying the Theme Style

The functionality of the basket is fine, but the appearance is terrible. Fortunately, jQuery UI provides a framework of CSS styles that you can apply to elements to give them the same visual appearance as applied to the widgets by your theme. Listing 26-4 shows some simple additions to the HTML elements in the document.

Listing 26-4. Applying the jQuery UI CSS Framework Styles to the table Element

```
...
<body>
    <h1>Jacqui's Flower Shop</h1>
    <form method="post" action="http://node.jacquisflowershop.com/order">
        <div id="productWrapper">
            <div id="products"></div>
        </div>
        <div id="basket" class="ui-widget ui-widget-content">
            <table border=0 id="basketTable">
                <tr class="ui-widget-header">
                    <th>Product</th><th>Quantity</th><th>Remove</th></tr>
                <tr id="placeholder"><td colspan=3>No Products</td></tr>
            </table>
        </div>
        <div id="buttonDiv"><button type="submit">Place Order</button></div>
    </form>
</body>
...
```

You may have noticed that I have used the ui-widget class in some of the examples in preceding chapters. This is the basic jQuery UI style, and it is applied to the outer container of sets of elements that require an appearance that is consistent with the jQuery UI widgets. The ui-widget-content class is used for elements that contain content, and the ui-widget-header is, as its name suggests, used for header elements.

■ **Tip**   I describe the jQuery UI CSS framework classes in Chapter 35.

In addition to applying these classes, I disabled the border for the table element as follows:

```
...
#basketTable {border: none; border-collapse: collapse}
...
```

You can see the effect in Figure 26-7.

Figure 26-7. *Applying the jQuery UI CSS framework classes to the table*

Applying the CSS Framework More Widely

You can go further and apply the framework styles more widely. Listing 26-5 shows some useful additions to the document.

Listing 26-5. Applying the Framework Styles More Widely

```
...
<body>
    <div id="logoWrapper" class="ui-widget ui-widget-content ui-corner-all">
        <h1 id="logo">Jacqui's Flower Shop</h1>
    </div>
    <form method="post" action="http://node.jacquisflowershop.com/order">
        <div id="productWrapper">
            <div id="products"></div>
        </div>
        <div id="basket" class="ui-widget ui-widget-content">
            <table border=0 id="basketTable">
                <tr class="ui-widget-header">
                    <th>Product</th><th>Quantity</th><th>Remove</th></tr>
                <tr id="placeholder"><td colspan=3>No Products</td></tr>
            </table>
        </div>
        <div id="buttonDiv"><button type="submit">Place Order</button></div>
    </form>
</body>
...
```

I have placed the h1 element inside a div and applied several of the framework styles, including ui-corner-all, which creates the rounded corners that you can see in Figure 26-8. I also applied some new styles to this document to create the effect I wanted, overriding the styles in the styles.css file you have been using since Chapter 3:

```
...
<style type="text/css">
    .dcell img {height: 60px}
    #basketTable {border: none; border-collapse: collapse}
    th, td {padding: 4px; width: 50px}
    td:first-child, th:first-child {width: 150px}
    #placeholder {text-align: center}
    #productWrapper {float: left; width: 65%}
    #basket {width: 33%; text-align: left; float: left; margin-left: 10px;
        position: absolute; right: 10px}
    #buttonDiv {clear: both}
    #logo {font-size: 1.5em; background-size: contain; margin: 1px;
        border: none; color: inherit}
    #logoWrapper {margin-bottom: 5px}
</style>
...
```

Figure 26-8. *Applying the CSS framework styles to the document header*

Applying Rounded Corners to the Table

Applying the ui-corner-all class to table elements causes some problems, as shown in Figure 26-9. You will notice that the table element doesn't have rounded corners. This is caused by an interaction between the jQuery UI CSS framework classes and the way that tables are handled in most browsers.

Product	Quantity	Remove
	No Products	

Figure 26-9. *The effect of rounded corners on a table*

To get around this problem, you need to change the table element, apply the jQuery UI CSS framework classes slightly differently, and define a new custom style. First, you need to modify the table, as shown in Listing 26-6.

Listing 26-6. Modifying the table Element to Support Rounded Corners

```
...
<form method="post" action="http://node.jacquisflowershop.com/order">
    <div id="productWrapper">
        <div id="products"></div>
    </div>
    <div id="basket" class="ui-widget ui-widget-content ui-corner-all">
        <table border=0 id="basketTable">
            <thead id="theader" class="ui-widget-header">
                <tr>
                    <th class="ui-corner-tl">Product</th>
                    <th>Quantity</th>
                    <th class="ui-corner-tr">Remove</th></tr>
            </thead>
            <tr id="placeholder"><td colspan=3>No Products</td></tr>
        </table>
    </div>
    <div id="buttonDiv"><button type="submit">Place Order</button></div>
</form>
...
```

I have added a thead element to the table, separating the header from the body rows. It is important to assign the thead element an id and to apply the ui-widget-header class. Since the header is part of the ui-widget-header class, you can remove it from the tr element.

Next, you apply the ui-corner-tl and ui-corner-tr classes to the outer cells in the header row. These classes create rounded corners for the top-left and top-right corners of the elements to which they are assigned. (I describe all of the jQuery UI CSS framework classes in Chapter 35.)

Next, you need to use the id you gave to the thead element to disable the CSS border property in the style element and do the same for the table element, like this:

```
...
<style type="text/css">
    .dcell img {height: 60px}
    #basketTable {border: none; border-collapse: collapse}
    th, td {padding: 4px; width: 50px}
    td:first-child, th:first-child {width: 150px}
    #placeholder {text-align: center}
    #productWrapper {float: left; width: 65%}
    #basket {width: 33%; text-align: left; float: left; margin-left: 10px;
        position: absolute; right: 10px}
```

```
#buttonDiv {clear: both}
#logo {font-size: 1.5em; background-size: contain; margin: 1px;
    border: none; color: inherit}
#logoWrapper {margin-bottom: 5px}
#theader {border: none}
</style>
...
```

Finally, you need to make a small tweak to the removeTableRow function. Now that you have separated the header row and placed it in a thead element, you have one fewer row in the tbody. Here is the change:

```
...
function removeTableRow(row) {
    row.remove();
    if ($("#basketTable tbody").children(":visible").length == 0) {
        $("#placeholder").show();
    }
}
...
```

■ **Tip** The tbody element is created automatically by the browser when the table element is parsed. It is an oddity of HTML that you don't have to specify this element (although you can if preferred).

With these changes, you have a table with rounded corners that matches the other elements in the document, as Figure 26-10 shows.

Figure 26-10. A table with rounded corners

Creating the jQuery UI Button

The next step is to relocate the button and transform it into a jQuery UI widget. Listing 26-7 shows the changes to the document.

Listing 26-7. Relocating and Transforming the Button

```html
<!DOCTYPE html>
<html>
<head>
    <title>Example</title>
    <script src="jquery-2.0.2.js" type="text/javascript"></script>
    <script src="jquery-ui-1.10.3.custom.js" type="text/javascript"></script>
    <script src="handlebars.js"></script>
    <script src="handlebars-jquery.js"></script>
    <link rel="stylesheet" type="text/css" href="jquery-ui-1.10.3.custom.css"/>
    <link rel="stylesheet" type="text/css" href="styles.css"/>
    <style type="text/css">
        .dcell img {height: 60px}
        #basketTable {border: none; border-collapse: collapse}
        th, td {padding: 4px; width: 50px}
        td:first-child, th:first-child {width: 150px}
        #placeholder {text-align: center}
        #productWrapper {float: left; width: 65%}
        #basket {text-align: left;}
        #buttonDiv {clear: both; margin: 5px}
        #logo {font-size: 1.5em; background-size: contain; margin: 1px;
            border: none; color: inherit}
        #logoWrapper {margin-bottom: 5px}
        #theader {border: none}
    </style>
    <script id="flowerTmpl" type="text/x-handlebars-template">
        {{#flowers}}
            <div class="dcell">
                <img src="{{product}}.png"/>
                <label for="{{product}}">{{name}}:</label>
                <input name="{{product}}" value="0" />
            </div>
        {{/flowers}}
    </script>
    <script id="rowTmpl" type="text/x-handlebars-template">
        <tr id="{{name}}"><td>{{product}}</td><td>{{val}}</td>
            <td><a href="#">Remove</a></td>
        </tr>
    </script>
    <script type="text/javascript">
        $(document).ready(function () {

            $.getJSON("mydata.json", function (data) {

                var flowers = $("#flowerTmpl").template({ flowers: data }).filter("*");
```

```
                var rowCount = 1;
                for (var i = 0; i < flowers.length; i += 2) {
                    $("<a>").text(data[i].name + " & " + data[i + 1].name)
                        .appendTo("<h2>").parent().appendTo("#products");
                    $("<div>").attr("id", "row" + (rowCount++))
                        .appendTo("#products")
                        .append(flowers.slice(i, i + 2));
                }
                $("#products").accordion();

                $("input").change(function (event) {
                    $("#placeholder").hide();
                    var fname = $(this).attr("name");
                    var row = $("tr[id=" + fname + "]");

                    if (row.length == 0) {
                        $("#rowTmpl").template({
                            name: fname,
                            val: $(this).val(),
                            product: $(this).siblings("label").text()
                        }).appendTo("#basketTable").find("a").click(function () {
                            removeTableRow($(this).closest("tr"));
                            var iElem = $("#products").find("input[name=" + fname + "]");
                            $("#products").accordion("option", "active",
                                iElem.closest("div[id^=row]").index("div[id^=row]"));
                            iElem.val(0).select();
                        });
                    } else if ($(this).val() != "0") {
                        row.children().eq(1).text($(this).val());
                    } else {
                        removeTableRow(row);
                    }
                });
            });

            $("#buttonDiv, #basket").wrapAll("<div>").parent().css({
                float: "left",
                marginLeft: "2px"
            });

            $("button").button();

            function removeTableRow(row) {
                row.remove();
                if ($("#basketTable tbody").children(":visible").length == 0) {
                    $("#placeholder").show();
                }
            }
        });
    </script>
</head>
```

```
<body>
    <div id="logoWrapper" class="ui-widget ui-widget-content ui-corner-all">
        <h1 id="logo">Jacqui's Flower Shop</h1>
    </div>
    <form method="post" action="http://node.jacquisflowershop.com/order">
        <div id="productWrapper">
            <div id="products"></div>
        </div>
        <div id="basket" class="ui-widget ui-widget-content ui-corner-all">
            <table border=0 id="basketTable">
                <thead id="theader" class="ui-widget-header">
                    <tr>
                        <th class="ui-corner-tl">Product</th>
                        <th>Quantity</th>
                        <th class="ui-corner-tr">Remove</th></tr>
                </thead>
                <tr id="placeholder"><td colspan=3>No Products</td></tr>
            </table>
        </div>
        <div id="buttonDiv"><button type="submit">Place Order</button></div>
    </form>
</body>
</html>
```

I have wrapped the buttonDiv and basket elements in a new div element and adjusted some of the CSS styles to adjust the positioning of these elements. And, as Figure 26-11 shows, I call the button method to create a jQuery UI button.

Figure 26-11. *Repositioning and transforming the button element*

Adding the Completion Dialog

When the user clicks the Place Order button, I want to collect some additional information from them. I showed you how to display a multipart form using tabs in Chapter 20, so for some variety, I'll use a dialog widget this time. Listing 26-8 shows the changes to the document for the dialog.

Listing 26-8. Adding the Dialog

```
<!DOCTYPE html>
<html>
<head>
    <title>Example</title>
    <script src="jquery-2.0.2.js" type="text/javascript"></script>
    <script src="jquery-ui-1.10.3.custom.js" type="text/javascript"></script>
    <script src="handlebars.js"></script>
    <script src="handlebars-jquery.js"></script>
    <link rel="stylesheet" type="text/css" href="jquery-ui-1.10.3.custom.css"/>
    <link rel="stylesheet" type="text/css" href="styles.css"/>
    <style type="text/css">
        .dcell img {height: 60px}
        #basketTable {border: none; border-collapse: collapse}
        th, td {padding: 4px; width: 50px}
        td:first-child, th:first-child {width: 150px}
        #placeholder {text-align: center}
        #productWrapper {float: left; width: 65%}
        #basket {text-align: left;}
        #buttonDiv {clear: both; margin: 5px}
        #logo {font-size: 1.5em; background-size: contain; margin: 1px;
            border: none; color: inherit}
        #logoWrapper {margin-bottom: 5px}
        #theader {border: none}
        #completeDialog input {width: 150px; margin-left: 5px; text-align: left}
        #completeDialog label {width: 60px; text-align: right}
    </style>
    <script id="flowerTmpl" type="text/x-handlebars-template">
        {{#flowers}}
            <div class="dcell">
                <img src="{{product}}.png"/>
                <label for="{{product}}">{{name}}:</label>
                <input name="{{product}}" value="0" />
            </div>
        {{/flowers}}
    </script>
    <script id="rowTmpl" type="text/x-handlebars-template">
        <tr id="{{name}}"><td>{{product}}</td><td>{{val}}</td>
            <td><a href="#">Remove</a></td>
        </tr>
    </script>
```

```javascript
<script type="text/javascript">
    $(document).ready(function () {

        $.getJSON("mydata.json", function (data) {

            var flowers = $("#flowerTmpl").template({ flowers: data }).filter("*");

            var rowCount = 1;
            for (var i = 0; i < flowers.length; i += 2) {
                $("<a>").text(data[i].name + " & " + data[i + 1].name)
                    .appendTo("<h2>").parent().appendTo("#products");
                $("<div>").attr("id", "row" + (rowCount++))
                    .appendTo("#products")
                    .append(flowers.slice(i, i + 2));
            }
            $("#products").accordion();

            $("#products input").change(function (event) {
                $("#placeholder").hide();
                var fname = $(this).attr("name");
                var row = $("tr[id=" + fname + "]");

                if (row.length == 0) {
                    $("#rowTmpl").template({
                        name: fname,
                        val: $(this).val(),
                        product: $(this).siblings("label").text()
                    }).appendTo("#basketTable").find("a").click(function () {
                        removeTableRow($(this).closest("tr"));
                        var iElem = $("#products").find("input[name=" + fname + "]");
                        $("#products").accordion("option", "active",
                            iElem.closest("div[id^=row]").index("div[id^=row]"));
                        iElem.val(0).select();
                    });
                } else if ($(this).val() != "0") {
                    row.children().eq(1).text($(this).val());
                } else {
                    removeTableRow(row);
                }
            });
        });

        $("#buttonDiv, #basket").wrapAll("<div>").parent().css({
            float: "left",
            marginLeft: "2px"
        });

        $("button").button();

        $("#completeDialog").dialog({
            modal: true,
            buttons: [{ text: "OK", click: sendOrder },
```

729

```
                        {
                            text: "Cancel", click: function () {
                                $("#completeDialog").dialog("close");
                            }
                        }]
        });

        function sendOrder() {

        }

        function removeTableRow(row) {
            row.remove();
            if ($("#basketTable tbody").children(":visible").length == 0) {
                $("#placeholder").show();
            }
        }
    });
    </script>
</head>
<body>
    <div id="logoWrapper" class="ui-widget ui-widget-content ui-corner-all">
        <h1 id="logo">Jacqui's Flower Shop</h1>
    </div>
    <form method="post" action="http://node.jacquisflowershop.com/order">
        <div id="productWrapper">
            <div id="products"></div>
        </div>
        <div id="basket" class="ui-widget ui-widget-content ui-corner-all">
            <table border=0 id="basketTable">
                <thead id="theader" class="ui-widget-header">
                    <tr>
                        <th class="ui-corner-tl">Product</th>
                        <th>Quantity</th>
                        <th class="ui-corner-tr">Remove</th></tr>
                </thead>
                <tr id="placeholder"><td colspan=3>No Products</td></tr>
            </table>
        </div>
        <div id="buttonDiv"><button type="submit">Place Order</button></div>
    </form>
    <div id="completeDialog" title="Complete Purchase">
        <div><label for="name">Name: </label><input name="first" /></div>
        <div><label for="email">Email: </label><input name="email" /></div>
        <div><label for="city">City: </label><input name="city" /></div>
    </div>
</body>
</html>
```

I have added a div element with the content that will be displayed to the user in the body element, along with some CSS styles to override those that are in the styles.css file that is imported into the document using a link element. Here is the call to the dialog method that creates the dialog widget:

```
...
$("#completeDialog").dialog({
    modal: true,
    buttons: [{ text: "OK", click: sendOrder },
            {
                text: "Cancel", click: function () {
                    $("#completeDialog").dialog("close");
                }
            }]
});
...
```

I have created a modal dialog that has two buttons. Clicking the Cancel button will close the dialog. Clicking the OK button will call the sendOrder function. This function doesn't do anything at the moment.

As you will remember from Chapter 22, the dialog widget is open by default, which means that it is shown to the user as soon as it is created. You can see how it appears in Figure 26-12.

Figure 26-12. *The dialog used to complete the purchase*

■ **Tip** Notice that I have narrowed the selection when I set up the change event on the input elements. I limit the selection to exclude those input elements in the dialog. If I had not done this, entering a value in the Complete Purchase dialog would have added a new item in the basket.

Handling the Place Order Button Click

I don't want the user to see the dialog box until they click the Place Order button. I use the autoOpen setting to hide the dialog until it is needed and use the click method to handle the button click, as Listing 26-9 shows.

Listing 26-9. Hiding the Dialog and Handling the Button Click

```
...
<script type="text/javascript">
    $(document).ready(function () {

        $.getJSON("mydata.json", function (data) {

            var flowers = $("#flowerTmpl").template({ flowers: data }).filter("*");

            var rowCount = 1;
            for (var i = 0; i < flowers.length; i += 2) {
                $("<a>").text(data[i].name + " & " + data[i + 1].name)
                    .appendTo("<h2>").parent().appendTo("#products");
                $("<div>").attr("id", "row" + (rowCount++))
                    .appendTo("#products")
                    .append(flowers.slice(i, i + 2));
            }
            $("#products").accordion();

            $("#products input").change(function (event) {
                $("#placeholder").hide();
                var fname = $(this).attr("name");
                var row = $("tr[id=" + fname + "]");

                if (row.length == 0) {
                    $("#rowTmpl").template({
                        name: fname,
                        val: $(this).val(),
                        product: $(this).siblings("label").text()
                    }).appendTo("#basketTable").find("a").click(function () {
                        removeTableRow($(this).closest("tr"));
                        var iElem = $("#products").find("input[name=" + fname + "]");
                        $("#products").accordion("option", "active",
                            iElem.closest("div[id^=row]").index("div[id^=row]"));
                        iElem.val(0).select();
                    });
                } else if ($(this).val() != "0") {
                    row.children().eq(1).text($(this).val());
                } else {
                    removeTableRow(row);
                }
            });
        });

        $("#buttonDiv, #basket").wrapAll("<div>").parent().css({
            float: "left",
            marginLeft: "2px"
        });
```

```
$("button").button().click(function (e) {
    e.preventDefault();
    if ($("#placeholder:visible").length) {

        $("<div>Please select some products</div>").dialog({
            modal: true,
            buttons: [{
                text: "OK",
                click: function () { $(this).dialog("close") }
            }]
        })
    } else {
        $("#completeDialog").dialog("open");
    }
});

$("#completeDialog").dialog({
    modal: true,
    autoOpen: false,
    buttons: [{ text: "OK", click: sendOrder },
            {
                text: "Cancel", click: function () {
                    $("#completeDialog").dialog("close");
                }
            }]
});

function sendOrder() {

}

function removeTableRow(row) {
    row.remove();
    if ($("#basketTable tbody").children(":visible").length == 0) {
        $("#placeholder").show();
    }
}
});
</script>
...
```

When the user clicks the button, I check to see whether the placeholder element is visible. I do this using jQuery, using a selector that produces a jQuery object that will contain elements only if the placeholder is visible.

I am using the visibility of the placeholder as a proxy for the user having selected some products. The placeholder is hidden if there are any selections in the basket, and so a visible placeholder tells me that there are no selections.

■ **Tip** This is a nice example of the way you can layer functionality in a document, but it does mean that my simple test for product selection depends on the implementation of the basket and will need to change if I ever modify the way that the basket works.

I create and display a dialog widget dynamically if the user clicks the button without having selected any products. You can see how this appears in Figure 26-13. If selections have been made, then the completion dialog is shown to capture the final information I want from the user.

Figure 26-13. *Displaying a dialog if there is no product selection*

Completing the Order

All that remains is to implement the sendOrder function. I have already shown you the different ways that you can send data to the server via Ajax, so to keep this chapter simple, I will simply collect the values from the various input elements and create a JSON object that can be sent to a server for processing. Listing 26-10 shows the additions to the document.

Listing 26-10. Completing the Order Process

```
...
function sendOrder() {
    var data = new Object();
    $("input").each(function(index, elem) {
        var jqElem = $(elem);
        data[jqElem.attr("name")] = jqElem.val();
    })
    console.log(JSON.stringify(data));
    $("#completeDialog").dialog("close");
    $("#products input").val("0");
    $("#products").accordion("option", "active", 0);
    $("#basketTable tbody").children(":visible").remove();
    $("#placeholder").show();
}
...
```

In this function I get the value from each of the input elements and add them as properties to an object that I then convert to JSON and write to the console.

More usefully, I then reset the document, closing the dialog, resetting the values of the input elements, switching to the first panel of the accordion, and resetting the basket. Figure 26-14 shows the document with some product selection. I'll use these to generate the JSON string.

Figure 26-14. *Selecting products using the example document*

When I click the Place Order button, I am presented with the dialog requesting additional information, as shown in Figure 26-15.

Figure 26-15. *Providing additional information to complete the order*

Finally, clicking the OK button generates the JSON and resets the document. The JSON for this example is as follows:

{"aster":"12","daffodil":"7","rose":"5","peony":"2","primula":"0","snowdrop":"0",
 "first":"Adam Freeman","email":"adam@my.com","city":"London"}

And, as Figure 26-16 shows, you are back where you started, ready to go through the process again.

Figure 26-16. *Resetting the document*

Summary

In this chapter, I refactored the example document to incorporate features from jQuery UI. I added some of the widgets, such as accordion, dialog, and button, as well as gave an initial look at how you can apply the jQuery UI CSS framework classes to manage the appearance of other elements. I give more detail about these CSS classes in Chapter 35. In Part 5, I turn to jQuery Mobile, which you can use to create web applications that are targeted at mobile devices.

■ ■ ■

CHAPTER 27

Getting Started with jQuery Mobile

In this chapter, I show you how to obtain jQuery Mobile and add it to an HTML document. I also explain that jQuery Mobile takes a different approach to creating widgets and how you must adapt to accommodate this approach. Touch-enabled devices provide some unique challenges for web application developers, and I explain some of the core features that jQuery Mobile provides to help simplify the process and set out some general guidance for the development and testing of mobile web apps. Table 27-1 provides the summary for this chapter.

Table 27-1. *Chapter Summary*

Problem	Solution	Listing
Add jQuery Mobile to an HTML document.	Add a script element to import the jQuery and jQuery Mobile libraries and a link element to import the CSS.	1
Create a jQuery Mobile page.	Use the data-role attribute with a value of page.	2
Disable the browser virtual page.	Configure the viewport.	3
Defer the execution of custom JavaScript code until after jQuery Mobile has enhanced a document.	Use the pageinit event.	4
Simplify touch event handling.	Use the jQuery Mobile gesture and virtual mouse events.	5–7
Respond to changes in device orientation.	Handle the orientationchange event or use CSS media queries.	8, 9

■ **Note**   As I explained in Chapter 1, the jQuery Mobile API changed with the release of version 1.3, and I highlight these changes in the chapters that follow.

Setting Up jQuery Mobile

To start this chapter, I'll show you how to obtain and install jQuery Mobile. jQuery Mobile is built on the foundation of jQuery and jQuery UI, so you'll see some common patterns that are consistent with these libraries.

Obtaining jQuery Mobile

The first thing you need is jQuery Mobile, which is available from `http://jquerymobile.com`. As I write this, the current version of jQuery Mobile is 1.3.1, and you can get a zip file from the download page. For version 1.3.1, this is called `jquery.mobile-1.3.1.zip`.

■ **Tip** Just as with jQuery and jQuery UI, jQuery Mobile can be loaded via a content distribution network (CDN). I described CDNs in Chapter 5, and they can be a great idea for Internet-deployed web applications (but rarely for intranet applications). The jQuery Mobile download page includes details of the links you will require to use jQuery Mobile via a CDN.

Creating a Theme

jQuery Mobile supports a theme framework, which is like a simplified version of the one that jQuery UI uses. There is a default theme included in the jQuery Mobile package, but if you want to create a custom theme, you can do so at `http://jquerymobile.com/themeroller`. Using the ThemeRoller application generates a zip file that contains a CSS file to include in your web documents. I describe how to use the theme framework in Chapter 28, but I'll be using the default theme rather than creating a custom one in this part of the book – in part because the jQuery Mobile ThemeRoller doesn't have a library of convenient themes available.

Getting jQuery

You also need jQuery. Version 1.3.1 of jQuery Mobile is intended to work only with versions 1.7.0 through 1.9.1 of jQuery. jQuery Mobile tends to lag behind releases of jQuery, and support for jQuery 2.0 is not available as I write this. However, you can use the latest 1.x release without any problems, and so I will use jQuery 1.10.1 for the examples in this part of the book.

■ **Tip** Even though jQuery Mobile is built on jQuery UI, you don't need to install the jQuery UI library. Everything you need is included in the jQuery Mobile download.

Installing jQuery Mobile

You need to copy three items from the jQuery Mobile download into the directory from which you serve your web content:

- The `jquery.mobile-1.3.1.js` file (the jQuery Mobile JavaScript library)
- The `jquery.mobile-1.3.1.css` file (the CSS styles jQuery Mobile uses)
- The `images` directory (the jQuery Mobile icons)

You also need the jQuery library, of course, and once everything is in place, you can create an HTML document that uses jQuery Mobile. As with the earlier chapters, I called my file `example.html`, and I saved it in the same directory as the items in the previous list. Listing 27-1 shows the contents of this file.

Listing 27-1. The Contents of example.html

```html
<!DOCTYPE html>
<html>
<head>
    <title>Example</title>
    <meta name="viewport" content="width=device-width, initial-scale=1">
    <script type="text/javascript" src="jquery-1.10.1.js"></script>
    <script type="text/javascript" src="jquery.mobile-1.3.1.js"></script>
    <link rel="stylesheet" href="jquery.mobile-1.3.1.css" type="text/css" />
</head>
<body>
    <div data-role="page">
        <div data-role="header">
                <h1>Jacqui's Shop</h1>
        </div>
        <div data-role="content">
            This is Jacqui's Flower Shop
            <p><button>Press Me</button></p>
        </div>
    </div>
</body>
</html>
```

The elements I highlighted are required for jQuery Mobile. The two `script` elements import the jQuery and jQuery Mobile JavaScript libraries, and the `link` element imports the CSS that jQuery Mobile relies on. Since my HTML file is in the same directory as the JavaScript and CSS files, I am able to refer to these files simply by name.

■ **Tip**   Ignore the rest of the document for the moment. I'll explain shortly what the `meta` element does and how the contents of the `body` element are.

Understanding the jQuery Mobile Approach

Although jQuery Mobile is based on jQuery UI, there are some significant differences that you need to be aware of. Before you start digging into the capabilities of jQuery Mobile, I need to explain those differences to provide a context for the information in the following chapters.

TIERED SUPPORT

jQuery Mobile offers different levels of support for different mobile browsers. There are three grades of support available and a long list of the supported devices and browsers in each. At the high end, *A-grade* support provides the richest experience and implements all of the features that I describe in this part of the book.

B-grade support provides everything except Ajax navigation, which I describe in Chapter 28. This is still a good level of functionality, but the movement between pages in an application won't be as smooth as for an A-grade device.

The *C-grade* category is basic. Only old devices fall into this category, and jQuery Mobile is unable to provide much functionality for these devices.

Happily, most modern mobile devices fall into the A-grade category of support. You can see a detailed list of supported devices at `http://jquerymobile.com/gbs`.

Understanding Automatic Enhancement

The most striking difference when using jQuery Mobile is that widgets don't have to be created explicitly. When using jQuery UI, you use jQuery to select one or more elements and then apply a method such as `button` or `tabs` to create a specific jQuery UI widget in the document. If you look at Listing 27-1, you will notice that I have not added a `script` element to the document to create any widgets. The only `script` elements are there to import jQuery and jQuery Mobile libraries. And yet, as Figure 27-1 shows, I get formatted content. (This figure shows the Opera Mobile emulator that I use extensively in this part of the book and that I properly introduce later in this chapter.)

Figure 27-1. *The example document*

> ■ **Note**   For most of the figures in this part of the book, I'll be using the Opera Mobile browser emulator in a landscape resolution, which lets me pack more examples into each page.

When you bring the jQuery Mobile library into a web page with a `script` element, the page is enhanced automatically. First jQuery Mobile looks for elements that have a `data-role` attribute. The value of these attributes tells jQuery Mobile what enhancements should be applied to the elements. Listing 27-2 highlights the `data-role` attributes in the example document.

> ■ **Tip**   Attributes whose name begins with *data-* are known as *data attributes*. Data attributes have been an informal convention for defining custom attributes for some time and have been included in the official standard for HTML5.

Listing 27-2. The data-role Attributes in the Example Document

```
<!DOCTYPE html>
<html>
<head>
    <title>Example</title>
    <meta name="viewport" content="width=device-width, initial-scale=1">
    <script type="text/javascript" src="jquery-1.10.1.js"></script>
    <script type="text/javascript" src="jquery.mobile-1.3.1.js"></script>
    <link rel="stylesheet" href="jquery.mobile-1.3.1.css" type="text/css" />
</head>
<body>
    <div data-role="page">
        <div data-role="header">
                <h1>Jacqui's Shop</h1>
        </div>
        <div data-role="content">
            This is Jacqui's Flower Shop
            <p><button>Press Me</button></p>
        </div>
    </div>
</body>
</html>
```

One of the unusual features of jQuery Mobile is that a single HTML document can contain multiple pages (a feature that I demonstrate in Chapter 28). The page is the building block of a jQuery Mobile application. There is only one page in this example, and it is denoted by the div element whose data-role value is page. Because the page is nested inside an HTML document, you also need to provide jQuery Mobile with additional information about the purpose of the elements contained within the page. There are two other data-role attributes, which tell jQuery Mobile which element contains the header information for page and which element contains the content. Table 27-2 summarizes the three data-role values in this example and their significance. You can readily correlate the div elements and their data-role values with the structure of the page shown in Figure 27-1.

Table 27-2. *Data-Role Attribute Values in the Example Document*

Value	Description
page	Tells jQuery Mobile to treat the content of the element as a page.
header	Tells jQuery Mobile that the element represents the page header.
content	Tells jQuery Mobile that the element contains the content for the page.

■ **Tip** jQuery Mobile will automatically insert the wrapper for the content part of a page. This means that any elements that are not part of another section are treated as content, allowing you to explicitly skip defining an element for that section.

You don't have to take any explicit action to make jQuery Mobile find the elements with `data-role` attributes and generate a page. This all happens automatically when the HTML document is loaded. Some elements, such as `button`, are automatically styled (although, as I demonstrate in later chapters, you can configure most widgets using other data attributes).

■ **Tip**   jQuery Mobile goes to great lengths to minimize the amount of custom JavaScript that is needed to create a mobile web application. In fact, it is possible to create simple applications without any custom JavaScript at all. This doesn't mean you can build jQuery Mobile applications for browsers that have JavaScript disabled, however. jQuery Mobile is a JavaScript library and requires JavaScript support to perform automatic enhancement of pages.

Understanding the Viewport

Although not part of jQuery Mobile, an important element to add to your HTML documents is the one highlighted in Listing 27-3.

Listing 27-3. The meta Element That Configures the Viewport

```
...
<head>
    <title>Example</title>
    <meta name="viewport" content="width=device-width, initial-scale=1">
    <script type="text/javascript" src="jquery-1.10.1.js"></script>
    <script type="text/javascript" src="jquery.mobile-1.3.1.js"></script>
    <link rel="stylesheet" href="jquery.mobile-1.3.1.css" type="text/css" />
</head>
...
```

I have highlighted the `meta` element whose name attribute is `viewport`. Many mobile browsers use a *virtual page* to display web content in order to improve compatibility with web sites that have been designed with desktop browsers in mind. This is generally a sensible idea because it provides the user with an overall sense of the page structure, even though the details are too small to read. Figure 27-2 shows the jQuery Mobile home page as it is displayed initially and zoomed so that the text is readable.

Figure 27-2. *The mobile browser virtual page*

The first frame shows the jQuery Mobile web site in a portrait orientation (which accentuates the effect). The text is too small to read, but mobile browsers have support for zooming in to regions of the page, as the second frame shows. The virtual page is a compromise, to be sure, but it's an understandable one given that relatively few web sites are tailored to mobile devices.

The problem is that the virtual page is applied without much discrimination and causes problems for jQuery Mobile applications. Figure 27-3 shows how the example document is displayed when the virtual page is used.

Figure 27-3. *The example document displayed in a wide virtual page*

As the figure demonstrates, the jQuery Mobile elements are displayed so small that they are unusable. The meta element in the example document tells the browser that the width of the page should be the width of the screen. This causes the browser to display your jQuery Mobile elements at a sensible size.

Understanding jQuery Mobile Events

There are two important pieces of information about events as they relate to jQuery Mobile. In the sections that follow, I describe each of them.

Understanding the Page Events

jQuery Mobile defines a series of events that describe the life cycle of pages. The most important of these is the pageinit event. jQuery Mobile automatically enhances pages by registering its functions to handle the jQuery ready event that you have been relying on in earlier parts of the book. If you want to include custom JavaScript in a document, you have to take care not to have your code executed before jQuery Mobile has finished processing the document. This means you have to wait for the pageinit event, and then it is triggered when jQuery Mobile has finished initializing the document. There is no convenient method like there is for the ready event, so you have to use the bind method to associate your function with the event, as demonstrated in Listing 27-4.

Listing 27-4. Using the pageinit Event

```
<!DOCTYPE html>
<html>
<head>
    <title>Example</title>
    <meta name="viewport" content="width=device-width, initial-scale=1">
    <script type="text/javascript" src="jquery-1.10.1.js"></script>
```

```
<script type="text/javascript">
    $(document).bind("pageinit", function () {
        $("button").click(function () {
            console.log("Button pressed")
        })
    });
</script>
<script type="text/javascript" src="jquery.mobile-1.3.1.js"></script>
<link rel="stylesheet" href="jquery.mobile-1.3.1.css" type="text/css" />
</head>
<body>
    <div data-role="page">
        <div data-role="header">
                <h1>Jacqui's Shop</h1>
        </div>
        <div data-role="content">
            This is Jacqui's Flower Shop
            <p><button>Press Me</button></p>
        </div>
    </div>
</body>
</html>
```

The arguments to the bind method are the name of the event you are interested in and the function that should be executed when the event is triggered. Your function will be executed only when the event is triggered for the element or elements you have selected and applied the bind method to.

In this example, I have used the bind method to register a function that will be executed when the pageinit event is triggered. Inside that function, I place the statements that I want performed when the document has been loaded and processed. In this case, I have used jQuery to select the button element in the document and used the click method to register another function that will be performed when the button is clicked, just as I have been doing throughout this book.

■ **Tip** Notice that I have inserted my new script element *before* the jQuery Mobile JavaScript library is imported into the document. This isn't essential for the pageinit event but is required for the mobileinit event that you use to change some jQuery Mobile settings (I demonstrate how to do this in Chapter 28). I find it a good idea to always put the custom code before importing the jQuery Mobile library, even if I am only responding to the pageinit event.

Understanding Touch Events

There is a specification for touch events in a browser, but it is pretty low level because there is a lot of variety in the touch interaction model. Some devices support multi-touch, for example, and there is wide variety in the way that touch gestures are interpreted. Table 27-3 describes these low-level touch events.

Table 27-3. *The Standard Touch Events*

Event	Description
touchstart	Triggered when the user touches the screen. For multi-touch devices, this event will be triggered each time a finger touches the screen.
touchend	Triggered when the user removes a finger from the screen.
touchmove	Triggered when the user holds or moves a finger while it is touching the screen.
touchcancel	Triggered when a touch sequence is disrupted. The meaning of this is device specific, but a common example is when the user slides a finger off the edge of the screen.

The responsibility of interpreting these events and working out their significance falls to the developer. It is a painful task that is fraught with errors and one that I recommend you avoid wherever possible. It's something that jQuery Mobile helps with, as I explain shortly.

■ **Tip** If you do want to get into the details of touch events, then you can find the specification at www.w3.org/TR/touch-events. This includes full descriptions of the events and the properties that are available for getting the detail of each touch interaction.

Most web sites have not been designed with touch events in mind. To support the widest possible range of web site scripts, the mobile browsers synthesize mouse events from the touch events. This means the browser triggers the touch events and then generates corresponding (fake) mouse events that represent the same actions, but as though they had been performed with a traditional mouse. Listing 27-5 contains a useful script that demonstrates how this is done.

Listing 27-5. Monitoring Touch and Synthesized Mouse Events

```
<!DOCTYPE html>
<html>
<head>
    <title>Event Test</title>
    <meta name="viewport" content="width=device-width, initial-scale=1">
    <link rel="stylesheet" href="jquery.mobile-1.3.1.css" type="text/css" />
    <script type="text/javascript" src="jquery-1.10.1.js"></script>
    <style type="text/css">
        table {border-collapse: collapse; border: medium solid black; padding: 4px}
        #placeholder {text-align: center}
        #countContainer * {display: inline; width:50px}
        th {width: 100px}
    </style>
    <script type="text/javascript">
        $(document).bind("pageinit", function() {
            var eventList = [
                "mousedown", "mouseup", "click", "mousecancel",
                "touchstart", "touchend", "touchmove", "touchcancel"]
```

```
        for (var i = 0; i < eventList.length; i++) {
            $("#pressme").bind(eventList[i], handleEvent)
        }

        $("#reset").bind("tap", function() {
            $("tbody").children().remove();
            $("#placeholder").show();
            startTime = 0;
        })
    });

    startTime = 0;
    function handleEvent(ev) {
        var timeDiff = startTime == 0 ? 0 : (ev.timeStamp - startTime);
        if (startTime == 0) {
            startTime = ev.timeStamp
        }
        $("#placeholder").hide();
        $("<tr><td>" + ev.type + "</td><td>" + timeDiff + "</td></tr>")
            .appendTo("tbody");
    }
</script>
<script type="text/javascript" src="jquery.mobile-1.3.1.js"></script>
</head>
<body>
    <div data-role="page">
        <div data-role="content">
            <div id="tcontainer" class="ui-grid-a">
                <div class="ui-block-a">
                    <button id="pressme">Press Me</button>
                    <button id="reset">Reset</button>
                </div>
                <div class="ui-block-b">
                    <table border=1>
                        <thead>
                            <tr><th>Event</th><th>Time</th></tr>
                            <tr id="placeholder"><td colspan=2>No Events</td><tr>
                        </thead>
                        <tbody></tbody>
                    </table>
                </div>
            </div>
        </div>
    </div>
</body>
</html>
```

There are two buttons and a table in this example. The Press Me button is wired up so that a selection of mouse and touch events are displayed in the table when the button is clicked. For each event, the event type and the number of milliseconds since the last event are shown. The Reset button clears the table and resets the timer. You can see the effect in Figure 27-4.

Figure 27-4. *Observing the sequence of touch and mouse events*

Table 27-4 shows the sequence of events and timings that arise when clicking the button in the Opera Mobile browser.

Table 27-4. *The Event Sequence from Opera Mobile*

Event	Relative Time
touchstart	0
touchend	96
mousedown	315
mouseup	315
click	321

You can see that the touchstart and touchend events are triggered first, responding to the moments when I touched and then released the screen. The browser then generates mousedown and mouseup events and then a click event. Notice that there is quite a delay between the touchend and mousedown events being triggered, roughly 300 milliseconds. This is enough of a delay to make relying on the synthesized events problematic because your web application will lag behind the user's touch interactions. Not all browsers have this problem, but it is common enough to be an issue, and I recommend you measure the latency on the browsers you intend to target.

Using the jQuery Mobile Gesture Methods

jQuery Mobile does two things to make working with events easier. The first is a set of gesture events that are triggered in response to certain sequences of low-level touch events, meaning that you don't have to analyze the touch sequence yourself to make sense of what gesture the user was making. These events are described in Table 27-5.

Table 27-5. *The Standard Touch Events*

Event	Description
tap	Triggered when the user touches the screen and then removes her finger in quick succession.
taphold	Triggered after the user touches the screen, keeps her finger in place for about a second, and then releases.
swipe	Triggered when the user performs a horizontal drag of at least 30 pixels with a vertical variation of less than 20 pixels within a one-second period.
swipeleft	Triggered when the user swipes in the left direction.
swiperight	Triggered when the user swipes in the right direction.

These events make dealing with basic gestures simple. Listing 27-6 adds these events to the timing example.

Listing 27-6. Adding the jQuery Mobile Gesture Events to the Timing Example

```
...
<script type="text/javascript">
    $(document).bind("pageinit", function() {
        var eventList = [
            "mousedown", "mouseup", "click", "mousecancel",
            "touchstart", "touchend", "touchmove", "touchcancel",
            "tap", "taphold", "swipe", "swipeleft", "swiperight"]

        for (var i = 0; i < eventList.length; i++) {
            $("#pressme").bind(eventList[i], handleEvent)
        }

        $("#reset").bind("tap", function() {
            $("tbody").children().remove();
            $("#placeholder").show();
            startTime = 0;
        })
    });

    startTime = 0;
    function handleEvent(ev) {
        var timeDiff = startTime == 0 ? 0 : (ev.timeStamp - startTime);
        if (startTime == 0) {
            startTime = ev.timeStamp
        }
        $("#placeholder").hide();
        $("<tr><td>" + ev.type + "</td><td>" + timeDiff + "</td></tr>")
            .appendTo("tbody");
    }
</script>
...
```

Figure 27-5 shows what happens when I click the button in the browser.

Figure 27-5. Adding the jQuery Mobile gesture events to the timing example

Table 27-6 shows the event sequence in an easy-to-read table. Since I am clicking a button, the only gesture event that appears is tap. The important thing to note is that the tap event is triggered quickly, usually within a couple of milliseconds of my releasing from the screen.

Table 27-6. The Event Sequence from Opera Mobile

Event	Relative Time
touchstart	0
touchend	63
tap	**63**
mousedown	317
mouseup	321
click	328

The nice thing about the gesture events is that jQuery Mobile will trigger them even in browsers that don't support touch events or that are running on devices without touch interfaces. Figure 27-6 shows the example running in the Google Chrome desktop browser.

Figure 27-6. The event sequence in a desktop browser

Table 27-7 shows the sequence of events and their relative timings more clearly.

Table 27-7. The Event Sequence from Google Chrome

Event	Relative Time
mousedown	0
mouseup	79
click	80
tap	**80**

As you might expect, there are no touchstart and touchend events in this sequence, and the order of the events is different (because the mouse events are real, rather than synthesized). Even so, the tap event is still triggered immediately after the click event.

■ **Tip** I use the tap event instead of click in mobile web applications because it avoids the timing issue that comes from the synthesized events and because it is also generated on non-touch platforms.

Using the jQuery Mobile Virtual Mouse Events

Browsers are not required to synthesize mouse events, meaning that a web application that works on touch and non-touch devices should listen for both mouse events and touch events. For mobile browses that do synthesize events, you end up with touch and mouse events for each interaction. To help simplify this process, jQuery Mobile defines a set of virtual mouse events. When you register for these events, jQuery Mobile takes care of removing the duplicates and ensuring that the appropriate events are triggered, irrespective of whether you have touch support. Table 27-8 describes the virtual events.

Table 27-8. *The Standard Touch Events*

Event	Description
vmouseover	Triggered in response to mouseover events (there is no equivalent touch event because the user's finger isn't always in contact with the screen).
vmousedown	Triggered in response to touchstart or mousedown events.
vmousemove	Triggered in response to touchmove or mousemove events.
vmouseup	Triggered in response to touchend or mouseup events.
vclick	Triggered in response to the click event.
vmousecancel	Triggered in response to touchcancel or mousecancel events.

The way that these events are generated creates a mouse-like sequence, even on touch devices. To explain what I mean, I have added some of the virtual events to the timing example, as shown in Listing 27-7.

Listing 27-7. Adding the jQuery Mobile Virtual Events to the Timing Example

```
...
<script type="text/javascript">
    $(document).bind("pageinit", function() {
        var eventList = [
            "mousedown", "mouseup", "click", "mousecancel",
            "touchstart", "touchend", "touchmove", "touchcancel",
            "tap", "taphold", "swipe", "swipeleft", "swiperight",
            "vmouseover", "vmousedown", "vmouseup", "vclick", "vmousecancel"]

        for (var i = 0; i < eventList.length; i++) {
            $("#pressme").bind(eventList[i], handleEvent)
        }

        $("#reset").bind("tap", function() {
            $("tbody").children().remove();
            $("#placeholder").show();
            startTime = 0;
        })
    });

    startTime = 0;
    function handleEvent(ev) {
        var timeDiff = startTime == 0 ? 0 : (ev.timeStamp - startTime);
        if (startTime == 0) {
            startTime = ev.timeStamp
        }
        $("#placeholder").hide();
        $("<tr><td>" + ev.type + "</td><td>" + timeDiff + "</td></tr>")
            .appendTo("tbody");
    }
</script>
...
```

When I touch the screen, jQuery Mobile generates the vmouseover and vmousedown events. These don't have any meaning in a purely touch environment. If you are writing an application that works across platforms, then you might want to perform some action when the user moves the desktop mouse over an element. The triggering of the synthetic vmouseover event in response to the real touchstart allows you to perform the same action seamlessly for touch devices. You can see the result in Figure 27-7.

Figure 27-7. *Adding the virtual events to the timing example*

Table 27-9 shows the event and timing sequence in a more easily readable form. Although the vclick event is triggered long before the synthetic click event, this isn't always the case, and I do not recommend using vclick as a substitute for click as a way to address the event latency issue.

Table 27-9. *The Event Sequence from Google Chrome*

Event	Relative Time
touchstart	0
vmouseover	**0**
vmousedown	**0**
touchend	64
vmouseup	64
vclick	**64**
tap	64
mousedown	320
mouseup	327
click	331

■ **Caution**   It is important not to make assumptions about the way that the real and virtual events are interleaved. This is because the event sequence on a non-touch device will be different. The order of the virtual events relative to one another will be the same; the intervening real events can change.

Responding to Device Orientation Changes

Most mobile browsers support an event called orientationchange, which is triggered every time the device is rotated through 90 degrees. To make life easier, jQuery Mobile will synthesize the orientationevent when it is not supported by the browser. This is done by listening for changes in the window size and looking at the ratio of the new height and width values. Listing 27-8 shows how you can respond to this event.

Listing 27-8. Responding to Changes in Orientation

```html
<!DOCTYPE html>
<html>
<head>
    <title>Example</title>
    <meta name="viewport" content="width=device-width, initial-scale=1">
    <link rel="stylesheet" href="jquery.mobile-1.3.1.css" type="text/css" />
    <script type="text/javascript" src="jquery-1.10.1.js"></script>
    <script type="text/javascript">
        $(document).bind("pageinit", function() {
            $(window).bind("orientationchange", function(e) {
                $("#status").text(e.orientation)
            })
            $("#status").text(jQuery.event.special.orientationchange.orientation())
        });
    </script>
    <script type="text/javascript" src="jquery.mobile-1.3.1.js"></script>
</head>
<body>
    <div data-role="page">
        <div data-role="header">
                <h1>Jacqui's Shop</h1>
        </div>
        <div data-role="content">
            <p>Device orientation is: <b><span id=status></span></b></p>
        </div>
    </div>
</body>
</html>
```

You must select the window object in order to bind to the orientationchange event. In this example, I change the text of a span element indicating the new orientation. This information is available through the orientation property of the Event object that is passed to the handler function.

jQuery Mobile also provides a method for determining the current orientation, as follows:

```
...
jQuery.event.special.orientationchange.orientation()
...
```

I use this method in the example to set the contents of the span element, since the orientationchange event isn't fired when the page is processed, only when the device is subsequently reoriented.

If you don't have a real mobile device to test this example with, then you can use one of the emulators that I describe later in this chapter. Most of them have the ability to simulate a rotation, triggered by a particular key stroke or button press. For the Opera Mobile emulator that I am using, pressing Ctrl+Alt+R triggers the effect, which is shown in Figure 27-8.

Figure 27-8. *Responding to a change in orientation*

The synthesized event that jQuery Mobile produces means you can get the same effect when you resize the window of a browser that doesn't support orientation changes, such as a desktop browser. In this case, the orientation is determined by the width and height of the window.

Using Media Queries to Manage Orientation

The orientationchange event allows you to respond to changes in orientation using JavaScript. An alternative approach is to use CSS, applying different styles to elements for each orientation, something you can achieve using a CSS *media query*. Listing 27-9 shows how this can be done.

Listing 27-9. Responding to Orientation Using CSS Media Queries

```
<!DOCTYPE html>
<html>
<head>
    <title>Example</title>
    <meta name="viewport" content="width=device-width, initial-scale=1">
    <link rel="stylesheet" href="jquery.mobile-1.3.1.css" type="text/css" />
    <script type="text/javascript" src="jquery-1.10.1.js"></script>
    <script type="text/javascript" src="jquery.mobile-1.3.1.js"></script>
    <style type="text/css">
        @media screen and (orientation:portrait) {
            #pstatus {display: none}
            #lstatus {display: inline}
        }

        @media screen and (orientation:landscape) {
            #pstatus {display: inline}
            #lstatus {display: none}
        }
    </style>
</head>
<body>
    <div data-role="page">
        <div data-role="header">
                <h1>Jacqui's Shop</h1>
        </div>
        <div data-role="content">
            <p>Device orientation is:
                <span id=pstatus><b>Portrait</b></span>
                <span id=lstatus><b>Landscape</b></span>
            </p>
        </div>
    </div>
</body>
</html>
```

CSS media queries allow you to define sets of styles that are applied under specific circumstances, in this case when the orientation is landscape or portrait. I use the CSS `display` property to show or hide elements, allowing me to create the same effect I had with JavaScript in the previous example. There is no need for any kind of synthesis in this situation. Media queries for orientation work equally well for desktop browsers and mobile browsers.

Working with Mobile Devices

Developing applications for mobile devices has some distinct differences from regular desktop development. In the sections that follow, I provide some guidance and information to help you get started and to highlight some of the key issues you will face.

IDENTIFYING MOBILE DEVICES

If you are offering an application to desktop and mobile users, you may want to tailor the interface you present. A common approach is to offer a jQuery UI interface to desktop browsers and a jQuery Mobile interface to mobile devices.

The difficulty is recognizing which browsers are running on mobile devices. There are various techniques for doing this, all of which are performed at the server, redirecting the browser to the appropriate HTML documents. I am not going to get into the detail of these, since they are outside the scope of this book. If you are new to this issue, then I suggest you look at `http://wurfl.sourceforge.net`, which contains a useful server-side component that can identify most mobile devices. You should also consider `https://github.com/kaimallea/isMobile`, which offers a client-side solution.

I recommend against automatically forcing the user to the mobile version of your application based on their browser. Some users prefer to use the desktop versions of applications, even on mobile devices, especially since mobile versions often have restricted functionality. My recommendation is to give the user a simple choice when he arrives at your site if you detect a mobile device and to make it easy to switch between the versions of your application even when the initial decision has been made.

Avoiding the Two Cardinal Sins of Mobile Development

There are two pitfalls to avoid when building web applications for mobile devices: *bad assumptions* and *unrealistic simulation*. I explain both and provide some context to help you avoid making some common mistakes.

Avoiding Bad Assumptions

The market for mobile devices is extremely vibrant, relatively immature, and lacking in standardization. When building web applications for desktops, there are some assumptions that are usually made (although they are often unstated). There is a general expectation about the minimum screen resolution, JavaScript support, the availability of certain plug-ins, and that the user will be able to point using a mouse and enter text using a keyboard.

That's not to say that these are reasonable assumptions. If you assume that JavaScript will be available, for example, then you eliminate potential customers who don't (or can't) enable JavaScript in their browser. You might decide that this is a good trade-off, that most users could enable JavaScript if they wanted, and that you'll just forgo users who don't meet the specification you require.

The situation in the mobile device market is more complicated because the market is so fragmented. The desktop space may seem diverse, but a Mac, a Windows PC, and a Linux box all have quite a lot in common. The same can't be said for mobile devices, and assumptions about screen size, network connectivity, and input method will eliminate some large segments of the market.

The World Is Not an iPhone

One of the worst assumptions I see made (and made often) is that the target market is the iPhone. The iPhone has been a wild success, but it isn't the totality of the mobile device market, and there are even variations between different iPhone models. A common target screen resolution is 320 by 480 pixels, which comes from the older iPhone models. A lot of devices have this resolution, but a growing number do not. Using a fixed-screen resolution in your mobile application will simply eliminate users who have screens that are too small and annoy users who have paid a premium to get a higher-resolution device.

The World Is Not a Phone at All

Another common assumption is that the target market is mobile phones, ignoring the success of the tablet market. Not only do tablets typically have higher screen resolutions, but the way that people hold them and use them is different. To see what I mean, head to any coffee shop and watch the customers. My (entirely unscientific but consistent) observation is that the greater size of tablets makes them slightly awkward to hold and so they are usually propped up against something else. This means they are somewhat unstable, and dragging a finger across the screen makes the tablet wobble slightly (making accuracy a problem) and obscures a lot of the screen (because the user's hand and arm are over the tablet itself).

My point is that the nature of mobile devices dictates a lot about how they are used and what kind of interactions are sensible and desirable. The best way to figure this out is to observe people interacting with a range of devices. If you have money and time available, then a usability lab is a fantastic resource. But even if you are in a hurry and on a budget, an afternoon spent in Starbucks can provide some valuable insights.

The World Is Not Touch Enabled

Not all mobile devices have touch screens. Some rely on a tiny mouse combined with a keyboard, and some have multiple input methods. One of my test machines is a small laptop that converts into a tablet. It has a touch screen as well as a full keyboard and mouse. Users expect to be able to use the best input method available to them, and making assumptions about the inputs available just leads to user frustration (which is why I rarely use the laptop/tablet combination device other than for testing).

Mobile Bandwidth Is Not Free and Not Infinite

The price of network connectivity goes through cycles, driven by the kinds of activities that the users of the network perform. At the moment, network providers are struggling to fund and build enough network capacity to satisfy demand, especially in densely populated urban areas. Eventually, the cost of capacity will fall and bandwidth available will increase, but at the moment, network providers are charging a premium for data access and applying low caps on the amount of data that a user can download in a month.

It is dangerous to assume that users are willing to dedicate a serious amount of their data to your web application. As a general rule, customers don't care as much about your application as you'd like them to. It may hurt to hear, but it is almost always true. Your application fills your world, as it should, but it is just one of many to a user.

In Chapter 28, I show you how jQuery Mobile can pre-fetch the content for a web application before the user needs it. It is a great feature, but it should be used with caution because it assumes that the user is willing to spend bandwidth on content they may never need. The same goes for automatic and frequent data updates. Use sparingly, cautiously, and only when the user has explicitly indicated that your application should be a heavy user of his network quota.

Equally, do not make assumptions about the data rate available to a mobile device. Think about your use of large resources such as images and video. Some users will have the capacity to quickly download such content, but many won't, and a low-bandwidth option is always welcome in my experience.

You should also be prepared to deal with the network being unavailable. I used to commute by train, and the network would drop out whenever I went into a tunnel. A well-written web application expects connectivity issues, reports them to the user, and recovers elegantly when the network becomes available again. Sadly, most applications are not well written.

■ **Tip** I once did some work for a global container shipping company, and the constraints they faced led them to create some of the most robust and adaptable applications I have seen. They had shipping agents at almost every port in the world, in places so remote that the agent's office was just a shack at the end of a pier. They could ship modern PCs to these locations (that didn't present a problem because they were a shipping company), but networking was often limited to a slow dial-up connection that worked for a couple of hours a day between power cuts, meaning that several days might pass between connections being established. Every application had to allow the local shipping office to carry on working even when there was no network link and synchronize the local data to the global network whenever a connection could be established. It took a lot of thought and testing, but the result was an IT infrastructure that helped them dominate global container shipping. I often think of these constraints when designing mobile applications – modern devices can usually expect better operating conditions, but the best applications always hope for the best, assume the worst, and deal with problems on behalf of the user.

Avoiding Unrealistic Simulation and Testing

The wide variation in mobile devices means you have to test thoroughly. Working with actual mobile devices during the early stages of development can be frustrating. The network requests are routed via the cell network, which requires the development machines to be publicly available. There are developer modes for some mobile devices, but they have their own drawbacks.

In short, you want a simulated environment in which to start your development, something that gives you the ability to build and test rapidly and conveniently and to do so without having to expose your development environments to the outside world. Fortunately, there are emulators that provide the facilities you require. I'll describe some of the available options later in this chapter, but they fall into two categories.

The first category of emulator is where the actual mobile browser has been ported to another platform. Everything about the browser is as close to the real thing as possible. The second category relies on the fact that most browsers use a common rendering engine for mobile and desktop machines. So, for example, if you want to get a rough idea of how the iPhone browser will handle a document, you can use the Apple Safari browser because it shares common roots. The emulator is little more than a visual wrapper and a screen size constraint around the desktop rendering engine.

Both approaches can be useful, and they are worth exploring. I use them often in the early stages of mobile product development. But once I have the basic functionality in place, I start including testing on real devices, and as the project nears completion, I switch to using only real devices and stop using the emulators altogether.

The reason for this is that the emulators have two main failings. The first is that they are not 100 percent accurate in their emulation. Even the best of emulators don't always present content the way that real devices using the same browser will. The second – and to my mind the most important – failing is that the touch inputs are simulated.

The mouse is used to make a touch-enabled browser work on a non-touch desktop PC, and a mouse just doesn't create the same effect as a finger. Three touch factors are missing in a desktop emulation: *tactility*, *obstruction*, and *inaccuracy*.

The Lack of Tactility

The lack of tactility means that you don't get a good idea about how using the web application will *feel*. Tapping and sliding on a glass display is an odd activity. When the application is properly responsive, the effect is elegant and enjoyable. The result is frustration when the application lags behind the input or misconstrues the touch interaction. The mouse isn't capable of giving you feedback about how well you are dealing with touch.

759

The Lack of Obstruction

I have already alluded to the issue of obstruction. When you use touch devices, even small ones, your finger and hand cover up part of the screen. You need to take this into account when designing a web application for a touch device. You need to place controls carefully so that the user can still see what's happening while she is touching the screen, and you need to bear in mind that roughly 10 percent of the population is left handed and so a different part of the screen will be obscured for these users. Only touching the buttons and links with your own hands gives you a true understanding of how easy your web application is to use.

■ **Tip** If you go and do some user observation at the coffee shop, look out for users following a distinctive pattern. They touch the screen and then move their hand completely out of the way for a second, before reaching back in and making another touch gesture. This is often indicative of an application that has located its widgets so that the visual feedback resulting from an action is under the user's hand. The user has to move her hand out of the way to see what happened before moving back in for another gesture, a tiring and frustrating experience.

The Lack of Inaccuracy

With the mouse, the user can be exceptionally accurate hitting a target on the screen. Per-pixel accuracy can be achieved with a modern mouse and a little practice. This is not the case with the human finger, and the most accuracy you can expect is "roughly in the area" of the target. This means you have to select widgets that are easy and create layout that takes inaccuracy into account. You can't get a feel for how easy it is to hit your widgets in the emulator. The mouse is not a good-enough proxy. You need to test on a range of different screen sizes and resolutions to understand what your users will face. This information provides essential cues as to the size and density of the widgets on your pages.

A PERSONAL TALE OF INACCURACY

My personal frustration goes back to when I used to commute to work by train. I live in the United Kingdom where the timely arrival of a train is seen as an unobtainable goal. In the summer, I didn't really mind when the train was late. I could linger in the sunshine. I never wanted to linger in the winter, and after a few minutes I would want to check to see just how late the train was going to be, which is possible with an online application.

Imagine the scene. The sun hasn't yet come up, the wind is bitter, and the ground is icy. I am wrapped up warm, but the heat I carried with me from the car is quickly ebbing away. I want to load the application, navigate to the information for my local station, and get an idea of how long I will be waiting (and if it is going to be a while, return to my car and consider driving to the office).

As soon as I take off my gloves, my fingers start to feel cold. After a few minutes, I can't flex my fingers properly and my hands start to shake, which is unfortunate because the widgets I need to hit are *tiny*; they are just regular web links displayed in a small font. I *never* managed to easily navigate to the information I wanted. I would hit the wrong link, be forced to wait for the wrong information to load, and then navigate back to try again. All the while, my ability to hit a widget accurately is getting worse as my hand gets colder. I grew to *hate* mobile web applications that assume pixel accuracy and that application in particular.

Using a Mobile Browser Emulator

Even though they have limitations, mobile browser emulators have a useful role to play. In the previous edition of this book, I described a range of different emulators and the benefits and drawbacks of each. Since then, my development style has changed, and I only use two tools: the Opera Mobile Emulator and BrowserStack.

USING DESKTOP BROWSERS TO TEST MOBILE APPLICATIONS

Desktop browsers are obviously not the same as the mobile versions, but share common underpinnings and can be useful for quick and dirty testing prior to deploying to real devices. I often use these browsers when I have the major building blocks of an application in place and I am fleshing out the functional areas. The main benefit of using the desktop browsers is that they have excellent development tools, including JavaScript debuggers and, for the most part, desktop browsers make excellent development tools for the early stages of a mobile project or when you are trying to track down problems in your code or markup.

Using the Opera Mobile Emulator

I use the Opera Mobile Emulator during the initial stages of my projects, at which point it tends to be the only testing I do. This browser allows me to simulate devices with different screen sizes, including tablets and landscape orientations.

The Opera Mobile browser that is being emulated is widely used, and the emulator does a reasonable (if not perfect) job of accurately laying out the content. Some jQuery Mobile features, such as navigation transitions (which I describe in Chapter 28), are not supported. This is the emulator that I used to obtain the screen shots for the figures earlier in the chapter.

The main benefit of this kind of testing is that it is fast, allowing for the quick write-and-test style of development style that I prefer. One nice feature is that you can debug the mobile emulator using the debugger built into the desktop version of Opera. The process for setting this up is a little clunky, but it can be a helpful feature. The Opera Mobile emulator is available without charge at http://www.opera.com/developer/mobile-emulator.

Using BrowserStack

BrowserStack is a commercial service that provides virtual machines running a wide range of browsers on common operating systems. I have started using this service because it is simpler than maintaining my own testing environments. It is not a perfect solution – the mobile browsers are emulators rather than actual hardware, for example, but the service is quick, easy to use, and pretty comprehensive. You can get a trial account at http://browserstack.com, and there are competing services available that offer similar functionality.

■ **Note** I have no affiliation with BrowserStack other than as a regular user – I pay for my account just like anyone else would and I don't receive any special treatment or discounts.

Summary

In this chapter, I explained how to obtain jQuery Mobile and add it to an HTML document and set out the basic approach that jQuery Mobile takes for automatically enhancing HTML documents and separating pages from those documents. I described the custom events that jQuery Mobile provides to make it easier to create touch applications, and I set out some basic guidance about how to approach mobile development and testing.

CHAPTER 28

■ ■ ■

Pages, Themes & Layouts

In this chapter, I describe one of the key building blocks for jQuery Mobile applications: *pages*. I touched on pages in Chapter 27, but now I'll go into the detail and show how to define, configure, and navigate between pages. I'll also show you two useful jQuery Mobile features for styling and structuring the content in pages: themes and grid layouts. Table 28-1 provides the summary for this chapter.

Table 28-1. Chapter Summary

Problem	Solution	Listing
Define a jQuery Mobile page.	Apply the data-role attribute to an element with a value of page.	1
Add a header or footer to a page.	Apply the data-role attribute to elements using a value of header or footer.	2
Define multiple pages in a document.	Create several elements whose data-role is page.	3
Navigate between pages.	Create an a element whose href element is the id of a page element.	4
Specify a transition effect for an a element.	Apply the data-transition attribute.	5
Set a global transition effect.	Assign a value to the defaultPageTransition setting.	6
Link to a page in another document.	Specify the URL of the document as the href value of an a element.	7, 8
Disable Ajax for a single link.	Set the data-ajax attribute to false.	9
Disable Ajax globally.	Set the ajaxEnable event to false.	10
Prefetch a page.	Use the data-prefetch attribute.	11, 12
Change the current page.	Use the changePage method.	13
Control the direction of the transition effect.	Use the reverse setting for the changePage method.	14
Specify the delay after which the loading dialog is shown.	Use the loadMsgDelay setting.	15
Disable the loading dialog.	Use the showLoadMsg setting.	16

(continued)

Table 28-1. (*continued*)

Problem	Solution	Listing
Determine the current page.	Use the activePage property.	17
Load pages in the background.	Use the loadPage method.	18
Respond to page loading.	Use the page loading events.	19
Respond to page transitions.	Use the page transition events.	20
Apply a swatch to a page or an element.	Use the data-theme attribute and set the value to the swatch that should be used.	21, 22
Lay out elements in a grid.	Use the jQuery Mobile layout CSS classes.	23

Understanding jQuery Mobile Pages

In Chapter 27, I showed you how to define jQuery Mobile pages within an HTML document using elements with specific roles. To recap, Listing 28-1 shows a simple page.

Listing 28-1. A Simple jQuery Mobile Page in an HTML Document

```
<!DOCTYPE html>
<html>
<head>
    <title>Example</title>
    <meta name="viewport" content="width=device-width, initial-scale=1">
    <link rel="stylesheet" href="jquery.mobile-1.3.1.css" type="text/css" />
    <script type="text/javascript" src="jquery-1.10.1.js"></script>
    <script type="text/javascript" src="jquery.mobile-1.3.1.js"></script>
</head>
<body>
    <div data-role="page">
        <div data-role="content">
            This is Jacqui's Flower Shop
        </div>
    </div>
</body>
</html>
```

This is a minimal page, which consists of two key elements, each of which has a data-role attribute. The element whose role is page denotes the region of the HTML content that contains the jQuery Mobile page. As I mentioned in Chapter 27, one of the key characteristics of jQuery Mobile is that the pages that are displayed to the user are not directly related to the HTML elements that contain them.

The other important element has a role of content. This denotes the part of the jQuery Mobile page that contains the page content. A page can contain different sections of which the content is only one, as I'll demonstrate shortly. You can see how the HTML in the listing is displayed in the browser in Figure 28-1.

Figure 28-1. *Displaying a minimal jQuery Mobile page in the browser*

Adding Headers and Footers to a Page

In addition to a content section, a jQuery Mobile page can contain a header and footer, denoted by elements whose data-role attributes are set to header and footer, respectively. Listing 28-2 shows both of these sections added to the example page.

Listing 28-2. *Adding a Header and a Footer to the Example Page*

```
<!DOCTYPE html>
<html>
<head>
    <title>Example</title>
    <meta name="viewport" content="width=device-width, initial-scale=1">
    <link rel="stylesheet" href="jquery.mobile-1.3.1.css" type="text/css" />
    <script type="text/javascript" src="jquery-1.10.1.js"></script>
    <script type="text/javascript" src="jquery.mobile-1.3.1.js"></script>
</head>
<body>
    <div data-role="page">
        <div data-role="header">
            <h1>Jacqui's Shop</h1>
        </div>
        <div data-role="content">
            This is Jacqui's Flower Shop
        </div>
        <div data-role="footer">
            <h1>Home Page</h1>
        </div>
    </div>
</body>
</html>
```

You can see the effect of these additions in Figure 28-2.

■ **Caution**   Headers and footers can occupy a lot of space on a small screen, as the figure shows.

Figure 28-2. Adding a header and footer to the page

■ **Tip**   Notice that the footer is displayed at the end of the content section, rather than at the bottom of the page. You can fix the position of headers and footers by setting the data-position attribute to fixed – this has the effect of keeping the header and/or footer in place while allowing the rest of the content to scroll freely. Test thoroughly when using this option: not all browsers support the CSS features that fixed headers and footers require.

Adding Pages to a Document

You can define multiple jQuery Mobile pages in a single document. This can be useful for simple web applications because you can bundle everything you need into a single HTML file, which can reduce the number of requests that have to be made to the server and the overall amount of data that has to be transferred (because some elements – like those in the head section – are only specified once for multiple pages). Listing 28-3 shows a multipage document.

Listing 28-3. Defining Multiple jQuery Mobile Pages in an HTML Document

```
<!DOCTYPE html>
<html>
<head>
    <title>Example</title>
    <meta name="viewport" content="width=device-width, initial-scale=1">
    <link rel="stylesheet" href="jquery.mobile-1.3.1.css" type="text/css" />
    <script type="text/javascript" src="jquery-1.10.1.js"></script>
    <script type="text/javascript" src="jquery.mobile-1.3.1.js"></script>
</head>
```

```
<body>
    <div id="page1" data-role="page">
        <div data-role="header">
            <h1>Jacqui's Shop</h1>
        </div>
        <div data-role="content">
            This is Jacqui's Flower Shop
        </div>
    </div>
    <div id="page2" data-role="page">
        <div data-role="header">
            <h1>Jacqui's Shop</h1>
        </div>
        <div data-role="content">
            This is page 2
        </div>
    </div>
</body>
</html>
```

This example defines two pages in the document. I have used the id attribute to assign each page a unique identifier, and these values form the basis for navigating between pages. Only the first page is shown when the HTML document is loaded. To let the user navigate between pages, I add an a element whose href is the id of the target page, as shown in Listing 28-4.

Listing 28-4. Navigating between Pages

```
<!DOCTYPE html>
<html>
<head>
    <title>Example</title>
    <meta name="viewport" content="width=device-width, initial-scale=1">
    <link rel="stylesheet" href="jquery.mobile-1.3.1.css" type="text/css" />
    <script type="text/javascript" src="jquery-1.10.1.js"></script>
    <script type="text/javascript" src="jquery.mobile-1.3.1.js"></script>
</head>
<body>
    <div id="page1" data-role="page">
        <div data-role="header">
            <h1>Jacqui's Shop</h1>
        </div>
        <div data-role="content">
            This is Jacqui's Flower Shop
            <p><a href="#page2">Go to page 2</a></p>
        </div>
    </div>
    <div id="page2" data-role="page">
        <div data-role="header">
            <h1>Jacqui's Shop</h1>
        </div>
```

```
        <div data-role="content">
            This is page 2
            <p><a href="#page1">Go to page 1</a></p>
        </div>
    </div>
</body>
</html>
```

In this example, I have added links between the pages. When a link is clicked, jQuery Mobile takes care of displaying the appropriate page from the document, as demonstrated in Figure 28-3.

Figure 28-3. *Navigating between pages in a document*

Configuring Page Transitions

When the user navigates between pages, jQuery Mobile uses an animation effect to transition between one page and the next. The default effect is called `slide`, which has the outgoing page slide to the left while the new page slides in from the right. jQuery Mobile defines a number of different effects, as follows:

- `slide`
- `pop`
- `slideup`
- `slidedown`
- `slidefade`
- `fade`
- `flip`

- turn

- flow

- none (meaning no effect, also expressed as null)

Not all mobile devices support all of the transitions correctly and you may encounter flickering and stuttering. Each new release of jQuery Mobile improves the number of devices that can support all of the transitions, but you should always test thoroughly to make sure that you don't see any problems on the devices you are targeting. If in doubt, try the fade or slide transitions, which I have found have problems on the fewest devices.

■ **Tip** The mobile browser emulators don't handle transitions well and generally ignore them. They work just fine on real mobile devices, however. If you want to see the transition on the desktop, then use either Google Chrome or Apple Safari, both of which handle the effects well.

You can change the way that an individual page transition is animated by using the data-transition attribute on the a element, setting the value to the effect you want. Listing 28-5 provides an example.

Listing 28-5. Using the data-transition Attribute

```
<!DOCTYPE html>
<html>
<head>
    <title>Example</title>
    <meta name="viewport" content="width=device-width, initial-scale=1">
    <link rel="stylesheet" href="jquery.mobile-1.3.1.css" type="text/css" />
    <script type="text/javascript" src="jquery-1.10.1.js"></script>
    <script type="text/javascript" src="jquery.mobile-1.3.1.js"></script>
</head>
<body>
    <div id="page1" data-role="page">
        <div data-role="header">
            <h1>Jacqui's Shop</h1>
        </div>
        <div data-role="content">
            This is Jacqui's Flower Shop
            <p><a href="#page2" data-transition="turn">Go to page 2</a></p>
        </div>
    </div>
    <div id="page2" data-role="page">
        <div data-role="header">
            <h1>Jacqui's Shop</h1>
        </div>
        <div data-role="content">
            This is page 2
            <p><a href="#page1">Go to page 1</a></p>
        </div>
    </div>
</body>
</html>
```

■ **Note**   I can't easily show you the different animation effects using figures. This example is one that requires experimentation in the browser. You can avoid having to type in the HTML by downloading the source code that accompanies this book and is freely available from Apress.com.

When the user clicks the highlighted link, the turn transition is used to display the target page. The turn effect is applied only to that single link. Other links in the page or in other pages in the same document will continue to use the default. Set the data-transition attribute to none if you want to disable the animation effect.

■ **Tip**   You can change the direction in which the effect is played by applying the data-direction attribute to the a element with a value of reverse. In the "Changing the Current Page" section, I give an example of reversing the transition direction and explain why it can be useful.

If you want to change the animation effect used for all navigation, then you need to set a global option. jQuery Mobile defines the defaultPageTransition setting, which you can set when the mobileinit event is triggered. Listing 28-6 shows how this is done.

Listing 28-6. Changing the default page Transition

```
<!DOCTYPE html>
<html>
<head>
    <title>Example</title>
    <meta name="viewport" content="width=device-width, initial-scale=1">
    <link rel="stylesheet" href="jquery.mobile-1.3.1.css" type="text/css" />
    <script type="text/javascript" src="jquery-1.10.1.js"></script>
    <script type="text/javascript">
        $(document).bind("mobileinit", function() {
            $.mobile.defaultPageTransition = "fade";
        })
    </script>
    <script type="text/javascript" src="jquery.mobile-1.3.1.js"></script>
</head>
<body>
    <div id="page1" data-role="page">
        <div data-role="header">
            <h1>Jacqui's Shop</h1>
        </div>
        <div data-role="content">
            This is Jacqui's Flower Shop
            <p><a href="#page2">Go to page 2</a></p>
        </div>
    </div>
    <div id="page2" data-role="page">
        <div data-role="header">
            <h1>Jacqui's Shop</h1>
        </div>
```

```
            <div data-role="content">
                This is page 2
                <p><a href="#page1">Go to page 1</a></p>
            </div>
        </div>
    </body>
</html>
```

There is no convenient method for registering a handler function for the `mobileinit` event, so you have to select the document object and use the `bind` method. The arguments to this method are the name of the event you want to handle and the handler function to use when the event is triggered.

■ **Caution**   The `mobileinit` event is triggered as soon as the jQuery Mobile script library is loaded, which means you have to register the handler function to change the global jQuery Mobile setting before the jQuery Mobile library is referenced in a `script` element. You can see how I have done this in the listing. The function will never be executed if the call to the `bind` method is not defined before the `script` element that loads the jQuery Mobile code.

To change the value of a global setting, you assign a new value to a property of the `$.mobile` object. Since I want to change the `defaultPageTransition` setting, I assign a value to the `$.mobile.defaultPageTransition` property, like this:

```
...
$.mobile.defaultPageTransition = "fade";
...
```

This statement sets the default effect to fade. I can still override this setting with the `data-transition` attribute.

Linking to External Pages

You don't have to include all the pages in a single document. You can add links just as you would if using regular HTML. To demonstrate this, I have created a new file called `document2.html`, the content of which is shown in Listing 28-7.

Listing 28-7. The Content of the document2.html File

```
<!DOCTYPE html>
<html>
<head>
    <title>Document 2</title>
    <meta name="viewport" content="width=device-width, initial-scale=1">
    <link rel="stylesheet" href="jquery.mobile-1.3.1.css" type="text/css" />
    <script type="text/javascript" src="jquery-1.10.1.js"></script>
    <script type="text/javascript" src="jquery.mobile-1.3.1.js"></script>
</head>
<body>
    <div id="page1" data-role="page">
        <div data-role="header">
            <h1>Jacqui's Shop</h1>
        </div>
```

```
        <div data-role="content">
            This is page 1 in document2.html
            <p><a href="#page2">Go to page 2 in this document</a></p>
            <p><a href="example.html">Return to example.html</a></p>
        </div>
    </div>
    <div id="page2" data-role="page">
        <div data-role="header">
            <h1>Jacqui's Shop</h1>
        </div>
        <div data-role="content">
            This is page 2 in document2.html
            <p><a href="#page1">Go to page 1</a></p>
        </div>
    </div>
</body>
</html>
```

This document contains a pair of jQuery Mobile pages, following the same structure as in the other examples. Linking to pages in other documents is simple. You just define an a element whose href attribute contains the URL of the target document, as shown in Listing 28-8.

Listing 28-8. Navigating to a Page in Another HTML Document

```
<!DOCTYPE html>
<html>
<head>
    <title>Example</title>
    <meta name="viewport" content="width=device-width, initial-scale=1">
    <link rel="stylesheet" href="jquery.mobile-1.3.1.css" type="text/css" />
    <script type="text/javascript" src="jquery-1.10.1.js"></script>
    <script type="text/javascript" src="jquery.mobile-1.3.1.js"></script>
</head>
<body>
    <div id="page1" data-role="page">
        <div data-role="header">
            <h1>Jacqui's Shop</h1>
        </div>
        <div data-role="content">
            This is Jacqui's Flower Shop
            <p><a href="#page2">Go to page 2</a></p>
            <p><a href="document2.html">Go to document2.html</a></p>
        </div>
    </div>
    <div id="page2" data-role="page">
        <div data-role="header">
            <h1>Jacqui's Shop</h1>
        </div>
```

```
        <div data-role="content">
            This is page 2
            <p><a href="#page1">Go to page 1</a></p>
        </div>
    </div>
</body>
</html>
```

jQuery Mobile uses Ajax to load the specified document and displays the first page automatically, using a transition effect if one has been specified. You can see the result in Figure 28-4.

Figure 28-4. *Navigating to a page in another document*

■ **Tip**   jQuery Mobile automatically applies its styles and enhancements to remote documents that are loaded via Ajax. This means you don't have to include the jQuery and jQuery Mobile `script` and `link` elements in files such as the `document2.html` file I used in the example. That said, I recommend you do include those references because it is possible to prevent jQuery Mobile from using Ajax when making such requests, and if this is done, then the automatic processing of content isn't performed.

Dealing with the Ajax/Page ID Issue

It isn't all plain sailing when linking to pages in other documents. There is a conflict between the way that Ajax content is managed and the way that jQuery Mobile pages are defined. Both rely on the value of the `id` attribute of elements. Figure 28-5 shows the problem.

Figure 28-5. *The multipage Ajax issue*

In this figure, I click the link that *should* display the page2 element in document2.html, but what I get is actually the page2 element in example.html, a confusing and unexpected result.

You can address this in two ways. The first is to define only one jQuery Mobile page per HTML document – this is the advice from the jQuery Mobile team.

The second approach is to disable Ajax when loading multipage documents. This fixes the problem, but it does mean that jQuery Mobile is unable to apply a transition effect when showing the new page. You can disable Ajax for a single a element by setting the data-ajax attribute to false, as shown in Listing 28-9.

Listing 28-9. Disabling Ajax for a Single Link

```
<!DOCTYPE html>
<html>
<head>
    <title>Example</title>
    <meta name="viewport" content="width=device-width, initial-scale=1">
    <link rel="stylesheet" href="jquery.mobile-1.3.1.css" type="text/css" />
    <script type="text/javascript" src="jquery-1.10.1.js"></script>
    <script type="text/javascript" src="jquery.mobile-1.3.1.js"></script>
</head>
<body>
    <div id="page1" data-role="page">
        <div data-role="header">
            <h1>Jacqui's Shop</h1>
        </div>
        <div data-role="content">
            This is Jacqui's Flower Shop
            <p><a href="#page2">Go to page 2</a></p>
            <p><a href="document2.html" data-ajax="false">Go to document2.html</a></p>
        </div>
    </div>
```

```html
    <div id="page2" data-role="page">
        <div data-role="header">
            <h1>Jacqui's Shop</h1>
        </div>
        <div data-role="content">
            This is page 2
            <p><a href="#page1">Go to page 1</a></p>
        </div>
    </div>
</body>
</html>
```

In this example, I have disabled Ajax for the link that navigates to document2.html. As Figure 28-6 shows, this produces the expected navigation sequence.

Figure 28-6. *Disabling Ajax to avoid an element id conflict*

You can turn off Ajax by default using the ajaxEnabled global setting, which is demonstrated in Listing 28-10. When this setting is false, Ajax will not be used for navigation unless you apply the data-ajax attribute to an element with a value of true.

Listing 28-10. Using the global Setting to Disable Ajax

```html
<!DOCTYPE html>
<html>
<head>
    <title>Example</title>
    <meta name="viewport" content="width=device-width, initial-scale=1">
    <link rel="stylesheet" href="jquery.mobile-1.3.1.css" type="text/css" />
    <script type="text/javascript" src="jquery-1.10.1.js"></script>
    <script type="text/javascript">
        $(document).bind("mobileinit", function() {
            $.mobile.ajaxEnable = false
        })
    </script>
```

775

```
        <script type="text/javascript" src="jquery.mobile-1.3.1.js"></script>
</head>
<body>
    <div id="page1" data-role="page">
        <div data-role="header">
            <h1>Jacqui's Shop</h1>
        </div>
        <div data-role="content">
            This is Jacqui's Flower Shop
            <p><a href="#page2">Go to page 2</a></p>
            <p><a href="document2.html">Go to document2.html</a></p>
        </div>
    </div>
    <div id="page2" data-role="page">
        <div data-role="header">
            <h1>Jacqui's Shop</h1>
        </div>
        <div data-role="content">
            This is page 2
            <p><a href="#page1">Go to page 1</a></p>
        </div>
    </div>
</body>
</html>
```

Prefetching Pages

You can ask jQuery Mobile to prefetch documents so that the pages they contain are immediately available when the user clicks a link. The advantage of this is that you create a more responsive application, but you do so by downloading content that the user may not require. To demonstrate this feature, I created a document called singlepage.html, the content of which is shown in Listing 28-11.

Listing 28-11. The singlepage.html File

```
<!DOCTYPE html>
<html>
<head>
    <title>Single Page</title>
    <meta name="viewport" content="width=device-width, initial-scale=1">
    <link rel="stylesheet" href="jquery.mobile-1.3.1.css" type="text/css" />
    <script type="text/javascript" src="jquery-1.10.1.js"></script>
    <script type="text/javascript" src="jquery.mobile-1.3.1.js"></script>
</head>
<body>
    <div id="page1" data-role="page">
        <div data-role="header">
            <h1>Jacqui's Shop</h1>
        </div>
```

```
        <div data-role="content">
            This is the only page in this document
            <p><a href="example.html">Return to example.html</a></p>
        </div>
    </div>
</body>
</html>
```

DECIDING WHETHER TO PREFETCH CONTENT

The decision about prefetching content is a difficult one. From the point of view of the application, prefetching can be a great idea because it produces immediate responses when the user navigates between pages. This can be particularly important when mobile connections are slow and coverage is spotty. Users don't like waiting, and a connection that keeps dropping out will make your application unusable if the content isn't available.

On the other hand, you run the risk of downloading content in anticipation of navigation actions that the user may not make. This can be unwelcome when mobile data plans charge punitive amounts to download data and have low monthly bandwidth limits. By prefetching content, you are assuming that the user considers your application to be important enough to trade bandwidth (and cost) for performance, something that may well not be the case. The sad fact is that although you may have lived and breathed your project for the last year, it may be nothing more than a mild convenience to your user.

My recommendation is *not* to prefetch pages. For those users who *do* consider your application important enough, you can give them an option to enable prefetching.

You enable prefetching by applying the data-prefetch attribute to the a element and setting it to true. Listing 28-12 shows the data-prefetch attribute applied to the example.html document.

Listing 28-12. Prefetching Content

```
<!DOCTYPE html>
<html>
<head>
    <title>Example</title>
    <meta name="viewport" content="width=device-width, initial-scale=1">
    <link rel="stylesheet" href="jquery.mobile-1.3.1.css" type="text/css" />
    <script type="text/javascript" src="jquery-1.10.1.js"></script>
    <script type="text/javascript" src="jquery.mobile-1.3.1.js"></script>
</head>
<body>
    <div id="page1" data-role="page">
        <div data-role="header">
            <h1>Jacqui's Shop</h1>
        </div>
        <div data-role="content">
            This is Jacqui's Flower Shop
            <p><a href="#page2">Go to page 2</a></p>
```

```
        <p>
            <a href="singlepage.html" data-prefetch="true">Go to singlepage.html</a>
        </p>
        </div>
    </div>
    <div id="page2" data-role="page">
        <div data-role="header">
            <h1>Jacqui's Shop</h1>
        </div>
        <div data-role="content">
            This is page 2
            <p><a href="#page1">Go to page 1</a></p>
        </div>
    </div>
</body>
</html>
```

In this example, I have asked jQuery Mobile to prefetch the target of my URL. When I click the link, jQuery Mobile is able to navigate to the prefetched content, avoiding any delay.

■ **Tip** It can be hard to be sure that features such as prefetching are working when you are developing on a fast, reliable network. I like to check these features by using a debugging HTTP proxy, which shows me the requests that are sent from the browser. If you are a Windows user, then I recommend Fiddler, which is an excellent tool that can be endlessly configured and customized. Fiddler can be downloaded from `www.fiddler2.com`.

Using Scripting to Control jQuery Mobile Pages

You don't always want to rely on the user clicking links to manage page navigation. Fortunately, jQuery Mobile provides you with methods and settings that allow you to control navigation using JavaScript. In the sections that follow, I'll show you how to take advantage of these methods to get fine-grained control over the navigation in a jQuery Mobile web application.

Changing the Current Page

The changePage method allows you to change the page that jQuery Mobile displays. Listing 28-13 shows the basic use of this method, which changes the displayed page based when a button is clicked.

Listing 28-13. Changing the Page That jQuery Mobile Displays

```
<!DOCTYPE html>
<html>
<head>
    <title>Example</title>
    <meta name="viewport" content="width=device-width, initial-scale=1">
    <link rel="stylesheet" href="jquery.mobile-1.3.1.css" type="text/css" />
    <script type="text/javascript" src="jquery-1.10.1.js"></script>
```

```
    <script type="text/javascript">
        $(document).bind("pageinit", function() {
            $("button").bind("tap", function(e) {
                var target = this.id == "local" ? "#page2" : "document2.html";
                $.mobile.changePage(target)
            })
        });
    </script>
    <script type="text/javascript" src="jquery.mobile-1.3.1.js"></script>
</head>
<body>
    <div id="page1" data-role="page">
        <div data-role="header">
            <h1>Jacqui's Shop</h1>
        </div>
        <div data-role="content">
            <fieldset class="ui-grid-a">
                <div class="ui-block-a"><button id="local">Local</button></div>
                <div class="ui-block-b"><button id="remote">Remote</button></div>
            </fieldset>
        </div>
    </div>
    <div id="page2" data-role="page">
        <div data-role="header">
            <h1>Jacqui's Shop</h1>
        </div>
        <div data-role="content">
            This is page 2
            <p><a href="#page1">Go to page 1</a></p>
        </div>
    </div>
</body>
</html>
```

In this example, I have added two buttons that cause the changePage method to be called when clicked. The event that I listen for using the bind method is tap, which is one of a small set of helpful cusfom events that jQuery Mobile defines. This event is triggered when the user taps the screen (or clicks the mouse on a non-touch enabled device). I described this event, along with the rest of the jQuery Mobile events in Chapter 27.

The buttons are standard HTML elements that jQuery Mobile automatically converts into button widgets. I describe the options for configuring jQuery Mobile buttons in Chapter 30. Finally, you will notice that I have assigned some elements to the classes ui-grid-a, ui-block-a, and ui-block-b. These are part of the jQuery Mobile support for creating page layouts, which I describe later in this chapter. The result of this example is pretty simple, as Figure 28-7 shows. When the user clicks one of the buttons, the changePage method is called, passing either the id value of a local page or a URL of another document for jQuery Mobile to display. The content is loaded, and the transition effect is displayed, just as when I was using regular links.

Figure 28-7. *Using the changePage method*

That's the basic use of the changePage method, but there are configuration options available. To configure the page transition, you pass a settings object as the second argument to the changePage method, specifying values for one or more settings. Table 28-2 describes the settings that are available. Most of these settings are best left with their defaults, but in the sections that follow, I show two of the settings that it can be useful to modify more frequently.

Table 28-2. *Settings for the changePage Method*

Setting	Description
allowSamePage Transition	When set to false (the default), jQuery Mobile will ignore changePage requests where the target page is the current page. A value of true allows such requests, although this can cause some problems with the transition animations.
changeHash	When true, the hash fragment in the URL bar will be updated to the new location (so that the page identifier is included in the URL). The default is true.
data	Specifies data to be included in the Ajax request used to load a document.
dataUrl	Specifies the URL used when updating the browser URL bar. The default is no value, which means the value is taken from the id of an internal page or the URL of a remote document.
loadMsgDelay	Specifies the number of milliseconds after which the loading image will be displayed to the user. The default is 50.
pageContainer	Specifies the element that should contain the new page.
reloadPage	When true, jQuery Mobile will reload the contents of a remote document, even if the data is already cached. The default is false.
reverse	When true, the transition effect will be played backward. The default is false.
role	Sets the data-role value for the new content – you can see this setting in use in Chapter 29.
showLoadMsg	A value of true will show the loading image when loading remote documents. The default is true.
transition	Specifies the transition effect to be used when displaying the new page.
type	Specifies the HTTP method used to request a document. The allowed values are get and post. The default is get.

▪ **Tip** These options are also used by the loadPage method, which I describe later in the chapter.

Controlling the Direction of the Transition Effect

The reverse setting is the one I use most often. jQuery Mobile will always play transition effects in the same way, which doesn't always make sense when you have presented the user with an action that effectively sends them back to an earlier page or where you are responding to a jQuery Mobile swiperight event. Listing 28-14 shows how to address this problem.

Listing 28-14. Transition Effect Direction Mismatched with Navigation Intent

```html
<!DOCTYPE html>
<html>
<head>
    <title>Example</title>
    <meta name="viewport" content="width=device-width, initial-scale=1">
    <link rel="stylesheet" href="jquery.mobile-1.3.1.css" type="text/css" />
    <script type="text/javascript" src="jquery-1.10.1.js"></script>
    <script type="text/javascript">
        $(document).bind("pageinit", function() {
            $.mobile.defaultPageTransition = "slide";
            $("button").bind("tap", function(e) {
                var target = this.id == "forward" ? "#page2" : "#page1";
                $.mobile.changePage(target, {
                    reverse: (target == "#page1")
                });
            })
        });
    </script>
    <script type="text/javascript" src="jquery.mobile-1.3.1.js"></script>
</head>
<body>
    <div id="page1" data-role="page">
        <div data-role="header">
            <h1>Jacqui's Shop</h1>
        </div>
        <div data-role="content">
            This is page 1
            <button id="forward">Go to Page 2</button>
        </div>
    </div>
    <div id="page2" data-role="page">
        <div data-role="header">
            <h1>Jacqui's Shop</h1>
        </div>
```

```
        <div data-role="content">
            This is page 2
            <button id="back">Back to Page 1</button>
        </div>
    </div>
</body>
</html>
```

There are two pages in this document, each of which contains a button that navigates to the other page. The button on the second page is labeled Back to Page 1. When the button on the second page is clicked, I change the direction of the transition effect by using a reverse value of true. I can't show this effect on a static page, but the effect feels much more natural. There is some subconscious expectation formed about the animation should be played in based on the navigational cue that you are returning to a previous page, rather than progressing to a new one. You will understand exactly what I mean if you view this example in a browser.

Controlling the Load Animation

jQuery Mobile displays an animated image when it loads a remote document via Ajax for longer than 50 milliseconds. When using a mobile browser emulator and a fast network, jQuery Mobile is able to load the document so quickly that the dialog box is never shown. But if you use an actual mobile data network or, as I have done, introduce a delay into the request, then the dialog remains on the screen long enough to be seen, as Figure 28-8 illustrates.

Figure 28-8. *The jQuery Mobile loading dialog box*

You can change the period after which the dialog is displayed by providing a value for the loadMsgDelay setting, as shown in Listing 28-15.

Listing 28-15. Changing the Delay for the Loading Dialog

```
<!DOCTYPE html>
<html>
<head>
    <title>Example</title>
    <meta name="viewport" content="width=device-width, initial-scale=1">
    <link rel="stylesheet" href="jquery.mobile-1.3.1.css" type="text/css" />
    <script type="text/javascript" src="jquery-1.10.1.js"></script>
    <script type="text/javascript">

        $(document).bind("mobileinit", function() {
            $.mobile.loadingMessage = "Loading Data..."
        })

        $(document).bind("pageinit", function() {
            $("button").bind("tap", function(e) {
                $.mobile.changePage("document2.html",{
                    loadMsgDelay: 1000
                });
            })
        });
    </script>
    <script type="text/javascript" src="jquery.mobile-1.3.1.js"></script>
</head>
<body>
    <div id="page1" data-role="page">
        <div data-role="header">
            <h1>Jacqui's Shop</h1>
        </div>
        <div data-role="content">
            <button id="forward">Go</button>
        </div>
    </div>
</body>
</html>
```

In this example, I have specified that jQuery Mobile should wait for one second before displaying the loading dialog to the user.

■ **Tip**   You can change the text in the loading dialog by setting a new value for the global `loadingMessage` property, as shown in the example. As with all jQuery Mobile global properties, this should be set in a function executed when the `mobileinit` event is triggered.

You can disable this dialog by specifying `false` for the `showLoadMsg` setting when you call the `changePage` method. This is not something I recommend doing, because providing the user with feedback is always a good thing, but Listing 28-16 shows the setting in use.

Listing 28-16. Disabling the Loading Dialog

```html
<!DOCTYPE html>
<html>
<head>
    <title>Example</title>
    <meta name="viewport" content="width=device-width, initial-scale=1">
    <link rel="stylesheet" href="jquery.mobile-1.3.1.css" type="text/css" />
    <script type="text/javascript" src="jquery-1.10.1.js"></script>
    <script type="text/javascript">
        $(document).bind("pageinit", function() {
            $("button").bind("tap", function(e) {
                $.mobile.changePage("document2.html", {
                    showLoadMsg: false
                });
            })
        });
    </script>
    <script type="text/javascript" src="jquery.mobile-1.3.1.js"></script>
</head>
<body>
    <div id="page1" data-role="page">
        <div data-role="header">
            <h1>Jacqui's Shop</h1>
        </div>
        <div data-role="content">
            <button id="forward">Go</button>
        </div>
    </div>
</body>
</html>
```

Determining the Current Page

You can use the $.mobile.activePage property to determine the current page that jQuery Mobile is displaying. Listing 28-17 shows the use of the activePage property.

Listing 28-17. Using the activatePage Property

```html
<!DOCTYPE html>
<html>
<head>
    <title>Example</title>
    <meta name="viewport" content="width=device-width, initial-scale=1">
    <link rel="stylesheet" href="jquery.mobile-1.3.1.css" type="text/css" />
    <script type="text/javascript" src="jquery-1.10.1.js"></script>
    <script type="text/javascript">

        var eventHandlerCreated = false;
```

```
        $(document).bind("pageinit", function () {
            if (!eventHandlerCreated) {
                $("button").bind("tap", function (e) {
                    var nextPages = {
                        page1: "#page2",
                        page2: "#page3",
                        page3: "#page1"
                    }
                    var currentPageId = $.mobile.activePage.attr("id");
                    $.mobile.changePage(nextPages[currentPageId]);
                })
                eventHandlerCreated = true;
            }
        });
    </script>
    <script type="text/javascript" src="jquery.mobile-1.3.1.js"></script>
</head>
<body>
    <div id="page1" data-role="page">
        <div data-role="header">
            <h1>Jacqui's Shop</h1>
        </div>
        <div data-role="content">
            This is page 1
            <button id="forward">Go</button>
        </div>
    </div>
    <div id="page2" data-role="page">
        <div data-role="header">
            <h1>Jacqui's Shop</h1>
        </div>
        <div data-role="content">
            This is page 2
            <button id="Button1">Go</button>
        </div>
    </div>
    <div id="page3" data-role="page">
        <div data-role="header">
            <h1>Jacqui's Shop</h1>
        </div>
        <div data-role="content">
            This is page 3
            <button id="Button2">Go</button>
        </div>
    </div>
</body>
</html>
```

There are three pages in this example, each of which has a button. When the button is clicked, I read the activePage property to get the current page. The activePage property returns a jQuery object that contains the current page, so I use the jQuery attr method to get the value of the id attribute.

My script includes a simple map that tells me what the next page should be for each of the pages in my document, and I use the id value obtained from the activePage property as the argument to the changePage method, ensuring that I progress through my pages in the sequence defined by my map.

■ **Tip** Notice that I use a variable called eventHandlerCreated to ensure that I only create one handler function for the tap event. The changePage method triggers the pageinit event and this can lead to multiple handler functions being set up – a common problem in jQuery Mobile applications and the likely cause if a single button click results in multiple page transitions. The most reliable way to prevent this problem is to use a variable like the one in the example.

Loading Pages in the Background

You can use the loadPage method to load remote documents without displaying them to the user. This is the programmatic equivalent of the prefetching that I demonstrated earlier in the chapter. The loadPage method takes two arguments. The first is the URL of the document to load, and the second is an optional settings object. The loadPage method supports settings as the changePage method, which I described in Table 28-2. Listing 28-18 shows the loadPage method in use.

Listing 28-18. Using the loadPage Method

```html
<!DOCTYPE html>
<html>
<head>
    <title>Example</title>
    <meta name="viewport" content="width=device-width, initial-scale=1">
    <link rel="stylesheet" href="jquery.mobile-1.3.1.css" type="text/css" />
    <script type="text/javascript" src="jquery-1.10.1.js"></script>
    <script type="text/javascript">

        var loadedPages = false;

        $(document).bind("pageinit", function () {
            if (!loadedPages) {
                $.mobile.loadPage("document2.html", {}).done(function () {
                    $("#gobutton").button("enable").bind("tap", function () {
                        $.mobile.changePage("document2.html");
                        loadedPages = true;
                    })
                })
            }
        });
    </script>
    <script type="text/javascript" src="jquery.mobile-1.3.1.js"></script>
</head>
<body>
    <div id="page1" data-role="page">
        <div data-role="header">
            <h1>Jacqui's Shop</h1>
        </div>
```

```
        <div data-role="content">
            <button id="gobutton" disabled="disabled">Go</button>
        </div>
    </div>
</body>
</html>
```

■ **Tip**   Notice that I have passed an empty settings object ({}) as the second argument to the loadPage method. There is a bug in version 1.3.1 of jQuery that requires a settings object even if no settings are changed.

In this example, I use the loadPage method to preload the document2.html file. The loadPage method returns a deferred object that you can use to receive notification when the page has loaded. I explain deferred objects in Chapter 35, but for now it is enough to know that you can call the done method on the object returned by the loadPage method, specifying a function that will be executed when the Ajax request started by loadPage has completed.

In this example, I use the enable method on the jQuery UI button widget to enable a button in the page and to register a handle for the tap event. When the button is clicked, I call the changePage method to navigate to the prefetched document. (I describe the jQuery Mobile support for buttons in Chapter 30.)

Notice that I have defined a variable called loadedPages. This addresses the same problem I had when using the changePage method (which calls loadPage internally): the pageinit event is triggered whenever jQuery Mobile initializes a page. This means the event is triggered when the document in the example is loaded and again when loadPage loads document2.html via Ajax. I use the loadedPages variable to ensure that I try to preload the content only once. It wouldn't be the end of the world to call loadPage twice (which is what would happen without the loadedPages variable) unless I enabled the reload setting. This would cause the cached copy of the document to be ignored and transfer document.html twice. I explain the set of jQuery Mobile page events in the following section.

Using Page Events

jQuery Mobile defines a set of events that you can use to receive notifications about change in pages. These events are described in Table 28-3, and I demonstrate some of the more useful ones in the sections that follow.

Table 28-3. *jQuery Mobile Page Events*

Event	Description
pagebeforecreate	Triggered when the page is being initialized.
pagecreate	Triggered when the page has been created but before most automatic enhancement has been performed.
pageinit	Triggered when the page has been initialized.
pageremove	Triggered before a page is removed.
pagebeforeload	Triggered before a page is requested via Ajax.
pageload	Triggered when a page has been successfully loaded via Ajax.
pageloadfailed	Triggered when a page has failed to load via Ajax.

(continued)

Table 28-3. (*continued*)

Event	Description
pagebeforechange	Triggered before a page transition is performed.
pagechange	Triggered after a page transition has been performed.
pagechangefailed	Triggered when a page change fails (this is usually because the requested document cannot be loaded).
pagebeforeshow	Triggered before a page is displayed to the user.
pagebeforehide	Triggered before a page is removed from the display.
pageshow	Triggered after a page has been displayed to the user.
pagehide	Triggered after a page has been hidden from the user.

Handling the Page Initialization Event

The pageinit event is the most useful of the jQuery Mobile page events, as described in Chapter 27. It is this event that you respond to when you want to configure your page using a script. I am not going to demonstrate this event again because you have seen it in every example so far, but I will emphasize that using the standard jQuery $(document).ready() approach is not reliable when working with jQuery Mobile.

Handling Page Load Events

The pagebeforeload, pageload, and pageloadfailed events can be useful for monitoring Ajax requests made for remote pages, either automatically generated by jQuery Mobile or programmatically via the changePage and loadPage methods. When demonstrating the loadPage method, I used a deferred object to respond when the page had been loaded, but you can achieve the same result using the pageload method (and, of course, the pageloadfailed method when things go wrong). Listing 28-19 shows the loadPage example updated to use the pageload event.

Listing 28-19. Using the pageload Event

```
<!DOCTYPE html>
<html>
<head>
    <title>Example</title>
    <meta name="viewport" content="width=device-width, initial-scale=1">
    <link rel="stylesheet" href="jquery.mobile-1.3.1.css" type="text/css" />
    <script type="text/javascript" src="jquery-1.10.1.js"></script>
    <script type="text/javascript">

        $(document).bind("pageload", function(event, data) {
            if (data.url == "document2.html") {
                $("#gobutton").button("enable").bind("tap", function() {
                    $.mobile.changePage("document2.html");
                })
            }
        })
```

```
                var loadedPages = false;
                $(document).bind("pageinit", function() {
                    if (!loadedPages) {
                        loadedPages = true;
                        $.mobile.loadPage("document2.html", {});
                    }
                });

        </script>
        <script type="text/javascript" src="jquery.mobile-1.3.1.js"></script>
    </head>
    <body>
        <div id="page1" data-role="page">
            <div data-role="header">
                <h1>Jacqui's Shop</h1>
            </div>
            <div data-role="content">
                <button id="gobutton" disabled>Go</button>
            </div>
        </div>
    </body>
</html>
```

In this example, I have specified a function that will be executed when the pageload event is triggered. jQuery Mobile provides information about the request by passing a data object as the second argument to the function. I use the url property to check that the document that has been loaded is the one I am expecting. The set of properties defined by the data object for the pageload event is described in Table 28-4. You can see from the table that most of the properties correspond to the jQuery Ajax support, which I described in Chapters 14 and 15.

Table 28-4. *pageload Data Object Event Properties*

Property	Description
url	Returns the URL passed to the loadPage method (this is method is used by jQuery Mobile when it requests pages and by the changePage method).
absUrl	The absolute URL that was requested.
options	The Ajax request options. See Chapters 14 and 15 for details of configuring Ajax.
xhr	The jQuery Ajax request object used for the request. See Chapters 14 and 15 for details of this object.
textStatus	The string description of the request status. See Chapters 14 and 15 for details.

Responding to Page Transitions

You can use the page transition events to be notified when the user navigates from one page to another (or when you do this programmatically using the changePage method). These events (pagebeforehide, pagehide, pagebeforeshow, and pageshow) are triggered for every page transition, even if the page has been displayed to the user before. Listing 28-20 shows the use of one of these events.

Listing 28-20. Responding to a Page Being Hidden

```html
<!DOCTYPE html>
<html>
<head>
    <title>Example</title>
    <meta name="viewport" content="width=device-width, initial-scale=1">
    <link rel="stylesheet" href="jquery.mobile-1.3.1.css" type="text/css" />
    <script type="text/javascript" src="jquery-1.10.1.js"></script>
    <script type="text/javascript">

        var registeredHandlers = false;
        $(document).bind("pageinit", function() {
            if (!registeredHandlers) {
                registeredHandlers = true;
                $("#page1").bind("pagehide", function(event, data) {
                    $.mobile.changePage($("#page1"));
                })
            }
        });

    </script>
    <script type="text/javascript" src="jquery.mobile-1.3.1.js"></script>
</head>
<body>
    <div id="page1" data-role="page">
        <div data-role="header">
            <h1>Jacqui's Shop</h1>
        </div>
        <div data-role="content">
            <a href="document2.html">Go to document2.html</a>
        </div>
    </div>
</body>
</html>
```

In this example, I register a handler function for the pagehide event on the page1 element, by selecting the element I want and calling the bind method. This means I will receive the event only when that selected page is hidden. This is a pretty dumb example, because it simply uses the changePage method to return to page1 whenever the pagehide event is triggered, but it does demonstrate the use of the event. Notice that I am still using a variable to ensure that I register my handler function only once. If I did not do this, then two functions would be registered for the same event on the same element when document2.html page is loaded.

Applying jQuery Mobile Themes

jQuery Mobile provides support for themes, rather like a simplified version of the themes support offered by jQuery UI. There is a default theme included in the jQuery Mobile files that you downloaded and installed in Chapter 27, and you can create custom themes using the jQuery Mobile ThemeRoller application, which is a variation on the application of the same name you used for jQuery UI.

■ **Note** As I mentioned in Chapter 27, I won't be creating and using a custom theme in this part of the book. The jQuery Mobile ThemeRoller application doesn't have a collection of pre-built themes, and it is difficult to describe the process to create a theme in writing. I'll be using the default themes in this chapter, but you can see the jQuery Mobile ThemeRoller at `http://jquerymobile.com/themeroller`.

A jQuery Mobile theme consists of one or more *swatches*, which is a set of styles that are applied to different kinds of elements. Swatches are identified by a single letter, starting with *A*. The default theme has five swatches, named A through E.

To view the default theme in ThemeRoller, navigate to `http://jquerymobile.com/themeroller`; click the Import link; and click on the `Import Default Theme` link, which imports the contents of the `jquery.mobile-1.3.1.css` file into the dialog (this is the CSS file that you downloaded and installed in Chapter 27). Click the `Import` button, and the ThemeRoller will process the CSS and display the default swatches, as shown in Figure 28-9.

Figure 28-9. *The swatches in the default theme*

You apply a theme to a jQuery Mobile page by using the `data-theme` attribute, setting the value to the name of the swatch you want. Listing 28-21 provides an example.

Listing 28-21. Using the Swatches in a Theme

```
<!DOCTYPE html>
<html>
<head>
    <title>Example</title>
    <meta name="viewport" content="width=device-width, initial-scale=1">
    <link rel="stylesheet" href="jquery.mobile-1.3.1.css" type="text/css" />
    <script type="text/javascript" src="jquery-1.10.1.js"></script>
    <script type="text/javascript" src="jquery.mobile-1.3.1.js"></script>
</head>
```

```
<body>
    <div id="page1" data-role="page" data-theme="a">
        <div data-role="header">
            <h1>Jacqui's Shop</h1>
        </div>
        <div data-role="content">
            This is Theme A
            <a href="#page2" data-role="button">Switch Theme</a>
        </div>
    </div>
    <div id="page2" data-role="page" data-theme="b">
        <div data-role="header">
            <h1>Jacqui's Shop</h1>
        </div>
        <div data-role="content">
            This is Theme B
            <a href="#page1" data-role="button">Switch Theme</a>
        </div>
    </div>
</body>
</html>
```

I have applied the data-theme attribute to the page element, which has the effect of applying the specified swatch to all of the child elements within the page. There are two pages in this example so that I can show how the same content is displayed by a pair of contrasting themes—and to make the point that there is no reliable way in jQuery Mobile to change the theme once a page has been through the automatic enhancement process. The data-theme attribute is transformed into a set of CSS classes that are applied to elements during page initialization, and so changing the value of the attribute doesn't do anything to change the classes. You can see the two-page example in Figure 28-10.

Figure 28-10. *Two pages in the same application using different swatches*

■ **Tip** There is also a swatch called `active`, which is used to highlight selected buttons. This is applied automatically by jQuery Mobile, but you can use it directly as well. If you do, be sure that you are not confusing the user by creating conflicting active elements.

Applying Swatches to Individual Elements

The previous example shows how you can style entire pages, but you can also apply swatches on a per-element basis, mixing and matching to get a specific effect. Listing 28-22 provides a demonstration.

Listing 28-22. Applying Swatches to Individual Elements

```html
<!DOCTYPE html>
<html>
<head>
    <title>Example</title>
    <meta name="viewport" content="width=device-width, initial-scale=1">
    <link rel="stylesheet" href="jquery.mobile-1.3.1.css" type="text/css" />
    <script type="text/javascript" src="jquery-1.10.1.js"></script>
    <script type="text/javascript" src="jquery.mobile-1.3.1.js"></script>
</head>
<body>
    <div id="page1" data-role="page" data-theme="a">
        <div data-role="header">
            <h1>Jacqui's Shop</h1>
        </div>
        <div data-role="content">
            <a href="document2.html" data-role="button" data-theme="b">Press Me</a>
            <a href="document2.html" data-role="button" data-theme="c">Press Me</a>
            <a href="document2.html" data-role="button" data-theme="e">Press Me</a>
        </div>
    </div>
</body>
</html>
```

In this example, I have applied the `data-theme` to the page and to the three button elements, each specifying a different swatch. You can see the effect in Figure 28-11.

Figure 28-11. *Applying different swatches to elements in the same page*

The jQuery Mobile support for themes is simple and easy to work with. It would be nice if you were able to change the swatches used by elements on the fly, but even with this omission, you can use swatches to tailor the appearance of your mobile applications.

Creating Grid Layouts

jQuery Mobile defines some useful CSS classes that you can use to lay out the contents of your mobile pages in grid form. This is something you could do yourself, but having them built into the library is useful and reduces the amount of custom development is needed, especially for simple mobile applications. jQuery Mobile defines four grid classes, each of which contains a different number of columns, as summarized by Table 28-5.

Table 28-5. *jQuery Mobile Layout Grid*

CSS Class	Columns
ui-grid-a	2
ui-grid-b	3
ui-grid-c	4
ui-grid-d	5

You apply one of the grid classes to a container element and then apply classes to each of the content items within, starting with ui-block-a, ui-block-b, and so on, for each column. Listing 28-23 shows the use of these classes to create a simple grid.

Listing 28-23. Creating a Grid Using the jQuery Mobile Layout Classes

```
<!DOCTYPE html>
<html>
<head>
    <title>Example</title>
    <meta name="viewport" content="width=device-width, initial-scale=1">
    <link rel="stylesheet" href="jquery.mobile-1.3.1.css" type="text/css" />
    <script type="text/javascript" src="jquery-1.10.1.js"></script>
    <script type="text/javascript" src="jquery.mobile-1.3.1.js"></script>
</head>
<body>
    <div id="page1" data-role="page" data-theme="b">
        <div data-role="header">
           <h1>Jacqui's Shop</h1>
        </div>
        <div data-role="content">
            <div class="ui-grid-b">
                <div class="ui-block-a"><button>Press Me</button></div>
                <div class="ui-block-b"><button>Press Me</button></div>
                <div class="ui-block-c"><button>Press Me</button></div>
            </div>
            <div class="ui-grid-a">
                <div class="ui-block-a"><button>Press Me</button></div>
                <div class="ui-block-b"><button>Press Me</button></div>
            </div>
            <div><button>Press Me</button></div>
        </div>
    </div>
</body>
</html>
```

In this example, I have created two grids: one with three columns and one with two columns. Each column contains a button element, and I have added a button outside of the grid to emphasize the default behavior, which is for elements to span the screen. You can see the result in Figure 28-12.

Figure 28-12. *Laying out elements in a grid*

Summary

In this chapter, I described pages, which are one of the key building blocks of jQuery Mobile. I also described the jQuery Mobile support for themes and grid layouts. These features provide the foundation for the most important jQuery Mobile features: the widgets. In Chapter 29, I start by describing the dialog and popup widgets.

CHAPTER 29

■ ■ ■

The Dialog & Popup Widgets

In this chapter, I introduce the first two jQuery Mobile widgets: the dialog and popup. jQuery Mobile widgets behave slightly differently from those in jQuery UI, but – as you'll learn – there is a common approach that underpins both libraries. Table 29-1 provides the summary for this chapter.

Table 29-1. *Chapter Summary*

Problem	Solution	Listing
Create a dialog widget.	Add the data-role attribute with a value of dialog to a div element that contains the dialog content or the data-rel attribute, also with a value of dialog, to a navigation link that will open the dialog.	1, 2
Create a dialog programmatically.	Use the changePage method.	3
Add buttons to the dialog.	Add a elements to the dialog element.	4, 5
Configure the dialog.	Use the configuration data attributes or call the dialog method and use the configuration options.	6, 7
Close the dialog.	Call the close method.	8
Create a popup widget.	Add the data-role attribute with a value of popup to a div element within the jQuery Mobile page that will display the widget.	9
Configure the popup.	Apply data attributes to the a element that opens the popup, or to the div element that contains the popup or call the popup method.	10–12
Control the popup programmatically.	Use the open, close, and reposition methods.	13
Respond to changes in the popup.	Handle the popup events.	14

Using the jQuery Mobile Dialog Widget

As its name suggests, the dialog widget presents the user with a dialog. Since this is the first of the jQuery Mobile widgets that I describe, I'll show you different ways in which widgets can be created and managed to set the scene for the rest of this chapter and the chapters that follow.

Creating the Dialog Widget

jQuery Mobile will automatically create dialog widgets when it encounters an element whose data-role attribute is set to dialog, as shown in Listing 29-1.

Listing 29-1. Creating a Dialog Widget Declaratively with the data-role Attribute

```
<!DOCTYPE html>
<html>
<head>
    <title>Example</title>
    <meta name="viewport" content="width=device-width, initial-scale=1">
    <link rel="stylesheet" href="jquery.mobile-1.3.1.css" type="text/css" />
    <script type="text/javascript" src="jquery-1.10.1.js"></script>
    <script type="text/javascript" src="jquery.mobile-1.3.1.js"></script>
</head>
<body>
    <div id="page1" data-role="page">
        <div data-role="header">
            <h1>Jacqui's Shop</h1>
        </div>
        <div data-role="content">
            <a href="#dialog1">Show the dialog</a>
        </div>
    </div>
    <div id="dialog1" data-role="dialog">
        <div data-role="header">
            <h1>You clicked the link!</h1>
        </div>
        <div data-role="content">
            This is the content area of the dialog
        </div>
    </div>
</body>
</html>
```

This example contains a page with an a element that, when clicked, will navigate to the element called dialog1. The data-role attribute for the dialog1 element is set to dialog, which causes jQuery Mobile to display the element and its contents as a dialog, as illustrated by Figure 29-1.

Figure 29-1. Displaying a page as a dialog

Dialogs can also be created through the application of the data-rel attribute to the navigation a element. In Listing 29-2, you can see how I have set the data-rel attribute to dialog in order to create an instance of the dialog widget from an element whose data-role attribute is set to page.

Listing 29-2. Using the data-rel Attribute to Create a Dialog Widget from a page

```
<!DOCTYPE html>
<html>
<head>
    <title>Example</title>
    <meta name="viewport" content="width=device-width, initial-scale=1">
    <link rel="stylesheet" href="jquery.mobile-1.3.1.css" type="text/css" />
    <script type="text/javascript" src="jquery-1.10.1.js"></script>
    <script type="text/javascript" src="jquery.mobile-1.3.1.js"></script>
</head>
<body>
    <div id="page1" data-role="page">
        <div data-role="header">
            <h1>Jacqui's Shop</h1>
        </div>
        <div data-role="content">
            <a href="#page2" data-rel="dialog">Show the dialog</a>
        </div>
    </div>
    <div id="page2" data-role="page">
        <div data-role="header">
            <h1>You clicked the link!</h1>
        </div>
        <div data-role="content">
            This is the content area of the dialog
        </div>
    </div>
</body>
</html>
```

799

In this example, there are two regular jQuery Mobile pages. The link in the first page is just like the links I was using for navigation in Chapter 28, with the exception that I have applied the data-rel attribute and set the value to dialog.

Creating the Dialog Widget Programmatically

The declarative approach is useful, but it requires you to fix the way that your content is displayed statically in the HTML. Sometimes you will want to decide to display a page as a dialog dynamically, which can be done through the changePage method and the role setting it supports. Listing 29-3 shows the use of the changePage method to create a dialog.

Listing 29-3. Creating a Dialog Programmatically with the changePage Method

```html
<!DOCTYPE html>
<html>
<head>
    <title>Example</title>
    <meta name="viewport" content="width=device-width, initial-scale=1">
    <link rel="stylesheet" href="jquery.mobile-1.3.1.css" type="text/css" />
    <script type="text/javascript" src="jquery-1.10.1.js"></script>
    <script>
        $(document).bind("pageinit", function (event, data) {
            $("#dialogLink").click(function (e) {
                $.mobile.changePage(this.href, {
                    role: "dialog"
                });
            });
        });
    </script>
    <script type="text/javascript" src="jquery.mobile-1.3.1.js"></script>
</head>
<body>
    <div id="page1" data-role="page">
        <div data-role="header">
            <h1>Jacqui's Shop</h1>
        </div>
        <div data-role="content">
            <p><a id="dialogLink" href="#page2">Show the dialog</a></p>
            <p><a href="#page2">Show the page</a></p>
        </div>
    </div>
    <div id="page2" data-role="page">
        <div data-role="header">
            <h1>You clicked the link!</h1>
        </div>
        <div data-role="content">
            This is page 2
            <a href="#" data-role="button" data-rel="back">Close</a>
        </div>
    </div>
</body>
</html>
```

This technique means you can use the same content in different ways. In the listing, I have defined two links, one of which I allow to use standard navigation to load a page defined in the same HTML document. I have defined a handler function for the click event from the other a element, which I process by calling the changePage method with a role setting of dialog. This means the way that the page is handled will depend on which link is clicked, as shown in Figure 29-2.

Figure 29-2. Creating a dialog programmatically

> ■ **Note** Caution is required when using this technique because jQuery Mobile caches the role associated with content – and that means that once you have displayed a page as a dialog, it will always be displayed as a dialog, even if you call changePage again with a role setting of page (or until the HTML document is reloaded).

Adding Buttons to the Dialog

You can add a close button to the dialog by adding a button element to the dialog's content, setting the data-role attribute to button and the data-rel attribute to back. I describe the jQuery Mobile button widget fully in Chapter 30, but you can see how it is applied for the dialog widget in Listing 29-4.

Listing 29-4. *Adding a Close Button to a Dialog*

```html
<!DOCTYPE html>
<html>
<head>
    <title>Example</title>
    <meta name="viewport" content="width=device-width, initial-scale=1">
    <link rel="stylesheet" href="jquery.mobile-1.3.1.css" type="text/css" />
    <script type="text/javascript" src="jquery-1.10.1.js"></script>
    <script type="text/javascript" src="jquery.mobile-1.3.1.js"></script>
</head>
<body>
    <div id="page1" data-role="page">
        <div data-role="header">
            <h1>Jacqui's Shop</h1>
        </div>
        <div data-role="content">
            <a href="#page2" data-rel="dialog">Show the dialog</a>
        </div>
    </div>
    <div id="page2" data-role="page">
        <div data-role="header">
            <h1>You clicked the link!</h1>
        </div>
        <div data-role="content">
            This is the content area of the dialog
            <a href="#" data-role="button" data-rel="back">Close</a>
        </div>
    </div>
</body>
</html>
```

I don't have to specify the target for the link. I just set the `href` attribute to # and leave jQuery Mobile to figure out what to do. This is useful because you may want to display a dialog from different pages, and you don't know which of them caused the dialog to be shown and therefore where the browser should return to. Figure 29-3 shows the effect of adding this element to the dialog.

Figure 29-3. *Adding a close button to a dialog*

You can additional buttons to a dialog with further a elements whose `href` attributes point to the pages that you want to display. This is what I have done in Listing 29-5, where I have added a link to another jQuery Mobile page in the same HTML document.

■ **Tip**   If you don't want to respond to a button by navigating to a new page, then you can handle the `click` event from the a element and use the `close` method to close the dialog – see the "Using the Dialog Methods" section later in the chapter for an example.

Listing 29-5. Adding a Navigation Button to a Dialog

```html
<!DOCTYPE html>
<html>
<head>
    <title>Example</title>
    <meta name="viewport" content="width=device-width, initial-scale=1">
    <link rel="stylesheet" href="jquery.mobile-1.3.1.css" type="text/css" />
    <script type="text/javascript" src="jquery-1.10.1.js"></script>
    <script type="text/javascript" src="jquery.mobile-1.3.1.js"></script>
</head>
<body>
    <div id="page1" data-role="page">
        <div data-role="header">
            <h1>Jacqui's Shop</h1>
        </div>
        <div data-role="content">
            <a href="#page2" data-rel="dialog">Show the dialog</a>
        </div>
    </div>
    <div id="page2" data-role="page" data-overlay-theme="d">
        <div data-role="header">
            <h1>You clicked the link!</h1>
        </div>
        <div data-role="content">
            This is the content area of the dialog
            <a href="#page3" data-role="button">OK</a>
            <a href="#" data-role="button" data-rel="back">Close</a>
        </div>
    </div>
    <div id="page3" data-role="page">
        <div data-role="header">
            <h1>Jacqui's Shop</h1>
        </div>
        <div data-role="content">
            This is page 3. You came here via the dialog.
        </div>
    </div>
</body>
</html>
```

In this example, I have added an a element that takes the user to page3, which I have also added to the document. Figure 29-4 shows the navigation from the dialog to the new page.

Figure 29-4. *Adding a navigation link/button to a dialog*

Configuring the Dialog Widget

The dialog widget defines a set of configuration options, which can either be set declaratively using `data` attributes or set using a JavaScript method call. I have listed both sets of options in Table 29-2, and below I describe how to use declarative and programmatic configuration.

Table 29-2. *Settings for the Dialog Widget*

Data Attribute	Setting	Description
data-close-btn	closeBtn	Gets or sets the position of the close button in the dialog header. The supported values are left, right, and none.
data-close-btn-text	closeBtnText	Gets or sets the text for the close button in the dialog header. This text is not displayed to the user, but it is detected by accessibility software.
data-corners	corners	Gets or sets whether the dialog should be displayed with rounded corners. The default value is true.
data-overlay-theme	overlayTheme	Gets or sets the theme over which the dialog is drawn. The setting is case sensitive and must be expressed in lower case.

    In most situations it is simpler and easier to configure widgets using data attributes and let automatic enhancement apply your settings. This is the standard jQuery Mobile approach to configuration, and you can see how I have used it for the `data-overlay-theme` attribute in Listing 29-6.

Listing 29-6. Configuring the Dialog Widget with a Data Attribute

```
<!DOCTYPE html>
<html>
<head>
    <title>Example</title>
    <meta name="viewport" content="width=device-width, initial-scale=1">
    <link rel="stylesheet" href="jquery.mobile-1.3.1.css" type="text/css" />
    <script type="text/javascript" src="jquery-1.10.1.js"></script>
    <script type="text/javascript" src="jquery.mobile-1.3.1.js"></script>
</head>
<body>
    <div id="page1" data-role="page">
        <div data-role="header">
            <h1>Jacqui's Shop</h1>
        </div>
        <div data-role="content">
            <a href="#dialog1">Show the dialog</a>
        </div>
    </div>
    <div id="dialog1" data-role="dialog" data-overlay-theme="d">
        <div data-role="header">
            <h1>You clicked the link!</h1>
        </div>
        <div data-role="content">
            This is the content area of the dialog
        </div>
    </div>
</body>
</html>
```

I have specified that the D swatch should be used as the overlay on which the dialog is displayed. You can see the effect in Figure 29-5: the dialog is displayed on a light-colored background instead of the black background associated with the default A swatch. (I described the jQuery Mobile approach to themes and swatches in Chapter 28.)

Figure 29-5. *Configuring a dialog widget with a data attribute*

You can configure a dialog widget after it has been created by calling the jQuery Mobile `dialog` method, passing in an object whose properties correspond to the settings from Table 29-2 that you want to change. In Listing 29-7, you can see how I have used the `dialog` method to configure the dialog.

Listing 29-7. *Configuring a Dialog Widget Programmatically*

```
<!DOCTYPE html>
<html>
<head>
    <title>Example</title>
    <meta name="viewport" content="width=device-width, initial-scale=1">
    <link rel="stylesheet" href="jquery.mobile-1.3.1.css" type="text/css" />
    <script type="text/javascript" src="jquery-1.10.1.js"></script>
    <script>
        $(document).bind("pageinit", function () {
            $("#dialog1").dialog({
                corners: false,
                overlayTheme: "e"
            });
        });
    </script>
    <script type="text/javascript" src="jquery.mobile-1.3.1.js"></script>
</head>
```

```
<body>
    <div id="page1" data-role="page">
        <div data-role="header">
            <h1>Jacqui's Shop</h1>
        </div>
        <div data-role="content">
            <a href="#dialog1">Show the dialog</a>
        </div>
    </div>
    <div id="dialog1" data-role="dialog" data-overlay-theme="d">
        <div data-role="header">
            <h1>You clicked the link!</h1>
        </div>
        <div data-role="content">
            This is the content area of the dialog
        </div>
    </div>
</body>
</html>
```

You can configure widgets in response to the pageinit event, and in the listing you can see how I select the element that underlies the widget and call the dialog method on it. The object that I pass to the dialog method has properties that correspond to the settings in Table 29-2, and you can see that I have defined new values for the corners and overlayTheme settings. The options passed to the dialog method override the data property values, and you can see the effect in Figure 29-6.

Figure 29-6. Configuring a dialog widget programmatically

■ **Caution**   The jQuery Mobile API documentation suggests that you can use the jQuery UI style `option` method call to configure dialog widgets, like this: `$("#dialog1"), dialog("option," "corners," false)`. However, if you use this approach, you will see an error message telling you that you can't call methods before widgets are initialized. This method call will only work once the widget has been displayed, but which time it is too late to perform configuration tasks. Instead, use the technique shown in the listing: pass in a configuration object to the `dialog` method in response to the `pageinit` event.

Using the Dialog Methods

The dialog widget only defines one method, which closes the dialog programmatically. I have described the method in Table 29-3 so that you can find it more easily when performing a quick search in the future.

Table 29-3. *Dialog Methods*

Method	Description
`dialog("close")`	Closes the dialog.

In Listing 29-8, I have created a dialog that is displayed for a fixed amount of time. In addition to the `close` method I have used the `data-close-btn` attribute to remove the close button from the menu bar.

Listing 29-8. Using the Dialog close Method

```
<!DOCTYPE html>
<html>
<head>
    <title>Example</title>
    <meta name="viewport" content="width=device-width, initial-scale=1">
    <link rel="stylesheet" href="jquery.mobile-1.3.1.css" type="text/css" />
    <script type="text/javascript" src="jquery-1.10.1.js"></script>
    <script>
        $(document).bind("pageinit", function () {
            $("#page1 a").click(function (e) {
                var duration = 15;
                $("#remaining").text(duration);
                var interval = setInterval(function () {
                    $("#remaining").text(--duration);
                    if (duration == 0) {
                        clearInterval(interval);
                        $("#dialog1").dialog("close");
                    }
                }, 1000);
            });
        });
    </script>
    <script type="text/javascript" src="jquery.mobile-1.3.1.js"></script>
</head>
```

```
<body>
    <div id="page1" data-role="page">
        <div data-role="header">
            <h1>Jacqui's Shop</h1>
        </div>
        <div data-role="content">
            <a href="#dialog1">Show the dialog</a>
        </div>
    </div>
    <div id="dialog1" data-role="dialog" data-close-btn="none" data-overlay-theme="d">
        <div data-role="header">
            <h1>Important</h1>
        </div>
        <div data-role="content">
            This in an important message that will be displayed
            for <span id="remaining"></span> seconds.
        </div>
    </div>
</body>
</html>
```

The script element in this example sets up a handler for the click event triggered when the link that opens the dialog is triggered. The only way to open a dialog programmatically is with the changePage method, so I just let the default event action take care of opening the dialog and start a timer that counts down 15 seconds. I update the contents of a span element displayed by the dialog every second and call the dialog close method when the timer expires. The result is the dialog shown in Figure 29-7.

> **Important**
>
> This in an important message that will be displayed for 13 seconds.

Figure 29-7. A self-closing dialog widget

There are a couple of points to note. The first is that I don't have to explicitly refresh the content of the dialog to reflect the changes in the span element – the dialog automatically updates itself. The second point is that while I have created a dialog that doesn't have close buttons, the user can still dismiss my dialog by using the browser back button.

Using the Dialog Events

The jQuery Mobile dialog widget defines a single event, which I have described in Table 29-4. I never use this event and tend to handle the page-level events that I described in Chapter 28 instead.

Table 29-4. Dialog Events

Event	Description
create	This event is triggered when the dialog widget is created.

Using the jQuery Mobile Popup Widget

The jQuery Mobile popup widget presents content in a popup. Popups are light-weight alternatives to dialogs but offer more programmatic control.

Creating the Popup Widget

Popups are created by applying the data-role attribute to an element and setting the value to popup. Popups are not displayed automatically but are opened when the user clicks on an a element that targets the popup element and whose data-rel attribute is also set to popup. The popup and the link that opens it must be within the same jQuery Mobile page, as shown in Listing 29-9.

Listing 29-9. Creating a jQuery Mobile Popup Widget

```
<!DOCTYPE html>
<html>
<head>
    <title>Example</title>
    <meta name="viewport" content="width=device-width, initial-scale=1">
    <link rel="stylesheet" href="jquery.mobile-1.3.1.css" type="text/css" />
    <script type="text/javascript" src="jquery-1.10.1.js"></script>
    <script type="text/javascript" src="jquery.mobile-1.3.1.js"></script>
</head>
<body>
    <div id="page1" data-role="page">
        <div data-role="header">
            <h1>Jacqui's Shop</h1>
        </div>
        <div data-role="content">
            <a href="#popup" data-rel="popup">Show the popup</a>
        </div>
        <div id="popup" data-role="popup">
            <p>This is the popup content</p>
        </div>
    </div>
</body>
</html>
```

Clicking the link causes the popup to appear, as shown in Figure 29-8. Clicking outside of the popup dismisses it.

Figure 29-8. *Creating a jQuery Mobile popup*

Configuring the Popup Widget

As you can see from the figure, the popup is positioned over the link that opened it, which is rarely the effect that you want. You can configure the popup in two ways – either by configuring the a element that opens the popup or by configuring the popup itself.

Configuring the Link That Opens the Popup

The advantage of configuring the a element is that you can use the same popup several times, but apply different configurations. The drawback is that there are only two configuration options – but, fortunately, they are the ones that you are likely to want to adjust. I have listed the data attributes that can be applied to the a elements in Table 29-5.

Table 29-5. *Data Attributes for a Elements That Open Popups*

Data Attribute	Description
data-position-to	Specifies the position of the popup relative to the a element that opens it. The options are described in Table 29-6.
data-transition	Specifies the transition used to display the popup – see Chapter 28 for the list of jQuery Mobile transitions.

The data-position-to attribute specifies the position of the popup relative to the a element and can be set to the values shown in Table 29-6.

Table 29-6. *Values for the data-position-to Attribute*

Value	Description
origin	Centers the popup over the a element.
window	Centers the popup in the window.
selector	Centers the popup on the first element that matches the selector. If that element is not visible, then the popup is centered in the window.

In Listing 29-10, you can see how I have used the data-position-to attribute to change the position of the popup using a selector.

Listing 29-10. Configuring the Popup via the Link That Opens It

```
<!DOCTYPE html>
<html>
<head>
    <title>Example</title>
    <meta name="viewport" content="width=device-width, initial-scale=1">
    <link rel="stylesheet" href="jquery.mobile-1.3.1.css" type="text/css" />
    <script type="text/javascript" src="jquery-1.10.1.js"></script>
    <script type="text/javascript" src="jquery.mobile-1.3.1.js"></script>
    <style>
        #anchor { position: absolute; right: 10px; }
    </style>
</head>
<body>
    <div id="page1" data-role="page">
        <div data-role="header">
            <h1>Jacqui's Shop</h1>
        </div>
        <div data-role="content">
            <a href="#popup" data-rel="popup"
                data-position-to="#anchor">Show the popup</a>
            <span id="anchor">Anchor</span>
        </div>
        <div id="popup" data-role="popup">
            <p>This is the popup content</p>
        </div>
    </div>
</body>
</html>
```

I have used the selector option, specifying #anchor for the value for the data-position-to attribute on the a element that opens the popup. This selector matches the id of a div element that I have positioned at the right edge of the window with CSS. You can see the effect in Figure 29-9.

Figure 29-9. *Configuring the position of the popup via the a element*

Configuring the Popup Directly

There are more configuration options available when you configure the widget directly. As with the dialog widget, you can configure the popup with data attributes or via the popup method, and I have listed both in Table 29-7. Most of the configuration options are self-evident or similar to those used by the dialog widget.

Table 29-7. *Settings for the Dialog Widget*

Data Attribute	Setting	Description
data-corners	corners	Specifies whether the popup is drawn with round corners. The default is true.
data-dismissable	dismissable	If set to false, the popup is not dismissed when the user clicks outside of the widget. The default is true.
data-history	history	Specifies whether a history item is created before the popup is open. The default is true, which means that the browser is closed when the browser back button is clicked.
data-overlay-theme	overlayTheme	Specifies the theme used for the overlay. The default is null, which presents a transparent background.
data-position-to	positionTo	Specifies the position of the popup using the values in Table 29-6.
data-shadow	shadow	Specifies whether the popup will be drawn with a shadow. The default is true.
data-tolerance	tolerance	Specifies the minimum distances between the popup and the edges of the window. The default values are 30, 15, 30, 15.
data-transition	transition	Specifies the transition used when the popup is opened and closed.

Using the History Setting

The setting that causes the most confusion with the popup widget is data-history, which determines if a new entry in the browser history is created before the popup is opened. The effect of this setting means that the popup is closed by the browser back button – but this is a feature that doesn't always make sense, especially when the popup is opened and closed in response to a touch event, as demonstrated by Listing 29-11.

Listing 29-11. The Effect of Popup History Entries and Mouse Triggers

```
<!DOCTYPE html>
<html>
<head>
    <title>Example</title>
    <meta name="viewport" content="width=device-width, initial-scale=1">
    <link rel="stylesheet" href="jquery.mobile-1.3.1.css" type="text/css" />
    <script type="text/javascript" src="jquery-1.10.1.js"></script>
    <script type="text/javascript" src="jquery.mobile-1.3.1.js"></script>
    <script>
        var mouseHandlerSet = false;
        $(document).bind("pageinit", function () {
            if (!mouseHandlerSet) {
                $("#page1 a").mouseenter(function (e) {
                    $("#popup").popup("open", {
                        x: e.pageX, y: e.pageY
                    });
                });
                $("#popup").mouseleave(function (e) {
                    $(this).popup("close");
                });
                mouseHandlerSet = true;
            }
        });
    </script>
</head>
<body>
    <div id="page1" data-role="page">
        <div data-role="header">
            <h1>Jacqui's Shop</h1>
        </div>
        <div data-role="content">
            <p><a href="#popup" data-rel="popup">Popup</a></p>
        </div>
        <div id="popup" data-role="popup" data-history="false">
            <p>This is the popup content</p>
        </div>
    </div>
</body>
</html>
```

This example uses the popup open and close methods, which I describe later in the chapter, so that the popup is shown when the user moves the mouse or pointer over the a element and hidden when the user moves the mouse out of the popup (I used a configuration option passed to the open method to ensure that the popup is opened under the mouse pointer).

In this situation, the user may not expect the back button to simply close the popup since no explicit navigation was performed to open it in the first place – and this is a good opportunity to consider the data-history attribute as to create a consistent experience.

■ **Tip**   I am qualifying the use of this configuration setting carefully because understanding the mechanism is only part of the confusion that surrounds the use of popups. The other issue is deciding which approach to take – and this is something that can only be decided in the context of the rest of your application. User expectations in this kind of situation are hard to predict, and only user testing will show you which approach creates a natural experience for your web app. Don't be tempted to skimp on testing and simply make this a configurable option – most users attribute inconsistent behaviors to bad implementation and won't make the effort to see if it can be changed.

Using Popups to Present Rich Content

Popups can be used to present rich content, and a common use for popups is to present the user with a set of image thumbnails that open the full-size image in a popup, which is what I have done in Listing 29-12. (I included the images from this example in the free download from Apress.com that accompanies this book.)

Listing 29-12. Using the Popup to Display Rich Content

```
<!DOCTYPE html>
<html>
<head>
    <title>Example</title>
    <meta name="viewport" content="width=device-width, initial-scale=1">
    <link rel="stylesheet" href="jquery.mobile-1.3.1.css" type="text/css" />
    <script type="text/javascript" src="jquery-1.10.1.js"></script>
    <script type="text/javascript" src="jquery.mobile-1.3.1.js"></script>
    <style>
        .smallImage { height: 40%; width: 40%; padding: 5px}
    </style>
    <script>
        $(document).bind("pageinit", function () {

            var data = ["beach.png", "clouds.png", "fishing.png", "storms.png"];

            for (var i = 0; i < data.length; i++) {
                $("<img>").addClass("smallImage").attr("src",
                    data[i]).appendTo("#contentHolder");
            }

            $("#popup").popup({
                corners: false,
                overlayTheme: "a"
            });

            $("#contentHolder img").bind("tap", function (e) {
                var maxHeight = $(window).height() - 10 + "px";
```

```
                $("#LgImage").attr("src", e.target.src).css("max-height", maxHeight);
                $("#popup").popup("open");
            });
        });
    </script>
</head>
<body>
    <div id="page1" data-role="page" data-theme="d">
        <div id="contentHolder" data-role="content"></div>
        <div id="popup" data-role="popup" data-history="true">
            <img id="LgImage" class="zoomImg" src="" />
        </div>
    </div>
</body>
</html>
```

I use a `for` loop to generate a set of four thumbnail `img` elements that I add to the jQuery Mobile page and use standard CSS to ensure that they are all the same size. I create a handler for the `tap` event (which I described in Chapter 27) that sets the selected image as the content of the popup and calls the `open` method to display it to the user (I describe the open method in the *Using the Popup Methods* section later in this chapter, but for now it is enough to know that calling it will display the popup). You can see the effect in Figure 29-10: the user taps one of the thumbnail images and a larger version is displayed in the popup.

Figure 29-10. Using a popup to display images

I have used a mix of data attributes and settings to configure the popup, just to show both in use. The `div` element that underlies the popup has the `data-history` attribute, as follows:

```
...
<div id="popup" data-role="popup" data-history="true">
    <img id="LgImage" class="zoomImg" src="" />
</div>
...
```

This is the default value for the data-history attribute, but I like to be specific about this setting since it causes so much confusion. I used the popup method in the script element to set other options, as follows:

```
...
$("#popup").popup({
    corners: false,
    overlayTheme: "a"
});
...
```

Using rounded corners would clip part of the large image, so I specify square corners using the corners setting. I want to focus the user's attention on the large image when the popup is displayed, and so I have used the overlayTheme setting to provide a dark background for the popup.

A little extra work is required when using a popup to display content that might be larger than the popup itself because, by default, the content will scroll. To avoid this, I get the height of the window and use it as the basis for setting the height of the image in the popup, like this:

```
...
var maxHeight = $(window).height() - 10 + "px";
$("#LgImage").attr("src", e.target.src).css("max-height", maxHeight);
...
```

I make the image 10 pixels smaller than the window, which gives me a small border around the image to emphasize the fact that the user is seeing a popup. In theory, I should align my border with the tolerance setting, but it is unreliable as I write this and so I just use an explicit value to get the effect I want. I made the beach.png image, which is the first thumbnail in the sequence, larger than the others, and in Figure 29-11 you can what happens if I don't set the setting for the CSS max-height property: the top and bottom of the image are not displayed and there is no visual cue to indicate that the user can scroll to see the rest of the image.

Figure 29-11. *The effect of displaying content that is larger than the popup*

Using the Popup Methods

The popup widget defines the methods shown in Table 29-8.

Table 29-8. *Popup Methods*

Method	Description
popup("open")	Opens the popup.
popup("close")	Closes the popup.
popup("reposition")	Changes the position of the popup.

I demonstrated the basic use of the open method in the previous example, but you can provide an optional argument that configures how the popup is opened, providing equivalent functionality to the data attributes that are used with a elements. The optional argument is an object whose property names are shown in Table 29-9.

Table 29-9. *Properties for the Optional Argument to the open Method*

Name	Description
x	Specifies the X coordinate where the popup should be displayed.
y	Specifies the Y coordinate where the popup should be displayed.
transition	Specifies the transition used to animate the popup opening – see Chapter 28 for details of the jQuery Mobile transitions.
positionTo	Specifies the position of the popup, using the values described in Table 29-6.

The reposition method also takes a configuration object argument and you can use the x, y, and positionTo properties to specify the new location for the popup. The close method doesn't take any arguments and just dismisses the popup. In Listing 29-13, you can see all three methods in use.

Listing 29-13. Using the Popup Methods

```
<!DOCTYPE html>
<html>
<head>
    <title>Example</title>
    <meta name="viewport" content="width=device-width, initial-scale=1">
    <link rel="stylesheet" href="jquery.mobile-1.3.1.css" type="text/css" />
    <script type="text/javascript" src="jquery-1.10.1.js"></script>
    <script type="text/javascript" src="jquery.mobile-1.3.1.js"></script>
    <script>
        $(document).bind("pageinit", function () {
            $("button").bind("vmousedown", function (e) {
                var pop = $("#popup");
                switch (e.target.innerText) {
                    case "Open":
                        pop.popup("open", {
```

```
                    x: 10, y: 10, transition: "fade"
                });
                break;
            case "Close":
                pop.popup("close");
                break;
            default:
                pop.popup("reposition", {
                    positionTo: e.target.innerText == "Window"
                        ? "window" : "#page1 button"
                });
                break;
            }
        });
    });
</script>
</head>
<body>
    <div id="page1" data-role="page" data-theme="d">
        <div data-role="content">
            <button>Open</button>
        </div>
        <div id="popup" data-role="popup" data-history="true"
                data-dismissible="false">
            <button>Selector</button>
            <button>Window</button>
            <button>Close</button>
        </div>
    </div>
</body>
</html>
```

The jQuery Mobile page in this listing contains a button whose vmousedown event I handle by calling the open method on the popup. I pass in the optional configuration object to specify that the popup should be shown at a specific location (10 pixels from the top-left corner on the x- and y- axis) with the fade transition.

The popup contains additional buttons. The Close button calls the close method to hide the popup, and the others call the reposition method to specify different locations that the popup should be moved to. You can see the results in Figure 29-12.

Figure 29-12. *Using the popup methods*

■ **Tip**   Notice that I have set the `data-dismissible` attribute to `false` in this example. Without this setting, the synthetically generated mouse events that most touch browsers produce (as described in Chapter 27) are interpreted as clicks outside of the popup, causing the popup to be closed just after it is open. Setting the `data-dismissible` attribute to `false` ensures that this won't happen, and the popup can only be dismissed by the button that calls the `close` method.

Using the Popup Events

The jQuery Mobile popup widget defines the events shown in Table 29-10.

Table 29-10. *Popup Events*

Event	Description
create	Triggered when the popup widget is created.
beforeposition	Triggered before the popup is repositioned.
afteropen	Triggered after the popup has been displayed.
afterclose	Triggered after the popup has been hidden.

I rarely find these events useful and my use of the popup widget is generally limited to the methods and configuration options. The one exception is when I want to display a popup for a limited period of time, in which case the `afteropen` event can be useful, as Listing 29-14 demonstrates.

Listing 29-14. Handling Popup Events

```
<!DOCTYPE html>
<html>
<head>
    <title>Example</title>
    <meta name="viewport" content="width=device-width, initial-scale=1">
    <link rel="stylesheet" href="jquery.mobile-1.3.1.css" type="text/css" />
    <script type="text/javascript" src="jquery-1.10.1.js"></script>
    <script>
        $(document).bind("pageinit", function () {
            $("#popup").popup({
                afteropen: function (e) {
                    setTimeout(function () {
                        $("#popup").popup("close");
                    }, 5000);
                }
            });
        });
    </script>
    <script type="text/javascript" src="jquery.mobile-1.3.1.js"></script>
</head>
<body>
    <div id="page1" data-role="page">
        <div data-role="header">
            <h1>Jacqui's Shop</h1>
        </div>
        <div data-role="content">
            <a href="#popup" data-rel="popup">Show the popup</a>
        </div>
        <div id="popup" data-role="popup" data-position-to="window">
            <p>This is the popup content</p>
        </div>
    </div>
</body>
</html>
```

■ **Caution**   I only use this technique when I can't negotiate an alternative approach with the client. My feeling is that popups should be solely under the control of the user and that making them appear and disappear in ways that are not directly linked to user interactions can cause confusion.

In this example I handle the afteropen method be calling the setTimeout function to register a callback that will be executed five seconds later. The callback calls the close method to dismiss the popup.

Summary

In this chapter, I introduced the first two jQuery Mobile widgets: the dialog and the popup. jQuery Mobile widgets follow the same basic structure and philosophy as jQuery UI widgets, but with the obvious optimizations for mobile devices. In Chapter 30, I describe the button and collapsible block widgets.

CHAPTER 30

■ ■ ■

Buttons and Collapsible Blocks

In this chapter, I describe two additional jQuery Mobile widgets: *buttons* and *collapsible blocks*. The jQuery Mobile button widget works in a similar way to the jQuery UI buttons you saw earlier in the book, with the exception that you can create and use simple buttons without using any custom JavaScript code at all, relying instead on data attributes.

A collapsible block is like a single panel from an accordion; in fact, you can use collapsible blocks on their own or combine several together to form a simple accordion. Table 30-1 provides the summary for this chapter. I also show you widgets that offer variations on the same theme – *Navbars*, which group buttons to provide consistent navigation support and *collapsible sets*, which can be used to create accordion widgets.

Table 30-1. *Chapter Summary*

Problem	Solution	Listing
Create a button widget automatically.	Add a button element or an input element whose type is submit, reset, or button.	1
Create button widgets from other elements.	Apply the data-role attribute with a value of button.	2
Create a group of buttons.	Use the data-role attribute with a value of controlgroup. Use the data-type attribute to change the orientation.	3, 4
Add and position icons on buttons.	Use the data-icon and data-iconpos attributes.	5
Create smaller buttons.	Use the data-mini and data-inline attributes.	6
Update a button to reflect changes in the underlying element.	Use the refresh method.	7
Respond to button events.	Handle events from the underlying element.	8
Provide consistent navigation buttons.	Use the navbar widget.	9
Position the icons in a navbar.	Use the data-iconpos attribute	10
Create a collapsible block.	Apply the data-role attribute with a value of collapsible. Ensure that there is a header element as the first child.	11, 12
Receive notifications when a block is collapsed or expanded.	Handle the collapse and expand events.	13
Create an accordion.	Use the data-role attribute with a value of collapsible-set value.	14

Using jQuery Mobile Buttons

I already used some button widgets in earlier examples, but now it is time to loop back and explain how they work.

Creating the Button Widget

As part of the automatic page-enhancement process, jQuery Mobile creates buttons widgets from button elements or from input elements whose type attribute is set to submit, reset, button, or image. You don't have to take any special action for these element types because jQuery Mobile does all the work for you. Listing 30-1 shows a page that contains some of these automatically enhanced elements.

Listing 30-1. Relying on the Automatic Creation of Button Widgets

```
<!DOCTYPE html>
<html>
<head>
    <title>Example</title>
    <meta name="viewport" content="width=device-width, initial-scale=1">
    <link rel="stylesheet" href="jquery.mobile-1.3.1.css" type="text/css" />
    <script type="text/javascript" src="jquery-1.10.1.js"></script>
    <script type="text/javascript" src="jquery.mobile-1.3.1.js"></script>
</head>
<body>
    <div id="page1" data-role="page" data-theme="b">
        <div data-role="header">
            <h1>Jacqui's Shop</h1>
        </div>
        <div data-role="content">
            <button>Button</button>
            <input type="submit" value="Input (Submit)" />
            <input type="reset" value="Input (Reset)" />
            <input type="button" value="Input (Button)" />
        </div>
    </div>
</body>
</html>
```

You can see how a button widget is created for each type of element in Figure 30-1.

Figure 30-1. *Button widgets created automatically by jQuery Mobile*

Creating Buttons from Other Elements

jQuery Mobile can also create buttons widgets from other elements. In earlier chapters, you saw me create a button widget from an a element by applying the data-role attribute with a value of button. You can also do this for other types of elements, such as div. Listing 30-2 contains an example.

***Listing 30-2.** Creating Buttons from Other Elements*

```
<!DOCTYPE html>
<html>
<head>
    <title>Example</title>
    <meta name="viewport" content="width=device-width, initial-scale=1">
    <link rel="stylesheet" href="jquery.mobile-1.3.1.css" type="text/css" />
    <script type="text/javascript" src="jquery-1.10.1.js"></script>
    <script type="text/javascript" src="jquery.mobile-1.3.1.js"></script>
</head>
<body>
    <div id="page1" data-role="page" data-theme="b">
        <div data-role="header">
            <h1>Jacqui's Shop</h1>
        </div>
        <div data-role="content">
            <a href="document2.html" data-role="button">A Element</a>
            <div data-role="button">DIV Element</div>
        </div>
```

```
        </div>
</body>
</html>
```

You can see how jQuery Mobile deals with the elements in this example in Figure 30-2.

Figure 30-2. *Creating button widgets using other elements*

Creating Grouped Buttons

You can create a group of buttons that have no spacing between them by creating a *control group*. You do this by applying the data-role attribute with a value of controlgroup to the parent element for two or more button widgets. Listing 30-3 provides a demonstration.

Listing 30-3. Creating a Set of Grouped Buttons

```
<!DOCTYPE html>
<html>
<head>
    <title>Example</title>
    <meta name="viewport" content="width=device-width, initial-scale=1">
    <link rel="stylesheet" href="jquery.mobile-1.3.1.css" type="text/css" />
    <script type="text/javascript" src="jquery-1.10.1.js"></script>
    <script type="text/javascript" src="jquery.mobile-1.3.1.js"></script>
</head>
<body>
    <div id="page1" data-role="page" data-theme="b">
        <div data-role="header">
            <h1>Jacqui's Shop</h1>
        </div>
        <div data-role="content">
```

```
        <div data-role="controlgroup">
            <button>Back</button>
            <button>Home</button>
            <button>Next</button>
        </div>
    </div>
</div>
</body>
</html>
```

In this example, there are three buttons, all of which are children of a div element whose data-role is control group. You can see the effect in Figure 30-3. Notice how only the top and bottom buttons have rounded corners.

Figure 30-3. *A set of buttons displayed in a group*

You can change the orientation of the button group by setting the data-type attribute to horizontal, as shown in Listing 30-4.

Listing 30-4. Creating a Horizontal Button Group

```
<!DOCTYPE html>
<html>
<head>
    <title>Example</title>
    <meta name="viewport" content="width=device-width, initial-scale=1">
    <link rel="stylesheet" href="jquery.mobile-1.3.1.css" type="text/css" />
    <script type="text/javascript" src="jquery-1.10.1.js"></script>
    <script type="text/javascript" src="jquery.mobile-1.3.1.js"></script>
</head>
```

```
<body>
    <div id="page1" data-role="page" data-theme="b">
        <div data-role="header">
            <h1>Jacqui's Shop</h1>
        </div>
        <div data-role="content">
            <div data-role="controlgroup" data-type="horizontal">
                <button>Back</button>
                <button>Home</button>
                <button>Next</button>
            </div>
        </div>
    </div>
</body>
</html>
```

You can see how the browser displays a horizontal button group in Figure 30-4. Once again, notice how the rounded corners are applied only to the outside elements.

Figure 30-4. *Creating a horizontal button group*

Configuring jQuery Mobile Buttons

jQuery Mobile defines a number of data attributes and configuration settings you can use to configure buttons and to create buttons from different element types. These attributes are described in Table 30-2, and I demonstrate those that are unique to buttons in the sections that follow.

Table 30-2. *Data Attributes and Configuration Settings for Buttons*

Data Attribute	Setting	Description
data-corners	corners	When true, buttons are drawn with rounded corners. A value of false means that square corners will be used. The default is true.
data-icon	icon	Specifies an icon to be used in the button.
data-iconpos	iconpos	Specifies the position of an icon, if one is used.
data-iconshadow	iconshadow	Applies a shadow to the icon when set to true.
data-inline	inline	Creates a button that is sized to its contents (rather than filling the screen).
data-mini	mini	When set to true, displays a compact button.
data-shadow	shadow	When true, buttons are drawn with a shadow. A value of false means that no shadow will be used. The default is true.

Adding Icons to Buttons

jQuery Mobile includes a set of icons that can be used in buttons. These are included in a single image file in the images directory you installed in Chapter 27. Table 30-3 shows a list of the icon names and a brief description of each.

Table 30-3. *Icons Included in jQuery Mobile*

Icon Name	Description
arrow-l arrow-r arrow-u arrow-d	Arrows that are facing left, right, up, and down.
bars	A set of three horizontal lines.
edit	A pencil, used to indicate that the user can edit content.
check delete	A check and a cross.
plus minus	Plus and minus signs.
gear	A cog.
refresh forward back home search	Browser style icons to refresh, advance to the next page, return to the previous page, return to the home page, or search.
grid	A grid of small squares.
star	A star.
alert	A caution warning.
info	A stylized letter i.

You apply the icons to a button using the `data-icon` attribute, where the value specifies the name of the icon to use. You use the `data-iconpos` attribute to specify where the icon will be located in the button. The default is `left`, but you can also specify `top`, `right`, and `bottom`. If you set `data-iconpos` to `notext`, only the icon is displayed. Listing 30-5 provides an example of using both of these attributes.

Listing 30-5. Adding Icons to Buttons

```
<!DOCTYPE html>
<html>
<head>
    <title>Example</title>
    <meta name="viewport" content="width=device-width, initial-scale=1">
    <link rel="stylesheet" href="jquery.mobile-1.3.1.css" type="text/css" />
    <script type="text/javascript" src="jquery-1.10.1.js"></script>
    <script type="text/javascript" src="jquery.mobile-1.3.1.js"></script>
</head>
<body>
    <div id="page1" data-role="page" data-theme="b">
        <div data-role="header">
            <h1>Jacqui's Shop</h1>
        </div>
        <div data-role="content">
            <div class="ui-grid-b">
                <div class="ui-block-a">
                    <button data-icon="home">Home</button>
                </div>
                <div class="ui-block-b">
                    <button data-icon="home" data-iconpos="top">Home</button>
                </div>
                <div class="ui-block-c">
                    <button data-icon="home" data-iconpos="notext"></button>
                </div>
            </div>
        </div>
    </div>
</body>
</html>
```

In this example, I created three buttons, all of which display the home icon. The first button uses the default icon position, the second button uses the top position, and the last button uses the notext value, which creates an icon-only button. You can see how these buttons appear in Figure 30-5.

Figure 30-5. *Creating icon buttons*

You can see that each button has a distinctive style. The most striking is the last button, which displays no text. This looks visually appealing, but my experience with this kind of button is that they are hard to hit with a finger, and not all users immediately recognize them as a means of navigating elsewhere in the application.

Creating Inline and Mini Buttons

jQuery Mobile buttons span the entire width of the screen by default. You can see an example of the default button width in Figure 30-1. I used the layout grid to create smaller buttons in subsequent examples, but I could have achieved a similar effect using *inline buttons*, which are just big enough to accommodate their content and are created by setting the data-inline attribute to true.

I can also create mini buttons by setting the data-mini attribute to true. Mini buttons have the standard approach to width, but occupy less vertical space. Finally, you can combine both data attributes to create inline mini buttons, which are just wide enough to accommodate their content *and* occupy less vertical space than regular buttons. Listing 30-6 shows all three types of buttons.

Listing 30-6. *Using Inline and Mini Buttons*

```
<!DOCTYPE html>
<html>
<head>
    <title>Example</title>
    <meta name="viewport" content="width=device-width, initial-scale=1">
    <link rel="stylesheet" href="jquery.mobile-1.3.1.css" type="text/css" />
    <script type="text/javascript" src="jquery-1.10.1.js"></script>
    <script type="text/javascript" src="jquery.mobile-1.3.1.js"></script>
</head>
<body>
    <div id="page1" data-role="page" data-theme="b">
        <div data-role="header">
            <h1>Jacqui's Shop</h1>
```

831

```
        </div>
        <div data-role="content">
            <button data-icon="home" data-inline="true">Home</button>
            <button data-icon="home" data-mini="true">Home</button>
            <button data-icon="home" data-inline="true" data-mini="true">Home</button>
        </div>
    </div>
</body>
</html>
```

You can see the effect in Figure 30-6.

Figure 30-6. *Using inline and mini buttons*

Using the Button Methods

The button widget defines three methods, which I have described in Table 30-4.

Table 30-4. *Button Methods*

Method	Description
button("disable")	Disables the button so that it can't be clicked.
button("enable")	Enables the button so that it can be clicked.
button("refresh")	Refreshes the widget to reflect changes in the underlying HTML element.

The enable and disable methods are self-evident. The refresh method is required when the contents of the underlying button or input element changes, as demonstrated by Listing 30-7.

Listing 30-7. Updating the Contents of Button Widgets

```
<!DOCTYPE html>
<html>
<head>
    <title>Example</title>
    <meta name="viewport" content="width=device-width, initial-scale=1">
    <link rel="stylesheet" href="jquery.mobile-1.3.1.css" type="text/css" />
    <script type="text/javascript" src="jquery-1.10.1.js"></script>
    <script>
        $(document).bind("pageinit", function () {
            var counter = 0;
            setInterval(function () {
                var msg = "Counter " + counter++;
                $("#buttonElem").text(msg).button("refresh");
                $("#inputElem").val(msg).button("refresh");
                $("#divElem span.ui-btn-text").text(msg);
            }, 1000);
        });
    </script>
    <script type="text/javascript" src="jquery.mobile-1.3.1.js"></script>
</head>
<body>
    <div id="page1" data-role="page" data-theme="b">
        <div data-role="header">
            <h1>Jacqui's Shop</h1>
        </div>
        <div data-role="content">
            <button id="buttonElem">Button</button>
            <input id="inputElem" type="button" value="Input" />
            <div id="divElem" data-role="button">Div</div>
        </div>
    </div>
</body>
</html>
```

There are three button widgets in this example, created from a button element, an input element, and a div element. The script element handles the pageinit event (which I described in Chapter 29) by calling the setInterval function to update the contents of the elements that underpin the button widgets every second.

I have to call the refresh method for the button and input elements; otherwise the changes I make to the elements won't be reflected in the button widgets:

```
...
$("#buttonElem").text(msg).button("refresh");
$("#inputElem").val(msg).button("refresh");
...
```

A different approach is required when you create button widgets from other elements, such as a div element. In this situation, jQuery Mobile adds content elements so that it can apply CSS styles to shape the widget, and changing the content of the element affects the shape of the widget. Instead, you will need to look at the HTML that jQuery Mobile generates inside of the element and locate the textual content. The div element in my example is populated with span elements, and I can change the text content by locating the element that is part of the ui-btn-text class, like this:

```
...
$("#divElem span.ui-btn-text").text(msg);
...
```

■ **Tip** I located this element by using the browser F12 tools to explore the content that jQuery Mobile generates during the enhancement process.

Using the Button Events

The button widget defines the standard create event that is triggered when the widget is created, but the widgets that underpin the widget will still trigger their own events, which will be supplemented by the jQuery Mobile events that I described in Chapter 29. This means that you can create handlers for the tap event, for example, to receive notification when the button is clicked, as demonstrated in Listing 30-8.

■ **Tip** Don't forget that events can have a default action for some elements – for example, this means that button widgets created from input elements will submit the form they are part of. See Chapter 28 for details of jQuery event handling.

Listing 30-8. Handling Button Events

```
<!DOCTYPE html>
<html>
<head>
    <title>Example</title>
    <meta name="viewport" content="width=device-width, initial-scale=1">
    <link rel="stylesheet" href="jquery.mobile-1.3.1.css" type="text/css" />
    <script type="text/javascript" src="jquery-1.10.1.js"></script>
    <script>
        $(document).bind("pageinit", function () {
            $("button").tap(function (e) {
                $(this).text("Tapped!").button("refresh");
            });
        });
    </script>
    <script type="text/javascript" src="jquery.mobile-1.3.1.js"></script>
</head>
```

```
<body>
    <div id="page1" data-role="page" data-theme="b">
        <div data-role="header">
            <h1>Jacqui's Shop</h1>
        </div>
        <div data-role="content">
            <button>Button</button>
        </div>
    </div>
</body>
</html>
```

In this listing I use the tap method to register a handler function for the tap event on a button. When the button is clicked, I handle the event by changing the button text and calling the refresh method to update the widget content.

Using jQuery Mobile NavBars

NavBars are groups of buttons that present navigation support in a header or footer, allowing the users to move through a set of content pages. NavBars are pretty simple, but they can be a useful tool when you have a set of related pages to display and you need to give the user a clear signal about which of those pages is currently displayed. NavBars are created using a specific element structure, which you can see in Listing 30-9.

Listing 30-9. Creating a NavBar

```
<!DOCTYPE html>
<html>
<head>
    <title>Example</title>
    <meta name="viewport" content="width=device-width, initial-scale=1">
    <link rel="stylesheet" href="jquery.mobile-1.3.1.css" type="text/css" />
    <script type="text/javascript" src="jquery-1.10.1.js"></script>
    <script type="text/javascript" src="jquery.mobile-1.3.1.js"></script>
</head>
<body>
    <div id="page1" data-role="page">
        <div data-role="header">
            <h1>Jacqui's Shop</h1>
            <div data-role="navbar">
                <ul>
                    <li><a href="#page1"
                        class="ui-btn-active ui-state-persist">Page 1</a></li>
                    <li><a href="#page2">Page 2</a></li>
                    <li><a href="#page3">Page 3</a></li>
                </ul>
            </div>
        </div>
        <div data-role="content">This is page 1</div>
    </div>

    <div id="page2" data-role="page">
        <div data-role="header">
```

```
            <h1>Jacqui's Shop</h1>
            <div data-role="navbar">
                <ul>
                    <li><a href="#page1">Page 1</a></li>
                    <li><a href="#page2"
                        class="ui-btn-active ui-state-persist">Page 2</a></li>
                    <li><a href="#page3">Page 3</a></li>
                </ul>
            </div>
        </div>
        <div data-role="content">This is page 2</div>
    </div>

    <div id="page3" data-role="page">
        <div data-role="header">
            <h1>Jacqui's Shop</h1>
            <div data-role="navbar">
                <ul>
                    <li><a href="#page1">Page 1</a></li>
                    <li><a href="#page2">Page 2</a></li>
                    <li><a href="#page3"
                        class="ui-btn-active ui-state-persist">Page 3</a></li>
                </ul>
            </div>
        </div>
        <div data-role="content">This is page 3</div>
    </div>
</body>
</html>
```

The NavBar is defined by a div element whose data-role attribute is set to navbar. The individual buttons within the NavBar are defined as a elements contained in li elements contained, in turn, in an ul element. In the listing, I have used the Navbar in its most common form, which is where it is duplicated across multiple jQuery Mobile pages to give a consistent reference to the user, as shown in Figure 30-7.

Figure 30-7. *The NavBar widget*

The NavBar widget allocates the available screen space equally between the navigation buttons, and clicking one of the buttons displays the page identified by the href attribute of the underlying a element.

There are two CSS classes that must be applied to the a elements to indicate to the user that page is being displayed. The ui-btn-active class marks the button as active, and the ui-state-persist class ensures that the active state is displayed if the user navigates back to a previously displayed page.

Configuring jQuery Mobile NavBar

The NavBar supports just one data attribute/configuration option, which I have described in Table 30-5.

Table 30-5. *Data Attributes and Configuration Settings for NavBar*

Data Attribute	Setting	Description
data-iconpos	iconpos	Specifies the position of icons in the NavBar buttons. The supported positions are left, right, top (the default), and bottom. You can also use the notext value to display an icon without any text.

I listed the jQuery Mobile icons earlier in the chapter. Individual icons are applied to the a elements using the data-icon attribute, and you can see how I have positioned the icons with the data-iconpos attribute in Listing 30-10.

Listing 30-10. Positioning the Icons in a NavBar

```
<!DOCTYPE html>
<html>
<head>
    <title>Example</title>
    <meta name="viewport" content="width=device-width, initial-scale=1">
    <link rel="stylesheet" href="jquery.mobile-1.3.1.css" type="text/css" />
    <script type="text/javascript" src="jquery-1.10.1.js"></script>
    <script type="text/javascript" src="jquery.mobile-1.3.1.js"></script>
</head>
<body>
    <div id="page1" data-role="page">
        <div data-role="header">
            <h1>Jacqui's Shop</h1>
            <div data-role="navbar" data-iconpos="left">
                <ul>
                    <li><a href="#page1" data-icon="alert"
                        class="ui-btn-active ui-state-persist">Page 1</a></li>
                    <li><a href="#page2" data-icon="info">Page 2</a></li>
                    <li><a href="#page3" data-icon="gear">Page 3</a></li>
                </ul>
            </div>
        </div>
        <div data-role="content">This is page 1</div>
    </div>
</body>
</html>
```

You can see the effect of the icons in Figure 30-8.

Figure 30-8. *Adding and positioning icons in a NavBar*

Using the NavBar Methods & Events

The NavBar widget doesn't define any methods and supports only the create event, which is triggered when the widget is instantiated.

■ **Tip** Handle the events from the a elements to respond to user navigation.

Using Collapsible Content Blocks

jQuery Mobile includes support for creating *collapsible content blocks*, which are sections of content with a header that can be closed so that only the header is available. This is similar to a single panel of a jQuery UI accordion, which I described in Chapter 19.

Creating the Collapsible Block

A collapsible block has a specific structure you need to follow in order to give jQuery Mobile the elements it needs. Listing 30-11 contains an example.

Listing 30-11. Creating a Single Collapsible Block

```
<!DOCTYPE html>
<html>
<head>
    <title>Example</title>
    <meta name="viewport" content="width=device-width, initial-scale=1">
    <link rel="stylesheet" href="jquery.mobile-1.3.1.css" type="text/css" />
    <script type="text/javascript" src="jquery-1.10.1.js"></script>
    <script type="text/javascript" src="jquery.mobile-1.3.1.js"></script>
</head>
```

```
<body>
    <div id="page1" data-role="page" data-theme="b">
        <div data-role="header">
            <h1>Jacqui's Shop</h1>
        </div>
        <div data-role="content">
            <div data-role="collapsible">
                <h1>New Delivery Service</h1>
                <p>We are pleased to announce that we are starting a home delivery
                service for your flower needs. We will deliver within a 20 mile radius
                of the store for free and $1/mile thereafter.</p>
            </div>
        </div>
    </div>
</body>
</html>
```

The first thing you have to do is create a div element and apply the data-role attribute with a value of collapsible. This tells jQuery Mobile that you want a collapsible block and that it should look for a header element as the first child of the div. You can use any of the header elements, h1 through h6. I used an h1 element, but jQuery Mobile treats all of the headers equally for this kind of widget. The remaining child elements of the div are used as the content for the collapsible element, creating the effect that is shown in Figure 30-9.

Figure 30-9. *Expanding a collapsible block*

The block is collapsed when it is first displayed, meaning that the content is hidden and only the header can be seen. As a cue for the user, a plus icon is drawn at the left edge of the header area (which is styled in the same way as a non-inline button). Clicking on the header reveals the content and replaces the icon with a minus sign, indicating that the block can be collapsed again.

Configuring jQuery Mobile Collapsible Content Blocks

jQuery Mobile defines the data attributes and configuration settings shown in Table 30-6.

Table 30-6. *Data Attributes and Configuration Settings for Collapsible Blocks*

Data Attribute	Setting	Description
data-collapsed	collapsed	When true, the default value, the block is shown collapsed (that is, only the header is visible to the user). A value of false means that the block is shown expanded.
data-collapsed-icon	collapsedIcon	Specifies the icon displayed when the block is collapsed.
data-content-theme	contentTheme	Specifies the theme for the content area of the collapsible block.
data-corners	corners	When true, the collapsible block is drawn with rounded corners. A value of false results in square corners.
data-expanded-icon	expandedIcon	Specifies the icon displayed when the block is expanded.
data-iconpos	iconPos	Specifies the position of the icon in the header, using the same values as for the NavBar and Button widgets.
data-inset	inset	When set to false, the header will fill the window without any padding. The default is true.
data-mini	mini	When set to true, the header is drawn in a compact form.

In Listing 30-12, you can see how I have applied some of the data attributes to the example.

Listing 30-12. Configuring the Collapsible Block Widget

```html
<!DOCTYPE html>
<html>
<head>
    <title>Example</title>
    <meta name="viewport" content="width=device-width, initial-scale=1">
    <link rel="stylesheet" href="jquery.mobile-1.3.1.css" type="text/css" />
    <script type="text/javascript" src="jquery-1.10.1.js"></script>
    <script type="text/javascript" src="jquery.mobile-1.3.1.js"></script>
</head>
<body>
    <div id="page1" data-role="page" data-theme="b">
        <div data-role="header">
            <h1>Jacqui's Shop</h1>
        </div>
        <div data-role="content">
            <div data-role="collapsible" data-content-theme="e" data-collapsed="false"
                    data-inset="false" data-iconpos="top">
                <h1>New Delivery Service</h1>
                <p>We are pleased to announce that we are starting a home delivery
                service for your flower needs. We will deliver within a 20 mile radius
                of the store for free and $1/mile thereafter.</p>
            </div>
        </div>
    </div>
</body>
</html>
```

I have changed the values for the data-content-theme, data-inset, data-iconpos, and data-collapsed attributes. You can see the effect in Figure 30-10.

Figure 30-10. *Configuring the collapsible block widget*

Using Collapsible Block Methods

The collapsible block widget does not define any methods.

Using Collapsible Block Events

The collapsible block widget defines the events shown in Table 30-7.

Table 30-7. *Collapsible Block Events*

Event	Description
create	This event is triggered when the widget is created.
collapse	Triggered when the collapsible block is collapsed.
expand	Triggered when the collapsible block is expanded.

In Listing 30-13, you can see how I have handled the collapse and expand events to report on the status of a collapsible block. If this seems like a contrived example, it is because these events are rarely useful.

Listing 30-13. Using the Collapse and Expand Events

```html
<!DOCTYPE html>
<html>
<head>
    <title>Example</title>
    <meta name="viewport" content="width=device-width, initial-scale=1">
    <link rel="stylesheet" href="jquery.mobile-1.3.1.css" type="text/css" />
    <script type="text/javascript" src="jquery-1.10.1.js"></script>
    <script type="text/javascript">
        $(document).bind("pageinit", function() {
            $('#colBlock').bind("collapse expand", function(event) {
                $('#status').text(event.type == "expand" ? "Expanded" : "Collapsed");
            })
        });
    </script>
    <script type="text/javascript" src="jquery.mobile-1.3.1.js"></script>
</head>
<body>
    <div id="page1" data-role="page" data-theme="b">
        <div data-role="header">
            <h1>Jacqui's Shop</h1>
        </div>
        <div data-role="content">
            The block is <b><span id="status">Expanded</span></b>

            <div id="colBlock" data-role="collapsible" data-content-theme="e"
                    data-collapsed=false>
                <h1>New Delivery Service</h1>
                <p>We are pleased to announce that we are starting a home
                delivery service for your flower needs. We will deliver within a
                20 mile radius of the store for free and $1/mile thereafter.</p>
            </div>
        </div>
    </div>
</body>
</html>
```

In this example, I use the bind method to listen for the expand and collapse events. I do this in a single call to the bind method by listing the events I am interested in, separated by spaces. When one of the events is triggered, I update the content of a span element to reflect the status of the collapsible block. You can see the change in status in Figure 30-11.

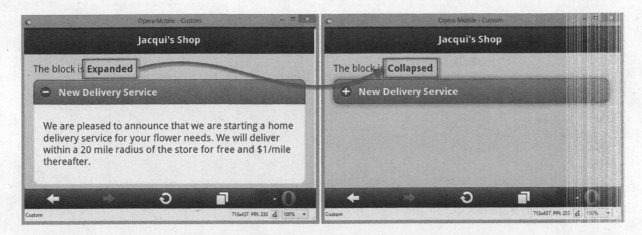

Figure 30-11. *Responding to the expand and collapse events*

Using jQuery Mobile Collapsible Sets (Accordions)

The collapsible set widget combines multiple collapsible blocks to create an accordion. Collapsible sets are defined by using a div element that wraps two or more collapsible blocks in a single parent element and applying the data-role attribute to the div element with a value of collapsible-set. You can see how this is done in Listing 30-14.

Listing 30-14. *Creating a jQuery Mobile Accordion*

```
<!DOCTYPE html>
<html>
<head>
    <title>Example</title>
    <meta name="viewport" content="width=device-width, initial-scale=1">
    <link rel="stylesheet" href="jquery.mobile-1.3.1.css" type="text/css" />
    <script type="text/javascript" src="jquery-1.10.1.js"></script>
    <script type="text/javascript" src="jquery.mobile-1.3.1.js"></script>
</head>
<body>
    <div id="page1" data-role="page" data-theme="b">
        <div data-role="header">
            <h1>Jacqui's Shop</h1>
        </div>
        <div data-role="content">
            <div data-role="collapsible-set" data-content-theme="e">
                <div data-role="collapsible">
                    <h1>New Delivery Service</h1>
                    <p>We are pleased to announce that we are starting a home
                    delivery service for your flower needs. We will deliver within a
                    20 mile radius of the store for free and $1/mile thereafter.</p>
                </div>
                <div data-role="collapsible" data-collapsed=false>
                    <h1>Summer Specials</h1>
                    <p>We have a wide range of special summer offers.
```

843

```
                        Ask instore for details</p>
                </div>
                <div data-role="collapsible">
                    <h1>Bulk Orders</h1>
                    <p>We offer discounts for large orders. Ask us for prices</p>
                </div>
            </div>
        </div>
    </div>
</body>
</html>
```

In this example, I defined a div element with the collapsible-set value for the data-role attribute, which contains three collapsible blocks.

■ **Tip**   Notice that I applied the data-content-theme attribute to the outer container. This has the same effect as using the attribute on each individual collapsible block.

The default is for all of the collapsible blocks to be collapsed initially, so I applied the data-collapsed attribute to one of the blocks with a value of false so that it is expanded when the page is first displayed. When the user clicks on a header, the presently expanded element is collapsed. You can see the effect in Figure 30-12.

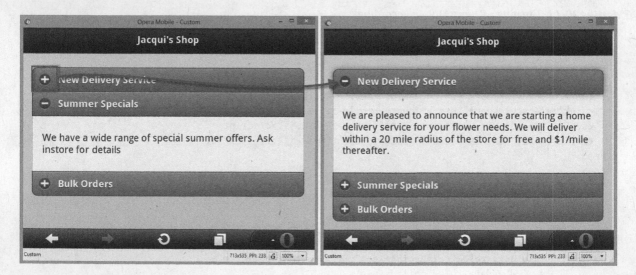

Figure 30-12. *Expanding a block in a jQuery Mobile accordion*

Configuring the Collapsible Set

The collapsible set supports the same set of data attributes and settings as the collapsible block widget.

Using the Collapsible Set Methods

The collapsible set widget supports one method, as described in Table 30-8.

Table 30-8. *The Collapsible Set Method*

Method	Description
collapsibleset("refresh")	Refreshes the widget to reflect changes in the underlying HTML element.

Using the Collapsible Set Events

The collapsible set widget only defines the `create` event, which is triggered when the widget is applied to an HTML element.

Summary

In this chapter, I described more jQuery Mobile widgets: buttons and collapsible blocks and widgets that offer variations on the same theme – NavBars and collapsible sets. In Chapter 31, I show you the jQuery Mobile form widgets.

■ ■ ■

Using jQuery Mobile Forms

There are particular difficulties when presenting a form on a mobile device. There is little enough screen real estate available to start with, and you need to give the user form elements that are easy to manipulate by touch without creating a page that requires endless scrolling to complete. In this chapter, I show you how jQuery Mobile enhances form elements so that they are consistent with other widgets and can be readily used on a touch screen.

jQuery Mobile does a lot of work automatically when the page is loaded. Form elements are enhanced without your intervention, and Ajax is automatically used when the form is submitted so that jQuery Mobile can smoothly transition to the results returned by the server.

I recommend careful thought when you are creating forms for mobile devices. By their nature, forms are intended to gather input from users, but this can be a tedious process on a mobile device, especially when it comes to typing. In addition, some mobile devices don't display scrollbars when the user isn't actively scrolling through a page. This means that the user isn't always aware there are form elements just off of the immediate display. To create the best possible experience for users, you need to follow some basic guidelines:

- *Require as little typing as you can.* Where possible, use alternative widgets that allow the user to make simple touch selections, such as check boxes or radio buttons. This can reduce the range of inputs that the user can make, but it might have the effect of increasing the number of users who are willing to complete the form.

- *Use navigation between pages to display sections of a form.* This gives users a clear indication of their progress through the form and doesn't require them to speculatively scroll to see if they are missing anything.

- *Eliminate any form elements that are not required.* Mobile forms should be as streamlined as possible, and that can mean accepting less data from mobile users than you get from desktop users.

Table 31-1 provides the summary for this chapter.

Table 31-1. *Chapter Summary*

Problem	Solution	Listing
Create widgets for form elements.	No specific action is required – jQuery Mobile will apply the widgets automatically.	1
Add a button that clears the contents of an input element or change the way that the widget for an input element is displayed.	Use the data-clear-btn and data-mini attributes.	2
Enable or disable an input element.	Use the enable and disable methods.	3

(*continued*)

Table 31-1. (*continued*)

Problem	Solution	Listing
Create a slider widget.	Define an input element with a type attribute of range.	4
Create a range slider widget.	Define a pair of input elements within a div element whose data-role attribute is set to rangeslider.	5
Configure the appearance of sliders.	Use the data-highlight, data-mini and data-track-theme attributes.	6, 7
Update a range slider to reflect changes in the underlying input elements.	Use the refresh method.	8
Receive notifications when a slider widget is used.	Handle the start, stop, and normalize events.	9, 10
Create a widget for a select element.	No specific action is required.	11
Configure the button displayed for a select element.	Use the data-corners, data-icon, data-iconpos, and data-mini attributes.	12
Configure the popup that allows users to pick a value for a select element.	Use the data-native-menu, data-overlay-theme, and data-divider-theme attributes.	13
Add a placeholder to a selectmenu.	Set the data-placeholder attribute to true on one of the option elements contained by the select element.	14
Control a selectmenu widget programmatically.	Use the open, close, disable, enable, and refresh methods.	15
Create a flip switch widget.	Define a select element that contains two option elements and that has the data-role attribute set to slider.	16
Create checkbox and radio button widgets.	No specific action is required.	17–20

Creating Form Element Widgets

jQuery Mobile uses automatic enhancement to create widgets for form elements when HTML pages are loaded, just as with the widgets I described in earlier chapters. Listing 31-1 shows a jQuery Mobile page that contains a form element and some form-related child elements.

Listing 31-1. A Simple Form in a jQuery Mobile Page

```
<!DOCTYPE html>
<html>
<head>
    <title>Example</title>
    <meta name="viewport" content="width=device-width, initial-scale=1">
    <link rel="stylesheet" href="jquery.mobile-1.3.1.css" type="text/css" />
    <script type="text/javascript" src="jquery-1.10.1.js"></script>
    <script type="text/javascript" src="jquery.mobile-1.3.1.js"></script>
    <style type="text/css">
        #buttonContainer {text-align: center}
        div[data-role=fieldcontain] { padding: 0 10px; }
    </style>
</head>
```

```
<body>
    <div id="page1" data-role="page" data-theme="b">
        <div data-role="header">
            <h1>Jacqui's Shop</h1>
        </div>
        <form method="get">
            <div data-role="fieldcontain">
                <label for="name">Name: </label>
                <input id="name">
            </div>
            <div data-role="fieldcontain">
                <label for="address">Address: </label>
                <textarea id="address"></textarea>
            </div>
            <div id="buttonContainer">
                <input type="submit" data-inline="true" value="Submit"/>
            </div>
        </form>
    </div>
</body>
</html>
```

This is a simple form, but it sets the scene for how jQuery Mobile handles forms overall. There are two form elements: a text input and a textarea, each of which is paired with a label element. You can see the result in Figure 31-1, which I created using the BrowserStack service because the Opera Mobile Emulator doesn't properly implement a feature that jQuery Mobile relies on for form elements, which I explain in the next section.

Figure 31-1. A simple form displayed by jQuery Mobile

849

■ **Tip**   Notice that I have used CSS to set the padding property for the div elements that contain the form elements. Without this setting, jQuery Mobile would have drawn the label and the form element right up against the left and right edges of the window.

jQuery Mobile will automatically submit the form when an input element whose type is submit is included within a form element. The form will be submitted using Ajax by default, but this behavior can be disabled by applying the data-ajax attribute with a value of false to the form element.

In the last example, each form element and its label are wrapped in a div element. I set the data-role of the div element to be fieldcontain, which tells jQuery Mobile that I want the label and the form element displayed in a single line, and you can see the effect in Figure 31-1.

The styles that jQuery Mobile applies to align the label and the form element are used only when the screen is at least 450 pixels wide. Below that width value, the label and the input/textarea element are displayed on separate rows, as illustrated by Figure 31-2. The Opera Mobile Emulator always reports that its screen is less than 450 pixels wide, which is why I had to generate the figures for these examples using a different browser. (This is just a problem with the emulator – the real Opera Mobile browser implements the feature correctly.)

Figure 31-2. *Displaying a form in portrait orientation*

Using the Textinput Widget

jQuery Mobile uses different widgets for each of the form elements that it supports and the first of these I describe is the *textinput* widget, which is used for textarea elements and input elements. This is the widget used in the previous example.

Configuring the Textinput Widget

The textinput widget defines the attributes and settings properties described in Table 31-2. The settings are applied via the textinput method.

Table 31-2. *Attributes and Configuration Settings for TextInput Widgets*

Data Attribute	Setting	Description
data-clear-btn	clearBtn	When set to true, the widget is displayed with a button that clears the contents. The default is false.
data-clearn-btn-text	clearBtnText	Sets the text for the clear button for accessibility software.
data-mini	mini	When set to true, creates a small version of the widget. The default is false.
data-prevent-focus-zoom	preventFocusZoom	When set to true, the browser is prevented from zooming while the widget has the focus.

In Listing 31-2, you can see how I have applied the data-clear-btn and data-mini attributes to configure the textinput widget on an input element.

Listing 31-2. Configuring the Textinput Widget

```
...
<form method="get">
    <div data-role="fieldcontain">
        <label for="name">Name: </label>
        <input id="name" data-clear-btn="true" data-mini="true">
    </div>
    <div data-role="fieldcontain">
        <label for="address">Address: </label>
        <textarea id="address"></textarea>
    </div>
    <div id="buttonContainer">
        <input type="submit" data-inline="true" value="Submit"/>
    </div>
</form>
...
```

You can see the result in Figure 31-3. The clear button isn't shown until the user starts to enter text into the input element, and clicking the button deletes any content that has been entered. If you use the clear button feature, then be sure to do so consistently for all of your input elements.

Figure 31-3. *Configuring the textinput widget*

Using the Textinput Widget Methods

The textinput widget defines the two methods shown in Table 31-3.

Table 31-3. *TextInput Methods*

Method	Description
textinput("disable")	Disables the widget, preventing the user from entering or editing content.
textinput("enable")	Enables the widget, allowing content to be entered or edited.

In Listing 31-3 I have used both methods to change the state of an input element.

Listing 31-3. Using the Textwidget Methods

```
<!DOCTYPE html>
<html>
<head>
    <title>Example</title>
    <meta name="viewport" content="width=device-width, initial-scale=1">
    <link rel="stylesheet" href="jquery.mobile-1.3.1.css" type="text/css" />
    <script type="text/javascript" src="jquery-1.10.1.js"></script>
    <script>
        $(document).bind("pageinit", function () {
            $("button").tap(function (e) {
                $("#name").textinput(e.target.id);
                e.preventDefault();
            });
        });
    </script>
    <script type="text/javascript" src="jquery.mobile-1.3.1.js"></script>
    <style type="text/css">
        #buttonContainer {text-align: center}
        div[data-role=fieldcontain] { padding: 0 10px; }
    </style>
</head>
```

```
<body>
    <div id="page1" data-role="page" data-theme="b">
        <div data-role="header">
            <h1>Jacqui's Shop</h1>
        </div>
        <form method="get">
            <div data-role="fieldcontain">
                <label for="name">Name: </label>
                <input id="name" data-clear-btn="true" data-mini="true">
            </div>
            <div id="buttonContainer">
                <button id="enable">Enable</button>
                <button id="disable">Disable</button>
            </div>
        </form>
    </div>
</body>
</html>
```

I added buttons to change the state of the input element, and you can see how a disabled element appears in Figure 31-4.

Figure 31-4. *Disabling a textinput widget*

Using the Textinput Widget Events

The textinput widget defines only the create event, which is triggered when the widget is applied to an element.

Using the Slider and Range Slider Widgets

The slider widget is applied to input elements whose type attribute is set to range. The value of the input element is used to set the initial position of a slider on a scale, which is defined by the values of the min and max attributes. Listing 31-4 shows a simple example of a range input element.

Listing 31-4. Using the Slider Widget

```
<!DOCTYPE html>
<html>
<head>
    <title>Example</title>
    <meta name="viewport" content="width=device-width, initial-scale=1">
    <link rel="stylesheet" href="jquery.mobile-1.3.1.css" type="text/css" />
    <script type="text/javascript" src="jquery-1.10.1.js"></script>
    <script type="text/javascript" src="jquery.mobile-1.3.1.js"></script>
    <style type="text/css">
        div[data-role=fieldcontain] { padding: 0 10px; }
    </style>
</head>
<body>
    <div id="page1" data-role="page" data-theme="b">
        <div data-role="header">
            <h1>Jacqui's Shop</h1>
        </div>
        <form method="get">
            <div data-role="fieldcontain">
                <label for="quantity">Quantity: </label>
                <input id="quantity" type="range" value="10" min="1" max="20">
            </div>
        </form>
    </div>
</body>
</html>
```

■ **Tip**   The range value for the type attribute was added in HTML5, as part of a broader set of enhancements to the input element. For full details, see my book *The Definitive Guide to HTML5*, which is also published by Apress.

I have defined an input element with the type attribute set to range, specifying that the initial value is 10 and the range of values is 1 to 20. You can see how jQuery Mobile enhances this element with the slider widget in Figure 31-5.

Figure 31-5. *Using the slider widget*

You can also create a *range slider* by pairing two input elements, allowing the user to select an upper and lower value in a single widget. In Listing 31-5, you can see how I have created a range slider.

Listing 31-5. Using the Range Slider Widget

```
<!DOCTYPE html>
<html>
<head>
    <title>Example</title>
    <meta name="viewport" content="width=device-width, initial-scale=1">
    <link rel="stylesheet" href="jquery.mobile-1.3.1.css" type="text/css" />
    <script type="text/javascript" src="jquery-1.10.1.js"></script>
    <script type="text/javascript" src="jquery.mobile-1.3.1.js"></script>
    <style type="text/css">
        div[data-role=fieldcontain] { padding: 0 10px; }
    </style>
</head>
<body>
    <div id="page1" data-role="page" data-theme="b">
        <div data-role="header">
            <h1>Jacqui's Shop</h1>
        </div>
        <form method="get">
            <div data-role="fieldcontain">
                <div data-role="rangeslider">
                    <label for="quantityLow">Quantity: </label>
                    <input id="quantityLow" type="range" value="10" min="1" max="20">
                    <input id="quantityHigh" type="range" value="15" min="1" max="20">
                </div>
            </div>
        </form>
    </div>
</body>
</html>
```

The input elements are contained in a div element whose data-role attribute is set to rangeslider. The min and max values of the input elements must be the same and the value attribute values are used to set the initial position of the handles that are used to select the range, as shown in Figure 31-6.

Figure 31-6. *Using the range slider widget*

■ **Tip**   The range slider widget doesn't change the way that form data is sent to the server. Separate values will be sent for both of the input elements.

Configuring the Slider and Range Slider Widgets

The slider and range slider widgets support the same set of data attributes and configuration settings, as described in Table 31-4.

Table 31-4. *Attributes and Configuration Settings for Slider and Range Slider Widgets*

Data Attribute	Setting	Description
data-highlight	highlight	When set to true, the section of the slider track that represents the selected value is highlighted. The default value is false.
data-mini	mini	When set to true, the widget is drawn in a more compact form. The default is false.
data-track-theme	trackTheme	Specifies the theme for the track part of the slider.

■ **Tip**   When setting options, use the slider method to configure slider widgets and the rangeslider method to configure range slider widgets.

You have seen the effect of the data-mini attribute in earlier widgets and so I won't repeat the description here. I usually set the data-highlight attribute to true because I think it makes the purpose of the slider – especially the range slider – more obvious. In Listing 31-6, you can see how I set the attribute on the div element of a range slider.

Listing 31-6. Using the data-highlight Attribute on a Range Slider Widget

```
...
<form method="get">
    <div data-role="fieldcontain">
        <div data-role="rangeslider" data-highlight="false">
            <label for="quantityLow">Quantity: </label>
            <input id="quantityLow" type="range" value="10" min="1" max="20">
            <input id="quantityHigh" type="range" value="15" min="1" max="20">
        </div>
    </div>
</form>
...
```

In Figure 31-7 you can see the range slider with and without the highlight enabled.

Figure 31-7. *The effect of the data-highlight attribute*

You can further emphasize the slider by combining the data-track-theme attribute with the globally available data-theme attribute. The data-theme attribute affects the slider handle or handles and data-track-theme affects the slider track. In Listing 31-7, I have applied both attributes to the range slider from the previous example.

Listing 31-7. Using Themes for Slider Handles and Tracks

```
...
<form method="get">
    <div data-role="fieldcontain">
        <div data-role="rangeslider" data-highlight="true"
            data-theme="b" data-track-theme="a">
            <label for="quantityLow">Quantity: </label>
            <input id="quantityLow" type="range" value="10" min="1" max="20">
            <input id="quantityHigh" type="range" value="15" min="1" max="20">
        </div>
    </div>
</form>
...
```

You can see the effect of the themes in Figure 31-8.

Figure 31-8. Applying Themes to a Range Slider and Its Track

Using the Slider and Range Slider Methods

The slider and range slider widgets define the methods shown in Table 31-5.

Table 31-5. Slider and Range Slider Methods

Slider Method	Range Slider Method	Description
slider("disable")	rangeslider("disable")	Disables the widget, preventing the user from changing the slider value or values.
slider("enable")	rangeslider("enable")	Enables the widget, allowing the user to change the slider value or values.
slider("refresh")	rangeslider("refresh")	Updates the widget to reflect changes in the underlying HTML elements.

The refresh method lets you change the value of the attributes on an underlying input element and have those changes reflected in the widget, as demonstrated by Listing 31-8.

Listing 31-8. Using the Refresh Method

```html
<!DOCTYPE html>
<html>
<head>
    <title>Example</title>
    <meta name="viewport" content="width=device-width, initial-scale=1">
    <link rel="stylesheet" href="jquery.mobile-1.3.1.css" type="text/css" />
    <script type="text/javascript" src="jquery-1.10.1.js"></script>
    <script>
        $(document).bind("pageinit", function () {
            $("button").tap(function (e) {
                var currentMax = Number($("#quantityLow").attr("max"));
                $("#quantityLow, #quantityHigh").attr("max", currentMax - 1);
                $("#slider").rangeslider("refresh");
                e.preventDefault();
            });
        });
    </script>
    <script type="text/javascript" src="jquery.mobile-1.3.1.js"></script>
    <style type="text/css">
        div[data-role=fieldcontain] { padding: 0 10px; }
    </style>
</head>
<body>
    <div id="page1" data-role="page" data-theme="b">
        <div data-role="header">
            <h1>Jacqui's Shop</h1>
        </div>
        <form method="get">
            <div data-role="fieldcontain">
                <div id="slider" data-role="rangeslider" data-highlight="true"
                        data-theme="b" data-track-theme="a">
                    <label for="quantityLow">Quantity: </label>
                    <input id="quantityLow" type="range" value="10" min="1" max="20">
                    <input id="quantityHigh" type="range" value="15" min="1" max="20">
                </div>
                <div id="buttonContainer">
                    <button>Change Range</button>
                </div>
            </div>
        </form>
    </div>
</body>
</html>
```

In this example I use a button to decrement the value of the max attribute of the input elements that underpin the slider and call the refresh method so that the widget is updated to reflect the changes.

Using the Slider Events

The slider and range slider widgets define different sets of events. In Table 31-6 I have described the events that are available for the slider widget.

Table 31-6. *Slider Events*

Event	Description
create	Triggered when the slider widget is created.
start	Triggered at the start of any interaction with the slider, including when the widget is tapped (to set a specific value) or when the handle is dragged.
stop	Triggered at the end of any interaction with the slider.

In Listing 31-9, I use the start and stop events to update the content of a span element.

Listing 31-9. Using the Slider Widget Events

```html
<!DOCTYPE html>
<html>
<head>
    <title>Example</title>
    <meta name="viewport" content="width=device-width, initial-scale=1">
    <link rel="stylesheet" href="jquery.mobile-1.3.1.css" type="text/css" />
    <script type="text/javascript" src="jquery-1.10.1.js"></script>
    <script>
        $(document).bind("pageinit", function () {
            $("#quantity").slider({
                start: function () {
                    $("#message").text("Sliding");
                },
                stop: function () {
                    $("#message").text(quantity.value);
                }
            });
        });
    </script>
    <script type="text/javascript" src="jquery.mobile-1.3.1.js"></script>
    <style type="text/css">
        div[data-role=fieldcontain] { padding: 0 10px; }
    </style>
</head>
<body>
    <div id="page1" data-role="page" data-theme="b">
        <div data-role="header">
            <h1>Jacqui's Shop</h1>
        </div>
```

```
            <form method="get">
                <div data-role="fieldcontain">
                    <label for="quantity">Quantity: </label>
                    <input id="quantity" type="range" value="10" min="1" max="20">
                </div>
                Value: <span id="message">Ready</span>
            </form>
        </div>
    </body>
</html>
```

When I receive the start event, I change the contents of the span element to indicate that the slider value is changing. When I receive the stop event, I update the span element to display the value that has been selected – notice that I get the value directly from the input element and not via the slider widget.

Using the Range Slider Events

In Table 31-7, I have described the events that are defined by the range slider widget.

Table 31-7. *Range Slider Events*

Event	Description
create	Triggered when the range slider widget is created.
normalize	Triggered when the widget has to normalize the values in the input elements, which happens when the user drags one handle past the other.

As I write this, the event handling for the range slider widget doesn't work consistently when using the rangeslider method. Instead, event handlers must be created using the bind method, which you can see used in Listing 31-10.

Listing 31-10. Using the Range Slider Widget Events

```
<!DOCTYPE html>
<html>
<head>
    <title>Example</title>
    <meta name="viewport" content="width=device-width, initial-scale=1">
    <link rel="stylesheet" href="jquery.mobile-1.3.1.css" type="text/css" />
    <script type="text/javascript" src="jquery-1.10.1.js"></script>
    <script>
        $(document).bind("pageinit", function () {
            $("#slider").bind("rangeslidernormalize", function () {
                alert("Normalized!");
            });
        });
    </script>
    <script type="text/javascript" src="jquery.mobile-1.3.1.js"></script>
    <style type="text/css">
        div[data-role=fieldcontain] { padding: 0 10px; }
    </style>
</head>
```

```
<body>
    <div id="page1" data-role="page" data-theme="b">
        <div data-role="header">
            <h1>Jacqui's Shop</h1>
        </div>
        <form method="get">
            <div id="slider" data-role="rangeslider" data-highlight="true"
                    data-theme="b" data-track-theme="a">
                <label for="quantityLow">Quantity: </label>
                <input id="quantityLow" type="range" value="10" min="1" max="20">
                <input id="quantityHigh" type="range" value="15" min="1" max="20">
            </div>
        </form>
    </div>
</body>
</html>
```

I have to use the name rangeslidernormalize in order to receive the event, which is an artifact of having to use the bind method. In this example I call the alert function when I get the normalize event – not least because I have yet to find a real-world situation when this event is useful.

Using the Selectmenu Widget

jQuery Mobile provides you with two ways to deal with select elements. The first is to use the selectmenu widget, which presents the user with a stylized version of the select element, with a drop-down button. The selectmenu widget is the default widget applied to select elements, as demonstrated by Listing 31-11.

Listing 31-11. A Page Containing a Select Element

```
<!DOCTYPE html>
<html>
<head>
    <title>Example</title>
    <meta name="viewport" content="width=device-width, initial-scale=1">
    <link rel="stylesheet" href="jquery.mobile-1.3.1.css" type="text/css" />
    <script type="text/javascript" src="jquery-1.10.1.js"></script>
    <script type="text/javascript" src="jquery.mobile-1.3.1.js"></script>
    <style type="text/css">
        #buttonContainer {text-align: center}
    </style>
</head>
<body>
    <div id="page1" data-role="page" data-theme="b">
        <div data-role="header">
            <h1>Jacqui's Shop</h1>
        </div>
        <form method="get">
            <div data-role="fieldcontain">
                <label for="name">Name: </label>
                <input id="name" placeholder="Your Name">
            </div>
```

861

```
        <div data-role="fieldcontain">
            <label for="speed"><span>Speed: </span></label>
            <select id="speed" name="speed">
                <option value="vfast">Very Fast</option>
                <option value="fast">Fast</option>
                <option value="normal" selected>Normal</option>
                <option value="slow">Slow</option>
            </select>
        </div>
        <div id="buttonContainer">
            <input type="submit" data-inline="true" value="Submit"/>
        </div>
    </form>
  </div>
</body>
</html>
```

You can see how jQuery Mobile enhances select elements in Figure 31-9. The Opera Mobile Emulator doesn't display the selectmenu widget correctly, so I obtained the screenshot using BrowserStack.

Figure 31-9. *A select element that has been enhanced by jQuery Mobile*

Configuring the SelectMenu Widget

The selectmenu widget defines data attributes and configuration settings shown in Table 31-8. The configuration options are applied via the selectmenu method. The configuration of the selectmenu widget can be broken down into two areas: configuring the button that is displayed most of the time, and configuring the popup that allows the user to make a selection. I describe both configuration areas in the sections that follow.

Table 31-8. *Attributes and Configuration Settings for Selectmenu Widgets*

Data Attribute	Setting	Description
data-corners	corners	Specifies whether the button that displays the list of options is drawn with rounded corners. The default value is true.
data-divider-theme	dividerTheme	Specifies the theme used for optgroup elements when the nativeMenu option is false.
data-icon	icon	Specifies the icon that will be displayed on the widget button.
data-iconpos	iconPos	Specifies the position of the icon on the widget button.
data-inline	inline	Specifies that the widget will be drawn in a compact style.
data-mini	mini	Specifies that the widget will be drawn in a smaller style.
data-native-menu	nativeMenu	Specifies whether the native selectmenu will be used. The default is true.
data-overlay-theme	overlayTheme	Specifies the theme used for the selectmenu popup when the nativeMenu option is set to false.

Configuring the SelectMenu Button

The selectmenu widget replaces the standard select element with a button that matches the rest of the jQuery Mobile theme. You can configure how the button appears using the data-corners, data-icon, data-iconpos, data-inline, and data-mini attributes or their configuration property counterparts. I have described all of these configuration options as they have appeared in earlier chapters, so I am not going to cover them in depth, but in Listing 31-12 you can see how I have applied some of the attributes to change the way that the button is displayed.

Listing 31-12. Configuring the Selectmenu Button

```
...
<div data-role="fieldcontain">
    <label for="speed"><span>Speed: </span></label>
    <select id="speed" name="speed"
        data-iconpos="left" data-icon="gear" data-mini="true">
        <option value="vfast">Very Fast</option>
        <option value="fast">Fast</option>
        <option value="normal" selected>Normal</option>
        <option value="slow">Slow</option>
    </select>
</div>
...
```

I have changed the icon that is displayed and moved it to the left side of the button with the data-icon and data-iconpos attributes and specified a smaller button size with the data-mini attribute. You can see the effect of these changes in Figure 31-10.

Figure 31-10. *Configuring the selectmenu widget button*

Configuring the SelectMenu Popup

By default, the selectmenu widget will display the native browser menu when the user clicks on the button to make a selection. This is a sensible idea, because it provides the user with access to whatever optimizations the browser offers to take advantage of the device features. In Figure 31-11, you can see the native menus for the iOS, Android, and Opera browsers and these are shown by default when the user clicks on the selectmenu widget button.

Figure 31-11. *The Native Select Menus*

You can disable the native menu and have the selectmenu widget display one that matches the rest of the jQuery Mobile theme by setting the data-native-menu attribute to false. This prevents the user from benefiting from the native enhancements, but has the advantage of offering consistency. In Listing 31-13, you can see how I have used the data-native-menu to disable the native menu and the data-overlay-theme attribute to set the theme used for the popup.

Listing 31-13. Configuring the Selectmenu Popup

```
...
<div data-role="fieldcontain">
    <label for="speed"><span>Speed: </span></label>
    <select id="speed" name="speed" data-native-menu="false" data-overlay-theme="e">
        <option value="vfast">Very Fast</option>
        <option value="fast">Fast</option>
        <option value="normal" selected>Normal</option>
        <option value="slow">Slow</option>
    </select>
</div>
...
```

You can see the effect of these changes in Figure 31-12.

Figure 31-12. *Disabling the native selectmenu*

Specifying Placeholders

You can use an option element as the placeholder for a select element by setting the value of the data-placeholder attribute to true. Placeholders are shown when the select element is initially displayed but isn't present in the list of options that the user chooses from. Listing 31-14 shows the use of the data-placeholder attribute.

Listing 31-14. Using the data-placeholder Attribute

```
...
<div data-role="fieldcontain">
    <label for="speed"><span>Speed: </span></label>
    <select id="speed" name="speed" data-native-menu="false" data-overlay-theme="e">
        <option value="placeholder" data-placeholder="true">Select a Speed</option>
        <option value="vfast">Very Fast</option>
```

```
        <option value="fast">Fast</option>
        <option value="normal">Normal</option>
        <option value="slow">Slow</option>
    </select>
</div>
...
```

You can see the effect in Figure 31-13. I generally like to use placeholders with select menus, but this is an especially useful technique for giving the user context when hiding label elements in portrait layouts.

Figure 31-13. *Specifying a placeholder element*

Using the Selectmenu Methods

The selectmenu widget defines the methods shown in Table 31-9.

Table 31-9. *Methods for the selectmenu Widget*

Method	Description
selectmenu("open")	Opens the selectmenu widget to display the popup.
selectmenu("close")	Closes the popup.
selectmenu("disable")	Disables the widget so that values cannot be selected.
selectmenu("enable")	Enables the widget so that values can be selected.
selectmenu("refresh")	Refreshes the widget to incorporate changes in the underlying select element.

Listing 31-15 shows how to use buttons to control the selectmenu.

Listing 31-15. Controlling the Selectmenu Programmatically

```
<!DOCTYPE html>
<html>
<head>
    <title>Example</title>
    <meta name="viewport" content="width=device-width, initial-scale=1">
    <link rel="stylesheet" href="jquery.mobile-1.3.1.css" type="text/css" />
    <script type="text/javascript" src="jquery-1.10.1.js"></script>
    <script type="text/javascript">
        $(document).bind("pageinit", function () {
            $("button").bind("tap", function (e) {
                e.preventDefault();
                if (this.id == "open") {
                    $("#speed").selectmenu("open");
                    setTimeout(function () {
                        $("#speed").selectmenu("close")
                    }, 3000);
                } else {
                    $("#speed").selectmenu(this.id)
                }
            });
        })
    </script>
    <script type="text/javascript" src="jquery.mobile-1.3.1.js"></script>
    <style type="text/css">
        [data-role=fieldcontain], .ui-grid-b { margin: 10px; }
    </style>
</head>
<body>
    <div id="page1" data-role="page" data-theme="b">
        <div data-role="header">
            <h1>Jacqui's Shop</h1>
        </div>
        <form method="get">
            <div class="ui-grid-b">
                <div class="ui-block-a">
                    <button id="open">Open</button>
                </div>
                <div class="ui-block-b">
                    <button id="enable">Enable</button>
                </div>
                <div class="ui-block-c">
                    <button id="disable">Disable</button>
                </div>
            </div>
            <div data-role="fieldcontain">
                <label for="speed"><span>Speed: </span></label>
                <select id="speed" name="speed"
                        data-native-menu="false" data-overlay-theme="e">
```

867

```
                    <option value="placeholder"
                        data-placeholder="true">Select a Speed</option>
                    <option value="vfast">Very Fast</option>
                    <option value="fast">Fast</option>
                    <option value="normal">Normal</option>
                    <option value="slow">Slow</option>
                </select>
            </div>
        </form>
    </div>
</body>
</html>
```

I have defined three buttons that call the open, enable and disable methods. When I call the open method, I also use the setTimeout function to call the close method after three seconds.

Using the Selectmenu Events

The selectmenu widget defines only the create event, which is triggered when the widget is applied to the underlying elements.

Using Flip Switches

If a select element contains only two option elements, you can elect to create a *flip switch* instead of a regular selectmenu widget. You create a flip switch by applying the data-role attribute to the select element with a value of slider, as shown in Listing 31-16.

Listing 31-16. Creating a Flip Switch

```
<!DOCTYPE html>
<html>
<head>
    <title>Example</title>
    <meta name="viewport" content="width=device-width, initial-scale=1">
    <link rel="stylesheet" href="jquery.mobile-1.3.1.css" type="text/css" />
    <script type="text/javascript" src="jquery-1.10.1.js"></script>
    <script type="text/javascript" src="jquery.mobile-1.3.1.js"></script>
    <style type="text/css">
        #buttonContainer {text-align: center}
        [data-role=fieldcontain] { margin: 10px; text-align: center }
    </style>
</head>
<body>
    <div id="page1" data-role="page" data-theme="b">
        <div data-role="header">
            <h1>Jacqui's Shop</h1>
        </div>
```

```
<form method="get">
    <div data-role="fieldcontain">
        <label for="speed"><span>Speed: </span></label>
        <select id="speed" name="speed" data-role="slider">
            <option value="fast">Fast</option>
            <option value="slow">Slow</option>
        </select>
    </div>
    <div data-role="fieldcontain">
        <label for="size"><span>Size: </span></label>
        <select id="size" name="size" data-role="slider">
            <option value="large">Large</option>
            <option value="small" selected>Small</option>
        </select>
    </div>
    <div id="buttonContainer">
        <input type="submit" data-inline="true" value="Submit"/>
    </div>
</form>
        </div>
    </body>
</html>
```

There are two flip switches in this example. You can see how they are displayed in the browser in Figure 31-14. The user can change the setting either by tapping or clicking on the exposed value or by dragging the slider into position.

Figure 31-14. *Using flip switches*

Using the Checkboxradio Widget

The checkboxradio widget is automatically applied to input elements whose type attribute is set to checkbox or radio.

Creating Check Boxes

The simplest way to create check boxes is to define an input element whose type is checkbox, followed by a label element, as shown in Listing 31-17.

Listing 31-17. Creating Simple Check Boxes

```
<!DOCTYPE html>
<html>
<head>
    <title>Example</title>
    <meta name="viewport" content="width=device-width, initial-scale=1">
    <link rel="stylesheet" href="jquery.mobile-1.3.1.css" type="text/css" />
    <script type="text/javascript" src="jquery-1.10.1.js"></script>
    <script type="text/javascript" src="jquery.mobile-1.3.1.js"></script>
    <style type="text/css">
        #buttonContainer {text-align: center}
        form { margin: 10px; }
    </style>
</head>
<body>
    <div id="page1" data-role="page" data-theme="b">
        <div data-role="header">
            <h1>Jacqui's Shop</h1>
        </div>
        <form method="get">
            <div data-role="fieldcontain">
                <label for="name">Name: </label>
                <input id="name" placeholder="Your Name">
            </div>

            <input type="checkbox" name="check" id="check"/>
            <label for="check">I agree</label>

            <div id="buttonContainer">
                <input type="submit" data-inline="true" value="Submit"/>
            </div>
        </form>
    </div>
</body>
</html>
```

You can see how this check box is presented in Figure 31-15. I have shown the checked and unchecked state of the check box in the figure.

Figure 31-15. A jQuery Mobile check box

870

Applying a Label to a Check Box

By default, check boxes span the entire width of their parent element, which means, in this case, that the check box is the entire width of the screen. You need to use a particular element structure if you want to make the check box fit into the layout so that it matches the textinput widget above it, as shown in Listing 31-18.

Listing 31-18. Changing the Layout of a Check Box

```
<!DOCTYPE html>
<html>
<head>
    <title>Example</title>
    <meta name="viewport" content="width=device-width, initial-scale=1">
    <link rel="stylesheet" href="jquery.mobile-1.3.1.css" type="text/css" />
    <script type="text/javascript" src="jquery-1.10.1.js"></script>
    <script type="text/javascript" src="jquery.mobile-1.3.1.js"></script>
    <style type="text/css">
        #buttonContainer {text-align: center}
        form { margin: 10px; }
    </style>
</head>
<body>
    <div id="page1" data-role="page" data-theme="b">
        <div data-role="header">
            <h1>Jacqui's Shop</h1>
        </div>
        <form method="get">
            <div data-role="fieldcontain">
                <label for="name">Name: </label>
                <input id="name" placeholder="Your Name">
            </div>

            <div data-role="fieldcontain">
                <fieldset data-role="controlgroup">
                    <legend>Terms & Conditions:</legend>
                    <input type="checkbox" name="check" id="check"/>
                    <label for="check">I agree</label>
                </fieldset>
            </div>

            <div id="buttonContainer">
                <input type="submit" data-inline="true" value="Submit"/>
            </div>
        </form>
    </div>
</body>
</html>
```

The outer element should be familiar by now—a div element with the data-role attribute set to fieldcontain. The problem that jQuery Mobile faces is that there is already a label element associated with the input element, so you have to take an alternative path to give jQuery Mobile the information it needs. You do this by adding a fieldset element whose data-role is set to controlgroup and adding a legend element before the input, containing the text you want displayed. You can see the effect in Figure 31-16.

Figure 31-16. *Changing the layout of a check box*

Grouping Check Boxes

You can use a fieldset element with a data-role of controlgroup to group multiple check boxes together. Listing 31-19 contains a demonstration.

Listing 31-19. Grouping Check Boxes Together

```
<!DOCTYPE html>
<html>
<head>
    <title>Example</title>
    <meta name="viewport" content="width=device-width, initial-scale=1">
    <link rel="stylesheet" href="jquery.mobile-1.3.1.css" type="text/css" />
    <script type="text/javascript" src="jquery-1.10.1.js"></script>
    <script type="text/javascript" src="jquery.mobile-1.3.1.js"></script>
    <style type="text/css">
        #buttonContainer {text-align: center}
        form { margin: 10px; }
    </style>
</head>
<body>
    <div id="page1" data-role="page" data-theme="b">
        <div data-role="header">
            <h1>Jacqui's Shop</h1>
        </div>
```

```
<form method="get">
    <div data-role="fieldcontain">
        <label for="name">Name: </label>
        <input id="name" placeholder="Your Name">
    </div>

    <div data-role="fieldcontain">
        <fieldset data-role="controlgroup">
            <legend>Choose Your Flowers:</legend>
            <input type="checkbox" name="roses" id="roses"/>
            <label for="roses">Roses</label>
            <input type="checkbox" name="orchids" id="orchids"/>
            <label for="orchids">Orchids</label>
            <input type="checkbox" name="asters" id="asters"/>
            <label for="asters">Asters</label>
        </fieldset>
    </div>

    <div data-role="fieldcontain">
        <fieldset data-role="controlgroup" data-type="horizontal">
            <legend>Font:</legend>
            <input type="checkbox" name="bold" id="bold"/>
            <label for="bold"><b>b</b></label>
            <input type="checkbox" name="italic" id="italic"/>
            <label for="italic"><em>i</em></label>
            <input type="checkbox" name="underline" id="underline"/>
            <label for="underline"><u>u</u></label>
        </fieldset>
    </div>

    <div id="buttonContainer">
        <input type="submit" data-inline="true" value="Submit"/>
    </div>
</form>
    </div>
</body>
</html>
```

There are two groups of check boxes in this example. The first set is laid out vertically, which is the default orientation. jQuery Mobile changes the style of the widgets so that there is no space between the individual input elements and only the outer corners of the block are rounded. For the second set, I set the data-type attribute to horizontal, which changes the direction of the layout and causes jQuery Mobile to hide the check box, creating a set of buttons that can be toggled on and off. You can see the result in Figure 31-17.

Figure 31-17. *Grouping check boxes*

Creating and Formatting Radio Buttons

You create radio buttons and format them in much the same way as you format check boxes. Listing 31-20 contains an example.

Listing 31-20. Creating a Group of Radio Buttons

```
<!DOCTYPE html>
<html>
<head>
    <title>Example</title>
    <meta name="viewport" content="width=device-width, initial-scale=1">
    <link rel="stylesheet" href="jquery.mobile-1.3.1.css" type="text/css" />
    <script type="text/javascript" src="jquery-1.10.1.js"></script>
    <script type="text/javascript" src="jquery.mobile-1.3.1.js"></script>
    <style type="text/css">
        #buttonContainer {text-align: center}
        form { margin: 10px; }
    </style>
</head>
<body>
    <div id="page1" data-role="page" data-theme="b">
        <div data-role="header">
            <h1>Jacqui's Shop</h1>
        </div>
```

```
<form method="get">
    <div data-role="fieldcontain">
        <label for="name">Name: </label>
        <input id="name" placeholder="Your Name">
    </div>

    <div data-role="fieldcontain">
        <fieldset data-role="controlgroup">
            <legend>Choose Your Flowers:</legend>
            <input type="radio" name="flowers" id="roses"/>
            <label for="roses">Roses</label>
            <input type="radio" name="flowers" id="orchids"/>
            <label for="orchids">Orchids</label>
            <input type="radio" name="flowers" id="asters"/>
            <label for="asters">Asters</label>
        </fieldset>
    </div>

    <div data-role="fieldcontain">
        <fieldset data-role="controlgroup" data-type="horizontal">
            <legend>Choose Your Flowers:</legend>
            <input type="radio" name="flowers" id="roses"/>
            <label for="roses">Roses</label>
            <input type="radio" name="flowers" id="orchids"/>
            <label for="orchids">Orchids</label>
            <input type="radio" name="flowers" id="asters"/>
            <label for="asters">Asters</label>
        </fieldset>
    </div>

    <div id="buttonContainer">
        <input type="submit" data-inline="true" value="Submit"/>
    </div>
</form>
    </div>
</body>
</html>
```

Once again, I created horizontal and vertical groups, and you can see how they are displayed in the browser in Figure 31-18.

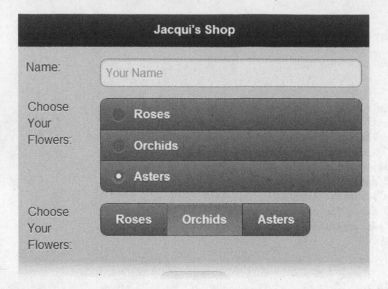

Figure 31-18. *Creating groups of radio buttons*

Configuring the Checkboxradio Widget

The checkboxradio widget supports only one configuration option, which I have described in Table 31-10.

Table 31-10. *Attribute and Configuration Setting for checkboxradio Widgets*

Data Attribute	Setting	Description
data-mini	mini	When set to true, the widget is created in a compact form.

Using the Checkboxradio Methods

The checkboxradio widget defines the methods shown in Table 31-11.

Table 31-11. *Methods for the checkboxradio Widget*

Method	Description
checkboxradio("disable")	Disables the widget so that values cannot be selected.
checkboxradio("enable")	Enables the widget so that values can be selected.
checkboxradio("refresh")	Refreshes the widget to incorporate changes in the underlying elements.

Using the Checkboxradio Events

The checkboxradio widget defines only the create event, which is triggered when the widget is applied to the underlying elements.

Summary

In this chapter, I showed how jQuery Mobile enhances form elements to make them consistent with the broader touch-enabled style. You don't have to take any special action to submit a form, which is done automatically using Ajax so that jQuery Mobile can smoothly manage the transition to the page returned by the server. You can rely on jQuery Mobile to automatically enhance form elements, but there are some good reasons to apply some additional elements and data-role attributes, especially when it comes to dealing with select elements. In Chapter 32, I continue my description of jQuery Mobile widgets, turning to the listview and panel widgets.

■ ■ ■

Using Lists and Panels

In this chapter, I describe the jQuery Mobile list and panel widgets. Lists are an important tool in building mobile web applications, and they often provide simple and obvious navigation around the different functional areas of a web application. The beauty of lists is that they are compact, even when the individual list items are large enough to be selected by touch. They are also extremely well understood by users. Simply placing an arrow icon at the right edge of a list item (which jQuery Mobile does by default) makes it clear to most users that selecting the item will cause some kind of selection or navigation to occur.

Panels are a general-purpose widget that brings content into context on the left or right side of the window. Panels can be used to display any content, but are most frequently used for settings or navigation features that are persistent throughout the application. Table 32-1 provides the summary for this chapter.

Table 32-1. *Chapter Summary*

Problem	Solution	Listing
Create a list.	Define a ul or ol element that contains one or more li elements and has the data-role attribute set to listview. The contents of the li elements should be links.	1
Create an inset list.	Set the data-inset attribute to true.	2
Create a list whose items are made of two distinct parts.	Add a second link to each li element.	3
Allow the user to filter the contents of the list.	Set the data-filter attribute to true.	4, 5
Add dividers to a list.	Set the data-role attribute to list-divider on individual li elements.	6
Add a count bubble to a list item.	Use the ui-li-count class.	7
Use different text emphasis.	Use the h1-h6 and p elements.	8
Add an aside to a list item.	Use the ui-li-aside class.	9
Create a panel.	Set the data-role attribute to panel on a div element contained within the page to which the panel relates.	10
Set the position and the display style of a panel.	Use the data-display and data-position attributes.	11
Specify how a panel can be dismissed.	Use the data-swipe-close and data-dismissable attributes.	12

Using the ListView Widget

jQuery Mobile provides flexible support for handling lists through the listview widget. Listing 32-1 shows a basic list that links to jQuery Mobile pages inside the same document. Each page describes a different flower, and the list provides the user with a mechanism to navigate to these pages.

Listing 32-1. A Basic List

```html
<!DOCTYPE html>
<html>
<head>
    <title>Example</title>
    <meta name="viewport" content="width=device-width, initial-scale=1">
    <link rel="stylesheet" href="jquery.mobile-1.3.1.css" type="text/css" />
    <script type="text/javascript" src="jquery-1.10.1.js"></script>
    <script type="text/javascript" src="jquery.mobile-1.3.1.js"></script>
    <style type="text/css">
        .lcontainer {float: left; text-align: center; padding-top: 10px}
        .productData {float: right; padding: 10px; width: 60%}
    </style>
</head>
<body>
    <div id="page1" data-role="page" data-theme="b">
        <div data-role="header">
            <h1>Jacqui's Shop</h1>
        </div>

        <ul data-role="listview">
            <li><a href="#roses">Roses</a></li>
            <li><a href="#orchids">Orchids</a></li>
            <li><a href="#asters">Asters</a></li>
        </ul>
    </div>

  <div id="roses" data-role="page" data-theme="b">
        <div data-role="header">
            <h1>Roses</h1>
        </div>
        <div>
            <div class="lcontainer">
                <img src="rose.png">
                <div><a href="#" data-rel="back" data-role="button"
                        data-inline=true data-direction="reverse">Back</a>
                </div>
            </div>
            <div class="productData">
                A rose is a woody perennial within the family Rosaceae.
                They form a group of erect shrubs, and climbing or trailing plants.
                <div><b>Price: $4.99</b></div>
            </div>
        </div>
    </div>
```

```
<div id="orchids" data-role="page" data-theme="b">
    <div data-role="header">
        <h1>Orchids</h1>
    </div>
    <div>
        <div class="lcontainer">
            <img src="orchid.png">
            <div><a href="#" data-rel="back" data-role="button"
                    data-inline=true data-direction="reverse">Back</a>
            </div>
        </div>
        <div class="productData">
            The orchid family is a diverse and widespread family in the order
            Asparagales. It is one of the largest families of flowering plants.
            <div><b>Price: $10.99</b></div>
        </div>
    </div>
</div>

<div id="asters" data-role="page" data-theme="b">
    <div data-role="header">
        <h1>Asters</h1>
    </div>
    <div>
        <div class="lcontainer">
            <img src="aster.png">
            <div><a href="#" data-rel="back" data-role="button"
                    data-inline=true data-direction="reverse">Back</a>
            </div>
        </div>
        <div class="productData">
            The name Aster comes from the Ancient Greek word meaning "star",
            referring to the shape of the flower head.
            <div><b>Price: $2.99</b></div>
        </div>
    </div>
</div>
</body>
</html>
```

Most of this document is given over to the pages that describe the flowers. The actual list is just a few elements, as follows:

```
...
<ul data-role="listview">
    <li><a href="#roses">Roses</a></li>
    <li><a href="#orchids">Orchids</a></li>
    <li><a href="#asters">Asters</a></li>
</ul>
...
```

■ **Tip**   I used the ul element in this example, but jQuery Mobile treats numbered lists (created with the ol element) in just the same way.

This is a standard HTML unnumbered list, expressed using the ul element, which contains three li elements. To apply the listview widget, I set the data-role attribute on the ul element to listview.

The basic use for a list widget is to provide navigation, and to this end, the content of each li element is an a element that links to one of the other pages in the document. Clicking or tapping the individual list items takes the user to the appropriate page. You can see the listview widget and one of the content pages in Figure 32-1. I added a link-based button to each content page that takes the user back to the list, using the standard transition (but in reverse).

Figure 32-1. *A simple jQuery Mobile listview widget*

Configuring the Listview Widget

The listview widget supports a number of data attributes and configuration settings that can be used to change the appearance and behavior of the list. These are described in Table 32-2 and demonstrated in the sections that follow.

Table 32-2. *Attributes and Configuration Settings for Listview Widgets*

Data Attribute	Setting	Description
data-count-theme	countTheme	Specifies the theme for count bubbles.
data-divider-theme	dividerTheme	Specifies the theme for dividers.
data-filter	filter	When set to true, the listview is shown with a filter.
N/A	filterCallback	Specifies a function that is invoked by the filter.
data-filter-placeholder	filterPlaceholder	Specifies a placeholder for filtering.
data-filter-theme	filterTheme	Specifies the theme for the filter search bar.
data-header-theme	headerTheme	Specifies the theme for nested headers.
data-icon	icon	Specifies the icon used on headers.
data-inset	inset	When set to true, the listview is drawn in a style that suits nested lists.
data-split-icon	splitIcon	Specifies the icon for a split list.
data-split-theme	splitTheme	Specifies the theme for a split list.

Creating Inset Lists

The default layout for lists is to fill the width of the container element and to have square corners, which doesn't match the style of other jQuery Mobile widgets. To make the style consistent, you can create an inset list, which has rounded corners and can be used in elements that do not touch the edges of the screen. You create an inset list by applying the data-inset attribute with a value of true to the ul or ol element, as shown in Listing 32-2.

Listing 32-2. Creating an Inset List

```
...
<div id="page1" data-role="page" data-theme="b">
    <div data-role="header">
        <h1>Jacqui's Shop</h1>
    </div>

    <div id="container" style="padding: 20px">
        <ul data-role="listview" data-inset=true>
            <li><a href="#roses">Roses</a></li>
            <li><a href="#orchids">Orchids</a></li>
            <li><a href="#asters">Asters</a></li>
        </ul>
    </div>
</div>
...
```

In this example, I placed the ul element inside a div element. I used the CSS padding setting to inset the list from the edge of the parent element, and I used the data-inset attribute to change the style of the list. You can see the result in Figure 32-2.

Figure 32-2. *Creating an inset list*

Creating Split Lists

Split lists are useful when there are two actions that can be performed for each item in the list. The list item is split into two sections, and clicking or tapping on each part of the item leads to a different action. Listing 32-3 shows a split list that allows users to get information about a flower or simply add it to their shopping basket.

Listing 32-3. Using a Split List

```
<!DOCTYPE html>
<html>
<head>
    <title>Example</title>
    <meta name="viewport" content="width=device-width, initial-scale=1">
    <link rel="stylesheet" href="jquery.mobile-1.3.1.css" type="text/css" />
    <script type="text/javascript" src="jquery-1.10.1.js"></script>
    <script type="text/javascript" src="jquery.mobile-1.3.1.js"></script>
    <style type="text/css">
        .lcontainer {float: left; text-align: center; padding-top: 10px}
        .productData {float: right; padding: 10px; width: 60%}
        .cWrapper {text-align: center; margin: 20px}
    </style>
</head>
<body>
    <div id="page1" data-role="page" data-theme="b">
        <div data-role="header">
            <h1>Jacqui's Shop</h1>
        </div>

        <div id="container" style="padding: 20px">
            <ul data-role="listview" data-inset=true>
                <li><a href="#basket" class="buy" id="rose">Roses</a>
                    <a href="#roses">Roses</a></li>
                <li><a href="#basket" class="buy" id="orchid">Orchids</a>
                    <a href="#orchids">Orchids</a>   </li>
                <li><a href="#basket" class="buy" id="aster">Asters</a>
                    <a href="#asters">Asters</a>   </li>
            </ul>
        </div>
    </div>

    <div id="basket" data-role="page" data-theme="b">
        <div data-role="header">
            <h1>Jacqui's Shop</h1>
        </div>
        <div class="cWrapper">
            Basket will go here
        </div>
        <div class="cWrapper">
            <a href="#" data-rel="back" data-role="button" data-inline=true
                data-direction="reverse">Back</a>
        </div>
    </div>

    <div id="roses" data-role="page" data-theme="b">
        <div data-role="header">
            <h1>Roses</h1>
        </div>
        <div>
            <div class="lcontainer">
```

```
            <img src="rose.png">
            <div><a href="#" data-rel="back" data-role="button"
                    data-inline=true data-direction="reverse">Back</a>
            </div>
        </div>
        <div class="productData">
            A rose is a woody perennial within the family Rosaceae.
            They form a group of erect shrubs, and climbing or trailing plants.
            <div><b>Price: $4.99</b></div>
        </div>
    </div>
</div>

<div id="orchids" data-role="page" data-theme="b">
    <div data-role="header">
        <h1>Orchids</h1>
    </div>
    <div>
        <div class="lcontainer">
            <img src="orchid.png">
            <div><a href="#" data-rel="back" data-role="button"
                    data-inline=true data-direction="reverse">Back</a>
            </div>
        </div>
        <div class="productData">
            The orchid family is a diverse and widespread family in the order
            Asparagales. It is one of the largest families of flowering plants.
            <div><b>Price: $10.99</b></div>
        </div>
    </div>
</div>

<div id="asters" data-role="page" data-theme="b">
    <div data-role="header">
        <h1>Asters</h1>
    </div>
    <div>
        <div class="lcontainer">
            <img src="aster.png">
            <div><a href="#" data-rel="back" data-role="button"
                    data-inline=true data-direction="reverse">Back</a>
            </div>
        </div>
        <div class="productData">
            The name Aster comes from the Ancient Greek word meaning "star",
            referring to the shape of the flower head.
            <div><b>Price: $2.99</b></div>
        </div>
    </div>
</div>
</body>
</html>
```

To create a split list, add a second a element to the li elements. jQuery Mobile splits each list item in two and inserts a vertical divider between the parts. Clicking or tapping the left part of the item navigates to the target of the first a element, and clicking or tapping on the right part navigates to the second a element. You can see how the list items are presented in Figure 32-3.

Figure 32-3. *Creating split lists*

In this example, I set all of the left parts of the list items to point to a new page I added to the document called basket. I'll come back to this example in Chapter 33 and expand on it to put a simple shopping basket in place. For this example, the basket page is simply a placeholder.

■ **Tip**   jQuery Mobile uses the arrow icon for the split button by default. You can change this by applying the data-split-icon attribute to the ul or ol element, specifying the name of the icon you want. Chapter 30 contains a list of the available icons.

Filtering Lists

The listview widget provides a mechanism for filtering the content of lists, which is enabled by applying the data-filter attribute with a value of true to the ul or ol element, as shown in Listing 32-4.

Listing 32-4. Using List Filtering

```
<!DOCTYPE html>
<html>
<head>
    <title>Example</title>
    <meta name="viewport" content="width=device-width, initial-scale=1">
    <link rel="stylesheet" href="jquery.mobile-1.3.1.css" type="text/css" />
    <script type="text/javascript" src="jquery-1.10.1.js"></script>
    <script type="text/javascript" src="jquery.mobile-1.3.1.js"></script>
    <style type="text/css">
        .lcontainer {float: left; text-align: center; padding-top: 10px}
        .productData {float: right; padding: 10px; width: 60%}
    </style>
</head>
```

```
<body>
    <div id="page1" data-role="page" data-theme="b">
        <div data-role="header">
            <h1>Jacqui's Shop</h1>
        </div>

        <div data-role="content">
            <ul data-role="listview" data-inset=true data-filter=true>
                <li><a href="#roses">Roses</a></li>
                <li><a href="#orchids">Orchids</a></li>
                <li><a href="#asters">Asters</a></li>
            </ul>
        </div>
    </div>

    <div id="roses" data-role="page" data-theme="b">
        <div data-role="header">
            <h1>Roses</h1>
        </div>
        <div>
            <div class="lcontainer">
                <img src="rose.png">
                <div><a href="#" data-rel="back" data-role="button"
                        data-inline=true data-direction="reverse">Back</a>
                </div>
            </div>
            <div class="productData">
                A rose is a woody perennial within the family Rosaceae.
                They form a group of erect shrubs, and climbing or trailing plants.
                <div><b>Price: $4.99</b></div>
            </div>
        </div>
    </div>

    <div id="orchids" data-role="page" data-theme="b">
        <div data-role="header">
            <h1>Orchids</h1>
        </div>
        <div>
            <div class="lcontainer">
                <img src="orchid.png">
                <div><a href="#" data-rel="back" data-role="button"
                        data-inline=true data-direction="reverse">Back</a>
                </div>
            </div>
            <div class="productData">
                The orchid family is a diverse and widespread family in the order
                Asparagales. It is one of the largest families of flowering plants.
                <div><b>Price: $10.99</b></div>
            </div>
        </div>
    </div>
```

```
<div id="asters" data-role="page" data-theme="b">
    <div data-role="header">
        <h1>Asters</h1>
    </div>
    <div>
        <div class="lcontainer">
            <img src="aster.png">
            <div><a href="#" data-rel="back" data-role="button"
                data-inline=true data-direction="reverse">Back</a>
            </div>
        </div>
        <div class="productData">
            The name Aster comes from the Ancient Greek word meaning "star",
            referring to the shape of the flower head.
            <div><b>Price: $2.99</b></div>
        </div>
    </div>
</div>
</body>
</html>
```

As you can see in Figure 32-4, jQuery Mobile adds a search bar above the list. When the user enters characters into the search bar, jQuery Mobile removes all of the items from the list that don't contain that sequence of characters. (By default, filtering isn't performed until at least two characters have been entered into the filter.)

Figure 32-4. *Enabling list filtering*

■ **Caution** The ability to filter lists is a great feature, but it isn't always useful on small touch screens. To support character input, most mobile devices show a popup touch keyboard when the user activates a text input element such as the search bar. On small devices, the keyboard can occupy so much of the screen that the user can't easily see the results of the filter. This does not mean you should not support list filtering, but it is important to provide other navigation mechanisms if you are targeting devices with small screens.

Using a Custom Filtering Function

The default filter matches any list item that contains the set of characters the user has entered. These are matched anywhere in the list item text and are case insensitive. You can provide a custom filter function by using a jQuery UI-style method, as shown in Listing 32-5.

Listing 32-5. Using a Custom List Filter Function

```
...
<head>
    <title>Example</title>
    <meta name="viewport" content="width=device-width, initial-scale=1">
    <link rel="stylesheet" href="jquery.mobile-1.3.1.css" type="text/css" />
    <script type="text/javascript" src="jquery-1.10.1.js"></script>
    <script type="text/javascript">
        $(document).bind("pageinit", function () {
            $("ul").listview("option", "filterCallback", function (listItem, filter) {
                var pattern = new RegExp("^" + filter, "i");
                return !pattern.test(listItem)
            })
        })
    </script>
    <script type="text/javascript" src="jquery.mobile-1.3.1.js"></script>
    <style type="text/css">
        .lcontainer {float: left; text-align: center; padding-top: 10px}
        .productData {float: right; padding: 10px; width: 60%}
    </style>
</head>
...
```

You set the custom function by calling the option method and using the function as the value for the filterCallback setting. The arguments to the function are the text from a list item and the filter that the user has entered. The function is called once for each item in the list, and if you return true, the item for which the function has been called is hidden. In this example, I use a regular expression to restrict matches to list items that begin with the filter text. You can see the result in Figure 32-5, where typing the letter R into the filter box matches only the Roses item.

Figure 32-5. Using a custom filter

Adding Dividers

The listview widget can add dividers between list items. These dividers are specified by elements whose data-role attribute is set to `list-divider,` and they can be styled by the use of the `data-divider-theme` attribute applied to the ul or ol element that defines the list.

List dividers are useful for providing structure to long or complex lists without changing the way that the user navigates through the list. In Listing 32-6, you can see how I have added some divider elements and applied the `data-divider-theme` attribute to the example.

Listing 32-6. Using List Dividers

```
...
<div id="page1" data-role="page" data-theme="b">
    <div data-role="header">
        <h1>Jacqui's Shop</h1>
    </div>

    <div data-role="content">
        <ul data-role="listview" data-inset=true data-theme="c"
            data-divider-theme="b">

            <li data-role="list-divider">A</li>
            <li><a href="#asters">Asters</a></li>
            <li data-role="list-divider">C</li>
            <li><a href="document2.html">Carnations</a></li>
            <li data-role="list-divider">D</li>
            <li><a href="document2.html">Daffodils</a></li>
            <li data-role="list-divider">L</li>
            <li><a href="document2.html">Lilies</a></li>
            <li data-role="list-divider">O</li>
            <li><a href="#orchids">Orchids</a></li>
            <li data-role="list-divider">P</li>
            <li><a href="document2.html">Peonies</a></li>
            <li><a href="document2.html">Primulas</a></li>
            <li data-role="list-divider">R</li>
            <li><a href="#roses">Roses</a></li>
            <li data-role="list-divider">S</li>
            <li><a href="document2.html">Snowdrops</a></li>
        </ul>
    </div>
</div>
...
```

You can see the effect that the dividers create in Figure 32-6.

Figure 32-6. *Adding dividers to a list*

■ **Tip** You can apply the `data-theme` attribute directly to individual list items if you want a different appearance for just one element.

Using Convention-Based Configuration

Some configuration options are handled by convention rather than configuration. You already saw an example of this when you looked at split lists. If you add a second a element to the content of an li element, jQuery Mobile automatically creates a split list item. You don't have to apply a data attribute to create this effect – it just happens. In this section, I show you three different conventions you can use to format list items: count bubbles, text emphasis, and asides.

Adding Count Bubbles

You can add a small numeric indicator to a list item. These are called *count bubbles*, and they can be useful when list items represent a category of some sort and you want to provide information about how many are available. For example, if your list items represent e-mail folders, you can use count bubbles to indicate how many messages are in each folder. You might also use count bubbles to show how many items are in stock in an e-commerce application.

Although this effect is typically used to present numeric values, you can display any information you like. The meaning of the value needs to be self-evident, because you don't have room to provide an explanation to the user – just the value.

You create a count bubble by adding an additional child element to the contents of an li element. This child element must contain the value and be assigned to the `ui-li-count` class. You can see examples of count bubbles defined in Listing 32-7, including one that uses a nonnumeric value.

Listing 32-7. *Adding Count Bubbles to List Items*

```
...
<div id="page1" data-role="page" data-theme="b">
    <div data-role="header">
        <h1>Jacqui's Shop</h1>
    </div>
```

```
        <div data-role="content">
            <ul data-role="listview" data-inset=true data-filter=true>
                <li><a href="#roses">Roses<div class="ui-li-count">23</div></a></li>
                <li><div class="ui-li-count">7</div><a href="#orchids">Orchids</a></li>
                <li><a href="#asters">Asters</a><div class="ui-li-count">Pink</div></li>
            </ul>
        </div>
</div>
...
```

Notice that you can position the child element anywhere within the li element. It doesn't have to be the last element (although this is a common convention). You can see how the count bubbles are displayed in Figure 32-7.

Figure 32-7. *Using counter bubbles*

Adding Text Emphasis

The listview widget will apply different levels of emphasis when you use content that is wrapped in a header element (the h1 through h6 elements) instead of a p element (indicating a paragraph). This allows you to create a list item that contains a headline and some supporting details text, as shown in Listing 32-8.

Listing 32-8. Adding Text Emphasis

```
...
<div id="page1" data-role="page" data-theme="b">
    <div data-role="header">
        <h1>Jacqui's Shop</h1>
    </div>

    <div data-role="content">
        <ul data-role="listview" data-inset=true data-filter=true>
            <li>
                <a href="#roses"><h1>Roses</h1>
                    <p>A rose is a woody perennial within the family Rosaceae.</p>
                    <div class="ui-li-count">$4.99</div></a>
            </li>
```

```
        <li><div class="ui-li-count">7</div><a href="#orchids">Orchids</a></li>
        <li><a href="#asters">Asters</a><div class="ui-li-count">Pink</div></li>
    </ul>
  </div>
</div>
...
```

In this example, I used the h1 element to denote the name of the product and the p element to denote the detailed information. I included a count bubble, indicating the price of the item. (Prices are ideally suited to count bubbles because the currency symbol provides immediate meaning to the numeric value.) You can see the effect in Figure 32-8.

Figure 32-8. *Using text emphasis in a list item*

Adding an Aside

An *aside* is an alternative to using count bubbles. To create an aside, you add a child to the li element that contains the information you want to display and that is assigned to the ui-li-aside class. You can see the use of an aside in Listing 32-9.

Listing 32-9. Creating an Aside in a List Item

```
...
<div id="page1" data-role="page" data-theme="b">
    <div data-role="header">
        <h1>Jacqui's Shop</h1>
    </div>

    <div data-role="content">
      <ul data-role="listview" data-inset=true data-filter=true>
        <li>
          <a href="#roses">
              <h1>Roses</h1>
              <p>A rose is a woody perennial within the family Rosaceae.</p>
              <p class="ui-li-aside">(Pink) <strong>$4.99</strong></p>
          </a></li>
```

```
        <li><div class="ui-li-count">7</div><a href="#orchids">Orchids</a></li>
        <li><a href="#asters">Asters</a><div class="ui-li-count">Pink</div></li>
    </ul>
  </div>
</div>
...
```

You can see the style with which an aside is displayed for the Roses item in Figure 32-9.

Figure 32-9. *Using an aside*

Using the Listview Methods

The listview widget defines the two methods shown in Table 32-3.

Table 32-3. *Listview Methods*

Method	Description
listview("refresh")	Updates the listview widget to reflect changes in the underlying elements.

Using the Listview Events

The listview widget defines only the create event, which is triggered when the widget is applied to an element.

Using the Panel Widget

The panel widget appears to the left or right of the current page – you can use a panel to display any content, but the frequent uses are to provide access navigation options and application settings. Panels are created by setting the data-role attribute to panel on a div element, as shown in Listing 32-10.

Listing 32-10. Creating a Panel Widget

```
<!DOCTYPE html>
<html>
<head>
    <title>Example</title>
    <meta name="viewport" content="width=device-width, initial-scale=1">
    <link rel="stylesheet" href="jquery.mobile-1.3.1.css" type="text/css" />
    <script type="text/javascript" src="jquery-1.10.1.js"></script>
    <script type="text/javascript" src="jquery.mobile-1.3.1.js"></script>
    <style>
        .buttonContainer { text-align: center; }
    </style>
</head>
<body>

    <div id="page1" data-role="page" data-theme="b">
        <div data-role="header">
            <h1>Jacqui's Shop</h1>
        </div>

        <div data-role="content" class="buttonContainer">
            <a data-role="button" data-inline="true" href="#panel">Open Panel</a>
        </div>

        <div id="panel" data-role="panel" data-theme="a">
            <div data-role="panel-content">
                <h3>Simple Panel</h3>
                <p>This is the the panel</p>
                <button data-rel="close" data-inline="true">Close</button>
            </div>
        </div>
    </div>
</body>
</html>
```

The elements for the panel widget are defined within the page that will show the panel. In the example, I have defined a panel that contains some simple HTML elements, wrapped in a div element whose data-role attribute I have set as panel-content, which ensures that the content is positioned properly within the panel.

The main page in this example contains an a element whose href element specifies the id of the panel element. Clicking the link – or the button since I have set the data-role attribute to button on the a element – opens the panel. You can see the effect in Figure 32-10.

Figure 32-10. *Using the popup widget*

This is an example that you need to experience firsthand to properly appreciate, but clicking on the Open Panel button slides the main page to the right to reveal the panel. I can close the panel by clicking on the Close button in the panel (which I configured by setting the data-rel attribute to close) or by clicking in the part of the main page that remains visible.

Configuring the Panel Widget

The panel widget defines the data attributes and configuration settings shown in Table 32-4.

Table 32-4. *Attributes and Configuration Settings for Panel Widgets*

Data Attribute	Setting	Description
data-animate	animate	Specifies whether the panel will be animated when it is opened or closed. The default is true.
data-dismissable	dismissable	Specifies whether the panel can be closed by tapping the page that opened it. The default is true.
data-display	display	Specifies the relationship between the panel and the page. The values are reveal, push, and overlay and are described below
data-position	position	Specifies where the panel is shown. The values are left and right. The default is left.
data-position-fixed	positionFixed	Specifies whether the contents of the panel will remain visible even if the user scrolls down the page. The default is false.
data-swipe-close	swipeClose	Specifies whether the panel can be closed by swiping it. The default is true.

Positioning and Displaying the Panel

The data-display and data-position attributes determine where the panel is displayed (the left or right side of the window) and how it is displayed relative to the page that opened it. There are three values for the data-display attribute, which I have described in Table 32-5.

Table 32-5. *Values for the data-display Attribute*

Value	Description
reveal	The default value: the panel pushes the page out of the way.
push	The page is resized to share space with the panel.
overlay	The panel slides over the page.

In Listing 32-11, you can see how the effect of both settings, demonstrating all of the permutations of display and position options.

Listing 32-11. Positioning the Panel

```
<!DOCTYPE html>
<html>
<head>
    <title>Example</title>
    <meta name="viewport" content="width=device-width, initial-scale=1">
    <link rel="stylesheet" href="jquery.mobile-1.3.1.css" type="text/css" />
    <script type="text/javascript" src="jquery-1.10.1.js"></script>
    <script type="text/javascript" src="jquery.mobile-1.3.1.js"></script>
    <script>
        $(document).bind("pageinit", function () {
            $("#pageContent button").tap(function (e) {
                $("#" + this.id + "Panel").panel({
                    display: $("input[type=radio]:checked").attr("id")
                }).panel("open");
            });
        });
    </script>
</head>
<body>
    <div id="page1" data-role="page" data-theme="b">
        <div data-role="header">
            <h1>Jacqui's Shop</h1>
        </div>

        <div id="pageContent" data-role="content">
            <div class="ui-grid-a">
                <div class="ui-block-a"><button id="left">Left</button></div>
                <div class="ui-block-b"><button id="right">Right</button></div>
            </div>

            <div data-role="fieldcontain">
                <fieldset data-role="controlgroup" data-type="horizontal">
                    <input type="radio" name="display" id="reveal" checked="checked"/>
                    <label for="reveal">Reveal</label>
                    <input type="radio" name="display" id="push"/>
                    <label for="push">Push</label>
```

```
                <input type="radio" name="display" id="overlay"/>
                <label for="overlay">Overlay</label>
            </fieldset>
        </div>
    </div>

    <div id="leftPanel" data-role="panel" data-theme="a" data-position="left">
        <div data-role="panel-content">
            <h3>Left Panel</h3>
            <p>This is the the left panel</p>
            <button data-rel="close" data-inline="true">Close</button>
        </div>
    </div>

    <div id="rightPanel" data-role="panel" data-theme="a" data-position="right">
        <div data-role="panel-content">
            <h3>Right Panel</h3>
            <p>This is the the right panel</p>
            <button data-rel="close" data-inline="true">Close</button>
        </div>
    </div>
    </div>
</body>
</html>
```

I use a pair of buttons to open left and right panels (using the open method, which I describe later in this chapter) and a set of radio buttons (as described in Chapter 30) to select the display mode. You can see some of the permutations in Figure 32-11.

Figure 32-11. *Changing the display and position options*

The panel widget can't display the same elements to the left and the right of the window: the process for preparing the content aligns it one way or the other. It is for this reason that I have used two separate panels in this example.

Dismissing the Panel

The `data-swipe-close` and `data-dismissable` attributes allow you to control how the user can close the panel, either by making a swipe gesture or by tapping the page that opened the panel. Setting these attributes to `false` creates a panel that can only be closed when the user interacts with the panel content (or programmatically using the open or toggle methods, which I describe later in the chapter).

I am wary of taking control of widgets away from users and if you decide to use these attributes, then you should ensure that you do so consistently throughout your web app – having panels that are dismissed in different ways just causes frustration. In Listing 32-12, I have created a panel that is displayed for a fixed period and then dismisses itself – not something that I would recommend in a real application, but useful for demonstrating the widget features. The user can't dismiss the panel by tapping the page that opened it or by swiping, but the button can still be used to close the panel.

Listing 32-12. Creating Panels That Cannot Be Dismissed by Tapping the Page or Swiping

```
<!DOCTYPE html>
<html>
<head>
    <title>Example</title>
    <meta name="viewport" content="width=device-width, initial-scale=1">
    <link rel="stylesheet" href="jquery.mobile-1.3.1.css" type="text/css" />
    <script type="text/javascript" src="jquery-1.10.1.js"></script>
    <script>
        $(document).bind("pageinit", function () {
            $("a").tap(function (e) {
                var timeRemaining = 15;
                var intervalId = setInterval(function () {
                    $("#remaining").text(timeRemaining--);
                    if (timeRemaining == 0) {
                        $("#panel").panel("close");
                        clearInterval(intervalId);
                    }
                }, 1000);
                $("#panel").panel("open");
            });
        });
    </script>
    <script type="text/javascript" src="jquery.mobile-1.3.1.js"></script>
</head>
<body>
    <div id="page1" data-role="page" data-theme="b">
        <div data-role="header">
            <h1>Jacqui's Shop</h1>
        </div>

        <div data-role="content" class="buttonContainer">
            <a data-role="button" data-inline="true">Open Panel</a>
        </div>
```

```
            <div id="panel" data-role="panel" data-theme="a"
                    data-dismissable="false" data-swipe-close="false">
                <div data-role="panel-content">
                    <h3>Simple Panel</h3>
                    <p>This panel will close in
                        <span id="remaining">15</span> seconds.</p>
                    <button data-rel="close" data-inline="true">Close</button>
                </div>
            </div>
        </div>
    </body>
</html>
```

I use the open and close methods to control the visibility of the panel – I describe these methods properly in the next section – and use the JavaScript setInterval function to manage a countdown that closes the panel 15 seconds after it has been opened. The user can close the panel early by using the button element displayed in the panel – if you want to prevent the user from closing the panel, then you must ensure that the panel contains no such elements. The panel widget reflects changes in the underlying elements as they happen, as shown in Figure 32-12.

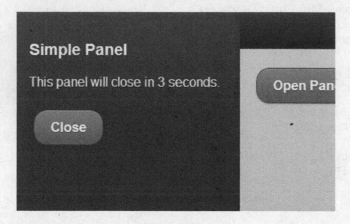

Figure 32-12. *A self-closing panel*

Using the Panel Methods

The panel widget defines the methods shown in Table 32-6. The open and close methods are demonstrated in the previous example.

Table 32-6. *Panel Methods*

Method	Description
panel("open")	Shows the panel.
panel("close")	Hides the panel.
panel("toggle")	Toggles the visibility of the panel: hidden panels are shown and visible panels are hidden.

Using the Panel Events

The panel widget defines the events shown in Table 32-7. I don't find these events useful in my own projects because I prefer to deal with the events from the elements that lead to the panel being shown or hidden.

Table 32-7. Panel Events

Event	Description
create	Triggered when the widget is created.
beforeopen	Triggered before the panel is shown.
beforeclose	Triggered before the panel is hidden.
open	Triggered after the panel is shown.
close	Triggered after the panel is hidden.

Summary

In this chapter, I described the jQuery Mobile list widget, which can be an essential navigation tool for mobile web applications. I showed you the different kinds of lists you can create, the different styles of list you can present to the user, and the configurations and conventions you can use to manage the content of individual list items.

■■■

Refactoring the Example: Part IV

In prior chapters in this part of the book, I introduced you to jQuery Mobile. In this chapter, I'll build a more complete example that uses the jQuery Mobile functionality. By its nature, jQuery Mobile is a lot simpler than jQuery UI, and there are a lot fewer design choices available. Your development efforts with jQuery Mobile are further constrained by the unique issues that face mobile device development.

Starting with the Basics

In Chapter 32, I showed you an example that used split lists. This example is the starting point for this chapter and I'll use it to build out some additional functionality. Listing 33-1 shows the initial example document for this chapter.

Listing 33-1. The Starting Point for This Chapter

```
<!DOCTYPE html>
<html>
<head>
    <title>Example</title>
    <meta name="viewport" content="width=device-width, initial-scale=1">
    <link rel="stylesheet" href="jquery.mobile-1.3.1.css" type="text/css" />
    <script type="text/javascript" src="jquery-1.10.1.js"></script>
    <script type="text/javascript" src="jquery.mobile-1.3.1.js"></script>
    <style type="text/css">
        .lcontainer {float: left; text-align: center; padding-top: 10px}
        .productData {float: right; padding: 10px; width: 60%}
        .cWrapper {text-align: center; margin: 20px}
    </style>
</head>
<body>
    <div id="page1" data-role="page" data-theme="b">
        <div data-role="header">
            <h1>Jacqui's Shop</h1>
        </div>

        <div id="container" style="padding: 20px">
            <ul data-role="listview" data-inset=true>
                <li><a href="#basket" class="buy" id="rose">Roses</a>
                    <a href="#roses">Roses</a></li>
                <li><a href="#basket" class="buy" id="orchid">Orchids</a>
                    <a href="#orchids">Orchids</a>  </li>
```

```
                <li><a href="#basket" class="buy" id="aster">Asters</a>
                    <a href="#asters">Asters</a>  </li>
          </ul>
      </div>
  </div>

  <div id="basket" data-role="page" data-theme="b">
      <div data-role="header">
          <h1>Jacqui's Shop</h1>
      </div>
      <div class="cWrapper">
          Basket will go here
      </div>
      <div class="cWrapper">
          <a href="#" data-rel="back" data-role="button" data-inline=true
             data-direction="reverse">Back</a>
      </div>
  </div>

  <div id="roses" data-role="page" data-theme="b">
      <div data-role="header">
          <h1>Roses</h1>
      </div>
      <div>
          <div class="lcontainer">
              <img src="rose.png">
              <div><a href="#" data-rel="back" data-role="button"
                      data-inline=true data-direction="reverse">Back</a>
              </div>
          </div>
          <div class="productData">
              A rose is a woody perennial within the family Rosaceae.
              They form a group of erect shrubs, and climbing or trailing plants.
              <div><b>Price: $4.99</b></div>
          </div>
      </div>
  </div>

  <div id="orchids" data-role="page" data-theme="b">
      <div data-role="header">
          <h1>Orchids</h1>
      </div>
      <div>
          <div class="lcontainer">
              <img src="orchid.png">
              <div><a href="#" data-rel="back" data-role="button"
                      data-inline=true data-direction="reverse">Back</a>
              </div>
          </div>
```

```
        <div class="productData">
            The orchid family is a diverse and widespread family in the order
            Asparagales. It is one of the largest families of flowering plants.
            <div><b>Price: $10.99</b></div>
        </div>
    </div>
</div>
<div id="asters" data-role="page" data-theme="b">
    <div data-role="header">
        <h1>Asters</h1>
    </div>
    <div>
        <div class="lcontainer">
            <img src="aster.png">
            <div><a href="#" data-rel="back" data-role="button"
                data-inline=true data-direction="reverse">Back</a>
            </div>
        </div>
        <div class="productData">
            The name Aster comes from the Ancient Greek word meaning "star",
            referring to the shape of the flower head.
            <div><b>Price: $2.99</b></div>
        </div>
    </div>
</div>
</body>
</html>
```

Inserting Products Programmatically

The first thing I'll do is replace the static pages that describe each flower with some that are created dynamically. This change allows me to have a more compact document and to easily add more flowers for the user to pick from without duplicating HTML elements. I will generate the pages using a data template, which I described in Chapter 12. Data templates work with the core jQuery library and so fit nicely into a jQuery Mobile application as well. I created a file called data.json that contains the data I need for the flowers. Listing 33-2 shows the contents of data.json.

Listing 33-2. The Content of the data.json file

```json
[{  "name": "aster",
    "label": "Asters",
    "price": "$2.99",
    "text": "The name Aster comes from the Ancient Greek word meaning star..."
},{ "name": "carnation",
    "label": "Carnations",
    "price": "$1.99",
    "text": "Carnations require well-drained, neutral to slightly alkaline soil..."
},{ "name": "daffodil",
    "label": "Daffodils",
    "price": "$1.99",
    "text": "Daffodil is a common English name, sometimes used for all varieties..."
```

```
},{ "name": "rose",
    "label": "Roses",
    "price": "$4.99",
    "text":  "A rose is a woody perennial within the family Rosaceae. They form a..."
},{ "name": "orchid",
    "label": "Orchids",
    "price": "$10.99",
    "text": "The orchid family is a diverse and widespread family in the order..."
}]
```

The data describes five flowers. For each of them, I defined the product name, the label to display to the user, the price per unit, and a text description.

■ **Note**   I did not show the full text description in the listing, but it is included in the data.json file that is part of the source code download for this book (which you can get from apress.com).

Now that I have the data, I can integrate it into the document. Listing 33-3 shows the changes from static to programmatically generated pages using a data template.

Listing 33-3. Adding Pages Dynamically

```
<!DOCTYPE html>
<html>
<head>
    <title>Example</title>
    <meta name="viewport" content="width=device-width, initial-scale=1">
    <link rel="stylesheet" href="jquery.mobile-1.3.1.css" type="text/css" />
    <script type="text/javascript" src="jquery-1.10.1.js"></script>
    <script src="handlebars.js"></script>
    <script src="handlebars-jquery.js"></script>
    <style type="text/css">
        .lcontainer {float: left; text-align: center; padding-top: 10px}
        .productData {float: right; padding: 10px; width: 60%}
        .cWrapper {text-align: center}
    </style>
    <script id="flowerTmpl" type="text/x-handlebars-template">
        {{#products}}
      <div id="{{name}}" data-role="page" data-theme="b">
            <div data-role="header">
               <h1>{{label}}</h1>
            </div>
            <div>
                <div class="lcontainer">
                    <img src="{{name}}.png">
                    <div><a href="#" data-rel="back" data-role="button"
                            data-inline=true data-direction="reverse">Back</a>
                    </div>
                </div>
```

```
            <div class="productData">
                {{text}}
                <div><b>Price: {{price}}</b></div>
            </div>
        </div>
    </div>
    {{/products}}
</script>

<script id="liTmpl" type="text/x-handlebars-template">
    {{#products}}
    <li>
        <a href="#basket" class="buy" id="A1">{{label}}</a>
        <a href="#{{name}}">{{label}}</a>
    </li>
    {{/products}}
</script>

<script type="text/javascript">
    var initComplete = false;
    $(document).bind("pageinit", function () {
        if (!initComplete) {
            $.getJSON("data.json", function (data) {
                $("#flowerTmpl").template({ products: data })
                    .filter("*").appendTo("body");
                $("ul").append($("#liTmpl").template({ products: data })
                    .filter("*")).listview("refresh")
            });
            initComplete = true;
        }
    })
</script>
<script type="text/javascript" src="jquery.mobile-1.3.1.js"></script>
</head>
<body>
    <div id="page1" data-role="page" data-theme="b">
        <div data-role="header">
            <h1>Jacqui's Shop</h1>
        </div>
        <div id="container" style="padding: 20px">
            <ul data-role="listview" data-inset=true></ul>
        </div>
    </div>

    <div id="basket" data-role="page" data-theme="b">
        <div data-role="header">
            <h1>Jacqui's Shop</h1>
        </div>
        <div class="cWrapper">
            Basket will go here
        </div>
    </div>
```

```
        <div class="cWrapper">
            <a href="#" data-rel="back" data-role="button" data-inline=true
                data-direction="reverse">Back</a>
        </div>
    </div>
</body>
</html>
```

I removed the per-flower pages and used data templates to generate what I need from the data, which I obtain using the getJSON method (described in Chapter 14). The key to this change is the simple custom JavaScript code, as follows:

```
..
<script type="text/javascript">
    var initComplete = false;
    $(document).bind("pageinit", function () {
        if (!initComplete) {
            $.getJSON("data.json", function (data) {
                $("#flowerTmpl").template({ products: data })
                    .filter("*").appendTo("body");
                $("ul").append($("#liTmpl").template({ products: data })
                    .filter("*")).listview("refresh")
            });
            initComplete = true;
        }
    })
</script>
...
```

When I obtain the data, I use a template to generate elements form the data and add the dynamically generated pages to the body element in the document. I also use a template to generate the items for the main list of flowers. I tell jQuery Mobile that I have modified the contents of the list, which I do by calling the refresh method on the listview widget, like this:

```
...
$("ul").append($("#liTmpl").template({ products: data })
    .filter("*")).listview("refresh");
...
```

The data templates are simple and use the standard techniques I described in Chapter 12. You can see the result in Figure 33-1—a list whose items are generated programmatically and link to pages that have been added to the document programmatically.

Figure 33-1. *Programmatically generated list items and pages*

Reusing Pages

I like the data template approach because it shows how jQuery underpins such a wide range of functionality, allowing you to bring together features like templates with an interface toolkit like jQuery Mobile.

That said, you can adopt a more elegant approach for dealing with the per-flower pages. Rather than generate a set of elements for each flower you want to show, you can generate one set of elements and modify them to show the flower that the user has selected. Listing 33-4 shows the changes to the document that make this possible.

Listing 33-4. *Reusing a Single Page for Multiple Products*

```
<!DOCTYPE html>
<html>
<head>
    <title>Example</title>
    <meta name="viewport" content="width=device-width, initial-scale=1">
    <link rel="stylesheet" href="jquery.mobile-1.3.1.css" type="text/css" />
    <script type="text/javascript" src="jquery-1.10.1.js"></script>
    <script src="handlebars.js"></script>
    <script src="handlebars-jquery.js"></script>
    <script id="liTmpl" type="text/x-handlebars-template">
        {{#products}}
        <li>
            <a href="#basket" class="buy" id="{{name}}">{{label}}</a>
            <a class="productLink" data-flower="{{name}}" href="#">{{label}}</a>
        </li>
        {{/products}}
    </script>
<script type="text/javascript">
    var initComplete = false;

    $(document).bind("pageinit", function () {
```

```
            if (!initComplete) {

                $.getJSON("data.json", function (data) {

                    $("ul").append($("#liTmpl").template({ products: data })
                        .filter("*")).listview("refresh");

                    $("a.productLink").bind("tap", function () {
                        var targetFlower = $(this).attr("data-flower");
                        for (var i = 0; i < data.length; i++) {
                            if (data[i].name == targetFlower) {
                                var page = $("#productPage");
                                page.find("#header").text(data[i].label);
                                page.find("#image").attr("src", data[i].name + ".png");
                                page.find("#description").text(data[i].text);
                                page.find("#price").text(data[i].price);

                                $.mobile.changePage("#productPage");
                                break;
                            }
                        }
                    })
                });
                initComplete = true;
            }
        })
    </script>
    <script type="text/javascript" src="jquery.mobile-1.3.1.js"></script>
    <style type="text/css">
        .lcontainer {float: left; text-align: center; padding-top: 10px}
        .productData {float: right; padding: 10px; width: 60%}
        .cWrapper {text-align: center}
    </style>
</head>
<body>
    <div id="page1" data-role="page" data-theme="b">
        <div data-role="header">
            <h1>Jacqui's Shop</h1>
        </div>
        <div id="container" style="padding: 20px">
            <ul data-role="listview" data-inset=true>

            </ul>
        </div>
    </div>

    <div id="productPage" data-role="page" data-theme="b">
        <div data-role="header">
            <h1 id="header"></h1>
        </div>
        <div>
            <div class="lcontainer">
                <img id="image" src="">
```

```
            <div><a href="#" data-rel="back" data-role="button"
                    data-inline=true data-direction="reverse">Back</a>
            </div>
        </div>
        <div class="productData">
            <span id="description"></span>
            <div><b>Price: <span id="price"></span></b></div>
        </div>
      </div>
    </div>

    <div id="basket" data-role="page" data-theme="b">
        <div data-role="header">
          <h1>Jacqui's Shop</h1>
        </div>
        <div class="cWrapper">
            Basket will go here
        </div>
        <div class="cWrapper">
            <a href="#" data-rel="back" data-role="button" data-inline=true
                data-direction="reverse">Back</a>
        </div>
    </div>
</body>
</html>
```

■ **Tip**   This is an approach that is particularly suited to jQuery Mobile because multiple pages are contained within a single HTML document. As a rule, you want to keep your HTML documents as simple as possible because of the limitations inherent in mobile devices.

I removed one of the data templates from the document and added a new page (whose id is productPage) that I use for each flower. I modified the template used to generate the list items so that there is no target page in the href attribute and to add my own data attribute so that I know which flower any given link relates to. When the data has been retrieved from JSON, the revised script selects all of the per-product links from the list elements I just created using the template and binds to the tap event. When a list item is tapped, I find the appropriate data item and use its properties to configure the productPage page, setting the text and image to display to the user, as follows:

```
...
<script type="text/javascript">

    var initComplete = false;

    $(document).bind("pageinit", function () {
        if (!initComplete) {
            $.getJSON("data.json", function (data) {

                $("ul").append($("#liTmpl").template({ products: data })
                    .filter("*")).listview("refresh");
```

```javascript
            $("a.productLink").bind("tap", function () {
                var targetFlower = $(this).attr("data-flower");
                for (var i = 0; i < data.length; i++) {
                    if (data[i].name == targetFlower) {
                        var page = $("#productPage");
                        page.find("#header").text(data[i].label);
                        page.find("#image").attr("src", data[i].name + ".png");
                        page.find("#description").text(data[i].text);
                        page.find("#price").text(data[i].price);

                        $.mobile.changePage("#productPage");
                        break;
                    }
                }
            })
        });
        initComplete = true;
    }
})
</script>
...
```

After I configure the page, I use the changePage method to trigger the navigation. There is no change in the appearance of the example, but you have a smaller set of elements for the mobile browser to manage, and it's a nice example of how you can manipulate the page structure of a jQuery Mobile document.

Creating the Shopping Basket

I am using a split list in this example, and the left side of the list item leads to the basket page. In this section, I'll define the elements for the page and add some JavaScript so that there is a simple basket in place. Listing 33-5 shows the changes to the document.

Listing 33-5. Implementing the Shopping Basket

```html
<!DOCTYPE html>
<html>
<head>
    <title>Example</title>
    <meta name="viewport" content="width=device-width, initial-scale=1">
    <link rel="stylesheet" href="jquery.mobile-1.3.1.css" type="text/css" />
    <script type="text/javascript" src="jquery-1.10.1.js"></script>
    <script src="handlebars.js"></script>
    <script src="handlebars-jquery.js"></script>
    <script id="liTmpl" type="text/x-handlebars-template">
        {{#products}}
        <li>
            <a href="#" class="buy" id="{{name}}">{{label}}</a>
            <a class="productLink" data-flower="{{name}}" href="#">{{label}}</a>
        </li>
        {{/products}}
    </script>
```

```html
<script id="trTmpl" type="text/x-handlebars-template">
    <tr data-price="{{price}}" id="{{name}}"><td>{{label}}</td><td id="count">1</td>
        <td id="subtotal">0</td></tr>
</script>
<script type="text/javascript">
    $(document).ready(function () {
        $.getJSON("data.json", function (data) {
            $("ul").append($("#liTmpl").template({ products: data }))
                .filter("*").listview("refresh");

            $("a.productLink").bind("tap", function () {
                var targetFlower = $(this).attr("data-flower");
                for (var i = 0; i < data.length; i++) {
                    if (data[i].name == targetFlower) {
                        var page = $("#productPage");
                        page.find("#header").text(data[i].label);
                        page.find("#image").attr("src", data[i].name + ".png");
                        page.find("#description").text(data[i].text);
                        page.find("#price").text(data[i].price);
                        $.mobile.changePage("#productPage");
                        break;
                    }
                }
            });

            $("a.buy").bind("tap", function () {
                var targetFlower = this.id;
                var row = $("#basketTable tbody #" + targetFlower);
                if (row.length > 0) {
                    var countCell = row.find("#count");
                    countCell.text(Number(countCell.text()) + 1);
                } else {
                    for (var i = 0; i < data.length; i++) {
                        if (data[i].name == targetFlower) {
                            $("#trTmpl").template(data[i])
                                .appendTo("#basketTable tbody")
                            break;
                        }
                    }
                }
                calculateTotals();
                $.mobile.changePage("#basket")
            });
        })
    })

    function calculateTotals() {
        var total = 0;
        $("#basketTable tbody").children().each(function (index, elem) {
            var count = Number($(elem).find("#count").text())
            var price = Number($(elem).attr("data-price").slice(1))
```

```
                var subtotal = count * price;
                $(elem).find("#subtotal").text("$" + subtotal.toFixed(2));
                total += subtotal;
            })
            $("#total").text("$" + total.toFixed(2))
        }
    </script>
    <script type="text/javascript" src="jquery.mobile-1.3.1.js"></script>
    <style type="text/css">
        .lcontainer {float: left; text-align: center; padding-top: 10px}
        .productData {float: right; padding: 10px; width: 60%}
        .cWrapper {text-align: center}
        table {display: inline-block; margin: auto; margin-top: 20px; text-align: left;
            border-collapse: collapse}
        td {min-width: 100px}
        th, td {text-align: right}
        th:nth-child(1), td:nth-child(1) {text-align: left}
    </style>
</head>
<body>
    <div id="page1" data-role="page" data-theme="b">
        <div data-role="header">
            <h1>Jacqui's Shop</h1>
        </div>
        <div id="container" style="padding: 20px">
            <ul data-role="listview" data-inset=true></ul>
        </div>
    </div>

    <div id="productPage" data-role="page" data-theme="b">
        <div data-role="header">
            <h1 id="header"></h1>
        </div>
        <div>
            <div class="lcontainer">
                <img id="image" src="">
                <div><a href="#" data-rel="back" data-role="button"
                        data-inline=true data-direction="reverse">Back</a>
                </div>
            </div>
            <div class="productData">
                <span id="description"></span>
                <div><b>Price: <span id="price"></span></b></div>
            </div>
        </div>
    </div>

    <div id="basket" data-role="page" data-theme="b">
        <div data-role="header">
            <h1>Jacqui's Shop</h1>
        </div>
```

```
    <div class="cWrapper">
        <table id="basketTable" border=0>
            <thead>
                <tr><th>Flower</th><th>Quantity</th><th>Subtotal</th></tr>
            </thead>
            <tbody></tbody>
            <tfoot>
                <tr><th colspan=2>Total:</th><td id="total"></td></tr>
            </tfoot>
        </table>
    </div>
    <div class="cWrapper">
        <a href="#" data-rel="back" data-role="button" data-inline=true
            data-direction="reverse">Back</a>
        <button data-inline="true">Checkout</button>
    </div>
</div>
</body>
</html>
```

I added a table to the basket page, which shows one row for each selected product. Each row shows the name of the product, the quantity, and the subtotal. There is a footer in the table that shows the overall total. I bound to the tap event so that when the user clicks on the left side of the split button, either a new row is added to the table or the quantity is incremented if there is already a row for this product in the table. New rows are generated using another data template, and everything else is handled by reading the contents of elements in the document.

I determine and maintain the entire state of the customer's basket using the DOM itself. I could have created a JavaScript object to model the order and driven the contents of the table from the object, but in a book about jQuery, I like to take every opportunity to work with the document itself. The result is a simple basket, which is shown in Figure 33-2.

Jacqui's Shop		
Flower	**Quantity**	**Subtotal**
Roses	2	$9.98
Daffodils	1	$1.99
Carnations	1	$1.99
Orchids	2	$21.98
Total:		$35.94

Back   Checkout

Figure 33-2. *The basket page*

Adding for Quantity Changes

The basket is functional, but if the user wants two roses, for example, she has to tap the Rose list item, tap the Back button, and then tap the Rose item again. This process is pretty ridiculous, so to make it easier to change the quantity of a product, I added some input elements to the table. You can see the changes in Listing 33-6.

Listing 33-6. Adding Range Sliders to the Basket Table

```html
<!DOCTYPE html>
<html>
<head>
    <title>Example</title>
    <meta name="viewport" content="width=device-width, initial-scale=1">
    <link rel="stylesheet" href="jquery.mobile-1.3.1.css" type="text/css" />
    <script type="text/javascript" src="jquery-1.10.1.js"></script>
    <script src="handlebars.js"></script>
    <script src="handlebars-jquery.js"></script>
    <script id="liTmpl" type="text/x-handlebars-template">
        {{#products}}
        <li>
            <a href="#" class="buy" id="{{name}}">{{label}}</a>
            <a class="productLink" data-flower="{{name}}" href="#">{{label}}</a>
        </li>
        {{/products}}
    </script>
    <script id="trTmpl" type="text/x-handlebars-template">
        <tr data-theme="b" data-price="{{price}}" id="{{name}}"><td>{{label}}</td>
            <td id="count"><input type=number value=1 min=0 max=10></td>
            <td id="subtotal">0</td>
        </tr>
    </script>
    <script type="text/javascript">

        var initComplete = false;

        $(document).bind("pageinit", function () {
            if (!initComplete) {
                $.getJSON("data.json", function (data) {

                    $("ul").append($("#liTmpl")
                        .template({ products: data })).listview("refresh");

                    $("a.productLink").bind("tap", function () {
                        var targetFlower = $(this).attr("data-flower");
                        for (var i = 0; i < data.length; i++) {
                            if (data[i].name == targetFlower) {
                                var page = $("#productPage");
                                page.find("#header").text(data[i].label);
                                page.find("#image").attr("src", data[i].name + ".png");
                                page.find("#description").text(data[i].text);
                                page.find("#price").text(data[i].price);
```

```javascript
                        $.mobile.changePage("#productPage");
                        break;
                }
            }
        })

        $("a.buy").bind("tap", function () {
            var targetFlower = this.id;
            var row = $("#basketTable tbody #" + targetFlower);
            if (row.length > 0) {
                var countCell = row.find("#count input");
                countCell.val(Number(countCell.val()) + 1);
            } else {
                for (var i = 0; i < data.length; i++) {
                    if (data[i].name == targetFlower) {
                        $("#trTmpl").template(data[i])
                            .appendTo("#basketTable tbody")
                            .find("input").textinput()

                        break;
                    }
                }
            }
            calculateTotals();
            $.mobile.changePage("#basket")
        })

        $(document).on("change click", "input", function (event) {
            calculateTotals();
        })
    });
    initComplete = true;
        }
    })

    function calculateTotals() {
        var total = 0;
        $("#basketTable tbody").children().each(function (index, elem) {
            var count = Number($(elem).find("#count input").val())
            var price = Number($(elem).attr("data-price").slice(1))
            var subtotal = count * price;
            $(elem).find("#subtotal").text("$" + subtotal.toFixed(2));
            total += subtotal;
        })
        $("#total").text("$" + total.toFixed(2))
    }
</script>
<script type="text/javascript" src="jquery.mobile-1.3.1.js"></script>
<style type="text/css">
    .lcontainer {float: left; text-align: center; padding-top: 10px}
    .productData {float: right; padding: 10px; width: 60%}
    .cWrapper {text-align: center}
```

```
        table {display: inline-block; margin: auto; margin-top: 20px; text-align: left;
            border-collapse: collapse}
        td {min-width: 100px; padding-bottom: 10px}
        td:nth-child(2) {min-width: 75px; width: 75px}
        th, td {text-align: right}
        th:nth-child(1), td:nth-child(1) {text-align: left}
        input[type=number] {background-color: white}
        tfoot tr {border-top: medium solid black}
        tfoot tr td {padding-top: 10px}
    </style>
</head>
<body>
    <div id="page1" data-role="page" data-theme="b">
        <div data-role="header">
            <h1>Jacqui's Shop</h1>
        </div>
        <div id="container" style="padding: 20px">
            <ul data-role="listview" data-inset=true></ul>
        </div>
    </div>

    <div id="productPage" data-role="page" data-theme="b">
        <div data-role="header">
            <h1 id="header"></h1>
        </div>
        <div>
            <div class="lcontainer">
                <img id="image" src="">
                <div><a href="#" data-rel="back" data-role="button"
                        data-inline=true data-direction="reverse">Back</a>
                </div>
            </div>
            <div class="productData">
                <span id="description"></span>
                <div><b>Price: <span id="price"></span></b></div>
            </div>
        </div>
    </div>

    <div id="basket" data-role="page" data-theme="b">
        <div data-role="header">
            <h1>Jacqui's Shop</h1>
        </div>
        <div class="cWrapper">
            <table id="basketTable" border=0>
                <thead>
                    <tr><th>Flower</th><th>Quantity</th><th>Subtotal</th></tr>
                </thead>
                <tbody></tbody>
```

```
                <tfoot>
                    <tr><th colspan=2>Total:</th><td id="total"></td></tr>
                </tfoot>
            </table>
        </div>
        <div class="cWrapper">
            <a href="#" data-rel="back" data-role="button" data-inline=true
                data-direction="reverse">Back</a>
            <button data-inline="true">Checkout</button>
        </div>
    </div>
</body>
</html>
```

I inserted an input element into the quantity cell in the template, which is used to generate rows for the table. The type of this input element is number, which causes some browsers to insert small up and down buttons alongside the text entry area. These buttons are too small to be useful for touch, but the browser will also filter the characters to discard anything that isn't appropriate for a number. Although it's acceptable for this chapter, this isn't a perfect approach for real projects because floating point numbers are supported, which means that the user can input fractions of products.

I call the textinput method when I add input elements to the document after the pages have been enhanced by jQuery Mobile:

```
...
$("#trTmpl").template(data[i]).appendTo("#basketTable tbody").find("input").textinput()
...
```

If I do not add this method call, the browser displays the native input element. Calling the textinput method causes jQuery Mobile to enhance the element, although it doesn't properly assign the swatch. So I defined a style for the input element to set the background color consistently:

```
...
input[type=number] {background-color: white}
...
```

I need to calculate the subtotals and totals more frequently now that the user can change the quantity of a product in the basket page. Because I add input elements to the document throughout the life of the application, I use the jQuery on method to handle events. The on method is described in Chapter 9. Here is the event handler code:

```
...
$(document).on("change click", "input", function (event) {
    calculateTotals();
})
...
```

I use the on method to associate my handler function with both the change and click events. The browsers that add up and down buttons to numeric input elements trigger the click event when those buttons are pressed, so I need to handle this event in addition to the more expected change event. My handler function calls the calculateTotals function when either event is triggered. You can see how the basket looks in Figure 33-3.

Figure 33-3. *Adding input elements to the basket page*

Adding a Button to the Information Page

The product information describes the flower the user has selected, but it doesn't provide any way for the user to add it to the basket. To round out the basic basket functionality, I added a button to the product page that adds the item to the basket. Listing 33-7 shows the changes to the product page.

Listing 33-7. Adding a Button to the Product Page

```
...
<div id="productPage" data-role="page" data-theme="b">
    <div data-role="header">
        <h1 id="header"></h1>
    </div>
    <div>
        <div class="lcontainer">
            <img id="image" src="">
            <div><a href="#" data-rel="back" data-role="button"
                    data-inline=true data-direction="reverse">Back</a>
            </div>
        </div>
        <div class="productData">
            <span id="description"></span>
            <div>
                <b>Price: <span id="price"></span></b>
                <a href="#" id="buybutton" data-flower="" data-role="button"
                    data-inline=true>Buy</a>
            </div>
        </div>
    </div>
</div>
...
```

I defined an a element that jQuery Mobile will transform into a button widget. I added a data attribute (data-flower) so that I can keep track of which flower is being displayed when the user taps the button. To support this button, I made some changes to the script. These changes are shown in Listing 33-8.

Listing 33-8. Adding Support for the Buy Button in the Script

```
...
<script type="text/javascript">

    var initComplete = false;

    $(document).bind("pageinit", function () {
        if (!initComplete) {
            $.getJSON("data.json", function (data) {

                $("ul").append($("#liTmpl")
                    .template({ products: data })).listview("refresh");

                $("a.productLink").bind("tap", function () {
                    var targetFlower = $(this).attr("data-flower");
                    for (var i = 0; i < data.length; i++) {
                        if (data[i].name == targetFlower) {
                            var page = $("#productPage");
                            page.find("#header").text(data[i].label);
                            page.find("#image").attr("src", data[i].name + ".png");
                            page.find("#description").text(data[i].text);
                            page.find("#price").text(data[i].price);
                            page.find("#buybutton").attr("data-flower", data[i].name);
                            $.mobile.changePage("#productPage");
                            break;
                        }
                    }
                })

                $("#buybutton").bind("tap", function () {
                    addProduct($(this).attr("data-flower"));
                })

                $("a.buy").bind("tap", function () {
                    addProduct(this.id);
                })

                function addProduct(targetFlower) {
                    var row = $("#basketTable tbody #" + targetFlower);
                    if (row.length > 0) {
                        var countCell = row.find("#count input");
                        countCell.val(Number(countCell.val()) + 1);
                    } else {
                        for (var i = 0; i < data.length; i++) {
                            if (data[i].name == targetFlower) {
                                $("#trTmpl").template(data[i])
                                    .appendTo("#basketTable tbody")
                                    .find("input").textinput()
```

```
                            break;
                        }
                    }
                }
                calculateTotals();
                $.mobile.changePage("#basket")
            }

            $(document).on("change click", "input", function (event) {
                calculateTotals();
            })
        });
        initComplete = true;
    }
})

function calculateTotals() {
    var total = 0;
    $("#basketTable tbody").children().each(function (index, elem) {
        var count = Number($(elem).find("#count input").val())
        var price = Number($(elem).attr("data-price").slice(1))
        var subtotal = count * price;
        $(elem).find("#subtotal").text("$" + subtotal.toFixed(2));
        total += subtotal;
    })
    $("#total").text("$" + total.toFixed(2))
}
</script>
...
```

These changes are pretty straightforward. When the user selects a product from the main list, I set the value of the data-flower attribute on the a element. I register a function to handle the tap event for the button and use the value data-flower to call the addProduct function, which contains code I extracted from another handler function. With these changes, the user can add products to the basket from the main list (by tapping on the left side of the split list item) or from the information page (by tapping the Buy button). Figure 33-4 shows the addition of the Buy button to the page.

Figure 33-4. Adding a button to the product information page

Implementing the Checkout Process

To round out this example, I'll demonstrate gathering the data from the various jQuery Mobile pages in a form that can be used to make an Ajax request. I will not make the request itself or implement the server. jQuery Mobile uses the core jQuery support for Ajax, which I described in Chapters 14 and 15. Listing 33-9 shows the addition of a page that is shown to the user when the Checkout button is tapped and the handler function that gathers the data.

Listing 33-9. Implementing the Checkout Process

```
<!DOCTYPE html>
<html>
<head>
    <title>Example</title>
    <meta name="viewport" content="width=device-width, initial-scale=1">
    <link rel="stylesheet" href="jquery.mobile-1.3.1.css" type="text/css" />
    <script type="text/javascript" src="jquery-1.10.1.js"></script>
    <script src="handlebars.js"></script>
    <script src="handlebars-jquery.js"></script>
    <script id="liTmpl" type="text/x-handlebars-template">
        {{#products}}
        <li>
            <a href="#" class="buy" id="{{name}}">{{label}}</a>
            <a class="productLink" data-flower="{{name}}" href="#">{{label}}</a>
        </li>
        {{/products}}
    </script>
    <script id="trTmpl" type="text/x-handlebars-template">
        <tr data-theme="b" data-price="{{price}}" id="{{name}}"><td>{{label}}</td>
            <td id="count"><input type=number value=1 min=0 max=10></td>
            <td id="subtotal">0</td>
        </tr>
    </script>
    <script type="text/javascript">
        var initComplete = false;
        $(document).bind("pageinit", function () {
            if (!initComplete) {
                $.getJSON("data.json", function (data) {
                    $("ul").append($("#liTmpl")
                        .template({ products: data })).listview("refresh");

                    $("a.productLink").bind("tap", function () {
                        var targetFlower = $(this).attr("data-flower");
                        for (var i = 0; i < data.length; i++) {
                            if (data[i].name == targetFlower) {
                                var page = $("#productPage");
                                page.find("#header").text(data[i].label);
                                page.find("#image").attr("src", data[i].name + ".png");
                                page.find("#description").text(data[i].text);
                                page.find("#price").text(data[i].price);
```

```javascript
                                page.find("#buybutton")
                                    .attr("data-flower", data[i].name);
                            $.mobile.changePage("#productPage");
                            break;
                        }
                    }
                })

        $("#buybutton").bind("tap", function () {
            addProduct($(this).attr("data-flower"));
        })

        $("a.buy").bind("tap", function () {
            addProduct(this.id);
        })

        function addProduct(targetFlower) {
            var row = $("#basketTable tbody #" + targetFlower);
            if (row.length > 0) {
                var countCell = row.find("#count input");
                countCell.val(Number(countCell.val()) + 1);
            } else {
                for (var i = 0; i < data.length; i++) {
                    if (data[i].name == targetFlower) {
                        $("#trTmpl").template(data[i])
                            .appendTo("#basketTable tbody")
                            .find("input").textinput();
                        break;
                    }
                }
            }
            calculateTotals();
            $.mobile.changePage("#basket")
        }

        $(document).on("change click", "input", function (event) {
            calculateTotals();
        })

        $("#submit").bind("tap", function () {
            var dataObject = new Object();
            $("#basketTable tbody").children().each(function (index, elem) {
                dataObject[elem.id] = $(elem).find("#count input").val();
            })
            dataObject["name"] = $("#name").val();
            dataObject["wrap"] = $("option:selected").val();
            dataObject["shipping"] = $("input:checked").attr("id")

            console.log("DATA: " + JSON.stringify(dataObject))
        })
    });
```

```
                    initComplete = true;
                }
            })

        function calculateTotals() {
            var total = 0;
            $("#basketTable tbody").children().each(function (index, elem) {
                var count = Number($(elem).find("#count input").val())
                var price = Number($(elem).attr("data-price").slice(1))
                var subtotal = count * price;
                $(elem).find("#subtotal").text("$" + subtotal.toFixed(2));
                total += subtotal;
            })
            $("#total").text("$" + total.toFixed(2))
        }

    </script>
    <script type="text/javascript" src="jquery.mobile-1.3.1.js"></script>
    <style type="text/css">
        .lcontainer {float: left; text-align: center; padding: 10px}
        .productData {float: right; padding: 10px; width: 60%}
        .cWrapper {text-align: center}
        table {display: inline-block; margin: auto; margin-top: 20px; text-align: left;
            border-collapse: collapse}
        td {min-width: 100px; padding-bottom: 10px}
        td:nth-child(2) {min-width: 75px; width: 75px}
        th, td {text-align: right}
        th:nth-child(1), td:nth-child(1) {text-align: left}
        input[type=number] {background-color: white}
        tfoot tr {border-top: medium solid black}
        tfoot tr td {padding-top: 10px}
    </style>
</head>
<body>
    <div id="page1" data-role="page" data-theme="b">
        <div data-role="header">
            <h1>Jacqui's Shop</h1>
        </div>
        <div id="container" style="padding: 20px">
            <ul data-role="listview" data-inset=true></ul>
        </div>
    </div>

    <div id="productPage" data-role="page" data-theme="b">
        <div data-role="header">
            <h1 id="header"></h1>
        </div>
        <div>
            <div class="lcontainer">
                <img id="image" src="">
```

```html
                <div><a href="#" data-rel="back" data-role="button"
                        data-inline=true data-direction="reverse">Back</a>
                </div>
            </div>
            <div class="productData">
                <span id="description"></span>
                <div>
                    <b>Price: <span id="price"></span></b>
                    <a href="#" id="buybutton" data-flower="" data-role="button"
                        data-inline=true>Buy</a>
                </div>
            </div>
        </div>
    </div>

    <div id="basket" data-role="page" data-theme="b">
        <div data-role="header">
            <h1>Jacqui's Shop</h1>
        </div>
        <div class="cWrapper">
            <table id="basketTable" border=0>
                <thead>
                    <tr><th>Flower</th><th>Quantity</th><th>Subtotal</th></tr>
                </thead>
                <tbody></tbody>
                <tfoot>
                    <tr><th colspan=2>Total:</th><td id="total"></td></tr>
                </tfoot>
            </table>
        </div>
        <div class="cWrapper">
            <a href="#" data-rel="back" data-role="button" data-inline=true
                data-direction="reverse">Back</a>
            <a href="#checkout" data-role="button" data-inline="true">Checkout</a>
        </div>
    </div>

    <div id="checkout" data-role="page" data-theme="b">
        <div data-role="header">
            <h1>Jacqui's Shop</h1>
        </div>

        <div data-role="content">
            <label for="name">Name: </label>
            <input id="name" placeholder="Your Name">

            <label for="wrap"><span>Gift Wrap: </span></label>
            <select id="wrap" name="wrap" data-role="slider">
                <option value="yes" selected>Yes</option>
                <option value="no">No</option>
            </select>
```

```
            <fieldset data-role="controlgroup" data-type="horizontal">
                <legend>Shipping:</legend>
                <input type="radio" name="ship" id="overnight" checked />
                <label for="overnight">Overnight</label>
                <input type="radio" name="ship" id="23day"/>
                <label for="23day">2-3 days</label>
                <input type="radio" name="ship" id="710day"/>
                <label for="710day">7-10 days</label>
            </fieldset>

            <div class="cWrapper">
                <a href="#" data-rel="back" data-role="button" data-inline="true"
                    data-direction="reverse">Back</a>
                <a href="#" id="submit" data-role="button"
                    data-inline="true">Submit Order</a>
            </div>
        </div>
    </div>
</body>
</html>
```

The new page is called checkout. I kept this form simple, prompting the user for a name and providing choices for gift wrapping and the shipping method. You can see how the page appears in Figure 33-5. I have shown the page in the portrait orientation because it allows me to display all of the elements without having to scroll.

Figure 33-5. *The checkout page*

When the user taps the Submit Order button, I gather the data from the different pages in the HTML document and write the result as a JSON string to the console. The following is an example of such a string:

```
{"carnation":"3","rose":"1","orchid":"1",
    "name":"Adam Freeman","wrap":"yes","shipping":"23day"}
```

Summary

In this chapter, I took some of the core features of jQuery Mobile and combined them to create a simple mobile implementation of the flower shop example. By its nature, jQuery Mobile is a lot simpler than jQuery UI. The main challenge is to design an approach that gives the user the information he requires within the confines of a small screen.

■ ■ ■

CHAPTER 34

Using the jQuery Utility Methods

jQuery includes a number of utility methods that perform advanced operations on jQuery objects or which supplement the JavaScript language to provide features that are usually present in programing languages. You may never need any of these methods, but they are used internally by jQuery, and making them publicly available means that you can save time and effort when you come across an odd problem that the jQuery team has already solved.

Some of these methods are applied to jQuery object and some are called against the main jQuery function, which I have illustrated using the $ notation (described in Chapter 5). Table 34-1 provides the summary for this chapter.

Table 34-1. *Chapter Summary*

Problem	Solution	Listing
Queue operations for later execution.	Use the general purpose queues.	1, 2
Filter the contents of an array.	Use the grep method.	3, 4
Determine if an array contains a specific object or value.	Use the inArray method.	5
Project the contents of an array.	Use the map method.	6, 7
Concatenate two arrays.	Use the merge method.	8
Remove duplicates from a jQuery object and sort those that remain by the order they appear in the document.	Use the unique method.	9
Determine the type of an object.	Use the isXXX or type methods.	10, 11
Prepare the contents of a form for submission.	Use the serialize or serializeArray methods.	12
Parse data into a more useful form.	Use the parseJSON or parseXML methods.	13
Remove the leading and trailing whitespace from a string.	Use the trim method.	14
Determine if one element contains another.	Use the contains method.	15

Queues Revisited: Using General Purpose Queues

In Chapter 10, I showed you how to use the jQuery effects queue to manage a chain of effects to apply to a set of elements. In fact, the effects queue is just one queue and the feature is a general purpose one that can be use more widely. Table 34-2 restates the queue-related methods, tweaked for general purpose use.

Table 34-2. *Queue Methods*

Method	Description
clearQueue(<name>)	Removes any functions that have not yet been run in the specified queue.
queue(<name>)	Returns the specified queue of functions to be performed on the elements in the jQuery object.
queue(<name>, function)	Add a function to the end of the queue.
dequeue(<name>)	Removes and executes the first item in the queue for the elements in the jQuery object.
delay(<time>, <name>)	Insert a delay between effects in the specified queue.

When these methods are used without specifying a queue name, jQuery defaults to fx, which is the queue for visual effects. I can use any other queue name to create a queue of functions.

When applying jQuery queues to general use, I use the clearQueue method instead of the stop method – stop has special support for jQuery effects that are not appropriate for broader use. Listing 34-1 provides an example of using a general purpose queue.

Listing 34-1. Using a Queue

```html
<!DOCTYPE html>
<html>
<head>
    <title>Example</title>
    <script src="jquery-2.0.2.js" type="text/javascript"></script>
    <link rel="stylesheet" type="text/css" href="styles.css"/>
    <script type="text/javascript">
        $(document).ready(function() {

            var elems = $("input");

            elems.queue("gen", function(next) {
                $(this).val(100).css("border", "thin red solid");
                next();
            });

            elems.delay(1000, "gen");

            elems.queue("gen", function(next) {
                $(this).val(0).css("border", "");
                $(this).dequeue("gen");
            });

            $("<button>Process Queue</button>").appendTo("#buttonDiv")
                .click(function(e) {
                    elems.dequeue("gen");
                    e.preventDefault();
                });

        });
    </script>
</head>
```

```html
<body>
    <h1>Jacqui's Flower Shop</h1>
    <form method="post">
        <div id="oblock">
            <div class="dtable">
                <div id="row1" class="drow">
                    <div class="dcell">
                        <img src="aster.png"/><label for="aster">Aster:</label>
                        <input name="aster" value="0" required />
                    </div>
                    <div class="dcell">
                        <img src="daffodil.png"/><label for="daffodil">Daffodil:</label>
                        <input name="daffodil" value="0" required />
                    </div>
                    <div class="dcell">
                        <img src="rose.png"/><label for="rose">Rose:</label>
                        <input name="rose" value="0" required />
                    </div>
                </div>
                <div id="row2"class="drow">
                    <div class="dcell">
                        <img src="peony.png"/><label for="peony">Peony:</label>
                        <input name="peony" value="0" required />
                    </div>
                    <div class="dcell">
                        <img src="primula.png"/><label for="primula">Primula:</label>
                        <input name="primula" value="0" required />
                    </div>
                    <div class="dcell">
                        <img src="snowdrop.png"/><label for="snowdrop">Snowdrop:</label>
                        <input name="snowdrop" value="0" required />
                    </div>
                </div>
            </div>
        </div>
        <div id="buttonDiv"><button type="submit">Place Order</button></div>
    </form>
</body>
</html>
```

■ **Tip**   The styles.css file that I reference in this example is the one I used in Part 2 of this book.

In this example, I add three functions to a queue called gen that operates on the input elements in the document. First, I use the val method to set all of the input values to 100 and the css method to add a border. Second, I use the delay method to add a one-second delay to the queue. Finally, I use the val and css methods to reset the input elements to their original state.

I also added a button to the document, which calls the dequeue method – unlike the effects queue, I am responsible for starting queue processing ourselves. You can see the effect in Figure 34-1.

931

Figure 34-1. *Using a general purpose queue*

The functions that I place in the queue work in the same way as for the events queue and, as before, I am responsible for either calling the dequeue method or invoking the function that is passed as an argument. I tend to use the function argument – just because I often forget to specify the queue name when calling the dequeue method, which means that my queue grinds to a halt.

Manually Processing Queue Items

Of course, you don't have to trigger one queued function from another – you could rely on an external trigger to dequeue each item, such as the user pressing the button I added to the document. Listing 34-2 shows how to do this.

Listing 34-2. Dequeuing Functions Explicitly

```
...
<script type="text/javascript">
    $(document).ready(function() {

        $("input").queue("gen", function() {
            $(this).val(100).css("border", "thin red solid");
        }).queue("gen", function() {
            $(this).val(0).css("border", "");
        }).queue("gen", function() {
            $(this).css("border", "thin blue solid");
            $("#dequeue").attr("disabled", "disabled");
        });
```

```
$("<button id=dequeue>Dequeue Item</button>").appendTo("#buttonDiv")
    .click(function(e) {
        $("input").dequeue("gen");
        e.preventDefault();
    });
    });
});
</script>
...
```

In this script, I have chained the queue calls together and added a function that sets a border on the selected elements and disables the button element, which must be clicked to process each item in the queue – there is no automated chaining.

Utility Methods for Arrays

jQuery provides a number of useful methods for working with arrays – these methods are described in Table 34-3. For the most part, there are better ways of working with HTMLElement arrays – just use the standard jQuery methods for handling and filtering elements. For other kinds of arrays, these methods can be helpful.

Table 34-3. Utility Methods for Working with Arrays

Method	Description
$.grep(<array>, function) $.grep(<array>, function, <invert>)	Filters the contents of an array based on a function.
$.inArray(<value>, <array>)	Determines if a particular item in contained in an array.
$.map(<array>, function) $.map(<array>, <map>)	Projects an array or map object using a function.
$.merge(<array>, <array>)	Appends the contents of the second array to the first.
$.unique(HTMLElement[])	Sorts an array of HTMLElement objects into document order and removes any duplicates.

Using the Grep Method

The grep method allows us to find all of the elements in an array that are matched by a filter function. Listing 34-3 provides a demonstration of this method.

Listing 34-3. Using the Grep Method

```
...
<script type="text/javascript">
    $(document).ready(function() {
        var flowerArray = ["aster", "daffodil", "rose", "peony", "primula", "snowdrop"];

        var filteredArray = $.grep(flowerArray, function(elem, index) {
            return elem.indexOf("p") > -1;
        });
```

```
        for (var i = 0; i < filteredArray.length; i++) {
            console.log("Filtered element: " + filteredArray[i]);
        }
    });
</script>
...
```

Our filter function is passed two arguments – the first is the element in the array, and the second is the array index of that element. Our function is called for each item in the array and returns true if the current item to be included in the filtered results.

In this example, I use the grep method on an array of strings, filtering out those that don't contain the letter p. I write the contents of the filtered array to the console, producing the following results:

```
Filtered element: peony
Filtered element: primula
Filtered element: snowdrop
```

You can supply an additional argument to the grep method – if this argument is true, then the filtering process is inverted and the result contains those elements that the function filtered out. Listing 34-4 shows the effect of this argument.

Listing 34-4. Inverting the Selection Using the Grep Method

```
...
<script type="text/javascript">
    $(document).ready(function() {

        var flowerArray = ["aster", "daffodil", "rose", "peony", "primula", "snowdrop"];

        var filteredArray = $.grep(flowerArray, function(elem, index) {
            return elem.indexOf("p") > -1;
        }, true);

        for (var i = 0; i < filteredArray.length; i++) {
            console.log("Filtered element: " + filteredArray[i]);
        }

    });
</script>
...
```

This change produces the following results:

```
Filtered element: aster
Filtered element: daffodil
Filtered element: rose
```

Using the inArray Method

The inArray method determines if an array contains a specified value – the method returns the index of the item if it is in the array and -1 otherwise. Listing 34-5 demonstrates the inArray method.

Listing 34-5. Using the inArray Method

```
...
<script type="text/javascript">
    $(document).ready(function() {
        var flowerArray = ["aster", "daffodil", "rose", "peony", "primula", "snowdrop"];
        console.log("Array contains rose: " + $.inArray("rose", flowerArray));
        console.log("Array contains lily: " + $.inArray("lily", flowerArray));
    });
</script>
...
```

This script checks to see if the array of flowers contains rose and lily. The results are as follows:

```
Array contains rose: 2
Array contains lily: -1
```

Using the Map Method

The map method uses a function to project the contents of an array or a map object into a new array, using a function to determine how each item is represented in the result. Listing 34-6 shows the use of the map method with an array.

Listing 34-6. Using the Map Method to Project an Array

```
...
<script type="text/javascript">
    $(document).ready(function() {
        var flowerArray = ["aster", "daffodil", "rose", "peony", "primula", "snowdrop"];

        var result = $.map(flowerArray, function(elem, index) {
            return index + ": " + elem;
        });

        for (var i = 0; i < result.length; i++) {
            console.log(result[i]);
        }
    });
</script>
...
```

Our mapping function is executed for each item in the array and is passed the item and its index in the array as arguments. The result from the function is included in the array returned by the map method. In this script, I transform each item in the array by concatenating the value with its index, producing the following results:

```
0: aster
1: daffodil
2: rose
3: peony
4: primula
5: snowdrop
```

You can use the map method to selectively project an array – there will be no corresponding item in the result if you don't return a value from the function for the item being processed. Listing 34-7 shows how you can selectively project from an array.

Listing 34-7. Selectively Mapping an Array

```
...
<script type="text/javascript">
    $(document).ready(function() {
        var flowerArray = ["aster", "daffodil", "rose", "peony", "primula", "snowdrop"];

        var result = $.map(flowerArray, function(elem, index) {
            if (elem != "rose") {
                return index + ": " + elem;
            }
        });

        for (var i = 0; i < result.length; i++) {
            console.log(result[i]);
        }
    });
</script>
...
```

Results are generated for all of the array values except rose, which gives rise to the following results:

```
0: aster
1: daffodil
3: peony
4: primula
5: snowdrop
```

Using the Merge Method

The merge method concatenates two arrays, as demonstrated in Listing 34-8.

Listing 34-8. Using the Merge Method

```
...
<script type="text/javascript">
    $(document).ready(function() {

        var flowerArray = ["aster", "daffodil", "rose", "peony", "primula", "snowdrop"];
        var additionalFlowers = ["carnation", "lily", "orchid"];

        $.merge(flowerArray, additionalFlowers);

        for (var i = 0; i < flowerArray.length; i++) {
            console.log(flowerArray[i]);
        }
    });
</script>
...
```

The items from the second array are appended to the first array, and the array specified by the first argument is modified by the merge process. The script in the example produces the following results:

```
aster
daffodil
rose
peony
primula
snowdrop
carnation
lily
orchid
```

Using the Unique Method

The unique method sorts an array of HTMLElement objects into the order in which they appear in the document and removes any duplicate elements. Listing 34-9 shows how to use this method.

Listing 34-9. Using the Unique Method

```
...
<script type="text/javascript">
    $(document).ready(function() {

        var selection = $("img[src*=rose], img[src*=primula]").get();
        $.merge(selection, $("img[src*=aster]"));
        $.merge(selection, $("img"));

        $.unique(selection);
```

```
        for (var i =0; i < selection.length; i++) {
            console.log("Elem: " + selection[i].src);
        }


    });
</script>
...
```

The sorting process is done in-place, meaning that the array passed as the argument to the unique method is modified. In this example, I created an array of HTMLElement objects that contain duplicates and which are not in document order and then apply the unique method.

Utility Methods for Types

jQuery provides a set of methods that are useful for determining the nature of a JavaScript object – these methods are described in Table 34-4.

Table 34-4. *Utility Methods for Working with Types*

Method	Description
$.isArray(Object)	Returns true if the object is an array.
$.isEmptyObject(Object)	Returns true if the object doesn't define any methods or properties.
$.isFunction(Object)	Returns true if the object is a function.
$.isNumeric(Object)	Returns true if the object is a number.
$.isWindow(Object)	Returns true if the object is a Window.
$.isXMLDoc(Object)	Returns true if the object is an XML document.
$.type(Object)	Returns the built-in JavaScript type for the object.

Most of these methods are simple – you pass an object to the method, which returns true if the object is of the type that the method detects and false otherwise. As a simple demonstration, Listing 34-10 contains an example using the isFunction method.

Listing 34-10. Using the isFunction Method

```
...
<script type="text/javascript">
    $(document).ready(function() {

        function myFunc() {
            console.log("Hello!");
        }

        console.log("IsFunction: " + $.isFunction(myFunc));
        console.log("IsFunction: " + $.isFunction("hello"));
    });
</script>
...
```

In this example, I use the `isFunction` method to test two objects. The results are as follows:

```
IsFunction: true
IsFunction: false
```

Using the Type Method

The type method is slightly different in that is returns the base JavaScript type of an object. The result will be one of the following strings:

- boolean
- number
- string
- function
- array
- date
- regexp
- object

Listing 34-11 shows the use of the type method.

Listing 34-11. Using the Type Method

```
...
<script type="text/javascript">
    $(document).ready(function() {

        function myFunc() {
            console.log("Hello!");
        }

        var jq = $("img");
        var elem = document.getElementById("row1");

        console.log("Type: " + $.type(myFunc));
        console.log("Type: " + $.type(jq));
        console.log("Type: " + $.type(elem));
    });
</script>
...
```

In this script, I use the type method on a function, a `jQuery` object, and an `HTMLElement` object. The results are as follows:

```
Type: function
Type: object
Type: object
```

Utility Methods for Data

jQuery defines a number of utility methods that can be useful for working with various kinds of data – these methods are described in Table 34-5.

Table 34-5. *Utility Methods for Working with Data*

Method	Description
serialize()	Encodes a set of form elements into a string suitable for submission to a server.
serializeArray()	Encodes a set of form elements into an array ready for encoding into JSON.
$.parseJSON(<json>)	Creates a JavaScript object from JSON data.
$.parseXML(<xml>)	Creates an XMLDocument object from an XML string.
$.trim(String)	Removes all whitespace from the beginning and end of a string.

Serializing Form Data

The `serialize` and `serializeArray` methods are a convenient way to extract the details from a set of form elements in a way that is useful for regular or Ajax form submissions. Listing 34-12 shows both methods in use.

Listing 34-12. Serializing Form Data

```
...
<script type="text/javascript">
    $(document).ready(function() {

        $("<button>Serialize</button>").appendTo("#buttonDiv").click(function(e) {

            var formArray = $("form").serializeArray();
            console.log("JSON: " + JSON.stringify(formArray))

            var formString = $("form").serialize();
            console.log("String: " + formString)

            e.preventDefault();
        });

    });
</script>
...
```

In this example, I serialize the form elements in the document using both methods and write the results to the console. The `serializeArray` method returns a JavaScript array that contains one object for each form element in the document. These objects have two properties: the `name` property contains the value of the `name` attribute of the element, and the `value` property contains the element's value. Here is the output from the example document:

```
[{"name":"aster","value":"1"},{"name":"daffodil","value":"0"},
 {"name":"rose","value":"0"},{"name":"peony","value":"0"},
 {"name":"primula","value":"2"},{"name":"snowdrop","value":"0"}]
```

By contrast, the serialize method creates an encoded string, as follows:

```
aster=1&daffodil=0&rose=0&peony=0&primula=2&snowdrop=0
```

Parsing Data

The parseJSON and parseXML methods are especially useful when dealing with the results of Ajax requests. For most web applications, JSON has taken over as the data format of choice, for the reasons I outlined in Chapter 14. XML is still used, but I only find myself using this XML data when integrating new applications with legacy back-end systems. Listing 34-13 shows the parseJSON method in use.

Listing 34-13. Parsing JSON Data

```
...
<script type="text/javascript">
    $(document).ready(function() {

        $("<button>Serialize</button>").appendTo("#buttonDiv").click(function(e) {

            var jsonData = '{"name": "Adam Freeman", "city": "London", "country": "UK"}'

            var dataObject = $.parseJSON(jsonData)

            for (var prop in dataObject) {
                console.log("Property: " + prop + " Value: " + dataObject[prop])
            }

            e.preventDefault();
        });

    });
</script>
...
```

In this example, I define a simple JSON string and use the parseJSON method to convert it into a JavaScript object. I then enumerate the properties in the object and their values to the console, producing the following output:

```
Property: name Value: Adam Freeman
Property: city Value: London
Property: country Value: UK
```

Trimming Strings

The trim method removes all of the whitespace from the start and end of string – this includes spaces, tabs, and newlines. This is a feature that most programming languages support as part of their core handling of character data, but which is missing from JavaScript for some reason. Listing 34-14 shows the trim method in use.

Listing 34-14. Using the Trim Method

```
...
<script type="text/javascript">
    $(document).ready(function() {

        $("<button>Serialize</button>").appendTo("#buttonDiv").click(function(e) {

            var sourceString = "\n  This string contains whitespace     ";
            console.log(">" + sourceString + "<")

            var resultString = $.trim(sourceString);
            console.log(">" + resultString + "<")

            e.preventDefault();
        });

    });
</script>
...
```

In this example, I use the `trim` method and write the original and trimmed strings to the console, producing the following results:

```
>  This string contains whitespace     <
>This string contains whitespace<
```

Other Utility Methods

There are a number of jQuery methods that don't neatly fit into another category, but which can still be useful – these are described in Table 34-6.

Table 34-6. Other Utility Methods

Method	Description
`$.contains(HTMLElement, HTMLElement)`	Returns `true` if the first element contains the second element.
`$.now()`	Returns the current time, shorthand for `new Date().getTime()`.

Checking Element Containment

The `contains` method checks to see if one element contains another. Both arguments are expressed as `HTMLElement` objects, and the method returns `true` if the element represented by the first argument contains the element represented by the second argument. Listing 34-15 provides a demonstration of the `contains` method.

Listing 34-15. Using the Contains Method

```
...
<script type="text/javascript">
    $(document).ready(function() {
        $("img").hover(function(e) {
            var elem = document.getElementById("row1");
            if ($.contains(elem, this)) {
                $(e.target).css("border", e.type == "mouseenter" ?
                                          "thick solid red" : "");
            }
        });
    });
</script>
...
```

In this script, I obtain an HTMLElement object using the DOM API and check to see that it contains the element passed to an event handler method – if it does, I set a border for the element that triggered the event.

■ **Tip** This method only works on HTMLElement objects – if you want to perform the same check on jQuery objects, then consider using the find method, which I described in Chapter 6.

Summary

In this chapter, I have described the jQuery utility methods – an eclectic set of helpful functions that can be used to perform advanced operations on jQuery objects or which supplement the JavaScript language features to provide support that programmers commonly need. These are the kinds of methods that you are glad exist when you need them, but can be safely forgotten about for most web application projects.

■ ■ ■

The jQuery UI Effects & CSS Framework

In this chapter I describe two utility features that jQuery UI provides. The first is a set of enhancements to existing jQuery methods that can animate colors, changes in element visibility, and the application of CSS classes. The other feature is a set of CSS classes that to apply a jQuery UI theme to the rest of our HTML documents in order to create a consistent look across an entire web application. Table 35-1 provides the summary for this chapter.

Table 35-1. *Chapter Summary*

Problem	Solution	Listing
Animate changes in color.	Use the enhanced `animate` method.	1
Animate the application of classes.	Use the enhanced `addClass`, `removeClass` and `toggleClass` methods and the `switchClass` method.	2, 3
Animate visibility transitions.	Use the enhanced `show`, `hide` and `toggle` methods.	4
Apply an effect without changing element visibility.	Use the `effect` method.	5
Style an element as a widget.	Use the widget container classes.	6
Apply rounded corners to an element.	Use the corner classes.	7
Apply the styles of a clickable widget to an element.	Use the interaction state classes.	8
Provide the user with cues about the state of an element.	Use the cue classes.	9, 10

Using the jQuery UI Effects

jQuery UI extends some core jQuery methods to animate different transitions for an element – this ranges from the animation of color changes through to the application of CSS classes. These can be valuable additions to a web application when used carefully, and to supplement these features, jQuery UI also defines some additional animation effects.

Animating Colors

jQuery UI extends the jQuery animate method, which I described in Chapter 10, to add support for animating colors. You can animate one of several CSS properties that define an element's colors. Table 35-2 describes the CSS properties that the animate method supports.

Table 35-2. *CSS Properties Supported by the jQuery UI Animate Method*

Property	Description
backgroundColor	Sets the background color of the element.
borderTopColor borderBottomColor borderLeftColor borderRightColor	Sets the color for individual sides of the element border.
color	Sets the text color for the element.
outlineColor	Sets the color for the outline, used to emphasize the element.

To animate colors, pass a map object as the argument to the animate method, detailing the properties to animate and the target values. Listing 35-1 contains an example.

Listing 35-1. Animating Colors

```
<!DOCTYPE html>
<html>
<head>
    <title>Example</title>
    <script src="jquery-2.0.2.js" type="text/javascript"></script>
    <script src="jquery-ui-1.10.3.custom.js" type="text/javascript"></script>
    <link rel="stylesheet" type="text/css" href="styles.css"/>
    <link rel="stylesheet" type="text/css" href="jquery-ui-1.10.3.custom.css"/>
    <style type="text/css">
        #animTarget {
            background-color: white;
            color: black;
            border: medium solid black;
            width: 200px; height: 50px;
            text-align: center;
            font-size: 25px;
            line-height: 50px;
            display: block;
            margin-bottom: 10px;
        }
    </style>
    <script type="text/javascript">
        $(document).ready(function() {
            $("button").click(function() {
                $("#animTarget").animate({
                    backgroundColor: "black",
```

```
            color: "white"
        })
    })
    });
    </script>
</head>
<body>
    <h1>Jacqui's Flower Shop</h1>

    <div id=animTarget>
        Hello!
    </div>

    <button>Animate Color</button>
</body>
</html>
```

I style the div element in this document so that it has an initial background color of white and a color of black. When the button in the document is clicked, I call the animate method, specifying that these properties be changed to black and white respectively. The transition from one color to another is done gradually and both properties are animated simultaneously. You can see the effect in Figure 35-1.

Figure 35-1. *Animating colors*

___

■ **Tip** Notice that I use the standard CSS property names in the style element – background-color, for example. But when specifying the same property in the map object, I switched to using camel case – backgroundColor. This allows me to specify the CSS property as a JavaScript object property without having to enclose the term in quotes.

___

In this example, I specified the colors I wanted using the CSS color shorthand values, black and white. There are shorthand values for a wide range of colors, but the animate method will also accept hexadecimal colors (#FFFFFF, for example) and RGB function colors, such as rgb(255, 255, 255).

___

■ **Tip** Aside from the support for the color properties, you can use the animate method just as I described in Chapter 10.

___

Animating Classes

jQuery UI provides a convenient way of animating sets of CSS properties using classes. Rather than specify each property, you simply define properties and values in a class and tell jQuery UI to add the class to one or more elements. jQuery UI will animate the transition from one state to another. Listing 35-2 provides a demonstration.

Listing 35-2. Animating Using Classes

```
<!DOCTYPE html>
<html>
<head>
    <title>Example</title>
    <script src="jquery-2.0.2.js" type="text/javascript"></script>
    <script src="jquery-ui-1.10.3.custom.js" type="text/javascript"></script>
    <link rel="stylesheet" type="text/css" href="styles.css"/>
    <link rel="stylesheet" type="text/css" href="jquery-ui-1.10.3.custom.css"/>
    <style type="text/css">
        .elemClass {
            background-color: white;
            color: black;
            border: medium solid black;
            width: 200px; height: 50px;
            text-align: center;
            font-size: 25px;
            line-height: 50px;
            display: block;
            margin-bottom: 10px;
        }
        .myClass {
            font-size: 40px; background-color: black; color: white;
        }
    </style>
    <script type="text/javascript">
        $(document).ready(function() {

            $("button").click(function() {
                if (this.id == "add") {
                    $("#animTarget").addClass("myClass", "fast")
                } else {
                    $("#animTarget").removeClass("myClass", "fast")
                }
            })
        });
    </script>
</head>
<body>
    <h1>Jacqui's Flower Shop</h1>

    <div id=animTarget class="elemClass">
        Hello!
    </div>
```

```
    <button id="add">Add Class</button>
    <button id="remove">Remove Class</button>
</body>
</html>
```

Once again, jQuery UI extends an existing jQuery method to add functionality. In this case, it is the addClass and removeClass methods that have been enhanced. I described the standard versions of these methods in Chapter 8. The jQuery UI versions do exactly the same thing: the second argument to the method to the duration and jQuery UI animates the transition from one class to the other.

In this example, I have defined a class called myClass, and there are buttons in the document that add and remove this class using the duration shorthand of fast. You can see the effect in Figure 35-2.

Figure 35-2. *Animating elements using classes*

■ **Tip**   The standard CSS style cascading rules apply, which means that the properties in a class will only be applied if the class is the most specific for the target element or elements. In the previous example I styled the initial state of the element by id, but in this example I use a class so that my modifications have effect. See Chapter 3 for details of CSS style cascading.

jQuery UI also enhances the toggleClass method – this works in the same way as the standard toggleClass method that I described in Chapter 8, but takes a duration argument and animates the transition, just as in the addClass and removeClass example above.

Switching Classes

In addition to enhancing some of the standard methods, jQuery UI also defines the switchClass method, which removes one class and adds another, animating the transition from one state to the other. Listing 35-3 contains a demonstration.

Listing 35-3. Using the switchClass Method

```
<!DOCTYPE html>
<html>
<head>
    <title>Example</title>
    <script src="jquery-2.0.2.js" type="text/javascript"></script>
    <script src="jquery-ui-1.10.3.custom.js" type="text/javascript"></script>
    <link rel="stylesheet" type="text/css" href="styles.css"/>
    <link rel="stylesheet" type="text/css" href="jquery-ui-1.10.3.custom.css"/>
    <style type="text/css">
        .elemClass {
            border: medium solid black;
            width: 200px; height: 50px;
            text-align: center;
            line-height: 50px;
            display: block;
            margin-bottom: 10px;
        }
        .classOne {
            font-size: 25px; background-color: white; color: black;
        }
        .classTwo {
            font-size: 40px; background-color: black; color: white;
        }
    </style>
    <script type="text/javascript">
        $(document).ready(function() {

            $("button").click(function() {
                $("#animTarget").switchClass("classOne", "classTwo", "fast")
            })
        });
    </script>
</head>
<body>
    <h1>Jacqui's Flower Shop</h1>

    <div id=animTarget class="elemClass classOne">
        Hello!
    </div>
    <button>Switch Class</button>
</body>
</html>
```

The arguments to the switchClass method are the class that should be removed, the class that should be added and the duration for the animation. In the example, my two classes define the same properties, but this need not be the case.

Using the jQuery UI Animations

jQuery UI includes a number of animation effects that can be applied to elements, much as with the core jQuery effects in Chapter 10. My recommendation is to use these effects sparingly. Animations applied carefully can be a genuine enhancement to the user experience – but all too often, they become a source of annoyance and frustration to the user. There are many different animation effects available, including blind, bounce, clip, drop, explode, fade, fold, highlight, puff, pulsate, scale, shake, size, and slide.

■ **Note** In this chapter, I am going to show you how to apply these effects, but I am not going to get into the detail of each individual effect. There is a good summary of the effects and the settings that can be applied to some of them at http://docs.jquery.com/UI/Effects.

Using Effects to Show and Hide Elements

jQuery UI enhances the jQuery UI show, hide, and toggle methods to apply animation effects. I described the original versions of these methods in Chapter 10. To use the enhanced jQuery UI versions of these methods, provide additional arguments specifying the effect you want to use and the duration over which it should be applied. Listing 35-4 shows the use of these enhanced methods.

Listing 35-4. Using the Enhanced Show, Hide, and Toggle Methods

```
<!DOCTYPE html>
<html>
<head>
    <title>Example</title>
    <script src="jquery-2.0.2.js" type="text/javascript"></script>
    <script src="jquery-ui-1.10.3.custom.js" type="text/javascript"></script>
    <link rel="stylesheet" type="text/css" href="styles.css"/>
    <link rel="stylesheet" type="text/css" href="jquery-ui-1.10.3.custom.css"/>
    <style type="text/css">
        .elemClass {
            font-size: 25px; background-color: white; color: black;
            border: medium solid black; width: 200px; height: 50px;
            text-align: center; line-height: 50px; display: block; margin-bottom: 10px;
        }
    </style>
    <script type="text/javascript">
        $(document).ready(function() {

            $("button").click(function() {
                switch (this.id) {
                    case "show":
                        $("#animTarget").show("fold", "fast");
                        break;
                    case "hide":
                        $("#animTarget").hide("fold", "fast");
                        break;
```

```
                        case "toggle":
                            $("#animTarget").toggle("fold", "fast");
                            break;
                    }
                })
            });
        </script>
    </head>
    <body>
        <h1>Jacqui's Flower Shop</h1>

        <button id="hide">Hide</button>
        <button id="show">Show</button>
        <button id="toggle">Toggle</button>

        <div id=animTarget class="elemClass">
            Hello!
        </div>
    </body>
</html>
```

There are three buttons in this example and clicking them leads to the show, hide, or toggle methods being called. For all three buttons, I have specified that the fold animation should be applied, using the fast duration. These methods work just like their core jQuery counterparts, except that the transition is animated.

Applying Standalone Effects

jQuery UI defines the effect method, which allows us to apply an animation to an element without having to show or hide it. When used with the right animation, this can be a useful way of drawing the user's attention to an element in the document. Listing 35-5 contains an example.

Listing 35-5. Using the Effect Method

```
<!DOCTYPE html>
<html>
<head>
    <title>Example</title>
    <script src="jquery-2.0.2.js" type="text/javascript"></script>
    <script src="jquery-ui-1.10.3.custom.js" type="text/javascript"></script>
    <link rel="stylesheet" type="text/css" href="styles.css"/>
    <link rel="stylesheet" type="text/css" href="jquery-ui-1.10.3.custom.css"/>
    <style type="text/css">
        .elemClass {
            font-size: 25px; background-color: white; color: black;
            border: medium solid black; width: 200px; height: 50px;
            text-align: center; line-height: 50px; display: block; margin-bottom: 10px;
        }
    </style>
```

```
<script type="text/javascript">
    $(document).ready(function() {

        $("button").click(function() {
            $("#animTarget").effect("pulsate", "fast")
        })
    });
</script>
</head>
<body>
    <h1>Jacqui's Flower Shop</h1>

    <div id=animTarget class="elemClass">
        Hello!
    </div>
    <button>Effect</button>
</body>
</html>
```

When the button in this example is clicked, the effect is applied in situ, without any permanent changes to visibility. In this case, I have used the pulsate effect, which causes the element to pulse on and off.

Using the jQuery UI CSS Framework

jQuery UI manages the appearance of widgets by applying a set of classes to elements that apply some complex CSS styles. Some of these classes are exposed to programmers so that elements that are not part of widgets can be styled in a consistent manner – I used some of these classes in the examples in Part IV of this book.

Using the Widget Container Classes

The three most basic classes in the CSS framework apply the core styles that are used on widgets. These classes are described in Table 35-3.

Table 35-3. *jQuery UI Widget Container Classes*

Class	Description
ui-widget	Applied to overall container elements.
ui-widget-header	Applied to header container elements.
ui-widget-content	Applied to the content container element.

These classes are applied to *container* elements – that is, those elements that contain all of the header and content elements (or, in the case of ui-widget, the outermost element). Listing 35-6 shows how to apply these classes.

Listing 35-6. Using the jQuery UI Widget Container Classes

```html
<!DOCTYPE html>
<html>
<head>
    <title>Example</title>
    <script src="jquery-2.0.2.js" type="text/javascript"></script>
    <script src="jquery-ui-1.10.3.custom.js" type="text/javascript"></script>
    <link rel="stylesheet" type="text/css" href="styles.css"/>
    <link rel="stylesheet" type="text/css" href="jquery-ui-1.10.3.custom.css"/>
    <style type="text/css">
        body > div {float: left; margin: 10px}
    </style>
</head>
<body>
    <h1>Jacqui's Flower Shop</h1>

    <div>
        <div>
            Flowers
        </div>
        <div>
            <div class="dcell">
                <img src="peony.png"/><label for="peony">Peony:</label>
                <input name="peony" value="0" />
            </div>
        </div>
    </div>

    <div class="ui-widget">
        <div class="ui-widget-header">
            Flowers
        </div>
        <div class="ui-widget-content">
            <div class="dcell">
                <img src="peony.png"/><label for="peony">Peony:</label>
                <input name="peony" value="0" />
            </div>
        </div>
    </div>
</body>
</html>
```

There are two sets of elements in this example, to one of which I have applied the container classes. You can see the effect in Figure 35-3.

Figure 35-3. *Applying the jQuery UI Widget Container Classes*

Applying Rounded Corners

The next set of CSS framework classes lets us apply rounded corners to our widget-like elements. Table 35-4 describes the classes in this category.

Table 35-4. *jQuery UI Widget Rounded Corner Classes*

Class	Description
ui-corner-all	Rounds all of the element's corners.
ui-corner-bl	Rounds the bottom-left corner.
ui-corner-bottom	Rounds the bottom-left and bottom-right corners.
ui-corner-br	Rounds the bottom-right corner.
ui-corner-left	Rounds the top-left and bottom-left corners.
ui-corner-right	Rounds the top-right and bottom-right corners.
ui-corner-tl	Rounds the top-left corner.
ui-corner-top	Rounds the top-left and top-right corner.
ui-corner-tr	Rounds the top-right corner.

These classes only take effect when an element has a background or margin, which means that they can be applied to the ui-widget-header and ui-widget-content classes, as shown in Listing 35-7.

Listing 35-7. Using the Rounded Corner Classes

```
<!DOCTYPE html>
<html>
<head>
    <title>Example</title>
    <script src="jquery-2.0.2.js" type="text/javascript"></script>
    <script src="jquery-ui-1.10.3.custom.js" type="text/javascript"></script>
    <link rel="stylesheet" type="text/css" href="styles.css"/>
    <link rel="stylesheet" type="text/css" href="jquery-ui-1.10.3.custom.css"/>
    <style type="text/css">
        body > div {float: left; margin: 10px}
    </style>
</head>
<body>
    <h1>Jacqui's Flower Shop</h1>

    <div>
        <div>
            Flowers
        </div>
        <div>
            <div class="dcell">
                <img src="peony.png"/><label for="peony">Peony:</label>
                <input name="peony" value="0" />
            </div>
        </div>
    </div>

    <div class="ui-widget">
        <div class="ui-widget-header ui-corner-top" style="padding-left: 5px">
            Flowers
        </div>
        <div class="ui-widget-content ui-corner-bottom">
            <div class="dcell">
                <img src="peony.png"/><label for="peony">Peony:</label>
                <input name="peony" value="0" />
            </div>
        </div>
    </div>
</body>
</html>
```

In order to create an overall effect, I have rounded the top corners of the header element and the bottom corners of the content element. You can see the result in Figure 35-4. Notice that I have added a little padding to the header element – the rounded corners are applied within the element's content box, which can require some additional space to avoid clipping content.

Figure 35-4. *Applying rounded corners to elements*

Using the Interaction State Classes

You can also apply CSS framework classes to show different interaction states, which allows to create elements that respond to user interaction in the same way that jQuery UI widgets do. Table 35-5 describes the classes available.

Table 35-5. *jQuery UI Interaction Classes*

Class	Description
ui-state-default	Applies the default style for clickable widget.
ui-state-hover	Applies the style used when the mouse hovers over a clickable widget.
ui-state-focus	Applies the style used when a clickable widget has the focus.
ui-state-active	Applies the style used when a clickable widget is active.

Listing 35-8 applies these four classes. Notice that I have applied padding to an inner span element in each case. The interaction state classes define padding values, and the easiest way to create spacing between the container element and the content is to target an inner element.

Listing 35-8. Applying the Interaction State Classes

```
<!DOCTYPE html>
<html>
<head>
    <title>Example</title>
    <script src="jquery-2.0.2.js" type="text/javascript"></script>
    <script src="jquery-ui-1.10.3.custom.js" type="text/javascript"></script>
    <link rel="stylesheet" type="text/css" href="styles.css"/>
    <link rel="stylesheet" type="text/css" href="jquery-ui-1.10.3.custom.css"/>
```

```
    <style type="text/css">
        body > div {float: left; margin: 10px}
        span {padding: 10px; display: block}
    </style>
</head>
<body>
    <h1>Jacqui's Flower Shop</h1>

    <div class="ui-widget ui-state-default ui-corner-all">
        <span>Default</span>
    </div>
    <div class="ui-widget ui-state-hover ui-corner-all">
        <span>Hover</span>
    </div>
    <div class="ui-widget ui-state-focus ui-corner-all">
        <span>Focus</span>
    </div>
    <div class="ui-widget ui-state-active ui-corner-all">
        <span>Active</span>
    </div>
</body>
</html>
```

You can see the effect of each class in Figure 35-5. Some of these states are similar in the jQuery UI theme that I am using, but you can use ThemeRoller (described in Chapter 17) to create a theme with increased state emphasis if required.

Figure 35-5. *The effect of the interaction state classes*

Using the Cue Classes

Some CSS framework classes allow us to provide the user with cues about the state of elements in the document. These classes are described in Table 35-6.

Table 35-6. *jQuery UI Interaction Cue Classes*

Class	Description
ui-state-highlight	Highlights an element to draw the user's attention.
ui-state-error	Emphasizes an element that contains an error message.
ui-state-disabled	Applies the disabled style to an element (but doesn't actually disable the element itself).

Listing 35-9 shows the use of the highlight and disabled cues.

Listing 35-9. Using the jQuery UI highlight Class

```html
<!DOCTYPE html>
<html>
<head>
    <title>Example</title>
    <script src="jquery-2.0.2.js" type="text/javascript"></script>
    <script src="jquery-ui-1.10.3.custom.js" type="text/javascript"></script>
    <link rel="stylesheet" type="text/css" href="styles.css"/>
    <link rel="stylesheet" type="text/css" href="jquery-ui-1.10.3.custom.css"/>
    <style type="text/css">
        body > div {float: left; margin: 10px}
        span {padding: 10px; display: block}
    </style>
</head>
<body>
    <h1>Jacqui's Flower Shop</h1>

    <div class="ui-widget">
        <div class="ui-widget-header ui-corner-top" style="padding-left: 5px">
            Flowers
        </div>
        <div class="ui-widget-content ui-corner-bottom">
            <div class="dcell">
                <img src="peony.png"/><label for="peony">Peony:</label>
                <input name="peony" value="0" />
            </div>
        </div>
    </div>

    <div class="ui-widget ui-state-highlight ui-corner-all">
        <div class="ui-widget-header ui-corner-top" style="padding-left: 5px">
            Flowers
        </div>
        <div class="ui-widget-content ui-corner-bottom">
            <div class="dcell">
                <img src="peony.png"/><label for="peony">Peony:</label>
                <input name="peony" value="0" />
            </div>
        </div>
    </div>
```

959

```
    <div class="ui-widget ui-state-disabled">
        <div class="ui-widget-header ui-corner-top" style="padding-left: 5px">
            Flowers
        </div>
        <div class="ui-widget-content ui-corner-bottom">
            <div class="dcell">
                <img src="peony.png"/><label for="peony">Peony:</label>
                <input name="peony" value="0" />
            </div>
        </div>
    </div>
</body>
</html>
```

You can see the effect of the classes in Figure 35-6. Notice that I have also applied the `ui-corner-all` style when using the `ui-state-highlight` class. This class applies a border, which will be shown with square corners by default. If the child elements have rounded corners, then you need to round the corners of the highlighted element as well.

Figure 35-6. *Applying the highlight cue class*

Listing 35-10 shows the use of the error state.

Listing 35-10. Using the Error Cue

```
<!DOCTYPE html>
<html>
<head>
    <title>Example</title>
    <script src="jquery-2.0.2.js" type="text/javascript"></script>
    <script src="jquery-ui-1.10.3.custom.js" type="text/javascript"></script>
    <link rel="stylesheet" type="text/css" href="styles.css"/>
    <link rel="stylesheet" type="text/css" href="jquery-ui-1.10.3.custom.css"/>
```

```
    <style type="text/css">
        body > div {float: left; margin: 10px; padding: 20px}
    </style>
</head>
<body>
    <h1>Jacqui's Flower Shop</h1>

    <div class="ui-state-error">
        Oops! Something went wrong.
    </div>
</body>
</html>
```

You can see the effect in Figure 35-7.

Figure 35-7. *Using the error cue class*

Summary

In this chapter, I described the enhancements that jQuery UI provides for animating transitions for color, visibility, and CSS classes. These are useful features, but they must be used with caution to avoid bombarding the user with distracting and annoying effects. I also described the principle classes of the jQuery UI CSs framework, which allows us to style elements in a way that is consistent with jQuery UI widgets, allowing us to extend the appearance of our jQuery UI theme to the rest of our HTML documents.

■ ■ ■

Using Deferred Objects

Throughout this book, you have seen examples that relied on *callbacks* – you provide a function that is executed when something occurs. A good example is the way events are handled, using a method such as click, passing in a function as an argument. The code statements in the function are not performed until the user triggers the event – until that point our function is dormant.

Deferred objects is the jQuery term for a set of enhancements to the way callbacks are used. When using deferred objects, callbacks can be used in any situation and not just for events; and they provide a lot of options and control over when and how callback functions are executed.

In this chapter, I'll start with a reasonably simple example and then build upon it to show the features and some useful patterns for managing deferred objects and background tasks.

I say *reasonably* simply, because using deferred objects bring us into the world of *asynchronous* or *parallel* programming. Effective parallel programming is a difficult skill to master, and JavaScript makes it more difficult because it lacks some of the advanced features that are present in other languages, such as Java and C#. Most projects don't need to use deferred objects and, if you are new to parallel programming, my recommendation is to skip this chapter until you are working on a project that does. Table 36-1 provides the summary for this chapter.

Table 36-1. *Chapter Summary*

Problem	Solution	Listing
Use the basic features of a deferred object.	Register a callback function using the done method. Call the resolve method to trigger the callback.	1
Use a deferred object with a background task.	Use the setTimeout function to create a background task and call the resolve method when the task is complete.	2-4
Signal a task failure.	Use the reject method to trigger the handlers registered using the fail method.	5, 6
Register handlers for both deferred object outcomes in a single method call.	Use the then method.	7
Specify a function that will be executed irrespective of whether the deferred object is resolved or rejected.	Use the always method.	8
Use multiple callbacks for the same outcome.	Call the registration method multiple times or pass the functions as comma-separated arguments.	9

(*continued*)

Table 36-1. (*continued*)

Problem	Solution	Listing
Create a deferred object whose outcome is determined by the outcome of other deferred objects.	Use the when method.	10
Signal task progress.	Call the notify method, which will trigger callback handlers which have been registered using the progress method.	11, 12
Get information about the state of a deferred object.	Use the state method.	13
Use Ajax Promises.	Treat the response from the jQuery Ajax methods as you would a deferred object.	14

A First Deferred Objects Example

I am going to start by showing you how deferred objects work and then show you how to use them. Listing 36-1 is a simple example that contains a deferred object.

Listing 36-1. A Simple Deferred Object Example

```
<!DOCTYPE html>
<html>
<head>
    <title>Example</title>
    <script src="jquery-2.0.2.js" type="text/javascript"></script>
    <script src="jquery-ui-1.10.3.custom.js" type="text/javascript"></script>
    <link rel="stylesheet" type="text/css" href="styles.css"/>
    <link rel="stylesheet" type="text/css" href="jquery-ui-1.10.3.custom.css"/>
    <style type="text/css">
        td {text-align: left; padding: 5px}
        table {width: 200px; border-collapse: collapse; width: 50%; float: left}
        #buttonDiv {width: 15%; text-align: center; margin: 20px; float: left}
    </style>
    <script type="text/javascript">
        $(document).ready(function() {
            var def = $.Deferred();

            def.done(function() {
                displayMessage("Callback Executed");
            })

            $("button").button().click(function() {
                def.resolve();
            })
```

```
        displayMessage("Ready")
    })

    function displayMessage(msg) {
        $("tbody").append("<tr><td>" + msg + "</td></tr>")
    }
    </script>
</head>
<body>
    <h1>Jacqui's Flower Shop</h1>

    <table class="ui-widget" border=1>
        <thead class="ui-widget-header">
            <tr><th>Message</th></tr>
        </thead>
        <tbody class="ui-widget-content">
        </tbody>
    </table>

    <div id="buttonDiv">
        <button>Go</button>
    </div>
</body>
</html>
```

This is a simple demonstration of how a deferred object works. I will step through it to set the context for the rest of the chapter. First of all, I created a deferred object by calling the $.Deferred method, like so:

```
...
var def = $.Deferred();
...
```

The Deferred method returns a deferred object – I have assigned this one to the variable called def. Deferred objects are all about callbacks, and so my next step is to register a function with the deferred object using the done method, like this:

```
...
def.done(function() {
    displayMessage("Callback Executed");
})
...
```

When it is executed, the callback function will call the displayMessage function, which adds a row to the table element in the document.

The final step is to set things up so that I can trigger the callback function, which I do by calling the resolve method. Triggering the callback like this is known as *resolving the deferred object*. I want to be able to control when the deferred object is resolved, and so I have added a button to the document and use the click method to handle an event. The irony here is that I am using one callback mechanism to help describe another – for the purposes of this chapter I want you to ignore the event system and focus on the fact that the deferred object isn't resolved until the button is pressed. Here is the function that calls `resolve` and so triggers the callback function registered with the done method:

```
...
$("button").button().click(function() {
    def.resolve();
})
...
```

Until the resolve method is called, the deferred object remains *unresolved* and our callback function won't be executed. Pressing the button resolves the deferred object, executes the callback, and displays the message in the table, as shown in Figure 36-1.

Figure 36-1. *Resolving a deferred object*

The important thing to understand here is that the deferred object isn't doing anything special. We register a callback function using the done method and they won't be executed until the resolve method is called. In this example, the deferred object isn't resolved until the button is clicked, at which point the callback function is executed and a new message is added to the table element.

Understanding Why Deferred Objects Are Useful

Deferred objects are useful when you want to execute functions at the end of some task without having to monitor that task directly – especially when that task is being performed in the background. Listing 36-2 contains a demonstration, which I'll then start to modify to add features.

Listing 36-2. Using Callbacks with a Long-Lived Task

...
```
<script type="text/javascript">
    $(document).ready(function() {
        var def = $.Deferred();

        def.done(function() {
            displayMessage("Callback Executed");
        })

        function performLongTask() {

            var start = $.now();

            var total = 0;
            for (var i = 0; i < 500000000 ; i++) {
                total += i;
            }
            var elapsedTime = (($.now() - start)/1000).toFixed(1)
            displayMessage("Task Complete. Time: " + elapsedTime + " sec")
            def.resolve();
        }

        $("button").button().click(function() {
            displayMessage("Calling performLongTask()")
            performLongTask()
            displayMessage("performLongTask() Returned")
        })

        displayMessage("Ready")
    })

    function displayMessage(msg) {
        $("tbody").append("<tr><td>" + msg + "</td></tr>")
    }
</script>
...
```

The process in this example is defined by the performLongTask function, which adds together a series of numbers – I want something simple and which takes a few seconds to complete and this fits the bill.

■ **Tip** On my system, the for loop in the performLongTask function takes about 0.5 seconds to complete, but you may need to adjust the upper limit for the loop to get a similar result on your system. Anywhere up to 4–5 seconds is a good duration for these examples – long enough to demonstrate the deferred object features, but not so long that you have time to make coffee while waiting for the task to complete.

Clicking the button now calls the performLongTask function. That function calls the deferred object's resolve method when its work is complete, causing the callback function to be invoked. The performLongTask function adds its own message to the table element before it calls resolve, so we can see the sequence of progression through the script. You can see the results in Figure 36-2.

Figure 36-2. *Using a deferred object to observe task completion*

This is an example of a *synchronous* task. You push the button and then have to wait while each function that is called completes. The best indicator that you are working synchronously is the way that the Go button stays in its pressed state while the performLongTask function does its work. Definitive proof comes in the sequence of messages displayed in Figure 36-2 – the messages from the click event handler come before and after the messages from the performLongTask and the callback functions.

The major benefit of deferred objects comes when working with *asynchronous* tasks – tasks that are being performed in the background. You don't want the user interface to lock up like it did in the last example; and so instead, you start tasks in the background, keep an eye on them, and update the document to give the user information about the progress and result of the work.

The simplest way to start a background task is to use the setTimeout function, which means using yet another callback mechanism. This may seem a little odd, but JavaScript lacks the language facilities for managing asynchronous tasks that other languages are designed with and so we have do make do with those features that are available. Listing 36-3 shows the example modified so that the time-consuming part of the performLongTask function is done in the background.

Listing 36-3. Performing the Work Asynchronously

```
...
<script type="text/javascript">
    $(document).ready(function() {
        var def = $.Deferred();

        def.done(function() {
            displayMessage("Callback Executed");
        })

        function performLongTask() {
            setTimeout(function() {
                var start = $.now();

                var total = 0;
                for (var i = 0; i < 500000000 ; i++) {
                    total += i;
                }
                var elapsedTime = (($.now() - start)/1000).toFixed(1)
                displayMessage("Task Complete. Time: " + elapsedTime + " sec")
                def.resolve();
            }, 10);
        }

        $("button").button().click(function() {
            displayMessage("Calling performLongTask()")
            performLongTask()
            displayMessage("performLongTask() Returned")
        })

        displayMessage("Ready")
    })

    function displayMessage(msg) {
        $("tbody").append("<tr><td>" + msg + "</td></tr>")
    }
</script>
...
```

I use the setTimeout function to perform the for loop in the performLongTask function after a delay of 10 milliseconds. You can see the effect this has in Figure 36-3 – notice that the messages from the click handler function appear before those form the performLongTask and callback functions. If you run this example yourself, you will notice that the button pops back into its regular state immediately, rather than waiting for the work to complete.

Figure 36-3. *Performing the task in the background*

Callbacks are particularly important when working with background tasks because you don't know when they are complete. You could set up your own signaling system – updating a variable, for example – but you would need to do this for every background task that is performed, which quickly becomes tiresome and error prone. Deferred objects provide a standardized mechanism for indicating that tasks have completed and, as I'll demonstrate in later examples, they offer a lot of flexibility in how this is done.

Tidying Up the Example

Before I start digging into the feature of deferred objects, I am going to update the example to use the pattern that I tend to work with in real projects. This is purely personal preference, but I like to split out the workload from the asynchronous wrapper and integrate the production of the deferred object into the function. Listing 36-4 shows the changes.

Listing 36-4. Tidying Up the Example

```
<!DOCTYPE html>
<html>
<head>
    <title>Example</title>
    <script src="jquery-2.0.2.js" type="text/javascript"></script>
    <script src="jquery-ui-1.10.3.custom.js" type="text/javascript"></script>
    <link rel="stylesheet" type="text/css" href="styles.css"/>
    <link rel="stylesheet" type="text/css" href="jquery-ui-1.10.3.custom.css"/>
    <style type="text/css">
        td {text-align: left; padding: 5px}
        table {width: 200px; border-collapse: collapse; float: left; width: 300px}
        #buttonDiv {text-align: center; margin: 20px; float: left}
    </style>
```

970

```
<script type="text/javascript">
    $(document).ready(function() {

        function performLongTaskSync() {
            var start = $.now();

            var total = 0;
            for (var i = 0; i < 500000000 ; i++) {
                total += i;
            }
            var elapsedTime = (($.now() - start)/1000).toFixed(1)
            displayMessage("Task Complete. Time: " + elapsedTime + " sec")
            return total;
        }

        function performLongTask() {
            return $.Deferred(function(def) {
                setTimeout(function() {
                    performLongTaskSync();
                    def.resolve();
                }, 10)
            })
        }

        $("button").button().click(function() {
            if ($(":checked").length > 0) {
                displayMessage("Calling performLongTask()")
                var observer = performLongTask();
                observer.done(function() {
                    displayMessage("Callback Executed");
                });
                displayMessage("performLongTask() Returned")
            } else {
                displayMessage("Calling performLongTaskSync()")
                performLongTaskSync();
                displayMessage("performLongTaskSync() Returned")
            }
        })

        $(":checkbox").button();
        displayMessage("Ready")
    })

    function displayMessage(msg) {
        $("tbody").append("<tr><td>" + msg + "</td></tr>")
    }
</script>
</head>
<body>
    <h1>Jacqui's Flower Shop</h1>
```

```
<table class="ui-widget" border=1>
    <thead class="ui-widget-header">
        <tr><th>Message</th></tr>
    </thead>
    <tbody class="ui-widget-content">
    </tbody>
</table>

<div id="buttonDiv">
    <button>Go</button>
    <input type="checkbox" id="async" checked>
    <label for="async">Async</label>
</div>
</body>
</html>
```

In this example, I have broken out the workload into a function called performLongTasksync, which is just responsible for performing the calculations. It has no knowledge of background tasks or callback functions. I like to keep the workload separate because it makes testing the code easier during the early stages of development. Here is the synchronous function:

```
...
function performLongTaskSync() {
    var start = $.now();

    var total = 0;
    for (var i = 0; i < 500000000 ; i++) {
        total += i;
    }
    var elapsedTime = (($.now() - start)/1000).toFixed(1)
    displayMessage("Task Complete. Time: " + elapsedTime + " sec")
    return total;
}
...
```

I have separated out the code to perform the task asynchronously – this is in the performLongTask function, which is an asynchronous wrapper around the performLongTasksync function and which uses a deferred object to trigger callbacks when the work has completed. Here is the revised performLongTask function:

```
...
function performLongTask() {
    return $.Deferred(function(def) {
        setTimeout(function() {
            performLongTaskSync();
            def.resolve();
        }, 10)
    })
}
...
```

If I pass a function to the Deferred method, it is executed as soon as the object is created, and the function is passed the new deferred object as a parameter. Using this feature, I can create a simple wrapper function that performs the work asynchronously and triggers the callbacks when the work has finished.

> ■ **Tip** If you are observant, you will have noticed that there is a chance that calling the done method to register a callback function may occur after the task has been completed and the resolve method has been called. This may occur for short tasks, but the callback function will still be called, even if done is called after resolve.

The other reason that I like to create a wrapper like this is because deferred objects can't be reset once they are resolved or rejected (I explain rejection in a moment). By creating the deferred object inside of the wrapper function, I ensure that I am always using fresh, unresolved deferred objects.

The other change I have made to this example is to add a toggle button, which allows the task to be performed synchronously or asynchronously. I will take this feature out of future examples because this is a chapter about asynchronous tasks, but it is a good way to make sure that you are comfortable with the difference. You can see the output from both modes in Figure 36-4.

Figure 36-4. *Performing the same task synchronously and asynchronously*

Using Other Callbacks

Now that I have a basic asynchronous example in place, I can turn to some of the useful features that deferred objects provide. The first is that I can signal different outcomes from our tasks. Table 36-2 describes the methods available for registering callbacks and the methods that are called on the deferred object that trigger them. I have already explained the done and resolve methods, and I cover the others in the sections that follow.

Table 36-2. *Methods for Registering Callbacks*

Callback Registration Method	Triggered By
done	resolve
fail	reject
always	resolve or reject

Rejecting a Deferred Object

Not all tasks complete successfully. When they do, I *resolve* the deferred object by calling the resolve method. But when something goes wrong, we *reject* the deferred object using the reject method. Callbacks functions are registered for failed tasks using the fail method. The reject methods triggers callbacks registered with the fail method in the same way that the resolve method triggers callbacks registered with done. Listing 36-5 shows a task that will either resolve or reject its deferred object.

Listing 36-5. Rejecting Deferred Objects

```
<!DOCTYPE html>
<html>
<head>
    <title>Example</title>
    <script src="jquery-2.0.2.js" type="text/javascript"></script>
    <script src="jquery-ui-1.10.3.custom.js" type="text/javascript"></script>
    <link rel="stylesheet" type="text/css" href="styles.css"/>
    <link rel="stylesheet" type="text/css" href="jquery-ui-1.10.3.custom.css"/>
    <style type="text/css">
        td {text-align: left; padding: 5px}
        table {width: 200px; border-collapse: collapse; float: left; width: 300px}
        #buttonDiv {text-align: center; margin: 20px; float: left}
    </style>
    <script type="text/javascript">
        $(document).ready(function() {

            function performLongTaskSync() {
                var start = $.now();

                var total = 0;
                for (var i = 0; i < 5000000  ; i++) {
                    total += (i + Number((Math.random() + 1).toFixed(0)));
                }
                var elapsedTime = (($.now() - start)/1000).toFixed(1)
                displayMessage("Task Complete. Time: " + elapsedTime + " sec")
                return total;
            }

            function performLongTask() {
                return $.Deferred(function(def) {
                    setTimeout(function() {
                        var total = performLongTaskSync();
                        if (total % 2 == 0) {
                            def.resolve(total);
                        } else {
                            def.reject(total);
                        }
                    }, 10)})
            }
```

```
            $("button").button().click(function() {
                displayMessage("Calling performLongTask()")
                var observer = performLongTask();
                displayMessage("performLongTask() Returned")
                observer.done(function(total) {
                    displayMessage("Done Callback Executed: " + total);
                });
                observer.fail(function(total) {
                    displayMessage("Fail Callback Executed: " + total);
                });
            })

            displayMessage("Ready")
        })

        function displayMessage(msg) {
            $("tbody").append("<tr><td>" + msg + "</td></tr>")
        }
    </script>
</head>
<body>
    <h1>Jacqui's Flower Shop</h1>

    <table class="ui-widget" border=1>
        <thead class="ui-widget-header">
            <tr><th>Message</th></tr>
        </thead>
        <tbody class="ui-widget-content">
        </tbody>
    </table>

    <div id="buttonDiv">
        <button>Go</button>
    </div>
</body>
</html>
```

In this example, I have tweaked the task so that a small random number is added to the total in each iteration of the `for` loop. The asynchronous wrapper function `performLongTask` checks the total returned by the synchronous function and resolves the deferred object if the total is even. If the total is odd, then the `performLongTask` function rejects the deferred object, as follows:

```
...
if (total % 2 == 0) {
    def.resolve(total);
} else {
    def.reject(total);
}
...
```

After calling the performLongTask function, my click event handler registers callback functions for both outcomes, using the done and fail methods, as follows:

```
...
var observer = performLongTask();
displayMessage("performLongTask() Returned")
observer.done(function(total) {
    displayMessage("Done Callback Executed: " + total);
});
observer.fail(function(total) {
    displayMessage("Fail Callback Executed: " + total);
});
...
```

Notice that I pass arguments to the resolve and reject methods when I call them. You don't have to pass arguments to these methods, but if you do the objects you supply will be passed as arguments to the callback functions, which allows you to provide additional context or detail about what has happened. In this example, the status of the task is determined by the calculation total, which I have passed as the argument to both the done and reject methods. You can see the outcome of a resolved and rejected deferred object in Figure 36-5.

Figure 36-5. *A task that can succeed or fail*

Chaining Deferred Object Method Calls

The deferred object methods are chainable, meaning that each method returns a deferred object on which other methods can be called. This is something I have been doing with jQuery objects throughout this book. Listing 36-6 shows how the calls to the done and fail methods can be chained together.

Listing 36-6. Chaining Deferred Object Method Calls

```
...
$("button").button().click(function() {
    performLongTask().done(function(total) {
        displayMessage("Done Callback Executed: " + total);
    }).fail(function(total) {
        displayMessage("Fail Callback Executed: " + total);
    });
})
...
```

Covering Both Outcomes

If there are callbacks for each outcome, they can be registered in one go using the then method. The first argument is the callback to use if the deferred object is resolved, and the second argument is the callback to use if the deferred object is rejected. Listing 36-7 shows the then method in use.

Listing 36-7. Using the Then Method

```
...
$("button").button().click(function() {
    displayMessage("Calling performLongTask()")
    var observer = performLongTask();
    displayMessage("performLongTask() Returned")

    observer.then(
        function(total) {
            displayMessage("Done Callback Executed");
        },
        function(total) {
            displayMessage("Fail Callback Executed");
        }
    );
})
...
```

I tend to use method chaining because I find it produces code where the outcome each function is prepared to deal with is more obvious.

Using Outcome-Indifferent Callbacks

There are occasions when you will want to execute a callback function irrespective of the outcome of the task. A common pattern is to use the always method to register a function that removes or hides elements which indicate that some background task is being performed and use the done and fail method to display the next steps to the user. Listing 36-8 shows the use of the always method to register a function which behaves the same regardless of the task outcome.

Listing 36-8. Using the Always Method to Register an Outcome-Indifferent Function

```
<!DOCTYPE html>
<html>
<head>
    <title>Example</title>
    <script src="jquery-2.0.2.js" type="text/javascript"></script>
    <script src="jquery-ui-1.10.3.custom.js" type="text/javascript"></script>
    <link rel="stylesheet" type="text/css" href="styles.css"/>
    <link rel="stylesheet" type="text/css" href="jquery-ui-1.10.3.custom.css"/>
    <style type="text/css">
        td {text-align: left; padding: 5px}
        table {width: 200px; border-collapse: collapse; float: left; width: 300px}
        #buttonDiv {text-align: center; margin: 20px; float: left}
    </style>
    <script type="text/javascript">
        $(document).ready(function() {

            function performLongTaskSync() {
                var start = $.now();

                var total = 0;
                for (var i = 0; i < 5000000  ; i++) {
                    total += (i + Number((Math.random() + 1).toFixed(0)));
                }
                var elapsedTime = (($.now() - start)/1000).toFixed(1)
                displayMessage("Task Complete. Time: " + elapsedTime + " sec")
                return total;
            }

            function performLongTask() {
                return $.Deferred(function(def) {
                    setTimeout(function() {
                        var total = performLongTaskSync();
                        if (total % 2 == 0) {
                            def.resolve(total);
                        } else {
                            def.reject(total);
                        }
                    }, 10)})
            }

            $("button").button().click(function() {
                displayMessage("Calling performLongTask()")
                var observer = performLongTask();
                displayMessage("performLongTask() Returned")

                $("#dialog").dialog("open");

                observer.always(function() {
                    $("#dialog").dialog("close");
                });
```

```
            observer.done(function(total) {
                displayMessage("Done Callback Executed: " + total);
            });
            observer.fail(function(total) {
                displayMessage("Fail Callback Executed: " + total);
            });

        })

        $("#dialog").dialog({
            autoOpen: false,
            modal: true

        })

        displayMessage("Ready")
    })

    function displayMessage(msg) {
        $("tbody").append("<tr><td>" + msg + "</td></tr>")
    }
</script>
</head>
<body>
    <h1>Jacqui's Flower Shop</h1>

    <table class="ui-widget" border=1>
        <thead class="ui-widget-header">
            <tr><th>Message</th></tr>
        </thead>
        <tbody class="ui-widget-content">
        </tbody>
    </table>

    <div id="buttonDiv">
        <button>Go</button>
    </div>

    <div id="dialog">
        Performing Task...
    </div>
</body>
</html>
```

In this example, I have added a jQuery UI modal dialog that is displayed when the task is running. I use the always method to register a function that closes the dialog when the task is complete – this means that I don't have to duplicate the code for tidying up after the task has finished in my functions that handle resolved or rejected deferred objects.

■ **Tip**   Callbacks functions are called in the order in which they are registered with the deferred object. In this example, I call the always method before calling the done or fail methods, which means that a outcome-indifferent function is always called before the functions that handle the resolved or rejected outcomes.

Using Multiple Callbacks

One of the benefits that arise from using deferred objects is that we can partition our code up into small functions that handle specific activities. To allow further decomposition of our code, deferred objects provide support for registering multiple callbacks for the same outcome. Listing 36-9 provides a demonstration.

Listing 36-9. Registering Multiple Callback Functions with a Deferred Object

```
...
<script type="text/javascript">
    $(document).ready(function() {

        function performLongTaskSync() {
            var start = $.now();

            var total = 0;
            for (var i = 0; i < 5000000  ; i++) {
                total += (i + Number((Math.random() + 1).toFixed(0)));
            }
            var elapsedTime = (($.now() - start)/1000).toFixed(1)
            displayMessage("Task Complete. Time: " + elapsedTime + " sec")
            return total;
        }

        function performLongTask() {
            return $.Deferred(function(def) {
                setTimeout(function() {
                    var total = performLongTaskSync();
                    if (total % 2 == 0) {
                        def.resolve({
                            total: total
                        });
                    } else {
                        def.reject(total);
                    }
                }, 10)})
        }

        $("button").button().click(function() {
            displayMessage("Calling performLongTask()")
            var observer = performLongTask();
            displayMessage("performLongTask() Returned")
```

```
        $("#dialog").dialog("open");

        observer.done(function(data) {
            data.touched = 1;
            displayMessage("1st Done Callback Executed");
        });

        observer.done(function(data) {
            data.touched++;
            displayMessage("2nd Done Callback Executed");
        }, function(data) {
            data.touched++;
            displayMessage("3rd Done Callback Executed");
        });

        observer.done(function(data) {
            displayMessage("4th Done Callback Executed: " + data.touched);
        });

        observer.fail(function(total) {
            displayMessage("Fail Callback Executed: " + total);
        });

        observer.always(function() {
            displayMessage("Always Callback Executed");
            $("#dialog").dialog("close");
        });


    })

    $("#dialog").dialog({
        autoOpen: false,
        modal: true
    })

    displayMessage("Ready")
})

function displayMessage(msg) {
    $("tbody").append("<tr><td>" + msg + "</td></tr>")
}
</script>
...
```

In this example, I have registered four callback functions using the done method. As the code shows, we can register functions individually or in groups by passing multiple functions, separated by commas, to the registration method. The deferred object ensures that the callback functions are executed in the order in which they were registered.

Notice that I have changed the argument passed to the resolve method in this example, making the result of the calculation a property in a JavaScript object. I did this to demonstrate that callback functions are able to modify the data passed via the deferred object. This can be useful for providing simple communication between handler functions (to declare that some particular action has been taken). You can see the effect of having multiple handlers in Figure 36-6.

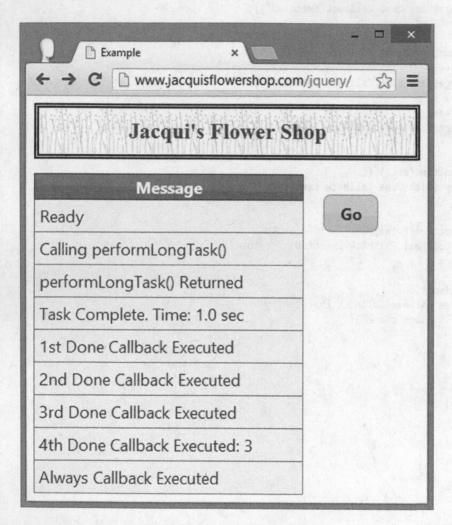

Figure 36-6. Using multiple callbacks for the same outcome

■ **Tip** You can specify multiple callbacks for each outcome using the then method by passing arrays of functions as arguments.

Using the Outcomes of Multiple Deferred Objects

We can use the when method to create deferred objects whose outcome is derived from several other deferred objects. This technique is useful when we are relying on the results from several background tasks, or when we don't want to start a task until we are sure that a set of other tasks have achieved a specific outcome. Listing 36-10 provides a demonstration.

Listing 36-10. Using the When Method

```
...
$("button").button().click(function() {

    var ob1 = performLongTask()
        .done(function() {
            displayMessage("1st Task <b>Resolved</b>")
        })
        .fail(function() {
            displayMessage("1st Task <b>Failed</b>")
        })

    var ob2 = performLongTask()
        .done(function() {
            displayMessage("2nd Task <b>Resolved</b")
        })
        .fail(function() {
            displayMessage("2nd Task <b>Failed</b>")
        })

    var ob3 = performLongTask()
        .done(function() {
            displayMessage("3rd Task <b>Resolved</b>")
        })
        .fail(function() {
            displayMessage("3rd Task <b>Failed</b>")
        })

    $.when(ob1, ob2, ob3)
        .done(function() {
            displayMessage("Aggregate <b>Resolved</b>")
        })
        .fail(function() {
            displayMessage("Aggregate <b>Failed</b>")
        })
})
...
```

In this example, I have three deferred objects, each of which was created calling the performLongTask function and to which I have attached callback functions using the done and fail methods.

I have passed all three deferred objects to the when method, which returns another deferred object (known as the *aggregate deferred object*). I have I have attached callback functions to the aggregate using the normal done and fail methods. The outcome of the aggregate is determined by the outcome of the other three deferred objects. If *all* three of the regular deferred objects are resolved, then the aggregate is also resolved and the done functions will be called. However, if *any* of the regular deferred objects are rejected, then the aggregate is rejected as well, and the fail functions will be called. You can see both outcomes for the aggregate in Figure 36-7.

Figure 36-7. Using the when method

■ **Caution**   If you look closely at the sequence of messages in the figure, you will spot a timing anomaly. The aggregate deferred object is rejected as soon as any of the underlying objects are rejected – this means that the callback functions registered with the fail method can be triggered while there are still tasks running. When dealing with a rejected aggregate object, you cannot assume that all of the tasks it depends on are complete.

Providing Progress Information

It is generally a good idea to provide the user with progress information when performing a long-lived task in the background. Deferred objects can be used to pass progress information from the task to callback functions, in much the same way we have been passing information about outcomes. We produce progress information using the notify method and register our callback function using the progress method. Listing 36-11 contains an example.

Listing 36-11. Producing and Consuming Progress Information via a Deferred Object

...
```
<script type="text/javascript">
    $(document).ready(function() {

        function performLongTaskSync() {
            var total = 0;
            for (var i = 0; i < 5000000  ; i++) {
                total += (i + Number((Math.random() + 1).toFixed(0)));
            }
            return total;
        }

        function performLongTask() {
            return $.Deferred(function(def) {
                setTimeout(function() {
                    var progressValue = 0;
                    for (var i = 0; i < 4; i++) {
                        performLongTaskSync();
                        progressValue += 25;
                        def.notify(progressValue)
                    }
                    def.resolve();
                }, 10)}
            )
        }

        $("button").button().click(function() {

            performLongTask().progress(function(val) {
                displayMessage("Progress: " + val + "%")
            }).done(function() {
                displayMessage("Task Resolved");
            })
        })

        $("#dialog").dialog({
            autoOpen: false,
            modal: true
        })

        displayMessage("Ready")
    })

    function displayMessage(msg) {
        $("tbody").append("<tr><td>" + msg + "</td></tr>")
    }
</script>
```
...

985

In this example, the task is to perform the calculation four times. After each calculation, I call the notify method on the deferred object and pass in my percentage progress (although you can pass any object or value that makes sense for your web application – I am using percentages for simplicity). In the click handler function, I have used the progress method to register a function that will be called in response to a progress update – I use this function to add a message to the table in the document.

This example demonstrates the basic ability to provide progress information, but it doesn't quite work in the way that we might hope. The problem is that the browser doesn't get the change to update the DOM with the new rows until after all four iterations are complete – this is a facet of the way that JavaScript tasks are managed and means that we get all of the progress updates in one go at the end of the task. To address this, we need to add small delays between each stage in the task to give the browser the time it needs to perform updates. Listing 36-12 shows how we can use the setTimeout function to introduce these delays and create a chain of deferred objects. I would usually use a for loop to set up the delays and the deferred objects, but to make this example clearer to read, I have defined all of the steps explicitly.

Listing 36-12. Breaking the Task Down to Allow DOM Changes

```
...
<script type="text/javascript">
    $(document).ready(function() {

        function performLongTaskSync() {
            var total = 0;
            for (var i = 0; i < 5000000  ; i++) {
                total += (i + Number((Math.random() + 1).toFixed(0)));
            }
            return total;
        }

        function performLongTask() {

            function doSingleIteration() {
                return $.Deferred(function(innerDef) {
                        setTimeout(function() {
                        performLongTaskSync();
                        innerDef.resolve();
                    }, 10)
                })
            }

            var def = $.Deferred();

            setTimeout(function() {

                doSingleIteration().done(function() {
                    def.notify(25);
                    doSingleIteration().done(function() {
                        def.notify(50);
                        doSingleIteration().done(function() {
                            def.notify(75);
                            doSingleIteration().done(function() {
```

```
                            def.notify(100);
                            def.resolve();
                        })
                    })
                })
            })
        }, 10);

        return def;
    }


    $("button").button().click(function() {

        performLongTask().progress(function(val) {
            displayMessage("Progress: " + val + "%")
        }).done(function() {
            displayMessage("Task Resolved");
        })
    })

    $("#dialog").dialog({
        autoOpen: false,
        modal: true
    })

    displayMessage("Ready")
})

function displayMessage(msg) {
    $("tbody").append("<tr><td>" + msg + "</td></tr>")
}
</script>
...
```

With this change, the progress updates are properly displayed. You can see the updates shown in Figure 36-8.

987

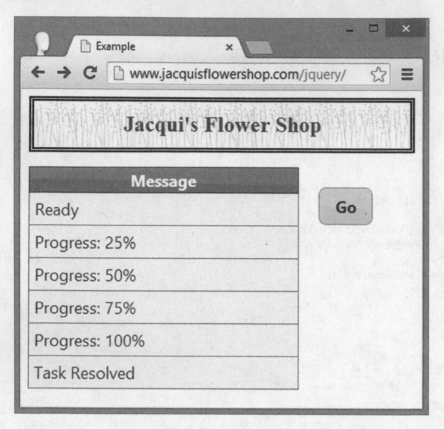

Figure 36-8. *Using a deferred object to provide progress information*

Getting Information about a Deferred Object

Deferred objects define the state method, which we can use to establish the state of the object and, by implication, the task that is being performed. The values that the method can return are described in Table 36-3.

Table 36-3. *Values for the State Object*

Value	Description
pending	Neither the resolve or reject method has been called on the deferred object.
resolved	The deferred object has been resolved (using the resolve method).
rejected	The deferred object has been rejected (using the rejected method).

■ **Caution**   Be careful when using this method. In particular, you should stop and think if you find yourself polling the status of a deferred object – you may have some design problems in your web application. Polling for status, especially in a while or for loop can mean that you have effectively made your task synchronous while incurring the overhead and complexity associated with asynchronous tasks.

The only time that I find the state method useful is when I have registered a callback using the always method and I am interested in the outcome of the task. Generally, I use the done and fail methods with separate callbacks functions, but there are times when I have code that is largely, but not quite, the same for both outcomes. Listing 36-13 contains a demonstration of using the state method.

Listing 36-13. Using the State Method

```
<!DOCTYPE html>
<html>
<head>
    <title>Example</title>
    <script src="jquery-2.0.2.js" type="text/javascript"></script>
    <script src="jquery-ui-1.10.3.custom.js" type="text/javascript"></script>
    <link rel="stylesheet" type="text/css" href="styles.css"/>
    <link rel="stylesheet" type="text/css" href="jquery-ui-1.10.3.custom.css"/>
    <style type="text/css">
        td {text-align: left; padding: 5px}
        table {width: 200px; border-collapse: collapse; float: left; width: 300px}
        #buttonDiv {text-align: center; margin: 20px; float: left}
    </style>
    <script type="text/javascript">
        $(document).ready(function() {

            function performLongTaskSync() {
                var start = $.now();

                var total = 0;
                for (var i = 0; i < 5000000  ; i++) {
                    total += (i + Number((Math.random() + 1).toFixed(0)));
                }
                var elapsedTime = (($.now() - start)/1000).toFixed(1)
                displayMessage("Task Complete. Time: " + elapsedTime + " sec")
                return total;
            }

            function performLongTask() {
                return $.Deferred(function(def) {
                    setTimeout(function() {
                        var total = performLongTaskSync();
                        if (total % 2 == 0) {
                            def.resolve(total);
                        } else {
                            def.reject(total);
                        }
```

```
                        }, 10)}])
                }

            $("button").button().click(function() {
                displayMessage("Calling performLongTask()")
                var observer = performLongTask();
                displayMessage("performLongTask() Returned")

                $("#dialog").dialog("open");

                observer.always(function() {
                    if (observer.state() == "resolved") {
                        $("#dialog").dialog("close");
                    } else {
                        $("#dialog").text("Error!")
                    }
                });

                observer.done(function(total) {
                    displayMessage("Done Callback Executed: " + total);
                });
                observer.fail(function(total) {
                    displayMessage("Fail Callback Executed: " + total);
                });

            })

            $("#dialog").dialog({
                autoOpen: false,
                modal: true

            })

            displayMessage("Ready")
        })

        function displayMessage(msg) {
            $("tbody").append("<tr><td>" + msg + "</td></tr>")
        }
    </script>
</head>
<body>
    <h1>Jacqui's Flower Shop</h1>

    <table class="ui-widget" border=1>
        <thead class="ui-widget-header">
            <tr><th>Message</th></tr>
        </thead>
        <tbody class="ui-widget-content">
        </tbody>
    </table>
```

```
        <div id="buttonDiv">
            <button>Go</button>
        </div>

        <div id="dialog">
            Performing Task...
        </div>
    </body>
</html>
```

Using Ajax Deferred Objects

Perhaps the most useful aspect of the deferred object functionality is the way it has been incorporated into the jQuery support for Ajax (which I described in Chapters 14 and 15). The jxXHR object that we get back from methods such as ajax and getJSON implement the Promise interface, which provides us with a subset of the methods defined by a regular deferred object. A Promise defines the done, fail, then, and always methods and can be used with the when method. Listing 36-14 shows how we can mix and match Ajax promises with deferred objects.

Listing 36-14. Using Ajax Promises and Deferred Objects

```
<!DOCTYPE html>
<html>
<head>
    <title>Example</title>
    <script src="jquery-2.0.2.js" type="text/javascript"></script>
    <script src="jquery-ui-1.10.3.custom.js" type="text/javascript"></script>
    <link rel="stylesheet" type="text/css" href="styles.css"/>
    <link rel="stylesheet" type="text/css" href="jquery-ui-1.10.3.custom.css"/>
    <style type="text/css">
        td {text-align: left; padding: 5px}
        table {width: 200px; border-collapse: collapse; float: left; width: 300px}
        #buttonDiv {text-align: center; margin: 20px; float: left}
    </style>
    <script type="text/javascript">
        $(document).ready(function() {

            function performLongTaskSync() {
                var start = $.now();

                var total = 0;
                for (var i = 0; i < 5000000   ; i++) {
                    total += (i + Number((Math.random() + 1).toFixed(0)));
                }
                var elapsedTime = (($.now() - start)/1000).toFixed(1)
                displayMessage("Task Complete. Time: " + elapsedTime + " sec")
                return total;
            }
```

```
            function performLongTask() {
                return $.Deferred(function(def) {
                    setTimeout(function() {
                        performLongTaskSync();
                        def.resolve();
                    }, 10)})
            }

        $("button").button().click(function() {
            displayMessage("Calling performLongTask()")
            var observer = performLongTask().done(function() {
                displayMessage("Task complete")
            });
            displayMessage("performLongTask() Returned")

            displayMessage("Calling getJSON()")
            var ajaxPromise = $.getJSON("mydata.json").done(function() {
                displayMessage("Ajax Request Completed")
            });
            displayMessage("getJSON() Returned")

            $.when(observer, ajaxPromise).done(function() {
                displayMessage("All Done");
            })
        })
        displayMessage("Ready")
    })

    function displayMessage(msg) {
        $("tbody").append("<tr><td>" + msg + "</td></tr>")
    }
    </script>
</head>
<body>
    <h1>Jacqui's Flower Shop</h1>

    <table class="ui-widget" border=1>
        <thead class="ui-widget-header">
            <tr><th>Message</th></tr>
        </thead>
        <tbody class="ui-widget-content">
        </tbody>
    </table>

    <div id="buttonDiv">
        <button>Go</button>
    </div>
</body>
</html>
```

■ **Tip** You can create your own Promise objects by calling the promise method on a deferred object. This can be useful if you are writing a JavaScript library and you only want to allow other programmers to attach callbacks and not to resolve or reject your deferred objects.

In this example, I have used the getJSON method and treated the result just as I would a deferred object. I attached a callback function using the done method and use it as an argument to the when method. You can see the output from this example in Figure 36-9.

Figure 36-9. Using Ajax promises

Summary

In this chapter, I have demonstrated the jQuery deferred object feature, which lets us signal progress and outcomes of tasks, typically tasks which are being performed in the background. Deferred objects are used within the jQuery support for Ajax, which lets us treat our Ajax requests and our custom background tasks in a consistent manner. Deferred objects are an advanced feature, and most web applications won't need them – but for those projects that do significant background tasks, they can help preserve a response experience for the user.

Index

■ D

Printed in the United States
By Bookmasters